504

WORKS ISSUED BY

THE HAKLUYT SOCIETY

ENGLISH PRIVATEERING VOYAGES
TO THE WEST INDIES

SECOND SERIES
No. CXI

ISSUED FOR 1956

COUNCIL AND OFFICERS
OF
THE HAKLUYT SOCIETY
1958

PRESIDENT
J. N. L. BAKER, Esq., M.A., B.Litt.

VICE-PRESIDENTS
Professor E. G. R. TAYLOR, D.Sc.
JAMES A. WILLIAMSON, Esq., D.Lit.
SIR ALAN BURNS, G.C.M.G.

COUNCIL
(*with date of election*)

K. R. ANDREWS, Esq., Ph.D. (1958)
Professor C. F. BECKINGHAM (1958)
Professor C. R. BOXER (1955)
EILA M. J. CAMPBELL, M.A. (1958)
G. R. CRONE, Esq., M.A. (1955)
E. S. DE BEER, Esq., Hon. D.Litt., F.S.A. (1956)
Sir MAURICE HOLMES, G.B.E., K.C.B. (1957)
Professor C. C. LLOYD (1958)
Sir HARRY LUKE, K.C.M.G., D.Litt. (1954)
Commander R. D. MERRIMAN, R.I.N., D.S.C. (1957)
J. V. MILLS, Esq., M.A. (1956)
G. P. B. NAISH, Esq., F.S.A. (1955)
N. M. PENZER, Esq., Hon. Ph.D. (1958)
Professor D. B. QUINN (1957)
Royal Geographical Society (General Sir JAMES MARSHALL-CORNWALL)
HELEN M. WALLIS, D.Phil. (1957)

TRUSTEES
J. N. L. BAKER, Esq., M.A., B.Litt.   E. W. BOVILL, Esq., F.S.A.
Sir GILBERT LAITHWAITE, G.C.M.G., K.C.B., K.C.I.E., C.S.I. (1956)

TREASURER: F. B. MAGGS, Esq.

HON. SECRETARY
R. A. SKELTON, Esq., B.A., F.S.A., British Museum, London, W.C. 1

HON. SECRETARIES FOR OVERSEAS
Australia: G. D. RICHARDSON, Esq.
Canada: Professor J. B. BIRD
New Zealand: C. R. H. TAYLOR, Esq., M.A.
South Africa: DOUGLAS VARLEY, Esq.
U.S.A.: W. M. WHITEHILL, Esq., Ph.D., F.S.A.

1. Sir Julius Caesar, Judge of the Admiralty

ENGLISH PRIVATEERING VOYAGES TO THE WEST INDIES
1588-1595

Documents relating to English voyages to the West Indies from the defeat of the Armada to the last voyage of Sir Francis Drake, including Spanish documents contributed by Irene A. Wright

Edited by
KENNETH R. ANDREWS

CAMBRIDGE
Published for the Hakluyt Society
AT THE UNIVERSITY PRESS
1959

PUBLISHED BY
THE SYNDICS OF THE CAMBRIDGE UNIVERSITY PRESS

Bentley House, 200 Euston Road, London, N.W. 1
American Branch: 32 East 57th Street, New York 22, N.Y.

©
THE HAKLUYT SOCIETY
1959

*Printed in Great Britain
by Robert MacLehose and Company Limited
at the University Press, Glasgow*

CONTENTS

CHAPTER III. THE VOYAGE OF JOHN CHIDLEY, 1589   page 59

13. William Magoths' account of the voyage of the *Delight*
14. The petition of the company of the *Delight*
15. *Querela* of John Chidley: deposition of Thomas Edwards
16. William Manby *contra* Elizabeth Chidley: deposition of Simon Furner
17. William Manby *contra* Elizabeth Chidley: deposition of James Robinson
18. William Manby *contra* Elizabeth Chidley: deposition of Benjamin Wood
19. Inventory of the *White Lion* after her return to England
20. Giles Fleming *contra* the *White Lion*: the libel
21. Giles Fleming *contra* the *White Lion*: deposition of Thomas Acton
22. Giles Fleming *contra* the *White Lion*: deposition of Thomas Campion
23. Giles Fleming *contra* the *White Lion:* deposition of Ellis Dobson
24. Giles Fleming *contra* the *White Lion*: deposition of Thomas Edwards
25. Elizabeth Chidley *contra* the *Wildman's Club*
26. Elizabeth Chidley *contra* the *Wildman's Club*: deposition of John Hearle
27. Elizabeth Chidley *contra* Richard Lewes: the libel
28. Elizabeth Chidley *contra* Richard Lewes: deposition of Thomas Fernley
29. Elizabeth Chidley *contra* Richard Lewes: deposition of John Hearle
30. Replies of Richard Lewes to articles of contempt brought against him
31. Deposition of Thomas Edwards concerning the *Robin*
32. Deposition of Simon Merrick concerning the *Robin*

CHAPTER IV. THE VOYAGE OF THE *BARK YOUNG*, 1590   86

33. Articles of a *querela* for George Bland, John Young and others
34. *Querela* of Bland, Young and others: deposition of William Irish
35. *Querela* of Bland, Young and others: deposition of Edmund Maynard
36. *Querela* of Bland, Young and others: deposition of John Kenney

CONTENTS

LIST OF ILLUSTRATIONS AND MAPS   *page* xix

LIST OF SOURCES CITED
    showing abbreviations used in the footnotes   xxi

NOTE ON EDITING   xxvii

INTRODUCTION   1
- I. The Materials   1
- II. Privateering during the Spanish War   16
- III. Privateering in the West Indies, 1588–95   28

CHAPTER I. THE VOYAGE OF THE *DRAKE*, THE *EXAMINER*, THE *HOPE* AND THE *CHANCE*, 1588   40
1. Thomas Watts *contra* Robert FitzWilliams: the libel
2. Thomas Watts *contra* Robert FitzWilliams: deposition of John Pocombe
3. Thomas Watts *contra* Robert FitzWilliams: deposition of Osborne Huntlowe
4. Thomas Watts *contra* Robert FitzWilliams: deposition of John Benson
5. Thomas Watts *contra* Robert FitzWilliams: deposition of Edward Hickman
6. Thomas Watts *contra* Robert FitzWilliams: deposition of Samuel Hearne

CHAPTER II. THE VOYAGE OF THE *BLACK DOG*, 1588–9   50
7. Richard Hakluyt's account of the voyage of the *Dog*
8. *Querela* of Arthur Michelson: deposition of Robert Abraham
9. *Querela* of Arthur Michelson: deposition of John Crokes
10. *Querela* of Arthur Michelson: deposition of John Fisher
11. *Querela* of Arthur Michelson: deposition of Thomas Webster
12. The appraisement of the *Black Dog*

PREFACE

the Honorary Secretary of the Hakluyt Society, whose practical help and encouragement at every stage in the preparation of the book have been invaluable.

My thanks are also due to Lord Hothfield, for permission to copy and publish the MS account of the seventh voyage of the Earl of Cumberland; to Sir John Lawes, Bart., for permission to reproduce the portrait of Sir Thomas Myddelton at Rothamsted; to Captain R. G. W. Berkeley for permission to reproduce the miniature of the second Lord Hunsdon at Berkeley Castle; to the Ashmolean Museum for permission to reproduce the portrait of Sir Julius Caesar; and to the British Museum for permission to reproduce a part of the Crace impression of Visscher's Long View of London. The sketch maps were drawn by Mrs Huhtala and Miss Moore of the Royal Geographical Society.

November 1958   K. R. A.

PREFACE

It was originally intended that the present volume should comprise a number of High Court of Admiralty documents relating to English privateering in the West Indies in the period 1585–1603, together with the relevant narratives from Hakluyt and Purchas. Before much progress had been made with the editing, however, the Hakluyt Society received from Miss I. A. Wright a bulky parcel of translations of documents in the Archivo de Indias, chiefly relating to English West Indies voyages in the years 1593–5. These were the materials for an intended sequel to her three volumes on English West Indies voyages already published by the Society, and it was with the utmost regret that we learned that Miss Wright would be unable to complete a fourth. All students of the period acknowledge the very great debt they owe to one who opened up and worked with unflagging zeal that rich quarry of information in Seville, hardly touched until then by writers on English maritime history. This debt is now to be increased, since much of Miss Wright's remaining material, which with great generosity she placed at my disposal, is incorporated in the present work. Most of all is this editor indebted, since the direct co-ordination of English and Spanish source material, though it necessitated ending this collection at the year 1595, enhances its interest and significance in no small degree. A few documents which are considered important and directly relevant have been added from other sources. For the checking, editing and annotation of all the documents herein the present editor takes full responsibility.

I wish to express my thanks to Dr José de la Peña, Director of the Archivo de Indias, for his co-operation in supplying microfilms of the Spanish documents, and to Mr G. P. B. Naish of the National Maritime Museum and Dr A. K. R. Kiralfy, reader in Law at King's College, London University, for reading the introduction before publication and offering some helpful suggestions. Above all I am indebted to Professor D. B. Quinn for his tactful encouragement and advice and to Mr R. A. Skelton,

CONTENTS

37. *Querela* of Bland, Young and others: deposition of John Cade

CHAPTER V. THE EXPEDITIONS OF 1591   *page* 95
38. The 'memorable fight' of the *Content*
39. Adjudication of the prizes: deposition of Roger Proude
40. Adjudication of the prizes: deposition of Edward Anthonison
41. Adjudication of the prizes: deposition of John de Calvete
42. Adjudication of the prizes: deposition of John Pouce
43. *Querela* of Robert Cobb concerning Watts' prizes: deposition of John de Calvete
44. *Querela* of Robert Cobb concerning Watts' prizes: deposition of John Pouce
45. Adjudication of the *Margaret*'s prize: deposition of Stephen Collomber
46. Adjudication of the *Margaret*'s prize: deposition of Diego López
47. Appraisement of the *Margaret*'s prize
48. Letter of Sir George Carey to Dr Julius Caesar
49. Carey *contra* Watts: deposition of William Lane
50. Carey *contra* Watts: deposition of Stephen Michell
51. Carey *contra* Watts: deposition of Ralph Lee
52. Carey *contra* Watts: deposition of Francis Lee
53. Carey *contra* Watts: deposition of John Brough
54. Carey *contra* Watts: deposition of John Mott
55. Carey *contra* Watts: deposition of Marmaduke Logan
56. Carey *contra* Watts: deposition of Noe Bailye
57. Carey *contra* Watts: deposition of William Drew
58. Carey *contra* Watts: deposition of James Bratholt
59. Carey *contra* Watts: deposition of Anthony Hooke
60. Carey *contra* Watts: deposition of Nicholas Dockerey
61. Carey *contra* Watts: deposition of William Bendes
62. Carey *contra* Watts: deposition of John Tilley
63. Carey *contra* Watts: deposition of Thomas Barlowe
64. Carey *contra* Watts: deposition of Robert Tilley
65. Carey *contra* Watts: deposition of John Froude
66. Carey *contra* Watts: deposition of Gideon Sanders
67. Carey *contra* Watts: deposition of Thomas Royall
68. Carey *contra* Watts: deposition of William Craston
69. Carey *contra* Watts: deposition of William Irish
70. Carey *contra* Watts: deposition of William Cradell
71. Carey *contra* Watts: deposition of Michael Geare

CONTENTS

72. Carey *contra* Watts: deposition of Thomas Gilbert
73. Carey *contra* Watts: deposition of Edward Waters
74. Carey *contra* Watts: deposition of Richard Die
75. Carey *contra* Watts: deposition of George Kennell
76. Carey *contra* Watts: deposition of Edward Pollard
77. Carey *contra* Watts: deposition of Ralph Gibson
78. Carey *contra* Watts: deposition of George Cocke
79. Carey *contra* Watts: deposition of Arthur Hill
80. Howard *contra* Watts: deposition of John Clercke
81. Howard *contra* Watts: deposition of Stephen Michell
82. Howard *contra* Watts: deposition of William Craston

CHAPTER VI. THE VOYAGE OF BENJAMIN WOOD, 1592   page 173

83. Warrant for the grant of letters of reprisal for the *Challenger*, the *Mineral* and the *Pilgrim*
84. Warrant for the grant of letters of reprisal for the *Flight*
85. Bonds taken for the good behaviour of the privateers
86. Deposition of Henry Reynolds
87. Letter to Dr Caesar from Sir John Hawkins
88. Declaration by the French ambassador concerning the *Florizant*
89. Warrant of the Lord Admiral for the grant of a commission of stay and arrest to Lord Thomas Howard

CHAPTER VII. CHRISTOPHER NEWPORT'S VOYAGE OF 1592   184

90. John Twitt's report of Newport's 1592 voyage
91. Warrant for the grant of letters of reprisal for the *Golden Dragon*, the *Prudence* and the *Virgin*
92. Bonds taken for the good behaviour of the privateers
93. The Lord Admiral *contra* Robert Thread: Thread's deposition
94. The part played by the *Golden Dragon* and the *Prudence* in the capture of the *Madre de Dios*
95. The Lord Admiral *contra* John Locke: deposition of John Estridge
96. Interrogatories for John Paul

CHAPTER VIII. THE VOYAGE OF WILLIAM KING, 1592   209

97. The Hakluyt account of King's 1592 voyage
98. Warrant for the grant of letters of reprisal for the *Salomon* and the *Jane Bonaventure*
99. Bonds taken for the good behaviour of the privateers
100. Deposition of Richard Sotherey

CONTENTS

CHAPTER IX. THE VOYAGES OF WILLIAM PARKER IN 1592
    AND 1593   *page* 219
  101. Report on the examination of prisoners captured by the
       Richard of Plymouth
  102. Interlocutory sentence of the *Catellina*
  103. Order for the delivery of the *Catellina* to Hutchins and
       Parker
  104. Report on the examination of prisoners captured by the
       Richard of Plymouth, 1593

CHAPTER X. THE VOYAGE OF SIR JOHN BURGH, 1593   225
  105. Warrant for the grant of letters of reprisal to Sir John
       Burgh
  106. Bonds taken for the good behaviour of Burgh's ships
  107. Appraisement of the *Golden Dragon*
  108. Deposition of Alonso de Ulloa de Toro
  109. Report of Francisco Gutiérrez Flores concerning Sir
       John Burgh

CHAPTER XI. THE VOYAGE OF JAMES LANGTON, 1593–4   236
  110. A report of Cumberland's seventh voyage
  111. Cumberland's prize taken by Frenchmen: deposition of
       John Yonge
  112. Langton at Cumaná: Spanish evidence
  113. Langton at Rio de la Hacha: Spanish evidence
  114. Langton on the Santo Domingo coast: Spanish report
  115. Langton on the Santo Domingo coast: deposition of
       Diego López
  116. Langton on the Santo Domingo coast: deposition of
       Alonso González
  117. Langton on the Santo Domingo coast: statement of Juan
       Caballero de Bazán
  118. Letter from the owner of an *ingenio* to his steward
  119. Report from Santo Domingo concerning the damage
       done by Langton
  120. General Spanish report on Langton's activities near
       Santo Domingo
  121. Trujillo report of Langton's raid on Puerto de Caballos

CHAPTER XII. THE *CENTAUR* AND THE LAST OF THE
    EDWARD BONAVENTURE, 1594   284
  122. Extract from Edmund Barker's narrative of the voyage

CONTENTS

of the *Penelope*, the *Merchant Royal* and the *Edward Bonaventure*

123. Tulier, Decuval and others *contra* the *Espérance* and the *Princess*: deposition of Roger Crampton
124. A prize taken by the *Centaur* near Havana: deposition of William Lane
125. Report from Santo Domingo to Spain concerning the wreck of the *Edward*
126. Further report from Santo Domingo to Spain concerning the wreck of the *Edward*

CHAPTER XIII. THE VOYAGES OF THE *GOLDEN DRAGON* AND THE *PRUDENCE*, THE *AFFECTION* AND THE *JEWEL*, 1594   page 298

127. Spanish report of raids by Langton and Newport on Puerto de Caballos
128. Interlocutory sentence of two Portuguese prizes captured by the *Dragon* and the *Prudence*
129. The consortship of the *Affection* and the *Dragon*: deposition of George Wattes
130. Watts, Myddelton and others *contra* a Spanish ship taken by the *Affection*: deposition of Thomas Sterkie
131. Watts, Myddelton and others *contra* a Spanish ship taken by the *Affection*: deposition of Thomas Pinchbacke
132. Spanish report of the capture of John Myddelton
133. Deposition of John Lawles relating to the voyage of the *Jewel*
134. Deposition of John Hammond relating to the voyage of the *Jewel*

CHAPTER XIV. THE VOYAGES OF WILLIAM PARKER, 1594 AND 1595   308

135. Deposition of Richard Bickford
136. Examination of Spanish prisoners
137. Examination of Spanish prisoners
138. Interlocutory sentence of the *Nuestra Señora de Loreto* of Cartagena
139. Interlocutory sentence of the goods taken at Puerto de Caballos
140. Trujillo report of three successive raids on Caballos
141. Official account of the Anglo-French capture of Puerto de Caballos, 1594

CONTENTS

142. Personal report of the governor, Gerónimo Sánchez de Carranza, concerning the Anglo-French capture of Puerto de Caballos in 1594
143. First report of Parker's movements in the Gulf of Honduras in 1595
144. Later report from Trujillo concerning Parker's movements
145. Further Spanish information on Parker in 1595

CHAPTER XV. THE VOYAGE OF JOHN RIDLESDEN, 1595   *page* 326
146. Deposition of John Ridlesden

CHAPTER XVI. THE VOYAGE OF MICHAEL GEARE, 1594–5   330
147. Deposition of Michael Geare
148. Deposition of James Bragge
149. The engagement with Geare's ships: report by Don Luis Fajardo from Havana
150. The engagement with Geare's ships: personal report by the Spanish commander
151. Interlocutory sentence of Geare's prize goods
152. Interrogatories for the examination of Michael Geare and his company

CHAPTER XVII. THE VOYAGE OF THE *ROSE LION*, 1594–5   338
153. Spanish prisoner's statement concerning the *Fortune*
154. Interlocutory sentence of the *Fortune* of Seville
155. Letter from Burghley and Howard to Dr Caesar
156. Appraisement of the cargo of the *Fortune*
157. Spirincke *contra* West: the libel
158. Spirincke *contra* West: deposition of William Starre
159. Spirincke *contra* West: West's allegation
160. Spirincke *contra* West: deposition of Bennet Boetto
161. Spirincke *contra* West: sentence against the plaintiffs

CHAPTER XVIII. THE VOYAGE OF PRESTON AND SOMMERS, 1595   377
162. Robert Davie's account of Preston's voyage
163. Preston at La Margarita: Spanish report
164. Preston followed by Raleigh at La Margarita: Spanish report
165. Preston at Caracas: Spanish report
166. A later Spanish account of the capture of Caracas

ILLUSTRATIONS AND MAPS

1. Sir Julius Caesar, Judge of the Admiralty   *Frontispiece*
   A portrait of 1633, copied in water colour by George Perfect Harding (d. 1853).—Illustrated Clarendon, vol. I, 39/90, Sutherland Collection, Ashmolean Museum.

2. The Thames eastward of London Bridge, about 1600   *facing p.* 20
   Claes Jansz. Visscher, Long View of London, Sheet 4.—British Museum, Department of Prints and Drawings, Crace Views, I. 16.

3. The West Indies about 1590   *facing p.* 37

4. George Carey, 2nd Lord Hunsdon   *facing p.* 86
   Miniature by Nicholas Hilliard, 1601.—Berkeley Castle.

5. Western Cuba in the late 16th century   *page* 96

6. The Gulf of Honduras   *facing p.* 196
   Detail from the map of the Audiencia of Guatemala by Juan López de Velasco, published in Antonio Herrera's *Descripcion de las Indias Occidentales* (Madrid, 1601).

7. Cumaná and La Margarita in the late 16th century   *page* 227

8. Hispaniola in the late 16th century   *page* 237

9. Sir Thomas Myddelton   *facing p.* 340
   Oil painting in the collection of Sir John Lawes, Bart., of Rothamsted.

LIST OF SOURCES CITED
showing abbreviations used in the footnotes

A. CONTEMPORARY MANUSCRIPTS

A. de I.—Archivo General de Indias, Seville:
42–1–9/4, Contratación 5109.
42–1–10/5, Contratación 5110.
53–1–15, Santo Domingo 15.
53–4–11, Santo Domingo 51.
53–6–7, Santo Domingo 73.
53–6–8, Santo Domingo 74.
53–6–15, Santo Domingo 81.
54–2–5, Santo Domingo 127.
54–2–6, Santo Domingo 128.
54–4–6, Santo Domingo 184.
54–4–8, Santo Domingo 186.
63–6–10, Guatemala 10.
63 6–39, Guatemala 39.
64–1–1, Guatemala 44.
73–1–32, Santa Fé 190.
147–5–15, Indiferente General 1866.
740–7–36, Indiferente General 742.

Appleby Castle:
'A Brief Relation of the severall voyages undertaken and performed by the right honorable George Earle of Cumberland'.

British Museum:
Additional MSS 11405, 12506, 12507, 36316, 36317.
Harleian MS 598.
Lansdowne MSS 67, 69, 70, 115, 130, 133, 134, 142, 143, 144, 145, 157, 158.
Sloane MS 2292.

Magdalene College, Cambridge:
Pepys MS 2870 (Miscellanea, vol. 2).

National Library of Wales:
Account Book: Thomas Myddelton, 'A jurnal of all owtlandishe accomptes begyninge this 14th May 1583.'

LIST OF SOURCES CITED

Public Record Office, London:
H.C.A. 1: High Court of Admiralty, Oyer et Terminer, 42, 43, 46.
H.C.A. 13: High Court of Admiralty, Examinations, 19, 22, 23, 24, 25, 26, 27, 28, 29, 30, 31, 32, 34, 35, 37, 101, 102, 143.
H.C.A. 14: High Court of Admiralty, Exemplifications, 25, 26, 27, 28, 29, 30, 31, 32, 33, 35.
H.C.A. 23: High Court of Admiralty, Interrogatories, 4.
H.C.A. 24: High Court of Admiralty, Libels, 56, 57, 58, 59, 60, 61, 62, 63, 64, 65.
H.C.A. 25: High Court of Admiralty, Letters of Marque, etc., 1 (packet 4), 2 (packet 5), 3 (packet 9).
Inquisitions Post Mortem (C. 142).
Requests 2: Court of Requests, Proceedings, 43, 240.
S.P. Dom. Eliz.: State Papers Domestic, Elizabeth, lxxvii, ccxxiv, ccxxxvii, ccxxxix, ccxlviii, cclix, cclxviii.

B. PRIMARY PRINTED SOURCES

Anderson, R. C. (ed.), *Letters of the Fifteenth and Sixteenth Centuries* (Southampton Records Society), 1921.
A.P.C. (N.S.): Dasent, J. R. (ed.), *Acts of the Privy Council (New Series)*, XVII–XX, 1898–1900.
Boteler's Dialogues: Perrin, W. G. (ed.), *Boteler's Dialogues* (Navy Records Society, LXV), 1929.
Bréard, C. et P. (ed.), *Documents rélatifs à la Marine Normande et à ses armements aux XVIᵉ et XVIIᵉ siècles pour le Canada, l'Afrique, les Antilles, le Brésil et les Indes*, Rouen, 1889.
Cal. Salis. MSS: Historical Manuscripts Commission, *Calendar of the Manuscripts of the Marquess of Salisbury Preserved at Hatfield House*, IV–V, 1892–4.
Cal. S. P. Dom. Eliz. 1595–7: *Calendar of State Papers, Domestic Series, Elizabeth, 1595–7*, 1869.
Corbett, *Spanish War*: Corbett, J. S. (ed.), *Papers relating to the Navy during the Spanish War, 1585–87* (Navy Records Society, XI), 1898.
Foster, *Voyages of Lancaster*: Foster, Sir William (ed.), *The Voyages of Sir James Lancaster to Brazil and the East Indies, 1591–1603* (Hakluyt Society, 2nd Series, LXXXV), 1940.
Further English Voyages: Wright, I. A. (ed.), *Further English Voyages to Spanish America, 1583–1594* (Hakluyt Society, 2nd Series, XCIX), 1951.
Hagthorpe, John, *England's Exchequer, or a Discourse of the Sea and Navigation*, 1625.
Hakluyt, Richard. See *Principal Navigations*.

LIST OF SOURCES CITED

Harlow, *Raleigh's Guiana*: Harlow, V. T. (ed.), *The Discoverie of the large and bewtiful Empire of Guiana, by Sir Walter Ralegh*, 1928.

Historical Manuscripts Commission, Report on the MSS of the Corporation of Southampton (11th Report, Appendix III), 1887.

Laughton, *Defeat*: Laughton, Sir J. K. (ed.), *State Papers relating to the Defeat of the Spanish Armada*, 2 vols. (Navy Records Society, I and II), 1894.

Marsden, *Law and Custom*: Marsden, R. G. (ed.), *Documents relating to the Law and Custom of the Sea*, 2 vols. (Navy Records Society, XLIX and L), 1915–16.

Marsden, *Select Pleas*: Marsden, R. G. (ed.), *Select Pleas in the Court of Admiralty*, 2 vols. (Selden Society, VI and XI), 1894 and 1897.

Monson's Tracts: Oppenheim, M. (ed.), *The Naval Tracts of Sir William Monson*, 5 vols. (Navy Records Society, XXII, XXIII, XLIII, XLV, XLVII), 1902–14.

Moule, H. J. (ed.), *Descriptive Catalogue of the Charters, Minute Books and other Documents in the Borough of Weymouth and Melcomb Regis, 1252–1800*, 1883.

Oviedo y Baños, Don Joseph de, *Historia de la Conquista y Población de la Provincia de Venezuela escrita por D. Joseph de Oviedo y Baños, vecino de la Ciudad de Santiago de León de Caracas, quien la consagra y dedica a su hermano el Señor D. Diego de Oviedo y Baños, Oidor de las Reales Audiencias de Santo Domingo, Guatemala y Mexico, del Consejo de S. M. en el Real y Supremo de las Indias*, Madrid, 1723.

Principal Navigations: Hakluyt, Richard, *The Principall navigations, voiages and discoveries of the English nation*, 3 vols., 1598–1600 (12 vols. Hakluyt Society, Extra Series, I–XII, 1903–5).

Purchas His Pilgrims: Purchas, Samuel, *Hakluytus posthumus or Purchas his pilgrimes*, 4 vols., 1625 (20 vols. Hakluyt Society, Extra Series, XIV–XXXIII, 1905–7).

Quinn, *Gilbert*: Quinn, D.B. (ed.), *The Voyages and Colonizing Enterprises of Sir Humphrey Gilbert*, 2 vols. (Hakluyt Society, 2nd Series, LXXXIII–LXXXIV), 1940.

Quinn, D. B. See *Roanoke Voyages*.

Raleigh, Sir Walter, *The History of the World*, 1614.

Roanoke Voyages: Quinn, D. B. (ed.), *The Roanoke Voyages 1584–1590*, 2 vols. (Hakluyt Society, 2nd Series, CIV–CV), 1955.

Rodríguez Demorizi, *Relaciones*: Rodríguez Demorizi, E. (ed.), *Relaciones históricos de Santo Domingo*, II (Archivo General de la Nación, IV), Ciudad Trujillo, Dominican Republic, 1945.

Simón, Fray Pedro, *Noticias Historiales de las Conquistas de Tierra Firme en las Indias Occidentales*, Bogotá, 1882.

LIST OF SOURCES CITED

Stevens, H. (ed.), *The Dawn of British Trade to the East Indies, 1599–1603* (Court Records of the East India Company), 1886.
Warner, G. F. (ed.), *The Voyage of Robert Dudley into the West Indies, 1594–5* (Hakluyt Society, 2nd Series, III), 1899.
Wright, I. A. (ed.), *Documents concerning English Voyages to the Spanish Main, 1569–1580* (Hakluyt Society, 2nd Series, LXXI), 1932.
—— ——, See *Further English Voyages*.
—— ——, *Historia Documentada de San Cristobal de la Habana*, 2 vols., 1927.

C. SECONDARY AUTHORITIES

Adams, Maxwell, 'A brief account of Ashton Church and of some of the Chudleighs of Ashton', *Transactions of the Devonshire Association*, XXXI (1899), 185–8.
Andrews, K. R., 'Appraisements of Elizabethan Privateersmen', *The Mariner's Mirror*, XXXVII (1951), 76–79.
—— ——, 'Christopher Newport of Limehouse, Mariner', *William and Mary Quarterly*, XI (1954), 28–41.
—— ——, 'The Economic Aspects of Elizabethan Privateering' (unpublished thesis in University of London Library), 1951.
Beaven, A. B., *The Aldermen of the City of London*, 2 vols., 1908–13.
Birch, J. G., *Limehouse through Five Centuries*, 1930.
Brown, Alexander, *The Genesis of the United States*, 2 vols., 1890.
Cokayne, G. E., *Some Account of the Lord Mayors and Sheriffs of the City of London*, 1897.
Cotton, R. W., 'An Elizabethan Adventurer', *Macmillan's Magazine*, LXXI (1894–5), 190–4.
D.N.B.: *Dictionary of National Biography*, 63 vols., 1885–1900.
Edwards, Edward, *The Life of Sir Walter Raleigh together with his Letters*, 2 vols., 1868.
Ewen, C. L'Estrange, *The Golden Chalice* (Paignton, privately printed), 1939.
Foster, Sir William, *England's Quest of Eastern Trade*, 1933.
Haring, C. H., *Trade and Navigation between Spain and the Indies in the Time of the Hapsburgs* (Harvard Economic Studies, XIX), 1918.
Kingsford, C. Lethbridge, 'The Taking of the Madre de Dios, Anno 1592', *The Naval Miscellany*, vol. *II* (Navy Records Society, XL), 1912.
Marsden, R. G., 'Early Prize Jurisdiction and Prize Law', *English Historical Review*, XXIV (1909), 675–97; XXV (1910), 243–63; XXVI (1911), 34–56.

NOTE ON EDITING

The nature of the High Court of Admiralty material has made it necessary to summarize certain documents and portions of others. Where this has been done it is indicated by the use of square brackets. The spelling has been left as in the original MSS, except for the modernization of the use of *i, j, u* and *v*, and the expansion of abbreviated words, with expansions shown in italics. Punctuation has been amended as little as possible, and only in the interests of clarity of meaning. In the translations from the Spanish, accents have not been added to the names of persons and places, since they are not used in the originals. Accents have been used, however, in the commentary. Dates are given in Old Style (the English usage), except in the Spanish documents, and elsewhere as indicated in the footnotes.

LIST OF SOURCES CITED

— —, 'The Vice-admirals of the Coast', *English Historical Review*, XXII (1907), 468–77.
Myddelton, W. H., *Pedigree of the Family of Myddelton* (Horncastle), 1910.
Nicholl, John, *Some Account of the Worshipful Company of Ironmongers*, 1851.
Pole, Sir William, *Collections towards a Description of the County of Devon*, 1791.
Ruddock, A., 'The Earliest Records of the High Court of Admiralty, 1515–1558', *Bulletin of the Institute of Historical Research*, XXIII (1950), 139–51.
Sluiter, Engel, 'Dutch-Spanish Rivalry in the Caribbean, 1594–1609', *Hispanic American Historical Review*, XXVIII (1948), 165–96.
Smyth, W. H., *The Sailor's Word-Book, an Alphabetical Digest of Nautical Terms*, 1867.
Swanton, J. R., *The Indians of the Southeastern United States* (Bureau of American Ethnology, Bulletin 137), Washington, 1946.
— —, *The Early History of the Creek Indians and their Neighbours* (Bureau of American Ethnology, Bulletin 73), Washington, 1922.
Taylor, E. G. R., *Late Tudor and Early Stuart Geography, 1583–1650*, 1934.
Williamson, G. C., *George, Third Earl of Cumberland*, 1920.

cases, rested in the last resort with the political authorities.[1]

We may now proceed to examine more closely the types of business dealt with by the court, before describing in detail the records thereby deposited.[2] An important source of revenue for the Lord Admiral were his droits, which were chiefly asserted by the vice-admirals and their deputies—officers appointed by the Lord Admiral for the maritime counties.[3] The Lord Admiral was entitled to unclaimed wrecks, flotsam, derelict property, deodand, whales and other royal fish and various other types of goods, including a share of goods legitimately captured from enemies. In the securing of these droits, however, the Lord Admiral met with many difficulties. The goods in question usually fell into other hands in the first place and the possessors were not easily persuaded to yield up their gains, however come by. As for the vice-admiralty officials, they had neither the resources nor, in many cases, the inclination, to apply the strict letter of the law. They were, of course, entitled to a share of the droits, but it often paid them better to come to terms with the possessors and forget the claims of the Lord Admiral. In the last resort, therefore, the Lord Admiral relied for the assertion of his droits upon the High Court of Admiralty. Where evasion of his jurisdiction was suspected the court instituted *ex officio* proceedings analogous to the inquisitions of office concerning the droits of the crown. Such proceedings are of particular interest to us when they concern the securing of the Lord Admiral's tenths of prizes.

[1] The interest of the Privy Council may be seen, for example, in chs. III and XVII below.

[2] The best account of the court is to be found in the introductions to the two volumes of R. G. Marsden, *Select Pleas in the Court of Admiralty* (Selden Society, VI and XI, 1894 and 1897). See also R. G. Marsden, *Documents relating to the Law and Custom of the Sea* (Navy Records Society, XLIX and L, 1915–16); R. G. Marsden, 'Early Prize Jurisdiction and Prize Law', *English Historical Review*, XXIV (1909), 675–97; XXV (1910), 243–63; XXVI (1911), 34–56; A. Ruddock, 'The Earliest Records of the High Court of Admiralty, 1515-1558', *Bulletin of the Institute of Historical Research*, XXIII (1950), 139–51.

[3] The vice-admirals were usually men of some importance and their work was normally carried out by deputies. These saw to arrests of ships and individuals, bound individuals to appear in court, made inventories of ships and cargoes, collected the Lord Admiral's tenths, examined witnesses by commission of the court, executed the sentences of the court, took bonds from privateers for good behaviour at sea, etc. Apart from such manifold activities, the vice-admiralties were chiefly concerned with the Lord Admiral's droits. See R. G. Marsden, 'The Vice-admirals of the Coast,' *English Historical Review*, XXII (1907), 468–77.

MATERIALS

it was the court of the Lord Admiral, through which he exercised the authority granted to him by the crown, and essentially the broad and varied character of Admiralty Court business reflected the breadth and variety of the powers and functions of the Lord Admiral. Thus it was not merely a court of law, but an administrative instrument with a considerable executive apparatus. This was the machinery used by the Lord Admiral to exert his control in matters of prize, spoil and piracy and to implement his droits in cases of wreck, deodand, etc. The proper execution of these functions was a source of profit to the Lord Admiral. Nor was the court's connection with a great officer a purely formal matter. The judge was the Lord Admiral's deputy and received instructions from him in matters particular and general. Even in the time of Dr Julius Caesar and Charles, Lord Howard of Effingham,[1] the court still bore the character of a great feudal franchise, a sphere of patronage and personal profit to the great nobleman, managed on his behalf by his servant, the eminent and learned judge.[2] The distinction between the judicial and administrative powers of the Lord Admiral is, however, largely theoretical; in practice they were connected in many ways, and in each particular sphere of the court's business the administrative and judicial functions are to be found side by side, or actually merging to become virtually indistinguishable. Many of the peculiarities of the court—and consequently of its records—have their origin in this characteristic duality.

The interest of the Lord Admiral in the court was also political. The prize jurisdiction of the court made it the arena of many a dispute between English and foreign merchants, behind whom stood their respective governments. Many a problem concerning the law of prize, the law of neutrality, the rights of belligerents and the freedom of the seas was involved in the deliberations of the court, and in all such matters the Privy Council (of which the Lord Admiral was a member) took a deep interest, repeatedly infringing the province of the court. In fact the decision in all such questions, whether concerned with general policy or individual

---

[1] Caesar was judge of the High Court of Admiralty from 1584 to 1636 and Howard was Lord High Admiral from 1585 to 1618.

[2] The correspondence between them vividly illustrates this (e.g. Lansdowne MS. 157, *passim*).

The Spanish documents, twenty-eight in number, are, with two exceptions,[1] selected from translations made by Miss I. A. Wright. All but one are from the Archivo General de Indias in Seville, and all relate to the last three years of the period, 1593 to 1595. The last of Miss Wright's Hakluyt Society volumes[2] included a number of Spanish documents relating to English West Indian voyages from 1588 to 1592—complementary to the English material in the first nine chapters of this present volume and frequently referred to herein. This Spanish evidence is not merely useful corroborative or additional information, but gives to the whole picture, as well as to individual voyages, something like an extra dimension. Official reports and investigations, as well as private letters, give us a measure of the impact, psychological and economic, naval and military, of ventures which, in the laconic accounts of English seamen, seem almost routine. The English may give more of the matter-of-fact details, and give them more accurately, but the Spanish provide more of the colour, the excitement and the heat of battle—more, too, of the parleys, illicit trading and intrigue. They tend to exaggerate the scale of the attack and enemy casualties, but rarely to such an extent as to discredit the substance of the story; only once or twice are panicky rumours repeated; far more often the authorities somehow obtained and forwarded valuable intelligence about the corsairs' strength and movements. Above all, the Spanish reports enable us, as no English material can, to weigh the significance of these depredations in the general struggle between Spain and England in the nineties and in the longer-term struggle for supremacy in the Caribbean.

The vast majority of the documents below, however, are drawn from the records of the High Court of Admiralty, and require for their understanding and interpretation some account of the court itself.

In the later sixteenth century the High Court of Admiralty had an extremely wide jurisdiction, and though the boundaries of its power were constantly being challenged by other courts, it dealt in practice with a great variety of business. As its name suggests,

[1] Documents 165 and 166 below.
[2] *Further English Voyages to Spanish America, 1583–1594* (Hakluyt Society, 2nd Series, XCIX, 1951).

INTRODUCTION

I. THE MATERIALS

ENGLISH voyages to the West Indies in the period 1588 to 1595, between the defeat of the Armada and the last voyage of Sir Francis Drake, were, as far as is known, all privateering ventures. Twenty-five of them are dealt with here, and though there were undoubtedly others, very little is known about them, with two important exceptions.[1]

Three main sources provide almost all the documents presented: contemporary printed narratives from Hakluyt; the Archivo General de Indias in Seville; and the records of the High Court of Admiralty in the Public Record Office, London. The Hakluyt narratives were all first published in 1600 in the third volume of the second edition of the *Principal Navigations*. Hakluyt in the dedication of this volume claimed to be revealing the 'secrets of the West Indies' fallen into English hands as a result of the wars with Spain; and such secrets he did reveal, not only in the Spanish rutters describing the West Indies proper, but in many reports relating to the 'West Indies' in the larger sense of the New World. In general, however, the privateering expeditions with which we are concerned were not of much geographical significance; Hakluyt included them rather to illustrate the valour of Englishmen and the glory of their exploits. Such patriotic inclinations did in one instance lead him to accept a somewhat tendentious version of one episode—the fight of the *Black Dog* and its ugly sequel—but as a rule his judgement was sound and the reports he published are strikingly corroborated by the other evidence.

---

[1] The two exceptions are the 1594 voyage of Sir Robert Dudley and the expedition promoted by John Watts in 1590, both of which have been fully described and documented in earlier volumes of the Hakluyt Society (G. F. Warner, *The Voyage of Robert Dudley into the West Indies, 1594–5* (Hakluyt Society, 2nd Series, III, 1899); D. B. Quinn, *The Roanoke Voyages 1584–1590* (Hakluyt Society, 2nd Series, CIV, CV, 1955), pp. 579–716).

MATERIALS

By long established custom the Lord Admiral had the right to a share of all prizes and during the war with Spain this share was fixed at one tenth. Although the details of how the tenths were levied and disposed remain in some respects obscure, it is quite certain that they were collected in our period.[1] Some of the proceeds, at any rate, came to the Lord Admiral, as is shown by a surviving account of the tenths received between 1587 and 1598.[2] However, there was a great deal of evasion of payment—the prize goods were sometimes sold abroad, but more often smuggled into the country.

In such circumstances the Lord Admiral would have great difficulty in recovering his droits, but his hand was strengthened to some extent in this particular context by the connection between the tenths and his general jurisdiction in matters of prize. For captains and masters were obliged to bind themselves, before departing on a privateering cruise, to render up a tenth of their prizes on returning to port. If they were suspected of evading this payment, the Lord Admiral could and often did institute proceedings against them. Essentially and in form the Lord Admiral in such proceedings was pursuing his droits, but the case involved the implication that the seaman concerned had violated the conditions laid down in his bond and would be liable to pay the value of the bond in penalty. The offender would be cited to appear before the judge and answer articles drawn up on behalf of the Lord Admiral. Statements might also be taken from those suspected of having received the 'embezzled' goods. Drafts and

---

[1] It was one of the tasks of the vice-admiralty officials to collect the tenths in their respective jurisdictions, but the job was sometimes taken over by other individuals. Sir John Hawkins, for example, collected the tenths for the Devon area for a time (Lansdowne MS 144, f. 36 and 157, ff. 430, 434).

[2] Harleian MS 598. This volume was evidently compiled by a personal secretary to Lord Howard and lay for some years at his home in Reigate, Surrey. It is an account of the goods received on behalf of the Lord Admiral as tenths. For each prize a separate entry is made, usually identifying the privateer, its owners, the captain and master, indicating the nature of the prize-goods and giving a more detailed inventory of that portion of the cargo allocated as the tenth. Some account of the sale and disposal of the tenth is included and the price for which it was sold. Alongside the price the following items for deduction are sometimes entered: the expenses of cartage, storage, etc., involved in dealing with the tenth; the amount of customs paid on the tenth; and the sum due to the author of the account for his twentieth share of the tenth. The account is not complete and the author is not known, but the manuscript is of great importance for the study of privateering.

copies of the articles for such examinations survive in the court records, as well as the related depositions, which are marginally marked 'Officium domini contra...' (giving the name of the offender). This kind of *ex officio* process was employed also in prosecuting individuals for contempt, often consisting in the denial of the court's jurisdiction.[1]

We have already alluded to the Lord Admiral's jurisdiction in matters of prize. This jurisdiction, which developed greatly in importance in the sixteenth century, originated in the disciplinary powers of the admiral over his fleet, which had been extended in various ways in the course of time, so that from 1589 the powers of the Lord Admiral included the right to issue letters of reprisal, to regulate the conduct of ships of reprisal and to adjudicate the prizes captured by them. These functions formed an important part of the work of the Admiralty Court during the war with Spain. General rules for their exercise were laid down by the Privy Council in 1585 and modified thereafter.[2]

Private citizens who wished to engage the enemy on their own account, by sending out what later came to be called 'privateers', were normally, from 1585 to 1603, entitled to do so only in redress of private wrongs suffered at the hands of Spain or Spanish subjects. A minority of privileged persons like the Earl of Cumberland and John Chidley were able to obtain special commissions from the Queen, issued as letters patent, but the majority had to obtain letters of reprisal from the Lord Admiral. The full procedure for obtaining letters of reprisal required the prospective grantee to submit to the court a *querela*, or complaint, in the form of a pleading, and to bring forward witnesses to support it.[3] The object of the *querela* proceeding was to prove that losses had been sustained at the hands of Spain or Spanish subjects and that the plaintiff was consequently entitled to letters of reprisal which would license him to recoup his losses upon Spanish shipping and

[1] Cp. the articles of contempt brought against Richard Lewes (ch. III below); also Marsden, *Select Pleas*, I, 83–8 and 206–10.

[2] For the 1585 regulations, see Corbett, *Spanish War*, pp. 36–8.

[3] In *querela* cases the process was *pro testibus ad perpetuam rei memoriam* and there was no defence. The aim of the process was to establish by witnesses a right or claim of some sort. The form of the pleading is indicated in document 25 below. In most instances we have no formal statement of the plaintiff's case, but frequently the articles, drawn up in the form of questions, upon which witnesses were examined, have survived, together with the depositions.

goods. In such suits there was, of course, no defence. But it is difficult to say how far this procedure was actually observed. That merchants did in fact appear before the court and make proof of losses is certain: a number of them had to enter into bonds in £100 to make proof of losses[1] and there exists a list, dated 1590, of 'men warned to make proofe of theare losses had in Spaine'; there are depositions in connection with such proceedings and sentences of the court in favour of the plaintiffs;[2] indeed, the warrants of the Lord Admiral authorizing the issue of letters of reprisal were often endorsed with a statement of the amount of losses sustained. But it is known that in some cases the obligation to prove losses was expressly waived; written pleadings in connection with such proceedings are very hard to find; and there is a great disparity between the number of sentences traceable and the number of grants of letters of reprisal. By and large it is evident that the obligation to prove losses became less serious soon after 1585 and that formal pleadings and sentences were increasingly dispensed with. In the circumstances of the time the laxity of the court in this respect is hardly surprising. There is no indication that anyone who applied for letters of reprisal was ever refused[3] and there is only one known case of the withdrawal of letters of reprisal on the grounds that the grantee had recovered more than he had lost.[4] Many of the merchant promoters of privateering must have recovered far more than their losses and yet apparently found no difficulty in getting their letters renewed.

When these preliminary formalities had been discharged, the Lord Admiral sent a warrant to the judge, requesting him to make out letters of reprisal in favour of the person or persons concerned. These warrants were usually endorsed with some particulars concerning the proposed expedition; items frequently mentioned were: the names and tonnages of the vessels, the number of their crews, the number of pieces of ordnance, the period for which they were victualled and the amount of the losses

---

[1] For such a bond see Marsden, *Law and Custom*, I, 251–2.
[2] A sentence in such a case is given in Marsden, *Select Pleas*, II, 165–7.
[3] Perhaps the judge's attitude was influenced by the fee of 13/4d. which he received for every grant. The grants were usually made for six months, so that the court derived a regular income from this aspect of its activities.
[4] Marsden, *Law and Custom*, I, 289. In this instance it is clear that the privateer was abusing his grant and becoming a nuisance.

claimed by the promoters. The warrants are not always endorsed, however, and those that are endorsed do not often give all this information.

Having acquired, in letters of reprisal, licence to set forth a vessel or vessels, those responsible for the venture, or simply the captains and masters, had to enter into bonds, in the form of recognizances, to pay to the Lord Admiral a specified sum (in our period usually £3000 for each ship) unless they adhered to certain rules. These obliged them to repair with all possible speed, after putting to sea, to the coasts of Spain and Portugal, the Azores and other remote places where Spanish and Portuguese subjects most frequently traded; not to attempt anything against her majesty's subjects or the subjects of princes in league and amity with her; to bring their prizes into such port of her majesty's realm as should be most convenient for them; not to break bulk before the vice-admiralty or other authorized officials had inventoried and appraised the prize goods; and to surrender a tenth of the prize goods to the Lord Admiral's officers. From 1589 the recognizances contained the additional proviso that the prize goods should be adjudicated and from 1591 a further emendation obliged captors to bring home with the prize goods members of the crew of each prize. Such a bond would be made out by the court and submitted by an officer of the court or vice-admiralty to the captain and master of the ship concerned, to be signed by them.[1] If there were several ships in an expedition there would be an equivalent number of bonds. These bonds were not very effective in regulating the conduct of expeditions. Seamen who risked their lives for booty were not as a rule scrupulous about leaving it intact until it had been taxed and pilfered by admiralty men. However, the machinery was not entirely futile: inventories and appraisements were made and tenths were in many, if not all cases paid.

In 1589 the Privy Council's regulations for the control of privateering were modified, provision being made for the adjudication of prizes. The full procedure, which took the form of a *querela*, required the claimant to appear personally before the judge, to make a statement and to produce witnesses to prove that the ship and goods taken belonged to the king of Spain or

[1] The full text of a recognizance is given below, pp. 178–9.

Spanish subjects, were captured by virtue of letters of reprisal and were therefore lawful prize. The witnesses were frequently Spanish seamen captured with the prize and their depositions would be duly recorded. In the statements of plaintiff and witnesses a brief description of the prize and its contents would be given. The judge, having duly considered these statements, would promulgate his interlocutory decree condemning the ship and goods as lawful prize.[1] This sentence was provisional, but if not challenged within a year would have the force of a final decree. The court would then issue instructions to the vice-admiralty or other local officials concerned, who were supposed in the meantime to have inventoried and appraised the prize, to deliver the same to the captors. Interlocutory sentences adjudicating prizes become quite frequent from 1589, but the perfunctory character of the proceedings prior to sentence is indicated by the poverty of the material relating to them, either in the form of summary reports of proceedings or in the form of depositions.[2] There survive a few depositions made before local officials and sent up to the court, these depositions being accompanied in the court records by a copy of the sentence, but how widely this procedure was employed it is impossible to say. The records of inventories and appraisements of prizes made by local officials are also rather thin and it seems likely that the indentures were frequently not (as it was stipulated they should be in the Privy Council regulations) returned to the court.

A large part of the business of the court consisted of spoil and piracy cases, concerned with attacks by English seamen upon foreign or English shipping. Usually the matter came to the notice of the court through the Privy Council or the Lord Admiral, to whom the plaintiff first submitted a petition. The plaintiff would then be granted a warrant for the arrest of the goods as his own, citing the detainers to appear and answer him in civil and maritime cause. The goods would be arrested on the authorization of the court and if the detainers failed to appear to defend the case, the goods would eventually be adjudged to the plaintiff. If the case was defended, the goods might be seques-

---

[1] The full text of an interlocutory sentence of a prize is given below, pp. 221–2.

[2] Depositions of this kind are not uncommon, but there are many sentences for which we have no related depositions.

trated by the court, appraised and, if perishable, sold. The case would continue as a civil action between the plaintiff and the defendant, and the goods, or their proceeds, would be adjudged to the successful party. All spoil cases, once the action was joined, were governed by the rules of practice obtaining in other civil suits, described below.

Independently of such civil proceedings, there might be a criminal prosecution of the spoilers for piracy, beginning with their arrest and imprisonment. The criminal jurisdiction of the court was, however, distinct from the civil, and most of the records relating to criminal cases were kept in a separate series.[1]

We have now broached a distinct and very important part of the court's business, a part less directly connected with the functions and rights of the Lord Admiral as an officer of state: civil suits in all kinds of mercantile and maritime affairs, including disputes relating to shipping, insurance, freight, bills of lading, seamen's wages and many other matters, some of them connected with privateering ventures. In these suits the High Court of Admiralty developed and administered its peculiar blend of civil and customary law, but the procedure and practice were chiefly characteristic of the civil law and closely resembled those of the ecclesiastical courts. The lawyers—judge, deputy judges and proctors—were civilians, the deputy judges being appointed from the doctors of Doctors' Commons.

The plaintiff initiated a civil action by securing the judge's warrant for the arrest of the defendant, who had to produce sureties to give bonds for his appearance before the judge at a time specified. If the defendant could not be found, goods of his within the court's jurisdiction might be arrested and the defendant cited to appear. If he failed to appear after the third proclamation, the arrested goods would be adjudged to the plaintiff. If he appeared, he could then produce sureties to give bonds for his appearance and would regain possession of the goods, the case proceeding normally. Both plaintiff and defendant had to produce sureties to enter into bonds that they would prosecute or defend the suit, appear as required in court, ratify the acts of their respec-

---

[1] As these records (H.C.A. 1) have yielded nothing of significance in connection with this particular period of privateering, there is little point in discussing them here. They are of course useful for other periods.

tive proctors and abide by the sentence of the court. These preliminaries were duly summarized, as they occurred, in the current Act Book, the detailed record of the business of the court.

The next stage was the submission of the *libel* by the plaintiff's proctor.[1] The libel, the plaintiff's pleading, began with a formal statement of the identity of the parties and of the nature of the pleading. A series of *articles*[2] followed, stating the case in detail, item by item; and at some stage, usually towards the end, the relief which the plaintiff sought was specified. Attached to the libel there might be one or more documents, such as schedules of goods, or other written evidence mentioned in the libel. The aim of the plaintiff was to prove the truth of the libel; the defendant's aim was to demonstrate its falsity. The libel would first be put to the defendant, who would have to admit or deny the truth of each article in turn, and might do so with comments, giving his reasons for denying this or that article. These *responsa personalia* of the defendant would be taken down in writing and signed by him.

It now rested with the plaintiff to prove the truth of the articles denied by the defendant,[3] and this he would attempt by producing witnesses, who would be examined on oath as to the truth of each article of the libel in turn.[4] The *depositions* thus made were recorded by a clerk of the court and signed by the *deponents*. The witnesses also had to answer any questions (called *interrogatories*) put to them on behalf of the defendant, such interrogatories being submitted to the court by the defendant's proctor and put

[1] The full text of a libel is given below, pp. 345-52.

[2] These were sometimes called 'positions', but never consistently. For example, the defendant's reply to the libel might be headed 'responsa personalia ... facta posicionibus libelli', or 'posicionibus et articulis libelli', and in the course of the replies phrases such as 'non credit articulum esse verum' would be used. The reason for this inconsistency was that originally the libel had contained both positions and articles, the former stating the case and the latter being designed as a basis for the examination of witnesses. In the course of time the positions and articles of the libel became confused and in our period each paragraph of the libel, after the formal pleading, was usually called an article.

[3] If the defendant admitted the truth of any articles in the libel, the plaintiff would not need witnesses to prove them. In practice, of course, the defendant normally denied everything conceivably deniable.

[4] This was the normal procedure. Sometimes, however, articles in the form of questions based upon the libel would be drawn up and used for the examination of witnesses. For example, in Watts *contra* Morgan plaintiff's witnesses deposed, not on the libel, but on special articles. See below, pp. 306-7.

to the witnesses (now called *respondents*) by a clerk. The replies were likewise recorded and signed.

However, the defendant usually wished to bring forward witnesses of his own, and in order to do so he might submit a pleading of his own, called a *materia*, similar in form to the libel, which, without denying the contents of the libel, aimed to destroy its force, usually by showing that the libel was legally inapplicable. The procedure following the submission of the libel would now be repeated for the materia: the plaintiff had to reply personally to the articles of the materia, witnesses were examined on the truth of the articles and the plaintiff could have the defendant's witnesses cross-examined. A materia was a form of *allegation*—the term applied to all pleadings subsequent to the libel. A simpler type of allegation was a series of articles stating the defendant's case and implicitly denying the truth of the libel. The same procedure would be followed here. Further pleadings might follow, but there was rarely more than one after the libel. On the other hand either party might desire to bring forward fresh witnesses to make additional points during the course of an action, and they could evidently do this simply by submitting to the court a series of articles in the form of questions, in answer to which the witnesses made depositions.

After all this documentation had been completed, the case was heard before the judge on an appointed day, and later a day was appointed for the hearing of the sentence. This rehearsed briefly what had been proved and in due form promulgated the judge's decision, being signed by the judge.[1]

Such were the main types of business with which the court dealt, and we may now consider more closely the character and value of the records arising. The material itself, which is kept in the Public Record Office in London, is voluminous. The very nature of the proceedings, in which the court itself assumed direct control, required that the clerical record of a cause should make available to the judge a detailed knowledge of all its circumstances and judicial stages. Thus the court itself should have had at its disposal a full written record of every cause when it came up for

---

[1] The full text of a sentence is given below, pp. 373–6. It was apparently the practice for each party to submit the decree it desired, and for the judge to sign the one submitted by the successful party.

teering, is not widely realised, even today. This is partly due to the difficulty of the material, for although a number of scholars have used the simplest and most rewarding series, the Examinations, few have penetrated the Libels files. Nevertheless it is worth the effort to draw together the material from each of the main series, for the result often provides an illuminating picture of the background of a venture and sometimes of the voyage itself. As the documents printed below demonstrate, it is frequently possible to reconstruct, from High Court of Admiralty sources, the course of a voyage about which little or nothing was previously known.

II. PRIVATEERING DURING THE SPANISH WAR

'For they [the Spanish] have good cause to remember, how they were baited in the Queenes time: there being never lesse then 200 sayle of voluntaries and others, upon their coastes.' So wrote John Hagthorpe in 1625,[1] and this was no great exaggeration. In the years 1589 to 1591, for example, at least 235 English vessels made privateering voyages, ranging all the seas southward from the Channel to Cape Verde and westward to the Americas.[2] The majority haunted the coasts of Spain and Portugal, but there were usually some in the region of the Azores and a few cruising the Caribbean. They sailed most often singly or in twos, though consortships made at sea might bring together half a dozen or more and a large expedition would normally attract to itself a number of fellow-travellers. On the longer voyages, of course, particularly on West Indies voyages, the single ship rarely went without a pinnace, and expeditions of three or four ships were the rule rather than the exception.

The most common type of English privateer in the Spanish war was the ordinary merchantman of some fifty to a hundred tons burden, commonly referred to as a 'bark', strengthened in striking power by the addition of guns and men, but not converted by rebuilding or any major alterations. Such were the

[1] John Hagthorpe, *England's Exchequer, or a Discourse of the Sea and Navigation* (1625), p. 25.
[2] 'Elizabethan Privateering', pp. 39–43. The Ph.D. thesis here cited has been drawn upon to a considerable extent for this part of the introduction.

MATERIALS

Very occasionally, however, a personal reply may be of great historical interest.[1] The Interrogatories are files of the lists of questions submitted for the cross-examination of witnesses. They are incomplete, partly because many such lists have migrated to the Libels files.

The Exemplifications are smaller and neater files than the Libels, being compiled by much the same method, but containing only paper documents—often copies or drafts. Much of the material consists of correspondence: instructions to the vice-admiralty and other local officials concerning the arrest, inventory and appraisement of ships and cargoes, the delivery of goods as adjudged by the court, the arrest of pirates; letters from the Lord Admiral and the Privy Council concerning all manner of affairs, general and particular, within the scope of the court; but there are also interlocutory sentences of prizes, articles for the examination of witnesses and other miscellaneous documents. The majority of the documents in the files for our period are connected with matters of prize, and the series is of considerable value to the historian, though the state of preservation of the documents varies considerably and some, especially at the top and bottom of each file, have partly or wholly crumbled away.

The Letters of Marque, Bonds, etc., are large bundles containing warrants of the Lord Admiral for the grant of letters of reprisal, bonds of individuals to make proof of losses, bonds for the good behaviour of ships of reprisal, letters connected with such warrants and bonds, and various other documents relating to administrative matters.[2] Only one of these bundles[3] concerns our period, and some of the material in it could not be used, owing to its state of disrepair. The rest covers the period from March 1590 to February 1593. Similar material for the following years does not appear to exist. The available documents, however, are of great interest. They enable us to identify ships, promoters, captains and masters engaged in privateering ventures and often give definite information about the tonnage, armament and crew.

The importance of the records of the High Court of Admiralty for the study of maritime history, and more particularly of priva-

---

[1] For example, the personal replies of Martin Pring (H.C.A. 13/104, 8 July 1602).
[2] Appointments of vice-admiralty officers, for example.
[3] H.C.A. 25/3.

have either been folded to fit the file (with consequent damage) or blackened at the edges and bottom to the point of illegibility. Sometimes the articles presenting the substance of a case would be in English, as the attached documents often were, but normally pleadings and sentences were written in Latin. A pleading would often be endorsed with the title of the case (x *contra* y), the name of the proctor submitting it and the date of submission. Sentences were also endorsed as having been passed and read on a certain date. Interrogatories, articles for the examination of witnesses, appraisements of ships, interlocutory sentences of prizes, depositions forwarded to the court by local officials, and many other documents connected with the suits before the court are also to be found in the files. For the study of any particular civil suit a close search of these files is therefore necessary; but it will probably not yield all the connected documents, since the files are by no means complete; and the search may be tedious, because the documents relating to a particular case may be scattered throughout several files.

The volumes of Examinations were presumably compiled by a clerk, who appears to have written the depositions and replies one after another into the same volume in the order in which the witnesses were actually examined, noting (or forgetting to note) in the margin the suit to which each statement referred. Each deposition would be signed by the witness (and, if the witness could not speak English, by the interpreter). The importance of the depositions hardly needs stressing: in every type of admiralty cause the sworn testimony played a vital part. Although the record is not complete, as may be seen from a comparison of the entries in the Act Books with those in the Examinations, these volumes provide the historian with a wealth of fascinating detail concerning all kinds of maritime affairs. Deponents of course contradict each other as to the matters at issue, but there is always much that is incidental, assumed, agreed, or established beyond reasonable doubt.

The Answers are also volumes of signed statements—the personal replies of the parties to the pleadings of adverse parties. Again these are incomplete and the total bulk is very much smaller than that of the Examinations. Nor are the statements so interesting, for they are usually little more than denials with comments.

decision. A large bulk of material consequently accumulated, but unfortunately it was not carefully or systematically preserved and has come down to us in an incomplete, ill-sorted and unkempt state. No attempt seems to have been made at the time to sort or index the material and little has been done in these respects since.

Although there is some confusion and overlapping between the various classes of Admiralty Court records, the material did fall, like a kind of deposit, into certain main groups, as follows: the Act Books (the day to day record of all judicial business done in the court);[1] the Libels (pleadings, articles, sentences and a variety of other documents);[2] the Examinations (a continuous record of depositions of witnesses);[3] the Answers (personal replies of the parties);[4] the Interrogatories (questions for the cross-examination of the witnesses);[5] the Exemplifications (miscellaneous, often copies or drafts);[6] the Letters of Marque, Bonds, etc. (warrants, bonds and other material relating to letters of reprisal).[7]

The Act Books are the most complete and the best preserved of all the series. In these stout volumes was entered, in Latin, a day to day summary of every judicial act of the court: the appearance of parties before the judge, the swearing of witnesses, the appointment of days for hearing cases, the submission of pleadings—all stages up to the delivery of sentence were noted. These volumes therefore provide the best guide to the progress of any suit and can be of considerable help in tracing the relevant material in other series.

The Libels are large files of documents which were evidently, when no longer required, placed face upwards, in no particular order, on a steadily accumulating pile, tied together at the end of a year and numbered consecutively. The main documents in these files are pleadings, with attached schedules or other written evidence, and sentences. They are usually of parchment and vary in size, the pleadings in particular often being so large that they

---

[1] H.C.A. 3. [2] H.C.A. 24. [3] H.C.A. 13. [4] H.C.A. 13.
[5] H.C.A. 23. Interrogatories and special articles.
[6] H.C.A. 14.
[7] H.C.A. 25. The series known as *Miscellanea* (H.C.A. 30) does not contain anything of interest for this study; there are several other series containing matter relating to this period, but of little historical value, except perhaps to the legal historian.

of tonnage, the share of London would be considerably greater. And London merchants had a correspondingly large share in the financing and organization of privateering.

The setting forth of a privateer required considerable capital, particularly for the initial venture, when the ship, supposing it already existed as a merchantman, would have to be suitably equipped and armed, as well as provided with victuals, powder, shot and other stores sufficient for a six months cruise. Except in some of the large expeditions and trading ventures, the crews were not paid wages, but took between them a third share of prizes in addition to 'pillage'. But the other items were expensive. The lesser privateer, like the *Black Dog*, would be worth two or three hundred pounds without her armament and stores; her cast pieces and small arms, together with powder, shot, match, etc., would account for another hundred or so; and victuals, together with candles, wood and other stores, would bring the outlay for the initial venture up to five or six hundred pounds, including the value of the ship. Consequently, even in ventures consisting of one small ship, the joint-stock system of investment was used more often than not. In many cases there were two or more joint owners, and they would contribute proportionately to the setting forth—'every man for his part'. In other cases part or all of the victualling expenses would be met by other venturers—sometimes by the captain, who in any case might well be a part-owner.

The capital outlay required appears to have risen progressively with the size of the ship. Chidley's 340-ton *White Lion*, for example, probably cost the owner altogether four or five thousand pounds, including the cost of her rebuilding. This was perhaps excessive, even for such a large ship, but a total outlay of three thousand pounds for a three hundred ton privateer, including over a thousand for expendable provisions, was reasonable.[1] While the outport merchants rarely had such large vessels at their disposal, the Londoners were already using numbers of them in trade, and could easily convert them into powerful privateers. Expenses would still be high, however, and the London merchants formed joint stocks among themselves to meet them, similar in structure and practices to joint stocks for smaller ventures. The *Rose Lion* in 1595, for example, had eight share-

[1] 'Elizabethan Privateering', p. 71.

was probably superior to any merchantman in design and armament, particularly because Raleigh strongly opposed the older fashion of high-charged ships. The performance of the *Anthony* at Puerto de Caballos also suggests a well-armed man-of-war.[1] Such vessels, though few in number, were often to the fore in the more ambitious expeditions, including those to the West Indies.

The smallest type of privateer was the pinnace. The term was used vaguely to indicate any small ship of up to about fifty tons burden, but it had often the special implication that the vessel was equipped with oars as well as sails. In West Indies privateering pinnaces were most useful, for they could often carry out actions for which a major ship was unsuited, and much of the coastal raiding and inshore operations characteristic of Caribbean warfare inevitably fell to such light craft. Those of the larger kind— roughly from twenty to fifty tons burden—resembled in most respects the *Fortunatus* of London, which, with a saker, two minions and two falcons, was better armed than the *Black Dog*.[2] She also carried fifteen oars, her own boat, and nettings for defence against boarders. That such a pinnace could hold its own against very powerful ships was heroically proved by the twenty-three men of Carey's *Content*, armed with only a saker, a minion, a falcon and two port-bases, in the engagement off Cape Corrientes in 1591.[3] Even the smaller type of pinnace, like Cumberland's twelve-ton *Discovery*, could survive long separation from the parent ship.[4]

A feature of the shipping engaged in West Indian privateering which may cause surprise is the overwhelming predominance of Londoners. There are forty-one ships mentioned herein whose port of origin has been traced; thirty-one were from London, six from Southampton and the neighbouring ports, two from Plymouth, one from Bristol and one from Weymouth. The pattern here does not reflect the general distribution of privateers, but even among privateers in general London ships accounted for about a third of the numbers at the beginning of the war and for about half by the end of it. If the comparison were made in terms

[1] Document 110 below.
[2] *The Mariner's Mirror*, loc. cit.
[3] Document 38 below.
[4] Document 110 below.

growing during the war and the proportion of really large vessels also grew. The *Merchant Royal* (350 tons) and the *Edward Bonaventure*, both Levant Company ships and Londoners, were typical of the largest, the *Golden Dragon* (150–180 tons) and the *Salomon* (200 tons) of the intermediate class. They might be employed in trade or in privateering or even in major naval expeditions, such as Drake's raid on Cadiz in 1587. Several of them did valuable service in the Armada campaign. Sometimes they would be sent on a trading voyage with instructions to spend a part of the time cruising for prizes.

In fighting power they were probably little inferior to the Queen's ships of their size, and they certainly gave a good account of themselves in more than one encounter with Spanish galleys. The frequent references to such vessels as 'tall ships' and such pictorial evidence as is available suggest that they were high-charged, built up with high fore and aftercastles. The rig seems to have been of the conventional kind, with six sails—spritsail, foresail, foretopsail, mainsail, maintopsail and mizensail, as shown in the inventories of the *Golden Dragon* and the *White Lion*.[1] They carried substantial armament, occasionally including culverins (18 pounders), but usually headed by demi-culverins (10 pounders), backed by sakers (5½ pounders) and lesser guns, with numerous muskets, calivers, harquebuses, pikes, bills, swords and pistols. Thus they were equipped with some heavy battery guns, and the *Edward Bonaventure*, with her thirty-one pieces, six of them brass, must have been a formidable ship. Nevertheless the main reliance was usually placed upon lighter pieces and small arms. As might be expected, ships of this class played a major part in West Indies privateering.

There were also a number of private men-of-war, usually belonging to important individuals such as the Earl of Cumberland (the *Anthony* and the *Pilgrim*), Sir Walter Raleigh (the *Roebuck*), and Lord Thomas Howard (the *Challenger* and the *Mineral*). Precise information about these is lacking, but in some cases at least they were probably in the style of the Queen's own ships. The Lord Admiral's private ships, indeed, were occasionally included in Royal Navy lists; the *Ark Raleigh* became the *Ark Royal*, and the Queen had no better ship. Raleigh's *Roebuck*

[1] Documents 107 and 19 below.

majority of the Bristol privateers, which seem to have been turned over to privateering mainly because the war itself frustrated their normal employment. Privateers of this sort could be and were put back to merchant service when trade revived or seemed to offer a better profit than prize-hunting. Similarly from Plymouth, Weymouth, Southampton and lesser centres of privateering this was the typical 'ship of reprisal', and this term itself, which had not yet begun to yield to the modern 'privateer', expresses much better the nature of much of the activity—a private war of merchants and merchantmen. Ships of this kind did not often leave European waters and consequently do not figure so largely in our West Indies ventures. They were well represented, however, and the appraisement of the sixty or seventy ton *Black Dog*, built about 1572, gives us a closer view of one of them.[1] This, like the two rather similar appraisements printed in the *Mariner's Mirror*,[2] mentions the usual three masts, a foresail and foretopsail, mainsail and maintopsail, and a lateen mizensail. An interesting feature of all these appraisements is the absence of any mention of a spritsail. A minion and three falcons, firing 4 lb. and 2 lb. shot respectively, made up the sum of her artillery, and though this was undoubtedly weak for a vessel which had to fend for itself in the Caribbean, it was not significantly weaker than the armament of comparable privateers. In fact ships of this size did not carry anything that can be classed as a heavy battery gun. On the other hand the *Black Dog* probably carried more calivers, muskets and pikes than are mentioned in the appraisement, for we know that she set forth with forty men. This high proportion of men to tons burden—more than one to two—was normal for a privateer, for prizes had to be manned home.

Much more powerful and effective as privateers were the merchantmen normally employed in dangerous and long-distance trading to the Mediterranean and as far south as the Guinea coast. These were distinctly larger ships of over a hundred tons burden —some of them over three hundred. About one in four of the privateers fell into this class in 1590, but their numbers were

[1] Document 12 below.
[2] K. R. Andrews, 'Appraisements of Elizabethan Privateersmen', *The Mariner's Mirror*, XXXVII (1951), 76–9.

2. The Thames eastward of London Bridge, about 1600
From the Long View of London by C. J. Visscher

holders, and probably each victualled for his part. John Watts' 1591 expedition of four ships and a pinnace had seven shareholders: Watts himself owned two of the ships and had a half share in each of the other vessels, while four of the shareholders had no part in the ships themselves.

West Indies ventures were of course more expensive than the shorter and less hazardous cruises. The ships, which tended to be larger, had to be better equipped in every respect and victuals were sometimes provided for eight or twelve, instead of the usual six months. Sheathing of the hull against the ruinous teredo-worm was necessary. Extensive repairs and refitting would be required when ships returned, as many did, battered and mauled by weather or enemy action. Owners had, far more often in this than in other types of venture, to reckon with the complete loss of a ship: Chidley's *Robin*, Carey's *Bark Burr*, Lord Thomas Howard's *Flight*, Cumberland's *Discovery*, Cordell's *Edward Bonaventure* and Michael Geare's *Handmaid* were all lost in the West Indian ventures described below.

In such ways the superior financial resources of the London merchants gave them advantages over most of the outport men, and among the score of individuals who dominated the business of privateering, including one or two outport merchants[1] and a few men of prominence in the state,[2] were a dozen or so London merchants such as John Watts, Henry Cletherow, Robert Cobb, John More, Thomas Cordell, Thomas Myddelton, John Stokes and Paul Bayning. The Londoners not only organized their own expeditions, but frequently invested in those set forth by gentlemen commanders like Chidley or by outport merchants.[3] Some, like Myddelton, regularly bought prize cargoes, for which, as wholesale dealers in products like sugar, pepper and dyewoods, they could find a market;[4] others, like Henry Cletherow—an ironmonger and rope merchant—had a special interest in shipping.

---

[1] Thomas Heaton of Southampton, for example.
[2] Raleigh, Cumberland, Sir George Carey and Charles, Lord Howard of Effingham, the Lord Admiral, all played an important part in promoting many ventures.
[3] Cletherow and Watts, for example, invested in Chidley's expedition, and Myddelton invested in Richard Hawkins' famous venture to the South Sea (see below, p. 72, p. 340, n. 1).
[4] Myddelton was a sugar merchant—see pp. 338–40 below.

Merchants were not, of course, the only promoters of privateering. The contribution of gentlemen adventurers, particularly to the more ambitious and risky undertakings, hardly needs stressing. Nevertheless they invariably relied upon merchants for more or less financial support—more in the case of Sir George Carey's *Bark Young* or Sir John Burgh's expedition, less in the case of Chidley's fleet. Of the two greatest patrons of privateering, Cumberland and Raleigh, the former seems to have preferred to finance his own ventures, while the latter frequently acted in partnership with others. The voyages promoted by gentry and nobility do seem to have their own peculiar stamp. The ships themselves, as we have seen, were often superior. Soldiers were often sent in some numbers, and the seamen paid wages. The captains were, many of them, gentlemen themselves —Burgh, Langton, Slingsby, Vavasour, Preston, Sommers, Chidley. Sometimes, as with Chidley, some great exploit was intended; or, as with Preston and perhaps with Carey's 1590 venture, some service in matters more important than mere prize-hunting. And even when plunder was the main object, as in Langton's voyage, fame and honour were also prized, and damaging the king of Spain's empire was thought a thing worth while in itself. Thus such ventures were not strictly business enterprise in the sense that the merchants' ventures usually were.

The company of a privateer was normally headed by a captain and a master, though occasionally the master is found in sole command, as in an ordinary merchantman. The general responsibility for the venture lay with the captain, while the master's job was to sail the ship. In some of the West Indies voyages an officer called the 'pilot' appears—Kingsnode, for example, in Watts' 1588 voyage and again in the *Black Dog*. The pilot was appointed to advise on special problems of navigation for the whole expedition, not merely for one ship, and in our cases they were men with expert knowledge of Caribbean waters. The only other officer with a general responsibility for the expedition rather than for a particular ship was the 'general' in command. When soldiers were sent the captain was usually a gentleman and there was often a lieutenant, also a gentleman, to lead the soldiers and perform various social duties for which a rude, sea-bred master was considered unfitted. Correspondingly, there existed among the captains a broad division between those of gentle origin and those who owed their position only to ability, experience and an early apprenticeship to the sea. These, like Christopher Newport, Benjamin Wood and Michael Geare, came from the general seafaring stock and made their way from apprentice to mariner, mariner to master's mate, thence to master and finally to captain. But some of the captains and masters had other advantages: James Lancaster, himself a merchant and, like several other London captains, an English factor in Spain before 1585;[1] or Stephen Michell, brought up in the household of the great privateering magnate John Watts, and consequently a captain at twenty-one. And the social mobility of Elizabethan England was such as to allow a select few of the old salts to achieve respectability—even, in Geare's case, knighthood. Thus in many privateers there was no line of social division between captain and crew. The authority of the captain in such circumstances had to be based on respect for his ability as a seaman, a fighter and a natural leader, and it is something of a tribute to such men as Newport and Geare that they were able to command the loyalty of notoriously tough and undisciplined men on long and sometimes unrewarding ventures, offering nothing but bad food, disease, danger and the vague hope of loot.

Under the master the most important officers were the master's mate, the master gunner and the purser, followed by the carpenter, the surgeon, the boatswain and the quartermasters. Then there were the under-officers—the gunner's, carpenter's, surgeon's and quartermasters' mates, and the steward, who was in fact the purser's assistant. All ships of course carried a cook, and most a cooper. The grander type of venture, with a complement of soldiers, would be equipped with a trumpeter and a corporal. In addition there would be a number of ordinary seamen and one or two boys. Privateers were invariably overmanned in anticipation of losses by fighting, disease and the manning home of prizes.

The men who sailed the privateers came chiefly from the ports of southern England from Bristol round to the Wash, the largest group among them being those from St Katherine's, Wapping, Ratcliffe, Limehouse and Rotherhithe—that busy stretch of the

[1] H.C.A. 13/26, 3 June 1586, 7 July 1586.

Thames east of London Bridge which was already becoming one of the great centres of world commerce. The evidence of numerous Admiralty Court depositions[1] suggests that privateer crews were largely recruited among seamen of the merchant service, and that many of them took ship fairly regularly in privateers from 1585. Like the captains and masters, they could and did easily change their ship, but there was a natural tendency to form a connection and continue in the same ship, or at least in the service of the same owner, for several ventures. No doubt many landsmen also were newly won for sea-service in the privateers, though Monson probably exaggerates when he says, 'the number of sailors and seamen are increased treble by it [privateering], to what they are in the navigations of peaceable voyages.'[2] The recruitment itself was done by the captain or the master and was an entirely voluntary agreement, except in the very special instances when permission was given to impress. Ships of reprisal thus competed with the Queen's ships for their men, and there is ample testimony to the preference of the sailors for privateersmen.

There is no doubt what the attractions were—the promise of plunder and the looser discipline. Drunkenness and disorder were very common in ships of reprisal. The taking of a prize often led to quarrels, insults and stabbings, or, if there were wines aboard, to orgies of drinking. The passionate rage of the master, Robert FitzWilliams, against his captain in the 1588 venture;[3] the quarrel between Locke and Keble in Newport's 1592 voyage—of such violence as to lead to the suspicion of murder;[4] the terrible allegations against Matthew Hawlse in Chidley's voyage;[5] the dangerous moment in Watts' 1591 expedition, when Michell and Geare threatened to board their own admiral[6]—such incidents were almost commonplace. So were the 'braules that were on borde amongst the company' of Carey's *Swallow*, who 'had droncke that day well of the wynes which they founde in the

---

[1] All depositions give name, occupation and approximate age. Some, like those quoted in chapter V below, give more detailed personal histories.
[2] *Monson's Tracts*, IV, 21.
[3] Document 2 below.
[4] Document 95.
[5] Document 14.
[6] Lansdowne MS 67, f. 152.

prize & some more then did them good, and that made them lye togeathers by the eares the most parte of the day.'¹ On a London privateer, the *Tiger*, commanded by a Dutchman, one of the crew 'herde W*illia*m Ivey the m*aste*r at sea nere the Burlinges after the takinge of the said shippes, sett the Captaine at noughte, and when the captaine blamed him for breakinge bulcke and makinge spoile of the goodes, and tould him howe he was chardged by his commissions not to breake bulcke, the said M*aste*r in this ex*amina*tes hearinge sayde shite on thy commissions we have nothinge to doe therewithe, we knowe what Commission our owner M*aste*r Holliday hath geven us and that they would followe.' Further, 'the said Captaine Barnestrawe was not regarded by the englishe men but greatlye reviled and called coppernose and that he was fitter to drincke ale then to be a Captaine.' The master's mate and the quartermaster even threatened to cast him overboard, and one of them struck him with a dagger.²

It is no wonder that Texeda, governor of Havana, considered the English corsairs 'a lot of drunkards' and 'a low lot'.³ Their own commanders cannot have held a much higher opinion of men whose customary independence as craftsmen of the sea was now inflated by the circumstance of war and the rule of brute force. The complaints of Richard Hawkins about indiscipline were as caustic as Texeda's, and more precise, but attempts to impose order often led to mutiny. As for the owners and adventurers, they had good reason to curse and prosecute the men whose interest it was to secure, by fair means or foul, as great as possible a share of the plunder.

Here, of course, was the main source of trouble—the sharing of prize goods. In the first place, the victorious crew had customary rights of 'pillage'. This included all goods and valuables found above deck, together with the personal belongings of the crew and passengers of the prize. But it was stipulated that 'there shalbe nothinge made pyllage being above the value of fortie shillinges (excepte apparrell)'.⁴ All the pillage was brought to the mainmast and shared, according to customary rules, among the

¹ Document 60.
² H.C.A. 13/29, 7 December 1591.
³ *Further English Voyages*, p. 301.
⁴ H.C.A. 24/58, no. 96.

captors. The captain took the enemy captain's chest and was also entitled to the best piece of ordnance. The master took the best cable, in addition to the enemy master's chest. The gunner took the enemy gunner's possessions and the second best gun, and so on. These rules, however, did vary in practice, and several versions of them exist from this period.[1] In fact so many disputes arose that Trinity House in 1594 laid down its own interpretation.[2] Whatever regulations existed, they were scantly regarded by the sailors. When it came to the heat of boarding and rifling, it was each man for himself, and even the crude sense of fair play, arising as much out of mutual distrust as out of comradeship, was swept aside. Now mutinies might easily occur, like the 'greate turmoil' on board the *Examiner* in 1590, 'betwixte the Captaine and the company for that he chardged the company they had robbed him'.[3] Jewels, money, gold, silver and similar valuables were the most prized, for they could most easily be concealed. And it was now, if ever, that a sailor might fill his pocket. 'As for the business of pillage,' Boteler relates, 'there is nothing that more bewitcheth them, nor anything wherein they promise to themselves so loudly nor delight in more mainly.'[4]

Very often, moreover, the crew took a hand in the disposal of the cargo proper before it could be inventoried and legitimately divided. The fate of the almost fabulous cargo of the *Madre de Dios* is well-known; John Bird, one of the merchants interested, angrily wrote, 'yt is not tollerable to lett such spoyle be made. There is no good order usyd any way to incounter the theevery of these lewde Fellowes.'[5] So was the *Jewel's* prize 'embezzled' at Appledore, near Bideford;[6] at Cork and Waterford, Milford Haven and Mounts Bay, Mead Hole in the Isle of Wight and other places a more or less regular traffic was carried on; and the disposing of cargoes in Barbary grew so common that Dr Julius Caesar thought he would 'open a gap of greate proffitte' to the

[1] Cp. W. G. Perrin (ed.), *Boteler's Dialogues* (Navy Records Society, LXV, 1929), pp. 39–40; *Monson's Tracts*, IV, 19 and 201. Dr Julius Caesar even cast doubt on the claim of the crew to any pillage, 'as this is noe tyme of open warre' (Lansdowne MS 157, f. 318).

[2] Pepys MS 2870, Miscellanea, vol. 2, p. 101.

[3] H.C.A. 13/28, 23 December 1590.

[4] *Dialogues*, p. 37.

[5] Lansdowne MS 70, f. 206.

[6] Documents 133, 134 below.

Lord Admiral by confiscating the good behaviour bonds of those who resorted there.[1] In such ways it was possible to cheat the owners and victuallers, who rarely obtained intact the two thirds of the cargo to which they were entitled. It was also worth while thus to evade the payment of customs duties and the Lord Admiral's tenths.

As to their rightful third of the cargo proper, the crew were usually content to sell it to the owners and victuallers, who could then deal with the cargo as a whole. This gave the adventurers a chance to recoup themselves at the expense of the seamen, who in this matter could easily be beaten down, having no facilities for storing or finding buyers for such goods as hides, dyewood or unrefined sugar. The crew divided their third among themselves according to rank, and a detailed example of how the allocation might be made in practice occurs in the records of Andrew Barker's 1576 venture.[2] The booty was divided into a large number of shares, of which the captain took eight, the master seven, the master's mate six and a half, the two master gunners six and five, one of the quartermasters five and the other quartermasters four, the two boatswains and one of the surgeons four each, the other surgeon four and a quarter, and the remainder of the sailors between two and three each, the boys receiving half a share and the soldiers between one and four each. There is enough evidence from other voyages, however, to show that there was no standard scale of sharing, and it was this uncertainty that led Trinity House to deliver its opinion in this matter as upon the subject of pillage.[3] It is not likely that the scale was in fact adopted in privateers, for it would have meant a reduction of the two or three shares normally taken by the rank and file to a single share each—an infringement of customary rights few captains would have dared to attempt.

If we consider a seaman's share in the returns of a successful voyage, it is not difficult to imagine why they preferred privateers to the Queen's ships. To a crew of about fifty a two thousand pound prize would yield single shares worth about four pounds each. On this scale an ordinary seaman would get eight or twelve

---

[1] Lansdowne MS 157, f. 442.
[2] I. A. Wright, *Documents concerning English Voyages to the Spanish Main, 1569–1580* (Hakluyt Society, 2nd Series, LXXI, 1932), pp. 102–8.
[3] Pepys MS 2870, Miscellanea, vol. 2, p. 101.

pounds for his share of the thirds, apart from such pickings as he might get from pillage and embezzlement. Obviously the sailor was unlikely to share in such a prize on every cruise, but the incentive was there—a single share in Watts' 1591 venture was valued at over ten pounds even by Watts' men and was probably worth fifteen or twenty. The men in the Queen's ships were paid ten shillings a month. In other respects, of course, the conditions of service were worse in the privateers. Dysentery, scurvy and sheer starvation were more common. But in all vessels of war sickness carried off far more men than fighting, and the crudities of the barber-surgeons added their own toll, as it may have been with Robert Keble, 'shott throughe the buttocke and grevously wounded whereof he lay languisshinge about vj dayes & then dyed'.[1]

In spite of the greed, the squalor and the cruelty of life in the privateers, when prisoners were sometimes tortured with a knotted cord about the temples, there was a less disreputable side to it. Among the men themselves a certain rough justice held sway, like honour among thieves, and at the lowest level a man who stole from his fellows would have short shrift. There was a certain contempt for cowardice and treachery and a willingness to stand together against forbidding odds. On occasions, an extraordinary fighting spirit could be roused, as it was in Carey's men, and some of the captains at least, and no doubt some of the men, were partly inspired by national and religious sentiment. In the West Indian voyages dealt with here such inspiration often shows itself, but it is much less evident in the common run of privateering. So, too, piratical attacks upon neutrals and other illegal practices of the kind were much more widespread among those who confined their attentions to European waters. For the men of the privateers in general Texeda's judgement was a fair one; a minority were worthy of respect, but did not in any sense deserve the treatment they have had at the hands of romantic writers.

III. PRIVATEERING IN THE WEST INDIES, 1588–95

The privateering season in the West Indies was more or less fixed by the weather and the movements of Spanish shipping.

[1] Document 95 below.

The weather made it advisable to leave the Gulf of Florida well before the end of August to avoid hurricanes; and the movements of Spanish shipping made it desirable to double Cape San Antonio somewhat earlier, for the Tierra Firme and New Spain fleets, as well as shipping from Honduras and Santo Domingo, would be converging on Havana during June and July. Most of the privateers, therefore, left in March or April—some earlier, even as early as January—to leave themselves time for whatever activities they had in mind to perform before joining the irregular patrol of the approaches to Havana. Very seldom was this routine not observed. The route, too, was more or less invariable— southward to the Canaries, or further, and then westward with the north-east trades to landfall at Dominica or thereabouts. Thence the more common direction was towards Hispaniola, occasionally making a circuit of Puerto Rico. The coasts of the Greater Antilles offered much in the way of small prizes, illicit trading and occasional raids on cattle ranches, sugar mills or unprotected ports like La Yaguana. They also offered much needed opportunities for victualling, careening the vessels and recruiting the health of the crews. Thus the great bay of western Hispaniola from Cape Tiburon to Cape St Nicholas, and all the *Banda del Norte* of that island from Cape St Nicholas eastwards became the haunt and refuge of privateers and the despair of the authorities in Santo Domingo. From here the corsairs could work through the Old Channel to Havana, but this was a difficult piece of navigation. An alternative was simply to sail home through the Caicos Passage. It was more usual, however, to work out of the Windward Passage and drop south to Jamaica and so on to Cape San Antonio, or perhaps first to Honduras.

On the other hand some of the stronger expeditions were first attracted to the Pearl Coast, where the stakes were higher, from La Margarita and the nearby islands to Rio de la Hacha. Success was not easily obtained in this region, and as the privateers moved westward along the Main their demonstrations seem to have become more and more tentative and less and less effectual. From the Main they could proceed to Honduras or strike across the *Mar del Norte* to the soft underbelly of the Greater Antilles, or make for Cape San Antonio.

Once in the Caribbean, the main hope of prizes lay in haunting the capes and ports for the shipping which crept along the coasts. Most of the vessels so taken were comparatively small—boats, barks or caravels of anything up to a hundred tons burden. These were easy prey for a privateer in the open sea, but near the shore they often had to be cut out by pinnaces or boats, and if this were not done quickly the prize might escape by running itself aground, the crew unlading the valuable part of the cargo and setting fire to the rest, or scuttling the lot. Thus there was much work for the pinnaces and boats. If a prize was of fair size and a good sailer, and taken early on in the voyage, she would be manned with a small English crew and sent home. The Spanish crew would be put ashore, except for one or two who would be sent with the prize to testify to the identity of ship and goods in the Admiralty Court. If such a prize were taken late in the voyage it would return with the privateer. On the other hand goods from a small or unweatherly vessel were usually trans-shipped to the privateer or to a larger prize, the original vessel being burnt, or simply sent on its way. The larger merchantmen sometimes put up a stiff resistance, as the men of the *Black Dog* learned to their cost, but the bulk of privateering consisted of a multitude of small actions which involved little serious danger.

This is hardly less true of the shore actions which played an ever increasing part in the West Indies raids of these years. The attackers naturally concentrated on cattle farms, sugar mills and unprotected settlements along the coasts, where not only was there no resistance, but the inhabitants were usually glad to ransom their dwellings and equipment and to barter with the Englishmen. Newport's capture of Ocoa, described as a 'town' of forty or fifty houses, and Langton's depredations along the southern coast of Hispaniola were typical of such activities. An assault upon a larger settlement like La Yaguana or Puerto de Caballos could be a more serious matter. Newport's men, for example, only took La Yaguana on the second attempt, and then with losses; and on this, as on one or two other occasions, the corsairs seemed to display a certain nervousness when separated from their ships. But for the most part they had comparatively easy successes, particularly at Caballos, and refrained from attempting tasks beyond their powers. Apart from Preston's expedition, which was much more formidable than the rest, only the strongest forces—those of Sir John Burgh in 1593 and James Langton in 1593-4—attacked really important places, and in these instances, at Asunción and Cumaná, they suffered defeat. The wisdom of the lesser fry in confining themselves to minor objectives is thus evident. Such easy captures, however, rarely yielded much in the way of booty. Time and again the townspeople removed themselves and everything of value into the hills or the bush, out of reach of the raiders; time and again the English were reduced, in the absence of sufficient offers of ransom, to burning the houses. What they might have achieved with more concerted efforts it is difficult to estimate, but Preston's notable feats at Caracas and Coro, though they produced little plunder, did show what was possible.

Among the miscellaneous prize goods returned by West Indian ventures, hides were by far the commonest item, and a great deal of sugar was taken. Silver, gold, money, pearls and other precious stones and similar valuables were the most important item in some half a dozen cargoes and often figured in others. Wines, indigo, ginger, sarsaparilla, logwood, balsam, *cassia fistula*[1] and cochineal are all mentioned several times; tobacco only once. These commodities commanded a good market in England, and on the whole prizes taken in the West Indies were more valuable than those taken in European waters. Cargoes of varied European manufactures were occasionally captured in the Caribbean, but were not so highly prized. Foodstuffs—cassava bread,[2] hogs, turtles, and the like—were frequently captured, and were useful for revictualling, but were not brought home.

What was the value of these activities to the raiders themselves? Monson maintained that 'of twenty such ships as go out with letters of reprisal, not two, for the most part, make a saving voyage; like a lottery, where one lighting upon a good prize encourages others to venture in it till they make themselves penniless and derided for their pains'.[3] For Elizabethan privateering in general this statement was certainly not true, and Monson him-

---

[1] A shrub, the bark of which was used in tanning, the pods yielding a purgative drug.
[2] Bread made of flour produced from the roots of the cassava plant, from which tapioca is also made.
[3] *Monson's Tracts*, IV, 21: an assertion which he repeats, with little substantiation, elsewhere (e.g. II, 231).

self implied its contradiction when he observed: 'And if we descend to the towns, which for a time flourished by the goods so gotten, and examine the conditions of them and their inhabitants, we shall find not only the people but the places impoverished after the same manner they were enriched (that is to say) by rapine, spoil, and piracy.'[1]

It is, however, worth considering whether the statement was somewhat less wide of the mark with respect to Caribbean ventures in particular. We would need much more detail—and precise detail—than we have about costs and prizes to analyse the profitability of West Indies privateering with anything approaching accuracy, but there are certain indications worth noting.

The participation of leading merchants cannot be ignored. John Watts sent out individual vessels and fleets throughout the war, year in and year out, chiefly to the West Indies, and by 1603 he was a very rich man. John More, another prominent London merchant, backed expedition after expedition across the Atlantic. Paul Bayning, Thomas Cordell and Thomas Myddelton—no less than City magnates—each invested in several such ventures, and further similar examples could be cited. Enterprises underwritten by such men, who must be classed among the most successful business men of the age, were not as a rule unsound. It is significant, too, that this same element were in 1600 to form the nucleus of the East India Company.[2] Nor is it likely that captains of the calibre of Newport, Parker and Geare would sail again and again to the Indies in a fruitless quest.

Of course there were risks, and they were greater in the West Indies than nearer home. Ships were lost, as we have seen; captains were sometimes captured, as John Myddelton was twice; prizes were lost at sea, like Parker's prize in 1594, or fell into French hands, like Langton's in the same year; and expensive and ambitious projects like Chidley's were liable to meet complete

[1] *Monson's Tracts*, II, 297.
[2] More, Bayning and Cordell were 'committies', or directors, from the early days of the Company; Myddelton was an important contributor; Watts was especially called in to advise on the preparation of the first venture 'in respecte of the great experience of Master Alderman Wattes in shipping & other directions in viages.' Lancaster was himself one of the greatest privateer captains and many others of the adventurers had made money out of reprisal actions. See H. Stevens, *The Dawn of British Trade to the East Indies, 1599–1603* (1886), pp. 1–12, 67 et passim.

cient at least to balance costs. Parker in the same year (1594) did very well at Caballos, and though a large part of his plunder did not reach England, the loss was offset by another prize taken earlier in the voyage. In the 1595 ventures Ridlesden made a clear profit, though not a large one; Geare seems to have done well, though his men paid heavily for it; the *Rose Lion* took a very substantial cargo which was eventually adjudicated to the captors; but for Parker's voyage of this year we have no details as to prizes.

Thus, so far as we can tell from rather sketchy information, some fifteen of our twenty-five expeditions were financially successful, and three or four were very profitable. Five to the best of our knowledge failed to meet expenses and for the remainder we cannot hazard a guess. The record is neither surprisingly good nor surprisingly bad for the kind of enterprise, and it is clear that West Indian privateering was not quite such a gamble as Monson suggested. It was, indeed, a reasonably attractive business, and for the most part those who engaged in it did so for profit. With a few exceptions, they were interested not so much in damaging the Spanish Empire as in filling their pockets. To this end they took the easiest and least heroic courses and were satisfied with a comparatively small gain for a comparatively small risk, though they all of course hoped to capture a stray treasure ship—hope fed by the luck of Watts' men in 1591.

This largely explains the lack of co-operation between the different expeditions. The individual expeditions were often planned with some care, quite detailed instructions being issued by the owners to the captains as to the conduct of the voyage. Definite objectives were sometimes fixed in advance—Newport's raid on La Yaguana and Langton's on La Margarita, for example. Arrangements were made for rendezvous when there were several ships involved, and messages were left in secret hiding places. What was lacking was co-operation between different expeditions. Consortships were sometimes made at sea, but more often than not led to disputes over prizes. The result of this absence of co-ordination was that privateers were occasionally caught by superior enemy forces and badly beaten, as were Geare off Cabañas in 1595 and Carey's ships off Cape Corrientes in 1591. Above all, this dissipation of forces prevented the English

disaster. But the more routine venture, with limited aims and an experienced leader, could with reasonable luck make a saving voyage. It was unusual for an expedition to fail to pick up a few prizes. Of our voyages, those of John Chidley (1589), Benjamin Wood (1592), John Myddelton (1592), Sir John Burgh (1593) and Amyas Preston (1595) were probably unrewarding, but in each case there is an obvious reason. Chidley's venture was over-ambitious; Wood and Myddelton alike tried to tackle the Tierra Firme coast with insufficient forces; and Burgh and Preston were both out for something more important than petty plunder. The 1588 venture of Watts' ships may have had small success, too, for the crew were evidently disappointed with the results, but this again was possibly because the leaders were not concerned exclusively with taking prizes.[1]

Of the remaining ventures, the *Black Dog*, in spite of the loss of the captain and pilot, brought home sufficient prize goods to make a profit, apart from what her unknown consorts may have taken. The voyage of the *Bark Young* was perhaps unsuccessful, for she lost one prize to Leaguers and the prize goods she declared at Southampton were valued at a paltry £80. Nevertheless it is not unlikely that she sent home other prizes before leaving the West Indies, especially as she intended to take a long route home *via* Virginia and Newfoundland. The voyages of 1591 were, taken together, highly profitable, and even Carey, who lost a ship, gained prizes worth over £4000. Watts' prizes probably amounted to £40,000—the biggest haul of the period in the West Indies. In the following year Newport and King achieved reasonable returns, Newport's efforts being happily crowned by his share in the spoil of the *Madre de Dios*. Parker's recorded prizes for 1592 and 1593 were small, but we know little of these two voyages and it seems unlikely that he failed to make further captures. Langton's voyage of 1593–4 was, thanks to the haul at Caballos, undoubtedly profitable; Newport, who followed him at Caballos, obtained nothing there, but sent home two other prizes which alone would have 'made' the voyage; the *Affection* and the *Jewel* likewise returned valuable prizes; Lane in the *Centaur* took two valuable French merchantmen, and though he may subsequently have lost these at law, a third prize was suffi-

[1] They may have been interested in Virginia—see pp. 43–4 below.

tions totalling at least seventeen ships, leaving aside Raleigh's force, Lancaster's Pernambuco raid and the final incursion of the Queen's ships under Drake and Hawkins.

To the Spanish in the West Indies the corsairs, though not individually formidable, were an ever growing menace. Their numbers were never known with any certainty, nor their intentions, and every sail upon the horizon conjured up the memory of Drake. Their anxiety was entirely reasonable; a West Indies expedition of real force was intended by Raleigh in 1592 and contemplated by others long before it was eventually realized in 1595. Moreover, the privateers, even without help from stronger squadrons, might, as Lane demonstrated in 1591, capture at least one of the merchantmen bearing a private cargo of silver, if not one of King Philip's silver galleons or silver frigates. The tendency of the colonial authorities, therefore, to exaggerate the strength of the privateers was partly due to a genuine anxiety which disposed them to believe the worst. It was also due to their desire to impress higher authorities with the urgency of the need for more men, more fortifications, more coastal patrols. Thus the rising wave of privateering, of little direct importance, contributed to press forward the re-organization and improvement of Spanish defences in the West Indies and the creation of the 'light armada' of fast-sailing frigates, by means of which the treasure of the Indies eluded English clutches. Off Havana after the bold jeers, the love messages and compliments that Texeda had to endure in 1591 and 1592,[1] it grew perceptibly hotter for the English. Myddelton was captured in 1594 off that coast and Geare was severely beaten the following year. The privateers could still make a nuisance of themselves, but no longer with impunity. Above all, while the English achieved nothing of importance, the Spanish prepared themselves to throw back the long delayed onslaught of *El Draque*.

In their anxiety to protect the flotas, however, the Spanish neglected the islands, and here the activities of the privateers achieved some positive result, not of significance in the war itself, but important as a stage in the slow process of penetration of the West Indies which was to reach its height in the seventeenth century. It was, of course, virtually impossible to protect the vast

[1] *Further English Voyages*, pp. 266–7, 301.

attempting any really important *coup*. It was felt—and with considerable justification—that large-scale assaults upon important places were not only expensive in money and human life, but were unlikely to reward the promoters or the participants with a profit. To take one's own way with a smaller force and trust to luck seemed a much more attractive proposition. At least one would not then have to divide one's prizes and perhaps lose a large part of a good haul. A larger view could only be expected from men in the position of Cumberland or Raleigh: 'It became not the fortune in which I once lived,' wrote the latter, 'to goe journeys of picorie, it had sorted ill with the offices of Honour, which by her Majesties grace I hold this day in England, to run from Cape to Cape, and from place to place, for the pillage of ordinarie prizes.'[1] Nevertheless Raleigh and Cumberland alike had ships at sea throughout the war doing precisely this, and without a doubt these 'journeys of picory' offset the losses they incurred in more ambitious undertakings.

Were these raids, then, of no significance in the war with Spain? Were they no more than an extension of normal privateering from Spanish coasts in Europe to Spanish coasts in America? On the face of it, the damage they did was small, if not negligible, and after the great hopes of the Virginia enterprise and the resounding blows of Drake's 1585-6 raid, this petty pillage was an anti-climax. Nevertheless it had a value apart from the financial one we have examined.

Although our twenty-five ventures by no means represent the sum of English activity in the Caribbean in these years, they are sufficient to show that it was mounting in a more or less continuous crescendo from the year of the Armada to the last voyage of Drake and Hawkins. In 1588 we have only one expedition and in 1589 two, but 1590 saw not only the *Bark Young* and the *Falcon's Flight* in the Indies, but a squadron of four of Watts' ships, consorted with two others. In 1591 there were at least eleven English privateers in the Caribbean, and in 1592 there were thirteen off the Havana coast, apart from Newport's four. Our figures for the following year seem to indicate some recession, but the number rose again in 1594 to eleven (including two of Dudley's ships), and in 1595 there were five separate expedi-

[1] Harlow, *Raleigh's Guiana*, p. 4. 'Picorie', or 'pickery', means petty theft.

area of the Caribbean and all its shores against the raiders and the traders, logwood cutters and salt laders, pearl fishers and tobacco planters, and it was probably the best policy for Spain to concentrate on defending the mainland and the vital artery of the treasure route. This inevitably meant that eastern Cuba, Jamaica, Hispaniola, Puerto Rico and the Lesser Antilles, though by no means abandoned, were more and more exposed to all forms of infiltration and attack. Already by the end of our period the situation had grown very serious, particularly in Hispaniola. Spanish officials themselves provide the best evidence of this in their reports—for example this report by Diego de Ybarra, treasurer of Santo Domingo, dated 14 October 1595:[1]

> But for the last four years, as I have said, corsairs are as numerous and as assiduous as though these were ports of their own countries. They lie in wait on all the sailing routes to the Indies, particularly the courses converging on this city of Santo Domingo. Coming or going, we always have a corsair in sight. Not a ship coming up from the outside escapes them; nor does any which leaves the harbour get past them. If this continues, either this island will be depopulated or they will compel us to do business with them rather than with Spain. The special judge, sent by your majesty to deal with vessels departing from their lawful course and with contrabandists, is unable to prevent this trade from continuing, though he proceeds uprightly and with clemency. They make their incursions safely and find persons with whom to barter, for the land is sparsely settled and full of horned cattle, so that anywhere that they put in they find opportunity awaiting in the presence of negroes and other wretched delinquents who live outside the law in the bush, certain that neither the special judge nor any other representatives of justice can lay hands on them. Therefore the way to avoid the damage done by these thieves and culprits is to drive the corsairs from these seas, and this can only be accomplished by the galleys your majesty is entreated to send promptly in order to forestall the serious consequences which must otherwise ensue.

But such measures as were taken were not very effective, for it

[1] A. de I. 53–6–15, Santo Domingo 81. 1 *pliego*. Original. Extract. Translated.

was not only the English who were interfering. There were the French and the Dutch, both of whom concentrated upon trade rather than direct plunder. The English, moreover, were learning to combine plunder and trade, and after 1595 English merchants interested in the West Indies participated increasingly in the commercial penetration of the area, though not despising windfalls of pillage. By the end of the war, in fact, the situation in Hispaniola, particularly in the northwestern part of the island, had so far deteriorated that the Spanish decided upon the drastic operation of evacuating the coasts and removing the towns of La Yaguana, Bayaha and Puerto Plata to the south. Thus this part of the island was abandoned to the buccaneers, the direct successors of the Elizabethan corsairs.[1]

There were other particularly weak spots. Puerto de Caballos on the Honduras coast, exposed and largely unprotected, was subjected to attack year after year from 1592 to 1597, and the nearby Golfo Dulce attracted much attention from the corsairs. At La Margarita, it was reported in October 1595, 'winter and summer enemies hang off this island all the time, which is why the canoe owners do not dare fish' (i.e. for pearls) and meanwhile at Cumaná it was 'quite the usual thing' for a ship to spend 'two or three months quite as though in its home port, trading and treating with the inhabitants'.[2] Thus the area was being softened up for the salt lading operations of the Dutch at Punta de Araya in the later nineties.

The period between the defeat of the Armada and the end of the Spanish war has often been seen by historians as one of lost opportunities, when the war deteriorated into a series of inconclusive raids and minor skirmishes. Whether English financial, naval and military resources were great enough for the launching and maintenance of more decisive campaigns is a matter of doubt, but in any case the pursuit of war by private individuals and groups was by no means fruitless. Capital was being accumulated, more and larger ships were being built for the dual purpose of trade and war, and men like Newport and Sommers were

[1] Engel Sluiter, 'Dutch-Spanish Rivalry in the Caribbean, 1594–1609', *Hispanic American Historical Review*, XXVIII (1948), 165–96.
[2] Pedro de Salazar to the crown, La Margarita, 8 October 1595 (A. de I. 54-4-6, Santo Domingo 184. 1 *pliego*. Original).

developing and disseminating their knowledge of the ocean and American waters. All this, and the organizing experience of promoters like John Watts, was to play a large part in ensuring the success of the Virginia and East India Companies. Trade and war, in this intermediate stage between the strivings of the eighties and the achievements of the 1600's, were inextricably entangled. England was gathering strength and at the same time sapping the strength of the Spanish Empire.

CHAPTER I

THE VOYAGE OF THE *DRAKE*, THE *EXAMINER*, THE *HOPE* AND THE *CHANCE*
1588

DOCUMENTS 1–6 comprise almost all that is definitely known about the expedition of the *Drake*, the *Examiner*, the *Hope* and the *Chance* to the West Indies in 1588. The only other references to it occur in Michael Geare's rather obscure summary of his early privateering career[1] and in a list of bonds taken for the good behaviour of ships of reprisal,[2] where it is noted that Robert Fewilliams (or FitzWilliams) gave a bond for £5000 on 8 March 1587/8. It is also probable that these are the ships whose activities in the West Indies are mentioned in Spanish documents.[3]

Of the ships, the *Drake*—the admiral or flagship—belonged to John Watts, the London merchant and shipowner, who shared the ownership of the *Examiner* with his son John, Thomas Sewell and Robert FitzWilliams. These two ships had sailed in the Cadiz expedition in 1587 and later in the same year were cruising off the coast of Spain.[4] The identity of the other two—the *Hope* and the *Chance*—remains uncertain, but the latter may have been Sir George Carey's.[5] In any case the leading promoter of this venture was John Watts.

Although the privateering activities of John Watts are fairly well documented, only the bare outline of his private life can be sketched and the personality of the man, even as a business man, escapes us. Born about 1550, the son of Thomas Watts of Buntingford, Herts., he married the daughter of Sir James Hawes, Lord Mayor of London and leading member of the Clothworkers gild, about 1574–5. By this time Watts had already visited Cadiz

---

[1] Document 71 below.
[2] Lansdowne MS 142, f. 109.
[3] *Roanoke Voyages*, pp. 778–84; *Further English Voyages*, pp. 233–7.
[4] Lansdowne MS 143, ff. 8–46.
[5] He owned a ship of that name in 1591 (Harleian MS 598, f. 13).

in trade and in the later seventies and early eighties he is found trading to Spain, the Canaries and the Azores. Watts was one of the merchants who suffered by the arrest of English shipping in Spanish ports in 1585; he sued for redress in the High Court of Admiralty and was granted letters of reprisal in the summer of 1585. Thenceforth his privateers, singly and in substantial fleets, kept up a continuous war upon Spanish shipping. They are found at sea in every year of the war and in every theatre of operations, some of them being among the most powerful of their kind. Watts not only set forth his own expeditions, but co-operated with other merchants and gentlemen in privateering, notably in the important ventures of Drake in 1587, Lancaster in 1595 and Cumberland in 1598. Nor did he abandon trade. In 1592 he became a member of the Levant Company and in 1600 a leading figure in the East India Company, of which he was appointed governor in 1601. Meanwhile he had been elected an alderman of the City of London in 1594. In 1603 he was knighted and in 1606 became Lord Mayor. In the last years of his life his mercantile interests remained important and were even extended: he was an active member of the Virginia Company and in 1610 he set forth a ship to trade in the Orinoco region. He died in 1616, leaving the manor of Mardocks in Hertfordshire to his son John. The verdict of the Venetian ambassador, who described Watts as 'the greatest pirate that has ever been in this kingdom' was unjust, but Watts was certainly the greatest of the merchant promoters of privateering.[1]

Of the personnel of this particular voyage, Roger Kingsnode (or Kingson), the pilot, is an interesting though obscure figure. English pilots who knew the West Indies and could, for example, negotiate the Old Channel, from the Eastern end of Cuba along its northern shore, were rare indeed at this date. But Kingsnode appears only twice in the West Indies, and on the second occasion—in 1589—he met his death.[2] Michael Geare, in the *Drake*,

---

[1] *D.N.B.*; G. E. Cokayne, *Some Account of the Lord Mayors and Sheriffs of the City of London* (1897), p. 29; A. B. Beaven, *The Aldermen of the City of London*, II, 45; 'Elizabethan Privateering', pp. 242–3; A. Brown, *The Genesis of the United States*, I, 99; H.C.A. 13/19, 1 March 1572/3; H.C.A. 13/24, 2 February 1579/80; H.C.A. 13/25, 30 March 1584; H.C.A. 13/143. Other references to Watts' privateering interests occur throughout the H.C.A. records between 1585 and 1603.

[2] See below, pp. 53, 55.

was already an experienced privateer and had a long career of West Indies venturing ahead of him.[1] FitzWilliams was an old associate of John Watts, having commanded one of his ships in 1585.[2]

The *Examiner* and her consorts left the port of London for the West Indies in March 1588, but not before the 8th, according to the date of FitzWilliams' bond. They managed to get away, in fact, shortly before the stay of shipping which prevented Sir Richard Grenville from sailing for Virginia at the end of March. The next definite news of the expedition finds three of the ships homeward bound off the coast of Newfoundland at the beginning of August, Kingsnode in the *Drake* having departed for the Azores. In the meantime the four ships had visited the West Indies, evidently with little success, though they had at some stage taken a prize—probably the Frenchman to which Huntlowe refers.

The English materials tell us nothing more about events in the West Indies. However, Spanish reports of 7/17, 12/22 and 13/23 July and 3/13 August indicate the presence of four English privateers—two ships and two pinnaces[3]—in the Old Channel from towards the end of June to about 12/22 July. The English, who were clearly hoping to intercept some of the Santo Domingo ships bound for Havana to join the homeward fleet, achieved nothing but the partial plunder of a cargo of Canary wines. Could this have been Watts' expedition? There is no evidence that any other English ships reached the West Indies that summer, and in view of the general stay of shipping it is unlikely that another such fleet of four ships crossed the Atlantic. The number of the ships and their size (the *Examiner*, as its name implies, was a pinnace, and the *Hope* or the *Chance* may have been of small burden), the single prize, the criticisms of Kingsnode's direction of the voyage, arising perhaps after well-nigh fruitless weeks in the Old Channel—the coincidence of such details, though no proof, is remarkable. Again, the Englishmen in the Old Channel, cheated of their prey by about 12/22 July, seem to disappear from

---

[1] See document 71 below.
[2] H.C.A. 13/25, January–February 1585–6 *passim*.
[3] Pedro Menéndez Marqués says four ships and a pinnace (*Roanoke Voyages*, p. 780).

the ken of the Spanish colonials about that date. Thus they could have reached Newfoundland about the beginning of August. Alongside all this must be set the confident statement of Pedro de Avana that 'these English are the same who were here last year'— to wit, Carey's ships,[1] which in 1587 comprised the *Commander*, the *Swallow* and the *Gabriel*.[2] This assertion, unsubstantiated though it is, can neither be confirmed nor categorically rejected, since we know nothing of the exploits of Carey's ships in the year of the Armada. It is possible, however, that the *Chance* was one of Carey's ships, and in that case the Spanish may have recognised one or two of Carey's men and jumped to the conclusion voiced by Pedro de Avana. In the light of the admittedly scanty evidence, it appears likely that the Englishmen in the Old Channel were in fact the *Drake*, the *Examiner*, the *Hope* and the *Chance*, and that this expedition was jointly set forth by Watts and Carey.

It is of some interest that Kingsnode, if our reconstruction of his itinerary is approximately correct, can have spent little or no time in attempting to seek for or bring aid to the stranded Virginia colony. This was, presumably, the only expedition, in the absence of Grenville's fleet and White's two pinnaces, which had the opportunity to establish contact with the colonists that year. Watts, perhaps, would not have been unwilling to assist, as he assisted in 1590. It may be that Kingsnode and his ships left England in March, before Grenville was forbidden to sail, and that the vital necessity of using this, the sole West Indies expedition of the year, for the assistance of the colonists was therefore not foreseen. On the other hand, the ships might have put in at one of the western ports early in April, in which case they might have heard news of Grenville's frustration. The theory is tempting, for it would explain the presence of the ships off the coast of Newfoundland, to the northward of the island, between the mainland ('Norumbega') and the island.[3] To refer to ships in such a position as 'homeward bound' only makes sense if we assume that they had worked up the North American coast. The fact, too, that one of Carey's ships and some of Carey's men may have been associated with this voyage suggests some interest in Virginia,

---

[1] *Roanoke Voyages*, pp. 783–4; *Further English Voyages*, pp. 234–5.
[2] H.C.A. 25/2 (5), 29 January 1586/7.
[3] Documents 2, 3 and 5.

since his previous year's expedition seems to have intended visiting the settlement. For the time being the problem, in the absence of further information, must remain unresolved.

* * *

1. Thomas Watts contra Robert Fitz Williams: the libel[1]

[Thomas Watts, late captain of the *Examiner* of London, against Robert FitzWilliams, late master of the same, pleads as follows: That between March and September, 1588, John Watts, senior, John Watts, junior, Thomas Sewell and Robert FitzWilliams were owners of the *Examiner* of London, which they set forth in warlike manner on a voyage 'ad partes Indiarum'; while the ship was at sea, FitzWilliams stirred up sedition among the soldiers and sailors against Thomas Watts, and finally assaulted Watts with a knife, wounding him in the head and the left arm; Watts has now lost the use of that arm, upon which, being left-handed, he depended for his living; he has been a sailor for the past twelve years, and during the three years before his injury was captain of various ships, including the *Margaret and John*, in which he fought against the Spaniards and captured their goods on the high seas. He asks to be granted damages. This libel submitted to the court 12 November 1588.]

*2. Thomas Watts contra Robert Fitz Williams:
deposition of John Pocombe*[2]

Thomas Wattes contra Robertum FeeWilliams Primus testis super libello

JOH*AN*NES POCOMBE de Limehouse nauta ubi per sex annos maiori ex parte commoravit natus in oppido de Exmouth in comitatu Devon fungens etate xxiij annorum aut circiter Testis in hac parte productus iuratus et examinatus dicit se Thomam Wattes a mense Februarii ultimi et Robertum FeeWilliams per idem tempus respective novisse.

Ad primum articulum libelli ... he knoweth that the articulate John Wattes thelder John Wattes the yonger Thomas Sewell and Roberte FeeWilliams in the monethes and yeare articulate were

[1] H.C.A. 24/56, no. 72. Summary. Translated. For the full text of a libel, see document 157.

[2] H.C.A. 13/27, 13 November 1588. Extract. Deposition on the libel, followed by replies to defendant's interrogatories.

Robertum witheshawe in Com*itatu* Ebor*acum* ib*ide*m oriundus etat*is* xxv annor*um* aut circiter. . . .
Fewilliams
3ᵘˢ testis
*acto*ris

Ad Inter*r*ogatoria. . . .

Ad se*cun*dum respondet he was Cooke of thexaminer. . . .

Ad 9 he answerethe the s*ai*d Wattes used him selfe well that viadge to his knowledge and followed suche order & direction as tharticulate Kingesnode gave that viadge wh*i*che if he had not obayed he thinkethe the s*ai*d Watt*es* & company had taken better purchase then they dyd.

5. *Thomas Watts* contra *Robert Fitz Williams:*
deposition of Edward Hickman[1]

Thomas
Wattes
contra
Robertum
Fewilliams.

EDWARDUS HICKMAN Civi*tati*s London vietor[2] ubi habitavit p*er* spatiu*m* septem annor*um* aut eo circiter et antea in Pago de Whetamsteade in Com*itatu* Hareforde natus in oppido de Ste Albons in eodem Com*itatu* etatis viginti sex annor*um* vel circiter. . . .

Ad primu*m* . . . this ex*amina*te sayled from this porte of London in the articulate shippe the Examiner. . . .

Ad se*cun*dum [Watts was reputed and taken for captain] untill he & Fewilliams the ma*ster* fell out, that he lefte her & wente into the Hoppe. . . .

Ad tertiu*m* et quartu*m* dicit that the Captayne withe s*ai*d shippe & company comeinge homewarde betwixte Newfounde lande and Normanbege[3] as he rememberethe [the two men fell out].

Ad Inter*r*ogatoria. . . .

Ad se*cun*dum res*p*ondet that he was Cowp*er* & Stewardes matte in thexaminer that viadge. . . .

Ad nonu*m* respondet The s*ai*d Wattes followed the order of tharticulate Roger Kingesnode till suche tyme as he sayled from thexaminer to the Ilandes as the common reporte was amongeste the company.

Ad decimu*m* respondet That Fewilliams dyd leave thexaminer

---

[1] H.C.A. 13/27, 10 May 1589. Extract.
[2] Cooper.
[3] Norumbega. The name was usually applied to the New England region, but occasionally embraced Virginia itself (*Roanoke Voyages*, pp. 78, 90–1, 208, 310, 347, 389, 445–6, 461, 556, 719, 729, 731).

pilott of the foure shipps in that viadge' and that the quarrel took place when the ship was off the coast of Newfoundland 'in the beginninge of August laste'.]

3. Thomas Watts contra Robert Fitz Williams: deposition of Osborne Huntlowe[1]

OSBORNE HUNTLOWE de Newe Branforde in Comitatu Middlesex nauta ubi habitavit per spatium trium annorum, et ante in hac civitate London ubi oriundus esset etatis xliiij^{or} annorum....

Ad primum ... shee was furnished & wente to seas in marche the yeare articulate & this examinate wente in her as Stewarde.

Ad secundum ... the said Wattes showed furthe a Commission from the Lorde Admirall ... whereby it dyd appeare that he was Captayne....

Ad iij^{um} et quartum articulos dicit That the Captayne shippe & company haveinge taken a prize att the Seas that viadge, and beinge to the Norwarde of the Newe founde lande[2] the said Feewilliams Chardged the forsaid Thomas Wattes the Captayne, that he had taken out of here certayne thinges to his owne use whiche weare none of his, but the Companyes, And the Captayne denyed the same, where uppon there was very harde speches betwixte them sundrye times....

Ad interrogatoria secundo loco data....

Ad 7um he sayethe the Admirall of the Fleete called the Drake [did][3] borde suche a shippe as in this interrogatory is conteayned, And John and Edwarde Pocombe amongeste other of the Examiners company, in the other shippes companyes presence allsoe wente on borde the said Frenche shippe in the shippes boate.

Thomas Wattes Contra Robertum Fe-Williams 2us testis actoris

4. Thomas Watts contra Robert Fitz Williams: deposition of John Benson[4]

JOHANNES BENSON de Branford in Comitatu Middlesex nauta ubi habitavit per spacium unius anni et ante apud Beck-

Thomas Wattes contra

---

[1] H.C.A. 13/27, 15 April 1589. Extract.
[2] Cp. Hickman's deposition (document 5), which puts the scene between Newfoundland and Norumbega.
[3] Omitted in original.   [4] H.C.A. 13/27, 29 April 1589. Extract.

master from doinge him mischeife and shortly after as yt grewe darker, the master wente to his boy and borowed his kniffe, and came uppon the hatches agayne and fell in wordes with the Captaine and of a soddaine strake at him with the knife, and hurte him in the foreheade, on the eye browe, and uppon his nose, and thurste him into the left arme this examinate standing by and not thinking that the master had eany weapon aboute him or had hurte the Captaine untill he sawe the bloodde ron down his face, and then this examinate requested the Captaine to goe into his caban and he would staunche the bloode, and when he entered the Caban yt was soe loe that he could not sett uprighte soe as he requested him goe forward under the haulfe decke, and as he was comminge out of the Caban dore the said FeeWilliams had gotten uppon a pike, and was ronninge at the Captaine therewith, which the Captayne seeinge stepped backe, and this examinate wente owt before him and willed the master lay downe the pike which he did, and the same nighte the said master hoysed furthe the boate and lefte the shippe and his chardge and wente into the Chaunce. Whiche he affirmeth to be most trewe. Ac aliter nescit.

Ad quintum dicit he hath herd Thomas Wattes say he was lefte handed, and had more use thereof then of his righte. Ac aliter nescit.

Ad sextum nescit deponere.

Ad septimum dicit he verely thinketh both by the assaultes aforesaid and woundes geven by the master to the Captayne he thoughte to have slayne the said Captaine, and the rather for that this examinate herd him threaten him, and say he would have a pounde of his bloode, and after the gevinge of the said woundes he likewise heard the master say he was sory he had not killed the said Captaine Ut dicit.

Ad octavum nescit plura dicere quam prius dictum est.

Ad nonum affirmat the said Thomas Wattes behaved him selfe modestly and soberly duringe the said viadge towardes the company and offered not eany abuse to eany, and if the master had not first made quarrell he verely thinketh the said fallinge out had not byn Ac aliter nescit. . . .

[Replying to interrogatories, he confirms his previous statements, adding that 'Thomas Wattes was Captaine but appoyncted noe governemente or direction for the viadge as he thinketh but the viadge was wholy directed by Roger Kingesnode Cheife

THE 1588 VOYAGE

owners of the Examiner of London, and sett her to sea for a viadge to be made to the West Indies sufficiently appoyncted withall necessaries For this examinate was masters mate of the said shippe the same viadge.

Ad secundum dicit Thomas Wattes was appoyncted Captaine of the said shippe by the owners joyntlye as he taketh yt For that he ys named Captaine in the Articles sett downe by the owners and masters for the viadge beinge subscribed by the owners, and as Captaine he came on borde and proceeded on the viadge and soe was accompted of the company of the said shippe of this examinates knowledge beinge one of the masters mates that viadge.

Ad tertium et quartum affirmat Roberte FeeWilliams wente master of the said shippe the viadge aforesaid and in the viadge outwardes he disliked that Thomas Wattes tooke uppon him to be Captaine, and openly sayd he was noe Captaine there or had to doe with the men or victualls and that John Wattes his brother requested him to suffer the said Thomas Wattes to goe with him in the shippe whereby they were at sundry variances and many wordes passed betwixte them yet they were made freindes and remayned togeather untill homewardes bounde they fell uppon the quoaste of newefound lande where William Loggins one of the masters mates sayd to the master that was noe course for them to kepe and wisshed him caste aboute and alter the same and Roberte FeeWilliams the master asked him what he had to doe to controule his direction and blamed him for yt, Whereat the Captaine made answere sayenge if he knowe what course ys to be taken as well as you meaninge the master, why should he not speake and geve his advise. To whom the master replyed Sayeinge you ever take parte agaynst me with them that are not my freindes and soe further wordes passed betwixte them, and in the eveninge followinge the master called uppe the company uppon the halfe decke, and as they came uppe the boateswaine was wantinge, whom the master called for, and the Captaine sayd lett him alone he ys but one man yt ys noe matter for him what have you to say to the company, and the master answered agayne to him hould you your peace, I have nothinge to say to you, and with that the master flewe uppon the Captaine and stricke him on the face with his fiste, and this examinate and others standinge by put them a sunder once or twise and hardly could keepe the

1586. He was an adventurer in the *Golden Dragon* in 1592 and prospective captain of the *Thunderbolt* of London in September 1592.¹ Of William Michelson nothing more is known.

From Hakluyt's mention of 'consorts' it is evident that the *Dog* was not alone in the West Indies, but was probably one of a fleet of English privateers. It would be idle, in view of the large number of privateers known to have been at sea in 1589, to speculate as to the identity of the *Dog*'s consorts, but Kingsnode's presence might suggest the ulterior figure of John Watts, whose *Little John* took a prize in the Azores that year.²

* * *

7. Richard Hakluyt's account of the voyage of the Dog³

A briefe remembrance of a voyage made in the yeere 1589 by *William Michelson* Captaine, and *William Mace* of *Ratcliffe*, Master of a ship called the *Dogge*, to the Bay of *Mexico* in the *West India*.

The aforesaide ship called the Dogge, of the burthen of threescore and ten tunnes was furnished, and armed forth with the number of fortie men: it departed from the coast of England in the moneth of May, directly for the West India: It fell with the Bay of Mexico, and there met with divers Spanish ships at sundry times, whereof three fel into her lapse⁴ and were forced to yeeld unto the mercie of the English: the last that they met within the Bay was a Spanish man of warre, whom the English chased, and after three severall fightes, upon three divers dayes, pressed him so farre that he entreated a parle, by putting out a flagge of truce: the parle was granted, and certaine of the Spaniards came aboord the English. Where after conference about those matters that had passed in the fight betwixt them, they received reasonable intertainment and a quiet farewell. The Spanish, as if they had ment to requite the English courtesie, invited our men to their shippe who perswading themselves of good meaning in the Spanish, went aboord: but honest and friendly dealing was not their purpose, suddenly they assaulted our men, and one with a dagger

Spanish Treason.

---

¹ *Principal Navigations*, II (1599), pt. i, 285–9; VI (1904), 392; document 92 below; H.C.A. 25/3(9), 21 September 1592.
² Lansdowne MS 144, ff. 27 and 35; Harleian MS 598, f. 55; H.C.A. 13/27, 20 May 1589.
³ *Principal Navigations*, III (1600), 557; X (1904), 156–7.   ⁴ Lap.

May 1589. She may or may not have wintered there, but in any case Hakluyt's dating of the departure in the month of May can hardly be correct.[1] As to the operations in the West Indies, Abraham's testimony shows that Michelson was pursuing the conventional strategy of the English privateers, haunting the coast of Cuba from Cape San Antonio eastwards to Havana. In the treatment of the events leading to the act of treachery there are certain differences between the versions of Hakluyt and Abraham, and at every point the latter's first-hand account seems the more credible. Hakluyt tends to exaggerate the strength of the enemy, the duration of the fight and the achievement of the English crew. It is unlikely that a privateer of 60–70 tons would have attacked a Spanish man-of-war, and if, as Hakluyt suggests, the *Black Dog*'s company had virtually won the day, why did they not enter and take possession of the enemy ship in the usual way? It is more likely that the Spaniard was a merchantman and that the English, at the end of a day's fighting, were hardly in a position to enforce their demands. A note by Dr Julius Caesar concerning the prize goods brought home to Plymouth indicates that they were worth about £1800—probably at least twice the value of the *Black Dog* and all its victuals, armament and stores.[2]

Of the personnel, Roger Kingsnode, the pilot, has already been mentioned. William Mace, the master, a mariner of Ratcliffe, was master of the *Swiftsure* in 1590, and in 1591 accompanied Raymond and Lancaster on their East Indies voyage as master of the *Edward Bonaventure*. It was on this voyage that Mace, going ashore on the island of Great Comoro, was killed by the 'perfidious Moors'.[3] Edward Wilkinson of Tower Hill, the recipient of Mace's letters in 1589, had fought the Spanish as commander of the *Merchant Royal* in a Mediterranean voyage of

---

[1] Obviously the ship cannot have left England in the month of May and arrived off Cape San Antonio by the early days of the same month (documents 7 and 8 below). It is possible, however, that Crokes, Fisher and Webster (documents 9, 10 and 11) are referring not to their final, but to some earlier setting forth—Mansfield's libel and Cletherow's replies agree on the fact that the *Dog* put into Plymouth twice in the course of 1588. If they are speaking of their final departure, it seems likely that they did winter in the West Indies.

[2] Lansdowne MS 133, f. 23.

[3] See Mace's deposition concerning Mead Hole (H.C.A. 13/28, 15 November 1589); *Monson's Tracts*, I, 242; *Principal Navigations*, II (1599), pt. ii, 104; VI (1904), 51–2.

CHAPTER II

THE VOYAGE OF THE *BLACK DOG*
1588–9

Hakluyt's own account of this voyage—document 7—is disappointingly brief, and the fuller account given by Robert Abraham and others of the crew—documents 8–11—not only expands but in some details corrects the published version. William Mace's letters no doubt included much circumstantial matter which could find no place in what was clearly intended to be a telling piece of reportage. The process of 'extraction', in fact, was all too effective. The High Court of Admiralty documents printed here relate to the suit of Arthur Michelson, executor of the dead captain's will, but it is not clear whether he is merely laying claim to the ownership of the *Dog* and the prize goods or establishing the right of the heirs to compensate themselves in the usual way for wrongs or injuries done by the Spaniards. A further suit in the court arose from the claim of Stephen Mansfield (or Mansford) to ownership of a part or the whole of the *Black Dog*. The documents in this case show that Henry Cletherow, a London merchant who invested in several privateering ventures, was financially interested in Michelson's expedition and was perhaps part-owner of the *Dog*.[1]

The new evidence shows that the *Black Dog* of London left England in the Autumn of 1588 and reached the West Indies by

[1] Mansfield's libel, H.C.A. 24/60, no. 16; Cletherow's personal replies, H.C.A. 13/101, 20 May 1592; H.C.A. order for relaxation of arrest of the *Dog*, H.C.A. 14/26, no. 61. Henry Cletherow (Clitheroe, Cletherall, etc.) was an important London merchant, born about 1546; he was master of the Ironmongers Company in 1592, 1603 and 1606; he died in 1607 (John Nicholl, *Some Account of the Worshipful Company of Ironmongers* (1851), p. 552). His interest in shipping perhaps arose chiefly from his business as a rope merchant; he supplied rope for the Queen's ships, and was described as 'he that doth buy all things for Hawkyns' (Corbett, *Spanish War*, pp. 222, 249). He invested in various privateering ventures, including several to the West Indies. His son, Sir Christopher, became Lord Mayor, M.P. for the City and a leading merchant of his day.

wherein he was master & wente into the Chaunce but it was of his owne will.

6. Thomas Watts contra Robert FitzWilliams: deposition of Samuel Hearne[1]

SAMUEL HEARNE de Whitechapell in suburbiis Civitatis London nauta ubi habitavit et in hac Civitate London ubi natus fuit a nativitate, etatis viginti trium annorum aut circiter. .... *Thomas Wattes contra Robertum Fewilliams*

[To the 10th, 11th and 12th articles he says he has heard that Watts was captain of the *Margaret and John* before he was wounded] and of his sighte & knowledge he was a very loftye man. ...

   Ad Interrogatoria primo loco data. ....

Ad secundum respondet he was master Carpenters matte in the Examiner the said viadge.

[1] H.C.A. 13/27, 13 May 1589. Extract.

stabde Roger Kingsnod the Englishe Pilote to the heart and slewe him, and others were served with the like sauce, onely William Mace the Master & others, notwithstanding al the prepared trappes of the enemie, lept overboord into the sea, and so came safe to their own ship: and directing his course for England, arrived at Plimouth the tenth day of September 1589, laden with wines, yron, Roans, which is a kinde of linnen cloth, and other rich commodities, looking for the arrivall of the rest of his consorts, whereof one and the principall hath not long since obtained his Port. Thus much in generall termes onely I have as yet learned, and received touching this voyage, extracted out of letters sent from the aforesaid William Mace, to Master Edward Wilkinson of Towre-hill in London. My principall intention by this example is to admonish our nation of circumspection in dealing with that subtill enemie, and never to trust the Spanish further, then that their owne strength shall be able to master them: for otherwise whosoever shall through simplicitie trust curtesie, shall by tryall taste of their assured crueltie.

8. Querela *of Arthur Michelson: deposition of Robert Abraham*[1]

ROBERTE ABRAHAM of Ratcliffe mariner aged xlij yeares or thereaboutes sworne & examined before the righte worshipfull Master Doctor Cesar Judge of the Admiralty whether he wente not to William Michelson in the Blacke Dogge, what prizes they tooke, howe the same are disposed & what ys become of the said William Michelson & his company. Sayth he wente to sea with William Michelson in the Blake Dogge under Lettres of Reprisall and cominge to the quoast of High Spaniola they drove a Frigott ashore and had certaine canvas owt of her, and an other Frigott they tooke at sea havinge nothinge in her but balaste. And on the quoast of Cuba, and Campechio[2] they tooke viij or ix frigottes more wherein they had noe commodities but hennes & victualls bounde to the Galleyes at Avana. Savinge they had in one of the said Frigattes xvij or xviij pipes of spanishe wynes whiche wer broughte into England in the Blacke Dogge.

Querela Arthuri Michelson pro testibus examinandis.

Primus

[1] H.C.A. 13/28, 29 January 1589/90. Abraham was master of the *Flight* in the West Indies in 1592 (see below, p. 180).
[2] Campeche.

Also they tooke nere Cuba a spanishe shippe laden with Iron, horseshowes and other wroughte Iron certaine wynes, and packes of clothe beinge canvas and french cloth in his judgement, certaine Jarrs of oyles and other thinges which were broughte to Plimouth & there devided. And sayth that comminge to Cape St. Anthony on the quoaste of Cuba William Michelson the Captaine with x men of his company wente away from them in a Frigott sayenge they would goe to see the quoaste as high as the Avana and promised to returne againe within six dayes: and Roger Kingson the pilott who had the chardge of the Blacke Dogge in absence of the Captaine promised he would stay ten dayes for them and willed them thincke that if they were gon in that tyme that eyther they were driven away by the Galleyes, or else were gon to sea after some prize which was on the iiijth of Maye laste: and soe they departed from them, and on the viijth of the same moneth of May the said prize which they took with the Dogge and broughte to Plimouth came in sighte, where uppon the pilott & Master wayed anker and wente to sea after her and tooke her, and then plyenge towardes St. Anthony againe to seeke for theire Captaine, the Currant deceaved them, and drove them L leages to the westward on the quoast of Campechio, when as they thoughte they had byn to the Eastward on the quoast of Cuba, and by this meanes they could not fetch the said rode of St. Anthony although they did beate xx dayes upp & downe xx dayes to bringe yt to passe. And sayeth that beinge on the quoast of Campechio they escried a shippe of greate burthen takinge in her ladinge in a Rode which they attempted to take & foughte with her one whole day and not beinge able to take her, wantinge men & provition they came to Parla with the Spaniardes and demaunded fyve thowsand duckettes to departe & suffer them lade without doinge them harme: and the Captaine of the spanishe shippe requested respecte untill the nexte day to conferre with his partners and merchantes on lande; and came on bord the Dogge and had speeches with the pilott & company of the Dogge which was putt in writinge. And here uppon the pilott made the said spanishe Captaine and his company with him good cheare, and at his departure the pilott Roger Kingson, William Mace the Master, the surgion and thre or foure more would nedes goe in the shipp boate to bringe the Captaine on borde his shippe, and comminge to the shipp side by suger speeches were intised to goe on bord the spanishe shipp to be feasted by the Spaniardes in like sorte. And soe wente on board, and beinge in the Captaines cabon altogeather the Captaine made them good chere, and in the meane tyme concluded with his company to arme themselves and come to the cabon dore, and when he gave his token, to dispatche them: and thereuppon the Captaine came to the pilott & ymbracinge him with many thankes, drewe his dagger & stabbed the said pilott to the hart and presently a number more were redy at the cabon dore with rapiers and stabbed him likewise, togeather with John Hughes the Surgion & Edmund Bense the corporell: and William Mace the master & two others did leape over borde and were taken upp by by the boate & saved, althoughe all wounded by the said Spaniardes. By which treason they were berefte of theire said enterprize and forced to be gon with the Dogge: and her said prize before taken. And sayth that shortly after they tooke the said Frigott with wynes which ys before spoken of, and in the same was a spanishe merchant, who tould them he had byn a little more[1] taken by an Englishe man in a Frigott called Captaine Gulielm[2] as he termed him, and by signes and tokens both of him his frigott & company they verely thoughte yt should be theire Captaine William Michelson. And he tould them moreover the said Guliermo had first taken one ship of cxl tonnes with his said Frigott, and the same day tooke also an other shipp of Lx tonnes beinge Spaniardes one havinge viij caste peeces. With which prizes this examinate and company were in hope the said Captaine Michelson was gon towardes England for that they made no doubte by the tokens which the Spaniard gave of him, but yt should be he. And since that tyme he never herd of him. And more he cannot declare.

9. Querela of Arthur Michelson: deposition of John Crokes[3]

JOHN CROKES of Blackewall sayler of the adge of xxviij yeares or there aboutes. . . . Deposethe And sayethe That aboute

Querela Arthuri Michelson

[1] Before.
[2] Captain William—the Spanish frequently called English seamen by their Christian names.
[3] H.C.A. 13/28, 30 January 1589/90. Extract.

pro testibus examinandis.
2

xvj monethes a goe he wente to Seas withe the said William Michelson Captayne of the Blacke Dogge haveinge Commission agayneste Spaniardes & theire goodes as he toulde this examinate & the reste of the companye, in whiche shippe this examinate was that viadge quarter master's matte....

More he sayethe they toke of Cape Ste Anthony on the quoaste of Cuba a Spanishe shippe of the burthen of Cxx tons or there aboutes beinge laden withe wynes and wroughte iron as this examinate did heare for husbandry, for as he sayethe he was never on borde her. Which was broughte to Plymouth & ther dischardged & the Lord Admiralls tenthes ther payde to master Richarde Hawkins.[1]

10. Querela *of Arthur Michelson: deposition of John Fisher*[2]

Querela Arthuri Michelson pro testibus examinandis.
3

JOHN FISHER of Ratcliffe shippe Carpenter of thadge of xxiij yeares or there aboutes ... Sayethe as followethe, vizt That aboute xiiij or xv monethes a goe [he went to sea with Michelson in the] Blacke Dogge of London....

[This examinate recalls Michelson] sayeinge att his departure in this examinates hearinge farewell my masters, I will come agayne to morowe.

11. Querela *of Arthur Michelson: deposition of Thomas Webster*[3]

Querela Arthuri Michelson pro testibus examinandis.
4

THOMAS WEBSTER of Ratcliffe mariner of the adge of xvij yeares or there aboutes ... Sayethe as followethe vizt That aboute xvj monethes a goe he wente to Seas in the shippe the Blacke Dogge of London....

And was as he sayethe the sayde Michelsons boye that viadge.

12. *The appraisement of the* Black Dog[4]

The appraisemente and valewacion of the good shippe called the Blacke Dogge with here tacle and furniture and suche goodes as

[1] His father, Sir John, seems to have been responsible for the collection of the Lord Admiral's tenths in Plymouth at this time (Lansdowne MS 157, ff. 430, 434).
[2] H.C.A. 13/28, 30 January 1589/90. Extract.
[3] Ibid. Extract.
[4] H.C.A. 24/57, no. 27. The values given are almost certainly underestimated, as was usually the case in such appraisements.

THE *BLACK DOG*

is in here lately belonginge unto William Michelsonn and attached by the auchthority of this courte att the suite and instance of Arthure Michelson, executor of the Laste will and testamente of the saide William Michelson deceased, made by us, Edwarde Elliottes inferiores, Thomas Weste,[1] John Dowglas shippe masters, and Thomas Bodman shippwrighte the thirde of February 1589 as followethe:

Inprimis we the said appraysers dilligente vewinge and seinge the hull of the said shippe the blacke Dogge beinge of the burthen of Lx tons or there aboutes and of the adge of xviij yeares or there aboutes with here mastes and yeardes beinge very farre out of Repration doe esteame and valewe the same att	xiij^{li}	vj^s	viij^d
Item we valewe all the tacle above heade standinge and runninge wythe pulleys		xl^s	
Item one Cable halfe worne	vj^{li}		
Item a smale kedger[2] and an anker worthe	xl^s	vj^s	viij^d
Item, a mayne, for sayle, misen sayle 2 bonttett[3] for the mayne one for the forsayle, a mayne toppe sayle, and for toppe sayle all muche worthe		xx^s	
Item a minion and thre Falcons of caste iron containing thirty six hunderethe withe Ladell springes and cartridges we ratte att	xij^{li}		
Item an oulde boate and fowere oares		v^s	
Item 2 pickes & a boarespeare			xij^d
Item 20 shotte minion and faulcon		v^s	
Item 2 kettells of brase one naughte worthe		vj^s	viij^d
Item a Crowe of iron			xij^d
Item ij leade and Lyne			viij^d
Item 3 compasses and one Glasse			vj^d
Item a Fide[4]			ij^d

---

[1] See below, p. 338. [2] A kedge, or small anchor. [3] Bonnets.
[4] Fid—a square bar of wood or iron used to support the topmast at the head of the lower mast.

Item 5 muskettes and three Caliveres xvj^s
Item 64 endes of Lodgewood¹ cont*aining*
 iiijC weyghte we valewe att xl^s
Item fyve oxe hides in the heire xxv^s
Item two halfe pipes of Ilande wynes iij^{li}
Item 2 Sharons² of Brasill bedes³
 cont*aining* 42 beades xlij^s
Item certaine waxe in weyghte
 xx pound*es* xiij^s iiij^d
   Sum*m*a totalis xlvij^{li} ix^s vij^d

In witnes wherof we the saide appraysers to theyse presentes have putte our handes the daye and yeare a forsayde.

  T S W   Edward Eliot
   by me John Douglas
    Thomas Bodman

---

[1] Logwood.
[2] Serons or seroons: openwork baskets, probably of wood and hide.
[3] Brazil beds, or hammocks.

CHAPTER III

THE VOYAGE OF JOHN CHIDLEY
1589

JOHN Chidley was a young gentleman of Devon, born in 1565 into an old and well connected family.[1] His venture was evidently favoured in high quarters, for a special commission for the voyage was obtained from the Queen[2] and an order from the Privy Council prevented the appropriation of Chidley's victuals by the provisioners of the Portugal expedition.[3] At least one member of the Privy Council—Lord Hunsdon—invested in the venture,[4] and it may be that Sir Walter Raleigh, who was a kinsman of Chidley's, used his influence at Court to assist the project.[5]

It is clear from all accounts that Chidley hoped to repeat the recent successes of Cavendish in the South Seas and to return home via the East Indies. Although an ambitious project, of a kind promoted more often by gentlemen adventurers than by merchants, it probably attracted a large number of investors, of whom only a few are mentioned in the surviving documents.[6]

---

[1] See Sir William Pole, *Collections towards a Description of the County of Devon* (1791), pp. 170, 255, 260, 353; Maxwell Adams, 'A brief account of Ashton Church and of some of the Chudleighs of Ashton', *Transactions of the Devonshire Association*, XXXI (1899), 185–8; R. W. Cotton, 'An Elizabethan Adventurer', *Macmillan's Magazine*, LXXI (1894–5), 190–4. In the sixteenth century the name was usually rendered as 'Chidley'.

[2] For an undated copy of the commission see S. P. Dom. Eliz., ccxxxvii, f. 54. The Queen refused to sign the commission until a clause, committing the venturers to payment of customs duties on prizes, had been included (S. P. Dom. Eliz., ccxxiv, nos. 32, 39, 49).

[3] *A.P.C. (N.S.)*, XVII, 165–6.

[4] He owned two brass culverins in the *White Lion* (*A.P.C. (N.S.)*, XX, 114, 144–5; additional MS 12507, f. 146).

[5] Chidley's father's sister married one of Raleigh's half-brothers.

[6] The following are known to have invested in the voyage: John Chidley, Francis Manby, William Walton, Simon Furner, John Watts, Henry Cletherow, William Longe, Giles Fleming, Thomas Polwhele, Thomas Edwards, Ellis Dobson, and Lord Hunsdon. Furner, Watts, Cletherow and Fleming were London merchants, Walton and Edwards provincial merchants, the rest gentlemen.

But essentially it remained Chidley's own scheme, in which he and his chief partner, Francis Manby, held the decisive large shares. Manby, who was reputed to have sold the most part of his lands for the setting forth of the intended voyage,[1] and Chidley, who 'hassarded all his great estate unto ruyn',[2] were gambling for wealth and fame. Bad luck and bad management lost them their all, and Chidley his life. But John Watts and Henry Cletherow, who invested in the voyage, and Paul Bayning, who may have invested too, went on accumulating fortunes from more business-like kinds of venture.

Magoths[3] refers to three ships, the *Wilde man*, 300 tons, the *White Lion*, 340 tons, and the *Delight* of Bristol, and two pinnaces. The *Wildman* and one of the pinnaces, the *Wildman's Club*, had formerly been known respectively as the *Susan* and the *Susan's Handmaid* and had belonged to Paul Bayning, who sold the pinnace—and possibly the ship as well—to Chidley.[4] As for the *Delight*, this was a ship of 120 tons supplied by William Walton, one of the most prominent privateering merchants of Bristol. Chidley renamed her the *Robin* and gave Walton a bill of adventure in the voyage for £900.[5] The *White Lion*, formerly the *Elizabeth Bonaventure*, was bought from the London merchant Roland Odell for £1200.[6] No references occur in the High Court of Admiralty records or elsewhere to Magoths' second pinnace, but there is no reason to conclude from this silence that he was mistaken. On the other hand Simon Merrick's deposition[7] suggests that there may have been a sixth vessel, which was for some reason delayed in port and failed to join the rest of the fleet. With about 800 tons of shipping, this was one of the larger expeditions of our series. It was also one of the most expensive. The £600

[1] Document 16 below.

[2] Pole, op. cit., p. 255. He seems to have sold the manors of Broad Clist, Chidley and Clanton.

[3] Author of the account of the voyage of the *Delight* printed by Hakluyt (document 13 below).

[4] Documents 25–9 below. It is not clear whether the *Susan* was sold to Chidley by Bayning; the latter may have 'adventured' the ship, and thus become an important shareholder in the enterprise.

[5] Documents 31 and 32 below. According to Merrick's statement, Chidley became the owner; in this case Walton could claim a proportion of whatever the total assets of the joint stock might be at the end of the voyage.

[6] Documents 15, 20, 23, 24 below.

[7] Document 32 below.

Adams.[1] Chidley's widow, to whom possession of the *White Lion* was granted on the order of the Privy Council,[2] relied for her defence upon the plea that Thomas Polwhele was never in fact the owner of the *White Lion*, and could not therefore have disposed of any part of it. Meanwhile in June 1590 Elizabeth Chidley instituted proceedings to prove ownership and secure possession of the *Wildman's Club*, which had fallen into the hands of Richard Lewes.[3] A decree was soon issued in her favour, but possession itself was not so easily obtained. George Sydenham, who was authorized by the court to arrest the pinnace, sent in a pathetic report of his failure to get near her,[4] whereupon the court itself prosecuted Lewes for contempt of its jurisdiction.[5] Nevertheless the pinnace was still eluding the grasp of the authorities when Mistress Chidley began a suit against Lewes several months later.[6] Finally, in February 1592, depositions were made by witnesses in support of the widow's claim to the wreck of the *Robin*.[7] It is from the surviving material relating to these cases that the following documents and extracts have been selected— with the exception of Magoths' narrative and the petition of the company of the *Delight*, both of which were printed by Hakluyt.[8]

* * *

[1] Adams, a shipwright, sued for moneys expended in the repair of the *White Lion* before her departure. The documents relating to the case are: the libel (H.C.A. 24/58, no. 57); depositions on the libel by William Giddy, sailor, of Ratcliffe (H.C.A. 13/28, 8 February 1590/1), Francis Donning, servant to Richard Adams (ibid.), Rowland Downing, apprentice to Richard Adams (H.C.A. 13/28, 15 February 1590) and Henry Purey, servant to Richard Adams (ibid.).

[2] The Privy Council interested itself closely in the proceedings: *A.P.C.* (*N.S.*), XVIII, 439–40; XIX, 71, 75, 330; XX, 114, 144–5; Lansdowne MS 158, f. 103.

[3] The documents relating to the case are: Chidley's *querela* for the *Wildman's Club* (document 25 below); depositions on the *querela* by John Hearle (document 26 below), Paul Bayning, merchant, of London (H.C.A. 13/28, 1 July 1590) and Thomas Fernley, servant to Bayning (ibid.); sentence, for Chidley (H.C.A. 24/58, no. 183).

[4] H.C.A. 24/58 no. 148, 11 July 1590: 'A breyffe note of my proceadinges in thexecucion of the commission. . . . I repayred to the key of Mynhede . . . the said Barke lying a floyte in the Channell [but those in the bark] did wey Anker, and hoysed upe there sayles and drewe themselves farther into the Sea . . .'.

[5] Documents relating to the case are: articles of contempt brought against Lewes (H.C.A. 24/58, no. 152); personal replies of Lewes to the articles (document 30 below).

[6] Related documents are: Chidley's libel (document 27 below); depositions on the libel by Fernley and Hearle (documents 28 and 29 below).

[7] Documents 31 and 32 below. [8] Documents 13 and 14 below.

been destroyed by the defections of Wood and Kendall. Meanwhile the Spanish had by some means got wind of the English intentions. A letter of 10 March 1590, from Arica itself—the principal objective of Chidley and his companions—reported that the English had been expected for four months, and that substantial defence preparations had been made, 'for the viceroy hath intelligence that there are certeine Englishmen of war comming thither'.[1] Even had he survived to lead his force—or part of it—into the South Seas, Chidley's task would not have been easy. Drake and Cavendish had roused the enemy from their slumbers.

The legal wrangles which ensued were long and complicated, but what is known concerning the High Court of Admiralty proceedings may be summarized as follows. Not long after the *White Lion* returned, a suit was begun in the name of John Chidley, claiming ownership of the vessel, presumably in order to forestall the claims of the creditors of Thomas Polwhele, who had been the reputed owner of the *White Lion* before its departure.[2] Nevertheless claims upon the ship were later pressed by William Manby,[3] Giles Fleming,[4] John Watts[5] and Richard

---

[1] *Principal Navigations*, III (1600), 562; X (1904), 170. Hakluyt makes the marginal note: 'This was M. John Chidleys fleet.'

[2] The deposition of Thomas Edwards (document 15 below) is all that survives concerning this case.

[3] The documents relating to the case are the following: Interrogatories *ex parte* Manby (H.C.A. 24/58, no. 207); replies to the interrogatories by: Roland Odell (H.C.A. 13/28, 23 June 1590), Furner, Robinson and Wood (documents 16, 17 and 18 below); inventory of the *White Lion* (document 19 below). The case seems to have been brought by one William Manby, presumably because Francis Manby was dead.

[4] The documents relating to the case are the following: the libel (document 20 below); depositions on the libel by Acton, Campion and Dobson (documents 21, 22 and 23 below), and by the following: Richard Marshall, fishmonger, of London H.C.A. 13/28, 30 September 1590); Roland Odell, merchant, of London (H.C.A. 13/28, 1 October 1590); John Rider, scrivener, of London (H.C.A. 13/28, 2 October 1590); Richard Adams, shipwright, of Ratcliffe (H.C.A. 13/28, 13 November 1590). Personal replies of Elizabeth Chidley to the libel (H.C.A. 13/101, 2 November 1590). Elizabeth Chidley's allegation (H.C.A. 24/58, no. 114); depositions on the allegation by Thomas Edwards (document 24 below) and Richard Smith, yeoman (H.C.A. 13/28, 3 December 1590). Interrogatories *ex parte* Fleming for Chidley's witnesses (H.C.A. 23/4, f. 322).

[5] The documents relating to the case are: Watts' libel (H.C.A. 24/58, no. 132) with the attached schedule of goods; Chidley's allegation (H.C.A. 24/58, no. 120). Watts was suing for various nails, hoops, spikes, wines, oil and vinegar contributed by him to the fitting out of the *White Lion* and alleged in the libel to be worth £400.

we have only Magoths' narrative, though the eventual wreck of the vessel on the coast of Normandy was confirmed by Thomas Edwards and Simon Merrick.[1]

The *Wildman*, the *Wildman's Club* and the *White Lion* remained together until disease struck down the leader of the expedition on 6 November 1589,[2] near the Equator, about which time Polwhele also died.[3] These losses sealed the fate of the expedition. Soon afterwards Benjamin Wood and his company deserted with the *White Lion* and brought her into Weymouth shortly before 20 January 1590.[4] Meanwhile the *Wildman* and her *Club* made for Trinidad, which they reached probably in December or January. Here the crews stayed some time recruiting their healths, and here it was that Abraham Kendall and others stole away with the pinnace.[5] In April they put into Barry and disposed of the stolen vessel,[6] and about midsummer the *Wildman* herself returned.[7] The successive desertions of Wood and Kendall—two seamen who proved their capacity in later voyages—suggests that whoever remained in nominal command after Chidley's death[8] intended to continue operations and perhaps to resume the southward course. In any case, the nominal commander's authority in the circumstances must inevitably have been tenuous. The whole expedition was evidently weakened and demoralized by sickness and by the loss of its leader, and any remaining hope of pursuing the original objectives must have

---

[1] Documents 31 and 32 below.

[2] The date is given in the Inquisition Post Mortem on Chidley (Inquisitions Port Mortem (C. 142), 229, no. 137).

[3] Documents 21 and 29 below.

[4] The date of the inventory of the *White Lion* (document 19 below). See also document 21.

[5] Document 29 below. Kendall was one of the leading English navigators of his time. He accompanied Drake to the West Indies in 1585–6 and was recommended by Drake to Ralph Lane as a capable and experienced master (*Principal Navigations*, III (1600), 264; VIII (1904), 343–4). He was chosen in 1591 to be master of the *Merchant Royal* in George Raymond's expedition to the East Indies, but was sent home in charge of the sick before the expedition reached the Cape (*Principal Navigations*, II (1599), pt. ii, 103; VI (1904), 390). In 1594 he accompanied Dudley on his West Indies venture and afterwards wrote a rutter of the voyage. He died at sea in Drake's last voyage (ibid., III (1600), 575, 588; X (1904), 205, 241). For a general assessment of Kendall see Warner, *The Voyage of Robert Dudley to the West Indies, 1594–5*, pp. xv–xviii *et passim*.

[6] Document 30 below.

[7] Document 21 below.

[8] Perhaps Acton, perhaps Ellis (documents 21 and 29 below).

Chidley gave for the *Wildman's Club* was an exorbitant sum for a mere pinnace, and the *Robin* was probably worth far less than £900. The *White Lion* was not only re-sheathed and trimmed, but the shipwrights 'pulled her downe and builte her englishe like'.[1] With her victuals and elaborate equipment the *White Lion* must have cost some four or five thousand pounds to set forth, and if the other ships cost anything like as much in proportion the total outlay for the voyage must have exceeded £10,000.[2]

According to Magoths, the three ships and two pinnaces left Plymouth on 5 August 1589. Chidley commanded the admiral, the *Wildman*, in which John Ellis sailed as master, while in the *White Lion* Thomas Polwhele was captain and Benjamin Wood master.[3] Both Chidley and Polwhele had served with distinction at sea during the year of the Spanish Armada; Chidley was commended for his valour by the Lord Admiral himself[4] and Polwhele, though he seems to have had no part in the fighting, won praise by his devotion to his duties as a captain.[5] Wood, however, was probably a more experienced seaman than either of them; he had taken part in the expedition of Amadas and Barlow to Virginia in 1584 and in the voyage to the Azores set forth by Raleigh two years later, and had probably been at sea much of the time since then.[6]

The first setback—the separation of the *Robin* (under Andrew Merrick as captain and Robert Burnet as master) from the rest of the fleet—must have occurred in late August or September somewhere between Cape Blanco and the coast of South America. Of the subsequent hardships and misadventures of the *Robin*

---

[1] Deposition of Henry Purey in the case of Richard Adams *contra* the *White Lion* (H.C.A. 13/28, 15 February 1590/1).

[2] Document 23 below. Some indication of the scale of her fitting out is given by the inventory made shortly after her return (document 19 below).

[3] Magoths puts Ellis master of the *White Lion* and Wood master of the *Wildman* —evidently a mistake (see documents 18 and 29 below).

[4] Laughton, *Defeat*, II, 60.

[5] Ibid., I, 171–3.

[6] *Principal Navigations*, III (1600), 251; VIII (1904), 310; II (1599), pt. ii, 121; VI (1904) 437. The failure of 1589 does not seem to have damaged his reputation, for he next appears as commander of Lord Thomas Howard's expedition to the West Indies (documents 83, 85 below); he accompanied Sir Robert Dudley to the West Indies in 1594 and met his end as the leader of Dudley's Cathay venture of 1596 (*Principal Navigations*, III (1600), 574–8; X (1904), 205; III (1600), 852; XI (1904) 417; Sir William Foster, *England's Quest of Eastern Trade*, pp. 138–41).

ENGLISH PRIVATEERING VOYAGES

The names of us sixe that returned of all our company were these.

{ 1 William Magoths of Bristol.
2 Richard Bush.
3 John Reade.
4 Richard Hodgkins of Westburie neere Bristol.

The two strangers.

{ 5 Gabriel Valerosa a Portugal.
6 Peter, a Briton.

14. *The petition of the company of the* Delight[1]

A petition made by certaine of the company of the *Delight* of *Bristol* unto the Master of the said ship *Robert Burnet,* one of the consorts of M. *Chidley,* being in the Streights of *Magellan* the 12. of February 1589.[2]

We have thought good to shew unto you (being our Master) our whole mindes and griefes in writing: that whereas our Captaine Matthew Hawlse,[3] and Walter Street doe beginne to take into the Captaines cabin this 12. of Febr. both bread and butter, (such as was put in for the provision of the shippe and company) only to feed themselves, and a few others, which are of their messe: meaning thereby rather to sterve us, then to keepe us strong and in health: And likewise upon the same, hee hath taken into his cabin certaine furniture, as swords, caleevers, and musquets: We therefore not well knowing their intents herein, except by certaine wordes cast out unwares, wee may conjecture, that your death, which God forbid, by them hath bene determined: doe all most humbly desire you being our Master, and having charge of the shippe, and us, this present voyage committed unto you, to consider: First, that by Gods visitation wee have lost 16. men, and that so much the rather because they were not alotted such necessary provision, as was in the ship to be had. Also to consider the great losse of 15. of our men with our boat at Penguinyland within the Streights of Magellan: and of 7. good and ser-

---

[1] *Principal Navigations,* III (1600), 842–5; XI (1904), 385–9.
[2] 1589/90.
[3] Andrew Merrick, the captain at the outset of the voyage, had presumably died.

CHIDLEY'S VOYAGE

getting up in 8. houres. Thus after wee had spent 6. weekes in the Streight striving against the furie of the elements, and having at sundry times partly by casualtie, and partly by sicknes lost 38. of our best men, and 3. anckers, and nowe having but one ancker left us, and small store of victuals, and, which was not the least mischiefe, divers of our company raising dangerous mutinies: we consulted, though somewhat with the latest,[1] for the safegard of our lives to returne while there was some small hope remayning: and so set saile out of The Streight homeward about the 14. of Februarie 1590. We returned backe againe by The river of Plate; and sailing neere the cost of Brasill we met with a Portugal ship of 80. tunnes, which rode at an ancker upon the coast, who as soone as she descried us to chase her, incontinently weyed, & ran her selfe on ground betweene the yland of S. Sebastian and the maine land. But we for want of a good boat, and by reason of the foule weather, were neither able to bord her, nor to goe on shore. Thence in extreeme misery we shaped our course for the yles of Cape Verde, and so passing to the yles of The Açores, the Canaries being something out of our course; the first land that wee mette withall in our Narrow sea was The yle of Alderney. And having now but six men of all our company left alive, the Master and his two mates and chiefe Mariners being dead, wee ran in with Monville de Hage[2] eight miles to the west of Cherbourg in Normandie. Where the next day after our comming to an ancker, having but one in all left, being the last of August 1590. by the foule weather that rose the ancker came home, and our ship drave on the rocks: And the Normans which were commanded by the governor of Cherbourg (who came downe to us that night) to have layd out another ancker for her, neglecting his commandement, suffered her miserably to be splitted, with desire to enrich themselves by her wracke. Within few dayes after this last mischance foure of us being Englishmen departed from Cherbourgh, and passed home for England in a barke of Weymouth, leaving the two strangers there behinde us.

They returne homeward.

The yle of S. Sebastian in 24. degr. of southerly latitude on the coast of Brasil.

They land at Monville de Hage 8. miles West of Cherbourg.

The wracke of the ship by the malice of the Normans.

They arrive in England.

---

[1] Probably means that particular attention was paid to the point of view of the mutinous crew, whose petition to the master is dated 12 February—two days before the homeward course was adopted.

[2] Omonville-la-Rogue, between Cherbourg and Cap de la Hogue.

ENGLISH PRIVATEERING VOYAGES

there died of our company by Gods visitation of sundry diseases 16. persons. Wee stayed in this harborough 17. dayes to grave our ship & refresh our wearied people, hoping here to have met with our consorts: which fell out contrary to our expectations. During our abode in this place we found two little springs of fresh water, which were upon the Northwesterly part of the land, & lighted upon good store of seales both old and yong. From hence we sailed toward the Streight of Magelan, and entred the same about the first of January. And comming to Penguin yland within the Streight we tooke and salted certaine hogsheads of Penguins, which must be eaten with speed: for wee found them to be of no long continuance; we also furnished our selves with fresh water. And here at the last sending off our boat to the yland for the rest of our provision, wee lost her and 15. men in her by force of foule weather; but what became of them we could not tel. Here also in this storme we lost two anckers. From hence we passed farther into the Streight, and by Port famine we spake with a Spaniard, who told us that he had lived in those parts 6. yeeres, and that he was one of the 400. men that were sent thither by the king of Spain in the yere 1582. to fortifie and inhabit there, to hinder the passage of all strangers that way into the South sea. But that and the other Spanish colonie being both destroyed by famine, he said he had lived in an house by himselfe a long time, and relieved himselfe with his caleever until our comming thither. Here we made a boat of the bords of our chests; which being finished wee sent 7. armed men in the same on land on the North shore, being wafted on land by the Savages with certaine white skinnes; who as soone as they came on shore were presently killed by an 100. of the wilde people in the sight of 2. of our men, which rowed them on shoare, which two onely escaped backe againe to us with the boat. After this traiterous slaughter of our men, we fell backe againe with our ship to the Northeastward of Port famine to a certaine road, where we refreshed our selves with muskles, and tooke in water & wood. At this time wee tooke in the Spaniard aforesaid, and so sailed forward againe into the Streight. Wee passed 7. or 8. times 10. leagues Westward beyond Cape Froward, being still encountered with mightie Northwest winds. These winds and the current were so vehement against us, that they forced us backe asmuch in two houres, as we were

Two springs of fresh water found at Port desire.

They enter into the Streight of Magelan.

They loose 15. of their men by tempest.

A Spaniard taken at Port-famine.

Seven of our men killed by the treason of the Savages on the North shore.

They passed 7. or 8. times ten leagues Westward of Cape Froward.

13. *William Magoths' account of the voyage of the* Delight[1]

A briefe relation of a voyage of *The Delight*[2] a ship of *Bristoll* one of the consorts of M. *John Chidley* esquire and M. *Paul Wheele*,[3] made unto the Straight of *Magellan*: with divers accidents that happened unto the company, during their 6. weekes abode there: Begun in the yeere 1589. Written by *W. Magoths*.

The fift of August 1589. the worshipfull M. John Chidley of Chidley in the countie of Devon esquire, with M. Paul Wheele and Captaine Andrew Mericke set forth from Plimmouth with three tall ships, the one called The wilde man of three hundred tunnes, wherein went for General the aforesaid M. John Chidley and Benjamin Wood as Master, the other called The white Lion, whereof M. Paul Wheele was captaine and John Ellis Master,[4] of the burthen of 340. tunnes: the third The delight of Bristol, wherein went M. Andrew Merick as Captaine, and Robert Burnet Master, with two pinnesses of 14. or 15. tunnes a piece. The Generall in his ship had 180. persons: M. Paul Wheele had 140, in our owne ship we were 91. men and boyes. Our voyage was intended by the Streight of Magellan for The South Sea, and chiefly for the famous province of Arauco on the coast of Chili.[5] We kept company together to the yles of the Canaries and so forward to Cape Blanco standing neere the Northerly latitude of 20. degrees on the coast of Barbarie, where some of our people went on shoare finding nothing to their content. Within 12. dayes after our departure from this place The Delight, wherein I William Magoths was, lost the company of the other two great ships, and the two small pinnesses. Howbeit we constantly kept our course according to our directions along the coast of Brasil, and by the River of Plate, without touching any where on land untill we came to Port desire in the latitude of 48. degrees to the Southward of the Equinoctial. Before we arrived at this place

M. Chidleys voyage intended partly for Arauco in Chili.

Cape Blanco.

The Delight looseth the company of the rest of the fleet.

Port desire.

---

[1] *Principal Navigations*, III (1600), 839–42; XI (1904), pp. 381–4.

[2] Magoths uses her old name: Chidley had renamed her the *Robin*.

[3] Should read 'Thomas Polwhele'; the surname is variously spelt 'Powlwhele', 'Polewheel', etc.

[4] Wood was master of the *White Lion* and Ellis of the *Wildman* (documents 18 and 29 below).

[5] Arica, on the coast of Peru, more probably.

CHIDLEY'S VOYAGE

viceable men besides neere Port famine: and of three anckers, and our Carpenter. Over and besides all these calamities to consider how you have (without all reason and conscience) bene overthwarted, disgraced, and outcountenanced by your mate Street, and Matthew Hawlse: Also what danger you are now subject unto, your death having bene so often conspired, and what danger we should be in, if it were (which God forbid) effected. Furthermore, to weigh with your selfe the great want of many necessaries in our ship: namely that we have but 6. sailers, (besides your selfe and your mate Street, whom wee dare not trust,) Also that wee have but one ancker, likewise the lacke of our boate and a Carpenter, of ropes, of pitch, treynailes,[1] bolts, and plankes, and the want of a skilfull Chirurgian. And whereas a view being taken of our provision there was found but five moneths victuals of bread, meale, greets,[2] and pease, and also but three moneths victuals of beefe, penguins and porke, three hogsheads of wine, ten gallons of aquavitae (whereof the sicke men could not get any to relieve them,) foure hogsheads of syder and 18. flitches of bacon, &c. the company hath but three flitches. Also the said Captaine Hawlse and Street have taken and seased upon 17. potts of butter, with certaine cheese, and an hogshead of bread at a time, and have bene thereof possessed to their owne private uses: And have not onely immoderately spent the companies provision in butter, cheese, aquavitae, &c. but have also consumed those sweete meates, which were layed up in the shippe onely for the reliefe of sicke persons (themselves being healthy and sound, and withholding the said meates from others in their sickenesse) and even at this time also (by reason of the small store of our provision, wee being enforced to come to a shorter allowance) they the saide Captaine Hawlse and your mate Street, doe find themselves agrieved at the very same allowance, wherewith other men are well contented. And although (besides our ordinary allowance, and more then all the rest of the company) they only have their breakefasts permitted unto them, yet they complaine that the company goeth about to famish them, whereas indeed they doe what lyeth in them to famish the company by feeding themselves fat, which doe no labour at all. These things

---
[1] Tree-nails, or hard wood pins.
[2] Grit, or coarse oatmeal.

being well weighed, you ought likewise to consider the long time that wee have lien here in these Streights of Magellan, having bene at, and seven or eight times, tenne leagues beyond Cape Froward, we have had but a small gale of winde with us: neither could wee come to an ancker, the water being so deepe: and (you know) the place is so dangerous, that wee were once embayed, and coulde scarce get out againe: And likewise, What fogges and mists are here already? Much more here wil be, the winter and darke nights being at hand, & we having not so much as a boate to seeke out any roade to ride in, saving a small weake boate made of mens chestes, in which it is not convenient to goe on shoare in a forreine countrey, where wee must goe with force: and having but one ancker left us, there is but little hope of life in us, as you may sufficiently judge, if wee should lose either the saide ancker or our boate, and therefore wee dare not put the same in danger for feare of loosing them. Also wee having lien here these sixe weekes and upward, the winde hath continued in the North-west directly against our course, so that wee can no way hope to get through the Streights into the South sea this yeere, and if we could, yet our provision is not sufficient, having spent so much thereof, in this our lingering aboade. Nay wee have scarcely victuals ynough to cary us home into England, if they bee not used sparingly, and with very good government. Therefore wee doe againe most humbly desire you to consider and have regard unto the premisses, as you tender your owne safetie and the safetie of us which remaine alive, that wee may (by Gods helpe) returne backe into England, rather then die here among wilde and savage people: for if wee make any longer abode in this place, it will bee (without all doubt) to the utter decay and losse, both of our selves, and of the shippe: and in returning backe, it may please God, that we may finde our fifteene men, and our boat at Penguin-yland (although this bee contrary to the mindes of Matthew Hawlse, and your mate Street) and having found them, wee doe not despaire in Gods mercie, but that in our returne homeward, hee will send us purchase sufficient, if wee would joyne our selves together in prayer, and love one another. And thus doing (as wee shalbe bound) even so wee will also heartily pray for the continuance of your good estate, and welfare, and for the length of your dayes, to the pleasure of Almightie God.

Lastly, wee doe most humbly beseech you to consider, that (after the losse of so many men and all the casualties aforesaid, as we were taking in of water by Port Famine, our boate-swaine, the hooper,[1] and William Magoths being on shoare) Matthew Hawlse did hallow to have them in all the haste come on-bord: saying therewithall these words: He that will come in this voyage, must not make any reckoning to leave two or three men on shore behinde him, whereas we had so lately lost all the foresaide men, having then but sixe sailers left us on-bord. Also the saide Matthew Hawlse did cary a pistoll for the space of two dayes secretly under his gowne, intending therewithall to have murthered Andrew Stoning, and William Combe as by confession of Hawlse his man, William Martin, it is manifest: for the saide William Martine reported unto two of his friends, viz. Richard Hungate, and Emanuel Dornel, that he kneeled upon his knees one whole houre before Matthew Hawlse in his owne cabin, desiring him, for Gods cause, not to kill either of them, especially because the saide Stoning and Martin came both out of one towne. Also the said Hawlse, at our second time of watering in the place aforesaid, came into the Gunners roome to speake with you (your selfe with the master Gunner Thomas Browne, and his mate William Frier being then present) demanding of you, if he should send certaine men to Port famine being two leagues from the ship by land. Thomas Browne answered him presently, that he should send none, for feare least the wind might arise, and by that meanes we should loose so many of our men more: to whom Matthew Hawlse replied that it was not material, for that he had made choyce of a company for the very same purpose, whose names were Emmanuel Dornel, Richard Hungate, Paul Carie, John Davis, Gabriel Valerosa, a Portugall, and Peter a Britaine, and the Spaniard which we had taken in at the same place, at our first time of watering. And thus we end, desiring God to sende us well into our native countrey. In witnesse whereof wee have subscribed our names.

The Spaniard taken in at Port famine.

Thomas Browne, Gunner,
John Morrice, &c.

[1] Or cooper.

ENGLISH PRIVATEERING VOYAGES

15. Querela *of John Chidley: deposition of Thomas Edwards*[1]

Querela Johannis Chidley pro testibus examinandis

Primus testis

THOMAS EDWARDES of Exeter merchante of the age of xxxviij yeares or thereaboutes sworne and examined ... on the behaulfe of John Chidley....

[Deposes that Thomas Polwhele, having contracted to pay Roland Odell £1200 for the *Elizabeth Bonaventure*, defaulted in his payments; that John Chidley thereupon made the payments on behalf of Polwhele and with the latter's consent became owner of the whole ship.]

16. *William Manby* contra *Elizabeth Chidley: deposition of Simon Furner*[2]

SIMON FURNER of London mercer of the adge of xxxviij yeres or thereaboutes....

[To the first question, whether he knew Thomas Polwhele, Francis Manby and John Chidley and knew of their intended voyage, he replies that he knew of Polwhele's intended voyage] for that he was an adventurer with him Fifty poundes in the sayd voyadge....

[To the eighth question, who were the adventurers in the *White Lion*, what shares they had and whether he had heard Polwhele confess that Manby had a third share in the *White Lion*] he sayth that to his best remembraunce and as he hath herd that John Wattes of London merchant was an adventurer iiijC^{li}, Henry Cletherowe C^{li} and master Fraunces Manbye aboute xvj or xvijC^{li} and more....

[To the tenth question, what money did Manby spend upon furnishing and provisioning the ship] he sayth that aboute two or three monethes before the sayd master Powlewhele his goinge to sea the sayd Powlewhele and master Manbye came to this

---

[1] H.C.A. 13/28, 24 February 1589/90. Extract. The only known document relating to this case. Edwards made two other depositions for Elizabeth Chidley (documents 24 and 31 below).

[2] H.C.A. 13/28, 23 June 1590. Extract. This and documents 17 and 18 are depositions in the form of replies to interrogatories submitted by Manby. The interrogatories (H.C.A. 24/58, no. 207, headed 'Interrogatoryes to be ministred to the Witnesses produced on the parte & behalfe of William Manbye gent. Complainant against mistres Elizabeth Chidley widow defendaunt') are here summarized in the brackets.

ex*amina*te and desired him to deale frendly with them for that they were to buye some Corne Powder of him the provision of their shippe; and in the end bargayned with this ex*amina*te for the valewe of two hundreth and Forty poundes worth of Powder; for the which one m*aste*r williamson of Greys Inne whoe was a dealer for m*aste*r Manbye as this ex*amina*te herd entred into band for the payment. . . .

[To the eleventh question, what more he knows concerning Manby's expenses in and about the intended voyage] he sayth he hath herd that m*aste*r Fraunces Manbye hath sould the most p*ar*t of his land*e*s for the setting forth of the sayd p*re*tended voyadge.

17. William Manby contra *Elizabeth Chidley: deposition of James Robinson*[1]

JAMES ROBINSON of London marin*er* of the adge of xxviij^{ty} yeres or thereaboutes. . . .

[To the first question, whether he knew Polwhele, Manby and Chidley and knew of their intended voyage, he replies that he did] For that he was m*aste*rs mate of the shippe the White Lion and wente in the sayd p*re*tended voyadge.

18. William Manby contra *Elizabeth Chidley: deposition of Benjamin Wood*[2]

BENJAMYN WOODE of Ratcliffe m*aste*r of the shippe called the Elizabeth al*ia*s the White Lion of London of the adge of xxvj yeres or thereaboute*s*. . . .

[To the fifth question, how many men were hired to serve in the *White Lion* and whether Francis Manby did not pay £250 towards their wages] he sayethe there was hiered to serve in the s*ai*d shippe that intended viadge the number of eightey men, whate money was disbursed or layde out uppon them he cannot certaynely depose for that some ones had three poundes some xl^s some more some lesse as opportunity served wherof there was a note kepte but this ex*amina*te hathe loste the same. . . .[3]

---

[1] H.C.A. 13/28, 24 June 1590. Extract. Robinson was the author of the inventory of the *White Lion* (document 19 below).

[2] H.C.A. 13/28, 25 June 1590. Extract.

[3] Magoths puts the number of men in the *White Lion* at 140, which would include soldiers. Payment of wages in advance was usual only in voyages expected to be of long duration.

[To the eighth question, who were the adventurers in the *White Lion*, what shares they had and whether he had heard Polwhele confess that Manby had a third share in the *White Lion*] he sayethe m*aste*r John Chidley for xjC^{li} Fraunces Manbye for xvjC^{li} W*illia*m Longe for ijCxlv^{li} John Wat*te*s & diverse others whose names he knowethe not weare adventurers in the White Lion....

[To the ninth question, whether the ship and furniture has since come into the hands of Mistress Chidley and how much they are worth, he replies that on his return to Weymouth after the voyage he was very sick and asked Nicholas Jones of Portland Castle to look after the ship and the interests of the adventurers, with which request Jones complied.]

19. Inventory of the White Lion *after her return to England*[1]

20 Januarye 1590

A not of suche goods as wear deliverid out of the whyt Lion at wemouthe as foloiethe

Imprimis deliverid in to a lytter[2] of the towne 14 barrilles 240 stokefyshe.

Deliverid in to a barke of the towne 3800 stokfyshe 40 barrilles 23 musketes 6 calivers[3] 4 leadinge staves on[4] Ensinge stafe.[5]

Deliverid in to burttes lyter 17 emptye hogsheds on barrill wythe bred 12 bundell wooden hopes 8 doussen Iron houpes 5 Jars of tar 17 barnecoukes[6] wythe Iron houpes 2 nettinges.[7]

Deliverid in to gilbarts lyter 400 Round shot 140 crossebar shot

---

[1] This inventory, made immediately after the return of the *White Lion*, was produced as evidence in Manby *contra* Chidley, but was not a High Court of Admiralty appraisement (cp. document 12 above). With her six sails the *White Lion* was normally rigged, and her armament, headed by ten demi-culverins, was quite impressive. For the explanation of the technical terms used in this document, reliance has been placed upon: Corbett, *Spanish War*; *Monson's Tracts*; and Smyth, *Sailor's Word Book*.

[2] Lighter.

[3] A kind of light musket.

[4] The usual spelling for 'one' in this document.

[5] Ensign staff.

[6] Probably a corruption of 'barricoes'—small casks.

[7] Nets protecting the waist of the ship against boarders.

30 langerill shot[1] 2 grapenells[2] 2 dossen Iron houpes 13 ston shot 17 muskettes 22 calivers 39 bandeleris[3] 11 flaps[4] 5 tuchboxes[5] 18 musket moles[6] 6 dussen mussket arowes on baskett wythe shott. Deliverid in to henrye hebbers liter 12 emptye hogsheds on greate cettell[7] on drom 8 dossen pikes 2 dossen bills 10 ladells 11 spounges 3 fyer pickes[8] 3 crows of Iron 2 hamers for to beat stockfishe 2 flaskes 13 targets 2 pump brakes of Iron 3 dossen musket restes 12 empty carteriges 10 wythe pouder 22 casses wythe stone 6 stormers[9] 27 arrowes 29 muskit stickes.

Deliverid in to burtes lyter 3 anker stokes 4 fyshes for the mayne mast[10] 3 plankes on david[11] for the bote on bots thought[12] 19 hogsheds 2 kettells 3 small seckes[13] on bakynge pan wythe a cover on spyt on skelyt on pot haunger.

Deliverid the 24 of Januarye to a barke of wemouthe on great barill of poulder 2 small barilles of poulder on great coper pott to sethe pesse in[14] on brasse cettell 6 hydes to cover the poulder wythe all 4 barilles of mache[15] won chest of candelles won funill of poulder 7 foullears chambers[16] 2 demicoulverin shott[17] won ston

---

[1] Round shot: ordinary round-shaped shot; cross-bar shot: shot which expanded on leaving the muzzle into the shape of a cross, with four quarters of a shot at its radial points, and which was used to destroy rigging as well as personnel; langrel or langrange shot: shot consisting of fragments of iron bound together.

[2] Grappling irons.

[3] Bandaleers: wide leathern belts for the carriage of small, wooden, leather-covered cases, each containing a charge for a firelock.

[4] Covers for cartridge boxes.

[5] Receptacles for lighted tinders.

[6] Molls, or ramrods.

[7] Kettle.

[8] Fire-bearing pikes or lances, used in fighting or in signalling. 'Firepikes were made with a coating, along the pike head, of fine powder, sulphur, saltpetre, sal-ammoniac, powdered glass, resin, spirits of wine, and oil. Pieces of lead and iron were stuck in the mixture, which was lit by a wick fixed upon a needle imbedded in it' (*Monson's Tracts*, III, 44).

[9] Probably formers, or small cylindrical pieces of wood, on which the musket cartridge-cases were rolled and formed.

[10] Long pieces of hard wood, so shaped that they could be bound lengthwise and in pairs to the masts to strengthen them.

[11] Davit.

[12] One boat's thwart—a seat or bench set athwart the boat.

[13] Sacks.   [14] To boil pease in.   [15] Match.

[16] Fowlers' chambers. Powder chambers for fowlers, which were guns of about 5 inch calibre, firing a shot of about 8 lbs. weight (Corbett, *Spanish War*, pp. 331–2).

[17] A demi-culverin was a gun of about $4\frac{1}{2}$-inch calibre, firing a shot of about 10 lbs. weight (ibid.).

morter a sprit sall wythe a bonnit a mayne bonnit a fore bonnit a fore topsall a myson bonnit won bugd barrill[1] of muskyt shot won small barill of muskyt shot, 63 barrilles of peas meall and otmeall won wythe a nouthear[2] 2 barrilles of mustersed 12 Runninge glasses 4 compases won flage.

Deliverid the 26 of Januarye from a bord the shype—the mayne course, the four course the mayne topsall wythe the yeard the mayne yeard, the myson yeard, the mayne halleards wythe the tyes the mayne parrill,[3] the top sall sheats wythe the lyftes the mayne martenits[4] the top sayll parrill wythe the tye the mayne braces the myson halleards wythe the tye the sprit sall yeard 2 flag stafes won flagstafe for the myson the mayne top sall boulinges the clulines the mayne sheats the mysson sheates wythe outhe[5] 2 small ropes.

 A note of the Whyte Lions ordnaunce that was Remaninge a bord wythe the Rest of her provision as folowethe

Imprimis 2 demicoullverins of brasse[6]

8 demicoulverins of Iron

8 Sakers of Iron[7]

4 foullears of Iron

5 ankers 4 cabelles

2 new hausers

1 small warpe[8]

the fore yeard the fore topmast

the fore topsall yeard the for top

the mayne top the fore top sall sheates

the fore boulinges the lyftes the clulines

the fore martinets the for top sayll braces

the fore braces wythe the Rest of hyr provision Remaninge a borde

---

[1] A budge-barrel or small cask, one head of which was formed by a leather bag, drawing close by a string, for carrying powder in safety from sparks.

[2] One with another.

[3] Parral or parrel: bands of rope by which the centres of yards are fastened at the slings to the masts, leaving them free to slide up and down as required.

[4] Martnets—the leech-lines of the mainsail.

[5] Without the.

[6] Brass guns were by this time common in the Queen's ships, but still rare in privateers. These were probably the 'culverins' belonging to Lord Hunsdon.

[7] A saker was a gun of about 4 inch calibre, firing a shot of about $5\frac{1}{2}$ lbs. weight (Corbett, *Spanish War*, pp. 331–2).

[8] A rope or light hawser.

the viadge and returne for England, trymmed upp the said Pinnace, and secretly without knowledge of the said Ellys master of the Wildman stole away, from the shippe, and caryed foure with him in the Pinnace for England. Which he knoweth to be true for that he was in the Wildeman at such tyme as the said Kendall stole away with the said Pinnace.

Ad duodecimum dicit the Wildemans Clubbe had in her one sacre, haulfe a dozen muskettes & calivers as he taketh yt when Kendall did stele awaye with [her].

30. Replies of Richard Lewes to articles of contempt brought against him[1]

Responsa personalia Richardi Lewes facta articulis contemptus adversus eum pro parte Domini Admiralli Anglie datis sequuntur.

[Accused of contempt of the jurisdiction of the Lord Admiral and the High Court of Admiralty, in withholding the pinnace called the *Susan's Handmaid* alias the *Wildman's Club* from Admiralty Court officials with warrants for its arrest on behalf of Elizabeth Chidley, Lewes states] ...

that he never knewe or hearde of the articulate Pinnace or carvell untill Aprill laste at which tyme the same arrived at Barry & afterwardes mistress Chidley made clayme to the same. ...

that Abraham Kendall did pawne the said pinnace to this respondente for xxv^{li} and a sacre for iiij^{li}.

31. Deposition of Thomas Edwards concerning the Robin[2]

THOMAS EDWARDES of the City of Exon. merchante of the age of forty yeares or thereaboutes sworne and examined before the righte worshipfull master Doctor Cesar Judge of her Majesties high Courte of the Admiralty on the behaulfe of mistres Elizabeth Chidley widowe concerninge a shippe called the Robyn of Bristowe, and the property of the same Deposeth

---

[1] H.C.A. 13/101, 31 July 1590. Extract. In the articles of contempt (H.C.A. 24/58, no. 152) Lewes is accused of saying: 'Lett mistres Sydley and all the frindes shee hathe do what shee cann yf yt bee not a hanginge matter shee shall not have the pynnace...'.

[2] H.C.A. 13/29, 17 February 1591/2. No marginal indication of the nature of the case is given, but it is evidently another *querela*, this time for the *Robin*.

29. *Elizabeth Chidley* contra *Richard Lewes:*
deposition of *John Hearle*[1]

JOHANNES HERLE famulus magistri Pauli Baninge mercatoris London cum quo habitavit per quadriennium aut circiter etatis sue triginta aut circiter attingens annos....

Ad secundum dicit that master John Chidley died in the said viadge nere the Lyne of this examinates knowledge beinge presente on borde the same shippe when he dyed. Ac aliter nescit.

Ad tertium quartum et quintum affirmat that master Chidley of this examinates knowledge was by him selfe & his servantes in possession of the said shipp or Pinnace called the Wilde mans Clubbe at the tyme of his death and untill the same was caried away towardes Englande. And this examinate was presente in the Cabon when master Chidley made his laste will, and required John Ellys master of the Wildeman to deliver both the shipp & the said Pinnace to his wiffe togeather with the tacle furniture & other thinges belonginge to them, and soe the said Ellys promised yf yt lay in his power to doe yt. Ac aliter nescit.

Ad sextum et septimum affirmat that after the death of master Chidley: Abraham Kendall James Davys, and William Towers did stele awaye the said Pinnace the Wildmans Clubbe from John Ellys & his company who was putt in truste to bringe her to Englande: aboute the Sotherne parte of the West Indies, and soe lefte the company of the Admirall beinge the Wildman, and came away for England in the said Pinnace the Wildmans Clubbe, and since as he hath herde the said Kendall soulde the said Pinnace. Ac aliter nescit.

Ad octavum et nonum decimum et undecimum affirmat verum esse that Richard Glover was Captaine of the Wildemans Clubbe by the appoynctemente of master Chidley & soe continued untill sicknes happened amongst them both in the shipp & Pinnace, and soe they sayled to an Island called Trinidatho after the death of master Chidley where they remaynned a tyme to recover theire healthes, and the said Richard Glover beinge also sore sicke did leave the Pinnace for his healthes sake, and in the meane tyme Abraham Kendall & some others with him consultinge to leave

[1] H.C.A. 13/28, 19 November 1590. Extract. Deposition on the libel.

26. *Elizabeth Chidley* contra *the* Wildman's Club: *deposition of John Hearle.*[1]

JOHN HEARLE servaunte unto master Paule Baninge of London merchaunte of the adge of xxvj or there aboutes. ...

[Confirms the first three articles of the *querela*, adding] but suere he is the said master Chidley sayled therewithe unto the Weste Indies for this examinate wente the said viadge in the Suzanne otherwise the Wildemane in Company of the said Pinnace.

27. *Elizabeth Chidley* contra *Richard Lewes:* the libel[2]

[Pleads that John Chidley was rightful owner of the *Susan's Handmaid*, alias the *Wildman's Club*, and sailed with it on his voyage; that on his death, Richard Glover, gent., captain of the pinnace, was deputed to hold it on behalf of Elizabeth Chidley; that subsequently Glover was forced by illness to leave the pinnace, which was then stolen by Abraham Kendall, one of the crew; that Kendall later disposed of the pinnace to Richard Lewes, who refuses to deliver the pinnace to its rightful owner, Elizabeth Chidley. This libel submitted to the court 23 October 1590.]

28. *Elizabeth Chidley* contra *Richard Lewes:* *deposition of Thomas Fernley*[3]

Elizabetha Chidley contra Richardum Lewes Primus testis super Libello

THOMAS FEARNLYE famulus Pauli Baninge mercatoris Londinensis cum permansit[4] per triennium natus in oselworth in Comitatu Glocester annos agens xxij aut circiter. ...

[To the first article he states] that master John Chidley aboute whitsontyde in the yeare 1589 was lawfull owner & possessor of a Carvell or Pinnace called the Susans handmaide and as owner thereof did munite & furnishe the same with victualls provision & other necessaries for a viadge intended to the South seas ... [and that three of Paul Bayning's men sailed in that voyage.]

[1] H.C.A. 13/28, 1 July 1590. Extract. Deposition on the *querela*.
[2] H.C.A. 24/58, no. 122. Summary. Translated. For the full text of a libel, see document 157.
[3] H.C.A. 13/28, 18 November 1590. Extract. Deposition on the libel.
[4] Should read 'cum quo permansit'.

CHIDLEY'S VOYAGE

m*aste*r Polewhele say he was greatly beholdinge to m*aste*r watt*es* & that he had adventured with him in the s*ai*d viadge thre or foure hundreth pounds.

25. *Elizabeth Chidley* contra *the* Wildman's Club[1]

FRANCISCUS CLERK exhibuit p*rocu*r*ationem* suam pro gener*osa* muliere Elizabetha Chidlie ... dedit allegat*ionem* et articulos sequentes et petit Ius et Iustitia.

Imprimis That aboute iij or ij yeares last past Paull Bayninge of London grocer, was lawfull owner, of a certaine small pinnise of the purden of xxv tunes or theraboutes, then called the Suzans Handmaide, and now called the Wildmans clubb....

Item That above a yeare or ij last past the sayd Paule Bayninge being in possession of the sayd Penise did lawfullie barginge and sell the sayd Pinnise w*i*th her takle and furniture to m*aste*r John Chidlie Esquire now deceased....

Item That after And by reason of the premisses the sayd John Chidlie was lawfull owner of the sayd Pinnise & in possession thereof and made a Journie w*i*th her unto the West Indies, and in the same voyage in the West Indies, or in some partes beyonde the sayd seas being in possession of the sayd pinnise died....

Item that after the death of John Chidlie the administracion of all the goodes of the sayd John Chidlie, was com*m*itted by a competente Judge to Elizabeth Chidlie....

Item that by reason of the premisses ... the sayd m*istres*s Chidlie administratrix a foresaid or some other in her name did enter into and tooke possession of the sayd Pinnise....

Item the premisses not w*i*thstanding the same Pinnise is by force & violence kept fro*m* her and possession taken from her, And therfore she desireth that first and befor all things she may be but in possession by the auctoritie of this courte.

---

[1] H.C.A. 24/58, no. 197. Extract, undated. This document is a draft of the *querela*. There is appended a note from Mistress Chidley's proctor, presumably to the registrar of the Court, asking him to summon the witnesses, to make out a sentence for Chidley and to issue a warrant to give her possession. The judge, he writes, has authorized these proceedings, which are usual in such cases, and he ends: 'Theis things requier present dispatch or els it will not serve m*ist*res Chidleis turne'. Sentence was granted (H.C.A. 24/58, no. 183) and a warrant issued (referred to in H.C.A. 24/58, no. 148).

by chardge of his oath that master John Chidley at his goinge to sea two yeares & a haulfe paste had a shipp of one William Walton of Bristowe of the burthen of Cxx tonnes or thereaboutes which master Chidley called the Robyn and furnished with artillery & other provision for a viadge to the South sea, and apoyncted Andrewe Merrick captaine of the same: and this examinate knoweth that master Chidley caried the said shipp the Robyn with other shipps in a flete to sea with them, and since this examinate hath herde say that the said shippe is caste away at Mountfeld in normandy. And this he knoweth to be true for that this examinate was an Adventurer with master Chidley in that action and on borde him at his departure & followed him to the Landes ende of England whereby he knoweth he caried the said shipp to sea with him.

32. Deposition of Simon Merrick concerning the Robin[1]

SIMON MERRICK of London gent. aged xxv yeares or thereaboutes sworne & examined before the said Judge of the Admiralty deposeth that master Chidley of this examinates knowledge had the said shipp the Robyn with her furniture of William Walton of Bristowe about thre yeares past and furnished her with munition and provision to make a viadge to the South seas which he then entended with other shippes; and gave a bill of adventure to the said William Walton of ixC^{li} for the same: and thereuppon the said John Chidley proceeded on his said viadge in his shippe the Wildman haveinge the said shippe the Robyn in his company whereof Andrewe Merricke was Captaine of this examinates knowledge who sawe him sett sayle uppon his viadge & sayled after him to have overtaken him with intente to have gon with him whereby he knoweth that master Chidley caried the said shipp the Robyn to sea with him and was owner thereof and since he knoweth that the said shipp the Robyn is cast away in her returne towardes England nere Mountfeild on the quoast of normandy For this examinate hath byn there and hath sene the peeces of the shipp that are saved & had procuration from mistres Elizabeth Chidley the late wiffe & Administratrix of the said John Chidley to recover the same to her use.

[1] H.C.A. 13/29, 17 February 1591/2.

CHAPTER IV

THE VOYAGE OF THE *BARK YOUNG*
1590

OUR knowledge of the voyage of the *Bark Young* to the West Indies in 1590 is based primarily upon High Court of Admiralty materials. The chief documents are connected with the claim of the owners of the privateer that certain French ships had robbed the *Bark Young* of a Spanish prize captured by the English company in the West Indies.[1] Further light is thrown upon the voyage by some passing references made to it in later depositions in the dispute between Sir George Carey and John Watts over prizes taken in 1591.[2]

The chief adventurers in the voyage of the *Bark Young* of Chichester were John Young and John Crooke, her owners, and Sir George Carey. John Young, a Chichester man, was an old sea-dog. He had seen service in Mary's reign and had been deeply involved in the activities of those ambiguous cruisers who had sailed under the flag of Don Antonio in the early eighties. After the outbreak of the Spanish war in 1585 he is found combining his duties as customer of Chichester and captain in the Armada campaign with his private business as shipowner, promoter of reprisal ventures and dealer in prize-goods, and this many-sided concern with maritime warfare made him one of the key men in that large privateering base which comprised Southampton, Portsmouth, Chichester and the Isle of Wight.[3] His partner, John Crooke, was a merchant and shipowner of Southampton, another old hand at the game of maritime spoil, whose name had

[1] Documents 33-7 below.
[2] Documents 64 and 69 below.
[3] His 'notes on Sea-service' (*Monson's Tracts*, IV, 202-27), probably written in 1596, contain some biographical details as well as much valuable material on sea-fighting. See also S. P. Dom. Eliz., cclix, no. 48. There are many references to his activities in the H.C.A. records (e.g. his deposition in H.C.A. 1/43, 27 October 1583). In 1597 he was appointed special adviser to the Lord Admiral and Dr Caesar in prize causes (Lansdowne MS 157, f. 256).

4. George Carey, 2nd Lord Hunsdon
Miniature by Nicholas Hilliard, 1601. Berkeley Castle

been linked with Young's before this.[1] Sir George Carey, whose interest in the voyage is revealed in his letter to the mayor of Southampton,[2] was represented in the ensuing legal action by his steward, George Bland, and William Irish, captain of the privateer, was another of Carey's men. Although Carey's financial share in the venture may not have been large, his interest was, in another sense, the controlling one. For his was the dynamic and directing spirit in most of the operations based upon the Isle of Wight and the neighbouring ports in the early years of the war. Captain-general of the Isle of Wight, vice-admiral of Hampshire, kinsman of the Queen, son of the Lord Chamberlain, brother-in-law of the Lord High Admiral, his power in the region was overwhelming. His letters to Dr Caesar show him crude and forthright in manner, aggressive in spirit, a friend and abettor of pirates, a receiver of illegal spoil. He knew personally many of the captains of the privateers, some of whom wore his livery. He had many dealings with the merchants and shipowners of the region. He was a promoter of privateering ventures himself. The voyage of the *Bark Young* may be considered as one of the three West Indies expeditions which he set forth under the command of his servant Captain William Irish of the Isle of Wight.[3] This last, a man of about thirty in 1591, was one of Carey's retinue, a gentleman in the livery of a nobleman. He had been to sea in Carey's ships since 1585 and is last heard of in 1596, still a captain in the same service.[4]

It was in February or March, 1590, that the *Bark Young* sailed

---

[1] Crooke is frequently mentioned in the H.C.A. records. For depositions by him see H.C.A. 13/23, 7 June 1578, and H.C.A. 13/25, 1 April 1586.

[2] R. C. Anderson, *Letters of the Fifteenth and Sixteenth Centuries* (Southampton Records Society, 1921), p. 180: Sir George Carey to Peter Stonier, mayor of Southampton, dated Greenwich, 2 February 1589/90. Requests Stonier to permit the bearer, William Irish, captain of the *Bark Young*, to pass to the Isle of Wight with his bark, to take in at the Isle of Wight certain victuals for his provision, 'which is my adventure in this his pretended voiage.'

[3] George Bland's position is referred to in H.C.A. 13/26, 12 October 1586. For Carey's letters to Caesar, see Lansdowne MS 158, ff. 54–66. Many references to Carey's privateering interests occur in the H.C.A. records and elsewhere, notably in Additional MS 11405. For the 1587 West Indies voyage, see *Roanoke Voyages*, pp. 498–9; *Further English Voyages*, pp. lxx–lxxi and 233–5; *Monson Tracts*, II, 229. For the 1591 venture, see below, pp. 95–172. There may have been other West Indies ventures promoted by Carey (e.g. in 1588—see pp. 40–3 above).

[4] Documents 34 and 69 below, and Harleian MS 598, f. 40.

for the Caribbean.[1] On 5/15 May she captured a prize of sugar and hides off Santo Domingo.[2] Meanwhile on 3/13 May Diego Menéndez de Valdés reported from Puerto Rico that 'eight days ago ... there arrived [on the south side] ... an Englishman, 50 tons burden, 30 crew, six pieces of artillery, two being brass pieces. He said that he was going to Florida to take off 200 English cast away there with their ship ...'.[3] This event must have occurred about 25 April/5 May. It has been suggested that the English ship in question was the *John Evangelist*, one of the ships sent out this year by John Watts.[4] Indeed it is well known that Watts' ships did intend to visit the coast of Florida in search of the lost colonists. Nevertheless John White's account of the expedition shows that these ships did not leave Dominica, their first landfall in the West Indies, until 2/12 May, a full week after the English vessel was seen and spoken to on the coast of Puerto Rico.[5] On the other hand the English privateer could have been the *Bark Young*, which was of some 55 to 70 tons burden[6] and which might well have approached Santo Domingo by the route along the south coast of Puerto Rico. Furthermore, there is some evidence that Carey was interested in Florida, since Irish had apparently sailed thither in 1587.[7] The proximity of the *Bark Young* and Watts' ships on 5/15 May, when the latter were operating off Puerto Rico, suggests that there may have been some understanding between them, and a further coincidence makes this appear more likely. The *John Evangelist*, as we know from John White's report, arrived at Cape Tiburon, at the western extremity of Hispaniola, before 21/31 May and was joined there by the rest of Watts' fleet and later by the *Moonlight* and the *Conclude*. Cape Tiburon was in fact the rendezvous of the Virginia expedition of that year, and Watts' men remained there,

[1] After the date of Carey's letter to Stonier (2 February), but probably not later than the date of the departure of Watts' fleet (20 March—*Principal Navigations*, III (1600), 288; VIII (1904), 406).

[2] Documents 33–6 below. The dates are here given in old and new style, since we are referring to both English and Spanish sources.

[3] *Further English Voyages*, p. 244.

[4] Ibid., p. lxxvi. For a detailed examination of the 1590 expedition, see *Roanoke Voyages*, pp. 579–716.

[5] *Roanoke Voyages*, p. 600.

[6] Laughton, *Defeat*, II, 182; H.C.A. 25/1 (4) 29 October 1585.

[7] *Further English Voyages*, pp. lxx–lxxi and 233–5.

with the aim of intercepting the Santo Domingo fleet bound for Havana, until 2/12 July. Now it was later revealed that the *Bark Young* took another prize in the course of her 1590 voyage—a prize captured off Cape Tiburon with the aid of the *Falcon's Flight*, a ship of Barnstaple.[1] The prize-goods were shared between the captors and when the *Bark Young* returned to Southampton she declared 'divers small parcels', including two elephant's tusks, some linen cloth, coarse thread, hats and women's doublets.[2] It is at least possible that Irish at Cape Tiburon made contact, or intended to make contact, with Cocke, Newport and the rest. To sum up: Watts' fleet was certainly preceded by a ship, answering to the description of a bark, whose crew knew of the intentions of the larger expedition and evidently meant to play their part in rescuing the colonists. This ship could have been the *Bark Young*. There is no other ship known to have been in the vicinity of Puerto Rico at the time indicated by the Spanish report. The Cape Tiburon episode provides supporting circumstantial evidence, but whether the *Bark Young*'s 1590 voyage was or was not a 'North American' voyage must in the end remain largely a matter of conjecture.

As for the *Falcon's Flight*, she was owned by John Norris, a Barnstaple merchant who promoted numerous privateering ventures. In 1592 and 1593 this ship, although still owned by Norris, is found sailing with the Earl of Cumberland's expeditions.[3] There is no evidence, however, that Cumberland organized a West Indies venture in 1590, though two of his ships are known to have been at sea that year.[4]

The next news of the *Bark Young* finds her leaving the harbour of 'Noterdam'[5] in Newfoundland on 6/16 August. Thus the possibility that Irish did reconnoitre the mainland coast cannot

---

[1] Documents 64 and 69 below.
[2] Worth a mere £80 (Harleian MS 598, f. 8; Lansdowne MS 133, f. 23).
[3] H.C.A. 24/59, no. 103; H.C.A. 24/62, no. 176.
[4] The *Robert* of London, under Nicholas Downton, brought a prize of sugar, hides and ginger to Portsmouth on 28 November 1590 (Harleian MS 598, f. 10). The *Delight* of Southampton, under Thomas Covert, took various prizes this year (Lansdowne MS 133, f. 24; H.C.A. 13/29, 27 January 1591/2; H.C.A. 14/27, nos. 21 and 65/6).
[5] The Bay of Notre Dame on the north coast of the island.

be ruled out. The clash with the seven French ships now ensued, and the *Bark Young* was home by 2/12 October.[1]

* * *

33. *Articles of a querela for George Bland, John Young and others*[2]

Articles ministred in her Majesties high Courte of the Admiralty on the behaulfe of John Younge & John Crooke owners of the Barcke Younge of Chichester & George Blande gent. & others victualers of the same.

1. Inprimis whether ys yt not true that the said George Blande John Younge John Crooke and partners in respecte of theire losses sustayned in the Dominions of the Kinge of Spaine did this laste yeare of 1590 obtayne lettres of Reprisall of the Lord high Admirall of England against the Kinge of Spaine & his subjectes for recompence of theire said losses.

2. Item whether did not the said owners and victualers furnishe and sett furth the good shipp called the Barcke Younge of Chichester to the seas to serve under the said Commission and appoyncted William Irishe Captaine thereof, with a master & sufficiente number of men for that purpose.

3. Item whether ys yt not true that the said William Irishe with the said shipp & companye followinge the contentes of theire said commission did aborde & take aboute the vth of May 1590 nere St Domingo in the Weste Indies a spanishe shippe of aboute xl tonnes laden with suger & hides belonginge to the subjectes of the Kinge of Spaine & were lawfully possessed thereof untill aboute the vjth of Auguste followinge as of theire lawfull prize.

4. Item whether ys not true that the said Captaine and company beinge lawfully possessed of theire said prize duringe the tyme aforesaid did bringe the same as farre as newefound lande in theire returne for Englande.

---

[1] The date her prize goods were appraised (Lansdowne MS 133, f. 23); 3 October, according to Harleian MS 598, f. 8.
[2] H.C.A. 24/58, no. 29. Undated.

5. Item whether ys not true that beinge in the newefound lande and com*m*inge out of the harbor of Noterdam with the said prize seaven greate shippes of Newhavon & Humflewe[1] in Fraunce belonginge to the leage[2] beinge there in fisshinge did aboute the vj^th of Auguste 1590 violently aborde & take the said spanishe shipp & ladinge from the said W*illia*m Irishe & company with many other thinges then in theire possession, and soe spoyled them thereof wholy caryenge the same away.

6. Item ys not true that the said Spanishe shipp & her ladinge was worth at such tyme as she was spoyled by the said Leagers the some of ijm^li, or of what other valewe more or lesse were they of to your knowledge.

7. Item whether ys yt not true that the said spanishe shippe & ladinge of suger & hides was broughte by the said spoylers to Newhavon in Fraunce & the good*e*s there landed and disposed by the Inhabitant*e*s of that towne setters furth of the said vij shipps, and howe doe you knowe the same to be true.

34. Querela *of Bland, Young and others: deposition of William Irish*[3]

WILLIAM IRISHE of Westha*m*[4] gent. of the age of xxx yeares or thereabout*e*s sworne & examined before the righte worshipfull m*aste*r Doctor Cesar Judge of her m*aje*sti*e*s high Courte of the Admi*ra*lty & m*aste*r of the Request*e*s uppon certaine articles ministred on the behaulfe of George Bland John You*n*ge gent. & others Sayth thereunto as followeth.

*Querela Georgii Blande Johannis Younge et aliorum p*r*o testibus examinandis.*

Primus testis.

To the first and second articles he affirmeth the same to containe a truthe For this ex*amina*te was appoyncted Captaine of the articulate shippe the Barcke Younge the tyme articulate by the said George Blande John Younge John Crooke & theire p*ar*tners who victualed and sett furth the said shippe to serve against the Kinge of Spaine and his subject*e*s with le*tt*res of Reprisall which were obtayned from the Lord Admirall for that purpose.

[1] Le Havre and Honfleur.
[2] The Catholic League.
[3] H.C.A. 13/28, 22 January 1590/1.
[4] Westham, Susex. Cp. document 69 below, where Irish is said to be of the Isle of Wight.

To the thirde he affirmeth most true yt ys that this examinate and his companye with the said shipp followinge the contentes of theire said commission did aborde and take of of St Domingo in the West Indies aboute the vth day of May laste paste a spanishe shippe of aboute forty tonnes laden with suger & hides comminge from St Domingo bounde for the Avana beinge manned with Spaniardes, and the whole ladinge belonginge to Spaniardes for noe others are permitted to traphicque there. And havinge taken the said prize this examinate & company were lawfully & quietly possessed thereof from aboute the vth of May untill the vjth of Auguste followinge.

To the iiijth and vth he sayth truth yt ys that this examinate and company beinge possessed as aforesaid of the said spanishe shippe and her ladinge did bringe the same as farre as newe found lande in theire viadge towardes Englande, and comminge out of the Roade of Noterdam with the same seven greate shipps of newhavon and humfleur in Fraunce belonginge to the leage, and beinge there on fisshinge did violently assaulte and sett uppon the said prize and foughte with her and this examinate in his shipp of warre a whole daye and at laste this examinate beinge soe fiersly assaulted by the said vij shippes & xv pinnaces which they had manned out was inforced to take his men out of the prize to defende his man of warre from them, and soe they tooke the said prize from this examinate, and he hardly escaped with his man of warre from them, beinge chased by them soe longe as the day lasted which he affirmeth to be most true.

To the vjth he saythe the said spanishe shippe was full laden with suger & hides, and he verely thinketh the same was verey well worth xvC^{li} sterling when they were taken from this examinate by the said frenche men.

To the vijth he sayth he was tould by one Denise de Parcke of Garnesey who was in Newe found lande that the said vij shippes and pinnaces were of newhavon & humfleur in Fraunce And one Cade of Barstable who was lately in Fraunce hath tould this examinate soe much & that he was at newehavon in Fraunce & sawe the suger and hides landed there out of the said spanishe shippe thither broughte by the said vij shipps comminge from Newfound lande with fishe.

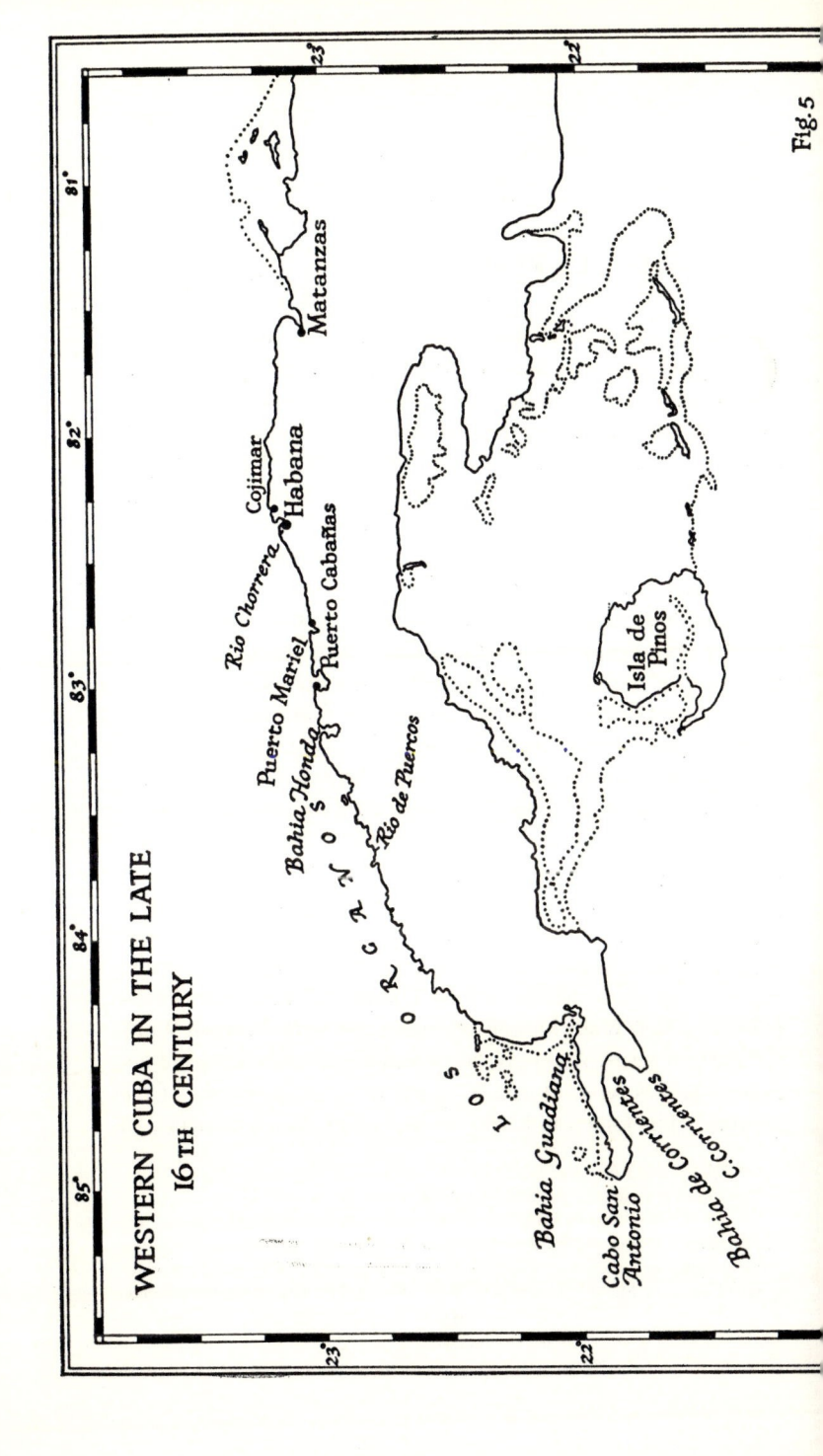

Fig. 5

CHAPTER V

THE EXPEDITIONS OF 1591

'CORSAIRS have been more numerous than usual this year', wrote a Spanish official from Santo Domingo in June 1591,[1] and English sources suggest that he was right. In this year there were at least eleven English privateers abroad in the West Indies, five set forth by John Watts and partners, two by another group of London merchants, three by Sir George Carey, and one other. These four separate expeditions had no plan of co-ordinated action, but as it happened their paths crossed and re-crossed and made their stories one.

Watts' fleet consisted of the *Centaur*, commanded by the leader of the expedition, William Lane, with John Gall master; the *Pegasus*, under Stephen Michell captain and Abicocke Perry master; the *Hopewell* (alias the *Harry and John*) under William Craston and George Kennell; the *John* (sometimes called the *Little John*) under Michael Geare and William Bendes; and the *Fifth Part*, a pinnace. This was a substantial force, totalling some five hundred tons burden of shipping,[2] and at its head there were men to be reckoned with. William Lane, who had sailed in reprisal voyages for five years, had already been a captain in Watts' 1590 venture and was to lead similar expeditions in 1592 and 1593–4. A responsible man, older than most of the privateering captains, he was a member of the London Clothworkers Company, to which Watts himself belonged, and he had known Watts for thirteen years. As might be expected, his statements and actions exhibit a sense of duty towards the chief promoter of the venture.[3] The same can hardly be said of his fellow captains, all

---

[1] *Further English Voyages*, p. 263.
[2] A modest estimate: see documents 49 and 50 below.
[3] Some personal details are given in document 49 below. Lane was also the author of three letters to Burghley giving a rather disjointed and inaccurate account of the voyage and the prizes taken and discoursing vehemently on his grudges against Geare and Michell (Lansdowne MS 67, ff. 152, 157, 163). One of these ends

foughte withall all one whole day in the newefound lande, and forced the englishemen to forsake her And sayth the Admirall of the said vij shipps was called John Blondell dwellinge in Newhavon to which place that shipp belonged The Captaine of the viceadmirall was called Captaine Bountainace[1] of Roane, the Captaine of the seconde Admirall ys called Peter Mabbile of Feckam,[2] and the shipp belonged to Feckamb also. The Captaine of the second viceadmirall was called Nicholas Mabbile of Feckam and the Captaines of the other thre shipps were named Peter de Mounte Nicholas Gaffey, and the third John Rokerell all of Fecambe and the shipps belonged to the same place which he knoweth to be true for that beinge at Newhavon and hearinge bragges made by the Frencheman of the takinge of the said prize from the englishe man of warre at Noterdam in Newe found lande this examinate harkened thereunto and tooke note of theire Captaines names which were as ys before declared Addinge also that the frenche men confessed that after they had taken out of the prize the suger & hides aforesaid and such other thinges as were in her, they soncke the Spanishe vessell in the bay of Noterdam or thereaboutes.

[1] A corruption of 'Boniface'?
[2] Fécamp.

THE BARK YOUNG

35. Querela of Bland, Young and others:
deposition of Edmund Maynard[1]

EDMOND MAYNARD of Ratcliffe mariner of the age of xxij yeares or thereaboutes sworne & examined before the said Judge of the Admiralty uppon the foresaid articles Sayth thereunto as followeth

[Affirms the truth of the articles, saying that the *Bark Young* was set forth] under the conduction of William Irishe Captaine thereof & Roberte Austyn master of the same [this examinate] beinge a quarter master of the said shipp.

36. Querela of Bland, Young and others:
deposition of John Kenney[2]

JOHN KENNEYE of Ratcliffe mariner of the age of xxviij yeares or thereaboutes sworne & examined before the said Judge of Admiralty uppon the foresaid articles Sayth thereunto as followethe

[Affirms the truth of the articles and states that] he was Trumpeter in the Barcke Younge.

37. Querela of Bland, Young and others:
deposition of John Cade[3]

JOHN CADE of Barnestable in the Countye of Devon merchante aged xlviij yeares or thereaboutes....

To the first second, third iiijth & vth vjth & vijth articles he deposeth by chardge of his oathe that aboute the monethe of October laste this examinate beinge at newhavon in Fraunce sawe there seven shippes arrived there before from the newefound lande laden for the most parte with dry fishe and he knoweth that there were landed in newhavon furth of the said shippes fyve hundreth & odde hides & eightene greate chestes of St Domingo suger whiche the Captaines and companye reported & commonly boasted of all aboute the towne that they had taken in a spanishe Carvell from an englishe man of warre which this examinate knewe to be the Barcke Yonge whom they

[1] H.C.A. 13/28, 22 January 1590/1. Extract.
[2] H.C.A. 13/28, 22 January 1590/1. Extract.
[3] H.C.A. 13/28, 27 March 1591.

Golden Noble, the *Moonshine* and the *Julian*, all of which were employed in privateering.[1]

There was at least one other ship involved in this 1591 complex of ventures: the *Lion* of Southampton, commanded by Captain John Oker. There is also mention of a Captain Richard Draper, who was evidently not the missing captain of the *Fifth Part*, since Lee distinguished him from the captains of Watts' ships: there may, therefore, have been another English privateer at Cape Corrientes on 25 June 1591.[2]

Carey's three ships sailed late in March or early in April and are next heard of between Dominica and Puerto Rico towards the end of May.[3] Meanwhile Lane and his men left Plymouth on 5 April in the company of Lord Thomas Howard, having agreed at least to serve under his command during the month of April.[4] Almost immediately, however, the *Hopewell* was left behind and never rejoined the main fleet. She cannot have been long delayed, for on 3 May she took a prize southward of the Canaries and late in May she encountered and consorted with Carey's men as they approached Puerto Rico by way of Guadeloupe, St. Kitts and the Virgin Islands.[5] Nor were the rest of Watts' ships—the *Centaur*, the *Pegasus* and the *John*—to remain long with Howard. About 20 April they lost him—probably intentionally—and a few days later, westward of Cadiz, they captured a substantial prize of hides containing some money, bullion, precious stones and other valuables. A violent squabble over the rich pillage arose between Geare and Michell on the one hand and Lane on the other, but

---

[1] 'Elizabethan Privateering,' p. 246.

[2] Document 51 below. This may have been Richard Draper of Southampton, merchant, who set forth a privateer in 1586 and again in 1587 and was indicted for piracy or some allied offence in 1587 (Lansdowne MSS 134; 142, f. 109; 144, f. 391).

[3] For the dating of the departure see documents 51, 52, 63 and 69 below.

[4] Howard was on his way to the coast of Spain and the Azores with a fleet of the Queen's ships and others. The nature of the conditions of the agreement between Howard and Watts' men was the crucial issue in the suit of Howard *contra* Watts.

[5] Mott (document 54) stated that the meeting took place between Guadeloupe and Puerto Rico on 23 May; Logan (document 55) put the place near the Virgins, but gave no date; Dockerey thought it occurred in June, after watering at Dominica (document 60); Craston, who kept a log of the voyage, put the meeting thwart of St. Kitts at the end of May (document 68); Kennell (document 75) put the place off Puerto Rico and the date at 9 June. The *Hopewell*'s previous itinerary is indicated in documents 81 and 82 below. Craston may have run aground deliberately, in order to give Howard the slip.

THE 1591 VOYAGES

Newport, now a man of thirty-one, had at least ten years of varied and eventful seafaring behind him and had won his way to a command in 1590, when his first appearance in the Caribbean led to the loss that marked him ever after as 'Captain Newport of the one hand'. During the remainder of the war Newport led no less than nine expeditions to the West Indies and when he was too sick to go himself he sent his henchmen. After the war he went twice again in trading ventures and between 1606 and 1611 commanded the Virginia Company's fleets. Then at fifty-two he entered the service of the East India Company and died in sea service at Bantam in 1617. Skilful and successful as a captain, loyal as a servant and later as a partner of the great London merchants who promoted his expeditions, Newport was one of the ablest of the privateers.[1] John Brough, haberdasher of London, captain of the *Prudence*, had been one of Robert Cobb's factors in Portugal in 1585 and since had been on three reprisal ventures, twice as captain.[2] Cuthbert Grippe of Ratcliffe was to spend the war privateering.[3] Of Newport's four merchant backers three—Cobb, More and Newton—played notable parts in the privateering war. Cobb was probably the dominant partner in this as in many previous enterprises, though his privateering activities seem to come to an end in 1594.[4] John More had a hand in numerous expeditions—including several to the West Indies—between 1590 and 1595.[5] John Newton was the owner or part owner of several powerful merchantmen—the *Bark Burr*, the

---

[1] K. R. Andrews, 'Christopher Newport of Limehouse, Mariner,' *William and Mary Quarterly*, XI (1954), 28–41.

[2] Document 53 below and H.C.A. 13/26, 27 May 1586.

[3] Cp. below, p. 185; H.C.A. 14/33, no. 278; H.C.A. 13/35, 23 January 1601/2 and 2 March 1601/2.

[4] Robert Cobb, girdler, of London, was interested in trade with Spain before 1585 (H.C.A. 13/25, 1 December 1584; H.C.A. 13/26, 27 May 1586). As owner or part-owner, he was interested in the privateering activities of the *Golden Dragon*, the *Prudence*, the *Brave*, the *Seraphim*, the *Samaritan*, the *Post*, the *Margaret*, the *Virgin*, the *Violet* and the *Roebuck*, all of London ('Elizabethan Privateering', p. 255).

[5] John More was a prominent London merchant, born c. 1548 (H.C.A. 13/27, 18 October 1588); alderman 1597–1603; master of the Skinners Company 1597 and 1601; committy of the East India Company 1599–1601; died 1603. He was one of the chief promoters of West Indies privateering in the early 1590's, helped to finance Lancaster's Pernambuco expedition and was one of the commissioners for Cumberland's 1598 voyage ('Elizabethan Privateering,' p. 255).

ventures.[1] The other investors were Henry Cletherow, part owner of the *Hopewell* and the *Fifth Part*, John Stokes, who had an interest in the *John*, Roland Stokes, Randall Symes and John Coken. All of these were London merchants and apart from the last, who cannot be identified, all at various times put money into privateering.[2]

Carey's expedition comprised the *Bark Burr* (130 tons burden) under Captain William Irish, the *Swallow* (35 tons burden), with Ralph Lee captain and Anthony Daniel master, and the *Content* (30 tons burden) under Nicholas Lisle and William King.[3] Irish we have already met; Lee was another such gentleman adventurer of the lesser sort, a man of some forty years of age wearing the livery of Sir George. He had done service at sea for the Prince of Orange and the Prince of Condé and had been on reprisal in Carey's shipping four or five times.[4] William King of Ratcliffe, master of the *Content* and possibly author of the story of her famous fight,[5] was to be the leader of an important expedition in 1592.[6]

The third expedition was that of the *Margaret* (sixty tons), under the command of Christopher Newport, with Cuthbert Grippe master, and the *Prudence* (fifty tons), under John Brough and Thomas Harding. But the first object of these ships, set forth by Robert Cobb, John More, John Newton and William Jones, merchants of London, was a trading voyage to Barbary.[7]

---

[1] There was some talk of 'wintering in the country'. For Raleigh's interest see Lansdowne MS 69, f. 60 (printed in E. Edwards, *The Life of Sir Walter Raleigh together with his Letters*, II, 43-4) and Lansdowne MS 67, f. 141.

[2] John Stokes had shared the ownership of the *John* with John Watts for some years. After 1591 the *John* disappears, but the *Michael and John*, owned by John Stokes, Thomas Scott and Michael Geare, makes its appearance in 1592 under Geare's command (see pp. 330-7 below). Roland Stokes' later interest in privateering is shown in H.C.A. 13/102, 4 February 1596/7. Randall Symes, a London clothworker, was an old associate of Watts (H.C.A. 13/24, 2 February 1579/80).

[3] See H.C.A. 25/3 (9), 17 February 1590/1—warrant of the Lord Admiral for the issue of letters of reprisal to Sir George Carey for the *Jason* (alias the *Bark Burr*), the *Swallow*, the *Content* and the *Jonas*. The last is not identifiable, unless this was the *Chance* (of Carey's), which brought home a West Indies prize in September 1591 (Harleian MS 598, f. 13).

[4] Document 51 below.

[5] Document 38 below.

[6] See pp. 209-18 below.

[7] H.C.A. 25/3 (9), 23 December 1590 (warrant for the grant of letters of reprisal).

three of whom were suspected of embezzling prize goods taken in this voyage. Watts, who often chose his captains from the circle of his close associates and dependants, was perhaps disappointed by the behaviour of Michell, a young man of twenty-one who had lived in his household, probably as an apprentice, for five years.[1] But Michell was the least delinquent of the three. Craston, who was perhaps at one time another of Watts' apprentices, was a typically unscrupulous privateering commander and eventually faced a charge of piracy in 1601.[2] He and Kennell in the *Hopewell* together with Geare and Bendes in the *John* were on bad terms with Lane, who clearly disliked their rough Limehouse ways.[3] Michael Geare was probably the leader among these turbulent spirits. Aged about twenty-six, he had been on reprisal voyages since 1585 and had twice already visited the West Indies. His ship, the *John*, was to the fore in much of the fighting and he, as her captain, had the pick of the pillage. He above all incurred Lane's dislike.[4]

In this enterprise Watts was the major shareholder, though the most eminent was Sir Walter Raleigh. The extent and form of the latter's interest can only be guessed, but there is little evidence of a connection between this voyage and Raleigh's colonizing

---

with the typically Elizabethan conceit: 'I beseeche your honor to thinke upon a pore sowldyer that nether hath had, nether hath, nether knoweth how to have, more then he hath, and must wyn, from this enymye...'—an interesting but no doubt misleading self-portrait. Lane evidently wrote Spanish, which suggests that he had been a factor in Spain before 1585 (*Further English Voyages*, p. 301).

[1] Document 50 below; Lansdowne MS 67, f. 154 (Michell's account of his share in the pillage).

[2] Document 68 below, where Craston, now aged 31, says he has known Watts for twenty years, suggests apprenticeship. He first appears as one of the crew of the *Examiner* in 1590, being involved in the embezzlement of gold from a prize (H.C.A. 13/28, 12, 23, 29 December 1590). He continued privateering after 1591 and in 1597 was master of the *Hopewell* in Charles Leigh's expedition to Cape Breton (*Principal Navigations*, III (1600), 195; VIII (1904), 166). For the piracy charge see H.C.A. 1/46, 17 March 1601/2 and following. In 1591 Craston and Kennell were thought to have deceived the customs and the adventurers to the tune of £1500 (Lansdowne MS 67, f. 197).

[3] Geare, Kennell and Bendes were of Limehouse, Craston of Rotherhithe. Of Geare and Michell Lane complained: 'I wrought like a man of warr but they piratlyke prayed upon me...' (Lansdowne MS 67, f. 152).

[4] For Geare, see p. 330 below. Kennell is found in command of a privateer in the West Indies in 1592 (p. 211 below). Gall had been to the West Indies in 1587 (document 49 below) and in 1590 (*Roanoke Voyages*, p. 711).

THE 1591 VOYAGES

eventually in May the prize was sold at Tenerife and course set for the West Indies.¹

It was in that same month that Newport, who had presumably made his intended trading visit to Barbary with the *Margaret* and the *Prudence*, took prize the *Nuestra Señora del Rosario* off La Yaguana in Hispaniola. The Spanish report from Santo Domingo dated 5/15 June 1591, which apparently refers to this incident, suggests that it occurred within the last ten days of May. It declares, however, that there were five corsairs and that four prizes were taken. Apart from the *Margaret*, the *Prudence* was presumably one of the five and since the *Prudence* (though not the *Margaret*) is found some three weeks later in company with the *Pegasus*, the *Centaur* and the *John*, it seems feasible that these three were also present at La Yaguana. Only the presence of the *Margaret* is certain, however, and of her there is no further news until her arrival in England shortly before 27 August.²

About the time that the *Margaret* was taking her prize Craston and Kennell in the *Hopewell* joined forces with Irish, Lee and Lisle and on 13 June these four ships reached a position between Cape Corrientes and Cape San Antonio.³ Here they were intercepted by a Spanish patrol which had been sent to Cape San Antonio to meet and escort to Havana the expected fleet from New Spain.⁴ The Spanish, under the command of Diego de la Ribera, had much the superior force and though the men of the *Content*, led by Lisle and King, fought back in desperation for a whole day and eventually escaped,⁵ the *Bark Burr* was set on fire and 'blown up', evidently by the explosion of her own powder.⁶ One man claimed to have been hurled overboard by the force of the explosion and though he and sixteen others of the crew, including Irish, were taken aboard the *Swallow*, it must be assumed that the majority perished with the ship.⁷ The sugges-

---

¹ Document 81 below, purporting to explain the separation from the main fleet, is not very convincing. For the prize, see documents 49, 50 and 81 and Lansdowne MS 67, ff. 152 and 157.
² Documents 45, 46, 47 below and *Further English Voyages*, p. 263.
³ They may not have kept together the whole of the intervening time (documents 55 and 60 below; but see also documents 54 and 68).
⁴ *Further English Voyages*, pp. lxxxiii–lxxxiv, 264–5, 306.
⁵ Document 38 below.
⁶ The phrase quoted is Hill's (document 79). The Spanish reference to the sinking of an English ship (*Further English Voyages*, p. 265) is thus not mistaken.
⁷ Documents 64 and 75 below.

tion, made by Craston and Kennell, that Irish basely deserted his ship and his men, may have been justified, but the two men who brought the charge were biased by the circumstances of the suit itself.[1] Nor did they themselves display much heroism during the engagement: they did as little as the *Swallow*'s men to assist the *Content* while she faced the onslaught of the greater part of the enemy force. During the fighting the *Content* was separated from the other privateers and apparently made good her escape by sailing north and east from Cape San Antonio. Damaged but not crippled, she returned to within five leagues of the cape and then sailed away to await her consorts at a pre-arranged rendezvous. She waited in vain for twenty-three days, for the *Hopewell* and the *Swallow* had returned to Cape Corrientes, there to find the *Centaur*, the *Pegasus* and the *John* together with the *Prudence* and the *Lion* of Southampton.[2]

This new junction of forces occurred on 19 June and on the 22, while the *John*, the *Hopewell* and the *Prudence* were in the bay watering and attending to other necessities, the remaining privateers took three prizes—the *Pegasus* and the *Centaur* one each (the *Katherine* and the *Gift of God*) and the *Lion* and the *Swallow* one between them. These prizes were all Santo Domingo men carrying hides, sugar and ginger and bound for Havana to join the main fleet. The prizes secured, the captains and masters of the seven ships (eight including the pinnace) agreed to consort together for eight days from 25 June (on which day the agreement was made).[3]

The English were thus in some strength (eight ships and three prizes) when they doubled the western point of Cuba and this, for the Swallow's men at least, was no doubt reassuring.[4] Thus

[1] Documents 68 and 75 below.

[2] 'The place according to the direction of our owner Sir George Carey' (document 38 below) was presumably not on the Cuban coast between Cape Corrientes and Matanzas, where the *Content* would have met with her consorts within twenty-three days. Nor could it have been to the south of Cuba, or on its southern coast, for the *Content* apparently did not redouble Cape San Antonio. Was the rendezvous, then, on the coast of Florida, and was Irish supposed to search again for the lost colonists?

[3] Document 49. Lee (document 51) said that the consortship was to last until 3 July, but did not attempt to substantiate the point, which in any event would not have helped Sir George Carey's case.

[4] Cp. document 71 below.

THE 1591 VOYAGES

the prizes were escorted past Havana as far as Matanzas and then, leaving the *Prudence* and the *Lion* to take the prizes through the Old Channel and so on homeward, Watts' four ships returned to lie in wait for further prey to the westward of Havana. The *Swallow*, although the consortship had now expired, accompanied them.[1] At this stage Watts' men were considering 'wintering in the country', but the events of the next few days scotched any such notions.[2]

On 5/15 July, early in the morning, the *John* and the *Pegasus* sighted, pursued and captured the *St. John* of Seville, a substantial prize with a lading of hides and cochineal which had strayed from Antonio Navarro's New Spain fleet.[3] The cochineal was removed and the rest of the cargo burnt with the vessel. The same day four more Santo Domingo men were taken, three with a normal cargo of sugar and hides and one laden with turtles; one of these fell to the *Swallow*, the rest to Watts' men. The following day, the sixth of July, saw the capture of the last and richest of the prizes—the *Trinity* (alias the *Michael*) of Seville. This was another of Navarro's New Spain fleet, belonging to Martín de Ygararan and Juan de Agustín.[4] The lading of silver, cochineal and hides was certainly very valuable, but estimates of its precise worth varied considerably: it was probably worth about £20,000.[5]

With such rich plunder in hand the Englishmen did not loiter in enemy waters. The *Prudence*, which had already left with two of the three prizes taken on 22 June, arrived at Plymouth by 26 August and Watts' ships with three more prizes were home by the middle of September. Watts' men had taken eight prizes in the course of their voyage;[6] one was sold at Tenerife on the outward voyage, another—the *St. John*—was burnt and a third was sunk on the homeward voyage; five were brought to England.

---

[1] Documents 56, 65, 66, 69 below.

[2] Documents 51, 65, 69 below.

[3] The master and owner was one Augustín de Paz (documents 42 and 44 below; *Further English Voyages*, pp. 270, 274).

[4] Documents 41 and 43 below and *Further English Voyages*, pp. 270, 274. Ygararan was master as well as part owner.

[5] Lane put the bullion and money alone at £18,000 (Lansdowne MS 67, f. 157). Myddelton and Carmarden, for customs purposes, estimated this part of the cargo at £20,000 (Lansdowne MS 67, f. 175). The Admiralty Court appraisal (H.C.A. 24/60, no. 159) was incomplete.

[6] Excluding one or two small vessels of little value.

The *Lion* and the *Swallow* also brought home one prize each. Financially the voyage was undoubtedly a great success for Watts and his partners, in spite of the embezzlement of some of the prize goods. Watts himself officially admitted the value of the goods (after pillage) at nearly £32,000.[1] The *Trinity* alone was worth about £20,000 and the first prize taken near Spain was substantial. Altogether the eight prizes probably made up some £40,000, after the crews had seized what they could by way of pillage and straightforward theft. Raleigh's complaint that the investors would only receive a 'one for one' profit on their capital is absurd on two counts. In the first place he took the total return of prize-goods at the official value. Secondly he miscalculated the net sum available to the principals by ignoring the fact that part of the initial capital outlay returned with scarcely diminished value at the end of the venture. A profit of one hundred per cent would not have been 'a small returne' for a privateering venture, but in this case the profit probably amounted to over 200 per cent.[2]

Almost inevitably—and fortunately for the historian—the very success of the voyage led to litigation. Immediately after their return the prizes were formally claimed by the principals and interlocutory sentences given accordingly.[3] The interest of Robert Cobb and partners, adventurers in the *Margaret* and the *Prudence*, was promptly and successfully asserted, not only in the *Margaret*'s prize, but also in Watts' prizes.[4] Next, on 13 October, Sir George Carey wrote to Dr Julius Caesar giving notice of his intention to sue Watts and his partners for a share in their profits.

[1] Lansdowne MS 67, f. 159. Watts gives a total of £31,380 and adds a variety of articles worth some £300. This estimate is confirmed by Lansdowne MS 69, f. 60, where the figures are not exactly the same, but quite close.
[2] See Raleigh's letter, Lansdowne MS 69, f. 60 (Edwards, *The Life of Sir Walter Raleigh together with his Letters*, II, 43–4).
[3] Documents 39–42 and 45–7. Also H.C.A. 24/60, nos. 150–2 and 161–2 (sentences and summaries of proceedings for the *Trinity*, the *St. John*, the *St. Katherine* and the *Gift of God*); H.C.A. 24/60, no. 165 (summary of proceedings and sentence of the *Margaret*'s prize); H.C.A. 24/60, no. 159 (appraisement of the cargo of the *Trinity*). Also depositions by Balthasar Rodríguez and Melchior Alonso (H.C.A. 13/29, 17 September 1591).
[4] For Cobb's case concerning the *Trinity* and the *St. John* see documents 43–4 below and depositions by Domingo Hernandes and Francisco Hernerowe (H.C.A. 13/29, 4 October 1591). For the *Margaret*'s prize, see documents 45–7 below.

The libel was submitted to the court on 12 November and in due course Watts submitted an allegation and additional positions; each party replied personally to the other's pleading and entered interrogatories for the cross-examination of the other's witnesses. The depositions and replies of both sets of witnesses—eleven for Carey and twenty for Watts—were made between 10 December 1591 and 13 March 1591/2.[1] The sentence of the court has not been traced, but it is fairly clear from the evidence that Carey's case was a weak one. His men were unable to show convincingly that any consortship agreement was in force when the prizes were taken; nor were they able to prove that the *Swallow* effectively assisted in the capture of any prizes other than those which actually came into Carey's possession. Thus Carey should in justice have found little consolation for the loss of the *Bark Burr* and the severe damage inflicted on the *Content*; but against the weakness of his case must be set the strength of his 'friendship' with Caesar and his family relationship with the Lord Admiral.[2]

If, as seems likely, Watts won this case, he was soon faced with fresh claims. In June 1592 Lord Thomas Howard began a prolonged suit for a share in the prizes, arguing that Watts' ships were legally consorted with the main fleet under his command. Although the case was pursued until 1594, decision was eventually given in favour of Watts.[3]

[1] Documents 48–79 below. Also H.C.A. 24/60, no. 21 (the libel), no. 20 (the *materia*), no. 19 (additional positions to the *materia*); H.C.A. 13/101, 1 December 1591 (replies of Watts to the libel) and 10 June 1592 (replies of Carey to the *materia*); H.C.A. 23/4, f. 274 (interrogatories *ex parte* Watts), f. 275 (interrogatories *ex parte* Carey) and f. 270 (interrogatories *secundo loco ex parte* Carey).

[2] There is more than suspicion of corruption in the relations between Challice the pirate, Carey and Caesar, as revealed in Carey's letter to Caesar in Lansdowne MS 158, f. 62. Carey's two prizes by the *Swallow* in 1591 were together worth perhaps £3000 (cp. documents 59 and 60 below) and a further prize by the *Chance* was worth about £1100 (Harleian MS 598, f. 13). Thus Carey, partly by reason of his scurvy treatment of the *Lion*'s men, gained something to offset the loss of the *Bark Burr* (cp. documents 59 and 66).

[3] Libel: H.C.A. 24/59, no. 162. Replies of Watts to the libel: H.C.A. 13/101, 23 June 1592. Interrogatories *ex parte* Watts and consortship agreement (the latter printed in Marsden, *Law and Custom*, I, 272–3): H.C.A. 23/4, ff. 252–3. Depositions on the libel: John Clercke (document 80 below); Richard Vavasour (H.C.A. 13/30, 16 February 1592/3); George Whitney (H.C.A. 13/30, 20 February 1592/3); Giles Porter (H.C.A. 13/30, 13 March 1592/3); John Duffield (H.C.A. 13/30, 23 March 1592/3); Walter Gore (H.C.A. 13/30, 14 April 1593); Robert Mansell (H.CA. 13/30, 19 April, 1593); John Linewray (H.C.A. 13/30, 3 May 1593); Thomas Coche (H.C.A. 13/30, 4 May 1593). Watts' allegation: H.C.A. 24/59,

Successful though he may have been in defending his booty against envious magnates, Watts fought a losing battle against his thieving sailors. The most prominent of the embezzlers were Michael Geare and William Bendes, captain and master of the *John*, who led the pillaging of the silver prize and of the prize taken near the Spanish coast. At Dartmouth Bendes disposed of substantial quantities of silver and gold, and others conveyed ashore and sold part of the cochineal. It is unlikely that Watts recovered the stolen goods or their equivalent in money.[1] Nor indeed did most of the sailors profit much from such dealings, for they were obliged to pass on the booty as quickly as possible and so made poor bargains. Thus one merchant boasted 'that he had boughte fifty hundreth of m*aste*r wattes ginger at Plimouth of the mariners for xxviij^s or xxx^s the hundrethe, and that he never made soe good a viadge all the days of his liffe . . .'.[2]

With the exception of document 38 (the Hakluyt account of the fight of the *Content*), the documents printed below are selected from those produced in the course of the legal proceedings. There are of course further materials relating to the venture, but these

no. 79. Additional positions to the allegation: H.C.A. 24/61, no. 156. Interrogatories *ex parte* Howard: H.C.A. 23/4, f. 205 (*secundo loco*) and ff. 239–44 (*primo loco*). Howard's replies to the allegation: H.C.A. 24/62, no. 5, and H.C.A. 24/61, no. 178. Depositions on the allegation: Stephen Michell (document 81 below); William Lane (H.C.A. 13/30, 26 January 1592/3); William Pousley (H.C.A. 13/30, 15 November 1593); William Drewe (H.C.A. 13/30, 16 November 1593); William Craston (document 82 below); Marmaduke Logan (H.C.A. 13/30, 23 November 1593); Walter Price (H.C.A. 13/30, 24 November 1593); William Roberts (H.C.A. 13/30, 26 November 1593); Michael Geare (H.C.A. 13/30, 12 December 1593). Replies of Drewe and Pousley to interrogatories: H.C.A. 13/30, 17 November 1593. Copy of consortship: H.C.A. 24/62, no. 6. Further replies of Watts to Howard's libel: H.C.A. 13/101, 21 March 1593/4. Sentence for Watts: H.C.A. 24/63, no. 241.

[1] The relevant documents are: Interrogatories on behalf of Watts and others concerning cochineal taken out of the *Michael* at Dartmouth (H.C.A. 24/60, no. 26). Replies to these by James Bratholt (H.C.A. 13/29, 19 January 1591/2); Harry Towers and Henry Dobson (H.C.A. 13/29, 24 January 1591/2). Articles on behalf of Watts and others concerning the disposal of valuables by Michael Geare, William Bendes and others (H.C.A. 24/59, no. 170/1). Depositions on these articles: Michael Geare (H.C.A. 13/29, 14 February 1591/2); Peter Anthony and Elias Anthony (H.C.A. 13/29, 24 February 1591/2); Robert Philpott (H.C.A. 13/30, 29 April 1592); William Snowe (H.C.A. 13/30, 10 March 1592/3). Deposition of John Smith concerning the embezzlement of Watts' prize goods in Ireland and at Bristol (H.C.A. 13/29, 4 February 1591/2). Deposition of Michael Geare on special articles (H.C.A. 13/29, 14 February 1591/2).

[2] H.C.A. 13/30, 29 April 1592.

do not in any considerable way amplify or modify the account given above.[1] It will be observed that several of the documents given in this chapter throw light upon earlier West Indies ventures.

*   *   *

38. The 'memorable fight' of the Content[2]

A relation of a memorable fight made the 13. of June 1591. against certaine Spanish ships & gallies in the West *Indies*, by 3. ships of the honorable sir George Carey knight, then marshall of her Majesties houshold, and captaine of the Ile of *Wight*, now Lord Hunsdon, lord Chamberlaine, and captaine of the honourable band of her Majesties Pensioners.

The 13. of June 1591, being sunday, at 5. of the clock in the morning we descried 6. saile of the king of Spaine his ships.[3] Foure of them were armadas, (viz. the Admirall and viceadmirall of 700. tuns apeece, and the other 2. of 600. apeece) and the other 2. were smal ships, each of them about 100. tuns. We met w^t them off the Cape de Corrientes, which standeth on the Iland of Cuba. The sight of the foresaid ships made us joyfull, hoping that they should make our voyage. But assoone as they descryed us, they made false fires one to another & gathered their fleet together, lying all close by a wind to the Southwards. We therefore at 6. of the clock in the morning (the wind being at East) having made our prayers to almighty God, prepared our selves for the fight: And (in hope they had bene of the Cartagena fleete) we bare up with our admirall and viceadmiral, to determine of the combate for the better direction thereof. Our parle being ended, our admiral, vice-admiral, & the Hopewel gave their admiral the prow, bringing themselves to leeward of him. We in the Content bare up with their viceadmiral, and (ranging along by his broad side aweather of him) gave him a voley of muskets and our great ordinance: then comming up with another small ship ahead of the

[1] The most important are: Lansdowne MS 67, ff. 141, 143, 148, 152, 154, 157, 159, 163, 175, 197; Lansdowne MS 69, f. 60; Harleian MS 598, f. 13.

[2] *Principal Navigations*, III (1600), 565–7; X (1904), 178–83. It may be that the author of this account was William King. He apparently wrote the account of his 1592 voyage which appeared in Hakluyt's collection in 1600. Moreover the 'memorable fight' is obviously the work of a sailor.

[3] Confirmed by Craston, who refers to eight ships, presumably including the two galleys (document 68 below).

former wee hailed her in such sort, that shee payd roome.[1] Thus being in fight with the little ship, we saw a great smoke come from our admiral, the Hopewel & Swallow forsaking him with all the sailes they could make: whereupon bearing up with our admiral (before we could come to him) we had both the small ships to windward of us, purposing (if we had not bene too hotte for them) to have layd us aboord. Thus (the fight continuing between us and them 3. houres) we were forced to stand to the Northwards, the Hopewel and the Swallow not comming in all this while to ayd us, as they might easily have done. Our admirall by this time being in fight with their viceadmiral, and another great ship of theirs, stood off to sea with his topgallant saile, and all the sailes he could make: then might the Hopewel & the Swallow have payd roome to second him, but they failed him as they did us, standing off close by a wind to the Eastward. All this time we were forced to the Northwards with 2. of their great ships and one of their small. They having a loom gale[2] (wee being altogether becalmed) w^t both their great ships came up faire by us, shot at us, and on the sudden furled their spritsailes & mainsailes, thinking that wee could not escape them. Then falling to prayer, we shipped our oars that we might rowe to shore, & anker in shallow water where their great ships could not come nie us, for other refuge we had none. Then 1. of their smal ships being manned from 1. of their great, & having a boat to rowe themselves in, shipped her oars likewise & rowed after us, thinking w^t their small shot to have put us from our oars, until ye great ships might come up with us: but by ye time she was within musket shot, the Lord of his mercie did send us a faire gale of wind at the Northwest off the shore. What time (they being all to leeward of us) wee stood to the East. The small ship was under our lee within Falcon shot, and another great shippe lay to the Westward, so that wee could no way possibly escape them upon that boord: then (we thinking to avoyd them by casting about to the Westwards) the other great shippe gate under our lee, and the small ship on our weather quarter, purposing to make us pay roome with the great ship, by force of her small & great shot.

---

[1] Probably a form of 'pay round'—to turn the ship's head or change course; but may be connected with the term 'going room' or 'going large', viz. from the wind.

[2] An easy gale of wind.

The names of the rest be these following.

John Pie.	John Twopenie.
John Smith.	Edmund Giggs.
John White.[1]	William Bateman.
John Butcher.	William White.
John Brooke.	Laurence Shellie.

39. *Adjudication of the prizes: deposition of Roger Proude*[2]

Querela Henrici Cletherowe Johannis Wattes Roberti Cobb et aliorum pro testibus ad perpetuam rei memoriam examinandis.

1. quoad the prizes.

ROGER PROUDE of London merchaunte of thadge of xxj yeares or there aboutes sworne & examined on the behalfe of Henry Cletherowe John Wattes Roberte Cobbe & company befor the worshipful master Thomas Steveington deputye Judge of Thadmiralty towcheinge twoe prizes broughte to Plymouthe by the Prudence, Sayethe

That in June laste the Centare and the Pegasus of London sette out by the forsaid merchauntes & company & in consorte withe the John & Prudence, tooke twoe Spanishe shippes laden withe hides Pepper Ginger & sugar broughte to Plymouthe by the Prudence as they weare comeinge from Ste Domange[3] & goeinge to the Havana, to wyndwarde of Cape Corinthus[4] whiche shippes and goodes as he hathe hearde the severall companyes therof beinge Spaniardes & Portingales confesse belonged onely to Spaniardes & Portingales, and the goodes weare laded att Ste Domingo, but by whome or for whose accompte by name he knowethe not.

40. *Adjudication of the prizes: deposition of Edward Anthonison*[5]

Querela Johannis Wattes et

EDWARDE ANTHONISON of Enchusen[6] in Northehollande late mariner in the shippe called the Ste Katheryne of

---

[1] Presumably not the White of Roanoke fame, who refers to his 1590 voyage as his last in his letter to Hakluyt (*Roanoke Voyages*, p. 712).

[2] H.C.A. 13/29, 26 August 1591. Deposition on the *querela* for the *Katherine* and the *Gift of God*. Cp. reports of proceedings (H.C.A. 24/60, nos. 151/2 and 162) and interlocutory sentences (H.C.A. 24/60, nos. 152 and 161).

[3] Santo Domingo.   [4] Cape Corrientes.

[5] H.C.A. 13/29, 16 September 1591. Deposition on the *querela*.

[6] Enkhuizen.

THE 1591 VOYAGES

from the cruell enemie, which hath beene more mightie by the providence of God, then any tongue can expresse: to whom bee all prayse, honour, and glory, both now and ever, Amen.

Appendix.

The barke called the Content had but one Minion, one Falcon, one Saker, & 2. port-bases. She continued fight (from seven in the morning til sunset) with 3. armadas of 600. and 700 tunnes apiece, and one small shippe of 100 tunnes, not being above musket shot from any of them. And before the sunne was set, there came up to her two of the kings gallies. Besides, the Armadas shot their great ordinance continually at her, not so few as 500. times. And the sides, hull, and mastes of the Content were sowed thicke with musket bullets. Moreover, all their sheats, tops and shrowdes were almost cut insunder with their great & small shot. There passed from the galies (each whereof came thrise up to her, & discharged five great pieces at a time, out of every their prowes forthright, within three yards of her poope) through her maine saile 19. great shot, through her maine top-saile foure: through her fore-saile seven: through her fore-top-saile five: and through her maine maste one. The upper part of the Content was hurt in five places. Onely 13 men continued this fight, the rest being in holde.

A frigat of the Spaniards (being afterward taken) confessed, that there were in the gallies above 40. Spaniards slaine, and many were hurt in that combate.

The names of those 13 persons that continued the fight.

Nicolas Lisle, Captaine.
M. Major, Lieutenant.
William King, Master.[1]
John Barwick, Mrs. mate.
William Clement, gunner.[2]
Thomas Houldships, Boteswaine.

Charles Creame.
Thomas Godfrey.
Giles Thornton.
John Pells.
John Bourel.
Ralph Grey.
William Heore.

[1] See pp. 209–18 below.
[2] A Weymouth man, master of the *Bark Randall* in 1590 and captain of the *Chance* of Weymouth in 1593 and 1595 (Harleian MS 598, ff. 23 and 37; H.C.A. 25/3 (9), 3 March 1591/2; H.C.A. 14/35, no. 160).

mending our estate into the hands of God) armed our selves, and resolved (for the honour of God, her majestie, and our countrey) to fight it out till the last man. Then shaking a pike of fire in defiance of the enemie, and weaving them amaine,[1] we bad them come aboord: and an Englishman in the gallie made answer, that they would come aboord presently. So managing our selves to our furniture,[2] and every moment expecting the assault, we heard them parle to this effect, that they determined to keepe us companie till the morning, and then to make an end with us: then giving us another shot from one of the gallies, they fell asterne. Thus our fight continued with the shippes and with the gallies, from seven of the clock in the morning till eleven at night. Howbeit God (which never faileth them that put their trust in him) sent us a gale of winde about two of the clocke in the morning at Eastnortheast, which was for the preventing of their crueltie, and the saving of our lives. Also (the Lord be praised for it) in all this dangerous fight, wee had not one man slaine, and but 2. hurt: but our sayles and ropes were so rent with their shot, that it was wonderfull to behold: our maine mast also was shot cleane through, whereby wee were in exceeding great danger. Thus our consortes forsooke us, and left us in these extremities. The next day being the 14. of June in the morning, wee sawe all our adversaries to lee-ward of us, and they espying us, chased us till 10. of the clocke, and then seeing they could not prevaile, gave us over. So that day about 5. of the clocke in the afternoone, we bare up to the Southwest, in hope to finde our consortes, but we had no sight of them at that time, nor afterward. Then stoode we in all that night for the Cape of S. Anthonie, hoping there to see our Admirall according to his direction. The 15. day of June early in the morning, we descryed the Spanish fleete againe, being within 5. leagues of Cape S. Anthonie. Then (having no sight of our consortes) we stoode for the place according to the direction of our owner sir George Carey, where we did plie for the space of 23. dayes, and never could see any sayle but two frigats, which wee gave chase unto the 24. of June, and could not fet them up.[3] Thus wee give God most humble thankes for our safe deliverance

A fight from 7. in the morning till 11. at night.

[1] Or 'waving amain'—brandishing a bright sword, or pike of fire, as a signal to the enemy to strike his topsail in token of submission.
[2] Preparing for action.
[3] Catch them up.

THE 1591 VOYAGES

Then (we being lerboord tacked, and they sterboord) we made her spring her looffe,[1] and by a fortunate shot which our gunner made, pierced her betwixt winde and water. Hereupon shee was forced to lay herselfe upon the carena,[2] and to stand with one of the other ships for ayde. Afterward (commending our selves to almightie God in prayer, and giving him thankes for the winde which he had sent us for our deliverance) we looked forth and descryed two saile more to the offen:[3] these we thought to have bene the Hopewell, and the Swallow that had stoode in to ayde us: but it prooved farre otherwise, for they were two of the kings gallies. Nowe having a loome gale of winde, wee shipped our oars, and rowed off the shore: and our watch was no sooner set, but wee espied one gallie under our lee hard by us, boging up[4] with us. Then (because it was evening) one of the great ships discharged sixe great shot at us, to the ende the gallies should knowe that wee were the shippe they looked for. Then the gallie came up, and (hayling us of whence our shippe was) a Portugall which wee had with us, made them answere, that we were of the fleete of Tierra firma, and of Sivil: with that they bid us amaine English dogs, and came upon our quarter star-boord: and giving us five cast pieces out of her prowe, they sought to lay us aboord: but wee so galled them with our muskets, that we put them from our quarter. Then they winding their gallie,[5] came up into our sterne, and with the way[6] that the gallie had, did so violently thrust in the boordes of our captaines cabbin, that her nose came into it, minding to give us all their prowe, and so to sinke us. But wee being resolute, so plyed them with our small shot, that they could have no time to discharge their great ordinance: and when they began to approch, wee heaved into them a ball of fire, and by that meanes put them off: whereupon they once againe fell asterne of us, and gave us a prowe. Then having a second time put them off, wee went to prayer, and sang the first part of the 25. Psalme, praysing God for our safe deliverance. This being done, we might see 2. gallies and a frigat all three of them bending themselves together to encounter us: hereupon we (eftsoones com-

---

[1] To spring a luff means to bring the ship's head up more to windward.
[2] To heel over to one side.   [3] In the offing.
[4] Perhaps from 'budge against'—to move against or act in hostility to.
[5] Turning it about.   [6] Momentum.

ENGLISH PRIVATEERING VOYAGES

testibus ad perpetuam rei memoriam.

aboutes sworne and examined before the wor*shipful* m*a*ste*r* doctor Cesar att the instance of Roberte Cobbe of London merchaunte by thinterpretac*i*on of Fraunces Marquino speakinge Spanishe sayethe as followethe viz*t*

That in the Trinity when shee was taken there was one pype as bigge as a pipe of wyne, and one greate Cheste filled w*i*the sillver uncoyned, and diverse other smale Chest*es* wherein weare silver, but howe muche was in every of them he cannot depose, but he thinkethe that there was in the whole to the valewe of fyve thowsand[1] Duckett*es* in the saide shippe belonginge unto the m*e*rchaunt*es* besides that whiche was and belonged to the company, w*hi*che was taken from them allsoe amongeste w*hi*che this ex*a*mina*t*e had taken from him seaven hunderethe pesos, every pesoe beinge worthe eighte Rialls. Allsoe there was in here xlvj Chest*es* of Cochenillo and fyve thowsande hides and noe other goodes.

Beinge demaunded whether any p*e*rson willed him to depose or saye that there was but xxx thousande ducatt*es* in the said shippe when shee was taken, and that the s*a*id parte[2] in regarde thereof would p*ro*cure his liberty and whate the s*a*id p*a*rtye was utterlye denyethe the same.

44. Querela *of Robert Cobb concerning Watts' prizes: deposition of John Pouce*[3]

Querela dicti Cobb pro testibus &c.

JOHN POUCE of Civill Late m*a*ste*r*s matte in the shippe called the Ste John, of the same place ... Sayethe

That to his knowledge, there was noe silver goulde presious stones, Pearle, or Jewells in the Ste John when shee was taken w*hi*che was laden for any marchaunte, to his knowledge, Butte he sayethe the company of the shippe wherof this ex*a*mina*t*e was one had taken from them amongeste them all w*hi*che was there owne aboute one thowsande duckett*es* in money.[4]

---

[1] A clerical error for 'fifty thousand'.
[2] Party.
[3] H.C.A. 13/29, 4 October 1591. Extract.
[4] For the rest Pouce merely repeats his former statement (document 42 above). Similar statements were made by Domingo Hernandes and Francisco Hernerowe, both mariners of the *St. John* (H.C.A. 13/29, 4 October 1591), though Hernandes says that the crew lost 7000 or 8000 ducats in money.

THE 1591 VOYAGES

42. *Adjudication of the prizes: deposition of John Pouce*[1]

JOHN POUCE of Sivill in Spayne marine*r* of thadge of thirtye fower yeares or there aboute*s* sworne and examined before the said ma*s*ter Doctor Hone by interpretac*i*on afor*s*aid ... Deposethe....

Querela Johannis Wattes &c quoad the Ste John.

4.

That the xv of July la*s*te paste accordinge to the newe still[2] neare unto the Havana, the shippe the John borded and tooke, the shippe the Ste John of Sivill of the burthen of iijC tons or there aboute*s* beinge laden withe sixe thow*s*ande hides, and fortye Che*s*tes of Cochenilo, in the presence of the Pegasus the Centaure and the Harye and John, wh*i*che goode*s* was laden in here att Ste John de Lowe[3] in nova Hispania, to be transported unto Sivill in Spayne, wh*i*che shippe the Ste John belonged unto Augustyne de Pace dwellinge in Civill,[4] to whom the goode*s* p*a*rticulerly & by name dyd belonge he knowethe not, but he is suere, the same belonged unto subjecte*s* of the Kinge of Spayne in Civill.

And he sayethe that after the Ste John was taken, twoe of the men of warre, tooke out of here the s*a*id Che*s*tes of Cochenilo, and for that shee was worme eaten and rotten soe that shee was not able, to kepe the Seas, they sette here on fiere withe all the hides in here. All wh*i*che he knowethe to be trewe because he was masters matte in the s*a*id Ste John that viadge, taken in here and broughte to Englande.[5]

43. Querela *of Robert Cobb concerning Watts' prizes: deposition of John de Calvete*[6]

JOHN CALVETTE of Ste Sebastian in Biskaye, late masters mate of the Ste Trinity of Civill, of the adge of 40 yeares or there

Querela Roberti Cobb pro

---

[1] H.C.A. 13/29, 17 September 1591. Deposition on the *querela*.
[2] 5 July, old style.
[3] San Juan de Ulua.
[4] Agustín de Paz (*Further English Voyages*, p. 270). He and Ygararan were both aboard their respective ships when they were taken; both were put ashore near Havana by the English.
[5] Cp. similar statements by Rodríguez and Alonso: H.C.A. 13/29, 17 September 1591.
[6] H.C.A. 13/29, 4 October 1591. Cobb, as owner of the *Prudence*, had an interest in Watts' prizes, and is here attempting to establish their value.

togeather beinge bothe manned withe Spaniardes & Portingales when they weare taken.

41. Adjudication of the prizes: deposition of John de Calvete[1]

Querela dicti Johannis Wattes pro testibus &c quoad navem the Trinity et oneracionem

3

JOHN DE CALVETE of St Sebastian, late mariner of the Ste Trinity, of the adge of xl yeares or there aboutes sworne and examined before the said master John Hone uppon an Allegacion given in this Courte on the parte & behalfe of the forsaid John Wattes Deposethe and sayethe there unto as followethe by interpretacion a forsaid vizt

That the St Trinitye of Civill of the burthen of ijCxl tons or there aboutes, laden att Ste John de Lowe[2] in nova hispania, withe hides Cochenile and silver to passe for Civill a forsaid was aboute the xvij of July Laste paste accordinge to the newe still[3] apprehended and taken in her said voyadge neare unto the Havana, by twoe shippes of Englande called the Centaure, and the John, whiche borded her in the presence of the Pegasus and the Harrye and John, and by the Centaure broughte to Englande, And he sayethe the said Trinity belonged unto Martyne de la Grande[4] and John de Augustine of Sivill, the Kinge of Spaynes subjectes, to whome the goodes belonged he knowethe not but he belevethe the same belonged unto the said Kinges subjectes. And parte of the said Coyne belonged unto the said owners. All whiche he knowethe to be trewe, because he was in the saide Trinity that voyadge for masters matte, and was taken and broughte in here into Englande. Addinge that the said fower men of warre after the takinge of the said shippe the Trinity dyd take out of her all the money in her, into them selves every shippe a portion, but howe muche every shippe had he cannot declare, but he sayethe there was in the holle[5] fiftye thowsande Duckettes platte and redye money, sixe and fortye Chestes of Cochenilo, and fyve thowsande hides in here when shee was taken.

[1] H.C.A. 13/29, 17 September 1591. Deposition on the *querela*. Summary of proceedings and interlocutory sentence: H.C.A. 24/60, nos. 150, 151.
[2] San Juan de Ulua.
[3] 7 July, old style.
[4] Martín de Ygararan (*Further English Voyages*, p. 270).
[5] Whole.

Cadiz, in Andolozia of thadge of xxxv yeares or there aboutes sworne and examined before the righte worshipful master John Hone Docter of Lawe Deputye Judge of Thadmiraltye by thinterpretation of Fraunces Marquino sworne trewly to enterprete, uppon an allegacion given in this Courte on the behalfe of John Wattes & others sayethe there unto as followethe, vizt *aliorum pro testibus ad perpetuam rei memoriam quoad the Katheryne et the Gifte of God.*

That the shippe the Ste Katheryne Late taken att the Seas by the Centaure neare unto Cape Corinthus, In July Laste,[1] and nowe att Plymouthe, wherof was master Martyne Franciscus of Armountye,[2] was the tyme when she was taken of Cadiz, in Andoluzia, and belonged unto a spaniarde there dwellinge whate his name was he knowethe not. And he sayethe the said shippe was laden withe sugar hides and Ginger, att Ste Domingo, bounde for Civill & Ste Lucar in Spayne, but for whose use he knowethe not. But he belevethe they weare all Spaniardes goodes exceptinge certayne goodes of this examinate whiche come to Lx^{li} sterling & coste him soe muche there. All whiche he knowethe to be trewe because was[3] a mariner in the same shippe and presente in her when shee was taken by the Centare & broughte to Plymouthe in here.

And he sayethe he sawe the shippe the Pegasus apprehende and take, neare unto the forsaid Cape Corinthus, an other shippe, her name he knowethe not,[4] within twoe howers before the said Catheryne was taken beinge Laden withe sugar hides and Ginger whiche shippe as he sayethe was of Civill and the master therof was called Ribrowle of Civill, whoe had parte of the said shippe and goodes withe other twoe younge men Spaniardes whate theire names weare he knowethe not, But he sayethe he sawe the saide shippe Laden att Ste Domingo, and was[5] to come to Sivill in company of the Ste Katheryne withe others. And more he cannot Depose Saveinge he sayethe the Katherin was of the burthen of one CL, and the other[6] of one hunderethe or there aboutes, And that they weare bothe broughte to Plymouthe

---

[1] June, in English style.
[2] Armentières?
[3] [Sic.]
[4] The words 'her name he knowethe not' are substituted for the words 'whiche he hathe since understoode to be called the Gifte of God', which are crossed out.
[5] [Sic.]
[6] The word 'other' is substituted for 'Gifte of God', which is crossed out.

45. *Adjudication of the* Margaret's *prize: deposition of Stephen Collomber*[1]

STEPHEN COLLOMBER of Eagwana,[2] in Highe spaniola[3] mariner of the adge of xxij yeares or there aboutes sworne and examined befor the righte worshipful master Thomas Skeffington Doctor of Lawe and Deputye Judge of Thadmiraltye towchinge the Nuestra Signiora De La Rosari late taken att the Seas by the Margarett of London Captayne Christopher Newporte and master Cutberte Grippe, by thinterpretacion of Benjamyn Hancocke speakinge the Spanishe tonge & sworne trewely to enterprete sayethe

Querela Roberti Cobb Johannis More George Sowthwicke et aliorum

That the shippe called the Nuestra Señora de La Rosara the tyme shee was taken by the Margarett was of Eagwana in highe Hispaniola by the Captayne & company therof belonged to Thomas Cardoza of Ste Domingo,[4] beinge laden withe vijC hides and xxviij Chestes of course Sugars some Casia fistula,[5] xx Jares of Mallasses, att Eaguana & there aboutes to be carryed to the Havana in the Weste Indies, and there to be dischardged. And he sayethe the said goodes belonged to one Pallasus of the Eagwana when they weare taken whiche he knowethe to be trewe because he was one of the companye of the said shippe and was taken withe here by the Captayne & Companye of the Margaret of London, and by them broughte into this Realme of Englande.

46. *Adjudication of the* Margaret's *Prize: deposition of Diego López*[6]

DIEGO LOPES of the Eagwana[7] in Hispaniola mariner, of thadge of xxiij yeares or there aboutes sworne and examined by interpretacion aforesaid before the saide Judge towchinge the said shippe and goodes.

Querela Roberti Cobb et sociorum pro testibus &c.

Sayethe, that the forsaid shippe nuestra Señora de la Rosara

---

[1] H.C.A. 13/29, 2 September 1591. Summary of proceedings and interlocutory sentence: H.C.A. 24/60, no. 165.
[2] La Yaguana. [3] Hispaniola.
[4] As it stands this makes no sense; if the second 'was' is omitted and the first 'of' is read as 'off', the result is reasonable. Cp. the clearer construction used in document 46 below.
[5] Cassia fistula.
[6] H.C.A. 13/29, 2 September 1591.
[7] La Yaguana.

beinge laden att the Eagwana or there aboutes withe vijC hides xxviij Chestes Course Sugars, some Cassia fistula and xx Jarres of mallasses to be carryed to the havana & there to be dischardged, dyd (the tyme they weare taken by the Margarett of London the Captayne & company therof, which was in Maye laste as he remembereth of the Eagwana) belonge, unto Thomas Cardoza of Ste Domingo, and Pallasus of the Eagwana was marchaunte of the said goodes, which he knowethe to be trewe because he was on of the companye of the same shippe and taken in here by the said Captayne & companye.

47. *Appraisement of the* Margaret's *prize*[1]

The Appraysment & Valuation of a small barcke Called the Equana[2] Laden with Sugars Hides and other thinges Late taken at Sea by a Barcke called the Margarett of London, Captaine xpoffer[3] Newporte made by us Nicholas Barnsley Thomas Pigott grocers Richard moorecocke salter,[4] John Cave Clothworker Robert Bragg and John Severne haberdasher the xxvijth of August Anno domini 1591 as Foloweth

Imprimis we the said Appraisers dilligently viewinge and perusinge the said Sugers beinge 28 chestes of St Domingo sugars in powder weyinge nett vjC one with an other we esteeme at xxviij^s the C which amounteth to	235^{ll} 04^s 0^d
Item 400 drye and merchauntable hides we esteme at vj^s the Hide one with an other which amounteth to	120. 00. 0
Item 353 wett Hides and Rotten withall we esteeme at ij^{s}vj^d the Hide which amounteth to	044. 02. 6
Item xjC Cashia Fistula beinge wett having taken sallt water we esteeme at x^s the C which amounteth to in the whole	005. 10.
Item fower thousand one hundreth Thre score peeces of silver plate of 8 Rialls spannishe	

[1] H.C.A. 24/60, no. 160. [2] Yaguana.
[3] Christopher. [4] Also a dealer in sugar.

the peece we esteeme at iiij⁸ ster*ling* w*hi*ch
am*ou*n*t*eth to   832. 00. 0
It*em* Forty pounde weight of Silver beinge
in platters sawsers and sall*t*es¹
we esteeme at iiij⁸viij*d* the ownce w*hi*ch
amoun*t*eth to   112. 00. 0
It*em* we esteeme the Hull of the said
shipp called the Equana beinge of the
burthen of 30 tonnes beinge olld & rotten
at   006. 13. 4
        Som*m*e Tottalls amounteth to   1355ˡˡ 9ˢ 10ᵈ

In wittnes whearof we the said appraisers have hereunto sett our hand*e*s the daye & yeare first above written.²

48. *Letter of Sir George Carey to Dr Julius Caesar*³

S*ir* I receved by my sarvant Burgley,⁴ a very kinde and frendly message from yow, in asseurans of your unfayned goodwill to me, and your desire to finde returne of the like. If you shall examine the cours of my Life, and belive what you shall finde most trew, my deeds have ever accumpanied my woords, and my frenship was never professed, where not firmely performed, untill cause was aparently geven to the contrary; your goodwill towrds me shall never dye unrequited to the uttermost of my powre, but have usery payde in dooble measeur. Now s*ir* you shall farder understande that I have a very poore prise c*um* into dartmowth, and m*aste*r watts a very riche on, in w*hi*ch I asseure my self as in the rest of his prises, I am to have by lawe on eygthe part, therfor in frenship I beseche and in Justice desire yow, to make no allowans of sale to him of his prises, nor to order any thinge that may prejudice me, untill he shall putt in sufficient asseurans in 10,000 pownde to answer me what by law shalbe

---

¹ 'Salvers'?   ² Signed.
³ Additional MS 12506, f. 285. Endorsed: 'To the Right woorshipfull Doctor Caesar Judge of the admiralty and of the requests to her ma*je*sty geve these.' Also endorsed by Caesar: '13 Octob*er* 1591. Sir George Carey. his kind love towards mee. that m*aste*r wats put in good suerties in 10000 lib. to answere to hi*m* in c*au*sa civili touching his last prises.'
⁴ Possibly John Burley of Newport, captain of the *Brave* of the Isle of Wight (H.C.A. 13/29, 24 April 1591).

approved mine, and that any arrest layd uppon this last prise be not descharged by you without the forsayd caution be put in for me, and so with my very harty commendations do committ you to the tuicion of the only almighty from the castell of carisbrooke this 13 of october 1591.

Your asseured lovinge frende
George Carey.

49. Carey contra Watts: deposition of William Lane[1]

Dominus Georgius Cary miles contra Johannem Wattes mercatorem London.

WILLIELMUS LANE Civitatis London pannorum ornator[2] ubi per xvij annos maiori ex parte commoravit, natus in pago de Melton in Comitatu Lecester annos agens xxxvj aut circiter Testis in hac parte productus iuratus et examinatus deponit se Johannem Wattes per xiij annos et Dominum Georgium Cary per tres menses respective novisse.

Primus testis super Materia Wattes.

Repetitus coram Domino Iudice 22 Ianuarii 1591

Ad primum articulum materie in hac causa date vigore sui iuramenti attestatur et affirmat verissimum That at such tyme as this examinate beinge Captaine of the Centaure and John Gale master of the same and the reste of the Captaines and masters of the articulate shippes the Pegasus the John & the Harry & John were sett to sea by master Wattes & his partners with lettres of Reprisall against the Spaniardes which was in the monethes of March or Aprill laste they had a speciall commission or order from master Wattes under his hande aucthorizinge them that what soever they did amongst them selves and the said iiij^{or} shipps he would complye & not further, and gave them greate chardge thereof and bound them in a greate penaltie to performe the same Ut dicit Et plura ad hunc articulum non deponit.

Ad secundum attestatur eundem continere veritatem For this examinate beinge Captaine of the said shipp the Centaure doth knowe that the articulate Captaines masters & shippes were sett furth to sea by master Wattes & his partners for noe other ende but to execute theire lettres of Reprisall against the Kinge of Spaine & his subjectes.

Ad tertium affirmat verum esse that the Captaines masters

---

[1] H.C.A. 13/29, 10 December 1591. Deposition on Watts' *materia*.
[2] Clothworker.

mariners & souldiers of the said foure shippes have noe other intereste or righte to eany parte of the prizes which were taken by them in the said viadge but only in one thirde parte, as both the lettres of Reprisall and the custome observed duringe theise troubles doth manifest, except eany of them were adventurers which ys more then this examinate knoweth if they were Ut dicit.

Ad quartam posicionem affirmat verum esse That two thirde partes of all the prizes taken by the said foure shippes and the Captaines masters mariners & souldiers thereof doth and did properly appertaine to the owners victualers and setters furthe of the same ships soe sone as the same prizes were taken, and noe parte thereof appertayned to the Captaines masters, mariners & souldiers, neyther had they or eany of them eany commission or aucthority to dispose of the said two thirdes but to sende them for Englande with all speede after the takinge Which he knoweth to be true For that the Captaines masters mariners & souldiers of the said shipps were appoyncted and placed in the said shippes to serve for thirdes and soe they did serve, and expected noe other parte of this examinates knowledge neyther is theire by the Commissions of Reprisall or the observed custome eany more due unto them more then pilladge, and theire thirdes.

Ad quintum affirmat verum esse that master Wattes did expresly in writinge geve order to this examinate, & to the reste of the Captaines and masters of the said foure shipps as he thinketh that they should kepe togeather soe nere as they could all the viadge and promised that what the said foure shipps & the Captaines, masters mariners & souldiers thereof should doe amongst them selves for the said iiij^{or} shipps he would stande unto, and he certenly knoweth he did expresly forbidde them that they should not consorte with eany other shippes but only with the said foure shipps sett out by the said John Wattes and his partners, and this commaundement was geven them before the settinge furth of the said shippes which he hath in writinge to shewe Affirminge that the Captaines masters and company had noe aucthority neyther could share for the owners and victualers of the said foure shippes, with eany other shippes, by his order, Ut dicit Ac plura nescit.

Ad sextum affirmat he never hearde of eany Reprisall that were[1]

[1] [Sic.]

graunted at eany tyme before this last Imbargo in Spaine which was in 1585 Ac ali*ter* nescit.

Ad septimu*m* attestatur [that he does not know of any such custom, whereby captains and masters can make consortships or agreements binding upon the owners and victuallers in the disposal of their thirds.]

Ad octavu*m* attestatur verissimu*m* that theire was noe consortshipp made betwixte the Hopwell, the Pegasus the Centaure & the John, and the Swallowe before the xxvth of June 1591 of this ex*amina*tes certaine knowledge For this ex*amina*te was Captaine of the Centaure and thereby knoweth that neyther he nor eany the company of that shipp consorted with the Swallowe before the said day.

Ad nonu*m* affirmat articulu*m* continere veritatem For this ex*amina*te was one of them that at the requeste of the Captaine of the Swallowe, and Captaine Irishe was contented to consorte for viij dayes nexte ensewinge the xxvth of June laste, and soe on the said xxvth day of June the Captaines & m*aste*rs of the said foure shippes sett out by m*aste*r Wattes & the Swallowe did consorte by worde of mouth only to continewe for viij dayes nexte ensewinge the xxvth of June aforesaid, and the same xxvth day was covenaunted to be one of the viijth[1] and other consorte there was not made of this ex*amina*tes certaine knowledge.

Ad decimu*m* affirmat veru*m* esse that betwixte the xxiiijth of June & the iiijth of July laste past the Hopewell, the Pegasus, the Centaure & the Little John or the companies thereof did not take eanye prizes whatsoever of his certaine knowledge For yf they or eany of them had taken eany such prizes this ex*amina*te beinge in companye with the other shipps all those days must ned*es* have knowen thereof.

Ad undecimu*m* attestatur veru*m* esse that theire was noe consorteshipp made on the xxvth of June laste betwixte the articulate shippes that after the viij dayes aggreed uppon should be expired, that eany devition of prizes to be taken should be made betwixte them accordinge to the burthen of theire shipps & nu*m*ber of the men, but that[2] after the said viij dayes expired yt should be lawfull for the said shipps to sever & the consorte &

---

[1] [*Sic.*]
[2] Probably means: '... of the men. On the contrary it was agreed that ...'.

aggreemente aforesaid to be utterly voide Which he knoweth to be most true for that he was presente at the said aggreemente and a principall actor therein.

Ad duodecimum affirmat that neyther this examinate nor eany his company of the Centaure of his certaine knowledge had noe speach or conference with the Captaine master or company of the Swallowe eyther on the second of July 1591 nor eany tyme else before the articulate prizes were taken, towchinge eany direction of saylinge or keepinge of eany course to meete with or take eany prizes What eany of the other shipps did he knoweth not.

Ad decimum tertium deponit that on the vth day of Julye laste past to his best remembraunce the John and the Pegasus in the morninge betymes tooke one greate spanishe shippe of thre hundreth tonnes laden with hides & some cochenill, and he doth not knowe that the Swallowe was in sighte or nere, nether gave eany aide to the takinge of the same prize and the same day in the after none this examinate & companye of the Centaure tooke an other spanishe shippe which came to Bristowe; without the healpe of eany other shippe, and at such tyme as they tooke the said prize the Swallowe was in chase of a shippe which she tooke and soe farre of that this examinate & company out of the Centaure could scarce see the said Swallowe of his certaine knowledge And sayth that aboute the vijth of July[1] in the morninge the Centaure & the John mett with an other spanishe shipp wherein the silver was beinge of most ritches, and after four houres fighte or thereaboutes tooke and subdued the said shippe without the aide healpe or assistaunce of eany other shippe of his certaine knowledge: and duringe all the tyme that the said spanish shippe was in sighte foughte withall and taken he is most assured that the Swallowe was not in sighte of the said prize: For if she had, this examinate beinge in the Centaure must nedes have seene her as he belevethe. And towchinge a smale prize taken by the Harry & John & the Pegasus he never hearde that the Swallowe gave eany aide to the takinge thereof Ut dicit Affirminge moreover that the Swallowe did not shotte at eany of the said foure shipps neyther was nere or could reach eany of them with shott when they were taken to his knowledge But when the two shipps that the Centaure where of this examinate was Captaine, was at the takinge of,

---

[1] Most of the witnesses say that the silver prize was taken on 6 July, a Tuesday.

were taken, this ex*amina*te assuredly knoweth that the Swallowe was not nere neyther shott at them or in eany sorte gave eany aide or healpe to the takinge of them. Ac plura non deponit.

Ad decimu*m* quartu*m* al*ia*s dictu*m* est et plura non deponit.

Ad decimu*m* quintu*m* attestatur he never knewe or hearde that the said shipp the Swallowe did geve chase to eany of the articulate two prizes or eany wayes healped to take them, neyther doth he knowe whether the Swallowe was in sighte when the two prizes taken by the Pegasus the Harry and the John were taken, or noe, But sayth he knoweth of his owne knowledge that when the other two prizes were taken by the Centaure & the John, the Swallowe was out of sighte when one was taken, and soe farre to leewarde when the other was taken that they could scarce see her Ut dicit ab eo predepositu*m* esse.

Ad decimu*m* sextum affirmat veru*m* esse That aboute the tyme that the said foure spanishe shippes were taken by the shippes of m*aste*r Watt*e*s & his p*a*rtners, the Swallowe gave chase to an other spanishe shippe and with the healpe of the Harry & John & Pegasus did take the same Spanishe shippe; and never did pursue or offer to geve chase to the said foure prizes which were taken by m*aste*r Watt*e*s shippes to this ex*amina*tes knowledge Reddendo rationem ut supra.

Ad decimu*m* septimu*m* dicit he was not presente & therefore cannot depose hereunto.

Ad decimu*m* octavu*m* dicit he hath herde the Hopwells company affirme that they did pursue the said spanishe shippe taken by the Swallowe, and endevored to take the same and shott att her and were within shott when she was taken, and beinge a greate shippe was the cheife cause that the Swallowe did take her, and thereuppon beinge pr*ese*nte at the takinge & within shott some of the Hopewells companye did enter on borde the said prize as he hath herd. Et al*ite*r nescit.

Ad decimu*m* nonu*m* attestatur he hath herd the company of the Hopwell affirme soe much as ys conteyned in this article viz[t] that althoughe they were presente and did healpe to take the said prize yet the Captaine & m*aste*r of the Swallowe denied them eany parte thereof Ac al*ite*r nescit.

Ad vicesimu*m* affirmat that this ex*amina*te & company of the Centaure did never claime or pretende eany title to eany parte of

Pegasus & the John in June laste came to a place in the Indies called Cape de Corientes founde[1] there the articulate shippe the Swallowe and the Hopewell beinge well beaten fewe dayes before as appeared by the Barcke Burre & the Contempt that were in theire companye,[2] and then the Swallowe beinge a smale shippe and weekly furnished & the company were gladde to shroude them selves amongst m*as*ter Wattes said shippes & soe intruded them selves into theire companye, and by meanes thereof the said shipp the Swallowe was in sighte righte to Leeward when the Pegasus tooke her prize but not within foure leages as he beleveth and certenly knoweth for that he sawe both the Swallowe & the Pegasus beinge betwixte them in the Centaure when the said prize was taken Notwithstandinge he sayth that when this ex*amina*te & his company in the Centaure tooke theire first prize in the Indies the Swallowe was not in company nor in viewe of his certaine knowledge.[3] Ac al*ite*r res*p*ondet negative.

[To the second and third he repeats that the *Swallow* played no part in the capture of the two prizes taken by the *Centaur* and the *Pegasus*]

Ad quartu*m* res*p*ondet and beleveth that the Swallowe did cause a spanishe shipp to strike which she pursued but that the same was entered & taken by the Lion of Hampton as he hath herde, beinge a thirde shipp and not eany of them which the Pegasus & Centaure tooke Ac al*ite*r res*p*ondet negative.

Ad quintu*m* res*p*ondet et fatetur that at the earnest request of Raph Lea Captaine of the Swallowe & Captaine Irishe beinge with him and Richard Drap*er* who came on borde the Harry & John there was a consorteshippe made betwixte this respondent W*illia*m Craston, Michaell Geere, Stephen Michell and John Broughe, and the said Raph Lee Captaine of the Swallowe to continue only for viij dayes then followinge, and did beginne uppon the xxvth day of June laste beinge the same day that they made the consorte. And sayth the said consorte was made by the said Captaines by worde of mouth, without the consente of theire severall companies tohis knowledge. Ac al*ite*r res*p*ondet negative.

Ad sextum respondet et credit that the said shippes duringe the

[1] Should read 'they founde'.
[2] They were in company at the time of the flight, but not afterwards.
[3] The *Swallow* was in company when the prizes were taken off Cape Corrientes. Lane may be referring to an earlier prize.

say that he had sayled to the Indies in the said shipp the Swallowe,[1] and that she was of xxxv tonnes and not bigger.

Ad xxix affirmat that the Harry and John al*ia*s the Hopewell is of the burthen of nynescore or thereabout*e*s The Centaure of Cxx tonnes, the Pegasus of Lxxx tonnes and the Little John of an Cxxx tonnes or thereabout*e*s and were furnished with thre hundreth and forty men or thereabout*e*s and seaventy peeces of ordinaunce of this ex*amina*tes knowledge at the tyme of the takinge of the said prizes.

Ad xxx^{um} attestatur verissimu*m* esse that the Swallowe was not presente at the takinge of eanye of the thre prizes which were laste taken by the Centaure the Pegasus the Hopewell & the John neyther gave eany aide, healpe or assistaunce at all in the takinge thereof to his knowledge. But most assured he is that when the prize taken north of the Avana by the Centaure & John was taken, the Swallowe was not in sighte neyther within foure leag*e*s at the leaste of this ex*amina*tes certaine knowledge But was soe farre to Leewarde in the currante at that tyme that this ex*amina*te & companye in the Centaure could not see the Swallowe which he affirmeth to be most true.

Ad xxxj deponit eundem continere veritatem reddendo rationem ut supra deposuit.

Ad xxxij dicit he is of opinion that the Captaine m*aste*r company & owners of the swallowe are not to clame in righte or to have eany p*a*rte of the said prizes taken by the Centaure the Hopewell, the Pegasus and the Little John in maner as ys before declared or in eany parte thereof, For that neyther the Swallowe nor the Captaine m*aste*r or companye thereof were presente at the takinge of eany of the said prizes neyther did shote at, fighte withall or geve aide succor or eany healpe to the vanquishinge and subduenge of the said prizes or eany of them as ys before declared. Ac ideo refert se ad iura in hac p*a*rte.

Ad ult*imum* dicit predeposita p*er* eu*m* esse vera.

Ad Interrogatoria ex p*a*rte D*omini* Georgii
Carie militis ministrata.

Ad primu*m* exposito sibi periculo p*er*iurii respondet that as this respondent and his company in the Centaure togeather with the

[1] Presumably in 1587.

ex*amina*te & his company of the Centaure for that as he confessed he was not in sighte when she was taken, nor was eany meanes or healpe in the takinge thereof But in the Pegasus prize he said he would clayme a p*art*e because he sawe her when she was taken Ac al*ite*r nescit.

Ad xxiiij^{um} affirmat he certenly knoweth that when the Pegasus tooke the articulate prize whiche was aboute the xxijth of June, the Swallowe was at the leaste foure leages of, and neyther did nor could geve eany aide or succor to the Pegasus in the takinge thereof, and the same prize would have escaped untaken for eany thinge the Swallowe could have don yf the Pegasus and Centaure had byn away Which he knowethe to be true for that the Pegasus was to windeward of the Centaure wherein this ex*amina*te was at the least thre lea*g*es at the takinge of the said prize, and at the same tyme the Swallowe was both to Leeward & a sterne of the Centaure aboute two leages of this ex*amina*tes sighte, this ex*amina*te in the Centaure beynge then betwixte them Ut dicit.

Ad xxv^{um} attestatur truth yt ys that the Swallowe and her company layde for the thirde Spanishe shipp which came in sighte and tooke her, and therein neyther this ex*amina*te nor the Captaines or m*aste*rs of the other thre shipps of m*aste*r Wattes claymed noe parte althoughe they were in company the nexte day, & mighte have byn theire owne carvers beinge the Stronger yf they had byn of that minde.

Ad xxvj dicit he hath herde that there were xxix hundreth hides in the said prize taken by the Swallowe before the said xxiiijth of June, which mighte be worth aboute xvC^{li} ster*ling* Ac al*ite*r nescit.

Ad xxvij dicit the prize which was taken by the Swallowe assisted by the Harry & John & Pegasus after the consorte aforesaid was expired, was of the burthen of nynty tonne and laden with ginger hides & suger and had some Jewells & pearle as he hearde and mighte by estimation of her grosse ladinge be worth foure thowsande poundes Ac al*ite*r nescit.

Ad xxviij dicit the Swallowe in his judgemente is of the burthen of xxxv tonnes little more or lesse and had in her about xx men & thre or fower peeces of ordinaunce at the tyme of the takinge of the said prizes. Ac al*ite*r nescit. Savinge he hath herde John Gale who was m*aste*r of the Centaure with this ex*amina*te the prize taken by the Swallowe neyther the Captaines masters & company of the Pegasus & Harry & John that ever he knewe of Ac aliter nescit.

Ad xxj attestatur [that consortships entered into by captains and masters are not binding on owners, etc.]

Ad xxij affirmat verum esse that aboute the xxijth or xxiijth of June laste & before eany consorteshippe was made by master Wattes his shipps with the Swallowe there came thre Spanishe shippes in viewe as the Centaure the Pegasus & the Swallowe were in company & togeather and the same shippes were firste escried by the company of the Centaure beinge a heade of the other shippes & nerest towardes the prizes, and the Centaure first gave chace to the said prizes, and the Pegasus followed nexte & the Swallowe was the laste of those thre that gave chase to the said shippes of this examinates certaine knowledge who then was in the Centaure & an eye witnes thereof, and because one of this examinates companye first escried the said prizes this examinate gave him forty shillinges in goulde for the same. Affirminge that at such tyme as this examinate & company in the Centaure did take one of the said prizes which was aboute xjth[1] of the clocke in the eveninge, the said shipp the Swallowe was nether presente nor gave eany aide or healpe to the takinge thereof, neyther did the company thereof see or knowe when the said prize was taken untill the morninge day lighte, and then the said shipp the Swallowe had a prize which she had taken that nighte, as also the Pegasus had an other Addinge moreover that this examinate & company in the Centaure were still a heade of the other two shipps in the pursuenge and takinge of the said prize, and thereby he knoweth that the Swallowe which was most to Leeward of all the thre & the hindermost, came not nere the said prize taken by the Centaure, neyther gave eany terror feare or healpe to the takinge thereof, for that she was not in sighte when the prize was taken of his certaine knowledge.

Ad xxiij^{um} deponit verum esse that Raph Lee Captaine of the Swallowe at such tyme as he came on borde the Harry John[2] to consorte with master Wattes shipps did confesse unto this examinate in the hearinge of sondry others that he could not neyther would clame eany parte of the said prize taken by this

---

[1] [Sic.]   [2] The *Harry and John*, alias the *Hopewell*.

contra Johannem Wattes.
2 testis super materia Wattes.
Repetitus coram Domino Iudice 22 Ianuarii 1591.

novem annos Dominum Georgium Carie ex visu per triennium respective novisse.

Ad primum articulum materie ... that this examinate beinge appoyncted by master Wattes his master, Captaine of the Pegasus and Abicocke Perry master [there were] ... foure severall copies of articles & directions made in writinge & one delivered to every of the Captaines. ...

Ad xxix^{um} attestatur verum esse that the Centaure is of Cxx tonnes, the Hopwell of CC tonnes the John betwene vij and viij score tonnes and the Pegasus of fourescore tonnes and upwards and are shippes of good service and were appoyncted with Lxviij peeces of ordenaunce or thereaboutes and aboute iiijC^{lli} amongst them. ...

Ad Interrogatoria. ...

Ad xxvij respondet master Wattes shippes tooke ten shippes and frigottes as he remembreth this laste sommer whereof two Frigottes were laden with turtells, and the Swallowe shott at one of those Fissher frigottes[2] when she was at least foure miles a sterne with a pott gonn, otherwise called a shorte saker and one other laden with hides was burnte, and nothinge was taken out of her, an other they lefte at Garrachico outwardes bounde & an one other was soncke homewardes bounde & fyve they broughte & sente home.

51. Carey contra Watts: deposition of Ralph Lee[3]

Dominus Georgius Carye miles contra Johannem Wattes.
Primus testis super Libello Domini Carie.
Repetitus viij^o

RADULPHUS LEE civitatis London generosus ubi per vij annos maiori ex parte commoravit natus in pago dicto Civerne Stoke[4] in Comitatu Worcester annos agens xL^{ta} vel circiter testis in hac parte productus iuratus et examinatus Dicit quod Dominum Georgium Carie militem per decennium et Johannem Wattes per quadriennium respective noverit.

Ad primum et secundum articulos libelli in hac causa dati in vim eius iuramenti attestatur eosdem continere veritatem For this examinate is the articulate Raphe Lee and was sett out for

[1] Weight.   [2] Turtle boats.
[3] H.C.A. 13/29, 21 December 1591. First deposition on Carey's libel.
[4] Severn Stoke.

THE 1591 VOYAGES

Ad xviij respondet negative.

Ad decimum nonum respondet the Swallowe mett with the Pegasus the Centaure & the John at Cape Corintes aboute the xixth of June laste as he remembreth But where she mett with the Hopewell he knoweth not.

[To the 20th, 21st, 22nd, 23rd and 24th he replies without adding to his former statements]

Ad xxv respondet that master Wattes sente this respondente his commission of restraincte articulate to Plimouth bearinge date the xxviijth of march laste where this respondent receaved the same, and the like restraincte master Wattes gave this respondent at Gravesende by worde of mouth in presence of William Craston Stephen Michell & Michaell Geere as he remembrethe Ac aliter nescit.

Ad xxvj respondet [he never heard of any consortship made at sea without the consent of the owners which bound the owners in the disposal of their thirds]

Ad xxvij respondet master Wattes his shipps tooke this laste viadge nyne prizes whereof one was laden with turtells, and some of them they eate, & soncke the reste with the Barcke, an other prize ran on shore nere the Avana which they fired, a thirde soncke comminge for England, and a fourth they sould in May laste at Teneriffe for the valewe of two thowsand duckettes because they were outwardes bounde on a longe viadge and could not cary the same with them, and fyve prizes they broughte home And sayth Sir George Cary his shipp the Swallowe was not presente or gave eany aide to the takinge of eany of all the said prizes But only was in sighte yet farre of at the takinge of one of them beinge the least prize, that came to Bristowe.

[His replies to the remaining six interrogatories add nothing to his former statements]

50. Carey contra *Watts: deposition of Stephen Michell*[1]

STEPHANUS MICHELL famulus Johannis Wattes cum *Dominus* quo habitavit per quinque annos vel circiter annos agens viginti *Georgius Carie* unum plus minusve testis... deponit se Johannem Wattes per *miles*

[1] H.C.A. 13/29, 14 December 1591. Extract. Deposition on the *materia*.

that the Hopwells company had eany goodes out of the said prize, but thinketh that they beinge on borde gott some pilladge yf eany were there to be had Ac al*ite*r nescit.

Ad undecimu*m* res*p*ondet the Swallowe was out of sighte when the silver prize was taken, and therefore he knoweth not whether she pursued after or noe. Ac al*ite*r nescit.

Ad duodecimu*m* res*p*ondet he hath for theise fyve yeares space gon*e* to sea with le*tt*res of Reprisall sondry tymes the first viadge was in a shipp of m*aste*r Wattes called the Margarett & John and the second tyme was in a shipp of m*aste*r Stephen Ridlesden, and since he hath gon*e* still in m*aste*r Wattes his shipps, and hath served as Captaine in two severall viadges.

Ad decimu*m* tertiu*m* R*es*p*o*ndet [that he cannot judge whether consortships made without the consent of the owners and victuallers are binding upon the owners and victuallers]

Ad decimu*m* quartu*m* respondet they broughte home fyve spanishe shippes which are noe better worth then for firewoode and he esteemethe them with theire furniture not worthe above an hundrethe poundes, nether would he geve more for them. Ac al*ite*r nescit.

Ad decimu*m* quintu*m* respondet he esteemeth all the good*e*s money bullyn pearle & other thing*e*s broughte to England by m*aste*r Wattes shippes this laste viadge to be worth aboute thirtye two thowsand poundes that ys come to this respondent*e*s knowledge, and soe they are valued. Ac al*ite*r nescit.

Ad xvj credit the Swallowe was sett furth by S*i*r George Carie Knighte and belongeth unto him For that he hath herde soe much Ac al*ite*r nescit.

Ad xvij*um* respondet that at sea they shared fyve thowsand and odd pound*e*s amongst the foure shippes vizt the Centaure the Pegasus the Hopewell and the John, whereof the Company of the Centaure had xiiij C^{li} amongst them w*h*ich came to vij^{li} a single share and since theire com*m*inge home they have had soe much more as with the vij^{li} aforesaid doth make uppe ten pound*e*s a single share with some odde moneye more And thereof this respondent for his p*ar*te beinge Captaine had viij single shares, vizt he had xxiiij^{li} in money of m*aste*r Wattes and Lvj^{li} at sea as he remembreth, and loketh for noe more for his owne p*ar*te Ac quoad alios ignorat. Ac al*ite*r respondet negative.

said viij dayes did keepe togeather accordinge to theire consorteshippe but in all that tyme they did not take eany prizes neyther geve chase to eany Notwithstandinge he grauntethe that two dayes after the expiringe of the said aggreemente of consorteshippe this Respondent & company in the Centaure tooke one smale prize with hides which they sett on fire & enjoyed not and aboute the vi^th of Julye[1] this respondente did take one other prize alone without eany healpe of the Swallowe beinge a leage of at leaste which was sente to Bristowe, and the Swallowe had soe much interest therein that the Captaine & company did not soe muche as offer one man to healpe to bringe her into Englande Affirminge also that the Centaure & the John tooke one other prize to the northward of the Avana wherein the silver was founde, and at the takinge thereof the Swallowe was out of sighte of his knowledge and did not assiste or geve eany aide to the takinge thereof, or of eany the other prizes. Ac aliter quam prius est responsum respondet negative Savinge he beleveth that the Swallowe was in sighte when the smale shippe broughte to Bristowe, and the greate shippe that was soncke, were taken.

Ad septimum respondet he hath herde as ys before answered that the Swallowe was in sighte when the Lesser shippe of St Domingo broughte to Bristowe was taken and made towardes her Ac aliter respondet negative.

Ad octavum respondet that the Swallowe as he belevethe with the healpe of the Hopwell and a Frigott did take one spanishe shippe laden with ginger hides & suger as he herde Ac aliter respondet negative.

Ad nonum respondet and belevethe that because the Hopewell was presente at the takinge of the said spanishe shippe togeather with the Swallowe, and the cheifest meanes and occasion of the takinge thereof therefore the Hopewell & the company thereof claymed parte therein as lawfully they mighte doe, and placed men in the same to bringe her for England But afterwardes the Swallowes companye as he hearde expelled the company of the Hopewell, sayenge they had noe righte therein, neyther should have share in the same.

Ad decimum respondet he neyther knoweth nor hath herde

---

[1] Probably on 5 July.

Captaine of the Swallowe by Sir George Carie owner thereof in some of the monethes articulate.

Iannuarij 1591 coram Domino iudice in Camera sua.

Ad tertium affirmat verum esse that Anthony Daniell wente master of the said shipp the Swallowe with this examinate.

Ad quartum dicit he hath herde yt commonly affirmed that John Wattes and his partners are owners of the articulate shipps the Centaure the Pegasus the Hopewell and the Little John and soe were accompted Ac aliter nescit.

Ad quintum sextum septimum octavum nonum decimum undecimum et duodecimum affirmat he knoweth the articulate Captaines & masters were in some of monethes[1] articulate Captaines & masters of the said shippes the Hopewell the Centaure the Pegasus & the John severally as theise articules declare For this examinate was at sea in the company of the said shipps Captaines & masters & therefore knoweth the same.

Ad decimum tertium attestatur verum esse That Sir George Carie, Knighte beinge owner of the said shippe the Swallowe in the monethes articulate did furnishe and sett furth the same with lettres of Reprisall in Aprill laste against the Subjectes of the Kinge of Spaine: and gave this examinate directions to doe what seemed best to this examinate & company for the betteringe of theire viadge & takinge of such prizes as they should meete with all.

Ad decimum quartum affirmat yt ys publickly reported that John Wattes & his partners did warlickly appointe furnishe and sett furthe the articulate shippes the Hopewell the Centaure, the Pegasus & the John with lettres of Reprisalls against the Spaniardes and appoyncted the persons articulate for Captaines & masters thereof but what aucthority or directions otherwise they gave theire Captaines & masters he knoweth not Ac aliter nescit.

Ad xv^{um} affirmat that this examinate & company of the Swallowe in the moneth of may or June laste beinge in the Indies followinge his commission of Reprisall in company of the Barcke Burre & the Contente, Shipps of Sir George Cary, mett with the Hopewell of master Wattes and soe they kepte company togeather & foughte with a fleete of Spaniardes and were putt to Flighte and severed Savinge the Swallowe & Hopewell which

---
[1] Definite article omitted.

kepte togeather for certaine dayes after and plyenge nere Cape Corantes[1] they mett with the Centaure the Pegasus & the John shipps of m*aste*r Wattes, and the Prudence and Lion of hampton,[2] and by reason some of them wanted water they wente into Corantes to water or doe some other necessaries and the Centaure, the Pegasus, the Swallowe & the Lion lay without, and thus lienge without there came thre spanishe shippes in sighte. Whereunto all the said foure shippes gave chase togeather in the forenoune and continued theire chase all the daye and in the sighte of this ex*amina*te & company of the Swallowe the Pegasus tooke one of the said shipps before nighte; and in the nighte followinge the Centaure tooke an other of them; and the thirde was forced to strike to the Swallowe but was first entered by the Lion Ac al*ite*r nescit Savinge he sayth he did geve chase to all the said iij shippes to the best advantadge he could to take them, and did his best endevor in the pursuite of them to take them.

Ad xvj nescit deponere.

Ad xvii^{um} dicit he hath used the sea theise xvj yeares space, and duringe that tyme he hath often hearde yt reported and affirmed that the Custome of the sea is and hath byn tyme out of minde that if diverse shippes beinge on warrefare doe pursue & followe and geve chase togeather to the ennimy, and some of them happen to take purchase, that then the other shipps beinge in sighte and followinge in chase oughte to share with the takers tonn for tonn & man for man Ac al*ite*r nescit.

Ad xviij^{um} dicit the Swallowe was in the yeare and monethes articulate well furnished and munited for a shipp of her burthen with ordinaunce and munition and had in her forty & odde men & boyes who made good fighte uppon the Spaniardes in that viadge. Ac al*ite*r nescit.

[To the 19th and 20th articles he does not depose.]

Ad xxj affirmat veru*m* esse That after the takinge of the said thre prizes all the foresaid foure shippes wente into Corantes where the other shippes of m*aste*r Wattes were and there this ex*amina*te and Captaine Irishe wente on borde the Hopewell, where the Captaines of the other shippes the Centaure the Pegasus & the John with the Captaines of the Lion & the Prudence

---

[1] Corrientes.
[2] The *Prudence* of London and the *Lion* of Southampton.

came on borde the said shippe the Hopewell, and there a consorteshippe was aggreed uppon by all the Captaines of the said shippes called the Centaure the Hopewell the Pegasus the John & the Swallowe to continewe untill the thirde of the nexte moneth of Julye betwene the said v shippes accordinge to the teanor of the articles that wer aggreed uppon before betwene master Wattes shipps whiche were then reade by Captaine Lane and there unto the said Captaines consented & aggreed. And uppon the makinge of the same consorteshippe Captaine Lane openly sayde before Captaine Draper Captaine Oker & others that they mente to winter in the Cuntrey, and that if they mente to continewe Consortes for longer tyme then the dayes aforesaid, that then they should not be soe farre a sonder but that they mighte call one to the other and acquainte them therewith. Ac plura non deponit.

Ad xxij attestatur yt was aggreed uppon by the Captaines of the said shipps of master Wattes and this examinate that what purchase soever should be taken by the said shipps or eany of them duringe the tyme of the said consorteshippe should be devided tonn for tonn & man for man: and further yt was aggreed uppon amongst them that whatsoever shipp was within shott at the takinge of eany prize shoulde have parte of the pilladge and such shippes as were not within shott should have noe parte thereof. Ac aliter nescit.

Ad xxiij^{um} deponit that accordinge to the said consorteshippe the said v shippes kepte company togeather and aboute the laste day of the consorteshippe, this examinate beinge betwene the Avana & the Mattances[1] Captaine Croston and Kennell haled this examinate and asked him if he were consorted with the Lion, and because this examinate was not well at ease he willed Captaine Irishe beinge on borde the Swallowe to speake aloude and tell them noe, and that they were consorted with none but with them, meaninge master Wattes shipps and soe he did and Craston or Kennell made answere yt was well, and Captaine Irish asked them agayne what the Centaure & Pegasus would doe and whether they would returne home agayne, and they replied agayne we cannot tell, but the Little John will doe as we doe. By occasion whereof this examinate made accompte to continue

[1] Matanzas.

consortes with them still and soe kepte company with them, and beinge in company and plyenge to & froe theye escried some thre or foure Spanishe shippes where unto all master Wattes shippes, being come togeather and the Swallowe gave chase, and every man shaped his course to the best advantadge some to cutt them of from the shore, other some plied to Seaward least by a winde they should escape away from them, and every man did his best endevor to annoy the ennimy as he thinketh for this examinate & company of the Swallowe for theire partes soe did Which he knoweth to be true For that he was Captaine of the Swallowe and sawe the said spanishe shipps and gave chase unto them in company and togeather with master Wattes shipps.

Ad xxiiij affirmat verum esse that the said shippes the Hopewell the Centaure the Pegasus the John and the Swallowe did geve chase togeather to the said Spanishe shippes, and endevored with all theire force and power to subdue & take them. Reddendo rationem ut supra that he was presente thereat, and did shote at the saint Domingo man a little before she was taken.

Ad xxv dicit verum esse That this examinate & company of the Swallowe did take one of the said spanishe shipps beinge laden with hides suger & ginger & some pearle.

Ad xxvj affirmat verum esse That the Centaure the Hopewell the Pegasus & the John and the Captaines & companies thereof did take thre other spanishe shipps on the vth of July as he remembrethe, and at the takinge of the said thre spanishe shippes this examinate and companye in the Swallowe were in sighte of them & sawe them taken and did followe after & geve chase unto them by all the meanes & healpe they coulde shewe of this examinates certaine knowledge, and he was within shott of two of the said prizes when they were taken; And sayth that the nexte day in the morninge this examinate caused some of his men to goe into the Topp to tell the shipps and to see whether there were eany chase geven, and they perceaved that the Little John had a shipp in chase to windewarde of them, and thereuppon this examinate spronge his loofe[1] and made after and in the after noone this examinate althoughe yt was somewhat farre of sawe the shott of the ordenaunce, and that the shipp was laide on borde & taken, and there uppon havinge men in the Topp &

---
[1] See p. 109, n. 1 above.

escryenge sayles to Leewarde as they thoughte, they bare a shorte sayle all nighte with intente to be in with them in the morninge. Which in truth fell out contrary to theire expectation. And sayth that when this examinate paid rome[1] as aforesaid he called to the master & Lieftenant in his prize & willed them to beare upp with the rest of the Flete, and by gods grace he would be with them the nexte day.

Ad xxvij^{um} attestatur verissimum esse that after this examinate and companye of the Swallowe had taken the said spanishe shippe whiche they possessed without shott of eany other of the shipps, the Hopewell sente as he thinketh a smale Carvell called the fifte parte to borde the said prize also whom this examinate resisted to come on borde Sayenge yt was contrary to theire aggreement that eany should have pilladge beinge without shott, and thereuppon they called to the Hopewell sayenge lay her aborde with the shippe, and soe the Hopewells Captaine called Croston & Kennell the master with others came on borde the said prize to this examinate; and this examinate asked them what they mente and whether they would make pilladge of them, and the said Craston and Kennell made answere that they mente noe such thinge but sayde to this examinate that he and his company should have as good parte of all such prizes as they tooke, as they made accompte to have with this examinate. Then this examinate requested that the company mighte be sente away, and such honest men lefte on borde with him as should be thoughte fittest And soe after they had pilladged and taken parrattes with other thinges from aborde they departed promisinge to leave but two of theire men, notwithstandinge there taried vj or vij of them. Which he affirmeth to be most true.

Ad xxviij dicit yt ys an ordinary matter at sea when shipps of warre doe meete to make consorteshipps for the better effectinge of such service as they entende; and he seeth noe reason but that the consorteshippe beinge made for the good aswell of the owners victualers and advanturers as the Captaines & company, should binde the owners & victualers beinge absente aswell as the Captaines & company, especially seinge the Captaines & masters are the owners deputies in those cases Ac aliter nescit.

Ad xxix dicit he hath herde the articulate prizes arrived at the

---

[1] See p. 108, n. 1 above.

articulate portes and were disposed of by m*aste*r Wattes & his company Ac al*ite*r nescit.

Ad xxx nescit deponere.

Ad xxxj dicit yt ys well knowen that a greate p*a*rte of the treasure & goodes broughte home in the articulate fyve prizes are come to the hand*e*s of m*aste*r Wattes and are disposed by him beinge the greatest owner & adventurer in the said foure shippes Ac al*ite*r nescit.

[Examinate's replies to the remaining eight articles add nothing to his above statement.]

Ad Interrogatoria

Ad primu*m* et secundu*m* exposito sibi periculo p*e*riurii et pena testis falcidici respondet he hath served at sea under the prince of Orange & the prince of Conde[1] and elswhere and made sondry viadges to sea duringe the space of theise xvj yeares past But howe many viadges he hath soe made he cannot recounte Ac al*ite*r r*es*p*o*nsum est supra.

Ad tertiu*m* respondet he hath served at sea with Reprisalls foure or fyve viadges in the shippinge of S*i*r George Carie Knighte and by vertue of Reprisalls graunted unto him in sondry yeares.

Ad quartu*m* r*es*p*o*ndet he hath not knowen of eany Reprisalls graunted to English men before theise troubles happened with Spaine.

Ad quintu*m* r*es*p*o*ndet yt ys com*m*only knowen that in theise cases of Reprisalls the use & custome is that two thirde p*a*rtes of all prizes taken doe belonge to the owners victualers & adventurers of such shipps as take them, and the other thirde p*a*rte to the companye. And noe more belongeth unto them to his knowledge.

Ad sextu*m* r*es*p*o*ndet he is ignorante what is lawfull or unlawfull in this case of consortinge For he sayth at theire goinge to sea they are forbidden many thinges which at theire beinge at sea they doe notwithstandinge Ac al*ite*r nescit.

Ad septimu*m* r*es*p*o*ndet se nescire.

Ad octavu*m* respondet he knoweth of noe consorteshipps made without the owners consent*e*s that have helde & byn avaylable against the owners ac ideo nescit r*es*p*o*ndere.

---

[1] Both in former times had issued letters of reprisal under which English adventurers sailed against Spanish or French Catholic shipping.

Ad nonum respondet that a consorteshipp was made betwene the Captaines of the Swallowe, the Hopwell, the Centaure the Pegasus & the John in the Roade of Corantes in the moneth of June laste, & was to continewe untill the third day of the moneth of July followinge And sayth the same Consorteshipp was made on borde the Hopwell in presence of Captaine Irishe, Captaine Draper & Captaine Oker, and the Captaines of master Wattes shipps, and this respondent and sondry others of the company of master Wattes shipps whom he cannot name. And at the makinge of the same consorteshipp this examinate would have had yt to be made for xiiij dayes or untill they wente to Winter, and Captaine Lane answered they should not be soe farre a sonder but that they mighte call one to an other, and accordingly, after they had broughte the shipps cleare of the Avana, this examinate happened to geve chase to the Lion and spake with her, and afterwardes meetinge with the Hopewell, she called to this respondent & asked whether he was consorted with the Lion and Captaine Irishe from the Swallowe made answere they were not consorted with eany but them meaninge master Wattes shipps & they replied sayenge yt was well, as ys before deposed.

Ad decimum respondet there was noe other but one consorteshippe made betwixte the Swallowe & master Wattes shippes beinge the same which ys before spoken of.

Ad undecimum respondet none of the prizes libellated were taken betwixte the xxiiij[th] of June & the iiij[th] of July 1591.

Ad duodecimum respondet there was noe such conference had betwixte this respondent & eany of master Wattes shipps eany of the dayes mentioned in this Interrogatory but every shipp tooke his best course to annoy the ennimy & lay as seemed fittest to take purchase Savinge on the vth of Julye when this respondent had taken his prize Captaine Craston, Kennell the master & others of the Hopewell came on borde his said prize & pilladged & tould this respondent that he should have as good share with them as they mente to have with him.

Ad xiij[um] respondet the Hopewell on the vth of July tooke a prize beinge the greatest & that which ys soncke as he taketh yt[1] and the same day the Centaure the Hopewell the Pegasus & the Fifte parte amongst them tooke two prizes more and this respon-

---

[1] Refers to the *St. John*, captured by the *John*, not by the *Hopewell*.

dents company shott at one of them out of the Swallowe before she was taken beinge the leaste of the St. Domingo men; and was in sighte when all the said thre shippes were taken and in chase of them as ys before declared, and the nexte day the John tooke an other prize thwart of or nere the Avana. Ac al*iter* nescit.

Ad xiiij^{um} res*p*ondet the Swallowe was within shott of that prize which the Hopewell tooke when she was taken, and also was within shott of the smale Domingo man which the Fifte *pa*rte foughte withall; and afterward*e*s taken by the other shipp*s*, and at the same later shipp the Swallowe made shott But what hurte they did them he knoweth not And sayth the Swallowe was without shott when the John tooke her prize But whether he was within shott or noe when the Centaure & Pegasus tooke theire thirde prize he remembreth not.

Ad xv res*p*ondet he was never on borde eany of the said prizes and therefore he knoweth not which of them was Ritchest Ac al*ite*r nescit.

Ad xvj^{um} res*p*ondet he was within shott of two of the said prizes and in sighte of them all when they were taken But which was Ritchest of them he knoweth not And sayth the Swallowe was to Leeward of that prize which the John tooke on the vjth day in the eveninge But howe farre of he cannot judge, and sayth he was not within shott of that prize at eany tyme before she was taken Notwithstandinge he sayth he gave chase after that prize untill he sawe she was taken & then he plied to Leeward after other sayles which he thoughte he had seene.

Ad xvij res*p*ondet he was to Leeward with the Swallowe when the Johns prize was taken But when the other prizes were taken he was in amongst them sometyme plyenge aboute on one tacke, sometyme on the other tacke soe as he cannot declare whether he was to windeward or Leeward of them.

Ad xviij res*p*ondet he beleveth that S*ir* George Cary Knighte hath righte to such parte of the two first prizes taken before the Consorteshippe, as the Lawe will geve him, as in sighte and chase, For the Pegasus tooke one of the said prizes in the sighte of this respondente and company of the Swallowe But the other was taken in the nighte tyme soe as they could not see yt althoughe they were in chase still.

Ad xix^{um} fatetur this respondent & companye did cause one

knoweth not that there was eany gould silver or pearle in the said prize the hides were thre thousand or thereaboutes that were taken in the said shipp & came to the handes of Sir George Cary knighte after composition made with the Captaines & owners of the Lion by reason the Lion first entered the said prize. . . .

Ad xxviij respondet the said second prize taken bye the Swallowe was laden with aboute two thousand hides and fifty Chestes of suger and some pearl howe much he knoweth not, the whole prize beinge worth xijC^{li} or thereaboutes as he belevethe. . . .

Ad xxxj respondet he was never servant nether tooke wages or livery of Sir George Cary Savinge as he served in his shippinge And sayth Captaine Irish and Raph Lee are servantes to Sir George.

53. Carey contra *Watts: deposition of John Brough*[1]

Dominus Georgius Carie contra Johannem Wattes.

3 testis Wattes.

JOHANNES BROUGHE Civitatis London haberdaisher ubi per omnem suam etatem commoravit annos agens xxxij aut circiter Testis . . . deponit quod Johannem Wattes per xij annos et Dominum Georgium Carye per septennium respective noverit. . . .

Ad octavum et nonum affirmat he knoweth that on the xxvth of June laste [when a consortship was made for eight days at the request of the Swallow's men] this examinate was present at the said Consorteshippe uppon occasion that this examinate was Captaine of an other shipp called the Prudence of London, and was on borde the Hopewell at dinner when Captaine Lee and Captaine Irishe came on borde & intreated for the said consorte and soe sawe the same concluded by worde only for viij dayes. . . .

Ad decimum et undecimum dicit that this examinate & his company were sente home with two prizes which were taken before the said Consorteshippe, and departed therewith from the company of the articulate shippes . . . on the first of Julye. . . .[2]

Ad Interrogatoria. . . .

Ad duodecimum respondet he hath gone to sea with Reprisalls

---

[1] H.C.A. 13/29, 31 December 1591. Extract. Deposition on the *materia*.
[2] Cp. document 59 below: the *Lion* left Watts' ships on the last of June.

THE 1591 VOYAGES

Ad xxxvij re*sp*ondet he hath answered when he hath byn asked a question Ac ali*ter* re*sp*ondet negative.

Ad xxxviij reddit causas scientie sue ut supra.

52. Carey contra *Watts: deposition of Francis Lee*[1]

FRANCISCUS LEE de Civerne Stoke in Comi*tatu* Worcester yoman ubi natus fuit annos agens xxxij aut circiter Testis.... Dicit q*u*od D*o*minum Georgiu*m* Carie per novem annos noverit Joha*nn*em Wattes non novit....

Dominus Georgius Carie miles contra Johannem Wattes.

Ad decimu*m* tertiu*m* affirmat eundem esse veru*m* For this exa*mina*te beinge Lieftenant of the articulate shipp the Swallowe knoweth that the said shipp was sett to sea by S*i*r George Cary in Aprill laste....

2 testis super Libello Domini Cary.

Ad xviij dicit the Swallowe is of the burthen of fortye or fifty tonnes in his judgemente, and was furnished with foure caste peeces and aboute forty men....[2]

Repetitus xxx⁰ Decembris coram Domino Iudice in camera sua.

Ad Interrogatoria....

Ad primu*m* et secundu*m* exposito sibi periculo p*er*iurii et pena testis falcidici respondet he is of the age of xxxij yeares, and hath used the seas fyve or six yeares and hath made in that tyme vj or vij viadges, and his first viadge was into the West Indies aboute v yeares paste in a shipp of S*i*r George Caries.[3]

Ad tertiu*m* re*sp*ondet he hath served at the seas with le*tt*res of Reprisall under m*aste*r Candish,[4] m*aste*r Sackford[5] S*i*r George Cary, m*aste*r Kinge of London[6] and others in severall viadges....

Ad xv re*sp*ondet the last prize w*hi*ch the Centaure tooke to the eastward of the Avana as he taketh yt was the best & ritchest prize, and the last prize that was taken....

Ad xxj re*sp*ondet that the said first prize which the Swallowe tooke was of the burthen of forty tonnes or thereaboute*s* and was laden with hides & nothinge else to his knowledge and he

[1] H.C.A. 13/29, 29 December 1591. Extract. Deposition on the libel.
[2] Probably an exaggeration of the tonnage and number of men. See H.C.A. 25/3 (9), 17 February 1590/1, where her burden is estimated at 35 tons.
[3] The 1587 voyage. [4] Cavendish.
[5] Henry Seckford, gentleman and merchant, of London, owner of the *Discharge* of London, and other privateers.
[6] Perhaps William King, though he is not known to have been engaged in privateering before 1591.

said prize but only by theire sighte and chase. And he denieth that he or his companye to his knowledge did expell them of master Wattes shipps out of the prize lefte there by the Captaine of the Hopewell. For they forsooke the shippe when this respondente was in the Swallowe & absente from the prize But he graunteth he did resiste them at the first to come on borde because by order of the consorte they were to have noe parte of the pilladge beinge without shott at the tyme of the takinge of the said prize. Ac aliter respondet negative.

Ad xxvij respondet negative.

Ad xxviij^{um} respondet the articulate prize was delivered to Sir George Cary at her arrivall in England beinge laden with hides suger & ginger & some money and pearle But howe muche he cannot declare neyther of what valewe the same were of.

Ad xxix respondet he hath served under the Prince of Orange and Prince of Condee at sea as a souldier But whether warrs were proclaymed by those princes or against them he knowethe not Ac aliter respondet negative.

Ad xxx^{um} respondet he knoweth not the burthen of eany of the articulate shipps or what men & ordinaunce they caried Ac aliter nescit.

Ad xxxj respondet he is servant to Sir George Cary and weareth his livery, and soe Captaine Irish is, and the rest of his contestes[1] were servantes to Sir George for the viadge Ac aliter respondet negative.

Ad xxxij respondet he was Captaine of the Swallowe and therefore he is in righte to have parte of the prizes which the Swallowe tooke: And he knoweth noe cause to the contrary but that he is to have parte of theise prizes in controversy if Sir George doe recover eany parte of them.

Ad xxxiij respondet viij shares is due unto him for his Captaine shippe accordinge to the use of Captaines.

Ad xxxiiij respondet in the equity of the cause he favorethe eyther parte alike.

Ad xxv respondet negative aliter quam supra.

Ad xxxvj respondet he hath questioned with Sir George Cary and tould him in some poinctes what he could say to such demandes as he asked of him. Ac aliter respondet negative.

[1] Fellow witnesses.

prize to strike which was borded by the Lion at the tyme the Centaure & Pegasus tooke theire prizes or shortly after which he beleveth had escaped untaken by the Centaure & Pegasus if the Swallowe had not byn there Ac al*iter* nescit.

Ad xx^um fatetur the Centaure was in chase of the said prize which was caused to strike by the Swallowe But whether she shott at the said prize yt ys more then this respondent can declare And sayth the Swallowe was as nere the said prize as the Centaure or Pegasus were when they first escried the said prizes and gave chase unto them, for they were all togeather when they first gave chase.

Ad xxj^um *res*p*o*ndet he knoweth not what quantity of good*es* or treasure was in the said prize for the Lion first entered her & had the riflinge of her: nether doth he knowe to whose hand*es* all the same good*es* have come Ac plura nescit.

Ad xxij^um *res*p*o*ndet that this respondent and his company of the Swallowe as he beleveth escried the thre prizes mentioned in this Interrogatory as sone as eany of the Centaure or Pegasus and gave chase all togeather to the said prizes.

Ad xxiij^um *res*p*o*ndet he & company in the Swallowe were not in sighte when the Centaure tooke her prize by reason of the nighte: And denieth that he made eany such confession as is conteyned in this Interrogatory to his nowe remembraunce, but if he did speake eany such thinge, yt was then by way of circumstance.

Ad xxiiij *res*pondet the Swallowe was to Leewarde of the articulate prize taken by the Pegasus when she was taken, But howe many leag*es* of he knoweth not.

Ad xxv^um that this respondent & company in the Swallowe did take the prize mentioned in this onterrogatory[1] without the healpe of eany other shipp, neyther was the Centaure, the Hopewell the Pegasus or the John within shott of the said prize when she was taken of his certaine knowledge howebeit he graunteth the said shippes were in sighte & chase as he beleveth at the takinge of the said prize.

Ad xxvj he sayth sondry of the company of the Hopewell forceably entered the prize which this respondente & company of the Swallowe tooke althoughe they were without shott, and gave noe aide or healpe to the Swallowe in the takinge of the

---

[1] [*Sic.*]

Repetitus coram Domino Iudice die predicto.

Ad septimum dicit he was never at sea before this late viadge.

59. Carey contra *Watts:* deposition of Anthony Hooke[1]

Dominus Georgius Carie contra Johannem Wattes.
8 testis Wattes.
Repetitus coram Iudice 24 Ianuarii 1591.

ANTHONIUS HOOKE Civitatis London pannorum ornator ubi per 27 annos maiori ex parte moram fecit, etatis sue xlij aut circiter attingens annos Testis ... dicit quod Johannem Wattes per xvj annos noverit et Dominum Georgium Carie militem per idem tempus etiam noverit. ...

Ad octavum et nonum dicit [he does not believe there was a consortship between the *Swallow* and Watts' ships] For that this examinate beinge purser of the Lion of Hampton & in company with the Swallowe ... harde the company of the Swallowe say they were not nether would be consorted with master Wattes shippes.

Ad decimum dicit that this examinate departed from the company of master Wattes shippes on the last of June last bounde homewardes in a prize which the Lion tooke....[2]

Ad xxv dicit verum esse that the Swallowe did lay for the thirde prize which was in chase and endevored to take the same But the same prize was taken by the Lion & kepte in her possession one nighte & parte of a day, & then the Captaine of Lion & Swallowe[3] did aggree to devide the same tonn for tonn & man for man, and thereuppon eyther shipp did putt like men & victualls into the prize to bringe her home (this examinate beinge one of them) by whom she was broughte to Southampton where Sir George Cary seazed on the said prize and tooke her wholy to him selfe, not allowinge the Lion or the owner Captaine or company thereof eany parte of the same but utterly denied that eany parte was due unto them; yet of his curtesy he gave them CC[li] whiche he swore they should not have excepte they would take yt of curtesy and soe acknowledge yt ... [and this examinate] harde him use the speeches aforesaid....

Ad xxvj dicit there were xxv hundreth hides in the said

---

[1] H.C.A. 13/29, 20 January 1591/2. Extract. Deposition on the *materia*. Deponent, like Lane and Watts, is a clothworker, and has known Watts for many years.
[2] Cp. document 53 above: the *Prudence* left Watts' ships on 1 July.
[3] [*Sic.*] Read: 'the captains of the *Lion* and the *Swallow*'.

THE 1591 VOYAGES

Swallow] of this ex*aminates* knowledge who wente surgion in the said shipp the said viadge. . . .

Ad xxiij xxiiij xxv et xxvj articulos affirmat that on the vth day of July laste to his best remembraunce (after m*aste*r Wattes shipps & the Swallowe had wafted the prizes before taken past the Avana and sente them homewardes) they escried [the other prizes]. . . .

*D*omini *Carie.*
Repetitus coram Domino Iudice in camera sua xij° Ianuarii 1591.

Ad Interrogatoria. . . .

Ad primu*m* et secundu*m* . . . res*p*ondet he was never at sea before this viadge in the Swallowe of S*i*r George Cary.

57. Carey contra *Watts: deposition of William Drew*[1]

WILL*IEL*MUS DREWE de Eastesmithfeilde iuxta Civitatem London Surgion annos agens xxxiij aut circiter Testis. . . . Dicit q*uo*d Joh*a*nn*e*m Wattes per biennium et D*o*minum Georgiu*m* Carie ex visu respective noverit.

Ad primu*m* et secundu*m* [he affirms that the ships were set forth by Watts] For this ex*amina*te was surgion in the articulate shipp the Cantaure. . . .

*D*ominus *Georgius Carie* contra *Joh*annem *Wattes.*
6 *testis Wattes.*

Ad Interrogatoria. . . .

Ad duodecimu*m* res*p*ondet he hath made thre or foure viadges to sea Under Reprisalls as a Surgion as namely in the Post belonginge to Alderman Sterky & others,[2] and two viadges in m*aste*r Wattes shipps.

58. Carey contra *Watts: deposition of James Bratholt*[3]

JACOBUS BRATHOLT Civi*tati*s London gonne maker ubi per septem annos com*m*oravit annos agens xxv aut circiter Testis . . . dicit q*uo*d Joh*a*nn*e*m Wattes per annu*m* noverit D*o*minum Georgiu*m* Carie militem non novit.

*D*ominus *Georgius Carie* contra *Johannem Wattes.*
7 *testis Wattes.*

Ad primu*m* et secundu*m* [he affirms that Watts set forth the ships] Which he knoweth to be true for that he wente to sea in the Little John the same viadge. . . .

---

[1] H.C.A. 13/29, 14 January 1591/2. Extract. Deposition on the *materia*.

[2] Alderman Thomas Starkey, a partner in some of Cobb's ventures.

[3] H.C.A. 13/29, 19 January 1591/2. Extract. Deposition on the *materia*. Bratholt on the same day answered articles ministered on behalf of Watts concerning the embezzlement of prize goods; his answers immediately follow the above deposition.

55. Carey contra *Watts: deposition of Marmaduke Logan*[1]

Dominus Georgius Carie miles contra *Johannem Wattes.*

5 testis Wattes.

Repetitus viij⁰ Ianuarii 1591 coram Domino Iudice in Camera sua.

MARMADUKE LOGAN de Redrith[2] nauta ubi per novem annos stetit natus iuxta oppidum Hullensem in Comitatu Eboracum etatis sue xxvj aut circiter attingens annos testis ... dicit quod Johannem Wattes per quatuor annos et Dominum Georgium Cary per novem annos respective noverit.

Ad primum et secundum [affirms the truth of the articles] For that this examinate was a quarter master in the said shipp called the Hopewell the said viadge....

Ad octavum dicit [there was a consortship made for eight days, to end on 2 or 3 July] for that the Lion of Hampton whereof John Oker was Captaine was also in consorte with the said shippes for the said viij dayes continuaunce and uppon the second or thirde of July last for that the consorteshipp was out he tooke his leave & departed from the said shippes....

Ad interrogatoria....

Ad duodecimum respondet that he hath served as a mariner in master Wattes shippes two viadges to the Indies with Reprisalls, and other viadges he hath not made with Reprisalls....

Ad xix respondet that the Hopewell mett with the Swallowe the Barcke burre & the Content of of[3] the Vergenes and kepte company thre dayes, and afterwardes they mett togeather, and at Cape Corantes the Swallowe mett agayne with the Hopewell & the rest of master Wattes shipps in June last but what day he knoweth not well but thinketh yt was about the xix[th] of June.

56. Carey contra *Watts: deposition of Noe Bailye*[4]

Dominus Georgius Cary contra *Johannem Wattes.*

3 testis

NOE BAILYE Civitatis London Barbichirurgus ubi per vij annos moram fecit, annos natus xxij vel circiter Testis ... deponit quod Dominum Georgium Cary militem per quinque annos et Johannem Wattes ex visu respective noverit.

Ad primum [he affirms that Sir George Carey set forth the

---

[1] H.C.A. 13/29, 7 January 1591/2. Extract. Deposition on the *materia*.
[2] Rotherhithe.
[3] [*Sic.*]
[4] H.C.A. 13/29, 11 January 1591/2. Extract. Deposition on the libel. Deponent is a barber surgeon.

foure viadges as he remembreth, and hath borne chardge as a Captaine thre tymes....

54. Carey contra *Watts: deposition of John Mott*[1]

JOH*ANN*E MOTT de Redrith[2] nauta ubi per sex annos moram traxit natus in villa de Lee in Com*itatu* Essex, annos natus xxvj aut circiter Testis.... dicit q*uo*d Joh*ann*em Wattes per duos annos novit et D*ominum* Georgiu*m* Carye non novit....

   Ad secundum affirmat eundem continere veritatem For this ex*amina*te beinge m*aster*s mate of the Hopewell [knows that the ships were set forth by Watts, etc.]

   Ad decimu*m* quartum dicit that the said vth of Julye this ex*amina*te wente out of the said prize wherein he was placed m*aste*r[3] into the John whereof michaell Geere was Captaine, and the nexte morninge beinge Tuesday this ex*amina*te out of the heade of the Toppe maste early in the morninge escried a sayle to the Northward of the Avana whereunto they of the John & the Centaure only gave chase and aboute one of the clocke in the after none this ex*amina*te & company of the John layde the said prize on borde & tooke her beinge the laste prize wherein the silver was, and shortly after the Centaures company came on borde the said prize....

Dominus Georgius Carie contra Johannem Wattes.

4 testis Wattes

Repetitus coram Domino Iudice quarto Ianuarii 1591 in Camera sua.

            Ad interrogatoria....

Ad duodecimu*m* res*p*ondet he was never at sea with le*tt*res of Reprisalls before this last viadge to the Indias in m*aste*r Wattes shipps....

   Ad xix^{um} res*p*ondet that this Respondent & company of the Hopewell mett with the Swallowe & the Barcke Burre betwixte a place called Guarre de Lope[4] & St John Porterico in the Indians, and kepte company with the Swallowe untill they came to Cape Corantes & there founde the other shippes and soe afterward*es* untill they came to the Avana as ys before answered and as he remembreth they first mett with the Swallowe aboute the xxiij of May last.

[1] H.C.A. 13/29, 3 January 1591/2. Extract. Deposition on the *materia*.
[2] Rotherhithe.
[3] He returned to Bristol as master of a prize, whereof one Phillip Hills was captain (Harleian MS 598, f. 13).
[4] Guadeloupe.

prize which the Lion & Swallowe had.... Which prize with her ladinge he esteemeth to be worth one thowsand fyve hundreth poundes....

Ad Interrogatoria....

Ad duodecimum respondet he hath byn at sea two viadges with lettres of Reprisalls, one aboute thre yeares past in the John Young of Chichester,[1] and nowe of Late in the Lion of Hampton....

Ad xxvj respondet [he knows nothing about the legal force of consortships made at sea] But sayth that Sir George toulde this respondent in the Wighte that he would not stande to eany consorte or covenant which his men made at sea, neyther should they geve away eany parte of that which was his which speeches were used uppon occasion that this respondent tould Sir George Cary that after the Lion had taken the said prize as ys before answered the company thereof aggreed with the captaine of the Swallowe because she was in chase to devide the same tonn for tonn & man for man, and yet Sir George tooke the same wholy away from the Lions company at Hampton as ys before declared.

60. Carey contra Watts: deposition of Nicholas Dockerey[2]

NICHOLAUS DOCKEREY Civitatis London nauta ubi per triennium moram fecerit et antea apud Wappinge per quinquennium annos agens quinquaginta duos aut circiter Testis... deponit quod Johannem Wattes per viginti annos et Georgium Cary per decem annos respective noverit. *Dominus Georgius Carie miles contra Johannem Wattes.*

Ad octavum et nonum dicit that Captaine Lee tould this examinate... that he had made a consorteshippe with master Wattes Captaines to continewe for viij dayes but uppon what daye yt was made he knoweth not For that he was not called to accompte at the makinge thereof althoughe was[3] masters mate in the Swallowe.... *9 testis Wattes. Repetitus coram Domino Iudice 24 Ianuarii 1591.*

Ad xxvij dicit the other prize taken by the Swallowe on the vth of Julye had in her when she was taken 2140 hides, fifty foure chestes of sugar whereof two whole chestes were consumed by a

[1] At sea 1588, 1589, 1590 and 1591 ('Elizabethan Privateering', p. 285)—not the same as the *Bark Young.*
[2] H.C.A. 13/29, 22 January 1591/2. Extract. Deposition on the *materia.*
[3] [*Sic.*]

leake ten serons[1] of ginger named to be a kintall[2] a peece, two serons of Indian pepper, and he hearde there were xiiij smale bagges of pearle which John Tilley of Wappinge delivered to one of the Hopewells company whose name he remembreth not to cary home for him, but he can not learne that eyther Tilley or Sir George had them. And besides there was a case of a foote and a haulfe longe or thereaboutes which was delivered to the Captaine of the Swallowe by the merchants of the prize which was sayde to be full of pearle but yt was broken open before yt came to Sir George his handes by the Captaine or some other at sea, and soe much pearle as this examinate sawe delivered to Sir George Cary, was seede pearle & lay in the bottome of the platters, and was not worth above xx^{li} in his judgemente: And sayth he herde the said prize was valewed at xvC^{li} or thereaboutes But what yt was worth he knoweth not. . . .

Ad posiciones additionales. . . .

Ad sextum attestatur verum esse that the Swallowe did not geve chase to eany prize all the vjth of July to his knowledge but lay nere her prize, and the Captaine of the Swallowe & others of the Swallowes cheife men were all that day untill the eveninge on borde theire prize pacifienge of braules that were on borde amongst the company. . . .

Ad Interrogatoria. . . .

Ad duodecimum respondet he hath byn at the takinge of prizes in Queene Maryes tyme in the Warrs betwixte Fraunce & Englande, and since theise troubles with Spaine he hath made some fower viadges as he remembreth with Reprisalls in the shipp the Diana with Captaine Hurde, in the Pasporte of London two viadges, and nowe in the Swallowe with Captaine Lee. . . .

Ad xix respondet the Swallowe met with the Hopewell in June laste after they had watered at Dominico & kepte with her untill they came to Cape Tabron[3] & there lefte her, and afterwardes they mett with the Hopewell agayne shorte of Cape Corantes & sayled togeather to Corantes where they mett with the Centaure the Pegasus & the John also. . . .

Ad Interrogatoria secundo loco ministrata. . . .

Ad secundum respondet he did not see the prize that was taken

---

[1] Crates or hampers.   [2] Or quintal, roughly a hundredweight.   [3] Tiburon.

on the vjth of July, by reason she was taken without sighte of the Swallowe & her prize as he belevethe. And sayth he was not sicke or diseased But graunteth that both Irishe, Lee this respondente & all the reste of the prize had droncke that day well of the wynes which they founde in the prize & some more then did them good, and that made them lye togeathers by the eares the most parte of the day.

61. *Carey* contra *Watts*: deposition of *William Bendes*[1]

WILL*IE*LMUS BENDES de Limehouse nauta ubi per xvj annos moram fecit annos agens xl^{ta} aut circiter Testis ... dicit quod Johannem Wattes per annum et Dominum Georgium Cary per mensem respective noverit.

Dominus Georgius Carie contra Johannem Wattes.
10. testis Wattes.

Ad primum articulum materie in hac causa date dicit he was master of the John....

Ad Interrogatoria....

Repetitus coram Domino Iudice 25 Ianuarii 1591.

Ad xij respondet he served master in the John this late viadge, and he wente master twice in master Sackfordes shipps, and hath made sondry other viadges to sea with Reprisalls with Captaine Fishebornc,[2] Captaine Barker & others....

Ad xvij respondet they shared at sea viij^{li} xiiij^s or thereaboutes a single share and xx^s a single share before out of the first prize taken by the Sotherne cape,[3] and this respondente since his comminge home hath receaved xxxvj^s for a single share out of all the goodes that were broughte home and noe more, for that which was shared at sea was in money & not for the goodes. And sayth that which he receaved, he had of Michaell Geare the Captaine.

62. *Carey* contra *Watts*: deposition of *John Tilley*[4]

JOH*ANN*ES TILLEY Civi*tat*is London sayler ubi permansit per xvij annos aut circiter Annos agens xxxiij aut circiter

Dominus Georgius Carie

[1] H.C.A. 13/29, 25 January 1591/2. Extract. Deposition on the *materia*.
[2] Captain Richard Fishbourne, a Plymouth owner-captain of privateers throughout the war and later one of the grantees of the Newfoundland Charter ('Elizabethan Privateering', p. 310).
[3] Cape St. Vincent.
[4] H.C.A. 13/29, 25 January 1591/2. Extract. Deposition on the libel.

contra
*Johannem
Wattes.*
*4 testis
Domini
Carey.*

Testis ... dicit quod Georgium Cary per annum et Johannem Wattes per xvj annos respective noverit.

Ad primum secundum et tertium articulos libelli affirmat eosdem continere veritatem For this examinate was one of the quarter masters of the articulate shippe the Swallowe....

Ad xxiij xxiiij xxv et xxvj affirmat verum esse that as the said shippes the Swallowe the Hopewell, the Centaure the Pegasus & the John were in company togeather betwene the Tartothos[1] and the high lande of the Avana they escried fyve sayles of Spaniardes uppon a monday....

Ad Interrogatoria....

Ad secundum respondet he is of the age of xxxiij yeares & hath byn at sea xix yeares and in that tyme hath made many viadges a greate many more then he can specify when, or in what shippinge he made them.

Ad tertium respondet he hath byn at sea foure viadges with Reprisalls viz in master Bassettes Flyboate,[2] in the Hare of Plimouth with Captain Turner, in the Centurion of London,[3] and nowe in the Swallowe of Sir George Caryes.

63. Carey contra *Watts: deposition of Thomas Barlowe*[4]

*Dominus
Georgius
Carie
contra
Johannem
Wattes.*
*5 testis
Domini
Carie.*
*Repetitus
coram
Domino
Iudice 28
Ianuarii
1591.*

THOMAS BARLOWE ville et Comitatus Southampton nauta ubi per quatuor annos moram fecit, natus in pago de Fingist in Comitatu Oxoniensis,[5] etatis sue xxv aut circiter annos agens testis ... dicit quod Dominum Georgium Cary per triennium noverit et Johannem Wattes non novit.

Ad primum articulum libelli affirmat Sir George Carye did sett furth the articulate shipp the Swallowe in warrefarre in marche or Aprill laste ... of this examinates knowledge who wente to sea in the Barcke Burre in the company of the Swallowe, & in the Indies when the Barcke Burre was sett on fier he came on borde the Swallowe & returned home in her....

---

[1] Tortugas.
[2] Probably the *Seadragon*, owned by George Bassett, fishmonger, of London, and others ('Elizabethan Privateering', p. 269).
[3] A powerful merchantman owned by Thomas Cordell.
[4] H.C.A. 13/29, 27 January 1591/2. Extract. Deposition on the libel.
[5] Fingest. At present in Buckinghamshire.

THE 1591 VOYAGES

Ad xiij affirmat veru*m* esse... and Captaine Irishe beinge Admirall of S*i*r George his shippes [had authority to make consortships.]

Ad Interrogatoria....

Ad primu*m* et secundu*m* ... res*p*ondet he hath byn at sea fyve yeares and went to sea first in the Gifte of God of Hampton of m*aste*r Goddardes¹ and since he hath made vj or vij viadges, twice to the Weste Indies with Captaine Irishe, in the Barcke Younge first,² & nowe in the Swallowe, and two viadges in the Lion of Hampton, and one viadge wi*t*h Captaine Hubbard in a smale Barcke of Salteaishe.

64. *Carey* contra *Watts: deposition of Robert Tilley*³

ROBERTUS TILLEY de Blanford in Com*itatu* Dorsett souldier ubi natus et educatus fuerit annos agens xlv aut circiter testis... deponit q*u*od D*ominum* Georgiu*m* Carie militem per quinquennium et Joha*n*nem Wattes per decennium respective noverit.

Ad primu*m* secundu*m* et tertiu*m* articulos libelli in hac causa dati ... attestatur eosdem continere veritatem For this exa*mi*nate wente to sea in the Barcke Burre in company of the Swallowe. . . .

Ad xvij affirmat that aboute two yeares past this exa*mi*nate was at sea with Captaine Irishe in the Barcke Younge of Hampton and in the Indies nere Cape Tabronne⁴ they mett with the Falcons flighte of Barstable belonginge to John Norris of Barstable & pr*e*sently after theire meetinge they escriede a sayle whereunto they gave chase togeather and the Barcke Younge beinge better of sayle layde the said prize on borde & tooke her, and notwithstandinge the Captaine & company of the Falcons Flighte came on borde the said prize & claymed theire p*a*rte in the same because they were in chase & sighte, and had p*a*rte thereof ton*n* for tonn & man for man....⁵

*D*ominus *G*eorgius *C*arie contra *J*ohannem *W*attes. 6 testis *D*omini *C*arie. *R*epetitus *eodem die* coram *D*omino *I*udice.

¹ Richard Goddard, merchant of Southampton and London, mayor of Southampton 1583, alderman of London 1595, interested in the ventures of the *Angel* of Southampton from 1593 ('Elizabethan Privateering', p. 292).
² In 1590.
³ H.C.A. 13/29, 28 January 1591/2. Extract. Deposition on the libel.
⁴ Tiburon.
⁵ See p. 89 above.

Ad Interrogatoria....

Ad primum et secundum ... respondet he hath used the seas ten or xij yeares and wente to sea first in the Flyeinge Harte with Courte Hecleboroughe,[1] then in the gallion Fenner,[2] the Bevis of Hampton John Challys Captaine,[3] and since in many other shippes on sondry viadges more then he can specifye.

Ad tertium respondet he wente to sea with Captaine Fenner first with lettres of Reprisalls, then in the Bevis, afterwardes in the Barcke Younge two viadges then in the William of Wells in the Portingall viadge[4] then in the Barcke Younge with Captaine Irishe[5] and lastly in the Swallowe of Sir George Caryes....

Ad xxxiij respondet he wente to sea in the Barcke Burre beinge consorted with the Swallowe and at sea was blowen over borde by powder at the firinge of the Barcke Burre, and soe gott on borde the Swallowe.

65. *Carey* contra *Watts: deposition of John Froude*[6]

*D*ominus *G*eorgius *C*arie contra *J*ohannem *W*attes.
*7 testis D*omini *C*arie.

JOH*ANN*ES FROUDE de Newporte in Insula Vectis nauta ubi per decennium commoravit etatis sue xliiij aut circiter attingens annos testis ... dicit quod D*o*minum Georgium Carie militem per septennium et ultra, noverit et Joh*ann*em Wattes non novit.

Ad primum secundum et tertium affirmat eosdem continere veritatem For that this ex*amina*te wente to sea in the Barcke Burre ... and at sea by reason the Barcke Burre was sett on fiere this ex*amina*te came on borde the said shipp the Swallowe....

Ad Interrogatoria....

Ad primum et secundum respondet he hath used the sea xvj yeares & upwardes, and hath made many viadges, and the first viadge that ever he made was with Captaine Turner a scottishe

---

[1] A notorious pirate, active in the late 1570's and early 1580's.

[2] The *Galleon Fenner* was privateering under the flag of Don Antonio in the early 1580's and Edward Fenner, her captain, was charged with piracy in 1584 (Lansdowne MS 134; H.C.A. 1/42, 30 March 1585 and 24 July 1585; S. P. Dom. Eliz., lxxvii, no. 46).

[3] Another pirate of the late 1570's and early 1580's (C. L'Estrange Ewen, *The Golden Chalice* (Paignton, privately printed, 1939) and Quinn, *Gilbert*, passim).

[4] The Portugal expedition of 1589.   [5] The West Indies voyage of 1590.

[6] H.C.A. 13/29, 1 February 1591/2. Extract. Deposition on the libel.

man under Commission of the Kinge of Navarre, the nexte viadge he made to Linxborne[1] & the Islandes in the Unity of London, afterwardes as he remembreth he served nexte under the Kinge of Portingall with Captaine Vaughan and since he wente to sea in the Muscatt of Sir George Cary two or thre viadges, and in the Lions Whelpe of the Lord Admiralls, and the Barcke Burre & Swallowe, besides sondry other viadges alongst the quoaste from porte to porte in trade of merchandizes....

Ad tertium respondet he hath made fower viadges with Reprisalls in the shippinge of Sir George Carye and one in the Lions Whelpe under Thomas Roche Captaine thereof, and none else to his remembrance....

Ad decimum respondet [he knows of no other consortship than the one made on 25 July] Savinge that as the Swallowe came backe towardes the Avana after the Hope[2] & the Little John, the Lion beinge gone into the Old Channell, the Captaine & master of the Hopewell haled the Swallowe and asked them if they were consorted with the Lion, & eyther Captaine Lee or Captaine Irishe answered sayenge Noe we are consorted with none but you, and soe asked what the John & Centaure would doe & whether they would winter in the Cuntrey, and some of the Hopewells men answered the John would doe as they did, what the Centaure would doe they knew not....

Ad xxv respondet true yt ys the Hopewell & the Vth Parte were in chase of the prize taken nere the Avana by the Swallowe....

Ad xxxiij respondet he wente to sea as masters mate of the Barcke Burre....

66. Carey contra *Watts: deposition of Gideon Sanders*[3]

GEDEON SANDERS de Bradinge in Insula vectis nauta ubi per quatuor menses ac antea Londini commoraverit annos natus xxxiiij[or] aut circiter Testis... deponit quod Dominum Georgium Cary per sexennium et Johannem Wattes per idem tempus noverit.... *Dominus Georgius Cary contra Johannem Wattes.*

[1] Lisbon.   [2] [Sic.]
[3] H.C.A. 13/29, 1 February 1591/2. Extract. Deposition on the libel.

Ad Interrogatoria. . . .

8 testis Domini Carie. Repetitus coram Domino Iudice tertio Ianuarii 1591.

Ad primum secundum et tertium . . . respondet he hath byn a sea ever since he was viij or x yeares of age, and hath made a hundreth viadges in his tyme both in trade of merchandize and warrefarre: whereof he had made ten or xij viadges with lettres of Reprisall, first with Captaine Fenton in the Gallion Lecester,[1] and afterwardes foure viadges with Captaine Riman[2] in the Lion and the Swiftsure,[3] and the Disdaine,[4] since he served in a carvell of one Pittes of Bristowe,[5] and the Diamonde of Bridgewater,[6] and two viadges in the Swallowe of Sir George Caries, two viadges in the Dischardge of master Sackfordes[7] & one viadge in the Earle of Harfordes pinnace[8] with others which he remembreth not. . . .

Ad duodecimum respondet [the *Hopewell* hailed the *Swallow* and asked if she were consorted with the *Lion*] Which passed as they came backe agayne when they had sente theire first prizes homewardes and broughte them past the Avana. . . .

Ad xxj respondet the said prize taken by the Swallowe first was of aboute Lx tonnes, and laden with thre thowsand hides and odde and noe other goodes to his knowledge, which Sir George receaved and gave the Lions company CC^ll out of the same.

67. Carey contra *Watts*: deposition of Thomas Royall[9]

Dominus Georgius Carie contra

THOMAS ROIALL de Bradinge in Insula vectis Sayler, ubi per tremestrem et antea Harwici per quatuor annos moram fecit annos agens xxviij aut circiter Testis . . . Dicit quod Georgium

---

[1] Edward Fenton's unsuccessful voyage of 1582.
[2] Captain George Raymond. For his activities in 1585, see Quinn, *Roanoke Voyages*, pp. 165–6, 171–3. He did noteworthy service with Drake in 1587 and as captain of the *Elizabeth Bonaventure* in 1588 (Corbett, *Spanish War*, p. 141). For his later career see 'Elizabethan Privateering', p. 262, and Foster, *Voyages of Lancaster*.
[3] Both of Chichester.
[4] The Lord Admiral's ship ('Elizabethan Privateering', p. 338).
[5] Christopher Pitts of Bristol, merchant, who set forth the *Seabright* in 1589 (ibid., p. 331).
[6] Ibid., pp. 321–2.   [7] See p. 143, n. 5 above.
[8] May have been the *Phoenix* or the *Frances*, both Hertford's ('Elizabethan Privateering', pp. 287, 341–2).
[9] H.C.A. 13/29, 3 February 1591/2. Extract. Deposition on the libel.

iiijth of July laste there was talke at dinner tyme where yt was best to ly to see the fleete com*m*inge for the Avana, and this respondente bye reason he had byn there two or thre viadges before sayde he thought the fittest lyeinge was betwixte the Avana & the Tortuthos,[1] and Captaine Geere affirmed the best lyeage was somewhat to Leeward of the Avana keepinge lande in sighte and accordingly they came thither & lay there, and before they came thither this respondente asked Captaine Craston many tymes when they shoulde goe to Leeward of the Avana....

Ad xxxj re*s*pondet he is servant to S*i*r George Carye & hath byn xiiij or xv yeares....

Ad xxxiij re*s*pondet he wente out Captaine of the Jason but by reason of mischance at sea he lefte the Jason & wente on borde the Swallowe, and had viij shares.

70. Carey contra *Watts: deposition of William Cradell*[2]

*D*ominus *G*eorgius *C*arie contra *J*oh*a*nnem *W*attes. *1 2 testis W*attes. *R*epetitus eodem die coram *D*omino *I*udice.

WILL*IE*LMUS CRADELL de Ratcliffe nauta ubi per quatuor aut quinque annos moram fecit natus in oppido de Arundell in Com*itatu* Sussex, annos agens xxiiij aut circa Testis. ... Dicit q*uo*d Joh*ann*em Wattes per bienniu*m* noverit et D*omi*n*u*m Georgiu*m* Cary non novit.

Ad primu*m* et secundu*m* [he affirms that Watts and his partners set forth the ships] Which he knoweth to be true For this ex*ami*nate was gonners mate in the said shipp the John....

Ad Interrogatoria....

Ad duodecimu*m* re*s*pondet he hath byn at sea thre viadges w*ith* lett*r*es of Reprisall viz*t* one with Captaine Riman in the Disdaine & two viadges in the Indies in m*aste*r Wattes shipps.

71. Carey contra *Watts: deposition of Michael Geare*[3]

*D*ominus *G*eorgius *C*arie

MICHAELL GEERE de Limehouse nauta ubi natus et educatus fuerit annos agens viginti sex aut circiter Testis...

---

[1] Tortugas.

[2] H.C.A. 13/29, 11 February 1591/2. Extract. Deposition on the *materia*.

[3] H.C.A. 13/29, 14 February 1591/2. Extract. Deposition on the *materia*. Geare also answered two sets of articles concerning embezzled prize goods on the same day; these answers immediately follow this deposition.

lickly appoincte furnishe & sett out the said shipp to sea aboute Aprill laste with le*tt*res of Reprisall togeather with the Barcke Burre & the Contente whereof this ex*amina*te wente Admirall....

Ad xvij^(um) dicit.... Also this ex*amina*te in the yeare 1590 beinge in the Indies in the Barcke Younge tooke a prize, and the Falcons Flighte of Barstable happeninge to escry the same saile & to be in chase & sighte had by reason thereof p*ar*te of the same prize ton*n* for ton*n* & man for man....[1]

Ad xxj affirmat [that consortship was made] betwixte this ex*amina*te, & Raph Lee for them selfe & the reste of the Swallowe, and Captaine Lane, Captaine Michell Captaine Geere Captaine Broughe Captaine Oker, Captaine Draper and the m*as*ter of the hopewell For them selves & theire companyes ... and Captaine Raph Lee requested that the consorteshippe mighte be for longer tyme, and Captaine Lane answered, that if they wente not to winter, but kepte togeather they should not be soe farre a sonder, but that theye mighte call one to an other and prolonge the tyme of consorteshippe....

Ad xxiij affirmat veru*m* esse that after the makinge of the said consorteshippe the said shippes ... kepte company togeather as high as the Mattances,[2] and broughte theire prizes taken before past the Avana to sende them away for Englande, and saylinge backe againe [were hailed by the *Hopewell*, etc.]....

Ad Interrogatoria....

Ad primu*m* et secundu*m* ... res*p*ondet he hath used the seas aboute viij yeares space, and hath made some viij or ix viadges to sea as namely first in the Muscatt of S*ir* George Caries, then in the Gabriell of S*ir* George Caries, then in the Swallowe of S*ir* George Caries, nexte in the Dischardge of M*as*ter Sackfordes two viadges,[3] afterwardes two viadges in the Barcke Yonge, then in the Jason[4] and Swallowe this laste viadge.

Ad tertiu*m* res*p*ondet he hath byn at sea with le*tt*res of Reprisalls all the viadges before sett downe, and such Reprisalls as he wente to sea with, were graunted to S*ir* George m*as*ter Sackford, and some to this respondente....

Ad duodecimu*m* res*p*ondet negative Savinge that as this respondente was on borde the Pegasus at dinner on sondaye the

---

[1] See above, p. 89.   [2] Matanzas.
[3] See p. 143, n. 5 above.   [4] Alias the *Bark Burr*.

Captaine an other viadge in master Wattes shippes servinge with lettres of Reprisalls, and more viadges he hath not made with Reprisalls or on Warrefarre but in the Queenes shippes, and in the Narrowe seas when the Spanishe fleete was there....[1]

Ad xix^{um} respondet that this respondente & company of the Hopewell mett with the Swallowe & her consortes thwart of St Christophers Islande in the Indies in the ende of May last as he remembreth, and remayned togeather untill they mett with a fleete of viij shipps of warre and foughte with them In which fighte the Barcke Burre beinge one of the Swallowes consortes was sett on fire, and the Captaine forsoke her, and gott on borde the Swallowe with others of his company. And sayth that afterwardes this respondent & company togeather with the Swallowe sayled to Cape Corantes, & there mett with the John the Pegasus & the Centaure....

   Ad Interrogatoria tertio loco ministrata....

Ad quartum respondet the persons that were lefte in the said prize taken by the Swallowe, by appoynctemente of this respondent were Marmaduke Logan John Battle, Hary Hankyn of this respondentes company & two others of the Frigott[2] whose names he knoweth not.

69. Carey contra Watts: deposition of William Irish[3]

Dominus Georgius Carie contra Johannem Wattes.
1o testis Domini Carie.
Repetitus dicto die coram Domino Iudice.

WILLIELMUS IRISHE Insule vectis[4] generosus ubi per septem annos et ultra commoravit annos agens triginta aut eo circiter Testis ... Dicit quod Dominum Georgium Cary per xiiij annos et Johannem Wattes per septem annos respective noverit.

Ad primum secundum et tertium articulos affirmat eosdem continere veritatem Reddendo rationem scientie that Sir George Cary hath possessed the articulate shipp the Swallowe vj or vij yeares space as lawfull owner thereof and aboute Aprill laste he sett out the said shipp ... this examinate wente to sea in her company as Captaine of the Barcke Burre sett furth the same tyme by Sir George also....

Ad xiij attestatur verum esse That Sir George Carie did war-

---
[1] There is no trace of Craston before 1590.   [2] The *Fifth Part*.
[3] H.C.A. 13/29, 10 February 1591/2. Extract. Deposition on the libel.
[4] Cp. document 34 above, where Irish is said to be of Westham (Sussex).

Carie per quinquennium et Johannem Wattes per idem tempus noverit.... *Johannem Wattes.*

Ad secundum et tertium [affirms the truth of the articles] For this examinate was a sayler in the Swallowe.... *9 testis Domini Carie.*

Ad Interrogatoria....

Ad primum et secundum... respondet he is of the age of xxviij yeares, and hath byn a sea xij yeares space or thereaboutes, and hath made many viadges on fisshinge fare and merchandizes more then he can recounte.

Repetitus eodem die coram Domino Iudice.

Ad tertium respondet he hath made thre viadges to sea with Reprisalls, the first was with Oliver Hilliarde in the Barcke Brave, and nexte in the shipp the Swallowe of Sir George Caries, and since of late he was in the Earle of Harfordes Pinnace whereof Phillipp Smith of Dartmouthe was Captaine & Master.[1]

68. *Carey* contra *Watts: deposition of William Craston*[2]

WILL*IEL*MUS CRASTON de Redrith[3] nauta ubi per tres annos et ultra moram fecit annos agens xxxj aut circiter Testis... Dicit quod Johannem Wattes per viginti annos et Dominum Georgium Carie per biennium aut circa respective noverit....

Dominus Georgius Carie contra Johannem Wattes.

Ad decimum attestatur verissimum esse that none of the prizes in question were taken betwixte the xxiiij[th] of June & the iiij[th] of July laste For that the same prizes were taken on the vth & vj[th] of July 1591 of his certaine knowledge as appeareth by his booke which he kepte of all that passed the whole viadge....

11 testis Wattes. Repetitus coram Domino Iudice V⁰ Ianuarii 1591.[4]

Ad decimum sextum affirmat verum esse that on the vth of July laste the Captaine master and company of the Swallowe did pursue & take a prize as ys before deposed, and also a frigott laden with turtells....

Ad posiciones Additionales....

Ad sextum nescit deponere but by reporte of his men that came out of the Swallowes prize who affirmed that both the Captaine & most of the company were droncke on borde the prize all the vj[th] day of July, and quarrellinge one with an other....

Ad duodecimum respondet he was Lieftenant one viadge and

[1] See p. 156, n. 8 above.
[2] H.C.A. 13/29, 4 February 1591/2. Extract. Deposition on the *materia*.
[3] Rotherhithe.   [4] [*Sic.*]

contra
Johannem
Wattes.
16 testis
Wattes.

dicit quod Johannem Wattes per novem annos et Dominum Georgium Carie per quinquennium respective noverit. . . .

Ad Interrogatoria. . . .

Ad sextum respondet that this respondent & company of the Hopewell mett with the Swallowe and the Barcke Burre of of Portorico and shortly after they foughte with the Kinge of Spaines men of warre on the xiijth of June betwixte Cape St Anthony & Cape Corantes, and in the fighte the Barcke Burre fell on fire & Captaine Irishe beinge Captaine of her with aboute xvj of the cheifest men like tale[1] fellowes ron away & gott on borde the Swallowe leavinge the shipp & the rest of theire men in greate distresse, and from that tyme the Swallowe sayled with the Hopewell to Cape Corantes plyenge of & on where they mett with the Centaure the Pegasus & the John. . . .

Ad xij respondet he hath gon master thre viadges with lettres of Reprisall and as a mariner diverse other viadges howe many he remembreth not For as he sayth he hath made no other viadges since Reprisalls began but in shipps warlickly sett out against the Spaniardes. As namly he hath served with Roberte Bradshawe[2] Captaine of a shipp of this porte of London whose name he hath forgotten and in the Canter of Hampton belonginge to master Cotton,[3] the Barcke Burre of London, the Roe Bucke & the Gallion Dudley of master Candishes, the Little Delite of master Barbors, the Greate Delite of the Lord Admiralls,[4] and the Hopewell of master Wattes & more he cannot remember. . . .

Ad xix responsum est supra that the Hopewell mett with the Swallowe aboute the ixth of June laste, and afterwardes they mett with the Centaure the John & the Pegasus aboute the xixth of the same moneth.

[1] 'Tall'? Cp. the frequent use of 'smale' for 'small'.
[2] Of Limehouse. Master of the *Centurion* of London in 1591 (*Principal Navigations*, II (1599), pt. ii, 168; VII (1904), 35), and of Watts' *Affection* in 1592 (p. 211 below).
[3] Edward Cotton, merchant, of Southampton, owner of the *Bevis* and the *Edward* of Southampton (H.C.A. 13/26, 3 January 1587/8; H.C.A. 25/1 (4), 2 October 1585; Lansdowne MS 115, f. 196; *Historical MSS Commission, Report on the MSS of the Corporation of Southampton* (11th Report, Appendix III, 1887), p. 121).
[4] For the *Little Delight* and the *Great Delight*, see 'Elizabethan Privateering', pp. 235, 337–8.

74. Carey contra *Watts: deposition of Richard Die*[1]

RICH*AR*DUS DIE de Ratcliffe naupegus[2] ubi per viginti annos mora*m* fecit annos agens xxxiij aut circiter Testis.... Dicit q*u*od Joha*n*nem Wat*t*es per xiij annos noverit et D*omi*num Georgiu*m* Carie per octo annos etia*m* noverit.

*D*ominus Georgius Cary Co*n*tra Joha*n*nem Wat*t*es.

Ad primum et secundum [affirms the truth of the articles] For this exa*min*ate was Carpenter of the said shipp called the John....

*15 testis Wat*tes. Repetitus coram *D*omino *I*udice eodem die.

Ad Interrogatoria....

Ad sextum r*es*pondet that when this respondente & companye came w*ith* the John to Cape Corantes they founde the Hopewell & the Vth parte beinge her pinnace, togeather w*ith* the Swallowe there....

Ad duodecimu*m res*pondet he hath made viij or nine viadges to sea with let*t*res of Reprisall as he remembreth first in the Goulden Dragon of W*illia*m Bigat*t*es beinge sett out by Alderman Sterky m*aste*r Cobbe & others, then in the barcke Burre belonginge to m*aste*r Burd & m*aste*r Newton one viadge, in the Margatt & John of m*aste*r Wat*t*es two viadges, in the Dischardge of m*aste*r Sackfor*d*es two viadges, in the Little John of m*aste*r Wat*t*es two viadges....

Ad decimu*m* quartu*m res*pondet he would have geven fourescore poun*d*es for the shipp the michaell[3] beinge the last prize that was taken, if he might have had her taclinge ankers cables ordenaunce & furniture that belonged to the same shippe. The other foure shippes w*ith* theire furniture were worth some L^{li} some xl^{li} and some lesse.[4]

75. Carey contra *Watts: deposition of George Kennell*[5]

GEORGIUS KENNELL de Limehouse nauta ubi per quinq*ue* annos moram fecit, annos natus xxxj aut circiter testis...

*D*ominus Georgius Carie

[1] H.C.A. 13/29, 28 February 1591/2. Extract. Deposition on the *materia*.
[2] Shipwright.
[3] Alias the *Trinity*.
[4] A more informed and reliable judgement than Lane's (document 49 above).
[5] H.C.A. 13/29, 2 March 1591/2. Extract. Deposition on the *materia*. Deponent sometimes appears as 'Kevill'.

Ad xiij re*sp*ondet... that noe consorteshipp made at sea by a captaine can binde them of his company to yelde thereunto For they have an interest in the matter as well as the Captaine, and if the Captaine doe not aske the consente of the m*as*ter, quarter m*as*ters, m*as*ter mattes gon*n*er & other cheife officers of the shipp, and soe be imparted by them to the reste of the company whereby a generall consente or of the greater p*ar*te be had to the same yt cannot stande good or be available soe farre as he hath knowen or seene since the tyme that he hath used the seas by way of Reprisall.

73. Carey contra *Watts: deposition of Edward Waters*[1]

*D*ominus *Georgius Carie* contra *Joh*annem *W*attes. *11 testis* *D*omini *Carie.* *Repetitus coram D*omino *Iudice in Camera sua xxiiij° februarii 1591.*

EDWARDUS WATERS de newporte in Insula vectis Ocopolarius[2] ubi per xv annos mora*m* fecit, natus in villa de Southampton, annos agens xxiij aut circiter testis.... Dicit quo*d* D*ominum* Georgiu*m* Carie militem per sex annos noverit Joh*ann*em Wattes non novit....

Ad secundu*m* et tertiu*m* [affirms the truth of the articles] For this ex*amin*ate as he sayth was gon*n*er of the Swallowe....

Ad Interrogatoria....

Ad primu*m* et secundu*m* re*sp*ondet he hath used the sea xvj yeares....

Ad tertiu*m* respondet he hath made viij viadges or ix wi*th* le*tt*res of Reprisall against the Spaniardes since the Imbargo viz[t] two out of London in the moneshine[3] & the Prudence,[4] two out of Hampton in the Minion,[5] & the W*illia*m,[6] foure out of the Wighte in the shippinge of S*i*r George Cary, & Captaine Jolliffe,[7] and one viadge in the Swiftesure wi*th* Captaine Waddon,[8] and more he remembreth not.

[1] H.C.A. 13/29, 23 February 1591/2. Extract. Deposition on the libel.
[2] Probably a corruption of *scopolarius*, a gunner (Latin *scopos*, a mark or aim).
[3] See p. 175, n. 2 below.   [4] See p. 98 above.
[5] For the voyages of the *Minion*, owned by Laurence Prowse and William Dudson, see 'Elizabethan Privateering', pp. 286–7.
[6] Probably the *William Bonaventure* of Thomas Heaton's (ibid., pp. 289–90).
[7] One of Carey's captains of the Isle of Wight, active since the seventies in all manner of sea fighting (ibid., pp. 279–80).
[8] Captain John Waddon, captain and part owner of the *Swiftsure* of Chichester (S. P. Dom. Eliz. ccxxix, no. 37; H.C.A. 24/57, no. 207; H.C.A. 13/26, 6–11 May 1587; H.C.A. 14/25, nos. 5, 45, 46; H.C.A. 24/65, no. 27).

Dicit quod Johannem Wattes per quatuor annos et Dominum contra
Georgium Carie per septem annos respective noverit.... Johannem
                                                       Wattes.
       Ad Interrogatoria.... *13 testis*
                                                       Wattes.
Ad xij respondet he hath gone to sea every yeare since Reprisalls began, with lettres of Reprisall, and hath byn Captaine
only this laste viadge and master two viadges before, As namely
he wente first to sea two viadges in the Marlyn of Sir George
Caries nexte the Drake of master Wattes in the Indies[1] and since
in the examiner & the John[2] of master Wattes & other shipps
which he remembreth not....

Ad xxj respondet affirmative, and especially in the Indies
where there is danger of the ennimy to be feared if men of warre
comminge thither be not stronge....

Ad xxiij respondet that the Swallowe had taken noe prizes in
the Indies this laste sommer as he beleveth if she had not byn in
the company of master Wattes shippes: For that of her selfe,
she durst not without company have come nere the Avana where
the Kinges Galleys and Armados laye.

72. Carey contra *Watts: deposition of Thomas Gilbert*[3]

THOMAS GILBERT de Ratcliffe nauta ubi per xij annos Dominus
moram fecit annos agens xxx^ta vel circiter testis ... dicit quod Georgius
Johannem Wattes per quatuor annos, et Dominum Georgium Carie
Carie ex visu respective noverit. contra
                                                     Johannem
Ad primum et secundum [he knows the articles to be true] For Wattes
that he was gonner of the said shipp the Centaure.... mer-
                                                     catorem.
       Ad Interrogatoria.... *14 testis*
                                                       Wattes
Ad xij respondet he hath made v or vj viadges to sea with
lettres of Reprisall against the Spaniardes in the George Bonaventure of master Cordells,[4] the Prudence belonginge to master
Ridlesden,[5] and ever since in master Wattes shippes.

---

[1] The West Indies voyage of 1588 (pp. 40–9 above).

[2] Geare was master of the *John* in the West Indies in 1590 (*Roanoke Voyages*, p. 580).

[3] H.C.A. 13/29, 19 February 1591/2. Extract. Deposition on the *materia*.

[4] Thomas Cordell, London merchant.

[5] John Ridlesden, owner and captain of the *Prudence* of Barnstaple, made at least two West Indies voyages (see p. 327 below).

THE 1591 VOYAGES

76. *Carey* contra *Watts: deposition of Edward Pollard*[1]

EDWARDUS POLLARD de Ratcliffe nauta ubi per tresdecim annos habitavit annos natus xxvij aut circiter testis... dicit quod Johannem Wattes per tres annos et Dominum Georgium Carie ex visu respective noverit.

Ad primum et secundum [affirms the ships were set forth] of this examinates knowledge who wente as quarter masters mate in the Little John that viadge....

Dominus Georgius Carie contra Johannem Wattes.
17 testis Wattes.
Repetitus coram Domino Iudice die predicto.

Ad Interrogatoria....

Ad duodecimum respondet he wente first to sea on warfarre with Sir Frances Drake to the West Indies in the Aide of her majesties,[2] and nexte he sayled in the Seadragon of william Hollidayes,[3] and then in the Unity of London[4] against the Spaniardes Afterwardes he served in the Lion with Captaine Polewhele,[5] and since in the Barcke Bery of Plimouthe Thomas Bery Captaine John Grimesby was master[6] and last in the John of master Wattes with lettres of Reprisall.

77. *Carey* contra *Watts: deposition of Ralph Gibson*[7]

RADULPHUS GIBSON de Tower Hill tormentator[8] ubi per xij annos moram fecit annos agens xxxiij aut circiter Testis... dicit quod Johannem Wattes per quatuor annos noverit et Dominum Georgium Carie non novit.

Dominus Georgius Carie contra Johannem Wattes.
18 testis Wattes.

Ad primum et secundum [affirms the articles] For this examinate wente gonner of the said shipp the Little John that viadge....

Ad Interrogatoria....

---

[1] H.C.A. 13/29, 3 March 1591/2. Extract. Deposition on the *materia*.
[2] Drake's 1585–6 expedition.
[3] London merchant, mercer. Interested in various privateering ventures during the war ('Elizabethan Privateering', pp. 267, 269).
[4] Possibly also Holliday's (ibid., pp. 267, 319).
[5] See above, pp. 59–85.
[6] 'Elizabethan Privateering', p. 306.
[7] H.C.A. 13/29, 7 March 1591/2. Extract. Deposition on the *materia*.
[8] Gunner.

Ad xij respondet he was never at sea in shipp of warre before this viadge in the John.

78. Carey contra Watts: deposition of George Cocke[1]

Georgius Carie miles contra Johannem Wattes.
19 testis Wattes.

GEORGIUS COCKE de Limehouse nauta ubi per biennium habitaverit et antea in villa de Lee per omnem suam etatem fungens etate viginti duorum annorum aut circiter Testis. ... Deponit quod Johannem Wattes per triennium noverit et Dominum Georgium Carie non novit.

Ad primum et secundum [affirms the articles] For this examinate was masters mate in one of the said shippes called the John. ...

Ad Interrogatoria. ...

Ad duodecimum respondet he hath only byn at sea two viadges with lettres of Reprisall once in the Hopewell & last in the John of master Wattes.

79. Carey contra Watts: deposition of Arthur Hill[2]

Dominus Georgius Carie contra Johannem Wattes.
20 testis Wattes.

ARTHURUS HILL de Wappinge Wall mariner ubi per triennium moram fecit, annos agens viginti sex aut circiter Testis ... dicit quod Johannem Wattes per quatuor annos noverit et Dominum Georgium Carie non novit. ...

Ad Interrogatoria. ...

Ad sextum respondet that this respondente & company mett with the Swallowe nere Cape Corantes havinge lost her Admirall which was blowen uppe before in fighte with the Spaniardes Armados. ...

Ad duodecimum respondet he hath byn at sea aboute xij viadges within theise thre yeares in shipps of warre, in the John of master Wattes he hath made vij or viij viadges to the quoast of Spaine & one to the Indies, and two or thre viadges in the Disdayne of the Lord Admirall, and two viadges in the Hare of Hampton of master Eatons.[3]

[1] H.C.A. 13/30, 9 March 1591/2. Extract. Deposition on the *materia*.
[2] H.C.A. 13/30, 13 March 1591/2. Extract. Deposition on the *materia*.
[3] Thomas Heaton, merchant and customer of Southampton, shipowner and promoter of privateering ('Elizabethan Privateering', pp. 278, 284).

80. *Howard* contra *Watts*: deposition of John Clercke[1]

JOHANNES CLERCKE Civitatis London generosus ubi permansit per viginti annos natus in villa de Safforne Walden in Comitatu Essex, etatis sue xxxiij aut circiter attingens annos testis in hac parte productus iuratus et examinatus dicit quod honorandum virum Dominum Thomam Howard per viginti annos et Johannem Wattes per octo annos respective noverit.

Dominus Thomas Howard contra Johannem Wattes mercatorem London.

Ad primum articulum affirmat eundem continere veritatem For this examinate uppon the grauntinge of her Majesties lettres pattentes articulate to the righte honorable Thomas Lord Howard for the purpose conteyned in this article had them delivered him by the Lord Thomas to peruse, which this examinate reade, and thereuppon by vertue of the same the said Lord Thomas appoincted & made this examinate his Lieftenante and as his Lieftenante served at sea under him the whole viadge whereby he knoweth the contentes of this article to be most true.

Primus testis super Libello.

Ad secundum attestatur eundem verissimum esse That her Majesty appoincted her highnes articulate shippes the Defyaunce the Revenge, the Elizabeth Bonaventure the Crane & the Moone to the said Lord Thomas Howard for the accomplisshinge of such service against the Spaniardes & others in enmity with her Majesty as he was by his Commission or lettres pattentes aforesaid assigned unto and the same shippes the said Lord Thomas had to sea with him of this examinates certaine knowledge beinge his Lieftenante that viadge.

[To the third he states he has seen the letters patent.]

Ad quartum attestatur verissimum esse that besides the lettres pattentes aforesaid under the greate seale of England graunted to the said Lord Thomas Howarde the Queenes most excellente Majesty delivered or caused to be delivered to the said Lord Thomas Howard certaine articles instructions or directions firmed with her Majesties owne hande which this examinate

---

[1] H.C.A. 13/30, 15 June 1592. Extract. Deposition on the libel. Clercke was a gentleman sea-captain. Commanded Oughtred's *Susan Fortune* on her Newfoundland voyage of 1582 (Quinn, *Gilbert*, pp. 85–6; H.C.A. 13/24, 25 April 1583, etc.). Captain of Raleigh's *Golden Noble* 1586 and of Cavendish's *Galleon Dudley* 1590 ('Elizabethan Privateering', pp. 246, 340–1). Commanded John Newton's *Julian* of London 1593 and 1594 (H.C.A. 24/62, no. 68; H.C.A. 13/102, 2 April 1595, 25 June 1595, 24 January 1595/6, 11 and 13 April 1598; H.C.A. 13/31, 11 June 1594).

also sawe & reade, & therby the said Lord Thomas was further aucthorized by her Majesty to take eanye shippes which he should happen to meete withall, if he should thincke them fitt to serve, to whom he should promise for such tonnadge & allowaunce for consorte as in reason they may challinge as by the said articles or instructions may more at lardge appeare.

Ad quintum et sextum affirmat [that the *Defiance*, the *Bonaventure*, the *Mermaid* of London and the *Disdain* were victualled by Lord Thomas].

Ad septimum deponit that when the Lord Thomas Howard came with his Fleete to Plimouth he founde there the articulate fower shippes the Hopewell the Centaure the Pegasus & the John, and a smale pinnace in the harbor beinge ready furnished & victualed to goe to sea, and this examinate talked with Captaine Lane & he tould this examinate that master Wattes his owner had geven him order to attende my Lord Thomas Howard & the Queenes shippes untill a certaine tyme and afterwardes there was a speeche in the Towne geven out by the mariners of master Wattes said shippes that if my Lord Howard commaunded them to attende on him they would ron awaye Whereof my Lord beinge certified, he caused the Queenes Commission & her highnes Instructions to be publickly reade at the High Crosse of Plimouth in presence of the Maior, master Heale the Counceler, proclamation beinge first made that all Captaines Masters mariners & souldiers that were in the Towne should repaire to the Crosse & heare the Queenes Commission reade and afterwardes in the harbor my Lord Thomas caused a flagge of Councell to be hunge out, whereuppon Captaine Lane & all the reste of master Wattes Captaines came on borde the Defiaunce when my Lord Howard by vertue of his Commission commaunded them to attende him and her Majesties shippes in the presence of this examinate & many others.

[To articles 8, 9, 10, 11, 12 and 13 he deposes that Watts' four ships went with Howard's fleet and followed the commander's instructions until they arrived off the coast of Spain. To article 14 he cannot depose.]

Ad xv affirmat verum esse that the Lord Thomas Howard beinge with his Fleete on the quoaste of Spaine & havinge then the Centaure the Pegasus & the Little John in his company did in hearinge of this examinate commaunde Captaine Lane to accompany the Minion of Hampton and to ply to the shoare there to seeke for Carvells of advise or eany other shippinge of the Kinge of Spaines & to take them as prize, and to repaire unto him the nexte day whom they should finde in the offinge, and the Minion of Hampton accordingely did that service & returned but Captaine Lane not regardinge my Lords commaundemente wente his wayes carienge with him my Lords articles & repayred now more to my Lord all that viadge of this examinates certaine knowledge.

Ad xvj deponit that the Hopewell, the Centaure the Pegasus & the John after theire departure from my Lord Thomas & his Fleete did take that viadge first one Ritch shipp on the quoaste of Spaine & caried her to the Canaries worth xxx thowsand pounde as yt was reported at sea, and then sayled into the West Indies & tooke theire thre or fower shipps more as he herde Ac aliter nescit.

Ad xvij^{um} affirmat he hath herde yt reported that the shipps and goodes which master Wattes shipps & Captaines tooke the laste Sommer were worth one hundreth thowsand poundes Ac aliter nescit....

Ad Interrogatoria....

Ad septimum et octavum respondet he knoweth that there was a consorteshippe made aboute the third of Aprill 1591 betwene the Lord Thomas Howard & the Captaines of the Hopewell the Centaure the Pegasus the John and theire smale Pinnace in such manner & forme as ys conteyned in the scedle[1] mentioned in theise Interrogatoryes and annexed to the same which he beleveth to be a true copy of the said consorteshippe and to be made and concluded on as in the said schedle is conteyned whereunto he referreth him selfe.

Ad nonum respondet he doth not knowe nether beleveth that my Lord Thomas Howard did putt his hande to the said consorteshippe....

Ad undecimum respondet that my Lord Thomas Howard with his Fleete whereof the Hopewell the Centaure the Pegasus & the John were a parte, departed from Plimouthe on the vth of Aprill 1591, and before the ende of the same monethe beinge on the quoaste of Spaine Captaine Lane... departed from the Fleete and returned not agayne.

[1] This 'schedule' of the consortship is printed in Marsden, *Law and Custom*, I, 272–3; it allows for the sharing of only those prizes taken 'in sight'.

81. Howard contra *Watts*: deposition of Stephen Michell[1]

Dominus Thomas Howard contra Johannem Wattes.
Primus testis super materia Wattes.
Repetitus coram Domino Thoma Crompton legum doctore Iudicis Surrogato die sabbato ix⁰ Decembris 1592 presente me Jo. Pulford.

STEPHANUS MICHELL nuper Capitaneus navis vocatae Pegasus annos agens xxij aut circiter Testis in hac parte productus iuratus et examinatus dicit quod Johannem Wattes per octo annos, et Dominum Thomam Howard per biennium aut circa respective noverit.

Ad primum articulum materie in hac causa date affirmat [that John Watts and his partners owned and set forth on reprisals the *Centaur*, the *Pegasus*, the *Hopewell* and the *Little John*, this examinate being captain of the *Pegasus*.]

Ad secundum affirmat [that the four ships went to the coast of Spain and the Indies to execute their commission.]

Ad tertium et quartum affirmat [that the four ships were at Plymouth ready to sail about 4 April 1591.]

Ad quintum et sextum attestatur et affirmat that the righte honorable the Lord Thomas Howard ... did make stay of the said foure shippes to joyne with his said Fleete, which Captaine Lane this examinate & the reste of the Captaines & masters of the said foure shippes would not yelde unto unlesse yt would please his Lordship to enter into consorteshippe with them. . . . [Lane and his fellow captains therefore had articles of consortship drawn up and submitted to Lord Thomas, who signed them; the same articles of consortship are annexed as a schedule to the materia.]

[To the 7th, 8th and 9th he affirms that Lord Thomas personally handed the signed articles to Captain Lane and that Watts' ships were not stayed for any other purpose than is expressed in the said articles.]

Ad decimum affirmat verum esse that the said foure shippes ... beinge furnished provided & sett furth for a particuler viadge to the West Indies muste nedes make saile to the quoaste of Spaine onwarde on the said viadge & therefore Captaine Lane, this examinate & the reste of the Captaines & masters of master Wattes shippes did the more willingly aggree to attende uppon the Lord Thomas & his fleete to the quoaste of Spaine duringe that moneth of Aprill 1591 accordinge to his Lordships aggreemente For that his Lordship promised not to stay them longer

[1] H.C.A. 13/30, 6 December 1592. Extract. Deposition on the *materia*.

[and so they attended Lord Thomas and his fleet towards the coast of Spain, with the intention of proceeding on their voyage to the West Indies after the end of April.]

Ad undecimum attestatur that as the said foure shippes... were in theire said course saylinge in company of the Lord Thomas, one of them called the Harry & John returninge into Falmouth came a grounde there, and soe was lefte behinde and within fewe dayes after followed after the said Lord Thomas & his fleete, and aboute the xxth daye of the said moneth of Aprill as the said Lord Thomas and his fleete togeather with the Centaure the Pegasus and the Little John were in company uppon the quoaste of Spaine, there happened a greate storme wherein the said thre shippes... were by force of the tempest severed from the said Lord Thomas & his fleete and inforced and driven out of sighte of the said Lord Thomas & his Fleete, and soe farre a sonder that they did never meete or come in sighte one of the other duringe the said moneth of Aprill....

[To the 12th and 13th he states that the three ships sought in vain for Howard's fleet after the storm.]

Ad decimum quartum deponit that of his certaine knowledge there was noe prize taken by eany the said foure shippes or the Captaines masters & companyes thereof before the xxiiijth day of the said moneth of Aprill 1591 howebeit he graunteth that aboute the xxiiij or xxvth of the said moneth of Aprill there was a prize taken by the Centaure the John & the Pegasus uppon the quoaste betwixte Spaine & Barbarye beinge laden with hides & other thinges....

[To the 15th, 16th and 17th he affirms that no prize was taken by any of the four ships in sight of Howard's fleet and that this was the only prize taken by any of the four ships in April 1591.]

[Replying to interrogatories, he states that he was born in Somersetshire and lives with John Watts, as he has done for five or six years. He admits that Lane was sent to the coast of Spain by Howard two days before the storm occurred, but does not know whether Lane rejoined the main fleet before the storm. The *Pegasus* and the *John*, having lost the fleet during the storm, happened by chance to meet the *Centaur* soon afterwards. The *Centaur*, the *Pegasus* and the *John* were hailed one night after the storm by the *Galleon Dudley*, which nevertheless departed without 'gevinge eany directions where the L*ord* Thomas was'.]

82. *Howard* contra *Watts: deposition of William Craston*[1]

D*ominus* Thomas Howard *contra* J*oh*annem *Wattes.* 5 *testis Wattes.* R*epetitus coram Jacobo Stopes iudicis Sur*rogato *xix novembris 1593.*

WILL*IE*LMUS CRASTON Civi*tatis* London nauta ubi per totam fere etatem habitavit annos agens xxxij aut circa testis. ...

Ad Interrogatoria. ...

Ad duodecimu*m* res*p*ondet that this ex*amina*te & his company in the Hopewell havinge gott theire said shippe cleare in Falmouth havon, followed after to the quoaste of Spaine to seeke the L*ord* Thomas & his flete & lay of & on there, but coulde not meete with the L*ord* Thomas his fleete or eany m*aste*r Wattes shippes untill he founde them in the Indies. ...

Ad xvij nescit plura dicere qua*m* prius dictu*m* est Savinge that this ex*amina*te & his company of the Hopwell tooke a crosse saile[2] to the Southwarde of the Isle[3] of the Canaries the thirde day of may 1591 wherein was a butt of wyne, a vessell of vinegar & some victualls not worth above V^{li} in the whole.

[1] H.C.A. 13/30, 17 November 1593. Extract. Deposition on the *materia*.
[2] A square sailed vessel.
[3] [*Sic.*]

ENGLISH PRIVATEERING VOYAGES

On 12/22 June the four English ships joined forces in an attempt to capture a frigate which had run itself aground. They failed, and thirteen of the landing party, including Robert Barrett, were captured, while others were drowned or killed by the enemy. Barrett's ship—the *Moonshine*'s consort—capsized and sank. After this disastrous action there is no news of Myddelton, but a later Spanish report says that he was captured by Alonso de Bazán in 1592.[1] Wood's two ships presumably made for Cape San Antonio, and thereabouts they must have fallen in with other Englishmen, including their old companions in the *Mineral* and the *Flight*. With them they worried the Havana coast until about the end of August, when the English corsairs appear to have left the scene.[2] Vavasour was home by 6/16 February 1592/3 and Coche by 24 April/4 May 1593,[3] but of Wood's return we hear nothing. As for the *Flight*, she returned early in 1593, but not to England. In short, Wood's venture can hardly have been successful, since no important prizes seem to have been taken to offset the misfortunes of the voyage.[4]

*   *   *

83. *Warrant for the grant of letters of reprisal for the* Challenger, *the* Mineral *and the* Pilgrim[5]

Ma*ste*r Ceasar I am contented you make oute comyssion of reprisall unto my very good Lorde the Lor*d* Thomas Howard to set forthe and furnishe to the seas the good shippes called the Challenger of London of the burthen of Cxth tonnes the Mynyrall of London of the burthen of C^{th6} tonnes and the

---

[1] Document 132 below.

[2] New style. *Further English Voyages*, p. 300.

[3] Both made depositions in the High Court of Admiralty in the case of Howard *contra* Watts (H.C.A. 13/30, under these dates).

[4] Reynolds refers to the rifling of sundry carvels in the Indies, a conveniently vague formula setting no limit to the damages claimed, but if any prize of considerable value had been taken he would no doubt have mentioned it.

[5] H.C.A. 25/3 (9), 6 March 1591/2. Endorsed: 'The Challenger of London of Cxx tonnes, Benjamyn Wood Captaine.'

[6] Abbreviation for 'hundreth', extended by some confused analogy to the 110 tons of the *Challenger*.

Trinidad, where by barter he obtained water and fruits. By 25 May/4 June he had reached La Margarita and, coasting westwards touching at Cape de la Vela, Rio de la Hacha and Santa Marta, he arrived at Hicacos Point, near Cartagena, on 12/22 June. Meanwhile he had acquired nothing of value and had even found difficulty in obtaining food and water; furthermore his fleet was now reduced to two ships, the *Mineral* and the *Flight* having disappeared in storms off Coro and Rio de la Hacha.[1]

It was at Hicacos Point that the *Challenger* and the *Pilgrim* met with two small vessels: the *Moonshine* (50 tons), under John Myddelton captain and John Hore master, together with a prize of some 30 tons—taken earlier off the coast of Spain—commanded by one Robert Barrett (alias Frost). The *Moonshine*, owned by the London merchant John Newton, had been on reprisal in 1586, 1590 and 1591, each time under John Myddelton, gentleman.[2] His fellow captain, Barrett, had commanded the *Salomon*, a London merchantman, in the Cadiz expedition of 1587 and the *Toby*, another London merchantman, in the Armada campaign.[3] Myddelton and Barrett had reached Hicacos Point by a route similar to that taken by Wood, and with more or less similar luck; they had left England a little before Wood's fleet, which they had met in the Canaries, and they had kept a day or two ahead of Wood's men all along the Spanish Main.

[1] This summary of events is based on the Spanish material.

[2] *Principal Navigations*, II (1599), pt. ii, 169–75; VI (1904), 35–8; 'Elizabethan Privateering', pp. 259–60; *Monson's Tracts*, I, 262, 271. She had also served against the Armada under John Brough (Laughton, *Defeat*, II, 327). John Myddelton of Westchester, aged 26 in 1589 (H.C.A. 13/27, 9 June 1589), was probably the eldest son of Richard, brother of Sir Thomas Myddelton (W. H. Myddelton, *Pedigree of the Family of Myddelton* (Horncastle, 1910)). It is often stated that the captain of the *Moonshine* in 1591 was William Myddelton, but there seems to be no evidence for this. In fact William, the elder brother of Sir Thomas, was in command of the *Riall* of Weymouth that year, and as the name of John Myddelton is on other occasions associated with the *Moonshine*, it is reasonable to assume that it was he who warned Howard of the approach of Bazán's fleet. He was captured by the Spaniards in 1592 and again when he visited the West Indies in the *Affection* in 1594 (document 132 below).

[3] H.C.A. 25/2 (5), 13 March 1586/7; Laughton, *Defeat*, II, 327. The *Toby* was a 200-ton London merchantman, set forth on reprisal by Richard Staper, the famous Levant trader, in 1592 (H.C.A. 25/3 (9), 15 August 1592). Barrett was also known as Frost among the Spaniards (*Further English Voyages*, pp. 290–1).

London, gentleman, gave his age in May 1593 as thirty-three and declared that 'he was his honors servante and wore his Livery some fowere or fyve yeares agoe and not since...'.[1] Nothing further is known of Thomas Turner of Saffron Walden, gentleman, but Abraham was of course the sailor who had given so lucid an account of the voyage of the *Black Dog*.[2]

As for the ships, the *Challenger*[3] and the *Mineral* do not recur in the annals of privateering. The *Pilgrim* had served with Howard's fleet in 1591 and was perhaps the ship employed by Cumberland in 1593.[4] The *Flight* was the French ship, the *Florissant*, which had been captured in 1591 by Richard Vavasour (then captain of the Queen's ship *Foresight* in Howard's fleet). The Frenchman and its lading of Newfoundland fish had been judged lawful prize on the ground that they belonged to 'Leaguers', and Howard had then bought the vessel from the Queen for £64. On her return from the West Indies early in 1593 the *Flight* put into port at the Ile de Ré and was there arrested at the request of its former owners and adjudged their property. Howard's efforts to regain the vessel were unavailing and in 1595 he was granted commission of stay and arrest to the value of £1000 against the shipping of the merchants of 'Olderney de Barges' and the Ile de Ré.[5]

Thus with some 350 tons of shipping and about 200 men[6]—a force not extraordinarily large for a privateering venture—Wood left England in April, 1592. At the Canaries he encountered other English privateers, but, effecting no consortships, pressed on to

[1] H.C.A. 13/30, 4 May 1593. His name appears in the Spanish records as 'Cuchi' or 'Escot'.

[2] See document 8 above.

[3] The Spanish version was 'La Chalandilla'.

[4] Lansdowne MS 67, f. 177; and pp. 236–83 below.

[5] Documents 86–9 below and Lansdowne MS 67, f. 183 (a further reference to the capture of a French ship by Vavasour in 1591). Ships hailing from ports under the control of the Catholic League were lawful prize from 1589, when Henry IV succeeded to the throne of France. 'Olderney' cannot be definitely identified, but was perhaps Oléron, the island to the south of the Ile de Ré. Hawkins' letter and the French ambassador's declaration appear in the records together with a badly damaged copy of the interlocutory sentence adjudging the French ship lawful prize; it is evident that all three documents were produced in connection with Howard's claim for restitution. Hawkins must have been asked his opinion and the other two documents must have been dug out from earlier files. The copy of the sentence is H.C.A. 24/60, no. 2.

[6] Perhaps more: cp. *Further English Voyages*, pp. 288, 290, 294.

CHAPTER VI

THE VOYAGE OF BENJAMIN WOOD
1592

IN June 1592 thirteen sail of English corsairs were haunting the coastline about Havana; four of these were ships set forth by Lord Thomas Howard under the command of Benjamin Wood.[1] Until recently, this was all that was known of Howard's 1592 expedition. The publication of relevant Spanish materials by I. A. Wright in 1951[2] provided much fresh detail about the events of the voyage and it is now possible, with the aid of several High Court of Admiralty documents,[3] to identify the ships and captains and thus to present a coherent account of the venture.

Lord Thomas Howard's fleet consisted of the *Challenger* of London (120 tons), Benjamin Wood captain and John Tomlyn master; the *Mineral* of London (100 tons), Richard Vavasour captain and Richard Cawson master; the *Pilgrim* of London (90 tons), Thomas Coche captain and William Elsemore master; and the *Flight* of Plymouth (50 tons), Thomas Turner captain and Robert Abraham master.[4] Benjamin Wood, in command of the expedition, is not known to have had any lasting connection with Howard, but two of the other captains—Vavasour and Coche—were Howard's men. Vavasour, on his return from this voyage, described himself as a gentleman of London, aged about twenty-five, who 'is attendante uppon the Lorde Thomas Howarde in his honors house and one of his gent*lem*en and doethe some tymes weare his honors Cloathe . . .'.[5] Thomas Coche of

---

[1] Document 97 below.
[2] *Further English Voyages*, pp. 280–1, 283–95, 297–304, 308–9.
[3] Documents 83–9 below.
[4] Documents 83–5 below. The estimates of tonnage which occur in the Spanish depositions do not vary significantly from the Admiralty Court figures.
[5] H.C.A. 13/30, 16 February 1592/3. His name appears in the Spanish records as 'Babisar' or 'Dababeres' (*Further English Voyages*, pp. 286, 289).

25 January 1591/2, for the good behaviour of the *Flight* of Plymouth, 50 tons burden, Thomas Turner captain, Robert Abraham master.]

(e) *John Myddelton and John Hore for the Moonshine.*

[A similar bond in £3000, jointly by John Myddelton and John Hore, dated 22 January 1591/2, for the good behaviour of the *Moonshine* of London, fifty tons burden, set forth by John Newton of London, merchant, Myddelton and Hore respectively captain and master.]

86. *Deposition of Henry Reynolds*[1]

HENRIE REYNOLDS servante to the righte honorable Thomas L*ord* Howard aged xxx yeares or thereabou*tes* sworne & examined before the righte worshipfull m*aste*r Doctor Cesar Judge of her m*aje*sties high Courte of the Admi*ral*ty on the behaulfe of the said L*ord* Thomas concerninge a French shipp called the Florizant of newhavon taken at the seas by m*aste*r Vavisor Captaine of the Foresighte of her m*aje*sties as belonginge to Leagers, & since stayed at St martyns in Poitowe nere Rochell by Viodett & others of Olderney Barges & others Sayth by chardge of his oathe that after takinge of the said shipp the Florizant from them of the leage, and judgemente geven in her m*aje*sties high Courte of the Admi*ral*ty wi*th* consente of the L*ord* Ambassador of Fraunce that the same was lawfull prize, the said shipp was furnished & victualed for a viadge to be made to the Indies, & Thomas Turner appointed Captaine thereof, who with his company aboute Aprill com*m*inge shalbe thre yeares[2] proceeded on that viadge and had the riflinge of sondry Carvells in the Indies out of the which by reporte of the Captaine & companye they had some gould portingall base money and sondry other good*es*, and homeward*es* bounde they stopped in St martyns Roade & there the shippe aforesaid was arrested by men of Olderney berges & St martyns as belonginge unto them, and uppon knowledge of the stay of the said shippe, the said Lord

[1] H.C.A. 13/30, 31 January 1593/4. Deposition on Howard's *querela*. Reynolds was captain of the Lord Admiral's *Lion's Whelp* in the West Indies in 1596–7 (Additional MS 12505, ff. 467–9).
[2] Should read 'two years'.

or merchandizes as they shall soe take and apprehend of the subjectes of the kinge of Spaine togeather with three or fower the cheifest persons of every such prize whereof the master and pilott to be two to some porte of this Realme of Englande as shalbe most convenient for them: And doe not breake bulcke wast spoile sell or diminishe anie parte or parcell thereof untill they shalbe adjudged in her majesties highe Courte of the Admiralty to be lawfull prize And thereuppon an Inventory taken by the viceadmirall of the place or his deputy where they shall soe arrive and other publicke officers of the same and appraysement made of the same goodes by some six honest men Inhabitantes of the saide porte and that the same Inventory and appraysement shalbe returned into her majesties highe Courte of the Admiralty within six weekes then next after ensewinge And also doe answere and paye or cause to be answered and payed in the highe Court of the Admiralty aforesaid to the use of the Lord Admirall aforesaide the full tenth parte of all such shippes goodes monies and merchandizes as they shall soe take and apprehend by vertue of the saide Commission at the tyme of exhibittinge the saide Inventory and appraysement as aforesaide; That then this obligacion to be void and of noe force or else to remaine in full power and vertue.

Signatum sigillatum et
diliberatum in presentiis   Beniemen Wood.
mei Johannis Webber
   Walteri Righte.

(b) Richard Vavasour for the Mineral.

[A similar bond in £3000 by Richard Vavasour, dated 6 March 1591/2, for the good behaviour of the *Mineral* of London, 100 tons burden, himself captain, Richard Cawson master.]

(c) Thomas Coche for the Pilgrim.

[A similar bond in £3000 by Thomas Coche, dated 6 March 1591/2, for the good behaviour of the *Pilgrim* of London, 90 tons burden, himself captain, William Elsemore master.]

(d) Lord Thomas Howard for the Flight.

[A similar bond in £3000 by Lord Thomas Howard, dated

85. Bonds taken for the good behaviour of the privateers[1]

(a) Benjamin Wood for the Challenger.

Noverint universi per presentes me Benjamin Woodd generosum capitaneum navis vocate the Challenger portus London teneri et firmiter obligari honorando viro Carolo domino Howard baroni de Effingham magno domino admirallo Anglie in ter mille libris monete Anglie solvendis eidem domino admirallo aut suo certo atturnato heredibus vel successoribus suis ad quem quidem solucionem bene et fideliter faciendam obligo me heredesque et executores meos firmiter per presentes sigillo meo sigillatas datas sexto die mensis martii Anno domini 1591 stilo Anglie Regni serenissime nostre Elizabethe Regine etc. anno xxxiiij°.

The Condicion of this obligacion is such That whereas the Right honorable Thomas Lord Howarde is aucthorized by vertue of lettres of Reprisall obtayned from the abovenamed Lord Admirall to send furth to the seas one shipp called the Challenger of London of the burthen of Cxx tonns or thereaboutes whereof the abovebound Ben. Woodd goeth as Captaine and John Tomlyn master with men ordinance and victualls sufficient for the same service for the apprehendinge and takinge the goodes of the kinge of Spaine or anie his subjectes as by the tenor of the said Comission more at lardge maye appeare; If therefore the said Captaine and master with their saide shipp and companie doe presently after their puttinge to sea with all possible spede repaire to the Coast of Spaine the Islandes or such other remote places where the Spaniardes and portingalls doe most use their trafficke and doe not attempt aniethinge against anie her majesties lovinge subjectes or the subjectes of the french king or the subjectes of the princes of Italy or the subjectes of the kinges of Scotland or Denmarke or the Inhabitantes of the united provinces of the lowe Countries or the hawnce Townes or molest or spoile anie Fleminge or frenchman under the color of Legars or the subjectes of anie other prince or potentate beinge in leage and amity with her majestie But only against the subjectes of the king of Spaine, And doe bringe or cause to be brought all such shippes goodes monies

[1] H.C.A. 25/3 (9). Signed, and sealed with the seal of one of the officials witnessing the signature.

Pilgryme of London of the burthen of iiij^{xx} tonnes or thereaboutes in warlike manner agaynste the kinge of Spayne & his subjectes and his or theire goodes under suche articles and conditions as are agreed one betwixte the Lords of the counsell & merchauntes on that behalfe And let this be yowre warraunte for the same From the courte at whitthall the 6. of Marche 1591

Youre Lovinge frende
C Howard

postcript you shall not neede
to take any other bandes then
the bandes of eiche one of the
captaines for eiche severall ship.

To my lovinge frende master Doctor
Ceasar Judge of the highe courte of
the Admyraltye.

84. *Warrant for the grant of letters of reprisal for the* Flight[1]

Master Ceasar I am contented you make oute comyssion of reprisall unto my very good Lord the Lord Thomas Howard to set oute & furnishe to the seas the good shippe called the Flyighte of Plymouth of the burthen of 50. tonnes or thereaboutes in warlike manner agaynst the kinge of Spayne & his subjectes & his or theire goodes under suche articles and conditions as are agreed on betwixte the Lords of the counsell & merchauntes on that behall[2] And let this be yowr warraunt for the same From the courte at whitehall the 25 of January 1591

youre lovinge frende
C Howard.

To my lovinge frende master Doctor
Ceasar Judge of the highe courte of
the Admyraltye.

[*Endorsed*] The Captain's name ys Thomas Turner of Safforn Walden gentleman xxx men, [ ] master, vj caste peeces, viij monethes victualled.

---

[1] H.C.A. 25/3 (9), 25 January 1591/2. In the endorsement the name of the master is omitted.

[2] [*Sic.*]

Thomas sente this ex*amina*te into Fraunce w*ith* l*ett*res from the Ambassador directed to the Lieftenante of the towne of St martyns for releace of the said shippe, and uppon examination of the cause before the Judge of that place he tould this ex*amina*te that l*ett*res were noe profe but if he had broughte over w*ith* him profe from the Ambassador & this Courte that the shipp had byn adjudged good prize in England he would have geven order for redelivery of the shippe, which without the same he could not doe, & therefore wisshed him to retorne into England for such proves & thereuppon he should finde justice ministred unto him. . . . [Examinate then procured the required proofs, but was told, when he presented them to the judge, that sentence had meanwhile been given in favour of the other claimants.] Soe as this ex*amina*te seeinge noe meanes to obtayne justice there thoughte good rather to returne for England then to consume more tyme & expence in followinge the said suite which he per‑ceaved would be endles there, & soe came away.

87. *Letter to Dr Caesar from Sir John Hawkins*[1]

after my very harty com*m*endac*i*ons, my lord thomas S*er*vaunt this bearer hathe requyred me to certefye you of a frenche pryse that was taken under my Lord thomas charge w*ith* the foresyght of her ma*jes*ties m*aste*r vaveser one of her ma*jes*ties pencyon*er*s beynge captayne

The ship as I lerned was of newhaven taken by the sayd fore‑syght laden w*ith* newfowndland fyshe, the frenche men that were taken in here were a certayne tyme relyvyd at plymouthe uppon the same fyshe tyll they gott passage for newhaven. they made no clayme to be restoryd eyther of ther ship or good*es* w*h*ich they myght have had for the demaundynge beynge taken [by her] ma*jes*ties shipe, yf they had not confessyd them [selves Leaguers.] the kyng of frances servant beyng the [ambassador] toke a porcyon of the fyshe for the kyng*es* ryght as may appere by m*aste*r vavesors accompt whereof I send you a coppy together w*i*th the coppy of the accompt w*h*ich my lord admyrall & my

---

[1] H.C.A. 24/60, no. 3. Endorsed: 'To the Ryght worshipfull m*aste*r doctor ceaser m*aste*r of the request*es* & Judge of thadmyrallty gyve this at london'. Also endorsed by Caesar: 'Concerning my L*or*d Thomas Howard'. In the places in‑dicated by brackets the writing is obliterated.

lord thomas dyd allow under ther Lordships handes.[1] & this ys all that I know of this matter, but that my lord thomas payd for the ship & her fornyture to her majestie & the Rest of the partners as she was praysed which praysment was lxiiij^{li} as apperethe by the accompt & this I leve to troble you from deptford the Last of July 1593.

Your very lovyng frind
John Hawkyns.

88. Declaration by the French ambassador concerning the Florizant[2]

NOUS JEAN DE LA FIN [SEIGNEUR] DE BEAUVOIR LA NOCKE conseiller du Roy treschrestien en son conseil d Estat Capitayne de cinquante homm [ ] ordonnances et son Ambassadeur pres La Serenissime Royne d Angletere certifions a tous qu'il [ ] que nous ayant apparu que sur L examen faict en La court de L admirautie d Angletere, touchant un navire francois nomme Le florissant, pris par un des navires de la Serenissime Royne ou commandoit pour Capitayne Le Sieur Vavvisser gentilhomme pensionnayer de Ladite Dame, revenant Ledit Navire de terre neufve charge de poisson: que Ledit Navire auroit este trouve appartenant a ceux du Havre de Grace, estand du nombre des subjetz Rebelles de sa Majeste treschrestienne et partant trouve par Ladite Court confisquable avec Les biens y contenus, Nous a ces causes avons consenty et consentons que sentence soit donnee contre Ledit Navire et marchandises pour estre confisque au proffit des preneurs par le juge de Ladite court en forme acoustume: en temoing dequoy aux presentes signees de nostre main nous avons faict appozer Le Cachet de nos Armes a Londres, ce vingtiesme septembre 1591.

---

[1] Neither account can be traced.

[2] H.C.A. 24/60, no. 4. In the places indicated by brackets the writing is obliterated. The document is signed and sealed. A note in the corner of the MS, signed by Julius Caesar, reads: 'John Pulford, Drawe a sentence according to this from the Ambassader, whereof you shall receive further instructions from this bearer master Reinolds, and bring it to me either this night or tomorowe morning that I may signe it.'

89. Warrant of the Lord Admiral for the grant of a commission of stay and arrest to Lord Thomas Howard[1]

Master Caesar wheras a ship apertayninge to my good Lord the Lord Thomas Howard named the Flighte of the burthen of 60. tonnes cominge from the Weste Indyes in Anno 1593 was stayed by the Leiftenant of the Isle of Re neare Rochell uppon an areste made by a Frenchman of Olderney de Barges named Viodett and since cold neaver have justice nor restitutione of his saied ship wherfore theise are to pray and require you to graunt out comissione unto his Lordship or his assignes to staye anie such ship or goodes of the saied island or of Olderney aforesaied as his Lordship or his assignes shall at anie time herafter find within anie of her Majesties dominions to the valewe of one thousand poundes for to that som did his Lordships losses extend And for the same let this be your warrant from the court at Grenwiche the 8. of June 1595

Your lovinge freind
C Howard.

[1] H.C.A. 14/32, no. 155. Endorsed: 'To my lovinge freinde Master Doctor Caesar Judge of the Highe Courte of the Admyraltie.'

CHAPTER VII

CHRISTOPHER NEWPORT'S VOYAGE OF 1592

JOHN TWITT's account of Newport's 1592 expedition, published by Hakluyt in 1600, remains the chief source for this voyage.[1] The other documents printed below almost invariably testify to the accuracy and perceptiveness of Twitt's report and merely fill out his story with some interesting details. The new matter falls roughly into three sections: materials giving details of the personnel, financing and equipment of the venture;[2] a deposition by one of the captains, which incidentally outlines the course of the voyage;[3] and documents relating to the part played by the *Golden Dragon* in the capture and looting of the *Madre de Dios*.[4] On the West Indies part of the voyage some valuable Spanish records have already been printed by I. A. Wright.[5]

In January 1592 letters of reprisal were granted for the *Golden Dragon*, the *Prudence*, the *Margaret* and the *Virgin*, all London ships. The *Dragon*, of some 150 tons burden,[6] was the 'admiral' and, to judge from her appraisement in 1593, fairly powerful and well-equipped for a privateer.[7] It seems doubtful whether she was, as her owners and victuallers later urged, a new ship on her first voyage, for a ship of the same name in which the same persons were interested appears to have been at sea in 1585 or 1586.[8]

[1] Document 90.
[2] Documents 91–2.
[3] Document 93.
[4] Documents 94–6.
[5] *Further English Voyages*, pp. 281–3, 294, 302.
[6] Estimates of her burden vary from 90 tons (document 91) to 180 tons (documents 94 and 106).
[7] See document 107 below. She was evidently well supplied with smaller guns and muskets, though with 19 cast pieces she was less powerful than King's 200-ton *Salomon*, with 26 (document 98 below).
[8] See document 74 above. The owners and victuallers, in document 94, are obviously interested in emphasizing to the utmost their 'great charges'.

The *Prudence* and the *Margaret*[1] were somewhat smaller vessels and the *Virgin*, of 20–40 tons, is sometimes referred to as a pinnace. In all a fleet of some 300–350 tons[2] with a complement of about 200 men[3] (overmanned, but no more than was usual in privateers) made up a substantial force.

Of the eleven shareholders mentioned seven were London merchants[4] and two were shipowning masters of London[5]—a typical syndicate for one of the larger London expeditions. With Newport in the *Dragon* went the ill-fated Robert Keble as master;[6] the *Prudence* was commanded by Hugh Merrick, an experienced seaman[7] and, as master, John Paul, a Ratcliffe man who had sailed with Gilbert in 1583;[8] in the *Margaret* Robert Thread of Harwich[9] went captain and James Bragge of Limehouse master;[10] in the *Virgin* Henry Kedgell captain and Cuthbert Grippe master.[11]

Newport manifestly set out on this voyage with the intention of capturing La Yaguana in Hispaniola—an intention no doubt formed on the basis of his experience at that place the previous year.[12] La Yaguana was a small settlement—'a towne of three

---

[1] Described as a 'flyboat' in H.C.A. 24/59, no. 79.

[2] *Further English Voyages*, p. 294.

[3] The figures given in the Spanish sources are probably exaggerated. Thread speaks of a total force of 150 men landed at La Yaguana, with presumably a few left to man the ships.

[4] John More, Henry Cletherow, Robert Cobb, John Newton, George Southwick and William Jones we have already met (ch. v above). These were now joined by Peter Houghton, one of the sheriffs of London in 1593.

[5] William Bygate, owner or part owner of the *Golden Dragon* and the *Anne Bonaventure* in 1586 and master of the *Golden Lion* in the Cadiz expedition of 1587 (H.C.A. 13/26, 4 June 1586; H.C.A. 13/29, 28 February 1591/2; Additional MS 12505, ff. 238–48); and Edward Wilkinson (pp. 51–2 above). The identity of the other shareholders—Thomas Gardener and Edmond Burton, mariner—has not been traced.

[6] Killed in the *Madre de Dios* action (documents 94 and 95).

[7] A seaman's boy in 1576 (H.C.A. 13/22, 4 August 1576).

[8] *Principal Navigations*, III (1600), 155; VIII (1904), 64. He made further West Indies voyages in the *Anthony* in 1593–4 (ch. XI below) and twice in the *Neptune* in 1598 (K. R. Andrews, 'Christopher Newport of Limehouse, Mariner', *William and Mary Quarterly*, XI (1954), 36–7).

[9] Sometimes Thridd or Fridde. Aged 31 in 1592. At the end of 1592 letters of reprisal were obtained for Thomas James' *Pleasure* of Bristol, Robert Thread master (H.C.A. 25/3 (9), 15 December 1592).

[10] Master of the *Michael and John* in 1595 (document 148 below).

[11] See p. 99, n. 3 above for details of Grippe's career.

[12] See ch. v above.

streetes having about 150. housholds'[1]—remote from the other townships of the island and difficult of access by sail save in May, October and November. Already it was one of the most notorious of those places in the north and west of Hispaniola where illicit trade with the French, English and others was openly carried on.[2] However, their friendly commercial relations with some of the heretics did not save such towns from being plundered or held to ransom by others.

Until the first repulse at La Yaguana everything went well for Newport and his men. Leaving London a day before King, they reached Dominica six days ahead and captured a prize of negro slaves, whom they eventually landed at La Aguada on the northwest of the island of Puerto Rico. Still making good time, they passed on to Mona, thence to Saona and thence along the south coast of Hispaniola.[3] The four or five frigates taken here, though of little cash value, proved a useful addition to the fleet and the sugar and cattle from Ocoa made a considerable prize. Thread's account of the attack on La Yaguana, though in most respects inferior to Twitt's, does suggest that the failure of the first onset may have been due not only to irresolution but also to the undisciplined rapacity so typical of the privateers. To leave the ships at the uninhabited island[4] and proceed stealthily with the frigates along the shore was an excellent plan; but Thread credibly declares that the Spanish frigate in harbour was attacked before the landing. If the Spanish crew had detected the marauders such an attack was necessary—but only to prevent the alarm being given. In the event the alarm was given and the English seem to have wasted time taking provisions from the prize while the Spaniards ashore prepared a spirited defence. The failure to

[1] Twitt (document 90). In 1598 there were eighty households (E. Rodríguez Demorizi (ed.), *Relaciones históricos de Santo Domingo*, II, 185). La Yaguana was the modern Léogane, sometimes referred to then as 'Laguna'.

[2] Rodríguez Demorizi, *Relaciones*, II, 129–33.

[3] King, a few days behind, followed almost exactly the same course as Newport as far as Cape Tiburon, capturing another slave ship at Dominica and, like Newport, landing them at La Aguada (reference to two distinct cargoes of negroes is made in *Further English Voyages*, p. lxxxix, n. 3). Although the London merchant John More was an important backer of both expeditions, there is no evidence of any collaboration between the two commanders.

[4] Not Guanabo, which was too far away to be reached in the time indicated by Twitt. Possibly an island near Guava (Goave)—cp. Thread's reference to 'theire shipps at the Aguava' (document 93).

take the town at the first attempt meant failure to secure the expected pillage when the town was eventually taken, and the burning of La Yaguana and likewise of Guava[1] can have afforded little consolation.

In the Bay of Honduras in May and June they fared better, taking two fairly valuable prizes and considerable spoil in quicksilver and iron at Puerto de Caballos. Nevertheless, as Diego Martín de Angulo reported from Caballos, there was nothing to brag of in the booty they took;[2] at Caballos they obtained no ransom and the best part of the valuables had been removed to the hills by the forewarned inhabitants. Returning to Trujillo, moreover, they were driven off in the attempt to take a prize 'close under the castle' and, leaving the bay, 'discovered great store of shot intrenched in those places where they suspected we would have landed.'[3] It was of course usual for larger expeditions to make landings and attack townships, but Newport was something of a pioneer among the ordinary privateers in undertaking this type of action. His triumphs therefore were small and his difficulties and setbacks not a few; up to this point, in fact, the expedition might be called moderately successful, but no more.

Now it was that the prizes were lost in a storm and the *Margaret* and the *Virgin*, sent to find them, came home with them to England.[4] After an interesting encounter with the natives of 'certeine islands within the point of Florida'—doubtless the Calusa Indians of southwest Florida, of whom relatively little is otherwise known[5]—Newport and Merrick, with the *Dragon* and the *Prudence* sailed for the Azores.

The account of the part played by these two ships in the capture of the *Madre de Dios* has been included below[6] in order to complete the record of the expedition and is of special interest because it adds significantly to the documents relating to that

[1] The modern Goave. Thread's 'place called the Aguanovo' remains unidentified.
[2] *Further English Voyages*, p. 283.
[3] Twitt (document 90).
[4] An assessment of the Lord Admiral's tenth of one of the prizes is given in Harleian MS 598, f. 18. The tenth consisted of quantities of hides, raw and tanned, sarsaparilla, Spanish iron, quicksilver and indigo to the value of £154 13s. 10d. This assessment shows that the *Margaret* and this prize arrived at Weymouth in August.
[5] See p. 194, n. 1 below.
[6] Document 94.

episode already in print.[1] In the fighting itself, indeed—and on this point none of the other accounts substantially contradict Newport's claims—the men of the *Golden Dragon* bore themselves well, and Newport's address to them before the engagement[2] shows him to have been a leader of no mean stature. Of course the pillage of this prize more than anything else 'made' the voyage for the seamen of both ships, and not least for those who sailed the great ship home under Newport's command.[3] Even the shareholders in the venture, for all their grumbles and civil actions, must have made a highly respectable profit.

* * *

90. *John Twitt's report of Newport's 1592 voyage*[4]

A true report of a voyage undertaken for the West *Indies* by M. *Christopher Newport* Generall of a fleete of three shippes and a pinnesse, viz. *The golden Dragon* Admirall, whereof was Captaine M. *Newport* himselfe; The *Prudence* Vice-admirall, under the conduct of Captaine *Hugh Merrick*; *The Margaret* under Captaine Robert Fred; and The Virgin our pinnesse under Captaine *Henry Kidgil*: Begun from London the 25. of Januarie 1591.[5]

[1] C. Lethbridge Kingsford, 'The Taking of the Madre de Dios, Anno 1592' in *The Naval Miscellany*, vol. II (Navy Records Society, XL) prints five reports; there are also accounts given in *Principal Navigations*, II (1599), pt. ii, 194–9; VII (1904), 105–18); *Purchas His Pilgrims*, XVI (1906), 13–17; and *Monson's Tracts*, I, 278–86. These add nothing to the story as far as the activity of the *Dragon* and the *Prudence* is concerned, but several of them confirm that the *Dragon* was second only to the *Dainty* in tackling the carrack.

[2] Document 95.

[3] Document 96 below shows that John Paul was strongly suspected of embezzling valuables from the carrack as well as prize goods taken earlier in the West Indies. Merrick was also examined concerning jewels smuggled in and sold (*Cal. Salis. MSS.* IV, 242). Thomas Favell, one of the men of the *Dragon*, confessed to have taken a variety of precious stones (ibid. IV, 233–4) and mentioned among his accomplices Thomas Johns, trumpeter of the *Dragon*. John Hampton, pilot of the fleet, who was responsible for one of the main accounts of the capture, maintained that the greatest spoil was committed with the consent of Captain Newport. As for the men of the *Prudence*, they fared no worse, in all probability, since, as Kingsford (op. cit., p. 94) notes, 'The *Prudence* reached Plymouth on 3rd September; she had indigo, cinnamon, cloves, calico, and some other things; but since they were all of no great value and much of it seeming to be pillage, Drake and his fellow-commissioners thought no action necessary.'

[4] *Principal Navigations*, III (1600), 567–9; X (1904), 184–90.

[5] 1592, new style.

Written by M. *John Twitt* of *Harewich*, Corporall[1] in the *Dragon*. In which voyage they tooke and burnt upon the coast of *Hispaniola*, within the bay of *Honduras*, and other places, 3. townes, and 19. saile of shippes and frigats.

The 12. daye of Februarie An. 1591. we set saile from Dover roade, and having a prosperous winde, the 27. day of the same moneth wee fell with Cape Cantin on the coast of Barbarie, and on the 28. wee arrived at Santa Cruz roade, where having refreshed our selves some 3. or 4. dayes, we put off to sea againe, and about the 5. of March wee passed by the Ilands of the Canaries: and having a favourable wind, the 4. of April An. 1592. we fell with Dominica in the West Indies: where making stay a day or two, wee bartred with the Salvages[2] for certaine commodities of theirs, viz. Tabacco, hennes, Potato rootes, &c.

Passing from thence to a watering place on the other side of the cliffe, wee tooke a Portugall ship of Lisbone of 300. tuns, which came from Guinie, and was bound for Cartagena, wherein were 300. Negros young and olde.[3] Which ship we tooke along with us to S. Juan de Puerto rico, where we landed the marchant and one Spaniard more within a league of the towne, and landing some 20. or 30. musketiers, some 20. horsemen made towards us; but wee retired to our boates without any service done.

The 9. we lay hovering all day before the towne, the castle making a shot or two at us.

The reason why wee set the Portugall marchant aland there was, for that he hoped to helpe us to some money for his Negros there, but he falsified his worde with us, so that passing along to the Westermost ende of the sayde Iland, about some 9. or 10. leagues from the towne wee landed the Negros,[4] and sunke their ship.

---

[1] He was probably one of the men who stayed with Ralph Lane at the Roanoke settlement until the abandonment of the colony in June 1586 (*Roanoke Voyages*, p. 196). It was presumably here that he acquired the interest in 'savages' which he displays in this report. The duties of a corporal in a ship are described by Monson: 'to see the soldiers and sailors keep their arms neat, clean, and yare, and to teach and exercise them every calm day, sometimes with shot, and sometimes with false fires. In a fight he is to have an eye over the rest of the shot, that they do their parts and not to start from the place they are assigned.' (*Monson's Tracts*, IV, 58).

[2] The Caribs of Dominica, though fierce and intractable, were accustomed to bartering with Europeans.

[3] The Portuguese at this time conducted most of the slave trade.

[4] They were apparently landed at La Aguada (*Further English Voyages*, p. lxxxix, n. 3).

The 11. of Aprill we passed from thence to Mona some 15. leagues off, where we landed: there were on the Iland about 19. soules, the children of an olde Portugall, and his wife who affourded us such fruits as their Iland yeelded, viz. swines flesh, Potato rootes, &c.

From thence along wee passed to Saona, a long Iland and very fruitfull, replenished with store of wilde beastes and swine, where we landed, hunted, and trained our men.

Passing from hence Westward along the South coast of Hispaniola, wee descryed a frigat, which wee chased and tooke: wherein were 22. jarres of copper-money, being bound for S. Juan de Puerto rico, to buy wine there.

The next day we tooke 2. small frigats more, but nothing of any value in them.

The 15. of Aprill at night wee sacked a towne in the sayde Iland of Hispaniola called Ocoa, where was an Ingenio,[1] wherein we found sugar & poultrie great store, but the people had discovered our ships over night, and were fled into the mountaines. This town standeth a league from the seaside, consisting of some fortie or fiftie houses.[2] They brought us much cattell, and two wayne loades of sugar, to ransome the towne. While this action was perfourmed, Robert Freed of Harwich, captaine of the Margaret, tooke two frigats with certaine Spaniards on the other side of the bay, which came to lade sugar there at an Ingenio.

After we had here refreshed our selves, wee stode along for Cape Tiburon, where we watered: and making no stay there, about the 23. of Aprill wee left our shippes in a faire road-sted under an Iland not inhabited,[3] and with our frigats which wee had taken before, wherein wee shipped all our strength which possibly wee could affourd, leaving onely so fewe aboord our shippes as could hardly if neede had bene, have wrought them; we passed along by the sayd Iland to the Northwest part of Hispaniola, to a towne called Yaguana; where the 27. in the morning 2. houres before day we landed; but wee were discovered by

[1] A sugar mill, possibly that of Juan Caballero de Bazán raided by Langton in 1594 (see ch. XI below).
[2] Ocoa was a port of call for privateers and illicit traders, who took away sugar and hides and supplied the place with slaves (Rodríguez Demorizi, *Relaciones*, II, 131).
[3] Possibly the Ile du Grand Goâve: see p. 197, n. 8 below.

meanes of a frigat that lay laden with victuals, bound for Carthegena, the men of which frigat recovering on lande before us, gave an alarme to the towne, who were presently up in armes to the number of a hundred & fiftie horses. Wee marched notwithstanding along to the towne, having a Spaniard for our guide, where by that time the day brake, we were before the towne, where upon a faire greene making a stand, we were encountred by the horsemen having no strength of foote, but certaine few loose shot[2] which lay in a low valley at the entrie of the towne. The horsemen charged us very fiercely, but seeing they could not prevaile, brought in a drove before them of two hundred beastes or more: and so forcibly thinking to have broken our array, it pleased God to cause their cattell to returne backe upon themselves: and thus their owne device sorted out to their owne detriment. In this skirmish wee slewe their governour, a man very hardy, and of great valure. *This towne standeth from the waters side a league.*[1]

In the end, by reason of the Spaniards brags which they gave out, (as by the life of their wives and children, &c. that not one of us should goe aboord againe) a greater doubt of intercepting of us and of our boates was stroken into our captaines hearts then needed: and so for that time we retired to our boates not entring the towne, and so passed with our boates to our ships againe; where the same night our captaine determined to goe up with our shippes, but it fell so calme, that all the next day untill night we could not get up, and they having discovered us, baricadoed up their way, and conveyed all they had into the mountaines, leaving their houses onely bare and naked, notwithstanding we landed, and with great difficultie wee passed their baricados with the losse of two men at both conflicts, entred their towne and fired it, leaving not an house unburnt, being a towne of three streetes having about 150. housholds.

The same night wee passed with our boates to a small village called Aguava,[3] where we found excellent fruites of the countrey, which by reason of their cowardly brags wee also set on fire.

Being thus frustrated of our pretended voyage, we stoode for the bay of Honduras, and about the ninth of May we discovered

---

[1] As does the modern Léogane.
[2] Snipers.
[3] Guava.

in the afternoone a saile thwart of the bay of Truxillo, with whome we stood, and having a Spanish flagge out, they mistrusted us not, untill we had almost fet them up: and then wee went off with our boate, and tooke them within shot of the castle, and with our boates wee went and fet three or foure frigats which rode afore the towne, the castle playing upon us with their ordinance.

They thought some fleete had bene come from Spaine, for so they expected.[1]

Our captaine having understanding by the Spaniards, that there were three shippes more at Puerto de Cavallos, stood along that night for that place, but it fell out to bee so calme, that it was the fifteenth day of May or ever wee came there, the shippes having peradventure discovered us, stole alongst the shoare towards Truxillo, so that being voyde of that hope, we landed; the inhabitants forsaking the towne, fled into the mountaines. Wee remained in the towne all night, and the next day till towards night: where we found 5. or 6. tuns of quick silver, 16. tuns of old sacke, sheepe, young kids, great store of poultrie, some store of money, & good linnen, silkes, cotton-cloth, and such like; we also tooke three belles out of their church, and destroyed their images. The towne is of 200. houses, and wealthy; and that yere there were foure rich ships laden from thence: but we spared it, because wee found other contentment. And having taken our pleasure of the towne, as aforesayd, wee returned aboord our ships, standing backe againe for Truxillo, we discovered one of the shippes which was laden at Puerto de Cavallos: but they had espied us before, as it should seeme; for they had conveyed away as much as possibly they could ashore, and set their ship on fire; which so soone as we had discried, we made to her with our boates, and quenched the fire, and loaded up with hides the shippe which we tooke at our first comming; for she had but a thousand hides in her, and certeine jarres of balsamum: which being accomplished, wee sunke the shippe with the rest of the goods, and so stood alongst againe for Truxillo. It fell out to be so calme, that we were two and twenty dayes sailing backe that we had sailed in sixe dayes, which was about forty leagues: so that when we came before Truxillo, which was about the sixth of June, we found another of the ships there, but close under the castle, her ruther unhanged,[2] her sailes taken from her yards, &c. notwithstanding

---

[1] On this same day (9/19 May) Luis Alfonso Flores arrived at Cartagena with a fleet from Spain (*Further English Voyages*, p. lxxxviii).

[2] Her rudder removed from its hinges.

Bygate, Edward Wilkinson and Edmond Burton, mariners, bind themselves to pay to the Lord Admiral £3000. This bond to be of no effect provided that the ship engages in no piratical activities, returns its prizes to port for the payment of customs duties and tenths, etc. Dated 19 January 1591/2].

(*b*) [Hugh Merrick and John Paul, captain and master respectively of the *Prudence* of London, of 70 tons burden, which is to be set forth with letters of reprisal by Henry Cletherow, John More, Robert Cobb, John Newton and William Jones, bind themselves to pay to the Lord Admiral £3000. This bond to be of no effect provided that the ship engages in no piratical activities, etc. Dated 21 January 1591/2].

(*c*) [Henry Kedgell and Cuthbert Grippe, captain and master respectively of the *Virgin* of London, of 40 tons burden, which is to be set forth with letters of reprisal by Robert Cobb, John More, George Southwick and Thomas Gardener, bind themselves to pay to the Lord Admiral £3000. This bond to be of no effect provided that the ship engages in no piratical activities, etc. Dated 21 January 1591/2].

(*d*) [Robert Thread and James Bragge, captain and master respectively of the *Margaret* of London, of 50 tons burden, which is to be set forth with letters of reprisal by Robert Cobb, John More, George Southwick and Thomas Gardener, bind themselves to pay to the Lord Admiral £3000. This bond to be of no effect provided that the ship engages in no piratical activities, etc. Dated 22 January 1591/2].

93. The Lord Admiral contra *Robert Thread:* Thread's deposition[1]

Officium Domini contra Robertum Fridde.

RO*BE*RTE FRIDDE of Harwiche late Captaine of the Margarett of London of the age of xxxj yeares or thereaboutes sworne & examined before the righte Worshipfull m*aste*r Doctor Cesar Judge of the Admiralty uppon certaine articles[2] ministred against

[1] H.C.A. 13/30, 4 December 1592. The Lord Admiral is interested in the possible evasion of payment of tenths and in any other contraventions of the terms of the rules referred to in the bond of good behaviour.

[2] 'Articles to be ministred in the behalfe of the L*ord* Admirall Robert Cobbe and other m*er*chantes of London to Roberte Fride late Capitayne of the margarett a flyboate of London' (H.C.A. 24/59, no. 79).

We shaped our course from Florida homeward by the isle of Flores one of the Açores, where we watered, finding sir John Burgh there, who tooke us to be Spanyards, and made up unto us; with whom wee joyned in the taking the mighty Portugall caracke called Madre de Dios, and our captain M. Christopher Newport with divers of us was placed in her as captaine by the Generall sir John Burgh to conduct her into England, where we arrived in Dartmouth the seventh of September 1592.

91. *Warrant for the grant of letters of reprisal for the* Golden Dragon, *the* Prudence *and the* Virgin[1]

Master Ceasar I am contented you make oute comyssion of reprysall unto John Moore of London merchaunte & William Jones master of the Trynytye howse to set oute & furnish to the seas the good shippes called the golden Dragon of London of the burthen 90. tonnes or thereaboutes & the Prudence of London of the burthen of 60. tonnes or thereaboutes with theire pynnes the virgin of London of the burthen of 20. tonnes in warlike manner agaynste the kinge of Spayne & his subjectes and his or theire goodes under suche articles and conditions as are agreed on betwixte the Lords[2] of the counsell and merchauntes on that[3] behalfe And let this be youre warraunt for the same From the courte at Whithall the 26 of December 1591

Youre lovinge frende
C Howard

To my Lovinge frende master doctor Ceasar Judge of the highe courte of the Admyraltye.

92. *Bonds taken for the good behaviour of the privateers*[4]

(*a*) [Christopher Newport and Robert Keyble, captain and master respectively of the *Golden Dragon* of London, of 100 tons burden, which is to be set forth with letters of reprisal by Henry Cletherow and John More of London, merchants, and William

---

[1] H.C.A. 25/3 (9), 26 December 1591.
[2] MS reads 'LLo'.   [3] MS reads 'yt'.
[4] H.C.A. 25/3 (9), under dates given. Cp. document 85 above for the complete form of such bonds.

forme like unto the bosse of a bridle. These Savages were farre more civill than those of Dominica: for besides their courtesie, they covered their privities with a platted mat of greene straw, about three handfuls deepe, which came round about their waste, with the bush hanging downe behinde.[1]

The next day in the morning very early, there came a frigat of the iland of Cuba of 30. tunnes, put in by weather, which was bound for Havana, wherein were fifty hogges; to which we gave chase all that day, passing the gulfe of Bahama,[2] and about five of the clocke in the afternoone, after a shot or two made at her, shee yeelded unto us: wee hoisted out our boat, and went aboord, where we found some five Spanyards, five and fifty hogs, and about some two hundred weight of excellent tabacco rolled up in seynes.[3] We lightened them of their hogges and tabacco, and sent the men away with their frigat.

In this voyage we tooke and sacked foure townes, seventeene frigats, and two ships, whereof eight were taken in the bay of Honduras; of all which we brought but two into England: the rest we sunke, burnt, and one of them we sent away with their men. And to make up the full number of twenty, the Spanyards themselves set one on fire in the bay of Honduras, lest we should be masters of it.

---

[1] These were Calusa Indians, 'A large tribe, or confederation of tribes, on the west coast of the Florida Peninsula south of Tampa Bay and occupying the Florida Keys and most of the interior.' (J. R. Swanton, *The Indians of the Southeastern United States* (Washington, 1946), p. 101). The gold and silver which appear so plentiful must have been obtained from Spanish vessels wrecked along the Calusa coast (J. R. Swanton, *The Early History of the Creek Indians and their Neighbours*, (Washington, 1922), p. 388) and the two pieces of fine silver plate were clearly of Spanish origin. The knee ornament described is of particular interest: ornaments worn 'just below the knees' were found among the Timucua Indians further north, but in the limited reports concerning the Calusa Indians there appear few references to ornaments at all, and none to any ornaments of this type (Swanton, *Creek Indians*, pp. 387–8; *Southeastern Indians*, p. 523). The garment described by Twitt was a breechclout, but of a type peculiar to the Indians of Southern Florida. It was described by a later writer in further detail: '. . . a piece of plaitwork of straws, wrought of divers colours, and of a triangular figure, with a belt of four fingers broad of the same, wrought together, which goes about the waist; and the angle of the other having a thing to it coming between the legs; and strings to the end of the belt, all three meeting together, are fastened behind with a horse tail, or a bunch of silk grass, exactly resembling it, of a flaxen colour; this being all the apparel or covering that the men wear' (Swanton, *Creek Indians*, p. 391).

[2] The Gulf of Florida.

[3] Fishing nets.

we entered her, but they had placed such a company of musketiers under a rampire, which they had made with hides and such like, that it was too hote for us to abide, and so betaking us to our shippes againe, and standing out of the bay into the sea, wee discovered great store of shot[1] intrenched in those places where they suspected we would have landed. That night there fell such a storme of rain, thunder, lightening and tempestuous weather, that our ships were dispersed either from other. And having determined all of us to meet at a certeine Island, where wee purposed to water and refresh our selves; by meanes of the storme and other contagious weather which followed, we were frustrated of that hope.

We had lost our prize, and certeine frigats with the men. Two of our shippes went to seeke our prize and our men: and other two of us came homeward. And so we parted, not hearing either of other untill we came into England.

Our place of meeting should have beene at the Tortugas neere unto the point of Florida,[2] but the Golden dragon and the Prudence were put to leeward of this place: neverthelesse wee fell with certeine islands within the point of Florida,[3] were[4] the captaine of the Dragon M. Christopher Newport sent his pinnesse on shore with certeine shot to seeke for fresh water, where wee found none; but found the Savages very courteous unto us, who came brest high into the sea, and brought us a line to hall in our boat on shore, and shewed us that up into the land Northward was fresh water, and much golde. And one Michael Bagge of Ipswich boatswaines mate of the Dragon, had given him by one of the Savages for an olde rusty hatchet, a piece of golde wound hollow, and about the bignesse and value of an English angell, which the Savage ware hanging about his knee, with two pieces of fine silver plate, whereof one the sayd Savage gave John Locke, masters mate of the Dragon, being foureteene groats in value, for an olde knife: the other piece he gave to one William Wright a sailer, for an olde knife: which pieces of silver were in

---

[1] Refers to men, not to ammunition.

[2] Actually about 100 miles from Cape Sable, the Tortugas constituted an important landmark for ships taking the Florida Channel course homeward.

[3] This may refer to one of the more westerly of the groups of Florida Keys, or to islands closer to the mainland, towards the southern end of the western coast of Florida.

[4] [Sic.]

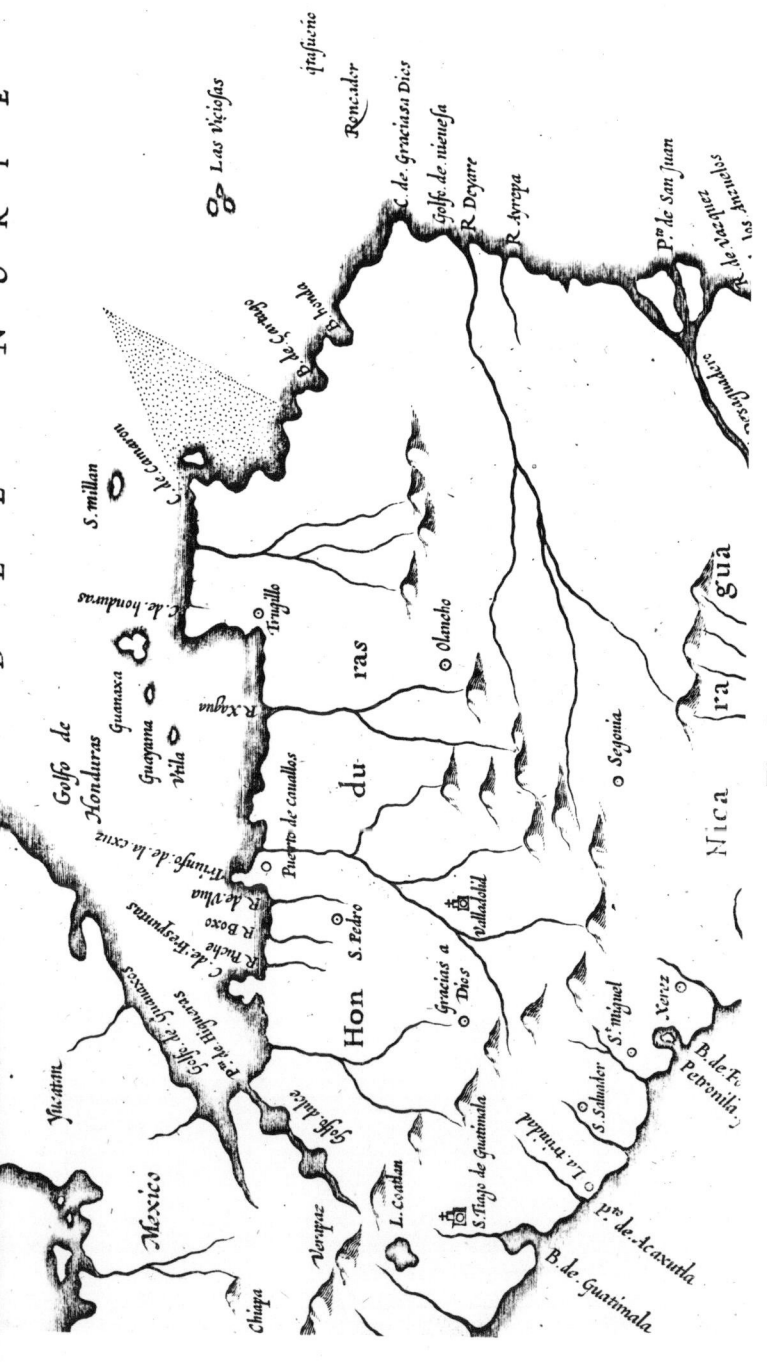

6. The Gulf of Honduras

From a map by Juan López de Velasco in the *Descripcion de las Indias Ocidentales* of Antonio de Herrera (1601)

him on the behaulfe of the Lord Admirall Roberte Cobbe & other merchantes of London Sayeth thereunto as followeth.

To the first article[1] he affirmeth that the Dragon the Prudence the Margarett & the Virgin beinge sett to sea by master Cobbe & other merchantes with lettres of Reprisall did first at Dominico[2] in the West Indies take a prize laden with negros and they sett the negros a shore at Porterico & burnte the shipp, & out of the same they had some rice & a smale provition of victualls & nothinge else. Afterwardes under the Isle Hispaniola[3] they tooke thre or fower empty frigottes & made pinaces of them & tooke them alonge with them, and at the Acoe they landed with the said pinnaces and tooke an Ingenio of sugers & broughte from thenc. aborde aboute two or thre hundreth suger loves for theire provition and made composition with the spaniardes for xx oxen not to burne theire Ingenions,[4] which oxen they receaved & soe departed. From thence they sayled to the Aguana[5] uppon the same Island of Hispaniola, and wente in with theire frigottes, & there tooke a frigott of xxx or xl tonnes laden with bredde of that Cuntrey, called Cassaba,[6] dry beefe and tallowe & thereof they tooke some parte for theire provition & burnte the reste & then wente on shore with a hundreth and ten men, and were incountred with aboute two hundreth horsemen & repulsed backe to theire frigottes after they had slayne the guvernor of the towne & some others in fighte, and thereuppon they rowed to a place called the Aguanovo not farre of[7] & burned the towne beinge a poore place inhabited by moores & spaniardes where they had nothinge but hens & victualls to his knowledge From thence they rowed to theire shipps at the Aguava[8] & by consente broughte

---

[1] 'Imprimis by charge of your oathe what shippe or shippes Frigottes Carvelles or other vesselles or pryses did you or any your Companye or Consortes take in the partes of India or elles where in this laste voyage and what severall goodes monny goulde silver plate Jewelles pearle or pretious stone or other thinges was founde in them or any of them at the takinge thereof And whoe tooke possession thereof how was it shared or devided and in whose handes doth it remayne?' (ibid.)

[2] Dominica. [3] [Sic.]
[4] Ingenios, or sugar mills. [5] La Yaguana.
[6] Cassava, bread made from the roots of cassava plants.
[7] Not identified. Thread may be thinking of Guava, which was burned, according to Twitt, after the capture and burning of La Yaguana.
[8] Presumably Guava, in which case the uninhabited island where the ships were left may have been the Ile du Grand Goâve.

them aboute to the Aguana¹ where they landed before & had the repulse, and landed agayne all theire force beinge aboute 150 men, and marched up to the towne and were encountred with, & at laste came to a parle with the Spaniardes to have them ransome the towne, which they would not for that they said they were sworne to the kinge, and thereuppon this examinate & his company entered the towne, & founde the spaniardes had caried all that ever they had into the woodes, and soe burned the towne, not gettinge eany pilladge there to his knowledge, and then marched backe to theire shippes & sayled away & directed theire course into the bay of the hondorous where under a towne of garrison called Tresillions² they chased a shipp under the walls of the towne & tooke the same beinge laden with hides and two or thre Chestes of Indico seven Jarrs of balsome,³ foure boultes of velvett & two or thre boultes of damaske & a peece of red cloth which shipp with theire ladinge they caried of into the sea and fett of two empty frigottes from the shore which they caried alonge with them, and entered further into the bay to a place called Porto de Cavallos, where they tooke a frigott laden with a thousand hides as yt was sayde, and also two or thre empty frigottes,⁴ and furwith wente a shore & tooke the towne, the people beinge fledde with most of their substaunce as yt appeared Notwithstandinge they gott there aboute xxviij Jarrs of quicksilver haulfe full or thereaboutes, vj or vij tonnes of Iron and some pilladge which was putt into the prize of hides taken before Also this examinate gott in ready money xij^{li}, and Captaine Newporte & Captaine Kedgell gott a smale quantity of plate there, and all the company had pilladge of apparell amongst them howe much he knoweth not: From thence they sayled away & overtooke a greate shippe of CC tonnes which came from the porte of Cavallos beinge laden with hides the company whereof fired them selves & shifted them selves a shore, notwithstandinge this examinate & his companye adventured to quenche the fire & with much travell & adventure slaked the fire & recovered out of the same aboute xij or xiij hundreth hides & viij fardells of

---

¹ La Yaguana. ² Trujillo.
³ Twitt says these were taken later, after leaving Puerto de Caballos, in the ship which the Spanish set on fire.
⁴ These prizes are mentioned neither by Twitt nor by the Spanish. It is most likely that Thread's memory failed him at this point.

Indico wherewith they filled upp the other two prizes taken before & sayled awaye[1] and beinge bounde to water this examinate in a storme loste the prizes, & by appoinctemente of Captaine Newporte wente to seeke them & founde them in the bay, and soe this examinate in the margarett & Captaine Kedgell in the Virgin came away for Englande. And other prizes this examinate tooke not this laste viadge nether was presente at the takinge of. And sayth he sawe noe pearles gould or Jewells that were taken duringe the viadge more then a Jewell which he hath & weareth in his hatt, nether was there eany sharinge or devidinge of eany goodes made in the viadge Savinge that this examinate founde out that two of this examinates company had gotten in money about xxx[s] which he tooke from them & gave to every one of the company xij[d] thereof.[2]

To the second[3] he sayth there were noe men of eany accompte taken in eany of the said prizes, but only mariners & of them viij were broughte to waymouth in the greate prize.

To the thirde[4] he sayth he broughte noe goodes gould silver plate pearle or merchandizes on shore at waymouthe or else where more then xij[li] in money which he spente in chardges. Savinge that all the goodes in the greate prize were landed there & inventaried by aucthority of the officers of that place. What others of his company have don he knoweth not.

To the iiij[th][5] he sayth there were noe more velvett damaske balsom or liquid amber taken more then ys before sett downe, whereof Captaine Newporte had thre Jarrs of balsome and all the damaske & velvett Captaine Merricke had two Jars of balsome,

---

[1] He completely omits reference to the second visit to Trujillo.

[2] A crew of thirty in the *Margaret* (50–70 tons) gives another indication of the total force, which cannot have been much greater than 200 men.

[3] 'Item at the takinge of the same prise what men of accompte were in the same prise or prises and whoe sett them ashore and why Came they not home with you in the prise?' (H.C.A. 24/59, no. 79.)

[4] 'Item what goodes gould silver plate pearle marchandizes or other thinges tooke you or any your Company on lande at waymouth or elles where and specifie the quantitye thereof and to whose possession or order came it and where doth it remayne or howe is the same or any parte thereof disposed?' (ibid.)

[5] 'Item what quantitye of velvet damaske Balsamon or Liquyde Ambore was there taken in any prise or pryses and howe was the same disposed and whether was there not a Jarr of Balsamon or Liquid Ambor conveyed awaye and bacon grease or such lyke putt in steade thereof by whome was it done and whoe hathe the balsamon or Liquid Ambor as you knowe or have harde?' (ibid.)

Kedgell had one Jarr & this ex*amina*te had an other Jarre which he delivered to his boy, and was stolen from him. And sayth he herde say that a Jarre of balsom was emptied in Captaine Newport*es* shippe & bacon greese putt in steede thereof but by whom yt was don he knoweth not. And more he cannot depose.

To the vth[1] he sayth he broughte in his shipp to Waymouth ten tanned hides which this ex*amina*t*es* company sould for aboute iiij^s a peece, & receaved money for them as for this ex*amina*te he sayth he soulde noe good*es* at all, nether knoweth of more to be sould then ys before declared.

To the vjth[2] he sayth he had only xij^{li} in money and a Jarre of balsome which money is spente & the balsome stolen from him & more he had not.

To the vijth[3] he sayth he gott noe more good*es* or money eyther on shore in the Indies or else where then is before settdowne.

To the viijth[4] he sayth there was noe good*es* delivered at waymouth or at eany other place into eany shipp or vessell that ever he knewe or hearde of out of the margarett or the prize.

To the ixth[5] yt was reported that a box with ringes was seene in the possession of Captaine Kedgell, but this ex*amina*te never sawe eany, nether knoweth what they were.

---

[1] 'Item what good*es* did you or any of your company give sell exchange or make awaye at waymouth or any other place, what quantitye, to what p*er*sone at what prises, and to what valew did the same extende and whoe receaved monny for the same?' (ibid.)

[2] 'Item what quantitye of the Balsome or other good*es* or mony taken in the prises aforesayde have you in your custodye or have you lefte in the custody of any other or whoe hath any of the same good*es*?' (ibid.)

[3] 'Item what quantitye of good*es* or monny more have you a shore at the In*d*yas or ell*es* where or otherwise got . . . [7 or 8 words illegible]?' (ibid.)

[4] 'Item whether did not there com one borde the margarett at waymouth where shee ryd or some other place a shippe or boate in the nyghte tyme and receaved indico Hides Salsaperill or other thing*es* into the same and howe much And what good*es* was put into the sayde shippe or boate and by whome and for whose accompte and whether were the sayde good*es* carryed and by whome receaved how often came such shippe or boate to and fro and what was the name of the sayde shippe or boate and the m*aste*r thereof w*hi*ch receaved the sayd good*es*?' (ibid.)

[5] 'Item what Jewell*es* plate pearle or other thing*es* came to the hand*es* of Capitayne Kidgell and to what valewe to your knowledge or as you have hard saye?' (ibid.)

NEWPORT'S 1592 VOYAGE

To the xth[1] he sayth he caried aboute iiij^{li} in money with him to sea outwardes bounde, on this viadge.

To the xjth[2] he sayth he broughte from Waymouth with him aboute fyve pounde in goulde which he had at hampton in his possession & shewed yt to John Taylor of Bristowe at hampton & to Richard Miller of Poole[3] uppon occasion that the said Tayler would have borowed money of this examinate, & he shewed them his money & tould them he had noe more then would cary him to London. And more gould or silver he had not nether shewed to eanye, and the same money was parte of that which he broughte from sea & ys spente in chardges since. And more he cannot depose.

94. *The part played by the* Golden Dragon *and the* Prudence *in the capture of the* Madre de Dios[4]

To the Righte Honorable the Lorde Willyam Burghlie Lorde Highe Threasorer of Englande

Righte honorable (accordinge to your Lordshipps commandemente) we have sett downe in wrytinge the moste parte of that which is affirmed conceminge the service performed by the Goulden Dragon and the Prudence aboute the takinge of the Carack moste humblie beseechinge your Honour to have consideration thereof.

Christopher Newporte Capitayne of the goulden Dragon of London, saythe and affirmeth to be true and credible that he and his Consorte came into the Isle of Flores, on the xxvth daye of Julye laste paste to take freshe water, and uppon an intended purpose to tarrye there for purchase, and that uppon the xxvjth daye of Julye laste paste Sir John Burrowes and his Fleete came *χροfer Newporte cap: of the goulden Dragon of 180 tonnes withe 81 men in her.*

---

[1] 'Item what store or stocke of monny or goulde carried you out with you at your goinge out uppon the voyadge?' (ibid.)

[2] 'Item what quantitye of goulde or silver did you bringe with you from Waymouth and whether had not you in your possession at Hampton or elles where since your comminge from Sea in reddy monny or gould the some of Two Hundreth Poundes or at leaste One Hundreth Poundes and how much monny did you showe at Hampton or elles where how came you by the same monny and what is becom of it?' (ibid.)

[3] A merchant and shipowner of Weymouth and Poole, who was interested in privateering.

[4] Lansdowne MS 115, f. 252. The claim is addressed to Burghley because he, as Lord Treasurer, took responsibility for the disposal of the prize.

ENGLISH PRIVATEERING VOYAGES

before that Ilande, and presentelie sente for this Capitayne aborde, to whome he wente, when Sir John Burrowes asked his oppinion, whether it were beste to staye there, or seeke further abroade for purchase, And that this Capitayne and Sir John Burrowes resolved to staye there, where theye stayed accordinglie, At which tyme Sir John Burrowes required this Capitayne and his companye to consorte them selves and theire shippes with him, which Consortemente was accordinglie made as by the true copie thereof herewithall delivered to your Honour dated the xxviijth daye of July laste paste appeereth.[1]

first sighte of the Carracke.

Uppon the Thirde daye of Auguste then nexte followinge, Sir John Burrowes with Capitayne Thompson Capitayne of a shipp called the Daintye, with this Capitayne (in the breke of the daye) espyed a farr of the greate Carack (whose cominge by before they expected) uppon sighte whereof, they all cutt sayle and in a shorte tyme had her in chase, And the Daintye and the Dragon (by reason theye sayled swifter then the reste) did firste incounter with her, and foughte with her a good space before Sir John Burrowes came, And that when Sir John Burrowes did come he and theye foughte with the Carack Three longe howres before any other shippes came at them, And concerninge the boardinge of her this Capitayne affirmyth that Sir John Burrowes boarded her at the Bowe and this Capitayne boarded her Thwarte the Hawse,[2] and Capitayne Thompson boarded her at the quarter, So that theis Three shippes were theye that firste boarded her,

goulden Dragons service Captein Newporte at the first bordinge the Carrack

goulden dragons hurte done in this service

And that when this Capitayne boarded her the sayde Dragons Maine sayle, and all her shrowdes were carryed awaye with the Borespritt[3] of the Caracke, and that in fighte beinge putt of againe, he retorned and boarded her under Sir John Burrowes quarter, and yett againe were putt of, so that this Capitayne was forced to putt on a newe maine sayle on the sayde Dragon which don theye with the reste forceablie boarded her againe and entred uppon her with all theire men, In which fighte this Capitayne affirmeth that Roberte Keble Master of the sayde Dragon with Three more of the sayde Dragons men were slaine oute righte

The Master of the dragon and 3 of her men slayne and more hurte in this

[1] No trace of the consortship has been found.
[2] The part of the bow in which are the hawse-holes for the cable.
[3] Bowsprit. One of the established techniques of boarding was to swing across the bows of the potential prize in such a way as to entangle her bowsprit with one's own rigging.

and divers others verie sore hurte in fighte And the same Dragon beinge a newe shipp and this her first voyadge[1] was verye sore beten toren and rente And that when the same Carack was fully wonne Sir John Burrowes placed this Capitayne for Capitayne in the Caracke under him and tooke oute of the sayde Dragon Fortye of her men into the sayde Caracke with vittells and furniture for them And that this Capitayne and his men came so home in her to Dartemouthe And that at the tyme of boardinge of the same Caracke there were in the sayde Dragon Fower skore and one men at the fighte the shipp beinge of the burden of Clxxx tonnes as aforesayde.

service and the shipp spoyled there

Newporte came home Cap: in the Carrack under Sir J: Borowes and 40 of the dragons men and 12 of the Prudence men

Moreover Hughe Merricke Capitayne of the prudence of London and John Paull Master of that shippe saye and affirme to be true and credible that the same Prudence contynewed in company with the Foresighte and other Shippes chasinge and fightinge with the same Caracke till shee was won And that before shee was won the same Capitayne adventuringe to take the Ensigne of the Poope of the Carack was thruste overboarde with a pycke and with muche adoe recovered him selfe into the Sampson and was saved and yett gave a newe assaulte and boarded her with the reste And that after shee was wonne this Capitayne putt into her Twelve of the prudence men to ayde Sir John Burrowes and Capitayne Newporte in bringinge her home And that theye came home in her and were vittelled and furnished with necessaryes oute of the Dragon And that there were in the sayde Prudence in fighte at wininge of the same Carack Fortye and Sixe men And that the same Prudence by the generalls appoyntemente carryed passengers a shore oute of the Carack[2] at Twoe severall tymes that is to saye CC at one tyme to the Ilande of Corvo and One hundreth Fower skore and Seaventene at an other tyme to the Ilande of Flores All which passengers were Three dayes aboarde the sayde Prudence and spente onelie of her vittayles.

Hughe Merrick Cap: of the Prudence of 100 tonnes with 46 men in her. their service.

Prudence imployed by the generall in carying passengers ashore

All this the sayde Capitaynes and master of the sayde Dragon and Prudence, and many more are redye to Justifie to your Honour uppon theire oathes to be verye true and muche more mighte be trulie alledged concerninge the same Twoe shippes

---

[1] This assertion may well be true, but a ship of the same name, in which the same persons were interested, is known to have been at sea in 1585 or 1586 (document 74 above).

[2] This is implicitly confirmed in document 96 below.

for further proofe service performed at the takinge of the same Caracke (yf it were not to tediouse and troblesome to your Honour) But yett yf your Lordship shall require further proofe and testimony what service the same Twoe shippes performed at the takinge of the same Carack we then referr ourselves to the reporte of Sir John Burrowes and all or any which were in the fleete at takinge her whoe by theire wordes or oathes will satisfye your Honour that nothing but truth is herein delivered.

[Signed]

χρofor newpote, Capten of the golden Dragon.
Hewgh Mericke Captaine of the Prudence.

John Loke masters mayt of the same.
John Paull master of the Prudence.

Jnº estrige his marke goner of dragon.
Richard Kayns marke the guner of the prudens.

Robarte allberrye gonners mate.

It maye please your good Lordship that we are many partenars of oure selves, and that the sayde Dragon and Prudence were sett fourthe at oure greate charges, and besydes that Twoe other shippes are consorted with them, the owners and vittellers of which Twoe other shippes muste be pertakers of what belongeth to us of the goodes of the sayde Caracke for the defrayinge of the greate charges theye were at in furnishinge and settinge fourthe of the same Twoe other shippes,[1] The Consideration of all which we humblie referr to your Lordships discretion.

Your Lordships most humble

P. Houghton
John More — Edmond Burton
Roberte Cobb — William Bygatt
George Sowthaicke — Per me Wm Jones
Henry Cletherow — John Newton
Thomas Gardyner

[Endorsed:] Proofes what servis the goulden Dragon and the Prudence performed at the takinge of the Carrack. 2. Dec. 1592.

---

[1] The only adventurer not subscribing here is Wilkinson, who in any case was interested in the *Golden Dragon*. Thus, unless there were shareholders of whom we have no knowledge, this plea is typical of the reckless disregard for fact which was so often displayed by Elizabethans involved in financial disputes. It no doubt was then, as now, virtually impossible for anyone outside a syndicate to reconstruct exactly who had contributed, and in what proportions, to a given enterprise.

9. Item what monny is owinge to you by any of the owners by youre owne deliverye what monny have any of them stopped of yours in theire handes what was the reason you delivered the same monny and whye is yt deteyned and kepte from you as you thincke.

10. Item what goodes wares marchaundizes or other thinges doe you knowe any other Capitayne Master or marryners have purloyned taken awaye or converted to theire owne use or uses the same havinge byn parte of the Weste Indye pryses or of the sayde Carracke goodes by whome and of what value as you remember.

11. Item goulde[1] ringes Cheynes silver treasure pearle pretioustones[2] or other thinges were there founde hidden in the Eves or elleswhere aboute your howse what the value thereof was whoe hid the same there and in whose handes dothe yt nowe remayne.

12. Item whether did you never saye to any person in talke with you aboute your owners troblinge you for goodes by them supposed to be of theires in your custodye that yf the hardeste fell you cold and wolde defraye the charge of your suitt and wage lawe with them with theire owne monny in your handes or what wordes did you ever use to that effecte.

[1] [*Sic.*] The word 'what' has been omitted.
[2] [*Sic.*]

vessells did you or any of your company or any of the other shippes or Pynnece (with you consorted) take in the Indyes ashore, or at Sea goinge to the Indyes or cominge from thence before the takinge of the Carracke.

2. Item what goodes wares, marchaundizes, gould, silver, treasure, pearle, pretious stones, or other thinges, were there in any shippe, vessell, or pryse by you or any of you taken, and what men of accompte were in them or any of them whoe discharged them, and whye broughte you them not home with you.

3. Item what goodes monny or other thinges were taken ashore, and broughte aboarde your shippes or any of them.

4. Item what goodes, monny, wares, or other thinges came to your handes or custodye, before the takinge of the Carracke or to your knowledge whoe ymbesselled or tooke any thinge oute of suche pryses or other thinges as you had taken before the Carracke.

5. Item whether were you not appoynted to carry passengers oute of the Carracke ashore, and whether carryed you them, And what goodes, monny, gould, cheynes Ringes, pearles dyamondes Rubyes or any other thinge did you your Capitayne or any of your company take from any of the passengers and to what value was yt as you remember.

6. Item what spices, drugges, wood or other thinges did you your Capitayne or any of your Company, take or converte to your owne use, or uses, of the Carracke goodes, and whatt broughte you home with you, and howe gott you yt home and the value.

7. Item wether did you not sell at dartmouth, or any other place in the Weste Contrye or since your cominge to London to any person or persons any kinde of spices drugges wood muske in Coddes[1] or otherwise, Amber greese Civitt goulde cheynes Ringes pearles dyamondes Rubyes or any other suche like marchaundize And to whome did you sell the same for how muche monny And what is become of the monny you made of the same.

8. Item whether was there any thinge taken from you or any of your company by any of the owners or other as supposed to be of the Carracke goodes what was yt was taken from you where by whome and of what value was yt as you remember.

[1] The natural pod or bag in which musk is found.

his muskett uppon the ennimy sondry tymes of this ex*amina*tes certaine knowledge who was gon*n*er of the said shipp.

To the vth he sayth true yt ys that the muskett which John Locke handled by often shotinge became hott & furred soe as Rob*er*te Keyball the m*aste*r p*er*ceavinge yt delivered him his peece beinge a snaphaunce[1] to continue his fighte wherewith he behaved him selfe verey stoutly and dischardged the same uppon the ennimye sondry tymes of his certaine knowledge.

To the vjth & vijth he affirmeth that as the said John Locke was busye chardginge & dischardginge his peece against the ennimy yt happened that fire fell into the pan of the muskett[2] which John Locke had in his handes of a soddayne & soe yt wente of of yt selfe, and as yt wente of the said Rob*er*te Keyball chaunced to crosse the ende of the muskett, & was shott throughe the buttocke and grevously wounded whereof he lay languisshinge aboute vj dayes & then dyed.

To the viijth he sayth he herde the said Rob*er*te Keyball say duringe the tyme he lay sicke by reason of the said wounde, that yt was a foule mischaunce & happened by misfortune & not of purpose as he well knewe, and soe acknowledged.

To the ixth & xth he sayth that all the company of the shipp generallye accompted the said facte to happen by mischaunce and not to be don of purpose, & that yt mighte as well have happened uppon this ex*amina*te or eany other of the company as uppon the said keyball at that tyme.

To the last he geveth reason of his knowledge as aforesaid.

96. *Interrogatories for John Paul*[3]

Interrogatoryes to be ministred to John Paull marryner (late m*aste*r of the Prudence in her laste voyadge to Sea in causes of Reprisall and in Consorte with the Goulden Dragon the Margarett and the Virgin) on the behalfe of Henry Cletherowe John More Rob*er*te Cobb and other marchaunt*es* as followeth viz.

    1. Imprimis what shipes frigot*es* Carvells or other vessell or

---

[1] A firelock or musket.

[2] Musgrave's explanation is that 'the cocke fell downe of yt selfe by reason the pin was worne' and this version is also favoured by Badge and Yonge.

[3] H.C.A. 24/61, no. 168.

95. *The Lord Admiral* contra *John Locke: deposition of John Estridge*[1]

JOHN ESTRIDGE of Lymehouse mariner of the age of 49 yeares or thereaboutes sworne & examined before the righte worshipfull master Doctor Cesar Judge of her majesties high Courte of the Admiralty uppon certayne articles[2] ministred on her majesties behaulfe concerninge the death of Roberte Keyball late master of the Dragon Sayth thereunto as followeth

Officium Domini contra Johannem Locke

To the first article he deposeth he knewe Roberte Keyball when he was livinge who was master of the Dragon of London for this examinate served as gonner in the same shippe And also he knoweth John Locke who was masters mate of the said shipp.

To the second he affirmeth Roberte Keyball was master of the Dragon & John Locke was his mate at such tyme as the Dragon amongst other shipps was in fighte with the Carracke whiche was afterwardes taken & nowe remayneth at Dartmouth For this examinate was gonner of the Dragon at that tyme.

To the third he affirmeth he knoweth of noe enmity that was betwixte the said Roberte Keyball & John Locke for that at such tyme as the Carricke came in sighte Xpofer Newporte the Captaine sayde masters nowe the tyme is come that eyther we must ende our dayes, or take the said carricke & wisshed all the company to stande to theire chardge like men and if eny displeasure were amongst eany of them to forgett & forgive one an other, which every one seemed willinge unto, & then the said Keyball tooke a canne of wyne & droncke to John Locke, & John Locke droncke to him agayne & soe throughe out the shipp every one droncke to the other whereby he is persuaded that all the company were good freindes one with an other.

To the iiijth he knoweth that John Locke duringe the fighte with the Carricke behaved himselfe verey valiantly & dischardged

---

[1] H.C.A. 13/30, 30 November 1592. On the same day depositions on the same articles were made by Robert Frances of Limehouse, mariner, aged about 50, a quartermaster in the *Dragon*; Edmund Musgrave of Harwich, mariner, aged about 23, coxswain of the *Dragon*; Michael Badge of Ipswich, sailor, aged about 26; and Edward Yonge of Southwark, musician, aged about 38. Their statements confirm the points made by Estridge, except as noted below.

[2] 'Articles or Interrogatories ministred touchinge and concerninge the death of Robert Keyball Maister of the shipp called the Dragon' (H.C.A. 24/59, no. 96). The substance of the articles is sufficiently evident from the replies.

certainly there were Englishmen haunting the Havana coast until about 20/30 August.¹ Clearly they hoped to pick a plum or two from the Tierra Firme or New Spain fleets, but eventually they were obliged to leave in order to avoid the hurricane season, disastrous to so many ships in the Florida Channel. The Spanish fleets did not converge on Havana until October and December of that year, having been advised to delay until the Cuban coast was clear.² Thus the English were thwarted of their real objective and had to be content with a few petty pickings. Nor were these at all plentiful, for the very numbers of the privateers helped to deter small Spanish vessels from sailing.

Indeed the English seem to have been more numerous in the West Indies this year than ever before. In addition to King, Wood, Myddleton, Lane and Newport, who between them commanded about fifteen sail, there were individual corsairs like Roberts, Kennell and Parker. Aware of each other's strength and intentions,³ such petty marauders may have collaborated when by chance they met, but it is unlikely that their operations were co-ordinated in any pre-arranged plan. They sailed independently to the West Indies, inspired, no doubt, by the success of the *Centaur* and her consorts the previous year. Perhaps too they were encouraged by the expectation that Raleigh or Cumberland or both would arrive with sufficient force to undertake a major *coup*, in which the lesser fry might with profit partake.⁴ In the event neither Raleigh's men nor Cumberland's reached the West Indies; but the bruit of their intentions was enough to scare the flotas into immobility and confine much other shipping to port. Thus of this year's West Indian privateers the only very successful one was Newport, who like a lone wolf followed his own devices—and even he found better fortune in the company of Raleigh's and Cumberland's fleets than in the Indies. Myddleton and Wood did poorly, as we have seen; King's prizes were small

---

[1] *Further English Voyages*, pp. 300–1. It was probably William Lane who wrote the 'letter full of compliments and menaces' to Texeda, for he and Geare had taken the treasure ship the previous year.

[2] Ibid., pp. xcii, 295.

[3] Cp. Barrett's revelations (ibid., pp. 294–5).

[4] Raleigh's first intention was a West Indies voyage (*Principal Navigations*, II (1599), pt. ii, 194; VII (1904), 105), and Cumberland's likewise (*Purchas His Pilgrims*, XVI (1906), 14). The latter at least was expected by the privateers according to Texeda (*Further English Voyages*, p. 300).

at Dominica. During the month of May he seems to have taken a few prizes of no great value on the Cuban coast, drifting eastwards as far as Matanzas and working back to Havana by the end of the month. Then occurred the fight with the galleys under Captain Pantoxa uncomfortably close to the Havana shore batteries commanded by Juan de Texeda, followed shortly by another inconclusive duel outside the harbour of Cabañas. It was about 5/15 June that King joined forces with other Englishmen: Wood, with the *Challenger*, the *Pilgrim*, the *Mineral* and perhaps the *Flight*;[1] Lane, leading a squadron of John Watts' ships— probably the *Centaur*, the *Affection* and the *John*;[2] Henry Roberts in the *Exchange* of Bristol, owned by William Winter;[3] and George Kennell in the *Bark Randall*, known as the *Canter*, of Weymouth, owned by John Randall.[4] After capturing the prize of wines, the thirteen sail[5] of privateers appeared off Havana about 18/28 June and shortly afterwards they cornered the vessel from Honduras at the mouth of the river Chorrera. Here, after a skirmish with galleys and a force of horse and muskets sent from the city, the English succeeded in making away with the prize, though the plate, coin and valuables, together with the crew, were safely removed ashore.[6]

This was probably the ship in which Richard Sotherey returned to England, arriving at Dartmouth before the end of August.[7] King may have followed a week later, as he states, but

[1] See ch. VI above.

[2] Monson refers to three ships (*Monson's Tracts*, II, 229) and Barrett to three vessels of 100 to 150 tons burden (*Further English Voyages*, p. 295). In September Lane, commanding the *Centaur* and Bradshawe, commanding the *Affection*, took a prize off Cape St Vincent (H.C.A. 13/30, 20 January 1592/3 and ult. February 1592/3). In December the *John*, under William Taverner, also took a prize in home waters (H.C.A. 13/30, 3 and 22 March 1592/3 and 28 April 1593; Harleian MS 598, f. 20).

[3] A prize taken by the *Exchange* reached Bristol on or before 5 July (Harleian MS 598, f. 17). The owner was probably the naval captain, son of the Sir William Winter who died in 1589. This was a Bristol family.

[4] A single-masted vessel, or smack. Bonds were taken for the good behaviour of the *Bark Randall* of 60 tons, captain George Kennell and master Thomas Smith, on 24 March 1591/2 (H.C.A. 25/3 (9), under this date). Randall was a privateering shipowner of Weymouth ('Elizabethan Privateering', p. 301).

[5] According to King. This may have included two prizes, or two more privateers.

[6] Eye-witness accounts of the fighting are given in *Further English Voyages*, pp. 304–7.

[7] Document 100 below.

tains of his day; he is first found commanding a squadron of the Queen's ships in 1576 and was knighted in 1587 while operating off Dunkirk; he again commanded a squadron in the Narrow Seas in 1588 and for many years after that remained in active and responsible service.[1] The other promoters of the expedition were three London merchants, who presumably shared ownership of the *Salomon*, for this ship sailed in Lancaster's expedition to Brazil and John More, Roger Howe and Simon Boreman are mentioned among the Londoners who subscribed to that enterprise.[2] The same three merchants were also interested in a projected cruise of the *Salomon* and the *Roebuck* in 1593.[3]

The *Salomon* was a fairly powerful ship for a privateer, armed with 26 pieces of ordnance and 90 men.[4] Her twelve-months supply of victuals was unusual, even for a West Indies cruise, the normal arrangement being to victual for six months only. The owners clearly meant business and they chose for their commander a man of some twenty-seven years who had proved his worth as a practical seaman and a fighter the previous year. For William King of Ratcliffe had been master of Carey's *Content* in 1591 and may well have written the account of her 'memorable fight' which was later to appear in Hakluyt's pages.[5]

The course of the voyage as far as the northern coast of Cuba is told straightforwardly enough by King and needs no further comment here. It must have been early in May (old style) that he rounded Cape San Antonio some three weeks after his arrival

[1] Laughton, *Defeat*, I, 25; II, 173–4; and several references to him in *Monson's Tracts*.

[2] Lansdowne MS 78, no. 59; Foster, *Voyages of Lancaster*, p. 58 (here Boreman is said to be the owner of the *Salomon*).

[3] H.C.A. 25/3 (9), 23 February 1592/3. Howe, together with one Jasper Moreman, another Londoner, also obtained letters of reprisal for the *Golden Lion*, captain William Persaye or Persett, early in 1592 (H.C.A. 25/3 (9), 26 February 1591/2 and 1 March 1591/2). Howe became a founder member of the East India Company. Simon Boreman, while resident in Seville, married Isabel de la Salde, returning to England with her and their infant son Simon in 1576. The younger Simon sailed with Lancaster in 1595, and in 1602 was captured in the Caribbean by the Spanish (I am indebted for this information to Professor Engel Sluiter).

[4] In 1593 she apparently carried only 18 pieces and 60 men (H.C.A. 25/3 (9), 23 February 1592/3).

[5] Document 38 above. He sailed as a captain in the Cadiz expedition of 1596 (*Monson's Tracts*, I, 358, 360) and is described in a deposition of 1598 as a gentleman of Ratcliffe, aged about 33 (H.C.A. 13/33, 21 June 1598). Wildes was prospective master of the *Salomon* in 1593 (H.C.A. 25/3 (9), 23 February 1592/3).

CHAPTER VIII

THE VOYAGE OF WILLIAM KING
1592

THE main narrative for this expedition was printed by Hakluyt in 1600 and there can be little doubt but that the author was the commander himself—William King. His account, reproduced below,[1] is supplemented here by three High Court of Admiralty documents[2] which fill out the story with details concerning the ships and personnel, the financing of the venture and the prizes. Further evidence is provided in various Spanish documents printed elsewhere.[3]

Howard's note to Caesar at the end of December 1592 shows that John More, Roger Howe and Simon Boreman probably intended setting forth, in addition to the *Salomon* and the *Jane Bonaventure*, a ship called the *Gertrude* and another pinnace.[4] Of these nothing more is heard, however, and in the middle of January bonds were taken from King and Wildes, captain and master of the *Salomon*, and from Richards and Perryman, captain and master of the *Jane*.[5] Ten days later the ship and pinnace set sail from Ratcliffe. In all these preliminary proceedings there is no mention of Sir Henry Palmer, who according to King was the owner of the *Jane*. Such silence need not surprise us, for men of position were sometimes reluctant to disclose their interest in a pursuit which, though legal, easily deteriorated into something less than respectable.[6] Palmer was one of the leading naval cap-

---

[1] Document 97.
[2] Documents 98–100.
[3] *Further English Voyages*, pp. 295–6, 300–1, 304–7.
[4] Document 98.
[5] Document 99.
[6] Caesar, for example, wrote in 1590 to the Earl of Hertford touching a prize matter: 'But I have had a speciall regarde to use the name of the Captayne & not of your *Lordship* in this cause,' so that Hertford's honour should not be touched, 'which is more deare to a noble man truely honorable then all the wealth of the Spanish king.' (Lansdowne MS 157, f. 30.)

and the better part of his best prize escaped him; Roberts sent a brazilman with sugar and brazilwood worth some £1700 to Bristol, but that was probably captured elsewhere.[1]

* * *

97. *The Hakluyt account of King's 1592 voyage*[2]

The voyage made to the bay of *Mexico* by M. *William King* Captaine, M. *Moore*, M. *How*, and M. *Boreman* Owners, with the *Salomon* of 200 tunnes, and the *Jane Bonaventure* of 40 tunnes of Sir *Henry Palmer*, from *Ratcliffe*, the 26 of January 1592.

The Salomon was manned with an hundred men, all mariners, and the Jane with sixe and twenty, all like wise mariners. Wee came first to the Downes in Kent, and never strooke saile in passing thence, untill we came to Cape S. Vincent on the coast of Portugall. From thence we shaped our course to Lancerota one of the Canarie islands, where we landed threescore men, and fetched a caravell out of an harborow on the South side, and from a small Island we tooke a demy-canon of brasse in despight of the inhabitants, which played upon us with their small shot at our first landing: of whom we slew three; and gave them the repulse. Thence we went to the Grand Canaria, where wee boorded a barke lying at anker: out of which wee were driven by great store of shot from the Island. From thence wee directed our course for the West Indies, and fell with the isle of Dominica about the tenth of April. There at a watering place we tooke a shippe of an hundred tunnes come from Guiny, laden with two hundred and seventy Negros,[3] which we caried with us to S. Juan de Puerto Rico, and there comming thorow El passaje,[4] we gave chase to a frigat which went in to S. Juan de Puerto Rico, and in the night we sent in our shallope[5] with fourteene men. And out of the harborow we tooke away an English shippe of seventy tunnes, laden with threescore tunnes of Canary-wines, in despight of the castle

---

[1] Harleian MS 598, f. 17.
[2] *Principal Navigations*, III (1600), 570-1; X (1904), 190-3. The use of the first person singular towards the end indicates that King himself wrote this account.
[3] Very much more crowded than the slaver Newport had captured a week earlier.
[4] Presumably the Virgin Passage.
[5] The *Jane*.

ENGLISH PRIVATEERING VOYAGES

and two new bulwarks, being within caliver shot. These two prizes we caried away to the Westermost part of the island, and put the Negros, except fifteene, all on land in a Spanish caravell which the Jane Bonaventure tooke: and we caried away one of the former prizes, and set fire on the other.[1] We passed thence by the isle of Mona, where we watered, and refreshed our selves with potatos and plantans, and so came to the isle of Saona: and from thence arrived at the mouth of the river of Santo Domingo. And as we sailed to Cape Tiburon, three leagues to the Westward of Santo Domingo we tooke a boate of fifteene tunnes, which had certeine jarres of malosses or unrefined sugar, with three men; which men with their boat wee caried with us to Cape Tiburon, which, in respect of service done unto us in furnishing us with fresh water, we dismissed. Thus contrary to other Englishmens courses we shaped ours to the Southward of Jamaica, and our shallop with 12 men ranged the coast but found nothing. Thence we ranged the three islands of the Caimanes, and landed at Grand Caiman, being the Westermost, where we found no people, but a good river of fresh water; and there we turned up threescore great tortoises; and of them we tooke our choise, to wit, fifteene of the females, which are the best and fullest of egges, whereof two served an hundred men a day. And there with stones we might kill turtle doves, wilde geese, & other good fowles at our pleasures. Thence we came to Cape de Corrientes on Cuba to water, and from thence to Cape S. Antonio, and so went over for the Tortugas, without taking of any new prize: and thence cut over to Rio de puercos on the coast of Cuba. There we tooke a small barke of twenty tunnes, with foure men and forty live hogs, with certeine dried porke cut like leather jerkins along, and dried hogs tongues and neats tongues, and 20 oxe hides. Then passing thence, within foure dayes we tooke a ship of 80 tunnes laden with hides, indico, & salsa perilla, North of an headland called Corugna: thence the current set us to the East to the old chanel. There we tooke a frigat of 20 tunnes, having certeine pieces of Spanish broad cloth & other small pillage: there continuing off the Matanças 12 dayes, with the winde so Westerly that we could hardly recover Havana in the moneth of May. Here we tooke two

Jamaica

A good river of fresh water in Grand Caiman.

Preserving of hogs-flesh.

[1] Cp. document 100 below. The wines, in a prize commanded by George Simson arrived at Rye before 25 August (H.C.A. 14/29, no. 101).

boats laden with tortoises, which we sunke, saving some of the tortoises, & setting the men on shore. Then at length we recovered up to Havana, where we came so neere to the forts, that for one houres fight they over-reached us with their long ordinance. Then came out the two gallies, having 27 banks on a side, and fought with us another houre; which for that time left us by reason of the increasing of the winde.[1] Then passing alongst nine leagues to the Westward we found out an excellent harbour, having three fadome water at the flood, able within to receive a thousand saile, where we found hog-houses, which they terme coralles, and tooke away certeine hogs and pigs. As we came out of this harbour, the weather being calme, we were incountered by the gallies, which had followed us, and fought with them three houres, oftentimes within caliver shot: but wee made such spoile of their men and oares, that they beganne to be weary, and gave us over, with their great losse. Here within foure dayes after, as we lay to the Northward sixe leagues off this harbour of Cavannas, we met with master captaine Lane, Generall of master Wats his fleet, and captaine Roberts, in the Exchange, a ship of Bristol, of an hundred and forty tunnes, and master Benjamin Wood with his foure ships which were set out by my Lord Thomas Howard with captain Kenel of Limehouse captaine of the Cantar of Weymouth. All we being heere together espied a ship of some 50 tunne, which we chased with their boats; but my shallope first boorded her, and tooke her: which had in her sacke, Canary-wine, muscadell, tent in jarres, and good store of oile in jarres. The ship we unladed and burned: the men ran on shore. Hence wee came all together, being about 13 sailes, before Havana; but passing by we gave chase to a ship of 60 tun, which entred into an harbour a league to the Northwest of Havana, which with boats was boorded, and found to be of Puerto de Cavallos in the bay of Honduras, laden with tanned hides, salsa perilla, Indico, raw hides, and good store of balsamum: and she had foure chests of gold, which they got on land before we could come to them.[3] We

The excellent haven of Cavannas.[2]

---

[1] Cp. the Spanish version, which seems to confuse this engagement with the later fighting at Chorrera and gives the impression that the galleys fought with a fleet of fourteen or sixteen privateers (*Further English Voyages*, p. 306).

[2] The modern Puerto Cabañas.

[3] The fighting is recounted in more detail in *Further English Voyages*, pp. 304-7.

brought this ship into England.¹ Thus spending a sevennight in lying off and on for purchase, and finding nothing come, I set saile for England, and arrived at Dover about the tenth of November 1592.

98. Warrant for the grant of letters of reprisal for the Salomon and the Jane Bonaventure²

Mr Cesar I am content that you make out Comission of reprisall for Symon Borman, John More, Roger Howe and company of London marchantes to sett out to the seas the Gartrude, the Salomon, and two small pinnaces³ in warlike sorte against the Kinge of Spayne, and his Subjectes in any of his dominions for recovery of goodes deteyned by him and them under such articles and conditions which are sett downe by the Lords⁴ of the privy Counsell and agreed upon on that behalfe, and Lett this be your warrant for the same. From the Court at whitehall this Last of December 1591.

Your Lovinge freind
C Howard.

To mr Doctor Cesar Judge of the Admeralty and to my servant Hareward Registre of the same.

[Endorsed]: A Commission for Simon Burman John Moore Roger Howe & Company of London merchantes to sett furth the Salomon of London of 200 tonnes William Kinge Captaine, John Wyldes master 26 peeces, 90 men victualls for xij monethes the losse 2m^{li5} to endure for xiiij monethes. An other for a Pinnace called the Jane Bonaventure of London of 30 tonnes Captaine William Richardes of Godmeston & master James Peryman 24 men, 6 peeces victualls for 12 monethes.

---

¹ Cp. document 100 below. The prize was commanded by Laurence Cocke and arrived at Dartmouth before 25 August (H.C.A. 14/29, no. 101). The parent ship in fact arrived much later, and the words 'we brought' can only mean that the prize was safely conducted home by some of King's men.

² H.C.A. 25/3 (9), 31 December 1591.

³ Only the *Salomon* and the *Jane* are mentioned in the endorsement. There is no other evidence of the existence of the *Gertrude*.

⁴ MS reads 'LLo.'

⁵ This means that the damages to be recovered by reprisal action are estimated at £2000.

KING'S VOYAGE, 1592

99. Bonds taken for the good behaviour of the privateers[1]

(a) [William King and John Wildes, captain and master respectively of the *Salomon* of London, which is to be set forth with letters of reprisal by Simon Burman, John More, Roger Howe and company of London, bind themselves to pay to the Lord Admiral £3000. This bond to be of no effect provided that the ship engages in no piratical activities, returns its prizes to port for payment of customs and tenths, etc. Dated 15 January 1591/2.]

(b) [William Richards of Goodmeston in Kent, gent., James Peryman of the City of London, sailor, and Robert Farley of Ratcliffe, sailor, the first two being captain and master respectively of the *Jane Bonaventure* of London, of 30 tons burden, which is to be set forth with letters of reprisal by Roger Howe and company of London, bind themselves to pay to the Lord Admiral £3000. This bond to be of no effect provided that the ship engages in no piratical activity, returns its prizes to port for payment of customs and tenths, etc. Dated 16 January 1591/2.]

100. Deposition of Richard Sotherey[2]

RICHARD SOTHEREY of Lymehouse mariner of the age of xxiij yeares or thereaboutes sworne & examined before the righte worshipfull master Doctor Cesar Judge of her majesties high Courte of the Admiralty concerninge the takinge of a prize by the Solomon[3] & the Jane her pinnace Sayth by chardge of his oath that he wente to sea quarter master in the Salomon of London with lettres of Reprisall and sealed[4] into the Indies where beyond the Avana nere the Isle of Cuba they mett with a spanishe shippe of aboute L. tonnes whereunto this examinate & company gave chase all the day and in the eveninge comminge nere the shore all the company in the said shipp tooke them into the boate & forsoke the shippe, soe as this examinate and company comminge on borde founde she was laden with hides noe livinge person beinge lefte on borde, which the Captaine & master

---

[1] H.C.A. 25/3 (9), under the dates given. See document 85 above for the complete form of such a bond.
[2] H.C.A. 13/30, 25 August 1592. A deposition concerning the prizes, such as was formally required for their adjudication.
[3] [Sic.]
[4] [Sic.]

caused to be manned & sent for England, and the same is arrived in Dartmouth¹ For this examinate came home in her: And he sayth the said shippe is a spanishe shippe builte of his certaine knowledge and was taken in the Indies soe as both the same shipp & her ladinge can belonge to noe others but the subjectes of the Kinge of Spaine for that noe other have trade in those partes And sayth that this examinate & company also entered the Rode of St John de Porterico in a shalloppe & there fetched furth a spanishe shippe of aboute Lx tonnes laden with Canary wynes havinge xiiij spaniardes on borde when this examinate & company entered noe² borde who for feare leepe³ over borde & gott on shore as he thinkethe, And because that shipp was verey weeke & spoyled they tooke out the wynes and putt them into an other spanishe shippe of aboute C tonnes whiche they tooke laden with negroes after they had put the negros ashore and the same shipp is also manned & sent for England but not arrived to his knowledge.⁴

[1] This was presumably the Honduras ship captured at the mouth of the river Chorrera. It was brought home under the command of Laurence Cocke (H.C.A. 14/29, no. 101).

[2] [Sic.]

[3] [Sic.] Viz 'did leepe'.

[4] The prize of wines had in fact arrived at Rye already under the command of George Simson (H.C.A. 14/29, no. 101).

CHAPTER IX

THE VOYAGES OF WILLIAM PARKER IN 1592 AND 1593

CAPTAIN William Parker himself recorded his two West Indian raids of 1596–7 and 1600–1 for publication in Hakluyt and Purchas.[1] It is a pity that we know so little of the man himself, for on both occasions he achieved remarkable results with small forces, using the technique of surprise attack with a mastery reminiscent of Sir Francis Drake. He first comes to notice, in fact, as one of Drake's captains in the 1587 raid on Cadiz.[2] A Plymouth man and a gentleman in rank, he was nevertheless not one of the regular captains of the Queen's ships, though he did serve under Essex in the other Cadiz expedition in 1596.[3] He was at this time described by Raleigh as 'sometime my servant and nowe attending on your Lordship' (the Lord Admiral).[4] The connection with Raleigh referred to here remains rather obscure. Parker, we now know, made reprisal voyages every year from 1590 to 1597, and from 1592 these voyages were always to the West Indies.[5] As a later chapter will show, he concentrated his attentions upon the region of Puerto de Caballos and the Golfo Dulce in 1594, 1595 and 1596–7, and on the last two occasions he was evidently probing for a land route to the South Sea. Thus Parker probably picked up as much information, first and second hand, reliable and unreliable, about the Caribbean and the Mainland, as any English sailor. The directions he passed on to Raleigh concerning the location of El Dorado

---

[1] *Principal Navigations*, III (1600), 602–3; X (1904), 277–80; *Purchas His Pilgrims*, XVI (1906), 292–7. Purchas misdated the later voyage, which took place in 1600–1, not 1601–2.
[2] Corbett, *Spanish War*, pp. xxiv, xxxiii, etc.
[3] *Monson's Tracts*, I, 359–60.
[4] *Principal Navigations*, III (1600), 628; X (1904), 340.
[5] For the voyages of 1590 and 1591, see Lansdowne MSS 142, f. 115 and 67, f. 190; H.C.A. 14/28, nos. 29 and 201; H.C.A. 24/60, nos. 22 and 23.

were, according to Raleigh, quite useless,[1] but Parker also obtained possession of a valuable Spanish rutter for West Indian navigation, which he likewise passed on to Raleigh.[2]

Parker was a shipowner as well as a captain, though in his earlier ventures his privateer, the *Richard*, belonged to Richard Hutchins, a Plymouth merchant. Parker presumably did tolerably well in these cruises, for he is found with his own ship in 1596, and in 1602—the year after his sensational raid on Puerto Bello—he became mayor of Plymouth. In 1606 he was one of the founding members of the Virginia Company, and in 1617 he was appointed vice-admiral of an East Indies expedition, only to die at Bantam in 1618.[3]

The documents printed in this chapter represent all that is known of Parker's West Indian voyages of 1592 and 1593.[4]

* * *

101. Report on the examination of prisoners captured by the Richard *of Plymouth, 1592*[5]

The examynacion of Anthony Martyn and others examyned before me John Sparcke merchant mayore of the boroughe of Plymouth the day and yeer heerunder written who say and confesse as followeth, to weet, they beinge shipped in a Frigott called the Katellyna of the Havana of the bourdon of xx tonnes belonginge to mathewe Luce of the Havana and the goodes also, which they tooke into her at Hattomanico[6] in the Ile of Hispaniola beinge about eight hundred hides, to be transported to the Havana, And by the way at Cape Taberon[7] were taken by the Richard of Plymouth william parker Captaine, about the xv[th]

---

[1] *Principal Navigations*, loc. cit.

[2] T. H. (Thomas Hariot in all probability) corrected his own copy (Sloane MS 2292, ff. 16–33) with one copied by John Douglas from the one given to Raleigh by Parker. Another version appears in *Principal Navigations*, III (1600), 603–13; X (1904), 280–306. See *Monson's Tracts*, II, 335; and E. G. R. Taylor, *Late Tudor and Early Stuart Geography, 1583–1650*, p. 201.

[3] *D.N.B.*

[4] All that is definitely known. It is possible that he was the 'William Finche' who raided a sugar mill at Ocoa Bay in 1592 or 1593. He was certainly off Hispaniola in both years (see pp. 240–1 below).

[5] H.C.A. 24/59, no. 139.

[6] Unidentified.

[7] Tiburon.

the Condatho[1] of thage of xix yeers thomas Andres of avero[2] of thage of xxxvj yeers and Sebastian of Tavalla[3] in Portugall of thage of xx yeers in like sorte examyned confesse and say as the above named Stephan Gonsalves hath sayd.

Interpreted by John venner of the towne
of plymoth aforsayd

[Signed] John Fenner.

John Gayer Mayore of the borough of plymoth abovesayd.

[1] Literally, the 'County'.
[2] Aveiro, Portugal.
[3] Probably Tavira.

Matthew Luce of Havana, a subject of the King of Spain, and as the same has been adjudged lawful prize to be delivered to Richard Hutchins and William Parker and their associates; therefore we order you, after inventory and appraisement of the same ship and hides and payment of tenths, to deliver them to Richard Hutchins and William Parker and their associates and to send the appraisement to us with all speed. 2 June 1592 in the 34th year of Elizabeth.]

104. *Report on the examination of prisoners captured by the* Richard *of Plymouth, 1593*[1]

The iiijth Day of June Anno Domini 1593.

An examynacion taken before John Gayer merchant mayore of the borough of Plymoth of certen spaniardes and portugalles brought into the porte of Plymoth aforsayd taken in the Indyas by the Richard of the same towne William Parker Captaine who sworne and examyned doe confesse and saye as followeth.

Stephan Gonsalves of Bayon in Galizia of thage of xxvj yers or theraboutes saith that he and his company about march last past were taken in a barcke of xxx tonnes laden with Turtells by the Richard aforsaid, in whom he remayned and was present in here when she tooke out of the harborough of Janico[2] a barcke called the St Anthony of the porte of portugall[3] without any men in here or any sayles or rother, who had in here half here ladinge of hides, which barcke the forsaid william parker did sayle with sayles of his owne & a rother[4] which he fette from the land. And also that he was with him at the takinge of a Frigott called the St Fraunces of Delinyhamo[5] of the Iland of Cuba bound for the havana with hides, whose men forsook here before they were borded & that he was brought home in the sayd shippe. Anthony Costo of the mathera[6] of thage of xxij yeers, Diego martyne of

---

[1] H.C.A. 24/61, no. 145. Nos. 146 and 147 in the same file are the interlocutory sentences of the two prizes here mentioned.

[2] Possibly the harbour of Monte Cristi, marked on De Bry's map (1594) as 'Guanique'.

[3] Oporto.

[4] Rudder.

[5] Unidentified.

[6] Madeira.

tain allegation of theirs, which allegation we wish to take and do take as read and inserted here; And that nothing effectual on the part and behalf of anyone having or claiming to have any right, title or interest in the above mentioned has been objected, elaborated, propounded or proved which does destroy or in any way weaken the case of the said Richard Hutchins, William Parker and partners on their part. Therefore we, Julius Caesar, doctor of laws, the judge aforesaid, having first invoked the name of Christ and turning our eyes to God alone and according to and with the advice of the learned men whom we have consulted in this cause, pronounce, decree and declare that the ship in question called the *Catellina* of Havana and its equipment and furniture, together with the eight hundred hides in her, captured by the said William Parker and his company with the said ship called the *Richard* of Plymouth and brought to the port of Plymouth, had pertained and belonged to Matthew Luce of Havana, subject or quasi-subject of the King of Spain by right of dominion, and did so pertain and belong at the time of their capture; and that the said Spanish ship with its furniture and the aforesaid hides were subdued and captured by the said William Parker and company with the aforesaid ship the *Richard* by lawful authority and by virtue of certain letters of reprisal granted by this illustrious court for that purpose; And we do adjudge by this our interlocutory sentence or decree, which we make and promulgate in these presents, that the ship and goods thus captured are the lawful prize of the said captors and should be delivered to them.

103. *Order for the delivery of the* Catellina *to Hutchins and Parker*[1]

[Charles Lord Howard to Sir John Gilbert, deputy vice-admiral of Devon and to John Sparke, mayor of Plymouth: as Richard Hutchins of Plymouth, owner of the *Richard*, and William Parker, captain of the same, and their associates, have given good proof before Julius Caesar, judge of the High Court of Admiralty, that the *Catellina* of Havana, together with its furniture and lading of 800 hides, lately taken and brought to Plymouth by William Parker by virtue of letters of reprisal, belonged to

---
[1] H.C.A. 24/59, no. 139. Summary. Translated. The MS is a copy.

of marche last by vertewe of his le*tt*res of reprisall, and arryved heer the xxth of this present may, w*hi*ch sayd prise by reason of leake hath wett and rotten many of the said hides. All w*hi*ch accordinge to order given in that behalf I have thought good to adve*r*tise, and doe heerby certyfye itt under my hand, yeven at plymoth aforsaid the xxvijth of may in the xxxiiijth yeer of the raigne of o*u*r sove*r*aigne Lady Elizabeth by the grace of god of England Fraunce and Irland Quene Deffendor of the Fayth &c 1592.

John Sparke maior of plymothe.

102. *Interlocutory sentence of the* Catellina[1]

In the name of God Amen, there having been heard, seen, perceived and fully discussed by us Julius Caesar, doctor of laws, legally constituted lieutenant, judge or president of the High Court of Admiralty of England and master of the Requests, the merits and circumstances of a certain civil and maritime cause and petition or matter, which before us in suit on the part of Richard Hutchins, owner of the ship called the *Richard* of Plymouth, and William Parker, captain of the same, and their associates, against the Spanish ship called the *Catellina* of Havana of twenty tons burden and eight hundred Indian hides captured in the same is proceeding and remains undecided, the party of the said Richard Hutchins, William Parker and partners lawfully appearing before us in trial and urgently pleading and claiming that sentence be given and justice be done for their party; And the whole and entire proceedings had and done before us in this cause having first been scrutinized and carefully reviewed by us; And having lawfully observed all that should be observed in this case, we consider we should proceed to the delivery of our interlocutory sentence or decree in the aforesaid cause and do proceed in the following manner: Wherefore, through what has been done, deduced, alleged, proved and likewise admitted we have discovered and clearly found that the party of the said Richard Hutchins, William Parker and partners have sufficiently and to the full founded and proved their intention as set forth in a cer-

[1] H.C.A. 24/59, no. 140 (wrongly numbered 130 in the file). Translated. Signed by Julius Caesar.

that Guiana was the main objective and that this may be taken as the first of the series of Raleigh's Guiana ventures.[1]

It is clear from Raleigh's statements that Burgh landed with a considerable force and was compelled to retire. He does not suggest that this was the occasion upon which the governor of La Margarita, Don Juan Sarmiento de Villandrando, met his death, though that event did occur in November 1593, in an encounter between a Spanish galley and a well-armed merchantman, which may have been Flemish or English.[2] Burgh seems to have arrived earlier, in July, August or early September.[3] The Spanish, as usual, exaggerate the strength of Burgh's shipping and manpower, but the governor put up a most effective resistance and compelled the English to retire before they had progressed far towards Asunción. In this minor conflict several Englishmen were killed and others wounded.[4] Nothing further is known about this voyage, except that the *Golden Dragon* arrived home before December 10, severely battered.[5]

*   *   *

---

[1] That the Guiana project was already occupying Raleigh's thoughts from the beginning of 1593 has been suggested by Edwards (*The Life of Sir Walter Raleigh together with his Letters*, 1, 159). As the voyage is barely mentioned by Raleigh himself, it would seem that it achieved nothing as far as Guiana was concerned.

[2] It has been suggested by V. T. Harlow, in his edition of Raleigh's *Discoverie of Guiana* (pp. lxxxiv, 22), that this incident (Venezuela Papers, Additional MS 36316, ff. 54–9) was the one involving Sir John Burgh, to which Raleigh twice referred. This is clearly a mistake, though it led to the right conclusion—the dating of Burgh's voyage in 1593.

[3] The Spanish report printed below (document 108) suggests early September, but another reference, apparently to the same event, places it four months before mid-November (Venezuela Papers, Additional MS 36316, f. 61). Announcing the recent death of Sarmiento, the report continues: 'four months before, an Englishman having sent four hundred men to lay waste this town, the most gallant gentleman [Sarmiento] compelled them to withdraw to the shore with the loss of many men, and to embark. Thus he delivered this island of your majesty's without risking any of his own men, except one, who rashly advanced into the enemy ranks and was killed.'

[4] Raleigh's estimate of sixteen lost is higher than the Spanish estimates. Some of the English probably died of wounds later. Among those killed ashore was one of the captains—presumably Kedgell or Wally.

[5] Document 107 seems to indicate damage from storm or from heavy fighting.

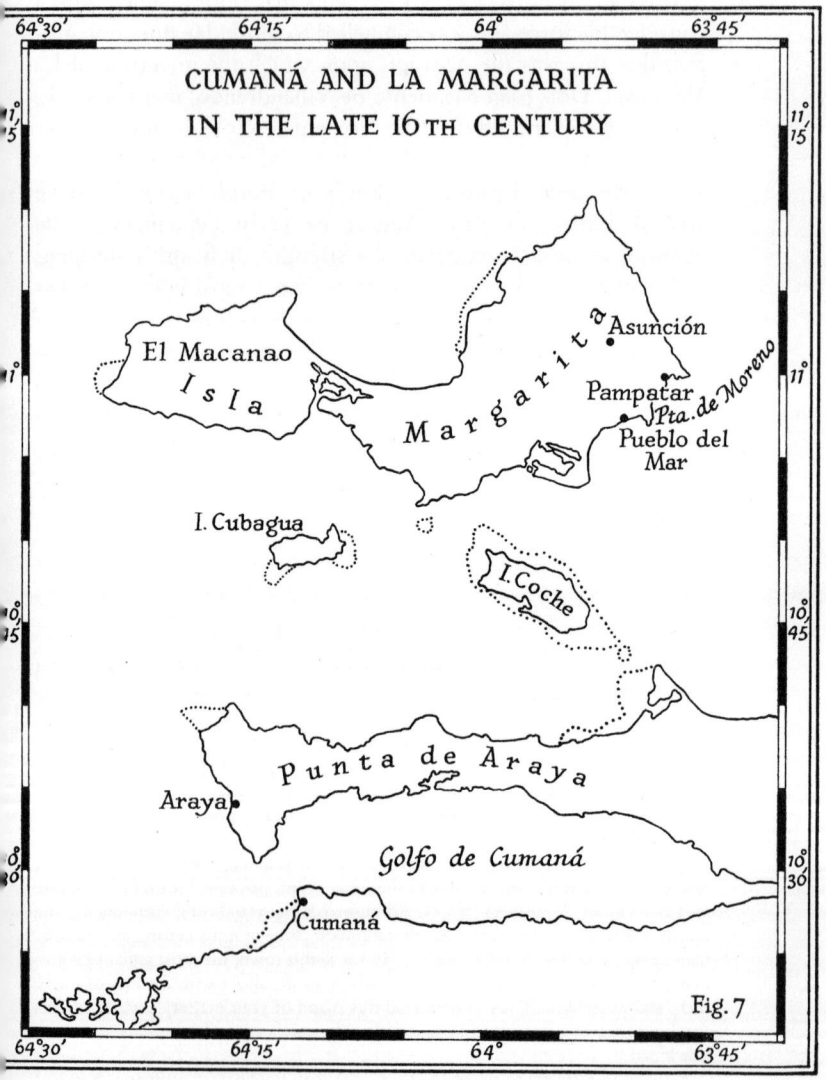

Fig. 7

attempted the Island.'[1] Later Raleigh again referred to the incident in his *History of the World*: 'Sir *John Borrowes* also, with a hundred *English*, was in great danger of being lost at Margarita, in the *West-Indies*, by having the grasse fired behinde him; but the smoke being timefully discovered, he recovered the Sea-shore with the losse of sixteene of his men.'[2] Sir William Monson also made two brief references to the voyage in his *Naval Tracts*: first, 'Sir John Burgh took a town in the island of Trinidad in the West Indies, and Sir Walter Ralegh another after'; secondly, '1595. Sir Walter Ralegh to Guiana, no profit at all; and the year before Sir John Burgh with the like success.'[3]

The documents published below show that the voyage took place in 1593. In March of that year letters of reprisal were obtained for the *Roebuck*, 300 tons,[4] to be commanded by Sir John Burgh, with John Bedford master;[5] the *Golden Dragon*, 150 tons,[6] captain Christopher Newport and master Andrew Shillinge; the *Prudence*, 100 tons, captain Thomas Wally and master Thomas Warne; and the *Virgin*, 50 tons, captain Henry Kedgell and master Cuthbert Grippe.[7] This fleet represents a combination of Newport's 1592 backers (More, Cobb, Southwick, Cletherow and other London merchants) with Sir Walter Raleigh, the owner of the *Roebuck*, who also provides the expedition with its general commander.[8] Monson is inaccurate as to the date of the voyage, and it is possible that he also mistook its objectives; nevertheless Burgh did visit La Margarita in 1593, as the Spanish records prove, and as he did so it is not unlikely that he also visited Guiana and Trinidad. What is more, the fact that this was in some sense a Raleigh venture makes it possible

---

[1] *Principal Navigations*, III (1600), 636; X (1904), 363.

[2] Book IV, ch. 2, p. 198 (1614 ed.).

[3] *Monson's Tracts*, II, 227, 230.

[4] This was the ship built by Raleigh and employed against the Armada, when its tonnage was given as 300 (Laughton, *Defeat*, I, 343; II, 326). Another ship of the same name belonged to Cavendish.

[5] Master of the *Moonlight* in her 1590 voyage (*Roanoke Voyages*, pp. 581, 648, etc.). He was then aged about 23.

[6] Estimates of her burden varied from 90 to 180 tons (documents 91, 94, 106, 107).

[7] Kedgell and Grippe held the same positions in the *Virgin* in Newport's 1592 voyage.

[8] The venture was probably financed out of the profits on the *Madre de Dios* prize goods, in which Raleigh, Burgh, Newport and Newport's backers all shared.

CHAPTER X

THE VOYAGE OF SIR JOHN BURGH
1593

Sir John Burgh, a younger son of William, the fourth Lord Burgh of Gainsborough, and a brother of Thomas, the fifth Lord Burgh, Lord-Deputy in Ireland, was born in 1562 and spent his early manhood soldiering in France and the Low Countries. On his return to England he became associated with Sir Walter Raleigh and was appointed by him in 1592 to command the land forces in the expedition which resulted in the capture of the great carrack. Soon after this, early in 1594, Sir John Burgh was apparently killed in a duel with John, the eldest son of Sir Humphrey Gilbert.[1]

Mystery, therefore, has long surrounded various brief references to a voyage to Guiana, Trinidad and La Margarita, which Burgh is alleged to have made in 1594. Raleigh first mentioned the attack upon La Margarita in his account of his first Guiana voyage, where he stated: 'for that he [Lope de Aguirre] there [at La Margarita] slew Don Juan de villa Andreda, governour of Margarita, who was father to Don Juan Sarmiento, governor of Margarita when sir John Burgh landed there, and

---

[1] *D.N.B.* and pp. 187–8 above. The only material referring to the duel is in S.P. Dom. Eliz. ccxlviii, f. 162. Here are given, without explanation, copies of the letters of challenge that passed between Sir John Burgh and Mr John Gilbert in London in March 1593/4. The first is a letter of challenge from Burgh, in which he refers to an earlier challenge, allegedly evaded by Gilbert. The latter now accepts, warning Burgh that 'the tyme of my depertupe for the low cuntries from hence is very shorte'. From these five letters the cause of the duel does not emerge, and Gilbert professes himself ignorant of it. Burgh, who stabbed the messenger that carried one of Gilbert's letters, must have been frantically enraged. His references to Gilbert as a 'young puppy', etc., make it practically certain that this was Sir Humphrey's eldest son John, now aged about 22 or 23, who was heir to his uncle Sir John and a nephew of Sir Walter Raleigh. He was naturally one of Raleigh's protégés, sailing with him to Guiana in 1595 and to Cadiz in 1596, where he was knighted. Burgh and he may have quarrelled over the spoil of the *Madre de Dios*, or over something connected with this West Indies venture of 1593.

105. *Warrant for the grant of letters of reprisal to Sir John Burgh.*[1]

After my hartie Comendacions. whereas Sir John Burghe knight hath obteined Leave to goe to the seas with certeine Ships to be imploied by him against the kinge of Spaine and his Subjectes, you shall therfore make Comissions unto him for such ships which he shall name unto you for the recovery of goodes deteyned by the said kinge of Spaine, and his Subjectes under such articles and conditions which are sett downe by the Lords of the Counsell, and agreed unto on that behalfe. and this shalbe your warrant for the same From Hampton Court this 27. of January. 1592.

your lovinge freind
C Howard

To master Docter Cesar Judge of Admeralty
and to my Servant Hareward Registre of the same.

106. *Bonds taken for the good behaviour of Burgh's ships*[2]

(a) [Sir John Burgh and John Bedford, captain and master respectively of the *Roebuck*, of 300 tons burden, which is to be set forth with letters of reprisal by Sir John Burgh, John More, Robert Cobb, Henry Cletherow, George Southwick and others, bind themselves to pay to the Lord Admiral £3000. This bond to be of no effect provided that the ship engages in no piratical activity, returns its prizes to port for the payment of customs and tenths, etc.]

(b) [Christopher Newport and Andrew Shillinge, captain and master respectively of the *Golden Dragon*, of 180 tons burden, which is to be set forth with letters of reprisal by Sir John Burgh, etc., bind themselves to pay to the Lord Admiral £3000. This bond to be of no effect provided, etc.]

(c) [Henry Kedgell and Cuthbert Grippe, captain and master respectively of the *Virgin*, of 50 tons burden, which is to be set forth with letters of reprisal by Sir John Burgh, etc. bind them-

---

[1] H.C.A. 25/3 (9), 27 January 1592/3.
[2] H.C.A. 25/3 (9), 3 March 1592/3. Summary. For the full text of such a bond see document 85 above.

selves to pay £3000 to the Lord Admiral. This bond to be of no effect provided, etc.]

(d) [Thomas Wallye and Thomas Warne, captain and master respectively of the *Prudence*, of 100 tons burden, which is to be set forth with letters of reprisal by Sir John Burgh, etc. bind themselves to pay to the Lord Admiral £3000. This bond to be of no effect provided, etc.]

107. *Appraisement of the* Golden Dragon[1]

An appraisemente and valuation of the Golden Dragon & the tacle aparell & furniture thereunto belonginge made by aucthority of her ma*jes*ties high Courte of the Admi*ral*ty at the requeste of the wor*shipful* ma*s*ter Peter Haughton one of the Sheriffes of the City of London: henry Cletherowe: & John Moore of London m*er*chante*s* by Thomas milton[2] Thomas white[3] w*illia*m hill maryn*ers* Thomas Bodman Thomas Groves, Edward Stephens shipwrightes the xth of December 1593 as followeth.

Inprimis we the said appraisers diligently
   viewinge the hull of the said shipp
     beinge by estimation of the burthen
     of 130 tonnes and without eany maste*s*
     savinge a bad foremaste & a Jewry
     maste doe esteeme & valewe the same   Cxlv^{li}

It*em* an old drabler an old bonnett an old
   mysen sayle an old topp sayle and an old

---

[1] H.C.A. 24/61, no. 51. It is not known why this appraisement was made. Were it not that the document is clearly dated 1593, appearing in the file among documents approximating to it in date, there would be good reason to connect it with the claim for a share in the carrack goods (document 94 above), particularly in view of the nature of the damage suffered on that occasion and the appearance of Houghton among those requesting the appraisement (he is known to have been interested in the 1592 venture, but his name is not otherwise connected with that of 1593). As the matter stands, it must be assumed that the *Dragon* did sail with Burgh, and encountered either a severe storm or a very powerful enemy. In any case she was home by 10 December 1593. The appraisement is of considerable intrinsic interest. For unusual terms not explained here, see document 19 above.

[2] Captain of the *Prudence* of London in 1585 (H.C.A. 25/1 (4), 27 July 1585).

[3] Captain of the *Amity* of London 1589–92 ('Elizabethan Privateering', pp. 229–30).

foresayle with a remnant of canvas we valewe at	vj^li		
Item a newe maine course & a bonnett eaten with Rottes	vj^li	xiij^s	iiij^d
Item two demiculveringes, vj sakers, vij minions & iiij^or fawcons of iron with the carradges wayenge togeather xij tonnes & xiijC waighte we valewe at viij^s per C makinge in the whole	lxi^li	iiij^s	
Item two ankers one lackinge a stocke	vij^li	xiij^s	iiij^d
Item thre old cables we appraise at	xvij^li	vj^s	viij^d
Item two boates ankers wayenge by estimation		xxiij^s	iiij^d
Item xxxj old muskettes whereof viij wante stockes at 3^s 4^d per peece	v^li	iij^s	iiij^d
Item thre olde hargubusshes a crocke[1] whereof one wanteth a stocke		ix^s	
Item xiij pistolls some havinge broken stockes	iij^li		
Item fower Iron targettes		xxxvj^s	
Item 1456 pounde waighte of powder at [5^d?][2] per pounde	xxix^li		xxij^d [3]
Item lxij crosse barre shott xj langringe shott & CCxx rounde shott & lxxij rounde shott more of Iron we valewe togeather	iiij^li	ij^s	
Item xxiiij old latten cartradges[4] & v formers[5] of woode		xx^s	

[1] The harquebus-à-crock was a caliver, the gun being suspended from its rest by a hook (*croc*).
[2] MS obscure.
[3] [*Sic.*] 1456 lbs. at 5d. per lb. would make £30 6s. 8d.
[4] With a casing of thin metal.
[5] 'The gunner's term for a small cylindrical piece of wood, on which the musket or pistol cartridge-cases are rolled and formed' (Smyth, *Sailor's Word-Book*).

Item xiij old springes & foure old
 ladells for ordinaunce					x^s

Item one broken bill & xv shorte pikes			iiij^s

Item haulfe a hundreth waighte of leade			iiij^s

Item one pease pott, xj muskett moldes
 & thre broken staves					xvij^s

Item ix tacles with old ropes for the peeces		x^s

Item a greate copper kettell & a smale kettell   iij^{li} x^s

Item thre peeces of waste clothes olde
 an old auncient[1] & an old flagge			iij^s

Item a Catt[2] for the shipp of wood &
 Iron & iiij old woodden boules				iiij^s

Item vij bundles of match spoyled with salte
 water							xij^d

Item two croes of Iron vij old lanternes,
 haulfe a hundreth base shott[3] and ten shivers
 of wood with brasse cockes[4] fyve pounde of
 sayle twyne vij old cumpasses, thre old
 runninge glasses we appraise at			xx^s

Item xxxj old rusty swordes xxv old bandeliers,
 two takles for ordinaunce and fower soundinge
 leades with rigginge ropes old & not
 serviceable						iij^{li}
			Summa—ijClxxxxix^{li} xiiij^s x$^{d\,5}$

[1] Ensign.

[2] 'The cat is a short piece of timber over the hawse, to which is fastened a great hook of iron to trice up the anchor from the hawse to the forecastle' (*Monson's Tracts*, IV, 48).

[3] Bases were guns of about 1¼" calibre, firing shot of some 6–8 ounces (Corbett, *Spanish War*, p. 322, 332).

[4] A shiver, or sheave, is 'the wheel on which the rope works in a block' (Smyth, *Sailor's Word-Book*).

[5] The sum should read £299 15s. 10d. This is a low figure for a ship of the burden of the *Dragon*, even taking into account her battered state.

In witnes whereof we the said appraysers have hereunto sett our handes the day & yeare above written.

108. Deposition of Alonso de Ulloa de Toro[1]

At San Lucar, Sunday, at six in the evening of the thirteenth day of the month of February in the year one thousand five hundred and ninety four, Señores Dr Pedro Gutierrez Flores, member of His Majesty's Council and president of the House of Trade with the Indies, situated in Seville, and Don Francisco Tello de Guzman, treasurer thereof, two flyboats having just anchored, said to have come from Santo Domingo in the Indies, gave order to Alonso Perez, sheriff of the said House of Trade to go and inspect them and to bring before them the master of the flyboat called the *Nuestra Señora del Rosario* and the pilot of the other flyboat called the *Nuestra Señora de Esperanza* and other mariners, who took the oath in legal form and deposed, each one, as follows.

The said master, who said that his name was Alonso de Ulloa de Toro, having taken the oath in legal form as aforesaid, and being questioned: Said that.....[2]

Item he said that at the beginning of October of last year, 'ninety-three, a frigate from the province of Caracas arrived at the port of Santo Domingo, bringing letters from the governor and private persons for the president [of the *audiencia*] and other residents, with news that three English galleons, of as much as four hundred tons each, had arrived a month before in the port of Pueblo del Mar in the island of Margarita and landed four hundred men with the intention of sacking the city of Asuncion (there being no other) in that island. They had a Portuguese for guide. It was before daybreak. They began to march towards that city. The governor of the island, Don Juan Sarmiento de Villandrando, had already been informed about these galleons and was ready to receive them in the port of Pampatar, where he supposed

---

[1] A. de I. 740–7–36. Indiferente General 742. 2 *pliegos*. Original. Translated. The Council of the Indies writes to the King, enclosing this record of an examination conducted by the House of Trade (it had been sent to them by the House of Trade). A transcript of the whole of the present document exists in the Venezuela Papers, Additional MS 36316, ff. 73–84.

[2] The first part of the deposition does not concern Burgh's voyage.

they would anchor. As soon as he heard that they had landed at Pueblo del Mar, he advanced on them, and a little after they had begun their march he fell upon them with the local defence force. Deponent does not know how many there were. It was then after daybreak. They killed a captain and some other English and wounded others and compelled them to re-embark. Some of the men of the island were also wounded. Antonio Muñon, accountant of the island of Margarita said the same; he was in Santo Domingo and after this event had received a letter from the island, in which it was said that another English ship had passed there and captured two men in a canoe, one of whom they tortured to find out where the pearl-fishers' camp was. They landed men at night, taking the same prisoner with them for guide, and caught the negroes and their overseers off guard. They seized more than a hundred negroes and all the boxes of pearls and re-embarked. Later they returned most of the negroes to their owners in exchange for ransom. The pearls they took in the said boxes were worth some five thousand pesos.[1]

Asked if the governor of Margarita was killed in the encounter with the English and how many were killed and wounded on each side and whether there were any important persons among them, deponent stated that there was no news that the governor had been killed.[2] On the contrary the report was that he had conducted himself like a very good captain and that there were not more than four or five wounded. He does not know who they were. Of the English, the aforesaid captain was killed; he was a very valiant soldier and in command of one of the galleons. The English dead were two or three men. He does not know how many were wounded, but it was said that there were wounded. The enemy re-embarked immediately.

Questioned as to the further doings of the ships of the English, whether they had attacked Cumana or other places and whether they had stayed to winter in the Indies or disembogued through the channel[3] to return to their country, deponent states that he does not know whether they attacked Cumana or other places or

[1] This second incident was of course Langton's raid—cp. pp. 236–83 below.

[2] The interrogators are clearly trying to establish whether this was the occasion upon which Sarmiento had met his death. In fact it was in November that he was killed—cp. above, p. 228.

[3] The Florida Channel, presumably.

ports, nor does he know what became of them. He knows nothing else about this matter.[1]

109. Report of Francisco Gutiérrez Flores concerning Sir John Burgh[2]

A corsair who passed by this island stated in Cumana that Don Juan de Amburgo, an Englishman who was here last year, was fitting out with the intention of returning to this island to accomplish what he then attempted, and that he is bringing a strong force.[3] I have endeavoured to strengthen the island by closing all but two roads which afford the best positions from which to offend the enemy. I hope in God for a happy outcome.

[1] Two shorter depositions, which add nothing to the master's statement, follow.
[2] A. de I. 54-4-8, Santo Domingo 186. 1 *pliego*. Original. Extract. Translated. Francisco Gutiérrez Flores is reporting to the King, 28 May 1594, being acting governor of Margarita, by the appointment of the *audiencia* of Santo Domingo, after the death of Sarmiento. The remainder of the document refers to the constant danger from privateers and the need to protect the island from attack.
[3] Gutiérrez Flores repeated this information in two later reports, rendering the name Don Juan de Anburs (A. de I. 54-4-6, Santo Domingo 184, 28 February and 17 March 1595).

CHAPTER XI

THE VOYAGE OF JAMES LANGTON
1593-4

THE Earl of Cumberland's privateering ventures have for a variety of reasons attracted considerable attention from historians, but what is usually known as the seventh voyage—that of the *Anthony*, the *Pilgrim* and the *Discovery* in 1593-4—has never been examined in detail. The narrative printed by Purchas[1] is evidently a contracted version of Richard Robinson's account of the voyage, a copy of which is reproduced below.[2] Either version provides a clear outline of the events and makes it unnecessary to rehearse them here. We can, however, in the light of a substantial body of fresh Spanish evidence, obtain a more intimate view of some of the episodes and register more precisely the impact of the expedition.[3] Some further information about the prizes taken is available from English sources.[4]

James Langton, the general commander, was a man well trusted by the Earl, who preferred him to William Monson for the leadership of his 1595 expedition, writing of him: 'I have left Langton the commander who, I know, if they meet anything, will have it, or I shall never see him.'[5] Again in 1598 he placed Langton in command of the flagship on the return voyage from Puerto Rico.[6] Such confidence appears to have been well placed, for Langton emerges from the Spanish records a figure worthy of respect. When there was fighting to be done, his men did not lack leadership; and he could not only write to an enemy commander in the elaborate manner of chivalry, but talk with petty traders in Spanish. One of the Spaniards described him as 'a

---

[1] *Pilgrims*, IV (1625), pt. iv, 1146-7; XVI (1906), 18-22.
[2] Document 110 below.
[3] Documents 112—21 below.
[4] Document 111 below and Harleian MS 598, ff. 28-9.
[5] G. C. Williamson, *George, Third Earl of Cumberland*, p. 146.
[6] Ibid., p. 178.

Juan Caballero de Bazán, through his steward Anton Catalán at the Ocoa sugar mill, was by now completely compromised. His first interest was to save his estate, or as much of it as possible, and for this he would readily make any concession to the English. Material offerings of sugar, honey, kids and the like would of course be received; but information was also valuable. In this case, however, Langton appears to have wished to convey information rather than to obtain it: this, at any rate, is the most likely explanation of the curious intrigue carried on by the Portuguese pilot, Diego Pérez.[1]

Pérez had established contact with Lope de Vega Portocarrero, governor of Santo Domingo, in December 1592, when he had written to him avowing his loyalty to the Spanish and Catholic cause.[2] When Pérez reappeared in Hispaniola at the end of 1593, the governor, in spite of some stirrings of suspicion, decided to take Pérez's information as reliable and duly reported it to Spain.[3] As the Spanish later realized, Pérez's intelligence concerning impending raids by Cumberland and Drake was simply fabricated.[4] In the light of these known facts, Anton Catalán's letter to his employer, Juan Caballero de Bazán, purporting to reveal that the English had detected their pilot's treachery, looks like yet another device for deceiving the Spanish. It was clearly necessary to give the governor some convincing evidence of Pérez's loyalty to Spain, and what better evidence could there be than a first hand report that the English were about to hang him?—particularly if that evidence were to be found in a letter ostensibly not intended for the eyes of the governor. What better messenger than Alonso González, who would certainly open the letter, particularly if Langton himself took pains to impress upon the messenger the grave importance of delivering the letter to the right person.[5]

The unfortunate owner of the plantation alleged in his letter to his steward that he had previously been plundered by English privateers in two different years—once by a Captain William Finch of Plymouth.[6] In his later statement before the judges, however, this part of the story became garbled and he now

[1] See documents 114–16, 119, 120.
[2] The translation of this letter is given in *Further English Voyages*, pp. 302–4.
[3] Document 114.
[4] Document 120.
[5] Document 116.
[6] Document 118.

LANGTON'S VOYAGE

from dwelling, and of the inconclusive exchanges, literary and military, at Rio de la Hacha.[1] The lesson was one which emerges again and again from the activities of the English in the Caribbean in the nineties: that places like Cumaná and Rio de la Hacha were quite capable of defending themselves against privateers, unless they were taken by surprise.

The next sphere of operations was Hispaniola. After making a clockwise circuit of the island, Langton plundered the coast east of the city of Santo Domingo, marching inland five leagues to raid Gregorio de Ayala's sugar mill about the middle of December. That month and January he spent in the area, providing his ships with supplies, adding ransom money and loot to his prize goods and 'loitering along that shore as safely as though it were his own country, because the very inhabitants there, whom he was despoiling, afforded him protection.'[2]

From his strategic position at Point Caucedo, on the eastern side of Santo Domingo Bay, he kept that city virtually blockaded for two and a half months, lying many a day athwart the harbour itself and capturing no less than nine vessels.[3] Meanwhile his pinnace ranged westward of the city to Ocoa Bay, where there were further estates to sack, and where his men learned of the wreck of the *Edward Bonaventure*, with its thirty-one guns, and of the frigate the Spanish had sent to salvage the ordnance. The Spanish seem to have been successful in salvaging and hiding most of the guns, which eventually reached Santo Domingo safely and went to strengthen the defences of the town; but their other expedition, in the early days of February 1594, was less fortunate. Its intention was to capture the English pinnace in Ocoa Bay, while Langton remained at Caucedo Point. At first all went well, and the pinnace was taken by two Spanish frigates; but the very next day Langton, who had been warned of the attack, intercepted the captors before they reached Santo Domingo, recaptured the pinnace and took prize the two frigates.[4]

---

[1] Document 113. The English lay off Rio de la Hacha three days—15–17/25–7 September.

[2] Document 120. The details are usefully summarized in document 119; and compare document 110.

[3] Document 120. See also A. de I., 53–6–15, Santo Domingo 81: City of Santo Domingo to the Crown, 20 May 1594.

[4] See documents 110, 115, 116, 119, 120.

good-sized, reddish man, with hair long in the old fashion, some thirty-five years of age,' and added, 'Captain Langton is the leader to whom regard must be paid.'[1] Francis Slingsby, the young captain of the *Pilgrim*, was a son of Francis Slingsby of Scriven and Mary Percy, only sister of the seventh and eighth Earls of Northumberland. Like Langton, he was one of Cumberland's following, and is found again in his service on the Puerto Rico voyage, as captain of the *Consent*.[2] Many years later, in 1619, it was he who read to Lady Anne, the Earl's daughter, the narratives of the Earl's voyages, prepared and compiled at her orders.[3]

This expedition also had the advantage of being piloted by Antonio Martín, a Spaniard who had been a canoeman at La Margarita, and it was no doubt he who provided the information necessary to make the raid on that island a success.[4] The loyalty of such adventurers was always dubious, but this very fact could be used to advantage, and in the case of Diego Pérez, the Portuguese pilot, Langton used it to considerable effect. The masters of the *Anthony* and the *Pilgrim* were respectively John Paul and John Dix.[5]

The expedition consisted of the 120-ton *Anthony*, the 100-ton *Pilgrim* and the pinnace *Discovery*. It appears to have been well manned and equipped, as might be expected of the Earl of Cumberland, but it was not unusually powerful for a privateering venture and its outstanding success must be accounted for by the combination of good leadership, good intelligence and good luck.

The first stage of the voyage, on the Pearl Coast, was moderately rewarding. The Spanish sources add little to our knowledge of the raid on La Margarita itself,[6] but do give details of the reverse at Cumaná,[7] on which the English narrative refrains

---

[1] Document 118. In the same document it is stated that Langton had been in Santo Domingo with Drake. His name is not mentioned in the lists of officers for the 1585 voyage, but he presumably went as a junior officer.

[2] Williamson, *George, Third Earl of Cumberland*, p. 178.

[3] Ibid., p. 21.

[4] This was presumably the notorious pirate who joined the English ships off Santo Domingo in 1590 (*Further English Voyages*, pp. 250–6).

[5] Harleian MS 598, ff. 28–9. John Paul had been with Newport in the West Indies in 1592, when they had visited Ocoa and Caballos (see ch. VII above).

[6] Document 108 above refers briefly to it.

[7] Document 112.

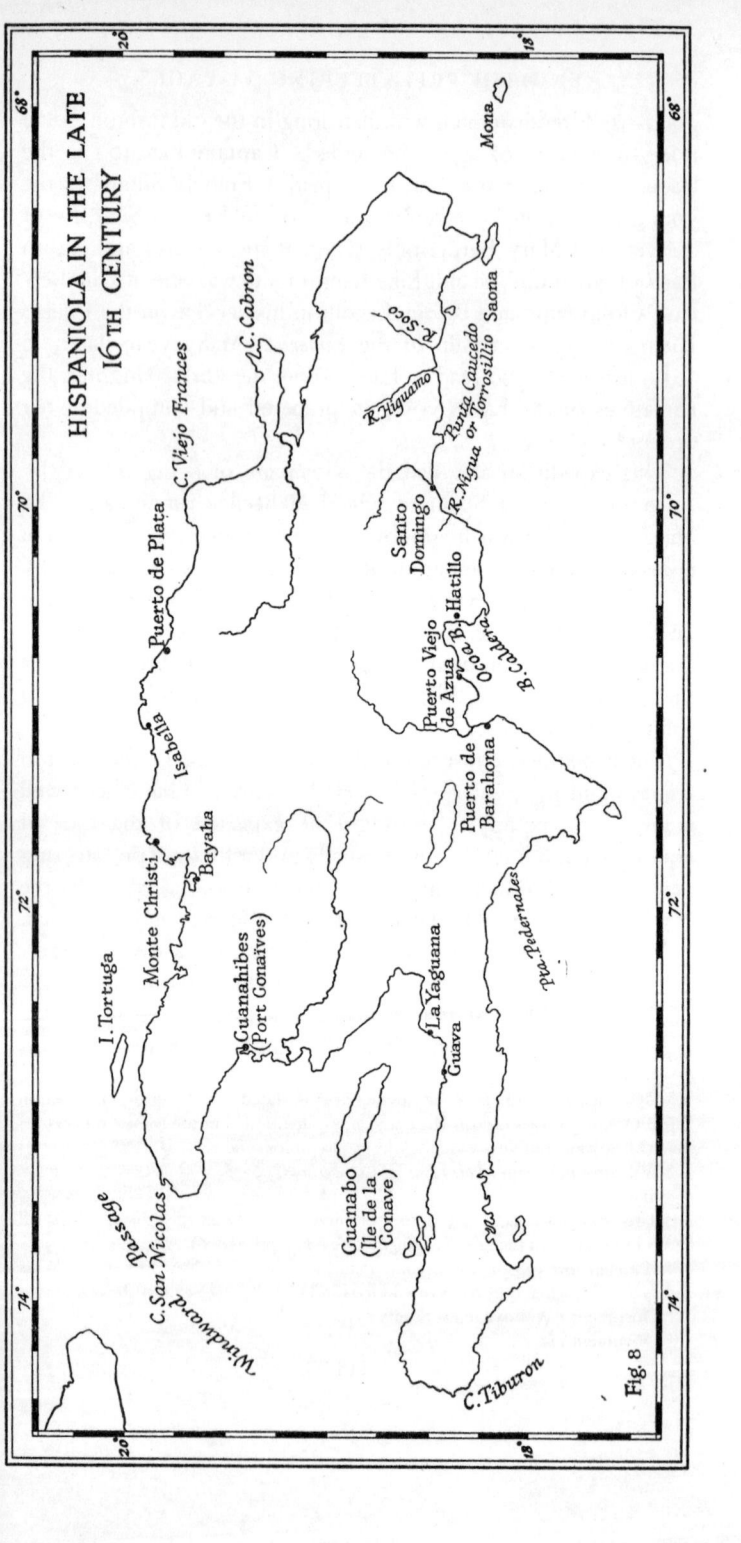

three Leagues from the water side.[1] But because the wealth of that place consisted most of Pearle which was so Portable a Comoditie, That if they should be discovered never so little before their Landing, they should be assured to finde nothing of value there. It was resolved therfore that they would Land in the Night, and so surprize them before they could convey those Shortt ends. To effecte which it was thought fitt to make the Eastermost part of *Margarita* as so to keepe out of sight of the Shoare untill the Evening, and then to make all the Saile they could to be in with the Shoare by Midnight or soone after, that then takeing their Boates they might Land and so surprize them in their Sleepe when they least suspected an Enemie and had no leisure to convey or hide their Riches.

And because it was unknowne at which of these *Rancheryas* they then remained. It was resolved to search the Eastermost first and so along westwards, if they failed there, knowing well (by reason of the Trade-Winde blowing there it was not possible to come from the west to the East[2].

Which Designe was putt in Execution accordingly, But when they Landed found the Towne Emptie and not one Creature in it. and so returned againe aboord their Shipps frustrate of that nights hopes: From thence with their Boates and Pynnaces went to search the next *Rancherya* (which was not above two Leagues) to see whether their Fishing was there or no. Commanding the Shipps to abide there returne. And when they came thither found that also destitute of people. And being then on Shoare, bethinking what was fitt to be done in this Case, doubting that either they were or should be discovered and so prevented of their Expectacion, espied a small *Canoa* from the *Island* of *Tortuga*s directing her course Streight to that Towne. This gave them some Comfort hopeing to have intelligence by them where the *Rancherya* was, and also good advise how to Compass the takeing of it. And to this ende lodged the Men close behinde the Houses, that they might Land before they were discovered, otherwise they would have rowed away, and given Intelligence to the prevencion of this Designe, In this *Canoa* there was one Spanyard and two Indyans, who little Expecting to have founde such Company to Entertaine them came boldly on Shoare and

[1] This refers to Asunción.   [2] [*Sic.*]

LANGTON'S VOYAGE

his lordshippe as he was determined before his comeing foorth of England dispatched awaie the *Anthony* the *Pilgrime* and the *Discoverie* in hope to make a voyadge there.

The *Anthony* a Shipp of one hundred and Twentie Tunnes[1] with Seaventie men in her was Commanded by Cap*tain* Langhton. *Antonio Marrino*[2] a *Spanyard* the *Pylott* in her who had lived long in those Indies, and was well acquainted with diverse Portts and places there and did Faithfullie Endeavour to make good the same according to his promise.

The *Pilgrime* a Shipp of about One hundred Tunnes with Fifty Five Men in her was Commaunded By Captaine *Francis Slingsby*, wherin was one *Diego Perrus*[3] a Spanyard for Pilott but not altogether So well acquainted in those parts as Antonio Maremo was.

And the *discovery* his Lordshipps owne being but a small Pynnace of Twelve Tunnes.

After they had don those Reverences accustomed at Sea to his Lo*rdshi*pp and the rest of his Fleet on the Coast of Spaine with vollies of great and small Shott of all parties, They Shaped their Course to the Southward. First for the Islands of the *Canaries* and then for the Islands of the *Antillas* in the *west Indies*. And the [ ][4] fell with the Island of *St. Lucya*, where and at the Island of *Matinyno*[5] they Stayed about three dayes to water & Refresh themselves, and to advise what Course to take from thence for the performeing of their intended voyadge, where it was agreed that they should first attempt the takeing of the *Rancheryas* of the Island of *Margarita*.

W*hi*ch *Rancheryas* are the Pearle fishing places of the said Island, containeing Six or Seaven severall villages wh*i*ch they inhabitt for that purpose but not above one of them at once: And when their Fishing doeth faile there, they remove to another place, and so the rest by Course, as they finde it most Convenient for them, haveing emptie houses alwayes ready standing for that purpose. And for more safety of the Pearle there gotten they Monethly carry them to the Towne of *Margarita* scituate about

---
[1] G. C. Williamson (p. 118) cites Robinson for a figure of 250 tons.
[2] Martino.   [3] Pérez.
[4] A gap of half a line in the MS.
[5] Modern Martinique. Here they captured a Portuguese caravel, which they took with them to Punta de Araya (document 112).

More important, however, was the impact of the voyage upon the Spanish, coinciding as it did with the depredations of several other privateering fleets. In Santo Domingo the authorities frankly admitted that he had kept the city beleaguered for two months and more and plundered with impunity the coast eastwards to Rio Soco and westwards to Ocoa. Worse still was the 'dealing and trading with these English,' which 'was so general and was conducted with such impunity during the time they lay off this coast that great damage has ensued to the *res publica* and business in general.'[1] Nor did the Trujillo report attempt to conceal the gravity of the blow at Puerto de Caballos: 'This affair has been very deeply felt throughout the country.'[2] Add to these the considerable success at La Margarita, and it is clear that Langton did all that could be expected of a small privateering venture: he made a thorough nuisance of himself.

* * *

110. A report of Cumberland's seventh voyage[3]

The Seaventh voyadge.

The Seaventh voyadge of the right hounorable the Earle of Cumberland to the West Indies in the years of our Lord 1593 and 1594.

buttons of gold set with emeralds, but these goods were not valued. The *Pilgrim*'s prize contained 821 raw hides, 115 tanned hides and 3 tons of blockwood, together valued at £570. These valuations were made in Portsmouth in May and June.

[1] Document 120.
[2] Document 121.
[3] This document is reproduced by kind permission of Lord Hothfield. It constitutes one section of a MS volume, now kept at Appleby Castle, entitled: 'A BRIEF RELATION of the severall voyages undertaken and performed by the right honorable GEORGE Earle of CUMBERLAND in his owne person, or at his owne charge, and by his direction against the King of Spaines fleetes territories & Dominions faithfully collected out of the Relations observations and Journalls of severall credible and worthy persons Actors and Commaunders under the said noble Earle in his severall voyages and Expiditions.' This volume is not that referred to by G. C. Williamson (*George, Third Earl of Cumberland*, pp. 24–5), which was compiled by one Richard Robinson, but is evidently a very imperfect copy thereof. It is obvious that Purchas must have used the original or a copy for his version of the voyage, contracting it quite drastically.

referred to a 'Captain John' and a 'Captain Philip Fiche'.[1] These persons cannot be identified with any certainty, but we may hazard that 'Philip Fiche' means 'William Finch', or 'William Fricke', or William Parker of Plymouth, who was certainly on or near the Santo Domingo coast in 1592 and 1593.[2]

It was probably in middle or late February that Langton relieved that coast of his unwelcome presence, thus fulfilling Juan Caballero's forecast[3] that he would tack back and forth there for a couple of months, to catch the canoes from the Pearl Coast or ships due from New Spain and the Azores; and, again as forecast, he moved south. Jamaica yielded little, and most of that little was captured by Frenchmen on its way home. Thus John Yonge's comment, that the prizes so far had been small and of little value, was not far from the truth.[4] The voyage had doubtless inconvenienced the Spaniards, but had brought no great material reward.

So from Jamaica the *Anthony*, with a frigate in her company, made first for Cape San Antonio and then for the Gulf of Honduras, where, off Puerto de Caballos, they dealt a shrewd blow at the enemy's communications and the flow of treasure. The English and Spanish accounts of the fighting,[5] which closely correspond, provide an interesting picture of the more serious kind of privateering action. The result was a distinct triumph for Langton and his men; they took the best of what there was in the seven ships and brought it away in the enemy flagship. Once again their hopes of treasure were disappointed, but it was a substantial cargo and made the voyage well worth while. Cumberland is usually said to have lost heavily by his expeditions, but on this one at least he must have made a handsome profit.[6]

[1] Document 117.
[2] Document 141 shows that 'Fricke' was a corruption of 'Parker'. But Newport was certainly at Ocoa Bay in 1592, and the reference to a captain who had lost one hand also suggests Newport (document 117 below).
[3] Document 118.
[4] Document 111.
[5] Documents 110 and 121 respectively. There are other references to the incident in documents 127, 140 and 141.
[6] Harleian MS 598, ff. 28–9 provides a record of the prize-goods, compiled in order to assess the Lord Admiral's tenth. The *Anthony* and her prize contained: 4333 Indian hides, raw and tanned, 57 chests and 64 bags of indigo, $6\frac{1}{2}$ tons of blockwood, six chests of sugar and 23 lbs. 8 oz. of pearl, together valued at £5340. The *Pilgrim* contained 4 chests of sugar, 7 lbs. of pearl, an ingot of gold and 9

drew upp their *Canoa* and begann to walk about their busyness, But when they were come so Farr on the Shoar as that they were without possibility to recover their *Canoa*, the Ambush seized and surprized them to their great Amazement: But the Captaines willed them not to Feare, promiseing them that they should receive no harme if they would faithfully assist them in the discoverie of the *Rancherya* then inhabited, and advise, or direct them the best way to surprize the same. To whom (the Spanyard being a Man of good discrecion) answered that for safety of his Life, he would deale truely with them, and told them that the presente Anchorya inhabitted by them was Five Leagues to the Westward, and that if they should goe by water assoone as their Boates should come about such a poinct they would bee discovered, and by that Meanes the place suddainly acquitted and emptied of all thinges of value: If they should goe by Land it was a very sore and long March in so hott a Clyme. And that there was in the Towne at least three hundred Spanyards and *Negroes* well armed whom he thought to strong for them. These things being thus delivered the Captaines entered into Consideracion and consultacion what was Fittest to be done in this Case.

To goe by Lande was thought the hopefullest waie, though the most dangerous, Wherupon they began to Examin the Estait of Men and Municion for the performance therof. In their Boates there were not above thirty Eight men, wherof some eight or Nyne were to goe along in those Boates to meet with them at the *Rancherya*. The *Anthonyes* Company Company[1] brought no Municion with them, but what was in their Flaskes and Bandeleers: From ye *Pilgrim* ther was brought about Fifteene poundes of Powder, with Match and Bulletts proporcionable besides what every Soldier had in his Flask and Bandileers. And notwithstanding the Former difficulties, ther rested yett one more of as great importance as any of the reste, That the shipps Stayed to the Eastwarde of them, expecting their comeinge againe that night, knowing that they were not provided either of Munycion or Victualls to stay or performe any matter of Consequence. And that if they proceeded they assured themselves in[2] must be in all likelyhood Five or Six dayes before they could recover their Shipps: And that the Shipps knowing their small force and

[1] [*Sic.*]   [2] [*Sic.*]

doubting that they might be Cutt of and themselves then weaklie Manned wanting the Captaines, their boates and best of their men might be made Instruments by the Spanyards to betraie them: And so either to Shape their Course for *England* or For some other place of the *West Indyes*.

Yett notwithstanding all these difficulties, knowing that *Fortuna audaces adiuvat*, they resolved to putt themselves to gods proteccion and to try their Fortunes on the Lands Journey, The Boates were commanded then to rowe along the Shoare and not to goe about that poinct till the Evening were come, and then to make what speed they might And the two Captaines with Eight and twenty men with their Armes and one to Carry that Little Municion they had began (by the direccion of the Spanish Guide) to march towards the Rancherya.

The day began to grow exceeding hott neither did they finde any water to refresh themselves in all this long March, untill they came within halfe a Myle of the R*ancherya*: in somuch that many of the men began to Faint and desired rather to be killed there, than to stirr one Foot further. Amongst which one Mr *Thomas Cholmley* who was in the Pilgrim fainted so much that if he had not found favour in Carrying his Armes he had beene left behinde: All these difficulties overcome they at last came to the said *Rancherya* soone after the day was gone: where they determined, that (notwithstanding their small Numbers) they must assault the Towne in three places at once least they might grow to a head in other places of the Towne if they should be assailed but in one: which resolucion was accordingly effected; The Spanyards little dreaming of an Enimie so nere them upon their First Entrance said: *Away with this Jesting* thinking it had beene the Governour of the Towne with a false Alarme to se how they would take it. But they were quicklie made beleive ther was no jesting meant; So that they then made all haste to quitt their houses, and gitt furth to the Woodes to save their Lives, there to take upp their Armes for their defence: whose personall harmes were not so much desired as their Estaites, Nether did they desire to take prisoners haveing so Few to Guard them, besides the dainger that the Enimie might by that Meanes discover their weakness in Makeing Escapes, and Encourage the Spanyards to make new Attempts upon them: Their Strength and Number being enough to have resisted three tymes so many assailants Notwithstanding so bravely did this small company bestirr them, that in small tyme they were wholly Masters of the Towne, makeing sure their Guardes, the better to gather together what wealth the place afforded: W*hi*ch (besides the Pillage the Soldjers gott) was not above the value of two thousand poundes in Pearle.

The Spanyards weapons were broken all that could be found least they should have drawne to a head against them. The Spanish guides by Negligence made an Escape and knew well the Number of them. The Hightowne[1] was well known could not in Fower and twenty houres come to annoy them. In the morneing after they had gotten all those things there found they drew to their Boates, and in them went aboard the *Canoaes* their Fishing for Pearle, who were all rideing hard by the Towne, with great Oysters in them, w*hi*ch they had gotten the night before: Here they began to refresh themselves with some Victualls gotten in the Towne haveing not Leisure to doe it all the night before: But now (this dainger by Gods Providence beyond Expectac*i*on overcome) It imported them to look diligently after their Shipps, who (not without reason findeing them so long absent) had cast all those doubts formerly spoken of, Nether had they above two dayes victualls in their Boates, if they should have missed them: But the shipps very Carefully came on Slowly to the westward, least they should overpass them, and about the 5th day after returned aboord their Shippes: Of w*hi*ch good fortune they were all very glad: Then did they come with their Shipps before the Towne and did ride there and willed them either to Ransome their houses and their *Canoes* or else they would come a Shoare and burne both: Now that they had their Forces altogether they haveing lost most of their Armes and knowing what they had Attempted with so few men did condicend to give two thousand *Duccatts* in Pearle for the Ransome of their Towne and Canoes: W*hi*ch being accepted and performed they departed: But now they had so fully discovered themselves *Carvills* of adviso went all the Coast along to give Inteligence of them: So that wheresoever the[2] came they found them already upon their Guardes to receive them. From thence they went to Cumeana a Towne upon

---

[1] Asunción.   [2] [*Sic.*]

the Maine not farr from *Margarita* with purpose ther to Land, but found it too hott and so returned againe aboorde their Shipps not without some loss:[1] From thence all along the Coast of *Terafirma* until they came to the *Islands* of *Aruba Carresao*,[2] where they Landed and refreshed themselves with Fresh water and victualls: From thence they went to the River *De Hache*, thinking to have taken that Towne and came to Achour[3] with their Shipps in the Road Shipped their Men into their Boates and Rowed towards the Shoare, wher they found the Enimie all ready in Armes to receive them, and had inteligence, that they had carryed all their Goods into the Mountaines, with purpose if they found not themselves strong enough to retire also thither spedyly, so that it was thought fitter to reserve their Men for some more hopefull service, then to hazard them for gaineing Empty houses: they returned aboord, Shott some great Ordynance into the Towne and weighed Anchour and sett saile for the *Islande* of *Hyspaniola*:[4] where the [   ][5] they came to *Cape Tyberoun* being the Southwest Cape of that Island: From thence they went to the Bay of St. Nicholas, (where the discovery being formerly lost about the *Islands* of the *Canaries* came to the Fleet, and not long after by reason of her Leakyness was cast off and her men taken into the other Shipps) thinking to have ridd there some tyme for Feare of the *Hirrocano*: which *Hurrocana* is a violent strong winde, and tho it come not every Yeare, Yett when doeth come is most comonly in November and December and is so furious that no shipp is able to resist the violence therof unless in very good harbours.

Here they had not remained above a Fortnight or three weekes but Impatient of their Idleness sett saile againe, and plyed all the Northside of *Hispanolia* to the Harbour of *Porta Plat*[6] and others where there was Little done worthy the Relacion: From thence they went to the *Islande* of *Mona* upon the Easter most part of *Hispaniola*, and so along the Southside of *Hispaniola* to the Island of *Sabona*[7] where they watered againe: where because it was in an Extraordinary Manner, and that it may hereafter be

---
[1] Document 112 gives a fuller account.
[2] Curaçao.   [3] [*Sic*.]
[4] For more detail see document 113.
[5] Gap of three or four words.
[6] Puerto Plata.   [7] Saona.

beneficiall for Men to know how to supply themselves in such cases, was, as hereafter is described. The *Island* of *Savona* is a very Low Flatt *Island* destitute of any Spring and to the Sea side a very fine Small Sand. Here not twenty Paces from the Wash of the Sea may be digged a hole some three foot deepe and knocking furth both the Heads of the Hoggshead being sett therin upright as out of a Well might asmuch Freshwater be taken as could be needfull: Nether could this water be any other then the Sea water Soaking through the Fyne small sand w*hich* had purged it selfe of the Saltness therwith. From thence they went to the River of *Soco* about Five Leagues to *Eastward* of *St. Domingo*, there tooke their boates and went in the night upp the River about Fower Leagues, where they Landed at an East Anchour[1] and suddainely surprized it with most of the people in it, an *Eastancha* is as it were a Country villadge, where the great men have their servants and Slaves to keepe their Cattle make their *Cassada* bread dress their Ginger and their fruites, keepe their Powltry and divers other services: being there possessed of their *Negroes* they came to Parley with them to make offers for the Ransome of their houses from burneing, and to restore them their *Negroes* againe, by whose Labour and Industry they had their great profitt. Upon this condic*i*on they agreed to give the Flesh of Thirty Beives and a good Quantitie of Cassada and such Fruits as the *Eastancha* yeilded, w*hich* was accepted, For that nothing else could be there expected, then supply of victualls. Beife will not keepe in those hott Countries above Fower & twenty houres, unless first salted and then dryed in the Sun being first cutt into two Sides like Bacon without a Boane left in it, and not a peice of Flesh left thicker then ones hand but must be stortched[2] with a knife, then must be rubbed Over with salt and remaine about twelve houres and after dryed in the Sun: So that Fower hott dayes drying will save it sufficiently: Other *East Anchaes* were ther taken upon the same River, w*hich* did Contribute the like provic*i*ons, From thence they went upon another River called *Marracava*, where ther was an *Ingenia* of *Sugars* w*hich* they took away for their provisions and caused the owner therof One

---

[1] Spanish *estancia*.
[2] Scorched, in the original sense of 'flayed'. The 'boucan' of the buccaneers was made in much the same way.

Gregorio Ayala to Ransome the same from burneing,[1] Thence went to the Mouth of the Harbour of *St Domingo* and ryd there at the East side of the same at a Poinct called the *Torrosillio*[2] to intercept any shipping should come from that harbour. here came the Serjeant Maior of the Towne aboord the *Pilgrim* upon (pledges given) to treat for the Ransome of some Prisoners remaineing with them: with whom came an *English Man* of Capt(ain) *James Lancasters* company who had lately comed into those partes out of the *East Indyes*, being one of Capt(ain) *George Reymardes* Fleet, whose shipp was newly cast away, a litle to the Westward of *St. Domingo* nere a place called the *Acoa*,[3] and in the Meane tyme they went betweene this and the River of *Soco* diverse tymes to Fetch those provisions of Beife and *Cassada* and other things which had beene prepared for them. Also whiles they abode there the[4] Fished with Sieve in the Mouth of that River and comonly made one Draught in the Morneing and the other at night, and tooke two kindes of Fishes wherof one Sort in the Morneing and the other in the Evening drawing all in one place, the one sort of Fish was a Mullet the other like a Sea Breame.

Understanding of two Ingenars more to the westward of *St Domingo*, the one called the *Acoa* the other *Saphasapea*[5] they went thither: and though they had left no Sugars nor anything of worth in them (as doubting their Comeing:) Yett were they content to Ransome them from Burneing with such provisions as they could gitt,[6] and so they returned to *St Domingo*: to which place their Boates went & came diverse tymes, but were at last observed by the Spanyards in *St Domingo*, from whence the Enimy Manned furth two *Carvills* full of soldiers and sent them foorth in the night privately to make after their Boates, and overtakeing them after some Fight tooke them, who by Chance weere recovered, The Shipps beareing in after them without any such distrust overtook them before they could goe cleare away with

---

[1] For more details see documents 117–19 below.
[2] Point Caucedo.
[3] Ocoa Bay. See below, p. 284, n. 5.
[4] [*Sic.*]
[5] Unidentified.
[6] The Ocoa mill belonged to Juan Caballero de Bazán: see documents 116–18 below for more detail.

their prizes, and fell in Fight with them, took those *Carvills* and their men and Boates againe, which rejoyced them more, then if they had taken a great purchase. There was in these *Carvills* two Fryers and in the Fight amongst others one of the Fryars was killed.[1] After this haveing Inteligence that they had saved the *Ordynance* of *Capt(ain) Lancaster his Shipp* they went to seeke them, and found drawne about halfe a Myle from the Waterside Fowerteene greate Peices of Iron all Calvering demi Calvering and *Sacar.* and Fower *Falcons* of *Brass*, the Iron peices were too heavy to deale with being so Far from the Waterside but the Fower Brass *Faulcons* were brought awaie with them. There also they tooke a very Fyne Friggat (being drawne upp under the Bowes of the Trees to be conceallced from them) which was manned and brought for England, and after made diverse voyadges for his Lordshipp.[2]

After a long tyme spent aboute *St Domingo* and no great profitt resolved to seek a New fortune in some other place and went to the *Island* of *Jamiaca* where they found two Barques laden with hydes & *Canifestula* which because they were not able to Mann them both took asmuch of the Goods as they could into their owne Shipps, and into one of the Shipps manned & sent fore England: But it was their ill fortune to be taken by a *Frenchman of Warr* in their voyadge homewards,[3] and left the other, hopeing that it might be a purchase after to some other Englishmen. From thence they went to the *Island* of *Cuba* to *Cape Corientes* and *Cape St Anthonio* to expect some Shipping comeing for the *Havana*, but none came: And now haveing spent about Eight Monethes in the Contry and made a good saveinge voyadge for his Lordshipp spent most of their victualls and growne weak of Men, haveing distributed some into their prizes, and lost divers in their severall Fights and conflicts (though Few or none by Sickness) they beganne to resolve to spend some tyme there and then to returne for *England, The Anthony* and the *Frygott* went to the Bay of of the *Honores*[4] *The Pylgrim* to the

---

[1] The incident is described in detail from the Spanish side in document 115 below; see also document 120.

[2] Cp. pp. 296–7 below. The prize was presumably the *Frigate* of the ninth voyage, which was cast away on her return from the Puerto Rico venture in 1598 (Williamson, pp. 142, 179).

[3] See document 111 below. [4] Honduras.

Havana, and lay there some Few dayes to Expect What should come thither, But findeing nothing and their victualls almost all Spent, the Winde Faire for England, and the Company weary and weak of their long voyadge, Sett Saile, and disimbogeing the *Gulfe* of *Bohamma* came for the *Islands* of the *Assores* and then arrived in the Harbour of *Plymouth* the Fowerteenth day of May haveing spent a full yeare and more since their departure thence.

The *Anthony* and the *Frygatt* went into the Bay of *Hundoros*, and when they were come to *Porticavalio*[1] within Fower Leagues descried seaven Shippes rideing in the Rode, wherof the Least was Ninescore, the winde came of the Shoare, so that they could not gitt in that night, And after they were comed to Anchour there, there came to them A *Canoa* with a Spanyard in her and hailed them. To whom *Antonio Martino* made Answer in Spanish and bidde y^m come aboord which they did. To whom he related[2] that they did looke for a Shipp and a *Frigatt* from y^e *Hauvana* and told they thought this had beene they, The Nexte Morneing they had the Sea turne, they sett saile and came in and Anchored within Caliver shott of the Spanish Shippes and mored their *Shipps* a head and Sterne and bent their Broad sides unto them and there they fought all that same day with those seaven Shipps and all that night now and then a Shott, And so about Sunsett Captaine *Langhton* sent the Boat and the *Shallopp* into the Shoare, From whence they brought a Frigatt of Twentie Tunne, The next Morneing betyme they Fyred the Frigatt and with their Boates purposed to bring her Cross the *Admyralls Hales*[3] But when they saw their comeing they all runne into the Boates and gott a Shoare. But the *Admyrall* she lett Slipp, For all the other Six Shippes unhanged their Rudders and Carryed them a Shoare, that none should be able to Saile the Shipps away if they should be taken. The Spanyard that came aboord of them told them that if they had stayed but Eight or Nine dayes longer, the kinges Treasure had beene brought thither out of the River of *Dulcye* to be brought home in these Shippes: And so they Loaded the *Admyrall* of the best out of all the Shipps and sent a Shoare to know whether they would Ransome the Rest, which

---

[1] Puerto de Caballos.
[2] The Spaniard told the Englishmen.
[3] Hawse: i.e. under her bows.

Vides, proprietary governor and captain-general for the King in this province....

I, Don Francisco Gutierrez Flores, lieutenant of the governor and captain-general in this city of Cumana, state that it is to my interest to establish by the testimony of witnesses ... the facts set forth in the questionnaire which I herewith present....

II. If they know that two ships manned by English enemies of our holy catholic faith, with a shallop and pinnaces, having raided the pearl fishery at El Macanao in the island of Margarita, word reached Cumana on the thirtieth day of the month of August last that they intended to come to this city and burn it. This was learned from certain Portuguese who accompanied the English of their own volition and were acquainted with all this coast. Because Governor Francisco Vides was absent, engaged in the conquest and pacification of the Indians of Cumanagoto province (in accordance with the agreement he entered into with his majesty), as soon as this news arrived, I, acting as his lieutenant, mustered all the people, reviewing the men and inspecting their arms; and I caused lookouts to be posted at Ancon de Refriegas Point, with smoke and fire signals to give warning as soon as they should sight the said ships, which warning was given.

III. If they know that the said lieutenant provided all the residents and transients who were in the town with powder, lead and match and other munitions necessary in war, supplying arms to those who had none; and set a watch in the ports where the enemy might do damage; and maintained a *corps de garde* nightly in the city square; and ordered to be closed all the roads by which the city might be entered; and built certain bulwarks and trenches at the entrance to the city, on a height from which the enemy might be molested without danger to our men. And in order that these men might be freer to carry out their orders, the said lieutenant Don Francisco commanded the women and children, old men and invalids to withdraw from the city, taking with them their clothing and what money there was in the place.

IV. If they know that since no-one remained in the city to feed the soldiers, particularly the non-residents who were there at the time, the said lieutenant provided these persons with rations of biscuit and wine, so that they responded promptly to

And sayth they tooke aboute fourtene hundreth hides out of the said prize into the French shippe with the mariners pilladge & apparell and soe departed leavinge the prize & the reste of her ladinge for that they could not stowe the reste otherwise he beleveth they would not have lefte a hide in the shippe And sayth that this examinate & his company made accompte & reckninge amongest them that the hides pilladge & mariners necessaries which the said frenche men tooke from them was worth nyne hundreth poundes & uppwardes And otherwise the valewe he knoweth not.

To the viijth he sayth the said French shippe was furred[1] on the sides with planckes from the stem before till within two yardes of the sterne, & her maine maste stoode uprighte which fewe french shipps use, and many of the company spake englishe, and he beleveth the said shippe was of Rochell althoughe they gave them selves out to be of newhavon For this examinate hearde one of the company thereof talkinge to an other in Englishe & sayeinge that those hides would sell well in Rochell And more to this article he cannot depose.

To the ixth he sayth he hath herde that the said French shipp arrived at Rochell & there secretly landed the hides aforesaid And more to this article he cannot depose.

To the xth he affirmeth truth yt ys that this examinate & his company of the said prize perceavinge the French men would rifle & spoile them, offered to goe with them into Fraunce with the said prize notwithstandinge they would not suffer them But tooke out as much goodes as they could store & then lefte them Which he affirmeth to be most true.

112. *Langton at Cumaná: Spanish evidence*[2]

(a) *Questionnaire*

In the city of Cumana, province of New Andalucia, in the Indies of the Ocean Sea belonging to the King our master, on the twentieth day of the month of September in the year one thousand five hundred and ninety three, before Francisco de

[1] Double planked.
[2] Questionnaire at Cumaná, 20 September 1593, with replies of several witnesses (A. de I. 54–4–6, Santo Domingo 184. 7 *pliegos*. Original). Extracts. Translated.

smale prizes of little valewe in the Indies, and namely they tooke two prizes in a harbor nere Geminico[1] beinge partly laden with hides, in February laste and laded all the hides into one of the shippes & caried the same awaye leavinge the other shipp in the harbor, and thereuppon the said Captaines placed this examinate and viij englishe men more into the said prize to bringe her for Englande.

To the iiijth he judgeth the said prize to be of the burthen of forty tonnes & had in her aboute xxij hundreth hides in his judgemente with some ebonye or blacke woode at such tyme as she was sente for Englande and he estemeth the said hides to be worth xiij^s iiij^d per hide And otherwise he cannot depose.

To the vth & vjth he sayth that this examinate & company of the said prize beinge in theire journey for Englande mett with a French shippe aboute one hundreth & fifty leagues to the eastwardes of Flowers[2] in 44[3] on the third of may laste beinge of the burthen of 80 tonnes in his judgemente. Which gave chase to the said prize all the nighte & aboute viij or nyne of the clocke in the morninge the said French shippe havinge a Rochell flagge in the sterne came uppe with the said prize & made one shott at this examinate & companye & haled them, & this examinate & his company answered them they were englishe men & theire shipp was a prize taken by the shipps of the Earle of Cumberlande Whereuppon the Frenche men havinge notice thereof tooke in theire Rochell flagge & putt out a blewe Leagers flagge in the toppe & soe layde this examinate & company on borde & entered theire men & tooke the shippe.

To the vijth he sayth the said Frenchemen after they came on borde gave out they were of newhavon[4] & for the leage & kepte the said shipp in theire possession from aboute ix of the clocke in the morninge untill aboute six or vij of the clocke in the eveninge Duringe which tyme they rifled all the shippe & company & romadged the goodes to looke for money, and greatly misused some of this examinates company and beate them to confesse for goulde or money and from some of them they tooke the verey stockinges from theire legges not leavinge them eanye thinge.

[1] Jamaica. [2] Flores.
[3] 44 degrees: an error of some five degrees.
[4] Le Havre.

they answered they would doe but came not: After which they Fyred one of the Shippes laden with Hydes & Logwood, ladeing part of her Ladeing in the Frigatt. A while after they Fired another (thinking to make them come) which ye most part of her Ladeing was *Sarsaparill* but they came not at all, For they were bound by an Oath By the *King* of *Spaine* not to ransome any, But all their Ordynance was Heaven Overboord saveing two or three Brass peices, which were left behinde in hope some Englishman might be the better for them hereafter. One of them was a Shipp of Five hundred Tunnes and the Least of the other were Nyne Score by Estimacion, From thence they brought away the Admyrall which was a Shipp of Two hundred and Fifty Tunnes and set saile from Portivalio[1] and so the Anthony and the Frigott came into Plymouth ye Fifteenth day of May being the next day after ye Pilgrims arrivall there.

111. *Cumberland's prize taken by Frenchmen: deposition of John Yonge*[2]

JOHN YONGE of Leverpole in the County of Lancaster mariner of the age of xxxv yeares or thereaboutes sworne & examined before master Doctor Cesar Judge of her majesties high Courte of the Admiralty uppon certaine articles ministred on the behaulfe of the righte honorable George Earle of Cumberland Sayth thereunto as followethe. *Querela Georgii Comitis Cumbrie pro bonis suis per gallos depredatis. Primus testis.*

To the first article he sayth by chardge of his oath that he served at sea since midsomer was xij monethes in a shipp called the Pilgryme sett to sea by the said Earle of Cumberlande, and in prizes taken that viadge in the Indies, and one Slingesby was Captaine of the said Pilgryme.

To the second he sayth that both the Pilgryme & the Anthony sett to sea by the said Earle of Cumberlande were directed to saile for the Indies whither they sayled & continued vij monethes space thereaboutes.

. To the third he sayth that Captaine Langton beinge Captaine of the Anthony & the said Slingesby & company tooke sondry

---

[1] For the Spanish version of this struggle see document 121.
[2] H.C.A. 13/31, 6 July 1594. The articles upon which this deposition was made are in H.C.A. 24/62, no. 122/4. Cumberland is attempting to establish a claim to the spoiled goods.

this present year he was struck by storm, which drove him to these parts. The caravel was dismasted and suffered other damage. He made the island of Matalino,[1] where the Englishman took him, seizing the caravel and its cargo. He brought the vessel along to Punta Araya. There the English made ready a round shallop and a canoe and two small vessels, in which a number of men embarked with muskets and other arms. Many of them wore corselets. Among them went their commander and his vice-admiral. As they embarked they said they were going to sack this city and they sounded their trumpets and other instruments and so set out. Deponent and his comrades remained at Araya as prisoners of the rest of the English. The next day the four vessels which had set out for this city from Punta de Araya, where the large ships lay, came back, and neither they nor the ships fired a salvo or gave other sign of rejoicing. Deponent and his comrades recognised that they were downhearted and had met with failure in this city's port. They were certain that the English had lost men, killed or wounded. Three or four times, as though he were flustered, and with an unpleasant expression, the English commander bade deponent tell the governor of this city that he had fought well. They then finished despoiling the caravel, the commander showing himself harsher with deponent and his fellows than he had been thitherto. He threatened to burn the caravel, but finally left it utterly ruined and went away. This is the truth and what he knows, on the oath he took. He affirms and ratifies his deposition and does not sign because he says that he cannot write. Before me, Domingo Hernandez.

113. Langton at Rio de la Hacha: Spanish evidence[2]

In this city on the twenty-fourth day of the month of September in the said year[3] there arrived and anchored in the harbour of this

[1] Martinino, or Martinique.

[2] Licentiate Francisco Manso de Contreras, services rendered at Rio de la Hacha, 24–7 September 1593 (A. de I. 73–1–32, Santa Fé 190). Extracts. Translated. This document is part of a dossier arising out of a petition of Licentiate Francisco Manso de Contreras, captain-general and governor of Santa Marta (including Rio de la Hacha) for reward of services. The papers are sewed into parts, and the selections translated here are from the part marked 'FF'.

[3] 1593.

and this amazed deponent because in all this city's existence no Frenchman has been known to enter as far as these enemies did. While this corsair lay waiting for a reply from his general, or so it seemed, a pinnace came out from the other side of the gulf, where the larger ships lay (at Ancon de Refriegas). Observing that this pinnace was at a distance, so that it would be difficult to relieve it, either from the ships or from the other vessels that were up the gulf, and recognizing a good opportunity, the lieutenant determined to send out a pirogue with soldiers. Among them was this deponent, to whom the undertaking was committed. Although they hurried after the pinnace, it hurried faster. The canoe and the pinnace which had gone ahead saw that the second pinnace was going to be taken and came back to its relief and so saved it. Otherwise the Spaniards would have captured it.

VII. In reply to the seventh question he said that when they saw they could not take the pinnace as they had desired to do, observing that the three vessels had joined up and that the enemy was strong, the Spaniards decided to withdraw to the port called Ostias. After a little, having taken on men and munitions from the canoe, the two pinnaces came after the pirogue to the city's harbour and deponent believes that their general ordered them to land and sack this city, as in effect they endeavoured to do. The two pinnaces bore down on the port; the canoe in the rear lay a gunshot off and began to bombard the port while the pinnaces opened musket-fire. Their purpose was to compel the men landing from the pirogue and the rest whom Don Francisco had on shore as support, to abandon the port, so that they might land without opposition. It did not fall out as they planned, because of Don Francisco's good exercise of command and the great devotion with which his troop obeyed him, doing their duty like honourable men. They defended the harbour and the enemy did not land there, although we had no cover whatever, for it is a flat saltbed. A stand here was temerity. And so the enemy departed.

(ii) *Domingo Diaz*

IX. In reply to the ninth question [he says that] as master of his caravel deponent left the port of Faro for Brazil. In August of

opened a heavy fire from their vessels with musketry and artillery and gave every indication of intention to effect a landing. They played martial music and Lieutenant Don Francisco Gutierrez encouraged his men to fight the enemy, as fight they did with such spirit and determination that the enemy turned away from the land and steered for the sea with their vessels, because of the damage our men were inflicting. The English returned to Port Araya, where they had left the two large ships mentioned.[1]

VIII. If they know that at the time when the English withdrew from the fight with our soldiers, they shouted for us to wait, that they would return with reinforcements and would not leave without burning the city of Cumana. And as a precaution, in consideration of what might occur later, Don Francisco built three earth bulwarks in Port Ostias, and from that time to the present watch is maintained regularly in the ports of this city. Don Francisco in this and in all else necessary for the safety of the city took particular care and saw to everything in person.

IX. If they know that as soon as he returned to Port Araya, where he had left his two large ships and a Portuguese caravel he had seized in the islands, the English corsair sailed away, releasing the caravel, together with certain Portuguese. These men came to anchor in the port of Hordoñez, within this city's jurisdiction. They said that the men of the four vessels which came to take this city were the major part of the corsair's strength; that among them was the commander himself and that when they returned to the ships which were left in Port Araya, they fired no salute nor gave any other sign of having been victorious, as they were accustomed to do when they rejoined after a separation, but appeared to the Portuguese to be much dejected at not having burned this city. The Portuguese understood that they had suffered loss in Englishmen killed. Don Francisco Gutierrez Flores.

(*b*) *Extracts from Replies*

(i) *Antonio Camacho*

VI. In reply to the sixth question [he says that] he saw the canoe and pinnace go up the gulf to a port called Aarayman. They discovered the principal port of this city, which is called Ostias,

[1] The *Anthony* and the *Pilgrim*.

orders issued to them. This made it unnecessary for the soldiers to scatter in search of food, for it would have been very inconvenient had they done so, since the enemy might have come upon the city without giving the men an opportunity to assemble in their places.

V. If they know that, Don Francisco having made these preparations and brought together a number of Indian bowmen to aid in the city's defence, on Saturday the fourth day of the present month of September, four enemy ships were sighted in the direction of Punta de Araya, which, when they arrived near the city, were seen to be a round ship[1] and one of the canoes which they had seized at the pearl fishery and two pinnaces. In person Don Francisco went with certain soldiers to the mouth of this city's river to damage the enemy and prevent him making a landing or obtaining water from the river, and to discover the said enemy's strength and purpose. Because they saw horse and foot at the river mouth the English did not enter, but that night lay at anchor a little above the river over towards the Gulf of Cumana.

VI. If they know that the next day, which was Sunday the fifth of the present month of September, the canoe and one pinnace went up the gulf to a point beyond Port Ostias, which is further than any other enemy ever entered. Presently another pinnace set out to row after the canoe and the first pinnace, and Don Francisco sent out a pirogue[2] with twenty soldiers to take the second pinnace before it could overtake the canoe. As soon as the pirogue set out, the canoe and pinnace which first entered the gulf returned under sail to protect the second pinnace, at which juncture the corsair's round ship did its best to come to the support of the canoe and pinnaces.

VII. If they know that when these three enemy vessels had joined forces in Port Ostias, they turned their bows to the place where the soldiers sent out in the pirogue had landed; and these men, with others who had accompanied Don Francisco to the said port, and some horsemen who also came up, made a stand, although in Port Ostias there is no place available where the enemy could be met on anything like equal terms. The English

[1] Presumably a prize.
[2] Spanish *piragua*: a large double canoe, formed of a hollowed trunk of a tree.

city a small craft belonging to Melchior Lopez, which a few days before had set out from this city for La Margarita. Those on board said that they had run for safety to this port, chased by an English pinnace and a canoe. This increased the alarm felt in this city and augmented vigilance for its protection and defence, for the enemy was now expected at any moment, and the governor set forth the situation by proclamations and by crier. He kept all the people under arms. They passed the night in the trenches, under heavy penalty for leaving these works. Before me, Luis Perez, notary.

On the twenty-fifth day of the said month of September in the aforesaid year one thousand five hundred and ninety three there appeared within sight of this city the said English pinnace and canoe. Inasmuch as the vessel which brought the news was in the harbour and without means of defence against these English, and as there was no way to protect or defend it because there is no artillery here, wherefore it must necessarily have fallen into the enemy's hands; therefore, in order that the enemy might not profit from it in any way whatsoever, the governor forthwith ordered that the vessel be set on fire, and this was done. Shortly afterwards the English canoe and pinnace entered and anchored in this port and sent their boat to the vessel, which was burning; but as far as could be observed from the shore, they got nothing from it, because everything had been destroyed. The boat returned to the canoe and pinnace. Immediately the governor ordered all men who were armed for the city's defence to keep out of sight, with their flags, behind certain bulwarks, in order that none might be seen or the enemy be able to discover their strength, so that he would conclude that he might land safely, and then receive the damage which his boldness deserved. Further, this was done in order to confuse him, in that he could see nobody. The enemy presently fired a few shots from his pinnace and canoe and the governor ordered the men who were behind the bulwarks to come forth and open fire with their small arms on the enemy on board the pinnace and the canoe. The enemy then hauled in his anchors and moved farther out to sea, out of musket range from the shore.

Presently the English canoe ran up a white flag in what seemed to be a signal of peace, and by the governor's order another such flag was shown on land and a boat came ashore from the English pinnace and canoe. On behalf of the governor a demand was made to know what they wanted and they said they came to fight and to take this city, and that they had no other message or order to discuss anything else or to make any other statement. The same boat returned to the shore later in the day with a white flag and those in the boat delivered a letter, as follows:

Letter from the English

'Most Illustrious Sir: Shortage of paper prevents me from showing due courtesy. I reached this city today, as your honours have seen, with the intention of taking it and whatever may be in it, and I have observed that your honours have carried everything away. I ran up a white flag when I first arrived, in order to parley with you, and you did not respond. Observing this, I fired three shots into the air, like a soldier, and your honours replied to me with small shot. I made sail lest any of my men should be unnecessarily hurt. If there were anything to be gained by it, the loss of half of them would not deter me.

'I had decided that as soon as my ships arrived here I would land and, though it profited me nothing more, at least burn the place for the greater fame and honour of my lord, the Earl of Cumberland, who would prefer this to all the treasure in the world. But I refrain from doing this on account of a Spanish pilot who is in my company, named Anton Martin. He was once a canoeman at La Margarita and worked for Señor Pedro de Peralta. The canoe captain was his negro Campos and he took the canoe *San Juan*, belonging to Señor Don Francisco Maldonado, from Rio de la Hacha to La Margarita when Señor Pedro de Peralta and Governor Don Juan de Villandrando went over. Because he has broken bread in your honours' houses this man entreats me to forgo my purpose, and so I have done and will leave in the morning if my ships come up and God so wills. Expect me within six years, when perchance we may meet again. Your honours have gravely affronted me by burning that vessel. Had I taken her at anchor and found her of no use to me, had she lacked cables and anchor, I would have furnished them, for I am no petty thief, nor stoop to burn the property of the poor which is their means of earning their daily bread. With this I kiss your honours' hands many times.

'From this canoe, and at your honours' service as a soldier in peace and in war. I do not sign my name, for I do not wish it known now, nor until God wills.[1]

'With the captain's consent I allow myself to add these lines to your honours, which are written that you may believe that I wish to serve you although I sail with these people. I might very well have come up at night and landed unobserved, for I know this coast, but I dropped anchor every night that you might see me coming by day. Last night I anchored off Punta de Piedras so that your honours might discover me in the morning. The captain desired to land and burn the town, but I have begged him to spare it and he has given me his word to do so.

'Good my lord marshal and your most reverend lordship, and Señor Don Luis de Leyva, captain-general, and Señor Pedro de Peralta and Señor Don Francisco and all the other gentlemen, I beg you to send refreshments out to the captain, that he may know that I have influence with your honours, as I have with him. Let Francisco de Lima y Meneses or his messenger come, and he will be as well treated as the captain himself. Your honours' servant, Anton Martin. To the illustrious gentlemen, Marshal Miguel de Castellanos, the bishop, the captain-general and other gentlemen of Rio de la Hacha, my lords.

'If your honours agree to do as Anton Martin says, send something. If not, reply with small shot, which will be well understood.'

The governor replied in another letter that there was no order in this city authorizing him to make presents such as were requested in this communication, although their restraint merited as much. Without any gifts, the boat returned to the pinnace and canoe. This took place in the presence of me, Luis Perez, notary. *The governor's reply. He refuses to send presents.*

After which the boat again came inshore with the white flag, and by the governor's order signals were made to it not to approach, for it was understood that it came only to reconnoitre the entrance to the river of La Hacha, for it was steering in that direction and it was now near nightfall. The boat turned back, and as night fell many cannon and musket shots were fired from on board the enemy pinnace and canoe, and they made sail for *The boat comes inshore.*

---

[1] Langton's faintly ridiculous letter ends here, and a postscript by Antonio Martín follows, with two further sentences added by the Englishman at the end, to authenticate it, as it were.

the open sea. The governor ordered every precaution to be taken. The Licentiate Manso de Contreras. Before me, Luis Perez, notary.

... On the twenty-sixth day of September in the same year, in the morning, the aforesaid pinnace and canoe were to be seen to the east of this city, and to the west appeared two other sails. The governor ordered many signals to be made to them, as was done, for the two sails to the westward seemed to be friends and steering for this port. In order that the English enemy might not seize them, smoke and fire signals were made and many shots were fired.

One of these two sails from the west turned on its course and fled from the enemy. The other made for this harbour and the pinnace and canoe came up to meet it in such manner that in order to save the people on board and the cargo it had to run aground. When the persons on board and some part of the cargo had been taken off, the vessel was set on fire. The English canoe came alongside immediately afterwards with the intention of seizing her. The canoe's rudder struck, and at the governor's order the men in the bulwarks and others along the beach opened fire and placed the enemy in such straits that only his good seamanship saved him from perishing there. He escaped from that danger and made for the open sea without obtaining any profit from that ship.

At this juncture two heavy tall ships, which later appeared to be English and consorts of the pinnace and canoe, were seen to be approaching this port, and they entered and anchored there. Before me, Luis Perez, notary.

The governor ordered the men into the trenches

Forthwith the governor ordered all his forces into the trenches and forts, to pass the night and keep watch there, with good order and vigilance, being himself present in person. He inspected the sentries with great care and diligence and was so engaged until next day dawned and showed two English ships, with the pinnace and the canoe, lying at anchor, where they remained all day.

During the day a small sail appeared to the eastward. By the governor's order and command, signals were made to her not to draw near the port, where the said two English ships, pinnace and canoe were anchored. This vessel steered for land, avoiding the port. Although the English canoe immediately set out in pursuit of her, she was aground when it came up, her cargo had been removed and she had been set afire, so that without obtaining any booty the canoe returned to where the two ships and the pinnace lay. So they remained all that day; and the next day they were not in the harbour.

Nevertheless the governor ordered the city to remain on the defensive and exercised extreme vigilance. All of which, as related, took place before me, the said Luis Perez, notary.

114. *Langton on the Santo Domingo coast: Spanish report*[1]

Sire

At the beginning of this month I wrote to your majesty by way of Puerto Rico. It was no little good fortune to be able to do so. This goes by the same route and in great danger of failing to arrive there. It leaves from here by night for fear of the enemies who for 60 days now have besieged this port. Not a vessel can enter or depart. This Englishman is called Captain Langton. He has two galleons, a shallop and two pinnaces and although these are few vessels, considering our forces here, they are a match for us on the sea.

I have information from a man in a position to know, unless he be deceiving me, and I think that he is not because of other advices which he has sent me and evidence he has given of a desire to return to the service of your majesty, whose subject he is. I have made him an offer on your majesty's behalf, for I desire to bring him back to allegiance because he is a man valuable in maritime matters in whom the English place great confidence and whom they esteem highly.

He has sent me word that this Captain Langton, who is here in these ships, is a servitor and creature of the Earl of....[2] About

---

[1] Lope de Vega Portocarrero to the crown, Santo Domingo, 30 January 1594 (A. de I. 53-4-11, Santo Domingo 51. 1 *pliego*. Original). Extract. Translated. The intelligence proved to be false, but this was not discovered by the Spanish until much later—cp. document 120 below. Their informant was Diego Pérez.

[2] Blank. Obviously Cumberland.

ten days ago a despatchboat came to him from England with an order for him not to leave here during the month of February because this earl is coming directly to this city with 40 ships. From here he will go to Havana to await the New Spain fleets and what money may come up from Cartagena. He also tells me that Francis Drake is coming at this same time with 20 ships. He will enter by way of La Margarita and run down all that coast as far as Cartagena, after which he will join up with these other 40 ships, making 60 in all, at Cape San Antonio. He assures me that this plan is definite. He sent me word to warn Havana at once and all the Main. I have done so. The ships leave tonight although at grave risk of being lost.

This informant warns me to put your majesty's strongbox in a safe place. This I have already done. It contained as much as 5000 ducats which were to be forwarded to Cartagena. This money will remain here until it be seen what comes of these things. He tells me that after the beginning of February I may expect the enemy any day. I am preparing in every possible way. The most that can be done is little because so strong an enemy cannot be resisted. I have here as many as 200 men, not all of them effective. I am obliged to divide this force to cover the three quarters from which the enemy might attack me. The informant who gives me these advices assures me that the enemy is bringing a landing force of 2000 musketeers. He tells me that in England they are abandoning the harquebus, so they are all musketeers. He informs me that the adviceboat which came from England brought this captain two despatches, one of which is not to be opened until February 1. He will let me know what it contains.[1]

115. Langton on the Santo Domingo coast: deposition of Diego López[2]

In the city of Santo Domingo on the ninth day of the month of February in the year one thousand five hundred and ninety-four,

---

[1] The continuation of this letter is given in document 125 below.
[2] A. de I. 53–1–15, Santo Domingo 15. 9 February 1594. Extract. Translated. One *pliego* of this *informacion* is in this *legajo*, the other three in Santo Domingo 51. In addition to Diego López, whose deposition is given here, Pedro Juan Justinian, Antonio and Alejo González, Diego Felipe, Alonso Fernández de Puga and Juan Montero made depositions.

Señor Doctor Don Simon de Meneses, judge of this royal *audiencia* and *alcalde de corte*[1] therein, stated that he is informed that when the two frigates left the river and harbour of this city to take and seize the pinnace belonging to the English corsairs who are off the coast of this island, of which frigates Juan Montero and Juan Fernandez de Santana were the captains, certain persons went out from this city and informed the English captain that the said frigates had set out to take his pinnace; for which reason the English captain went to its relief and defence with his ship and another pinnace and recovered the prize and took and captured the two frigates; in which matter the said captains were very culpable and negligent, and failed to do their duty as was their obligation; which was why the English recovered the prize and took the frigates and killed and wounded many persons; which has resulted in much damage, danger and risk. And in order to ascertain the truth and that the guilty may be punished, he ordered the following investigation to be made and evidence to be taken. Before me, Francisco Marmolejo, notary.

And thereupon, on the said day in the said month and year, in furtherance of the said investigation he took and received the oath in due legal form of Diego Lopez, resident and native of Garachico in the island of Tenerife, actually in this city, on which oath he promised to tell the truth, and ... said that he went as ship's boy on board of the frigate of which Juan Montero, resident in this city, was captain when it set out against the English corsairs.

The frigate left this harbour in pursuit of the English corsairs' pinnace, which was reported to be in the port of Ocoa, and, having arrived at the port of Ocoa, sighted the said pinnace which fled as soon as it recognized them. Juan Montero in his frigate and Juan Fernandez de Santana in his gave chase until they came to Pedernales Point where they came up with her and compelled her to strike sail in the name of the King, our master. They took her forthwith without a fight and Captains Juan Montero and Juan Fernandez de Santana boarded.

They quarrelled over the booty which they found in the pin-

[1] A qualified professional judge appointed by the crown, as distinct from a local magistrate.

nace and witness observed that certain seamen from the frigates, who were Alonso Perez Chinana and Alexos Diaz and Juan Dominguez and others then on board the pinnace, advised the captains, since they had taken the prize, to proceed with her to Puerto Viejo where they would be safer and could send the booty overland to this city. The captains declared that they would return by sea only and so the same night on which they took the prize—last Friday, the fourth of the current month—the said captains with the prize and the frigates steered for this city.

When they reached the point at Port Ocoa the next Saturday in the morning they sighted a large ship and a pinnace. The ship seemed to be the English flagship. As soon as the ship saw the frigates it summoned its pinnace, which the captain boarded with some thirty other men, it seemed, and in this pinnace he bore down on Juan Montero's frigate. When they saw that it was ready and carried artillery they sheered away and bore down on the other frigate, Juan Fernandez de Santana's, and gave it a sprinkling of musket- and gunshot and broke up the palisade with their pikes. Thereupon Santana leaped overboard and other seamen followed him. Juan Montero's frigate picked up seven and the pinnace saved others of them but Santana was drowned, as were three others who had leapt into the sea. From his pinnace the Englishman then boarded this frigate and took possession of it.

After he had so taken and captured it he steered for Juan Montero's frigate, flying a white flag and calling upon him to surrender and yield. The Englishman gave his word that he would do them no harm, but presently set them on land. To which Montero replied that he would surrender if permitted to retain the arms which were on board of his frigate. The Englishman answered that he would let him retain them if he saw fit and that he should prepare to fight unless he meant to surrender. And so witness saw that Montero surrendered because he had not men to resist. Most of his men were wounded. Only six or seven were sound, for they had fought the Englishman while he was taking the vice-admiral and the Englishman had damaged them with the artillery of the vice-admiral and wounded these men with musket and harquebus fire.

After he had taken the flag-frigate, being on board her, the English captain said to all who were in the vessel: 'What good

among themselves. Deponent could not understand what they said.

Anton Catalan had a letter in his hand and, trembling, said to deponent: 'Sir, for the love of God do me the favor to take this letter to Santo Domingo to my lord Juan Caballero. It is very important to me.' Deponent took the letter and again set out for shore with Captain Langton and his people. All the time they were in the boat the captain said nothing more to him except to beg deponent earnestly to try to have that letter delivered because it was very important to him that he get a reply to it.

Later, when deponent was alone on land, he was unfavourably impressed with what the captain had said to him, and in order that no evil might come of it, because they had a poor opinion of Anton Catalan, deponent and Juan Montero together opened the letter and read it and saw the information which Anton Catalan gave Juan Caballero, his employer. In this letter, among other things, he wrote: 'I gave the warning your honour ordered me to give these captains concerning the letter which the pilot of the vice-admiral wrote to the president. They thank your honour very much for the warning and beg your honour to send them the letter in evidence of the truth. They promise to respect your honour's property and to protect it from any other English who may arrive while they are here,' as will appear at greater length in the said letter signed by Anton Catalan. In view of its contents deponent and Juan Montero did not wish to deliver the letter to Juan Caballero. They sent it instead to the president that he might see it and discover in whom he placed confidence.

Deponent heard the English say that they were going to hang the pilot who wrote the letter betraying their plans and informing the president of them, because he was a traitor, as Juan Caballero had informed his steward, writing to him to tell them so. Deponent has seen that they are very angry and hold the pilot a prisoner because of it, declaring that they are going to hang him for betraying them.

Deponent saw how yesterday, Tuesday, about midday they burned his canoe and the other, belonging to Francisco Vides, in which Juan Montero and Santana set out to capture the English pinnace.

and begged him to tell, if he knew, which of the Spaniards in his company was traitor to him. Deponent assured him that he did not know, although Captain Langton promised him his canoe in exchange for the information and said that he would do anything deponent desired. He said to deponent: 'Go on, Spaniard! Why do you refuse to tell me what you know, when I would willingly pay you well for the information? Anyhow, you needn't tell me, for I know very well everything that goes on ashore at Santo Domingo. The night your canoe and the other one came to take my pinnace at midnight I knew of it immediately because a servant of the *sargento mayor*[1] and other soldiers came down to Point Caucedo where I was and talked with Pedro Juan and told him how two canoes had set out to take the pinnace and that they were going to hold them there in conversation to keep them from going after these canoes.' He said that the *sargento mayor's* servant was a young white man, well built, small. A little later the captain asked Pedro Juan what those young men wanted and whether they had brought him his *rescate*.[2] Pedro Juan answered, no, that they had told him they had come down to entertain him and discover whether the English were there. The captain demanded to know what they wanted and Pedro Juan replied: 'Your honour thinks they have come down to do business but they have come only to entertain you, to see if you are here and to detain you while they go to seize your pinnace.' And so he made sail on a course for Ocoa to capture the said canoes.

Anton Martin, pilot with the said English, told deponent the same thing that day (how Pedro Juan had repeated what the young servant of the *sargento mayor* had said to him) as he was bringing deponent to shore from the ship, or aboard the ship when deponent was talking with Anton Martin.

When deponent wished to go ashore Captain Langton came in the boat with him, saying that he wanted to come ashore alone with him to learn anything he could from deponent against the Spaniards he has with him. When they were near shore they were hailed from the vice-admiral and went to that ship to see what was wanted. Deponent saw Anton Catalan aboard the vice-admiral and the Englishmen began to talk in their language

[1] A high-ranking officer, who took direct command of the forces in the field.
[2] Ransom money.

Next morning, Saturday, deponent saw Anton Catalan, who they say is *mayordomo*[1] of Ocoa sugar mill and was held prisoner by the English, arrive at the said mill where deponent and the other men were. They asked him how it happened that the English had let him come ashore and he said that they had permitted it because the English master and some other Englishmen were acting as hostages for him in order that he might come to visit his wife and put on a clean shirt.

In talking with Anton Catalan deponent asked him among other things why he admitted to the said English that he had been ordered to put a poisonous herb[2] on the meat furnished them; and he replied that he had told them because they were about to hang him. The English captain assured him that he had learned all about that from the men he took with the canoes and that he could not deny it. When they were actually about to hang him, he admitted the charge for fear of losing his life. Thereupon they let him off.

Witness observed that Anton Catalan remained at the mill a while and went to Hatillo de las Cabras where his wife is. From there he returned shortly to the mill and said that he was going back to the English ships in fulfilment of his promise, and to date he has not returned. Deponent saw him on board the Englishman's flagship the day he left the estate and talked with him aboard the ship, for deponent went out to beg the said Englishman to release his canoe, because he is a poor man. Although deponent begged him to do so the Englishman would not return the canoe.

Next day deponent went down to the beach and called to the people on the ship, and the boat came ashore with some Englishmen, among them Captain Langton. When deponent begged him to return his canoe the captain bade him get into the boat and come aboard with him to discuss the matter. Deponent embarked and went to the frigate[3] . . . artillery they took at Azua which they were making ready.[4]

In the course of conversation Captain Langton asked deponent,

---

[1] Steward.
[2] Spanish *regalgar*—see document 117.
[3] A gap of one or two words in the MS.
[4] This was the artillery from the *Edward* (see pp. 296–7 below).

does it do you to come to do this, and to take the pinnace which you took, if your own people from Santo Domingo warn me immediately of what is on foot? For last Friday, which was the fourth of the present month, two merchants of that city came to my ship to trade and brought two bales of merchandise with them, and they warned me that an expedition had been raised in the city to take the pinnace.' He felt no alarm on its account because he had allowed it eight days in which to go whither he had sent it. And so he had made ready and gone to his vice-admiral and selected the best men there and with them come out to the relief of his pinnace....

Deponent said that in the fighting three or four persons were drowned and Fray Jorge de Acosta was killed and others wounded as he has stated. It was publicly known that they killed some eight of the English and wounded about fifteen.

This is the truth and what he knows on the oath he took and he signed his name and his age is fourteen years ... Diego Lopez.

116. Langton on the Santo Domingo coast: deposition of Alonso González[1]

Alonso Gonzalez, who said he was a householder of Rio de la Hacha, resident in the said Hatillo de las Cabras, being duly sworn ... said that he came to the sugar mill of Ocoa, which belongs to Juan Caballero Bazan, last Friday, the eleventh of the current month, to try to recover from the English a canoe belonging to deponent which the president sent out armed to take a pinnace of the said English, who were in Ocoa Bay; or to find out what they intended to do with it. After he had reached Ocoa Juan Montero arrived and Diego Felipe (son of Alonso Hernandez, merchant) and three or four other men with them. They said that they had come from the English ships and that they had been talking with the Englishmen. Deponent asked them how they dared to go aboard and they told him that the English had given Juan Montero their word to do no harm to him or anybody who came with him. Under this assurance they had gone out.

[1] A. de I. 53–1–15, Santo Domingo 15. Legalized copy. 9 folios. Extract. Translated. This deposition is extracted from the proceedings against Anton Catalán, being made, with other depositions, at Hato de las Cabras, 16–20 February 1594.

with a white flag and with the precautions I have laid down to you. Do not carry a lance or a dagger or a knife. Give them the presents I tell you and assure them that there is no need to go up to the plantation, because there is nothing more there to give them; and that you do not bring them fowls because the plantation has been sacked twice and there are none left to bring, for the negroes no longer raise chickens. Tell them that in addition to having sacked the estate twice before, they have seized two shipments of my sugar in two different years, so that, with the raids on the plantation, I have suffered more than 20,000 ducats damage. Therefore I trust in God's mercy that the three copper pans may be returned to place and all the water jars left where they are on the estate and in the purging house.

And bring back the new carts and the lumber to the carpenter's shop, but do not bring the grindstone. And, as I say, do not bring back anything appertaining to the forge—not a hammer—from where you have them hidden. Remove the screw from the smithy and hide it, so that if they go to the plantation they will find nothing to carry away. Leave out nothing unless it be a table cloth[1] and some handkerchiefs—things that can be hidden in a minute. Do not bring out my bedstead or your own, or anything else made of wood, for they will carry it off. In the meantime you may be cutting firewood and piling it up so that we may have it ready, for as soon as these thieves depart we can make sugar from this grinding, for the small copper pans can be be brought out as required, and so on.

Tell all the gang bosses to go back to their places and to be very vigilant. Be on the look-out and very careful to do as said, especially to collect the tools again from the negroes. Have them warn you, and you receive the English as well as you possibly can, and try to prevent them courteously from arriving at the mill. Tell them the president has stationed men at Cepicepi to come to do them damage, and that I did not want such a guard, although it was offered to me, because I want them to be my friends. Give them the enclosed letter and one of those you have there from William Finch, because although these people say they are from Ireland, Captain Langton is the whole thing and

[1] *Una tabla de mates:* perhaps a mistake for *tabla de manteles,* or 'table cloth'.

they declined to take all the ransom demanded, keeping only enough to satisfy the men. So he left I don't know how much, which is to be carried down this Friday, the twentieth of this month of December. They expect to tack back and forth there for a couple of months, for this is the season when the canoes come up from Caracas, Margarita and Coro; and ships are due from New Spain and from the islands. Afterwards they will move south. They inquired for Juan Caballero de Bazan and Ayala told them that he is poor, because his plantation has been raided twice and much sugar and many other things carried off, worth a lot of money. Captain Langton said that he knew it. So they let Ayala go again and returned to him his slave, whom they had seized, and promised to do everything they could for him. They said they had not set fire to the purging house; but all night long the negroes had beaten drums and blown whistles, keeping up a din and ringing the bell, and annoyed by this and believing that they might attack, the English had fired four shots and the blacks had all run away. In their annoyance the soldiers had set fire to the slaves' huts and the fire had spread to the purging house. From Francisco Ramirez and others they seized they demanded a ransom of a hundred loads of cassava and 40 beeves among them all (and they were many). This is what they will consume during their stay and on their voyage.

I have been equipping men, buying them powder. The president sent me word to spend 150 ducats on the men who demanded pay and he would make them go. I offered him two boxes of sugar, which were worth more. When Gregorio de Ayala heard this he came to advise me to do nothing of the sort. He said it was better to give four cases of preserves to the two captains and the two pilots; but he says that Captain Langton is the leader to whom regard must be paid. He says that if they are given kids, melons, oranges and beeves it will please them more and save me money. He says that Captain Langton was in this island with Francis Drake. With this and his letter and Captain William Finch's[1] which you have there, they will be satisfied; especially if in addition they are presented with a dozen loaves of sugar and another dozen jars of honey....

And before they set foot on shore, go out to speak to them

[1] *Finchi*. By 'his letter' Bazán means the enclosed letter *for* Langton.

wrote to him that he had shown the letter to Captain Philip Fiche who has lost one hand,[1] and when he read it he told Catalan that because of that letter he would refrain from breaking a half pike on his ribs, but he nevertheless wanted ransom or he would burn the mill. Whereupon out of abject fear (although deponent had ordered him to let it be burned rather than give anything), Catalan gave them two cases of sugar and certain kids, and this when he saw them marching on the mill to burn it. And so, Anton Catalan wrote, they refrained from burning it.

118. *Letter from the owner of an* Ingenio *to his steward*[2]

Praised be God for evermore, who in His infinite mercy improves conditions! Up to the present I have written you many letters full of misery and affliction, arising out of the false reports constantly circulating in this city, which penetrated into my very bedchamber to worry me. False, I say, because of what you will find set forth in this letter.

Yesterday, the 16th, Gregorio de Ayala returned from his plantation where he had gone to deliver the ransom, and he was with me here today. I do not know whether he gave them anything or not, but he went to El Soco and there Francisco Ramirez (who is under suspicion) made signals and the pinnace came up with the captains. One is called Captain Langton, a good-sized, reddish man, with hair long in the old fashion, some thirty-five years of age, with his pilot Anton Martin, a Canary Islander; and Captain Slingsby,[3] a young fellow, with his pilot, Diego Perez, a Portuguese. There Gregorio de Ayala talked with them, in French, and they took pity on him because they could see that he was old, and he pretended to them to be very poor. He says that

---

[1] 'Philip Fiche' is presumably to be identified with 'William Finch' in document 118, and this may be a corruption of 'William Parker'. However, the only one of the privateer captains who is known to have lost a hand is Christopher Newport, who did undoubtedly raid Ocoa Bay in 1592.

[2] Juan Caballero de Bazán to Anton Catalán, Santo Domingo, 17 December 1593 (A. de I. 53-4-11, Santo Domingo 51. 2 *pliegos*. Authenticated copy). Extract. Translated. The document consists of copies of several letters connected with the proceedings against Bazán and Catalán. One of these, a copy of a letter dated 18 December 1592, alleged to have been sent by Diego Pérez to Lope de Vega Portocarrero, is already printed in *Further English Voyages*, pp. 302-4.

[3] *Selinbed.*

117. Langton on the Santo Domingo coast: statement of Juan Caballero de Bazán[1]

In the city of Santo Domingo in La Española on Wednesday, the second day of the month of March in the year one thousand five hundred and ninety four, the president and judges, Licentiate Baltazar de Villafañe and Doctor Don Simon de Meneses, being in the royal jail of this city, ordered to be brought before them Juan Caballero de Bazan, prisoner, who, being duly sworn according to law, on his oath promised to tell the truth and was asked the following questions. . . .

[Asked why he wrote to his overseer Anton Catalan to supply the English with meat, preserves and other things, when he knows that it is forbidden to aid such persons] he said that he referred to the text of the letters which he admitted that he wrote. If he ordered meat and preserves to be given to them it was to save himself the vexation of having his plantation burned. He supposed that he might do this since publicly it was said in this city that this royal high court had authorized Gregorio de Ayala to ransom his mill and he delivered to the English gold and silver which are more valuable than meat and preserves. Other men also were seen to go forth to ransom their ships and they brought them into this port under the eyes of the royal court. He supposed that he could do the same and if he did so, if meat were furnished, it was, as he has said, to save himself the annoyance of having the mill destroyed; and so he ordered that the meat be poisoned with a herb that the enemy might die. . . .

Asked why he wrote to Anton Catalan (as appears from the letter he has admitted writing)[2] to hand Captain John's letter to Captain Langton, when he knows or should know that such letters exchanged with enemies may prove detrimental to this *res publica*, he said that he never saw Captain John's letter, but Anton Catalan wrote to him that Captain John had left a letter in which he asked any other English captains who might arrive with the intention of burning the mill, not to do so;[3] further, Catalan

---

[1] A. de I. 53–1–5, Santo Domingo 15. 5 *pliegos*. Authenticated copy. Extract. Translated. This is an extract from the record of an investigation into charges of illicit trading. Bazán is referred to throughout as *este confesante*.
[2] Document 118.
[3] This was perhaps John Myddelton.

speaks Spanish clearly and came from Plymouth, and it is not possible that he does not know Captain William Finch.[1]

Remove from the mill those jars in which we have water—do do not leave one—and all the other receptacles for water and the demijohns. Have water in only one place. Remove the copper pans and the drinking troughs for the dogs and oxen. With a single jug in each room everybody will have enough. Purge and prepare the sugar where it is and leave the boxes of sugar where you have hidden them. Tell Manuel Gonzalez as soon as he reaches Nigua to send me a large glass demijohn which he has there, empty; and to send it by somebody who is careful, lest it be broken. And for Christmas, send us a lot of kids and another of sugar.

Doña Menciana, my daughters send you greetings. And your wife kisses your hand. God preserve you. Santo Domingo, Friday, December 17, 1593. Although that bell is cracked, hide it where they will not find it. Juan Oran might well come up and bring the trumpet.

Juan Caballero de Bazan.

119. Report from Santo Domingo concerning the damage done by Langton[2]

Although by every ship that leaves we inform your majesty of what has been done to date of writing, so heavy and so continuous is the damage wrought by English and French to this island that even were these departing vessels more numerous than they are we would still have further damage and disaster to report.

About six days ago two ships with two pinnaces arrived in the ports of Yguamo and Cacui which lie east of this city on the course taken by ships returning to Spain. They landed men who went to the sugar mill belonging to Gregorio de Ayala, who is a councillor[3] of this city. They burned the church and the purging house and the negroes' huts together with their clothing. They

---

[1] William Parker was a Plymouth man.

[2] The City of Santo Domingo to the crown, 18 February 1594 (A. de I. 53–6–7, Santo Domingo 73. 1 *pliego*. Original). Extract. Translated. Ayala's estate was raided in mid-December, and this letter, or at least part of it, must therefore be a repetition of an earlier report.

[3] *Regidor*.

carried off what sugar there was and burned the hides. They carried off the small copper utensils used in sugar making and new small copper pans. They took the household furnishings even to the chairs. They carried off a negro slave and wrote to Gregorio de Ayala that within six days he should bring or send them a thousand ducats as ransom for what had not been burned, which was the standing cane and the mill, on penalty of their returning (from where they lay at the river's mouth) to burn it at the end of that period.

Off the river's mouth they took three vessels of the coasting trade, belonging to residents of this city. There were eight slaves on board of one. Another was a fishing-boat belonging to a man who was setting out to fish. They landed at other estates. From one which belongs to Catalina de Ciria, a widow, they carried off four or five slaves. They raided another estate belonging to Francisco Ramirez whom they robbed and made prisoner. In like manner they raided still another belonging to one Francisco Ramirez whom also they carried off.[1] One of these ships went down towards Ocoa where there are other mills and plantations which it is believed they will burn or loot. They say that these people are English and French and they have Portuguese with them, among whom is Antonio Martin, a seafaring man married in Portugal and in England. It is he who knows these ports and leads the enemy in.[2]

All this damage has been done (and worse will follow) daily since the two galleys were taken off this base. While they were on duty the enemy did not dare to come so close to land or venture half a league from his ships, much less the five leagues which lie between the sea and the sugar-mill above mentioned. Because of this island's great poverty we then besought your majesty to grant us the boon of making the galleys' appropriation payable in New Spain and it was so ordered. The money had just begun to come from that quarter when the galleys were ordered to be discontinued. Truly they were of great importance, for, in addition to preventing damage like that described, they checked the evil which is the cause of it, that is, the contraband trade done on

---

[1] Both Christian and surname are common, so that this may in fact mean two different men.
[2] Elsewhere Martín is always referred to as a Spaniard.

the north coast of this island with these people. As we wrote in our preceding communication to your majesty, this trade works a great decrease in your majesty's royal receipt of revenue and is ruining the island. Since the galleys have been discontinued this contraband has become more frequent and much more open than ever before was seen or dreamed of, for there have been nine ships at a time trading in these ports. Not a month ago there were three, of which two were these which have now appeared off this coast.[1]

While on the north coast they heard that the three ships, which left about a month ago with cargoes for Spain, were about to set out and they stationed themselves on the course these would take, with the intention of seizing them. Had these vessels delayed in doubling La Saona as long as is usual, there is no doubt at all that they would have captured them. They will repeat this, for while they are trading in the north they learn what vessels are preparing to leave this harbour and lie in wait for them, to take them. We entreat your majesty to deign to provide a remedy by stationing the two galleys here, paid from the royal treasury as are those on duty at Havana and at Cartagena[2]. . . .

Santo Domingo, 18 February 1594.
Don Pedro de Capilla
Baltazar de Figueroa
Juan Lopez Melgarejo
Gregorio de Ayala
Baltazar de Sepulveda
Juan Daca Davila
Adriano de Padilla
Geronimo Pedralves
  Alonso Ruiz, clerk of the council.

120. *General Spanish report on Langton's activities near Santo Domingo*[3]

Events we have to report to your majesty which have occurred since we wrote lately by way of Cartagena . . . are that an English

[1] Langton did make the circuit of the northern coast, and at that time the foreign traders there included the *Edward Bonaventure* and the French ships referred to in ch. XII below.
[2] The rest of the document refers to other matters.
[3] Juan de (?) and Diego de Ybarra to the crown, Santo Domingo, 17 March 1594 (A. de I. 53–6–8, Santo Domingo 74. 1 *pliego*. Original). Extract. Translated.

corsair named Captain James Langton appeared in the month of December last off Cape Caucedo which is five leagues east of this city. He had two armed ships and remained more than two months, laying siege to this city's maritime traffic and seizing vessels that approached this port. He was already master of the plantations along all the easterly coast and of a sugar mill there. He loitered along that shore as safely as though it were his own country because the very inhabitants there, whom he was despoiling, afforded him protection. Nor was anything done in this city to disturb him because of the negligence of the president and *audiencia*.

Their inactivity was due to false reports propagated by the English themselves to the effect that they were expecting an armada with which was to come the Earl of Cumberland[1] whose servants they were. Nor were the authorities moved by advices showing how weak these enemies were, furnished by prisoners they released and by two Englishmen who deserted. These deserters also declared to be false the report that the said earl was coming or any more ships expected.

Therefore, constrained by the damage they were with impunity inflicting, certain residents undertook to go out with vessels against these English. Don Antonio Pimentel, who lives in this city, offered to carry out the enterprise. Although his proposal was accepted and orders issued in preparation for it, nothing was accomplished because of the aforesaid remissness of the *audiencia*. Regret was general.

Observing which and realizing how safe he was, Captain Langton mustered the courage to raid still other estates on the westerly coast, at the same time maintaining his station, for he sent a pinnace thither with men, thus dividing his forces during periods of three, four and six days. This happened more than once and yet no effort was made at any time to sally against the ships at Point Caucedo, which he never doubled; nor to interfere with the pinnace which was detached to raid the coast.

Adverse criticism of this dereliction became so severe that it was decided to send two armed canoes after the pinnace. Their

---

The first surname could not be deciphered. A further extract from this report is given in document 126 below.

[1] *El Conde de Camorlan*.

preparation was entrusted to two seamen, who went out; but since those in command were incompetent the expedition fell into the Englishman's hands because of mismanagement after they had taken the pinnace they had gone after. From the land the English ships were warned of the danger it was in and they went to the relief of their pinnace.

Dealing and trading with these English was so general and was conducted with such impunity during the time they lay off this coast that great damage has ensued to the *res publica* and business in general.

121. Trujillo report of Langton's raid on Puerto de Caballos[1]

Wednesday, the 16th instant, an English corsair with a ship and a shallop arrived at Puerto de Caballos. According to advices we have received from there, he would seem to have few more than 120 men. He sent the shallop in to look over the vessels that were in the port. A canoe was sent out from shore carrying a Spaniard and two Indians. When they demanded to know whence the shallop came the enemy answered that it was an advice-boat from Havana and that the ship, which had remained off the Point, was from Cartagena. This satisfied the Spaniard and he went on board the shallop. Forthwith they seized him and the Indians and took them below deck. They detained the Spaniard but sent the Indians back with a letter for Diego Ramirez (in command of the ships which lay in the harbour), in which the enemy ordered him to surrender the ships and the town, or pay some ransom for them. Otherwise he would bombard the following Thursday. Since no answer was made to this demand he kept this word and battered them the next day in the morning. Both sides suffered damage from gunfire.

The day after, which was Friday, evidently knowing how few men there were on board our ships (it is a fact that some of them had not ten men on board), being advised by the Spaniard

---

[1] The City of Trujillo to Don Juan Maldonado Barnuevo, 31 March 1594 (A. de I. 147–5–15, Indiferente General 1866. 1 *pliego*. Copy. Duplicated in 42–1–10/5, Contratación 5110). This document was an enclosure in a communication from Juan de Ybarra to the Council of the Indies. Translated.

he captured with the canoe and by others whom he held prisoners, the enemy decided to lay fireworks on board of a frigate he seized in the port. Having converted the frigate into a fire-ship, he sent her against the flagship. At the same time musketeers attacked the pinnaces. Finding themselves endangered by fire, our people tried to slip their cables and so necessarily disclosed how few men they had kept below. So discovering their weakness, the pinnaces fired a round from their artillery and a round of smallshot which killed some persons and wounded many. This disheartened the rest. Diego Ramirez sought to do his duty and to persevere in the defence, but he could not because 20 men jumped overboard rather than fight. Therefore he and the rest were compelled to abandon the ships.

They did not leave in them any gold, silver or coin, because it had not yet been laded. The enemy got only some hides and dyewood and although on the Saturday following he took the town he found in it not even a hide, because in the three days that he was engaged with the ships the townspeople had opportunity to convey everything into safety. We have been advised that he set fire to the town and that he sent his shallop and a frigate to Golfo Dulce.[1] Although as soon as the enemy appeared the people there were warned to safeguard his majesty's money and that belonging to private persons, nevertheless if he reaches there it seems probable that he will do serious damage because of the large amount of merchandise he will find.

The ships he captured were the flagship belonging to Diego Ramirez (on board of which the master, Luis de Sevilla, was killed); Andres del Corro's ship (on board of which the boatswain was killed and eight or ten persons wounded); Benito Gonzalez Urraco's ship; Riberon's; and one belonging to Gregorio Delgado which came from the Canaries off her course; and another from the Canaries. The enemy felt very triumphant indeed with this haul. It is understood that they will carry away two of these vessels, laden and reinforced, and will burn the rest. This affair has been very deeply felt through the country, as is natural, both because of the damage to the province in general

---

[1] Document 140 below states that Langton did not take the town, and there is no mention of such an event in the English account. The brief summary of Langton's raid in document 127 below agrees well with the English account.

and also because of the individual loss suffered by the owners of the ships and their cargoes and by the inhabitants of Puerto de Caballos.

In this city we expect this corsair daily. In order to surprise that place he kept out of sight of this port as he went by, but upon his return he must necessarily pass here. In no matter what high spirits he may approach, we await him with the courage with which this city has invariably received others, especially since this courage will be increased by the arrival of the governor whom we expect hourly with reinforcements. He has advised us that he is coming. He has ordered us to inform your honour of the damage this enemy has done.

It would be very great even if he had done nothing more than prevent the forwarding to his majesty of more than 300,000 *pesos* which had been collected and were to have been shipped by these vessels. If there is any armada in that harbour or any other way to accomplish it, we entreat your honour to send armed ships to Cape Honduras or Cape San Antonio to punish this corsair, for it is not right that having, with a single small ship and a shallop, taken seven vessels, he should go unchastised and depart into his own country to boast of having sacked and burned the town and Golfo Dulce. As far as this city is concerned, we trust in God that the event will prove satisfactory because of the good spirit with which the householders and others are accustomed to resist even larger vessels.

To this end we are clearing Miguel Antonio Veneciano's frigate, of which Manuel Hernandez is pilot. He has our instructions to follow, in conveying this advice to your honour and to the generals of the royal armada and the New Spain fleet. Should they not be in that port your honour will do us the favour of delivering their despatches to them when they come.

We entreat your honour to send Veneciano back promptly with a reply to the letter he carries to your honour and to take measures addressed to the best good of God's and his majesty's services. Also to favour us with your honour's commands. Our Lord preserve your honour many years in greater estate, as we your honour's servants desire. Trujillo, in the province of Honduras, 31 March 1594. Pedro de Eguiça—Manuel de Leon—Martin de Solorzano.

CHAPTER XII

THE *CENTAUR* AND THE LAST OF THE *EDWARD BONAVENTURE*
1594

THE story of the *Edward Bonaventure*, one of three ships which set out under Captain George Raymond[1] for the East Indies in the spring of 1591, is recounted twice in the pages of Hakluyt—by Edmund Barker and Henry May. For the West Indies phase of the voyage Barker's account is fuller, since he remained with the ship almost to the end, and that part of his narrative is therefore reproduced below.[2] Some further details can now be added from the High Court of Admiralty records and from Spanish despatches from Santo Domingo.[3]

Barker relates how the *Edward*, after much travail, came to Mona for the second time in November 1593 and how nineteen of the crew, including himself and the captain—James Lancaster[4] —were left ashore, while five men and a boy sailed away in the ship, only to be wrecked where Langton found her, 'a little to the West of Saint Domingo at Acoa'.[5] Cumberland's men

---

[1] See above, p. 156, n. 2.   [2] Document 122.   [3] Documents 123–6.

[4] Not much can be added to the biographical sketch given in Foster, *Voyages of Lancaster*. He was probably born in 1554 and in 1581 was a factor at Seville; shortly before 1586 he represented Alderman Thomas Starkey of London at Seville, but by June 1586 he had returned to London (H.C.A. 13/26, 3 June and 7 July 1586). In 1587 he commanded the *Susan* of London in Drake's Cadiz raid (H.C.A. 25/2 (5), 13 March 1586/7); in 1589 the *Salomon* of London in the Portugal expedition (*Monson's Tracts*, I, 184); and in 1588 and 1590 the *Edward Bonaventure*, first against the Armada and later privateering in company with the *Merchant Royal*. On this latter cruise Lancaster and his fellow captain plundered a Dutch vessel and were charged with piracy (Lansdowne MS 134; H.C.A. 13/28, 8 October 1590, 15 November 1590, 3 December 1590 and 28 January 1590/1; H.C.A. 14/27, no. 50). Lancaster was a merchant himself, a member of the Company of Skinners, and pre-eminent among the commanders of the great London merchantmen.

[5] Document 110 above. The Spanish refer to Barahona (document 126) and to Azua (document 116) as the place of the wreck. Azua is situated on the north of Ocoa Bay, but Barahona is on the western side of Neiba Bay.

land. But before wee departed, there arose a storme the winde being Northerly, which put us from an anker and forced us to the Southward of Santo Domingo. This night we were in danger of shipwracke upon an Iland called Savona,[1] which is environed with flats lying 4 or 5 miles off: yet it pleased God to cleare us of them, & so we directed our course Westward along the Iland of Santo Domingo, and doubled Cape Tiberon,[2] and passed through the old chanell betweene S. Domingo and Cuba for the cape of Florida: And here we met againe with the French ship of Caen, whose Captaine could spare us no more victuals, as he said, but only hides which he had taken by traffike upon those Ilands, wherewith we were content and gave him for them to his good satisfaction.[3] After this, passing the Cape of Florida, and cleere of the chanell of Bahama, we directed our course for the banke of Newfound-land. Thus running to the height of 36 degrees, and as farre to the East as the Isle of Bermuda the 17 of September finding the winds there very variable, contrarie to our expectation and all mens writings, we lay there a day or two the winde being northerly, and increasing continually more and more, it grewe to be a storme and a great frete of wind:[4] which continued with us some 24 houres, with such extremitie, as it caried not onely our sayles away being furled, but also made much water in our shippe, so that we had sixe foote water in holde, and having freed our ship thereof with baling, the winde shifted to the Northwest and became dullerd: but presently upon it the extremitie of the storme was such that with the labouring of the ship we lost our foremaste, and our ship grewe as full of water as before. The storme once ceased, and the winde contrary to goe our course, we fell to consultation which might be our best way to save our lives. Our victuals now being utterly spent, & having eaten hides 6 or 7 daies, we thought it best to beare back againe for Dominica, & the Islands adjoyning, knowing that there we might have some reliefe, whereupon we turned backe for the said Islands. But before we could get thither the

The Ile of Savona environed with flats.
Cape de Tiberon. The old chanel passed.

---

[1] Saona.
[2] Tiburon, the western tip of Hispaniola.
[3] May's account shows that this second encounter took place in the large bay which stretches from Cape Tiburon to Cape St. Nicholas, where the *Edward* remained in the company of the French for about three weeks.
[4] Fret: squall.

THE *CENTAUR* AND THE *EDWARD*

the *Centaur* was about to sail with its precious gift to London.[1] Naturally, it is not clear from Lane's letter whether Cecil had a direct interest in the *Centaur*'s venture, whether there was some friendship between Cecil and Watts, or whether Watts was simply taking customary measures to insure dubious prize goods. The last is the most likely explanation.

* * *

122. Extract from Edmund Barker's narrative of the voyage of the Penelope, *the* Merchant Royal *and the* Edward Bonaventure[2]

... Our capitaine seeking to prevent this mischiefe,[3] being advertised by one of our companie which had bene at the Ile of Trinidada in M. Chidleis voyage,[4] that there we should be sure to have refreshing, hereupon directed his course to that Iland, and not knowing the currents, we were put past it in the night into the gulfe of Paria in the beginning of June, wherein we were 8 dayes, finding the current continually setting in, and oftentimes we were in 3 fadomes water, and could find no going out until the current had put us over to the Westernside under the maine land, where we found no current at all, and more deep water; and so keeping by the shore, the wind off the shore every night did helpe us out to the Northward.[5] Being cleare, within foure or five dayes after we fell with the Ile of Mona where we ankred and rode some eighteene dayes. In which time the Indians of Mona gave us some refreshing. And in the meane space there arrived a French ship of Cane[6] in which was capitaine one Monsieur de Barbaterre,[7] of whom wee bought some two buts of wine and bread, and other victuals. Then wee watered and fitted our shippe, and stopped a great leake which broke on us as we were beating out of the gulfe of Paria. And having thus made ready our ship to goe to Sea, we determined to goe directly for New-found-

The gulfe of Paria, or Bocca del Dragone passed. A good note.

The Ile of Mona.

[1] *Cal. Salis. MSS*, IV, 604.
[2] *Principal Navigations*, II (1599), pt. ii, 108–10; VI (1904), 403–7.
[3] The danger of mutiny, arising from shortage of victuals.
[4] See above, ch. III.
[5] The Gulf of Paria was a notorious trap for unwary captains.
[6] Caen.
[7] May, who spoke French, called him Barbotière.

The plaintiffs, owners of the two French ships, contended that they were merchantmen and had been attacked by the *Centaur*; further, that Le Havre was not subject to the Catholic League at the time of their capture, having been reduced to obedience to Henry IV on 30 March 1594. Watts and his associates contended that the French ships were men of war and had attacked the *Centaur* and that they were Leaguers, since the reduction of Le Havre had not been proclaimed in that city by the time of the capture of the two prizes. The evidence quoted below does not lend much substance to the claim that the Frenchmen were primarily men of war, who had crossed the Atlantic to prey upon English commerce. Nor does the English plea explain the readiness of the French to rescue Crampton and his shipmate, nor Crampton's failure to desert the French when he had the opportunity. In any case Crampton, who appears as chief witness against the French, cannot have inspired much respect.

Little else is known about the *Centaur*'s 1594 voyage. She sailed from England in January, set forth by John Watts, John Stokes, George Hanger[1] and others, and after her encounter with the Frenchmen, is found off Cuba, westward of Havana, where she took another prize on 21 June.[2] As the next chapter shows, Lane may well have had a pre-arranged rendezvous here with the *Affection* and the *Jewel*, both Watts' privateers. Soon after this the *Centaur* sailed for England, reaching Plymouth about the middle of August.[3]

On 5 September Lane wrote from Plymouth to Sir Robert Cecil concerning a 'muscat' or musk-rat 'taken in the Indias', which John Watts had evidently promised as a present to Cecil. The animal had been sold by the purser, but was now found, and

---

chingham (ibid.), all quartermasters in the *Centaur*; interrogatories put to all these witnesses save Crampton on behalf of the plaintiffs (H.C.A. 23/4, no. 176/7); a deposition concerning the prize goods by Richard Woodcocke (H.C.A. 13/31, 16 November 1594), who was placed in command of the *Espérance* and brought her to Plymouth; and various orders concerning the prizes (H.C.A. 14/31, nos. 65, 66, 101, 102, 139).

[1] A London merchant. Caesar includes one 'Davies' among the defendants.
[2] Document 124 below.
[3] The plaintiffs' case came before the court on 16 August (Lansdowne MS 130, f. 14). The *Espérance* and the *Princesse* arrived in England before 10 July, however, since an order for their stay and arrest was issued in the Admiralty Court on that date (H.C.A. 14/31, no. 139).

brought away four brass falcons and recaptured, for what they were worth, some of the damaged spices which the Spaniards had salvaged; but most of the *Edward*'s substantial artillery went to improve the fortifications of Santo Domingo.[1] The crew of five[2] surrendered and from them the Spaniards learned of the nineteen Englishmen stranded on Mona island.

About Christmas time, however, Barker, Lancaster and ten others were rescued by two French vessels. Of the seven remaining, three were killed by the Spanish who came to the island 'upon knowledge given by our men which went away in the *Edward*',[3] two were killed by accident and two escaped alive— again by the goodwill of Frenchmen. One of these last two survivors was Roger Crampton, a Ratcliffe sailor, who records that he left Mona in March 1594. He and his companion now sailed with their rescuers—the *Espérance* and the *Princesse* of Le Havre —to the north side of Hispaniola, where they found Barker and told him their news. It must have been shortly after this—about 23 April—that the two 'Newhaven' men were captured off Cape St. Nicholas by William Lane, captain of John Watts' *Centaur*.[4]

It is clear from the accounts of Barker and May, as well as from French and Spanish sources, that the French at this time were conducting a considerable trade in the area they called 'Perou', in the north and west of Hispaniola.[5] Loyalists and Leaguers alike took part, and their relations with the English, who, though primarily privateers, also traded in that region, seem to have been fairly amicable. Whether or not the ships of Le Havre were at the time of their capture Leaguers, and therefore lawful prize, was the issue of the admiralty case which ensued, of which we do not know the outcome. The notes made by the judge—Julius Caesar—indicate the essentials of the case.[6]

---

[1] Documents 125–6 below.
[2] The Spanish sources do not mention the boy.
[3] Barker (document 122 below).
[4] Document 123 below.
[5] The situation is described in document 119 above. Cp. Rodríguez Demorizi, *Relaciones*, II, 133, 145, etc. See also C. et P. Bréard (ed.), *Documents rélatifs à la Marine Normande*, pp. 144–67.
[6] Lansdowne MS 130, ff. 14–21. The other known documents relating to the case are few: the defendants' allegation (H.C.A. 24/62, no. 139); depositions thereto by Roger Crampton (document 123 below), Matthew Boise (H.C.A. 13/31, 15 October 1594), Robert Baker (H.C.A. 13/31, 16 October 1594) and George In-

Wattes.
Repetitus dicto die coram Domino Iudice hone legum doctore Iudicis Surrogato.

Princesse both of newehaven beinge shippes of warre & warlickely appointed both with men ordinaunce & other provision Which he knoweth to be true For that in march before this examinate beinge at an Island called Mona where he & others were lefte ashore when theire shipp the Edward of London which wente out with Captaine Riman perished: and understandinge of French shippes to be at that Islande soughte them out and founde the said shipp the Esperaunce & Princesse there, and first he gott passadge in the Esperaunce where he continued aboute vij dayes space, & then he wente on borde the Princesse & continued in her untill she was taken by Captaine Lane & broughte into Englande[1] Affirminge moreover that as men of warre they roved upp & downe to take purchase eyther of the Spaniardes or, englishe men if they could meete with eany.

Ad tertium[2] dicit the Captaines & companyes of the said shippes when he came first on borde them tould him they were of Deepe but afterwardes he understoode & they confessed they were of newehaven, and he verely beleveth they had commission from the governor of newhaven to take & would have taken englishe shippes & goodes as good prize if they could have overcome eany in that viadge For that they were men of warre & helde of the leage.[3]

[1] Baker, in reply to interrogatories, referred to Crampton's adventures and added: 'Captaine Lane tooke out of shippes of Deepe thre others of Captaine Rimans company which had likewise byn lefte on shore on the said Islande' [Mona] (H.C.A. 13/31, 16 October 1594).

[2] That the Frenchmen were commissioned by the governor of Rouen and Newhaven (Le Havre) to take reprisals against English shipping.

[3] The Catholic League. Decuval, captain of the *Espérance*, in a deposition summarized in Caesar's notes (Lansdowne MS 130, f. 20) declared 'that they had a passport from Viellarts, going from Newehaven in September 1593. with 35 men, burden 66 tons, for Perou, with charter partie, whether they carried iron, Linnens, & other marchandise specified in the charterpartie, & they trucked in the Indies for slaves & hides, where they found about Domingo the Princesse of Newehaven, who had trucked there for hides, and were laden therewith.' The rest of this deposition describes the capture of the two French ships by the *Centaur*. Caesar then notes that a charterparty is exhibited, containing an order from the merchants to the captains and masters 'for theire traffick'. Finally (f. 21) there is produced 'A passport to them from villarts, by which appereth amongst other things that they should not meddle or have to doe against them of the League or catholike union, but no word therein to war or offer violence to others, but rather to traffick quietly in the Indies & to transport from newehaven thether all lawefull merchandizes, & to bring from them the returne thereof to Newehaven as theire right port of discharge.'

Master Edmund Barker, shipped themselves in another shippe of Diepe, the Captaine whereof was one John La Noe, which was readie first to come away, and leaving the rest of their companie in other ships, where they were well intreated, to come after him, on sunday the seventh of Aprill 1594 they set homewarde, and disbocking[1] through the Cajicos[2] from thence arrived safely in Diepe within two and fortie dayes after, on the 19 of May, where after we had stayed two dayes to refresh our selves, and given humble thankes unto God, and unto our friendly neighbours, we tooke passage for Rie and landed there on Friday the 24 of May 1594.

M. Lancaster returneth to Diepe, and so to England.

123. Tulier, Decuval and others contra the Espérance and the Princesse: deposition of Roger Crampton[3]

ROGERUS CRAMPTON de Ratcliffe nauta ubi per decem annos moram fecit annos agens xxxij vel circa testis in hac parte productus iuratus et examinatus dicit quod Johannem Wattes et Willielmum Lane per octo annos Georgium hanger per duos menses respective noverit Ludovicum Tulier et Franciscum Decuvall a mense martio ultimo noverit.

Ad primum articulum[4] mediante suo iureiurando affirmat he certenly knowethe that William Lane was Captaine of the articulate shipp the Centaure in the Indies this laste yeare & sett to sea by master Wattes & his partners as he herde Ac aliter nescit.

Ad secundum[5] affirmat verum esse that Captaine Lane & his company of the Centaure in Aprill laste beinge in the Indies did there[6] meete with the articulate two shippes the Esperaunce &

Ludovicus Tulier Franciscus Decuvall et alii contra unas naves vocatas the Esperaunce et Princesse ac onerationes pro quibus Johannes Wattes et alii interveniunt. Primus testis

---

[1] Disemboguing.
[2] The Caicos Passage.
[3] H.C.A. 13/31, 15 October 1594. Deposition on the allegation.
[4] The first article of the allegation (H.C.A. 24/62, no. 139), which states that Lane was set forth on reprisal with the *Centaur* in January 1593/4 by John Watts, etc.
[5] That in April 1594 the *Centaur* met in the Indies with the two French ships, the *Espérance* and the *Princesse*, both men of war.
[6] Boise, in reply to interrogatories, stated that the Frenchmen were taken near Cape St Nicholas (H.C.A. 13/31, 15 October 1594). Baker, also in reply to interrogatories, stated that 'the place where the said shippe was taken ys tearmed by the Frenchmen Perrowe althoughe yt be hispaniola' (H.C.A. 13/31, 16 October 1594). Decuval (or Decqueville) in a statement summarized in Caesar's notes (Lansdowne MS 130, f. 20) refers to the destination of the voyage as 'Perou'.

ENGLISH PRIVATEERING VOYAGES

Great famine.

boyled in water, and now and then a pompion,[1] which we found in the garden of the olde Indian, who upon this our second arrivall with his three sonnes stole from us, and kept himselfe continually aloft in the mountaines. After the ende of nine and twentie dayes we espied a French shippe, which afterwarde we understood to be of Diepe,[2] called the Luisa, whose Captaine was one Mounsieur Felix, unto whom wee made a fire, at sight whereof he tooke in his topsayles, bare in with the land, and shewed us his flagge, whereby we judged him French: so comming along to the Westerne ende of the Island there he ankered, we making downe with all speede unto him. At this time the Indian and his three sonnes came done[3] to our Captaine Master James Lancaster, and went along with him to the shippe. This night he went aboord the French man, who gave him good entertainement, and the next day fetched eleven more of us aboord entreating us all very courteously. This day came another French shippe of the same towne of Diepe which remayned there untill night expecting our other seven mens comming downe: who, albeit we caused certaine pieces of ordinance to be shot off to call them, yet came not downe. Whereupon we departed thence, being devided sixe into one ship, and sixe into another, and leaving this Island, departed for the Northside[4] of Saint Domingo, where we remained untill Aprill following 1594, and spent some two monethes in traffike with the inhabitants by permission for hides and other marchandises of the Countrey. In this meane while there came a shippe of New-haven[5] to the place where we were, whereby we had intelligence of our seven men which wee left behinde us at the Isle of Mona: which was, that two of them brake their neckes with ventring to take foules upon the cliffes, other three were slaine by the Spaniards, which came from Saint Domingo, upon knowledge given by our men which went away in the Edward, the other two this man of New-haven had with him in his shippe, which escaped the Spaniards bloodie hands.[6] From this place Captaine Lancaster and his Lieutenant

Two ships of Diepe.

The French trafike in S. Domingo.

---

[1] Pumpkin.   [2] Dieppe.   [3] Down.
[4] May mean the north or west, for mariners seem to have envisaged the whole coastline north of Cape Tiburon as the north side of Hispaniola.
[5] Le Havre.
[6] These were Roger Crampton and his shipmate in either the *Princesse* or the *Espérance*.

winde scanted upon us, which did greatly endanger us for lacke of fresh water and victuals: so that we were constrained to beare up to the Westward to certaine other Ilandes called the Nueblas or cloudie Ilands,[1] towards the Ile of S. Juan de porto Rico, where at our arrivall we found land-crabs and fresh water, and tortoyses, which come most on lande about the full of the moone. Here having refreshed our selves some 17 or 18 dayes, and having gotten some small store of victuals into our ship, we resolved to returne againe for Mona: upon which our determination five of our men left us, remaining still on the Iles of Nueblas for all perswasions that we could use to the contrary, which afterward came home in an English shippe. From these Iles we departed and arrived at Mona about the twentieth of November 1593, and there comming to an anker toward two or three of the clocke in the morning, the Captaine, and Edmund Barker his Lieuetenant with some few others went on land to the houses of the olde Indian and his three sonnes, thinking to have gotten some foode, our victuals being all spent, and we not able to proceede any further untill we had obteyned some new supply. We spent two or three daies in seeking provision to cary aboord to relieve the whole companie. And comming downe to go aboord, the winde then being northerly and the sea somewhat growne, they could not come on shore with the boate, which was a thing of small succour and not able to rowe in any rough sea, whereupon we stayed untill the next morning, thinking to have had lesse winde and safer passage. But in the night about twelve of the clocke our ship did drive away with five men and a boy onely in it, our carpenter secretly cut their owne cable, leaving nineteene of us on land without boate or any thing, to our great discomfort. In the middest of these miseries reposing our trust in the goodnesse of God, which many times before had succoured us in our greatest extremities, we contented our selves with our poore estate, and sought meanes to preserve our lives. And because one place was not able to sustaine us, we tooke our leaves one of another, dividing our selves into severall companies. The greatest reliefe that we sixe which were with the Captaine could finde for the space of nine and twentie dayes was the stalkes of purselaine[2]

They returne backe to the West Indies.

Five English men left on the Nueblas.

The ship lost by driving away.

---

[1] Probably the Virgin Islands.
[2] Purslane—a type of herb or shrub.

THE *CENTAUR* AND THE *EDWARD*

Ad quartum[1] affirmat that whiles he was on borde he hath herde the french men call englishe men Lutheranos, and he is assured they would have taken & thoughte yt lawfull to take eany englishe mens goodes if they could. Ac aliter nescit.

Ad quintum[2] dicit there were on borde the Princesse when this examinate came first on borde two englishe muskettes & aboute xx peeces of englishe pewter where they had them or whether they tooke eanye englishe shipp that viadge he knoweth not *Ac* aliter nescit.

Ad sextum[3] attestatur verum esse that soe sone as the said two french shippes & the Captaines & companyes thereof escried the Centaure, they stayed one for the other & fitted them selves and prepared to sett uppon the Centaure & fighte with her when they perceaved she was an englishe shippe, and the company of eyther shippes aforseaid called the Esperaunce & Princesse with swordes drawen wayved the englishe men amaine, and one of the officers of the Princesse with a sworde drawen in his hande did bid the companye of the Centaure amaine englishe dogges, and shott two shott at the Centaure before she made eany shott at the Princesse Which he knoweth to be true For that he was in the Princesse at the same tyme & herde the wordes aforesaid & sawe the shottes made out of the same shipp before the Centaure shott at her & howe they prepared all thinges to fighte & mente to assaulte the said Centaure with all the force they had. Ac aliter nescit Savinge he sayth there were two shottes made before betwixte the Centaure & the Esperaunce but whether shott first he knoweth not.[4]

Ad septimum[5] dicit verum esse the said French shippes were shippes of warre & uppon sighte that the Centaure was an englishe shippe they putt them selves & theire shippes in redines & intended to assaulte & take the Centaure as he verely beleveth for that they tooke and accompted englishe men as ennimies and good prize unto them of his knowledge Ac aliter nescit.

Ad octavum[6] deponit verum esse that after the fighte began

---

[1] That the French in these ships considered themselves enemies of the English, etc.

[2] That they had made prize a certain English ship or ships and goods.

[3] That they prepared to attack and capture the *Centaur* as soon as they sighted her and set upon her before the English showed fight.

[4] Decuval of course maintains that the *Centaur* began the fighting, etc.

[5] That the French intended to capture the *Centaur*, etc.

[6] That the French persisted in the attempt to capture the *Centaur*, etc.

betwixte the said two frenche shippes & the Centaure, yt continued verey hotly and with greate fury the space of two howers, & the french men thinkinge the Centaure had not byn of such bignes and strength as she was, thoughte verely to have taken the Centaure & not to geve over excepte they were taken, as by theire heate in shotinge at the Centaure & theire behaviour on borde appeared which this ex*amina*te sawe beinge in the Princesse at that presente.

Ad nonu*m*[1] dicit veru*m* esse the said two Frenche shippes were taken bye the Centaure aforesaid in the said fighte in the moneth of Aprill laste, but on what day of the moneth he knoweth not certenly but thinketh yt was on the xxvj[th] of Aprill by the englishe stile and by reporte of the French men they had byn nyne monethes on that viadge before they were taken Ac al*iter* nescit.

Ad decimu*m*[2] affirmat the french men of the said two shippes did confesse to this ex*amina*te that they & theire shippes were of newhavon in normandye, & at such tymes as they were taken both shippes & good*es* belonged to them of newhavon as he thinketh Ac al*iter* nescit.

Ad undecimu*m*[3] dicit eundem esse veru*m* For the French men confessed them selves to be of the leage & Leagers & enimyes to the french kinge whiles this ex*amina*te was on borde them Ac al*iter* nescit.

Ad xij[4] nescit deponere.

Ad xiij[5] dicit veru*m* esse the French men and Captaine Lane beinge in the Indies could not understande of eany intreaty of peace that should be had betwixte the French kinge & the Inhabitant*es* of newhavon tempore articulato For that yt ys a matter unpossible for them to understand of there at that presente.

---

[1] That the French ships were taken prize on April 23rd (English style), having begun their voyage from one to five months previously.

[2] That the French ships and goods were of Newhaven ('nempe portu de Gratiis in normandia').

[3] That at the time when the *Centaur* and the French ships began their respective voyages, Newhaven was on the side of the rebels or Leaguers.

[4] That Newhaven and its inhabitants had not yet actually submitted to the King by 23 April 1594 (English style).

[5] That neither the Frenchmen nor the English in the Indies could have known about such a treaty by 23 April.

Ad xiiij[1] refert se ad edictum articulatum Et aliter quam prius dictum est nescit deponere.

124. *A prize taken by the* Centaur *near Havana: deposition of William Lane*[2]

WILLIAM LANE late Captaine of the Centaure of London aged xxxix yeares or thereaboutes sworne & examined in her majesties high Courte of the Admiralty Sayth he beinge sett to sea with lettres of Reprisall in January laste by master John Wattes & partners he proceeded to the Indies & betwixte the Avana & the Organos[3] he and his company aboute the xxj[th] of June laste tooke a Spanishe shippe which of his knowledge was builded in the Indies & called nra Seniora de Solidad of villa Rica[4] with aboute xj thowsande waighte of salsaperill and hides which he broughte to Plimouthe And sayth he certenly knoweth the said shippe was builded in the Indies & manned with Spaniardes which were all soe diseased that he durste not bringe them on borde his shippe or in company of his men for feare of infection whereby as also for that they tould this examinate that they were bounde from Tresilio[5] to the Avana he certenly knoweth both shipp & goodes belonged to the subjectes of the Kinge of Spaine as by theire lettres also remayninge with this examinate may appeare.

Johannes Wattes et socii contra navem hispanicam et onerationem tergorum.

125. *Report from Santo Domingo to Spain concerning the wreck of the* Edward[6]

In my last despatch to your majesty I reported concerning a ship from England, which with two others left there some two and a

---

[1] That by proclamation of the Queen of England, published before January 1593/4 (when the *Centaur* began her voyage), the Leaguers were proclaimed enemies to her majesty, and that at that time Newhaven adhered to the League.

[2] H.C.A. 13/31, 9 October 1594. On the same day a similar deposition was made by Robert Baker of London, quartermaster in the *Centaur*, aged 40 or thereabouts.

[3] Certain rocks lying off the coast of Cuba to the west of Havana.

[4] The *Nuestra Señora de Soledad* of Villa Rica in New Spain.

[5] Trujillo.

[6] Lope de Vega Portocarrero to the crown, Santo Domingo, 30 January 1594 (A. de I. 53–4–11, Santo Domingo 51, 1 *pliego*. Original). Translated. The extract is a direct continuation of that given in document 114 above. The remainder of the letter is not concerned with the activities of English privateers.

ENGLISH PRIVATEERING VOYAGES

half years ago for Portuguese India. After she had taken some prizes, this ship arrived in these parts and was wrecked some twenty leagues from here. There were only five men on board. The rest had gone on shore at an island called La Mona, near here, in search of food. The ship made sail in the meantime and because she was undermanned went aground. These English were brought before me and from them I learned that the ship carried 31 pieces of artillery. Immediately I sent a frigate with forty men to recover this artillery. They have already brought out 21 guns and taken them to a safe place. The rest have been left where they are because of this enemy.[1] Hearing of the matter, he went there, and I gave up my men and the artillery both as lost. They escaped by good management. Since I cannot use this artillery in this present emergency, I have sent them orders to leave it hidden in the bush and to return to this city because of my need of men.

126. Further report from Santo Domingo to Spain concerning the wreck of the Edward[2]

In the meantime two of the foreign ships which have appeared here were wrecked on this coast; one in an unpopulated port called Barahona,[3] sixteen leagues from this city by sea, 37 by land; and the other on the north shore near Bayaha.[4]

Measures were taken to salvage the cargo of the wreck nearest this port. It was an English vessel. Because it had broken up and gone to pieces many days before the news reached here, nothing much could be saved except the artillery, which was cast away in a position from which divers could bring it up, as well as the cannon balls. To date 21 pieces have been brought in, six of brass

[1] The writer is referring to Captain Langton, with whose activities the earlier part of the report is concerned.
[2] Juan de ... (undecipherable) and Diego de Ybarra to the crown, Santo Domingo, 17 March 1594 (A. de I. 53-6-8, Santo Domingo 74. 1 *pliego*. Original). The extract given here is from the same report as the extract given in document 120 above. Translated.
[3] Elsewhere the Spanish refer to Azua as the place of the wreck (document 116).
[4] Lope de Vega Portocarrero in his report also referred to this other wreck, saying that he had been told that this was the hulk which had fought the Cartagena galley at La Margarita, when the governor of the island, Sarmiento, had been killed (see ch. x above).

and fifteen of iron. Ten more which the vessel carried and the cannon balls the enemy had, as above stated, will be brought up as soon as he gives us an opportunity to do it.[1]

[1] The reference is to Langton, with whose activities the earlier part of the document is concerned. Further details about the salvage operations were given by Dr Don Simón de Meneses in a later report to the King (A. de I. 53-4-11, Santo Domingo 51, dated 20 December 1594): '... and how a large English ship went ashore at Azua, which is 20 leagues from this port. Prisoners taken stated that she was set out with two other large ships to take vessels trading to India and did take some so engaged ... the spices she carried were fetched in, although they arrived wet. A great part of them were seized by the English corsair as they were being brought to this city. Thirty-one pieces of heavy artillery were recovered, half brass and the rest iron, all very good guns, with which we have supplied all the forts of this city (they needed it) and still there are pieces to spare.'

CHAPTER XIII

THE VOYAGES OF THE *GOLDEN DRAGON* AND THE *PRUDENCE*, THE *AFFECTION* AND THE *JEWEL*
1594

THE *Golden Dragon*, which was evidently in poor shape in the early part of December 1593,[1] must have been refitted with all speed, for in the following January she left for yet another Caribbean cruise. Once again Newport was in command, with one Henry Ravens for master, and once again he was accompanied by the *Prudence* under Captain John Brough, and financed by the Cobb-More-Cletherow syndicate[2]. By 15/25 April they were at Puerto de Caballos, just a fortnight behind Langton, who had left them little in the way of plunder[3]. The Spanish governor and captain-general of Honduras, in his reports relating to the incident,[4] may seem over-anxious to justify himself, but English sources tend to corroborate his essential point—that all Newport succeeded in doing 'was to burn two ships he left behind and carry off another two.' The raid on the town itself was a failure. Nothing of value was found, since all the goods and valuables had been removed by the citizens, and Newport was tricked into beating a hasty retreat to evade a non-existent enemy force. The two Portuguese men, laden with hides and blockwood, which were adjudicated as prizes to Newport on their arrival at Dartmouth, were evidently taken at Bermuda on the way home.[5]

The next news of the *Golden Dragon* finds her in the company

---

[1] See document 107 above.
[2] Documents 128, 129, below.
[3] See ch. XI above. This was Newport's second raid on Caballos; the first took place in 1592—see ch. VII above.
[4] Document 127 below. Cp. documents 140 and 142 below.
[5] Document 128 below.

of John Watts' *Affection* on and perhaps before 4 June;[1] but there is no mention now of the *Prudence*, and it is to be presumed that she was escorting the two prizes home. Newport arranged a consortship with John Myddelton, the captain of the *Affection*, to last until 20 June, but probably parted company with his consort before that date;[2] and that is all we know of Newport's 1594 venture.

Myddelton, with Watts' man Robert Hutton as master, made two small captures on 20 June and a more substantial one on 26 June, this last being taken ten or twelve leagues westward of Havana and sent home, reaching London before 20 September.[3] The *Affection* remained near Havana to take another prize—of sugar, hides and ginger—in July, which she brought to London about the middle of October.[4] Meanwhile, however, the captain had been captured, with seven others, by pinnaces operating from Havana.[5]

When the *Affection* took her prizes on 20 June and 26th, she was probably in the company of two more of Watts' ships—the *Centaur* and the *Jewel*. For the *Centaur* also took a prize between Havana and the Organos on 21 June[6] and the *Jewel* took a small carvel coming out of Havana on the tenth of the same month.[7] It was of course common enough for privateers to meet in these waters, but in this case, since they were all Watts' ships (though sailing independently),[8] they presumably had instructions to rendezvous there.

The *Jewel*, a ship of 130 tons,[9] commanded by Richard Best, with Edward Farrier master, had made her way to the Indies via the Burlings and Cape Verde, reaching Havana in June. About

---

[1] This and the following dates in this introduction are given in English (old) style, as they are drawn entirely from English sources.

[2] Document 129 below.

[3] Ibid.

[4] Document 131.

[5] Document 132. Myddelton was taken to Spain in the Indies fleet in 1595 (*Cal. S.P. Dom. Eliz., 1595–7*, p. 51).

[6] Document 124 above.

[7] Document 134.

[8] It is possible that the *Centaur* and the *Affection* effected a consortship (H.C.A. 23/4, no. 14—interrogatories concerning such a consortship, but without any indication of the date).

[9] H.C.A. 25/3 (9), 6 March 1592/3. She was set forth in 1594 by John Watts, Henry Cletherow and John Stokes.

18 July she picked up a rich prize in the Bay of Mexico—an abandoned hulk of something above a thousand tons, with a miscellaneous cargo of dyes, drugs, silk, gems, etc. The items listed in the depositions represent but a fraction of the total lading of such a vessel, but the goods were valuable and of the type which invited embezzlement—easily transported, easily concealed, easily sold.[1]

* * *

127. Spanish report of raids by Langton and Newport on Puerto de Caballos[2]

Knowing how ill-prepared these ports are to resist even a pinnace, the enemy is no longer afraid. This year a large shallop of 60 tons burden and a large ship of 250 tons and three pinnaces appeared, all well armed with artillery and small shot. They opened fire on the flagship which was here in command of Diego Ramirez. Although this vessel and the other ships (which were five or six in all) defended themselves bravely, because they were short of men and those they had were sick and wounded, the enemy took them all and carried off the flagship, into which he loaded the best of the cargoes of the others. He left them stripped, without artillery or cordage, so that it will be impossible for them to sail this year. He burned two large shallops....

From Puerto Caballos, 25 April 1594

After I had written this to your lordship and as I lay in bed ill with fever, having been bled not five days before, the lookout made the smoke signal meaning large ships sighted. When they came in view they seemed to be English. I dressed at once and ordered that I should be carried to the beach in a chair. I caused many mules to be fetched and in good order with great haste

[1] See document 133 for details of the cargo. Voluminous depositions concerning the embezzlement of the goods by Sir Matthew Morgan and numerous accomplices high and low, are to be found in H.C.A. 13/31 and H.C.A. 13/32. See also H.C.A. 24/62, nos. 50, 61/7 and the document preceding no. 192; H.C.A. 24/63, no. 139. Sentence was eventually given for the owners against Morgan (H.C.A. 24/63, no. 151).

[2] Gerónimo Sánchez de Carranza, governor and captain-general of Honduras, to Don Francisco Coloma, Puerto de Caballos, 25 (26?) April 1594 (A. de I. 54–2–5, Santo Domingo 127. 1 *pliego*. A carelessly made copy, duplicated in A. de I. 63–6–10, Guatemala 10). Extract. Translated. Cp. documents 140 and 142.

westward of the Avana a spanishe shippe laden with nyne hundreth & seaventy hides xvj thowsand & odde hundrethes of salsaperill foure buttes of water & noe other goodes Which he knoweth to be true For that he was in the Affection at the takinge of the said prize.[1]

130. Watts, Myddelton and others contra a Spanish ship taken by the Affection: deposition of Thomas Sterkie[2]

Johannes Wattes Johannes Midleton et socii contra navem hispanicam et onerationem tergorum et salsaperill.

THOMAS STERKIE of London merchante of the age of xxvj yeares or thereaboutes sworne & examined before master Doctor Crampton Deputy to master Doctor Cesar Judge of the Admiralty concerninge the takinge of a prize by the Affection of London & the maner & order of the takinge of the same & to whom yt belongeth Sayth by chardge of his oath that on the xxvjth day of June laste the said shipp the Affection whereof John Midleton was Captaine & the company thereof aboute ten or xij leages to the westward of the Avana in the Indies escried a saile whereunto they gave chase & the winde blowinge scante they manned out theire boate & therewith aborded the shippe, and comminge aborde founde all the company fledde a shore in theire boate in the breake of the daye And sayth the said shippe soe taken is a Spanishe vessell builte of the burthen of L. tonnes or thereaboutes and was laden with salsaperill & hides the quantity he knowethe not, which the Captaine manned with sondry of his company & sente for Englande Which he knoweth to be true For that this examinate was presente at the takinge of the said prize & came home in the same to this porte of London where the goodes are landed Affirminge moreover that he certenly knoweth that the said shippe and ladinge did at the tyme of the takinge belonge to the Kinge of Spaines subjectes For that the shipp is a spanishe shippe & was taken in the Indies where noe nation may trade but the said Kinges subjectes.

[1] Baker adds that a turtle boat was driven ashore, out of which they had one turtle. A sixth article, originally included, but then crossed out, suggests the reason for the separation of the consorts: 'Item whether doe you knowe beleve or have hearde say that the Golden Dragon by extreamity of foule weather was severed from the Affection before the takinge of the said prize & for noe other cause.'

[2] H.C.A. 13/31, 20 September 1594. A shorter deposition was made on the same day and to the same effect by George Wattes, who also deposed concerning the consortship with the *Dragon* (document 129).

THE *DRAGON*, THE *AFFECTION* & THE *JEWEL*

January laste Christopher Neweporte wente Captaine of the Golden Dragon to sea & henry Ravens master with lettres of Reprisall against the Spaniardes & were sett out by master Cletherowe & his partners And more to this article he cannot depose, Savinge that in may or June laste the said Captaine Neweporte & his company mett in the Indies with the Affection whereof John Midleton was Captaine & Roberte Hutton master which he knoweth to be true For that he this examinate was masters mate of the Affection at that tyme.[1]

To the third he knoweth that the said Captaines & masters of the Golden Dragon & Affection after theire meetinge togeather in the Indies with consente of all the companyes did make & conclude of a consorteshippe betwixte the said shippes & the companyes thereof to endure untill the xxth of June laste in sighte & out of sighte both by day & nighte tonn for tonn & man for man, and the Captaines & masters sealed eche to other of this examinates knowledge.[2]

To the iiijth he sayth there were writinges interchangeably made of the said consorteshippe under the Captaines & masters handes althoughe he sayth he was not presente at the makinge & ensealinge thereof, beinge then in Carvell absente But at his comminge on borde he understoode by the company thereof & that yt was made in maner aforesaid And more to this article he cannot depose.[3]

To the vth he sayth that John Midleton Captaine of the Affection & his company on the xxth day of June laste stilo Anglie in the forenoone did take in the Indies a smale Spanishe Barcke laden with hides & two Chestes of candles & noe other goodes and after they tooke out the Candles they gave the barcke & hides to the Spaniardes againe For that they were not worth the sendinge home, and other prize or prizes they tooke not within the tyme of the consorteshippe of his certaine knowledge But graunteth that on the xxvjth day of the said moneth of June stilo Anglie beinge saturday they tooke aboute xij leages to the

---

[1] Baker says the ships met in June and were in company 'aboute a senightes space'.

[2] Baker says the consortship was made on 4 June.

[3] Baker says that after the agreement was sealed and delivered 'yt was reade to all the company on borde to knowe whether they liked thereof and would consente thereunto'.

are and how unable we are to defend ourselves without men or arms.

128. *Interlocutory sentences of two Portuguese prizes captured by the* Dragon *and the* Prudence[1]

(*a*) [Having duly considered the case of Henry Cletherow, John More and Robert Cobb, owners of the *Dragon* and the *Prudence* of London, and Christopher Newport and John Brough, respectively captains of the same, against the Portuguese ship the *Gift of God*, its furniture and its lading of 1230 dry hides, 220 crude Indian hides and three tons and eighteen kintalls of blockwood, captured by the said captains from the port of Vermuthos[2] in the Indies and brought to Dartmouth; we, Julius Caesar, judge of the High Court of Admiralty, find that they have given sufficient proof of their case; we therefore judge that the *Gift of God* and its furniture and lading belonged to subjects of the King of Spain, were legitimately captured by the aforesaid captains in the aforesaid ships by virtue of letters of reprisal issued by this court and should be delivered to Henry Cletherow, etc.]

(*b*) [A similar sentence of the Portuguese ship the *Blessing of God*, laden with 50 treated hides, 1670 Indian hides and twelve tons and five kintalls of blockwood, captured from the same place by the same ships and captains.]

129. *The consortship of the* Affection *and the* Dragon: *deposition of George Wattes*[3]

Henricus Cletherowe Johannes Moore et alii pro testibus examinandis.

Primus testis

GEORGE WATTES of Ratcliffe mariner aged xxxj yeares or thereaboutes sworne & examined in her majesties high Courte of the Admiralty uppon certaine articles ministred on the behaulfe of henry Cletherowe John Moore & company Sayth there unto as followeth.

To the first & second articles he knowethe that aboute

[1] H.C.A. 24/63, nos. 183, 184. Summary. For the full form of such interlocutory sentences see document 102 above.
[2] Bermuda?
[3] H.C.A. 13/31, 9 October 1594. Another deposition was made on the same day by Henry Baker of Limehouse, quartermaster of the *Affection*. The articles on which deponents were examined are in H.C.A. 24/62, no. 142.

caused the residents and merchants to remove their money and valuable merchandise from the town. I then ordered the crier to bid them, on penalty of death, to come to the defence of the place. Only twenty men, unarmed, responded. The five harquebuses they brought had neither powder nor shot.

Nevertheless I divided them into three squadrons and sent one to the right horn of the hill, one to the left and the other to the *corps de garde*. Though my fever was rising and the enemy fired heavily on the town, I did not leave the beach, but remained, so manoeuvring my few men that they might seem to be many.

The enemy now seized the ships that were loading in the bay and with four pinnaces came close to the shore, bombarding the town in such fashion that, seeing that I could not possibly defend the place, I ordered my people to fall back, without losing a man. About six o'clock in the afternoon they landed, and because in the first houses they found no money and saw that the townspeople had withdrawn so silently, they suspected some dangerous ambuscade and very hastily returned to their ships. I issued orders that no man should let himself be seen anywhere on the beach, which increased their suspicion.

Next day the English captain sent me a letter, in which he declared that he had taken the town and the ships in fair fashion, and bade me ransom them, or he would burn them. He demanded that I send him refreshment. I answered that a fortnight before Captain Langton had attacked the ships and taken them, but had done no damage to the town, for it is not legitimate warfare to burn deserted houses and ships. I said that I had now received reinforcements and that the refreshment they had brought consisted of horses and hamstringers, and that he might come and burn the town at his risk, for I would defend it. I assure your lordship that the reinforcements I had received amounted to a single man from San Pedro.

With this and other military stratagems I used, without troops, myself in bed and in the bush, I put such fear into him that I drove him out of the port, where the greatest damage he did was to burn two ships he left behind and carry off another two. Fear could not prevent this. He departed without obtaining a single *maravedi* from the town.

I report this that your lordship may know in what danger we

CHAPTER XIV

THE VOYAGES OF WILLIAM PARKER
1594 AND 1595

THE little settlement of Puerto de Caballos, exposed by its long beaches to attack and ill-equipped with arms or men to defend itself, was recognised as easy prey by the marauders. Before they had recovered from the successive shocks administered by Langton and Newport, the unfortunate citizens were to suffer further loss and humiliation at the hands of William Parker and his French consort Jeremias Raymond. Again in 1595 came Parker, and after him Raymond, and it is doubtful whether the place was any better prepared to resist. Only in 1597, when Sherley and Parker came in considerable force, was there serious opposition, which was nevertheless overcome.[1] Perhaps, after all, the town was not worth defending: the Spaniards considered removing it entirely to a safer place;[2] Parker in 1595 found nothing there worth the taking;[3] and Sherley in 1597 deemed it 'the most poore and miserable place of all India'.

Parker in 1594 sailed once again in the *Richard* of Plymouth, and was perhaps accompanied by the pinnace *Margery*.[4] Setting out early in the year, he joined forces with Raymond at Cape Verde. On April 7th they captured a cargo of hides off Saona, sending the prize home.[5] About a month later (5/15 May) four ships, two frigates and three pinnaces were sighted at Trujillo. Two of the pinnaces actually landed men, but presumably re-

---

[1] *Principal Navigations*, III (1600), 598–603; X (1904), 266–80. Trujillo was more strongly defended, as Newport found in 1592, Parker in 1594 and Sherley in 1597.

[2] Document 142 below.

[3] Document 144 below and *Principal Navigations*, loc. cit.

[4] Authority was given for the taking of bonds from the captains and masters of the *Richard* and the *Margery* on 26 November 1593 (H.C.A. 14/30, no. 34), but no other mention of the *Margery* occurs.

[5] Documents 136 and 138 below. The prize arrived at Plymouth by the end of June.

134. Deposition of Thomas Hammond relating to the voyage of the Jewel[1]

THOMAS HAMMONDE of London Cutler of the age of xxx yeares or thereaboutes sworne & examined before the said Judge of the Admiralty uppon the foresaid articles Sayth thereunto as followeth

Johannes Wattes Aldermanus et alii contra Dominus Matheum Morgan militem.

6

To the first article he deposeth that the Captaine & company of the Jewell aboute the xth day of June laste tooke a smale Carvell comminge out of the Avana wherein was 400 gammons of bacon ten buttes of meale, forescore Jarrs of hony, twenty serons of breade, and aboute the xviij of July followinge they founde in the bay of mexico a greate spanishe shipp of xjC tonnes[2]. . . . For he was Stewarde of the shippe & had more care to provide victualls then to regarde what goodes came on borde.[3]

---

[1] H.C.A. 13/31, 24 December 1594. Extract. Deposition on the libel.

[2] He goes on to describe the cargo, corroborating Lawles' account.

[3] The rest of the deposition concerns the embezzlement and disposal of the cargo.

ENGLISH PRIVATEERING VOYAGES

am holding him here along with another I had taken previously. I entreat your honour to tell me what to do with them. To deal with them harshly here would be detrimental to the many Spaniards the English capture every hour. By next year, if I am permitted and given a little support to enable me to add somewhat to the pinnaces, I venture to assert that they will accomplish good results. May God guide and keep your honour many years.

133. *Deposition of John Lawles relating to the voyage of the* Jewel[1]

Johannes Wattes Aldermanus et alii contra matheum morgan militem.

4

JOHN LAWLES of London mariner of the age of xxx yeares or thereaboutes sworne & examined before the said Judge of the Admira*l*ty uppon the foresaid articles sayth thereunto as followeth

To the first article he affirmeth by chardge of his oath that aboute Julye laste the captaine & company of the Jewell in the bay of Mexico founde a greate shippe of aboute xj or xij hundreth tonnes fleetinge[2] in the sea havinge her foremaste & bowspritt over borde, and noe man lefte in the same, and [in] the said shippe they founde xxiiij Chest*e*s & two bagges of cochenill seven chest*e*s & thre bagg*e*s of Indico, a ch*e*ste of balsom or Ile of spike,[3] a cheste & two barrells of drugg*e*s, two chest*e*s of threede two chest of rawe silke, twenty cases of marble stone, a cheste of smale blewe stones xiij peeces of brasse ordinaunce, & thre cupps of silver, which they tooke into the Jewell & then fired the shippe by com*m*aundemente of the Captaine. And other goodes or other thinges they tooke not duringe the viadge Savinge a frigott[4] wherein was hony meale & bacon w*h*ich they had for theire provition & happened unto them in good tyme, otherwise he thinketh they had byn greatly distressed for wante, which he knoweth to be true For that he was Boateswaine of the Jewell the said viadge.[5]

---

[1] H.C.A. 13/31, 23 December 1594. Extract. Deposition on the libel.
[2] [*Sic.*]
[3] [*Sic.*] Spike-oil.
[4] See document 134 below.
[5] The rest of the document concerns the embezzlement and disposal of the cargo.

131. Watts, Myddelton and others contra a Spanish ship taken by the Affection: deposition of Thomas Pinchbacke[1]

THOMAS PINCHBACKE of Ratcliffe mariner of the age of xix yeares or thereaboutes sworne & examined before the righte worshipfull Master Doctor Cesar Judge of her majesties high Courte of the Admiralty sayth he was a mariner of the affection of London whereof John Midleton was Captaine, and presente when as the said Captaine & his company to the westward of the Avana tooke aboute July laste a spanishe shipp laden with ginger suger & hides which was sente for Englande and is arrived in this porte of London, And sayth that he came not home in the prize, but continued in the man of warre which arrived here aboute thre weekes paste in company of the prize.

Johannes Wattes et alii contra navem hispanicam saccaro gingibore et tergoribus onustam.

Beinge asked what ginger suger or hides have byn imbeaceled or conveyed away since the takinge of the said prize sayth that at tymes he had gotten togeather aboute fifty poundes of ginger which master wattes seazed on at his oastes house[2] & more he had not savinge a cappe full of ginger which he sould for ij^s viij^d or iij^s to one Snowe in Limehouse.

And sondry others of the companye workinge under hould gott a pounde or two of ginger at tymes which they caried away in theire breeches, and more that hath byn conveyed away he knoweth not. As namely harry molliffe the masters man & Peter Robson had some ginger which this examinate sawe & more he cannot depose.

132. Spanish report of the capture of John Myddelton[3]

Lest my despatch of July 19 may have been lost, I will repeat what I then wrote, to the effect that with the two pinnaces I built I took an Englishman named John Myddelton,[4] a man of importance and a great corsair, whom Don Alonso de Bazan captured once before in the year '92,[5] and seven Englishmen with him. I

---

[1] H.C.A. 13/31, 5 November 1594.
[2] Probably means at deponent's lodgings.
[3] Extract. Translated. Don Juan Maldonado Barnuevo to Don Juan Ybarra, Havana, 19 August 1594 (A. de I. 54–2–5, Santo Domingo 127. 1 *pliego*. Original). Printed in full in I. A. Wright (ed.), *Historia Documentada de San Cristobal de la Habana*, II, 195.
[4] *Juan Midellon.*   [5] See above, ch. VI.

embarked them on finding the defenders alert. Whilst in the harbour, however, they captured the advice boat which had come from Caballos with news of the earlier raids and a request for help. Some of the advice boat's crew escaped ashore with the despatches, but among those captured the privateers found one at least—a certain Diego de los Reyes—willing to provide information about Caballos.[1]

Two days later, about midnight, a force of fifty-five men landed near Caballos and marched upon two decisive points— the governor's house and the house of the commander of the Honduras ships, Captain Diego Ramirez. It was a well-timed and well-organized assault, depending upon surprise, but above all it was prior knowledge of the situation that enabled Parker and Raymond to achieve more than Newport with fewer men. The governor's bravery and fortitude, to which he could find no better witnesses than himself and his comical secretary, the pathetic plight of half-dressed citizens taking refuge in the bush, the quarrels and accusations of treachery among them—these are well told in the Spanish documents below. The French and English kept the town for fourteen days and departed with substantial stores of hides, indigo, money and bullion, all of which had been brought back to the town when Newport withdrew.

The prize-goods were doubtless worth the trouble,[2] but of those allotted to the English few reached home. About the end of May the two commanders lost company and before the English had left the West Indies one of the two frigates laden with booty had sunk. The other parted from the *Richard* about the beginning of July off Newfoundland and, putting in at Kinsale with a leak, lost much if not most of its cargo by embezzlement and arrest. The *Richard* arrived at Plymouth on 21 July.[3]

In the absence of any High Court of Admiralty evidence, Parker's 1595 raid remains in a number of important respects obscure. The Spanish reports[4] differ as to the number of the

[1] Diego de los Reyes, sometimes known as Dieguillo el Mulato, is here embarking upon his career as a notorious pirate.

[2] The Spanish losses in the second and third raids on Caballos (those of Newport and Parker) were estimated at over 100,000 ducats by some witnesses, and the greater part of these were taken in the third raid (A. de I. 63-6-10, Guatemala 10, Licentiate Alvar Gómez de Abraunca to the crown, 18 February 1595).

[3] Document 137 below.

[4] Documents 143-5 below.

privateers, but it is clear that they included one ship and one or more smaller vessels. They evidently landed at Puerto de Caballos on 16 May, almost exactly the anniversary of the last assault, but found neither inhabitants nor goods; they may have taken a small prize or two in the harbour. Disappointed, they detached a part of their force to explore the Golfo Dulce for plunder and perhaps also for a route to the Pacific—the attempt to go inland on horseback seems to anticipate the long, weary and fruitless march of 1597, when Parker and Sherley were, as we know certainly, hoping to reach the South Sea.[1] On this occasion Parker did not press very far, and such probing yielded no more than a Spanish frigate in ballast and some victuals from ashore. The next move was to return eastwards to the island of Bonacca (Guanaja), north of Trujillo, where two other English ships joined them in setting course for Cape San Antonio.[2]

*   *   *

135. Deposition of Richard Bickford[3]

Richardus Hutchins et Willielmus Parker pro testibus examinandis.

Primus testis

RICHARD BICKFORD of Plimouthe souldier of the age of xxvj yeares or thereaboutes sworne & examined before master Doctor Hone Deputy to Master Doctor Cesar of her majesties high Courte of the Admiralty on the behaulfe of Richard hutchins & William Parker of Plimouth & partners concerninge a prize of hides & salsaperill disposed in Irelande & of the maner of the same Sayth by chardge of his oathe with william Parker beinge Captaine of the Richard of Plimouth & his company mett with Jeremias Raymond of Sherbrocke[4] in Normandye at Cape de Verde & consorted togeather & sayled in company to Porte de Cavalles in the Indies, & concluded togeather to make

---

[1] *Principal Navigations*, loc. cit.

[2] These two ships may well have been the two caravels detached by Dudley to go cruising in the West Indies while he explored the Orinoco. They were commanded by Captains Wood and Wentworth and on April 24/May 4 had been at Rio de la Hacha. Here Wood had sent a letter to the governor, Licentiate Manso de Contreras, offering to trade, but had received a sharp rebuff and forthwith departed (statement by Licentiate Manso de Contreras, 8 May 1595: A. de I. 73–1–32, Santa Fé 190 FF). See also *Principal Navigations*, III (1600), 575–6; X (1904), 205–7).

[3] H.C.A. 13/31, 28 August 1594.

[4] Cherbourg.

an assaulte the said Towne & sacke yt, and in the nighte tyme
with fifty fyve men they landed and tooke the watche first, and
then entered the towne & won the same, and were maisters
thereof the space of xiiij dayes, and in that tyme they laded foure
spanishe shippes founde there with hides & salsaperill founde in
the Towne, and some Anile & other goodes they laded also into
the Richard and the shipp of Captaine Raymonde, & made
equall devition of all the goodes betwixte the french men & the
said Parker & his company vizt the said Raymonde had two
barckes laden, and the said Parker two barckes laden, and thereuppon havinge taken theire pleasure of the Towne they departed
with the said goodes, and within x dayes followinge Captaine
Raymond & Captaine Parker lost company in a nighte, and as
Captaine Parker with his prizes was keepinge his course towardes
England one of his barckes laden with hides as aforesaid foundred
in the sea, and soncke, and out of the same they saved only thre
hundreth hides which they putt into the Richard, and aboute the
first day of July laste the other spanishe barcke laden also with
hides & salsaperill lost Captaine Parker on the bancke of Newe
found lande, beinge manned with xiij english men whom the said
Captaine Parker placed therein and made Phillipp Smith master
who with the reste of the company by reason of a leake fell with
Kinsale in Irelande where counsell was geven to make entry of
the shipp & goodes in the Custome House for feare of confiscation of the whole goodes if eany goodes were soulde with out
entry, which the master & company did for that they were to
make some sale for provision of victualls, and thereuppon henry
Williams masters mate conveyed a shore xvij hides, & hid them
in a wood, & the searcher seased on them for the Queenes use,
and a more quantity were imbeaseled but howe many he knoweth
not. And sayth that hereuppon the master & company were
examined before the Judge of the Admiralty there & the master
thinkinge to finde more favor sayde the same prize was taken by
a shipp of the Earle of Cumberlande, and the mariners confessed
the prize belonged to Captaine Parker & was taken by him
Uppon which contrarietye of speeches, Sir Thomas Norris
Knighte sente Alexander Clarck & John Bostocke to Kinsale to
stay the goodes, who with the assistaunce of Richard Roche
Sufferan of the Towne of Kinsale turned out all the companye of

the prize & put in such as they pleased to take chardge of the goodes, who conveyed away in the nighte tyme a greate quantity of the goodes & hid them in the woodes, whereof this examinate standinge in doubte with others of his company watched one nighte & founde forescore hides in the woodes which they that were placed in the prize had shifted away, and master Browne the viceadmirall seased on them & tooke them to his keepinge Whereuppon this examinate wente to the Sufferan & complayned of the said disorder & prayed him that those which were on borde mighte be examined what goodes more were made away, & he answered he had placed his man aborde, and knewe he would have better regarde to the goodes, and would not examyne them. And sayth the reste of the goodes not imbeaseled were landed & cellered in Kinsale by the said Clarcke & Bostocke by order of Sir Thomas Norris Knighte & there remaine as he thinketh. Which he knoweth to be true For that this examinate was one of the company of the Richard & presente at the takinge & sackinge of the said Towne of Porte de Cavalles, and was in the said prize at her arrivall at Kinsale & at the landinge of the said goodes.

136. Examination of Spanish prisoners[1]
The furste Day of Julye Anno Domini 1594.

The examynacion of Frauncisco Casatho of Vianna,[2] Frauncisco Vaze de porte,[3] John Domingos de Porte of St Maria,[4] examyned before me John Phellipps merchant mayore of the boroughe of Plymoth the day and yeer above written who severally and togithers confesse and saye as Followeth. They beinge shipped in a barcke of Carthagena in the Indyas called the nuestra Seignora de Loretta, departed there hence and went to St Domingo and there tooke in here ladinge of hides about the number of two thowsandes, which goodes did apperteyne to one Anthonio Gracia of Teneriff to be transported to Civill, and in comminge from St Domingo aforsayd to sayle towardes Civill,

---
[1] H.C.A. 24/62, no. 16.
[2] Vianna, Portugal.
[3] Oporto, Portugal.
[4] Puerto de Santa Maria, Spain.

PARKER'S VOYAGES, 1594-5

were taken by a barcke called the Richard of Plymoth william parker Capitayne, neer unto an Iland called Zoana[1] not farre from St Domingo aforsayd the vijth day of Aprill last past & were brought into the porte of Plymoth the xxvijth day of June now last past, by vertewe of lettres of reprisall graunted to the forsayd william parker. In witnes of this examinacion to be of a truthe I have heerunto putt to my hand the day and yeer furst above written.

Fco Cazado.
the signe of[2] Francisco Vaze.

John phillipes mayor.[3]

137. Examination of Spanish prisoners[4]
The xxxth Day of July Anno Domini 1594.

The examynacion of Alfonsa Ames of Lagust[5] of thage of xxvj yeers & Nicholas Alarte of St mary porte[6] of thage of xl^{tv} yeers, examyned before me John Phellipps merchant mayore of the boroughe of Plymoth the day and yeer above written who severally & togithers confesse & saye as followeth. That they beinge taken by one William Parker Captaine of a barcke called the Richard of Plymoth, in the Indyas, were present with him and with his Consorte one Jeremy Raymond a Frenche man when he tooke a towne called Porte de Cavalles in the Indyas where they tooke bitwixte the sayd william parker & the sayd Jeremy Reymond certen money bullen hides & anyle to what quantytye they knowe not, all which was equally devided bitwixte the said william parker & Jeremy Reymond, and that they loded the shipps of the sayd Jeremy Reymond with hides & two Frigottes for his portion & for william parker aforsayd two Frigottes with hides & the barcke sent home before was appointed & agreed uppon to be to the use of the abovesayd william parker in lieue & countervayle of the forsayd shipps of Jeremy Reymond laden also they testyfye that one of the Frigottes apperteyninge to the forsayd william parker was soncke in the Indyas in comminge, & that thother Frigott they lost company of the last day of June last, & that in a night they

---

[1] Saona.   [2] Signatory's mark.   [3] Signed.
[4] H.C.A. 24/62, no. 15.   [5] Lagos.   [6] Puerto de Santa Maria, Spain.

lost the company of the forsayd Jeremy Reymond theire consorte & stayed for him at lagonasho[1] 2 dayes or theraboutes, & not findinge him came away and arrived at plymoth the xxjth day of this Instant July 1594.

In witnes of this examynacion to be of troth I have examyned the prisoners above named uppon their othes, and have heerunto putt my hand the day and yeer above written.

John phillipes mayor.[2]

the signe of Nicholas[3] Alarte.

the signe of Alfonsa[4] Ames.

138. *Interlocutory sentence of the* Nuestra Señora de Loreto *of Cartagena*[5]

[Having duly considered the case of Richard Hutchins and William Parker, owners of the *Richard* of Plymouth, against the *Nuestra Señora de Loreto* of Cartagena in the Indies, its furniture, etc. and two thousand hides and other goods in her, recently taken at the seas by William Parker and his company and brought to Plymouth; we, Julius Caesar, judge of the High Court of Admiralty, find that they have given sufficient proof of their case; we find that the above ship and goods belonged to Anthonius Gratia of Tenerife, Spanish merchant, and other subjects of the King of Spain, and that they were therefore legitimately captured by William Parker in the *Richard* by virtue of letters of reprisal issued in this court, and should be delivered to the captors.]

139. *Interlocutory sentence of the goods taken at Puerto de Caballos*[6]

[Having duly considered the case of Richard Hutchins and William Parker, owners of the *Richard* of Plymouth, against

---

[1] Possibly a corruption of *Guanabo* (the modern *Gonave*) or of *Guanahibes* (the modern *Gonaïves*).

[2] Signed.   [3] Signatory's mark.   [4] Signatory's mark.

[5] H.C.A. 24/62, no. 17. Summary. Translated. For the full form of an interlocutory sentence see document 102.

[6] H.C.A. 24/62, no. 18. Summary. Translated.

silver, gold, money, hides, anil and other goods taken by William Parker and his company out of a certain town called Puerto de Caballos in the Indies and brought to Plymouth; we, Julius Caesar, judge of the High Court of Admiralty, find that the said goods belonged to subjects of the King of Spain and are therefore lawful prize.]

140. Trujillo report of three successive raids on Caballos[1]

+

On the 14th of the present month we received your honour's reply to the advice we sent[2] concerning the first seizure of the ships at Puerto de Caballos. After that event so many calamities have befallen the region, that to describe them augments the grief they inspire. For although the first Englishman did not burn the ships or take the town, and carried off only the flagship belonging to Diego Ramirez, he left the rest stripped and half laden; and on the 26th of last month another Englishman came and seized the ships and, after landing a hundred men, occupied the town. He took what cargo remained in the ships which the first had left, burned them and departed without taking anything of what there was on land.

In view of which, then supposing their labours were at an end, the governor and other residents and merchants came back into the town, bringing their merchandise and money which had been hidden in the bush, and decided to send an advice-boat to your honour and to the general commanding the royal armada, with despatches from the royal *audiencia*.

This they did, and the advice-boat had reached this city when, on the 15th of this month at dawn, as it was about to go out past the point, it sighted two pinnaces which had landed men, expecting to find the look-out on the point off guard. These pinnaces came alongside and the advice-boat's master, Francisco Rodriguez, and others made their escape with the despatches. They then saw four ships and two frigates and a pinnace off the

[1] City of Trujillo (Pedro de Eguiça, Manuel de León and Martín de Solórzano) to Don Juan Maldonado Barnuevo (governor of Havana), 29 May 1594 (A. de I. 54-4-6, Santo Domingo 184. 1 *pliego*. Copy). Translated.
[2] Document 121 above.

point, which, without entering this harbour, passed on to Puerto de Caballos. There similarly they sought to surprise the sentinel, as your honour will see by the enclosure,[1] written by a resident of Puerto de Caballos who happened to be at San Pedro, eight leagues away. This raid was worse than the two preceding because of the money they took. God turn all things to His purpose and by His hand apply the remedy!

Considering that the despatches which were saved from the advice-boat are of great importance and that to wait for further orders from the governor will mean long delay, because of the considerable disturbance which these hardships bring in their wake, and believing that such delay might entail certain inconveniences, we resolved to send this bark belonging to Antonio Veneciano to convey them and to report the ruin and destitution to which these three corsairs have in two months reduced this land. They fear nobody, knowing that there is none to offend them. If the armada, which they say will be in that city or off Cape San Antonio, would come out to meet and punish this corsair, it would be a valuable service, for it would give them to understand that they may not[2]... so entirely without risk.

In this city we stand ready daily, well prepared, although we presume that since the first two corsairs did not come here, neither will this one risk losing when he cannot win; and if he does attempt more than the others, we trust in God to defend us from him as He did from the preceding two....

Our Lord preserve your honour many years in His sacred service.

Trujillo, province of Honduras, 29 May 1594.

141. Official account of the Anglo-French capture of Puerto de Caballos, 1594[3]

I, Juan Ximenez, government notary of this province of Honduras, certify to those who may see this present that from evidence assembled by Gregorio de Alvarado, for his majesty

[1] This has not been found.
[2] MS torn.
[3] Official relation drawn up at Valladolid (Honduras), 4 July 1594 (A. de I. 42-1-9/4, Contratación 5109. 1 *pliego*. Legalized copy). Translated.

Caballos and merchants clad only in their shirts, without shoes, uncombed and without swords, among them Captain Diego Ramirez, commander of the Honduras ships, also undressed and without his sword. Of all of them, only the governor, though he was so ill and the enemy had surrounded his house, appeared attired in the black satin he usually wore to mass, wearing also his sword; but his left arm was badly hurt by the blow they gave him as he left his house. Seeing them all in this condition, the governor said that though the enemy had carried off all their belongings they might save their persons, and he ordered them to retire into the bush, where some thirty men assembled.

Being so assembled in the bush, and the governor stretched on the ground there, he ordered his slaves to bring him a package of biscuit and some cheeses which he had caused to be brought from his house when he was surrounded, giving no thought to any more valuable objects. When it had been fetched to him, he ordered that this food be portioned out to all the people three times daily, for two and a half days, when the supply was exhausted. The witnesses say that but for these rations the people would have perished of hunger.

At this juncture, the governor being in the bush with fever and almost at the end of his tether, they brought him warning that, chagrined that with his sword alone he should have cut his way through so many pikes and muskets, the enemy were assembling mules and horses to go and seize him in his camp. They could do this easily because the mulatto rower named Reyes, whom the enemy took in the advice-boat, was the one who arranged this treachery. He knew the way well, for he had been in the camp when the governor drove off the corsair Newport.[1]

Many indeed gave assurance that the enemy was certainly coming to capture the governor, and as there was no possible defence nor arms, nor even a sword besides the governor's, they all urged him to leave because he was so ill and too weak to handle the sword and all the rest were naked and unarmed. So the governor left the camp and went to the city of San Pedro. He provided horses and food at his own expense for the whole journey to that city. As a result of the hardship he endured, the governor relapsed into more serious illness when he arrived there.

[1] *neoporte.*

from all of them, but as he left they gave him a blow on the left shoulder which unjointed his arm. The musketeers kept firing at him.

Having come through this danger, the governor went up the street and met the notary, Gaspar Velazquez, at the corner of his house. As has been said, Velazquez had left by the hidden door and was waiting there to see how it might fare with the governor. In his deposition the notary states that he was amazed to see the governor emerge, sword in hand, because he had not believed that he could do it without being killed or captured, in view of the great number of the enemy who had surrounded him. All the witnesses agree that they did not believe that the governor could escape death or capture, so great was the danger he ran in leaving his house. God was pleased to spare him for his courage, as he was weak with fever and had recently been bled. All conclude by agreeing that they are sure nobody but the governor could have escaped from that danger and come forth as he came from the midst of so many enemies who surrounded his house and blocked his doorway.

When the governor had come out, as described, and met the notary, they went up the street together, still under heavy fire from the enemy's smallshot. The enemy pursued them closely, but were unable to take aim because it was a very dark night and they could not see them. The notary states that he was himself so agitated that, without his noticing, the papers he was carrying fell and scattered on the ground, and when the governor bade him pick them up he did not dare. Then, disabled as he was, the governor stooped and gathered up the papers, leaving not one. The notary was astounded and ran ahead of the governor, who called after him not to be afraid. All the witnesses who were the governor's neighbours and passed his house concluded their depositions by saying that they saw his residence surrounded by English and that the governor was ill, confined to his house; and some declare that they saw him come out by his front door, through the dangers described, sword in hand, beating down the enemies' weapons with his blade. Retiring in this fashion, the governor was the last to abandon the town, and he and the notary, Gaspar Velazquez, reached the bush along the river as day was breaking. There they found all the householders of Puerto de

governor's house, stopping nowhere so that there should be no time to warn him. As soon as they reached the governor's house many men, with pikes, halberds and smallshot, surrounded it, the governor lying ill within, as has been said. By this time people fleeing from the town to the bush were passing by all the time, and they kept calling out: 'Señor Governor, fly by the secret door, for the enemy has surrounded your house!' Witnesses state that they heard the governor respond, calling his household to fetch him clothing. The governor's house being thus surrounded by enemies and he inside, Gaspar Velazquez, clerk designate, who at that moment was passing in the street, fleeing from the enemy, came near the governor's house and heard him speak in his room. Astonished that the governor should not have been informed of what was happening and struck with pity for the governor sick in bed with the enemy at his door, he went in by a hidden door of the house and entered the chamber where the governor was. He found that the governor had just finished dressing and was as calm as if there had been no enemy in the land and no danger to himself.

After Gaspar Velazquez had come into the room where the governor was, he said to him: 'Señor Governor, why is your honour loitering here, when your house is surrounded by the English?' To which the governor replied, without being alarmed or disturbed, rather very quietly and calmly, that if the house was indeed surrounded by enemies the clerk should take an escritoire which was to hand, where the governor kept his majesty's despatches, and endeavour to save it, for which purpose he ordered a slave of his to fetch a light and delivered the escritoire to the notary, Gaspar Velazquez. The governor then ordered that the light be extinguished and took his sword and left the room, followed by the notary. The governor told Gaspar Velazquez to open the front door of his house, to which the notary replied that he dared not open it, because the enemy, who had the house surrounded, were there. So the notary went out by the secret door by which he had entered and the governor opened the front door where the English were. As he opened it they fired many musketshots into the house and drew together, blocking the entrance to the house. God granted that the governor, sword in hand, should pass through despite these enemies and escape

alcalde ordinario[1] of this city of San Pedro in the province aforesaid, in respect to what occurred in Puerto de Caballos on the occasion of the arrival there of Captain William Parker,[2] Englishman, and Captain Jeremias, Frenchman, corsairs, who entered the said port at midnight, I drew up this summary account from the statements made by very many witnesses who in the course of that investigation swore and deposed concerning events in the said port and the manner in which God was pleased to save the governor of this province[3] from the enemies who had surrounded the house where he lay sick in bed; and concerning what happened to other residents in the said port, which, drawn up in narrative form from this testimony, is as follows:

The governor cleared a frigate from the said port for Havana by order of the royal *audiencia* of Guatemala with despatches from that court and from Licentiate Pedro Mallen de Rueda, its president, with news of what had happened when Captain Langton,[4] the English corsair, came and looted and sacked the ships he found in the harbour and carried off the flagship. Within six days after this frigate left the port it was taken off Trujillo Point[5] by two corsairs, one English, named William Parker, and the other French, called Jeremias, who together and in agreement were coming up to sack the said port. Among others on board the frigate was a mulatto oarsman named something-or-other de los Reyes.[6]

Sentinels being on watch on the said port as usual, both on the beach and on the point, some two or three hours after midnight on the seventeenth of last May (the governor having been sick in bed for many days and bled the day before), these two corsairs, William and Captain Jeremias, seized the sentinel on the point and from two pinnaces silently landed men, unobserved. On the beach of the said port they formed these men into two squadrons, one of which went to Captain Diego Ramirez's house which was on the beach itself. With muffled drum the other marched on the

---

[1] Municipal magistrate.
[2] *Guillermo frique*. The corruption of English names is general in these records, but this is a particularly bad case.
[3] Gerónimo Sánchez de Carranza.
[4] *lanton*.
[5] Cape Honduras.
[6] *Fulano de los Reyes*.

ENGLISH PRIVATEERING VOYAGES

fortress or artillery, deserted by all and left alone at the post of danger. Being myself a man who understands war, I know that they would find no remissness to reprimand, but so much foresight to praise, that your majesty might show me favour. Our Lord preserve your majesty in good health and good fortune, as Christianity has need.

From Comayagua, 5 June 1595

143. *First report of Parker's movements in the Gulf of Honduras in 1595*[1]

An English ship and two pinnaces entered Puerto de Caballos on 16 May last and found neither the inhabitants nor their belongings, because everything had been removed to safety. Observing this after they had entered, they sent the two pinnaces towards Golfo Dulce on the 17th, and up to the 26th of that month they had not arrived at the establishment there, though they had appeared at an estate which is near it, belonging to one Antonio Jorge, where they took what foodstuffs they found. It was little. Thence they turned back without doing further damage.

144. *Later report from Trujillo concerning Parker's movements*[2]

For this year, early in May, Captain Parker,[3] an Englishman, arrived at the other port[4] with a ship and a pinnace. He landed, found nothing to steal and passed on to Golfo Dulce. Neither did

---

[1] The *audiencia* of Guatemala to the crown, Guatemala, 15 June 1595 (A. de I. 63–6–10, Guatemala 10. 1 *pliego*. Original). Extract. Translated. Signed by Doctor Francisco de Sandoval (president of the *audiencia*) and Licentiates Diego Carsate and Alvar Gómez de Abraunca. On the same day Doctor Francisco de Sandoval wrote to the king, referring to the corsair force as a ship of 200 tons, three others of 40 tons each and four pinnaces. He reported that the four pinnaces entered the Golfo Dulce and captured a frigate which had come from Campeche in ballast, and some food supplies (A. de I. 63–6–10, Guatemala 10. 2 *pliegos*. Original).

[2] City of Trujillo to the crown, 18 October 1595 (A. de I. 64–1–1, Guatemala 44. 1½ *pliegos*. Original). Extract. Translated. The earlier part of the document recapitulates the experiences of Trujillo in 1592 and 1594, referring to the successful rebuff administered to Newport in 1592 and to the nuisance caused by the presence of the 1594 corsairs, who obliged the Spanish at Trujillo to be on their guard all the time.

[3] *el Capitan Parc.*

[4] Puerto de Caballos.

324

serious allegations and taken evidence against me, asserting that from the bush I traded and bartered with the Englishman who made the raid. Although he could not prove this, as it was notoriously untrue, he has defamed me by attempting to do so; for, sire, instead of rewarding my services rendered at the point of greatest danger, which is Puerto de Caballos, not only have they not rewarded me, but they have harassed me with judges and receivers, spending my estate and ruining my reputation on the strength of allegations entered by a notorious delinquent. With what heart will my successor defend your majesty's interests when I, who have defended them, am attacked in my honour and compelled to spend what I have not in defending myself against calumny? How much better would my reputation have fared had I, if not aiding the treasurer, at least concealed his thefts, as the other governors here have done! Then, indeed, I would not now be suffering the penalties he merited by his conduct. As soon as I arrived in this province I informed your majesty of the impossibility of protecting Puerto de Caballos, because it is an open beach leagues long, where enemies may land at various points. I sent your majesty a map showing the topography of the land and also indicating the part and place to which the town was to be removed.[1] I asked that harquebuses be sent to me because there were not twenty in the whole province. Your majesty made no reply to me on these points, although I received answers to the other points brought up in my despatch. I have fulfilled my duty in every respect, both in peace and in war, as I have proved. No count of carelessness has been found against me. But I complain, sire, that my good name has less weight than Santiago's evil name, or his charges would not have been entertained. Your majesty conferred this office upon me on account of my services, to honour me; and it has been converted into an instrument to affront me. But these are the Indies, where virtue, honour, the sword and truth lie covered with rust, and only falsehood and deceit are valid currency. Misrepresentation and trickery are like the air—omnipresent. I would be glad indeed could this affair of mine be judged by veteran soldiers and experienced officers, that valour and justice might examine and pass judgement upon what I accomplished in Puerto de Caballos, sick, without troops, a

[1] The map has not been found.

your majesty's royal *audiencia* of Guatemala I sent an advice-boat to Havana, which within three days after it left Puerto de Caballos was taken by two corsairs, one English and one French, who were coming up to sack Trujillo. From persons on board[1] these enemies learned how weak this place was and of my poor health and of how well I had carried off the affair with Captain Newport. They advised the enemy not to enter by day, lest at my hands they should fare as the last Englishman had, but to enter at midnight, capturing the sentinel on the point and landing men. This they did, assaulting the town at midnight. They found me sick in bed and surrounded the house. In grave danger I dressed, and God delivered me, sword in hand, from the midst of them. At that hour I found everybody from the town in the bush, whither they had fled barefooted, uncombed, in their shifts and swordless. They were riled to see me, a sick man, clad and carrying my sword, come in among them, whose houses the enemy had not approached, as among so many women in their nightgowns. This did not worry me then, for I was sure that at no matter what hour he entered the enemy would find no booty, for at my orders everything had been carried into safety. But Santiago de Gregorio, treasurer of Honduras, against whom I proved the grave charges I reported to your majesty, persuaded these people to allege that it was owing to my negligence that the port was raided; and, though the witnesses were persons whose money and merchandise I had sent into safety, to accuse me of being responsible for the fact that the enemy had carried them off. The truth is that everyone saw these things removed from the port by my order and none saw them return. In order to remain in possession of other people's property, these people have conspired with Santiago and seek to prove that there was negligence—not because they think there was any, but to cover their own ill-doing. Since by my diligence the money was conveyed into safety, whereas its owners brought it back and it was captured, it would seem more just to bring suit against those who were at fault than against me, who have done nothing wrong. So far does Santiago go to avenge himself, because I proved that he had stolen from your majesty's treasury. Using the charge arising out of the raid as a cover, he has made very

---

[1] Dieguillo the Mulatto among them.

Immediately he ordered supplies to be sent to those persons who had remained in the bush. This and further details appear in the depositions and statements of witnesses to which I refer and from which this relation was drawn up at the request and command of the said governor.

Done in the city of Valladolid del Valle de Comayagua in the province of Honduras, on the third day of the month of July in the year one thousand five hundred and ninety four. I bear witness and in testimony thereof here sign my name in evidence of the truth. Juan Ximenez, government notary.

142. *Personal report of the governor, Gerónimo Sánchez de Carranza, concerning the Anglo-French capture of Puerto de Caballos in 1594*[1]

Sire

Nothing so chills the spirit of a faithful vassal as to see how some of your majesty's ministers appreciate loyal service. Instead of rewarding it and so encouraging the vassal to undertake greater things on your majesty's behalf, they annoy him on account of the good that he has done. I was sick in bed in Puerto de Caballos when news of enemies came. I got up and caused myself to be carried in a chair to the beach, where I remained the whole afternoon of the bombardment. By stratagem and ruse I, alone and unaided, drove from the harbour Captain Christopher Newport,[2] an Englishman, who landed with some 200 muskets. He went away again without taking anything of your majesty's royal treasury, because in good season I had conveyed it to a safe place. I also provided pack-mules for the *encomenderos*[3] and merchants, on which they removed their money and carried their belongings to safety. When the enemy landed he found nothing to steal. After God had vouchsafed me this happy outcome, by order of

---

[1] Gerónimo Sánchez de Carranza, governor of Honduras, to the crown, Comayagua, 5 June 1595 (A. de I. 63–6–39, Guatemala 39. 1 *pliego*. Original). Translated.

[2] *Cristoval Neoporta.*

[3] Grantees of *encomiendas*, having the right to levy tribute on the Indian settlements within areas specified in the grants.

he do any damage there, because he found nothing but some hides, which is a merchandise the English do not covet as the French do.[1] Thereupon, much displeased, he went to Guanaja,[2] at which island he found two other English ships which had come up from the Tierra Firme coast.[3] They spoke each other, and when the newcomers learned that there was no booty available, they all steered for Cape San Antonio. Then, on the sixteenth of July, Captain Jeremias the Frenchman appeared off this bay with three ships, a pinnace and a galiot.[4]

145. Further Spanish information on Parker in 1595[5]

Your majesty will see the account of the damage done in ninety-two and ninety-four and how this year, ninety-five, the corsairs found nothing to steal at Puerto de Caballos because I had cleared the ships in February. They burned and carried off what vessels they did find and with a pinnace and a galiot entered Golfo Dulce and carried off everything there. They made the settlers prisoner and tried to go inland on horseback. They were irked to find nothing of which to take possession as if it were their own. Really, given the condition of the ships which reached Havana from this province on 14 March, all of them would have been lost had they been here then. To get them off so early is a beginning of wise policy.

[1] The English did value hides and brought many cargoes of them home; but the extent of French trading in Hispaniola does suggest that they were more interested than the English.
[2] Donacca.
[3] Probably Benjamin Wood and company—see above, p. 310, n. 2.
[4] A small vessel combining oars and sails. The document goes on to relate the doings of Jeremy Raymond, who attacked and burned the settlement of Caballos, passing on to the Golfo Dulce and thence to the island of Utilla; here a force from Trujillo attacked and defeated the French, killing their leader.
[5] Doctor Francisco de Sandoval to the crown, Guatemala, 30 November 1595 (A. de I. 63–6–39 (155–z), Guatemala 39. 1 *pliego*. Original). Extract. Translated.

CHAPTER XV

THE VOYAGE OF JOHN RIDLESDEN
1595

ALTHOUGH Ridlesden in his deposition concerning this voyage refers to the *Bark Bond* as a ship and to the *Scorpion* and the *Violet* as his pinnaces, the *Bark Bond* and the *Violet* were of more or less equal burden—about 60 tons.[1] This was, then, a small-scale venture. The *Bark Bond* was a Weymouth privateer, owned by the Weymouth merchant John Bond, who had sent her on various expeditions before 1595 with the financial assistance of other Weymouth men.[2] On this occasion, however, the other adventurers were Londoners: John More, Edward Leckland and George Southwick, all London merchants; Stephen Ridlesden, one of the Lord High Admiral's officials, and Robert Bragge, another of Howard's men and a London merchant himself; and Bartholomew Matthewson, another London merchant, who contributed the *Violet* to the expedition.[3] John

---

[1] H.C.A. 25/3 (9), 2 September 1592 and 6 December 1592.

[2] 'Elizabethan Privateering', p. 294.

[3] This information about the financial backing of the venture comes from an action in the Court of Requests, brought against Matthewson by the other adventurers, who alleged that he had acquired more than his fair share of the prize goods (Requests, 2/240/61). Edward Leckland owned the *Globe* of London and sent her privateering in 1591 and 1592 ('Elizabethan Privateering', p. 245). Stephen Ridlesden was an official of the Lord Admiral's, frequently acting for him in prize matters (Harleian MS 598, *passim*; Lansdowne MS 145, f. 254); Lane refers to his setting forth a privateer in the later 1580's (p. 130 above) and he promoted (doubtless for Howard) the venture of the *Charles* in 1594 (H.C.A. 13/31, 25 November 1594). Robert Bragge was a receiver of the Lord Admiral's tenths of prizes (H.C.A. 13/33, 15 February 1598/9; H.C.A. 14/33, nos. 38, 39; Harleian MS 598 for the year 1590). He was one of the company of Amyas Preston's *Golden Riall* in 1585 (*Roanoke Voyages*, p. 237); was interested in the 1596 venture of Newport, Geare and John Ridlesden to the West Indies and in the post-war trade with the West Indies (K. R. Andrews, 'Christopher Newport of Limehouse, Mariner,' *William and Mary Quarterly*, XI (1954), 28–41). Matthewson owned the privateer *Orphante* in 1592 (H.C.A. 25/3 (9), 25 May 1592; H.C.A. 13/31, 7 November 1594; Requests, 2/46/6, 2/43/4).

Ridlesden, perhaps a Barnstaple seaman before he became 'of London gent.', had ten years of experience as a commander of privateers and this was not his last voyage to the West Indies.[1] The *Violet*, alias the *Why not I?* was commanded by William Towerson.[2]

Ridlesden took three prizes—the *St Francis* of Seville, the Azores prize and the cargo of hides taken in the Indies. The tenths of these were valued at £87 13s. 4d., £51 6s. 11d. and £13 6s. 8d. respectively, indicating a total return of about £1500. The cost of the expedition including some £600 for the capital value of ships and guns, was probably about £1200. This represents a low rate of profit for a privateering venture, for the adventurers would receive, after payment of customs and tenths and the crews' thirds, only about half of the total returns. Thus the profit to the adventurers would amount to a mere £150 on a total outlay of £1200.

Of the operations in the Indies little is known. They must have arrived in those waters in March or April and taken the prize in April or May. The *Bark Bond* then made her way home and the others stayed on until July, returning via the Azores in August and reaching Southampton in September.[3]

* * *

146. Deposition of John Ridlesden[4]

JOHN RIDLESDEN of London gent. Captayne of the Barque Bonde of Waymouthe of thadge of xxxv yeares or thereaboutes sworne and examined before the righte wor*shipful* ma*ster* doctor Cesar Judge of Thadmiralty Sayethe:

That aboute January was twelve monethe this ex*amina*te wente to Sea Captayne of the forsaid shippe for thexecution of Le*tt*res of Reprisall agayneste the Kinge of Spayne and his sub-

---

[1] Captain of the *Prudence* of Barnstaple in earlier years (Lansdowne MS 143 ff. 6-46; H.C.A. 13/26, 18 July 1587 and January 1587/8 *passim*; H.C.A. 25/3 (9), 15 July 1592; H.C.A. 13/29, 19 February 1591/2). For his 1596 West Indies voyage with Geare and Newport, see K. R. Andrews, 'Christopher Newport of Limehouse, Mariner,' loc. cit.

[2] Harleian MS 598, f. 35.

[3] Document 146 and Harleian MS 598, ff. 32, 34, 35.

[4] H.C.A. 13/32, 9 March 1595/6.

jectes & theire goodes together withe the Scorpion of London and the Violett his Pinnasses, And he sayethe that withe the sayd shippe and Pinnasses he tooke nere to the Isles of Canaryes a spanishe shippe of the burthen of sixescore tons or there aboutes, in February laste was twelve monethes, beinge laden withe Cordage, some forty or fifty tons of Canarye wynes some oyle, some iron workes, and sundrye other thinges, the particulers wherof he cannot specifye, But sayethe the shippe was of Civill and the goodes belonged to merchauntes of the same place, and shee was called the Ste Fraunces of Civill as the company toulde this examinate and his company: whiche prize this examinate sente into waymouthe, under the conducte of Alexander Coxe.[1]

Allsoe he sayethe that in Auguste was twelve monethes beinge homewardes bounde, he withe the Violette and Scorpion neare the Islandes meett withe and tooke a shippe of the burthen of Lxx[2] or there aboutes beinge laden withe some goate skinnes, hides, some sugare, myese[3] and others smale thinges the particulares wherof he cannot specifye. And he sayethe the same shippe was of Luxborne[4] and was thither bounde, and was laden att ste Iago in Cape de Verde, and belonged withe all the goodes to merchauntes of Luxborne as the company of here informed this examinate, And he belevethe the same to be true because shee and the other shippe were bothe manned withe Portingalles and Spaniardes And the latter shippe this examinate broughte to Sowthampton as he sayethe.[5]

Further more he sayethe that duringe his forsaid voyadge att the Seas he withe his shippe and Pinnasses aforsaid meett withe and tooke a smale Spanishe Frigotte in the Indies, out of whiche he and company tooke betwixte three and fower hunderethe

[1] Master of the *Violet* in 1592 (H.C.A. 25/3 (9), 2 September 1592). The details of the lading of the *St. Francis*, which was bound for Havana, are given in depositions by members of her crew (H.C.A. 24/63, no. 211) and in the estimate of the Lord Admiral's tenth (Harleian MS 598, f. 32). She reached Weymouth in April 1595, and was adjudicated as lawful prize in the Admiralty Court (H.C.A. 24/63, no. 209).
[2] [*Sic*.]   [3] Probably maize.   [4] Lisbon.
[5] The prize arrived at Southampton in September. She contained hides, goatskins, loaf sugar, cuskins (drinking cups), maize, guinea wheat, seed, goat butter, candles, 'elephants' teeth', wax, train-oil and three civet cats (Harleian MS 598, f. 35).

hides which he sente to waymouthe in the Barque bounde, And other goodes he had not out of the same Frigotte which belonged unto Spaniardes but theire names or of wheare they were he knowethe not, but the Frigotte was manned withe Spaniardes.[1]

[1] 300 hides, raw and tanned, came in the *Bark Bond* to Weymouth in June 1595 (Harleian MS 598, f. 34).

CHAPTER XVI

THE VOYAGE OF MICHAEL GEARE
1594–5

MICHAEL GEARE, born and bred in Limehouse, had been serving in voyages of reprisal regularly since 1585—that is, from about the age of nineteen. In the year of the Armada he sailed in John Watts' ship the *Drake* on what was probably his first visit to the West Indies. Two years later he was already a master, making a second West Indies voyage in Watts' 1590 expedition, and in 1591 he commanded the same ship—the *John*—again to the West Indies. On this voyage he emerged as a tough fighter, none too scrupulous in securing for himself an ample share of the proceeds. From 1592 to 1595 he commanded (and partly owned) the *Michael and John*, which may have been simply the *John* renamed.¹ After 1595 he made at least three more voyages to the West Indies—in 1596 with Newport, in 1601–2 with David Middleton, and in 1602–3 again with Newport.²

The 1594–5 venture of the *Michael and John* and the *Handmaid* was set forth by John Stokes, Thomas Scott and Michael

---

¹ It was of the same burden, 100–120 tons, and the *John*, owned by John Stokes and John Watts in 1591, vanishes from the records after that date. It seems likely that Geare, with Scott, bought Watts' share and had the ship appropriately renamed.
² For his earlier voyages, see document 71 above; *Roanoke Voyages*, pp. 579–716; H.C.A. 25/3 (9), 1 and 11 March 1591/2, 19 and 28 December 1592, 6 January 1592/3; H.C.A. 13/30, 12 June 1593; H.C.A. 13/31, 8 March 1593/4; H.C.A. 24/62, nos. 26, 37, 162/3, 166. For his later voyages, see Andrews, 'Christopher Newport of Limehouse, Mariner,' *William and Mary Quarterly*, XI (1954), 28–41. In later years he became an Elder Brother of Trinity House and was knighted—a respectable climax to a career of embezzling prize goods and similar dubious practices. His house in Stepney Green, called the Dagger House, from the dagger which hung outside, was bequeathed by his son in 1630 to the Corporation of Trinity House, with the proviso that out of the yearly rent the sum of £5 should be distributed among the poorest decayed seamen and seamen's widows inhabiting the hamlet of Limehouse (Birch, pp. 29–30).

Geare. After some success early in 1595 off Puerto Rico and Santo Domingo, Geare moved on to worry the coast near Havana. Here another prize fell to him—an empty ship, which he armed and manned to strengthen his own force. Then on 4/14 April Admiral Don Sebastián de Arencibia, patrolling the coast with a galleon and three shallops, sighted the English near Cabañas. A bitter struggle followed; of Geare's men about twenty were taken prisoner, many more were killed and only the *Michael and John* managed to escape. On the Spanish side the casualties were less heavy, but considerable.¹

Geare seems to have taken another prize in the Indies, and to have obtained in ransoms and direct plunder a valuable haul; but since he had smuggled this into the country without payment of customs and tenths, he had good reason not to mention it in his deposition.²

* * *

*147. Deposition of Michael Geare*³

MICHAELL GEERE late Captaine & parte owner of the Michaell & John of London sworne & examined before the righte worshipfull master doctor Cesar Judge of her majesties high Courte of the Admiralty what shipps or goodes he & company have taken by reprisall duringe this late viadge Sayth by chardge of his oathe that this examinates pinnace called the handmaide of London whereof Thomas Stookes was Captaine⁵ in January laste nere Porterico tooke a spanishe shipp of Civill called the Conception laden with ropes breade garlicke wynes oyle nayles okom pitche & other provision for the kinges fleete which this examinate with consente of his company sould to Nicholas Naflora a Spaniarde beinge Captaine of the said shippe for xvC duckettes

*Officium Domini contra Michaelem Geere.*⁴

---

¹ Documents 147–51 below.
² Document 152 below.
³ H.C.A. 13/31, 4 July 1595.
⁴ The exact nature of the Lord Admiral's case against Geare is not known, but the document itself suggests that he was suspected of concealing prize goods. Document 152 below indicates that he was probably interrogated again, and more precisely, later.
⁵ Presumably related to the owner, John Stokes. He was one of those captured by the Spanish.

but wantinge money he provided at St Domingo certaine pearle & plate as platters candlestickes & delivered the same unto this examinate not beinge of valewe above two hundreth poundes beinge all which he had for the said shipp & goodes.

Also he sayth that nere St Domingo the said Carvell & company a spanishe Frigott[1] comminge from St John de Porterico wherein was noe goodes but only foure hundreth & odde poundes in peeces of eighte v peeces of gould of xj ounzes & bagge[2] of seede pearle bounde for St Domingo, and nere the Havana they tooke an empty shipp which was goinge to lade hides, and the Kinges Fleete tooke the same from this examinate againe togeather with this examinates pinnace & xxv men,[3] And moore or other shipps or goodes he & company tooke not this viadge.[4]

148. Deposition of James Bragge[5]

JAMES BRAGGE of Limehouse mariner master of the Michaell & John of London aged xxxv yeares or thereaboutes sworne & examined before the said Judge of the Admiralty Sayth that in the Indies the handemaide beinge pinnace to the Margarett & John[6] tooke a spanishe shipp called the Conception of Civill and the same they sould to the spanishe Captaine by bargaine for xvC duckettes and they were fayne to take certaine old plate two smale chaines of gould & two chaines of pearle for paymente which they broughte home worth aboute two hundreth poundes sterling. Also he sayth that nere St Domingo they tooke a frigott comminge from St John de Porterico bounde for St Domingo wherein was foure hundreth & od poundes in peeces of viij & v smale peeces of gould wayenge xj ounzes & a bagge of seede pearle. And more shipps or goodes they tooke not but one empty shipp nere the havana which the kinges shipps tooke from them againe with their pinnace and xxv men.

[1] [Sic.] The word 'tooke' accidentally omitted.
[2] [Sic.] The indefinite article omitted.
[3] Compare the Spanish estimates in documents 149, 150 below.
[4] But see document 152 below.
[5] H.C.A. 13/31, 4 July 1595. James Bragge had been master of the *Margaret* in Newport's 1592 venture (document 92 above).
[6] [Sic.]

loose the shallop. They considered themselves fortunate to get away from her at a moment when I was so near that I had as good as boarded and taken the enemy. His flagship and mine were not 300 paces apart, but because he was a good sailer he broke out three in addition to his regular sails, whereas my flagship had not even its usual number and those it had were old. I tried to get new sails, but they were not to be procured in this city, for Don Francisco Coloma carried off everything when he went. So the enemy flagship got away from me, abandoning to me her vice-admiral and another shallop, with a couple of dozen living prisoners including the vice-admiral. We had killed about fifty others.[1] I lost sixteen or eighteen men killed.

Because there were many wounded and the shallops were in bad shape, I ordered one of them and the caravel and the two prizes to proceed at once to Havana, to care for the wounded and to overhaul the shallops. With my flagship and the remaining shallop I determined to follow the enemy flagship and his remaining shallop and to drive him from this coast, because of the damage a vessel of such great strength could do. I chased him three times; then, seeing I could not overhaul him, I decided to return to this harbour and here arm and fit out the shallops and ships that they might be better prepared and so overtake the enemy.

I entered Havana harbour on the 21st and found that the shallops which I had sent back had not yet arrived. That very day Don Luis Fajardo had received news that the enemy had bottled them up in Puercos river. He ordered me to return immediately to their relief with my flagship, a flyboat and a shallop. I set out at once and on the 23rd returned here with them all.

151. *Interlocutory sentence of Geare's prize goods*[2]

[Having duly considered the case Magdalene Stokes, widow of John Stokes, and of the other owners of the *Michael and John* of London, Michael Geare captain and James Bragge master, against certain plate, platters and candlesticks of silver, £400 and more in pieces of eight, five pieces of gold weighing eleven ounces, one

[1] Compare Geare's figure of 25 men lost (document 147 above).
[2] H.A.C. 24/63, no. 104. Undated. Summary. For the full form of an interlocutory sentence, see document 102 above.

would be ready, and so to clear the coast of any corsairs who might be about.

On which undertaking I left on the 3rd and, having proceeded to Cape Corrientes, reconnoitred the whole coast and spent four days off that cape and off Cape San Antonio, on the 11th of that month, ten or twelve leagues to sea, I met Don Francisco de Corral with four sails in his command. I left him to carry out my general's order, seeing that Don Francisco was so well armed that no corsair could trouble him, nor had I news of any on the coast.

The hulk I had for vice-admiral was such a laggard that with her in my company I could not possibly execute my orders and return to Havana by the specified date. Daybreak of the 14th found me off Pan de Cabañas in a dead calm two leagues from another ship of over 300 tons burden with three shallops.[1] I ordered my shallops to row out to reconnoitre these vessels and they saw that they were English.

As we left the harbour of Havana I had in writing ordered the commanders of these shallops to lay by the board any enemy they might meet, even if we encountered half a dozen together. Yet they came back to me because the enemy fired a few pieces. I issued them another order in writing, commanding all three shallops and the caravel to row to the enemy's flagship and attack her, on penalty of death, promising that I would support them immediately. They rowed towards the enemy and I followed in my flagship, towed by two shallops, in which I took my stand. In this fashion I covered nearly a league.

By this time the shallops, which were faster, came up to the enemy, and one shallop and the caravel laid the enemy's flagship by the board, as did the other shallop the enemy's vice-admiral. But because the enemy's flagship was so powerful, between her and one of her shallops they closed in on one of my shallops. The enemy flagship carried 200 men; my vessel, 50. They so maltreated my shallop that they had her almost beaten, and had I not come up as promptly as I did in my flagship they would have carried her off. But on seeing me approach, they made haste to

[1] A considerable exaggeration of the size of the *Michael and John*, though the figures mentioned in H.C.A. bonds for good behaviour, 100–120 tons, may well have been unduly low.

of the shallop which was their petty vice-admiral. They are given rations and well treated.

On this occasion, as in all others that come up in your majesty's service, I was aided by Admiral Don Sebastian with such care and punctuality that he deserves to be shown honour and favour by your majesty. He is at this very moment as I write ready, with yards across, to go out again to make the way safe for the New Spain fleet under Luis Alfonso Flores. He has three galleons and a flyboat, well manned with seamen and soldiers. These vessels are Luis Cestin's, the *Santo Tomas* and the *Bergoño*, in which Don Francisco de Corral came over. He also has the three available shallops in addition to the one taken from the Englishman, which I have also armed. He is therefore fully prepared for whatever may offer. These ships are fast enough to overhaul anything, and I therefore believe that any Englishman who may happen along here this year will leave punished with such damage as in other years they have inflicted. If it be understood that the enemy is stronger, I will go out with all the rest of my command.

150. The engagement with Geare's ships: personal report by the Spanish commander[1]

Sire

As soon as I had brought the Honduras ships safely into this port, Don Luis Fajardo ordered me to careen the two shallops and then, with them, a caravel and a galleon, to run along this coast as far as Cape Corrientes and between that cape and San Anton to remain three or four days and to return afterwards to Pan de Cabañas and to spend two or three days between that point and the Sonda de las Tortugas;[2] which done, to return to port without fail by the 20th of last month in order to set forth again to meet the New Spain fleet with the other vessels which by that time

[1] Don Sebastián de Arencibia to the crown, Havana, 3 May 1595 (A. de I. 54-2-6, Santo Domingo 128. 1 *pliego*. Original; duplicated). Translated.
[2] More or less due north of Cabañas.

149. The engagement with Geare's ships: report by Don Luis Fajardo from Havana[1]

Admiral Don Sebastian de Arencibia, who went out with a galleon and three shallops to protect this coast, returned to this harbour on the 23rd ultimo with two shallops which he took from an Englishman. One was the Englishman's vice-admiral and the other a vessel which he had seized some days before. It belongs to a householder of Havana. The Englishman had armed it. It has been returned to the rightful owner according to your majesty's provision contained in the ordinances for this course. This capture was of no further importance and the enemy's flagship got away. It was a 250 ton ship and the shallop *Coloma* and the caravel laid her by the board, but because it was calm the galleon, with the vice-admiral, Don Sebastian, on board, could not come up. Nevertheless the incident appeared important to the residents of this city, because this is the first prize the armada has made and because this corsair is the one who was doing the most damage along this coast; and because it was a hard-fought affair.

On the shallop *Coloma* alone, which carried 30 soldiers, thirteen persons were killed and seven or eight more wounded. Still others were killed and wounded on the other vessels. Ensign Guerrero of Captain Villaverde's company, who was in command of the shallop *Coloma*, fought well until he received three musket and two pike wounds. Some Englishmen boarded his vessel from the enemy's flagship, but, observing that Admiral Don Sebastian's ship was coming up, towed by two shallops for there was no wind, this vessel cut the cables which held her alongside the *Coloma* and made away, for she was the better sailer. It is understood that she was badly damaged.

Seventeen English were taken alive in the two shallops. All the rest died fighting. Some were drowned as they tried to get to their flagship. I have them here in prison along with the captain[2]

---

[1] Don Luis Fajardo to the crown, 3 May 1595 (A. de I. 54–2–6, Santo Domingo 128. 1 *pliego*. Original). The portions of the letter omitted, at the beginning and the end, do not relate to this incident. Don Luis Fajardo was left in command of the fleet at Havana after the departure of Don Francisco Coloma with his homeward bound armada in March 1595. Extract. Translated.

[2] Thomas Stokes (document 147 above).

ENGLISH PRIVATEERING VOYAGES

occupied with customs business and the management of official expeditions, and in close touch with men like Burghley and Sir John Hawkins. Among the gentlemen who borrowed money from him were Christopher Carleill and Thomas Cavendish. After 1585 Myddelton became interested in privateering. For him this was not merely a form of speculation, for he owned or partly owned a number of ships and had contact with the seamen of London and Weymouth. Above all, he was a sugar merchant, and sugar figured more largely than any other commodity in the prize goods of the Spanish war. Much of Myddelton's profit came from the purchase of the numerous cargoes of sugar taken by other privateers, but he also sent out his own expeditions and invested in others' ventures.[1]

In the voyage of the *Rose Lion*, as his account book reveals, Myddelton had an eighth share, and it seems to have been a profitable venture.[2] Of the voyage itself we know only that a prize—a ship called the *Fortune*, laden with ginger, sugar and other goods—was taken 'with smale fight' near Santo Domingo in March 1595 and brought to Plymouth in June.[3]

The documents relating to this voyage are chiefly concerned with the claim of certain Dutch merchants to the *Fortune* and a great part of her lading. The cause was fought at great length in the High Court of Admiralty and it was not until December 1597 that judgement was finally given in favour of the captors.[4] It

---

[1] One of his own privateers was the *Riall* of Weymouth. He refers also to some £300 laid out at Weymouth in the victualling of divers barks (Account Book, under date 5 October 1594), to an adventure of £150 in Richard Hawkins' South Seas expedition of 1593 (ibid., under date 8 December 1596) and to £300 invested in Raleigh's Guiana voyage of 1595 (ibid., under date 20 January 1594/5).

[2] Account Book, under dates 21 September and 5 October 1594, 4 June and 20 December 1595 and 10 May and 4 August 1596. The details given are tantalizingly incomplete and it is therefore impossible to be more precise than this.

[3] Documents 158 and 160 below. The allegation (document 159) gives January as the date of capture.

[4] Document 161 below. In this chapter the libel, the allegation, the sentence and a deposition from each side are given in full to illustrate the character of the H.C.A. documents. Further materials relating to this case are: depositions made at Plymouth by Spanish prisoners (H.C.A. 24/63, no. 219); depositions on the libel by Moreman, Le Bee and La Barre (H.C.A. 13/31, 23, 24, 25 September 1595 respectively) and Mucheron (H.C.A. 13/32, 21 May 1596); depositions on the allegation by Dias, Currea, Acton, Jennings, W. Weste and Ketchman (H.C.A. 13/31, 27 and 30 September, 16, 18 and 29 October 1595) and Stockes (H.C.A. 13/32, 21 January 1596/7); further pleading for West (H.C.A. 24/64, no. 32); interrogatories

he was also an important and representative figure in the privateering world some sketch of him is not out of place.[1] He was the fourth son of Richard Myddelton, governor of Denbigh Castle, and the elder brother of Sir Hugh Myddelton, who later undertook the New River project. Thomas, who was himself knighted in 1603, bought the estate of Chirk Castle in 1595, becoming M.P. for Merionethshire in 1597–8 and Lord Lieutenant of the county in 1599, Lord Mayor of London in 1613 and M.P. for the City in 1624, 1625 and 1626, living on to the age of about eighty at his manor of Stansted Mountfichet in Essex, where he died in 1631. He seems to have owed his success partly to native business ability and partly to the ramifications of his family. At an early age he entered the service of Ferdinand Poyntz, a merchant trading to the Netherlands, and by 1578 became Poyntz's factor at Flushing.[2] A few years later he married the daughter of Richard Saltonstall, governor of the Merchants Adventurers. In 1583 he was already a freeman of the Grocers Company and the chief partner in one of the two leading sugar refineries in London, trading on a large scale in sugar at Antwerp.[3]

Myddelton's commercial interests branched increasingly from this time, but the main stem remained the Mincing Lane sugar house. He was admitted to the Levant Company in 1592 and later invested in the East India Company, the Virginia Company and the Londonderry Company. He traded to Spain and to the Azores and, at the end of the war, to the West Indies.[4] During the nineties he was already a man of great influence, much

[1] The following biographical details are based on Cokayne, *Lord Mayors and Sheriffs*, pp. 60–5; the *D.N.B.*; the H.C.A. records; the MS account book of Myddelton's, entitled 'A Jurnal of all owtlandishe accomptes begyninge this 14th May 1583' (hereafter referred to as 'Account Book'), now deposited in the National Library of Wales; and Myddelton, *Pedigree of the family of Myddelton* (Horncastle, 1910).

[2] H.C.A. 13/23, 16 April 1578.

[3] Account Book, pp. 2–9 *passim*.

[4] He set forth a ship called the *Vineyard*, under his nephew Roger Myddelton, in 1602 and again in 1603, which together with a number of other English, French and Dutch ships, drove a brisk trade in the Indies, keeping their headquarters at Port Gonaïves (H.C.A. records for 1604, *passim*, and Account Book, p. 165, where the entry concludes: 'and so remayneth for my owne adventure in the said shippe and goodes as abovsaid ye some of 1568: 19; 9 starlinge beseechinge allmightie god to blesse and preserve the said ship with her pinace, and all the Company in them and send them saufely to retorne into England with all ther lading to gods glorie and our Comforte—I say my parte is—1568. 19. 9.').

CHAPTER XVII

THE VOYAGE OF THE *ROSE LION*
1594-5

THE *Rose Lion* was one of the powerful London merchantmen employed in the Levant trade, and like many of these ships she made several privateering voyages.¹ It was in late September and early October 1594 that she was fitted out at Plymouth by her captain, Thomas West,² at the expense of Thomas Cordell, William Garraway, Thomas Myddelton, Nicholas Farrar and others.³ The four mentioned were leading London merchants, and the name of Cordell connects this venture with Lancaster's almost exactly contemporary expedition to Pernambuco, Lancaster's chief backers being Cordell, Paul Bayning and John Watts.⁴

Thomas Myddelton is one of the few Elizabethan merchants of whom we know a little more than the usual formal details, and as

---

¹ For example in 1597 (H.C.A. 13/32, 22 December 1597 and 4 January 1597/8); 1598 ('Elizabethan Privateering', p. 362); 1599 (H.C.A. 13/34, 27 June 1599) and 1602 (H.C.A. 13/37, 25 June 1604).

² Captain of the privateer *Discharge* in 1590 ('Elizabethan Privateering', p. 236).

³ Cordell was a freeman of the Mercers Company and a leading figure in the Levant and East India Companies; as owner of two of the largest English merchantmen afloat—the *Merchant Royal* and the *Edward Bonaventure*—and as owner or part-owner of various other vessels, including the *George Bonaventure*, the *Royal Exchange* and the *Centurion*, he was one of the most important promoters of privateering. Garraway was of the Drapers Company and a member of the Levant and East India Companies. He partly owned the *Royal Defence*, the *Royal Exchange* and the *Merchant Royal*, and was thus associated with Cordell in Mediterranean trade and in privateering; unlike Cordell, he seems never to have become an alderman ('Elizabethan Privateering', pp. 233, 350). Farrar was in partnership with Myddelton. Others known to have been interested in this voyage were Christopher Baker, who was probably a member of the great shipbuilding family (Corbett, *Spanish War*, p. 298) and seems to have had a permanent interest in this ship, perhaps because he built her; and Richard Allett.

⁴ Lancaster set sail in October 1594 and returned in July 1595, but there is no evidence of any direct connection between the two voyages. A curious coincidence is that one of Lancaster's captains and the pilot of the *Rose Lion* had the same name: John Adey.

bag of pearls and other goods recently taken at the seas by Geare, Bragge and their company; we, Julius Caesar, judge of the High Court of Admiralty, find that they have given sufficient proof of their case; we judge that the above goods belonged to a certain Nicholas Naflora and other subjects of the King of Spain, and that they were therefore legitimately captured by Geare and Bragge in the *Michael and John* by virtue of letters of reprisal issued by this court, and should be delivered to the captors.]

152. *Interrogatories for the examination of Michael Geare and his company*[1]

Imprimis whether you did not take in the Indies a Carvell laden with passingers what quality they were what goodes they had aboute them severally every person viz. pearle Bullion precious stones, Corroll, reddy money, muske Civett or ambergreese and lett them specify the particulers of them and from whome they had the same.

Item what ransome they made of every particuler person.

Item whether there were not a noble woman a passinger in the same boate whome they ransomed at a thowsand pounde more or lesse, & what was her ransome. *Michaell Geere & company*

Item uppon what daye and tyme of the daye or night did you arrive uppon this quoast and which of your Company went ashoare uppon your arryvall, what his or their names are and what caried they ashoare with them.

Item uppon your arrivall in the narrowe seas whether you mighell Geere did not repayer upp to London what pearle gould Jewells etc. brought you upp with you to whome sould or disposed you the same and for what price.

Item what somme or sommes of money caried you from London back to your shippe and for what purpose caried you the same & of whome receaved you the same here in London.

Item what Gouldsmithes went downe with you in your Company or came aborde you before your coming upp to London & what plate money Jewells pearle Bullion precious stones muske Civett ambergreese or any other thinges whatsoever did they or any other whatsoever buy of you.

[1] H.C.A. 24/63, no. 195. Undated and unheaded, a very rough draft.

9. Sir Thomas Myddelton
Oil painting in the collection of Sir John Lawes, Bart

seems probable, however, that a part of the plaintiffs' case was in substance true—that they were trading covertly to the West Indies under the names of 'some assured friends in Spain' in order to evade the laws which forbade foreign merchants to take part in such trade. The widespread character of Dutch participation in the West Indies trade was and is generally known,[1] but the documents below provide some interesting details about it.

*   *   *

153. Spanish prisoner's statement concerning the Fortune[2]

To all Christian people to whom this presente writinge of true Testymonyall shall Come, George Baron gentleman Maior of the Bourroughe of Weymouthe sendeth greetings Sygnyfyenge and witnessinge by these presentes, That on the daie of the date hereof there came before him John Peritha of Viana in Portingale of the adge of lvij^{tie} yeres or thereabout whoe was latelie taken att Sea in a shippe of St Domingo Called the Roseave by a shippe of Dartmouth Called the Dyamonde, and beinge voluntarilie deposed upon the holie Evangeliste sayeth, That the shippe called the Fortune of Cyvyle nowe within the haven of Plymouthe, which was lately taken att the Seas by the Rose Lyon of London, and by her broughte in here laden with gynger Sugers and other merchandizes, doth belonge to John Aurikes of Cyvyle aforesaid who althoughe he be a Fleminge borne, yett he hath knowen hym to dwell in Cyvyle and in St Domingo where he was marryed by the space of Twentie and one yeres, and to Dego Peres de Purres as it was sayd att tharryvall of the said shippe in St Domyngo about a yere scynce, And also the said Deponent uppon his othe sayeth, That the said shippe after her sayd arryvall in St Domingo aforesaid, landed there Certayne wynes, oyles, olyfe, Capers,

---

for West (H.C.A. 24/63, no. 155, and 24/64, no. 73/4); depositions on West's further pleading by Garraway, Poyntell, Davies, Allett, Cordell, Myddelton and Farrar (H.C.A. 13/32, 8, 9 and 17 July 1596); letter from Burghley to Caesar asking him to hasten proceedings (Additional MS 12505, ff. 473–4, dated 22 May 1597).

[1] Documents 157 and 158 below contain open admissions of colouring. See also Haring, *Trade and Navigation*, pp. 107–12. (That some English merchants acted with the Dutch is also suggested—see p. 349 below).

[2] H.C.A. 24/63, no. 218. Statements to similar effect were taken from a passenger on the *Fortune* and a member of her crew, on 4 June 1595 (H.C.A. 24/63, no. 219).

figges, nuttes, and such like Commodities and greate store of lynnynge Cloth and silke, the which as appeared by the Cocquettes regesters and bills of ladinge which were in the said shippe that came from Cyvyle did belonge to the said John Aurikes and Dego Peres de Purres, and other Spaynishe merchauntes, as namely Pedro Alves, Pedro Ortes St Davale dwellinge in St Domingo aforesaid and divers other Spaynishe marchauntes there dwellinge. And farther he sayeth uppon his othe, That the sayd Gynger Sugers and other marchaundizes that were brought into Plymouthe haven in the said shippe were imbarqued into the same shippe in St Domingo aforesaid, by the foresayd Pedro Alves & Pedro Ortes St Davale to the use of theymeselfes and such as were partners with theym in the foresaid wynes & other marchaundizes that came from Cyvyle, to be therehence transported to Cyvyle aforesaid, he knoweth all this to be true for that he was present in St Domingo aforesayd, in the sayd shippe wherein he was taken, which did also there lade, when the sayd shippe did both discharge and recharge as aforesaid, and was made acquaynted with the register and bills of ladinge which the said shippe brought from Cyvyle to St Domingo, and hadd this favor amongest the merchaunts to lade into the sayd shippe a Chest of blewe stons for paynters worth there Two hundred duckettes, which because he was a Portingale borne, & therefore meight not be knowen to deale for anye thinge, he did direct it to byn delyvered to the foresayd John Aurikes att tharryvall of the sayd shippe att Cyvyle aforesaid, He noteth this withall, that the sayd shippe discharged & recharged att St Domingo aforesayd att a kaye within the Castell, which is a greate favor & none can be suffered so to do unles he be a Spaynyard, He affirmeth uppon his othe that there maie nott be anie (unles he be a Spaynyard or att least a subject allowed of the kinge of Spayne) permytted to trade or trafique into anie parte of the west Indyes uppon payne of lost of goodes and his bodye att the kinges pleasure, which hath byn a thinge alwaies duely observed, and is att this tyme, Besydes he sayeth that these Gyngers Sugers and other marchaundizes that were brought in hether in the sayd shippe were nott the retorne, or of the monies made of the said wynes and other merchaundizes that were brought to St Domingo in the said shippe as aforesayd, but was of the retorne and of the monyes made of Certayne other marchaundizes belonginge to the foresayd marchauntes and theire partners, which this Deponent Carryed to St Domingo about two yeres scynce. And Certaynely knoweth the same, but referreth it to the register, sayenge there it appeareth what everye man is and where he dwelleth. The sayenges of the said John Peritha were interpreted by Anthonie Goddard of Plymouthe marchaunte whoe can the language and did interprete the same uppon his othe. AS WITNES of the more trueth in this behalf the sayd Maior hath nott onlie hereunto subscribed his name, but also to the same hath fixed the seale of office of Maioraltie of the said Bourroughe Dated the Twelth daie of June in the seaven and Thirtith yere of the Raigne of our soveraigne ladye Elizabeth by the grace of god of Englande Fraunce & Irelande Quene defendor of the fayth &c.

George Barron Maior.[1]

154. *Interlocutory sentence of the* Fortune *of Seville*[2]

[Having duly considered the case of Thomas Cordell, alderman of the City of London, Thomas Myddelton, Christopher Baker, Nicholas Farrar and Richard Allett, merchants, John Adey, pilot, Thomas West, sailor, and their associates, owners of the *Rose Lion* of London, against the Spanish ship the *Fortune* of Seville and her lading of sugar, ginger and other goods, taken by Thomas West, captain of the said ship, and her crew and brought to Plymouth; we Julius Caesar, judge of the High Court of Admiralty, find that they have given sufficient proof of their case; we declare that the said ship was laden in the port of Santo Domingo in the Indies and was bound for Seville and that at the time of capture the goods in her belonged to John Aurikes, Jerome Pedraldes, Diego Perez de Purres, Peter Alves, Peter Ortes Sandavall, merchants of Seville, and other subjects of the King of Spain and were legitimately captured by the said captain by virtue of letters of reprisal issued by this court and should be delivered to the captors as lawful prize.]

[1] Signed.
[2] H.C.A. 24/63, no. 217. Summary. For the full form of an interlocutory sentence, see document 102 above.

155. Letter from Burghley and Howard to Dr Caesar[1]

After our hartie Comendacions Whereas a shippe of *Armeror*[2] in *Zeland* called the *fortune* hath latelie bene taken att the seas by Captayne West by waie of reprisall, beinge sett to the seas by Mr *Garwaie* and other englishe marchantes and the same so taken by them for good and lawfull pryse in asmuch as they alleage that the goodes in the saied shippe shoulde belonge to Spanyardes, and for proofe therof they have alleadged divers reasons, as shewinge the bookes of ladinge and other bookes which is denyed by certayne marchauntes of the Lowe Countries, and pretended by them to belonge to marchauntes of *Amsterdam* and other places of *Holland* & *Zeland*. Wee have therfore thought good to praie and requyre you to examyn the wittnesses and proofes on either side, aswell for the prysers to mayntayne theire clayme and tytle to be good and lawfull prise, as what can be saied by Witnesses or proofes on the contrarie parte to mayntayne and prove the goodes or any parte therof to belonge to marchauntes of *Holland* and *Zeland*, and herein to use such Convenyent speed as you maie, as the proofes on either side maie be had and accordinglie to advertise us of your proceedinges, And so fare you well from the Courte att Greenewich the xjth of August 1595.

Your verie lovinge freindes
W. Burghley.   C. Howard.

Judge of the Admyraltie.

156. Appraisement of the cargo of the Fortune[3]

The appraysement and valuacion of certen Ginger, Suger, and Cassia fistula lately attached by aucthority of this Courte at the

[1] Additional MS. 12505, f. 442. The procedure by which foreign merchants lodged complaints with the Privy Council, or members thereof, who referred them to the Admiralty Court, was quite normal. The document is endorsed: 'To our lovinge freinde Master Doctor Caesar, Judge of the highe Courte of the Admyraltie' and further endorsed by Caesar: '11 Aug. 1595. My L. Tresorer & my L. Admirall touching the cause of the Dutch ag. the goods brought in by capten West.'

[2] Armewe or Arnemuiden.

[3] H.C.A. 24/63, no. 122. Endorsed: 'Thappraysement of ginger & other goodes browght in by West.' No quantities are given and no totals on the right. The valuations are, as usual in H.C.A. appraisements, very low. The appraisers were

suite of John Cornelius Corffe, William Arenson, Starr & others —and taken at the seas by Thomas west Captaine of the Rose Lion of London and brought into this porte of London praysed by us John Burd, Robert Cobb, John Archer, George Southwick and Henry TopField merchauntes the third daye of October 1595: as followeth:

Inprimis we the sayd Appraysers havinge viewed and seene the sayd ginger beinge St Domingo Ginger very ill conditioned, ungarbled, full of Dust, worme eaton and rotten wett and Drye, good and badd one with another we valewe at iij^{li} vj^s 8^d per C.[1]

Item Domingo Suger in powders very moyste and packed of Divers sortes in each Cheste vizt pannells muscavadoes and in some of them sprinckled with course whites beinge all in Chestes we doe valewe and esteame one with another at xl^s per C.[2]

Item Cassia fistula ungarbled much broken and Drye we valewe and esteame worth xxx^s per C.

In witness whereof we the sayd Appraysers have hereunto putt our handes the daye and yere abovewritten.[3]

157. Spirincke contra West: the libel[4]

IN THE NAME OF GOD AMEN, before you, the honourable and eminent Julius Caesar, doctor of laws, lieutenant, judge or president of the High Court of Admiralty of England as well as of petitions of appeal to our serene lady the Queen, or before one or other of the masters surrogate president of the said court, the party of John Spirincke, Rowland Fawkner, William Williamson, John Cornelius Corffe, Peter Vanake and

all important London merchants and undoubtedly were acquaintances, if not friends, of the defendants.

[1] Myddelton's price for the ginger was £6 3s. 4d. per hundredweight (Account Book, under date 20 December 1595).
[2] Myddelton's price was 48/- (ibid).
[3] Signed by the appraisers.
[4] H.C.A. 24/63, no. 169. Endorsed: 'Johannes Spirincke Rowlandus Fawconer Willielmus Williamson Johannes Cornelius Corffe et alii contra Thomam Weste Clercke Senior Clercke Junior: Datum per Clercke Senior die Jovis xviij Septembris 1595.' In the original, items 4 to 15 inclusive are in English (except the formal pleadings in items 11 and 12) and the rest is in Latin.

associates against Captain Thomas West and against whomsoever else before you shall lawfully intervene on his behalf, by way of petition of complaint and bringing this action before you in whatever manner and form of law may be the best and most effectual and also to every and whatsoever effect of the law that is able howsoever to follow thereupon, states, alleges and in these writings propounds in law item by item as follows.

1. FIRSTLY, that in the months of March, April, May, June, July, August, September, October, November, December, January, February and March in the years of our lord 1593 and 1594, and in the months of March, April, May and June in the present year of our lord 1595, or in one or other or several of those months and years, the aforesaid John Spirincke and Rowland Fawkner were owners and lawful possessors of a certain ship called the *Fortune* of Armew in Zeeland and of all and singular the equipment and furniture whatsoever howsoever belonging and pertaining to it, and were and are commonly said, taken, held, named and publicly, openly and notoriously reputed to be owners and lawful possessors thereof. And he propounds severally, conjointly and separately.

2. ITEM, That agreement, peace and concord have been entered into, kept and concluded for several years and at present exist between our illustrious lady the Queen and her progenitors and this realm of England and the chiefs, leaders, heads or governors of the aforesaid town of Armew and the parts of Holland and Zeeland and particularly those neighbouring and adjoining parts of Holland and Zeeland in which the said plaintiffs at the said time lived and resided and at present live and reside, and that no war nor hostilities nor enmity came between or exists at present between the said illustrious Queen and the said chiefs, leaders, heads or governors of the respective parts of Holland and Zeeland or the dominions or provinces of the same.

3. ITEM that in the aforesaid years and months or one or other or several of them the aforesaid Rowland Fawkner in his own proper name and for his own account and profit, as well as in the name and for the account and profit of the aforesaid William Williamson, John Cornelius Corffe and Peter Vanake and their associates, living in the parts of Holland and Zeeland then being in league and accord with this realm of England, did lade the

aforesaid ship called the *Fortune* of Armew with goods, wares and merchandise for the making of a maritime expedition from the said port of Armew to the port of San Lucar in Spain, and for the furthering of this voyage obtained and procured from the magistrates of the said town of Armew a certain licence and authority to sail to the aforesaid parts and conduct trade there. And he propounds as above.

4. ITEM That the said shipp & goodes laden as aforesaid by the appoyntment of the said Merchauntes or of some of them were directed to John Erricus and Egbert Vandemate dutchmen dwellinge in Cyvill in Spayne with a purpose & intent that by their or one of their meanes furtheraunce help assistaunce & direction the said shipp Called the Fortune of Armew with the prosedeu[1] & monies made of all her Commodities wares goodes & Marchaundizes & such other monies & goodes as remained in the handes of the said Erricus and Vandemate might bee furnished from Cyvill aforesaid for a voyadge to bee had from thence to St. Domingo to the use of the said Merchauntes & their Companie as aforesaid. And he propounds as above.

5. ITEM that the said shipp Called the Fortune of Armew arryved about the moneth of Februarie Anno domini 1593 at St. Lucar in Cyvill aforesaid, and that at the time of the Arrivall of the ship aforesaid as also longe before the said John Erricus & Egbert Vandemate & ech of them were & ar accompted the factors of the said Williamson, Corffe, Vanake & companie & that they have and had the yeres & monethes aforesaid or in some of them in their possession wares goodes & Marchandizes to the valew of 10000[li] belonginge to the partics plaintiffes in this Cause. And he propounds as above.

6. ITEM that in the yeres & monethes aforesaid or in some or one of them the said Spirincke & Fawkner Williamson Corffe & Vanake & Companie or most or some of them were & are principall Merchauntes of Holland & Zeland & borne subjectes & inhabitantes in thoes Countries, & have used & doe at this tyme use the help direction & assistaunce of the foresaid John Erricus & Egbert Vandemate for their trade & traphicke in Marchandizinge from the partes of Holland & Zeland unto Cyvill in Spayne & from thence unto India. And he propounds as above.

---

[1] Proceeds.

7. ITEM that accordinge to direction given from the said Spirincke, Fawkner, Williamson, Corffe, Vanake & other the parties plaintiffes in this Cause the said John Erricus & Egbert Vandemate in the yeres & monethes aforesaid or in some one of them as their or some of their factors at St. Lucar aforesaid & to the use & Accompt of the said Marchaunts or some of them furnished the said shipp called the Fortune of Armew with a greate quantitie of oyle, wyne, lynnen Cloth & valnze[1] as the proper goodes of the said Marchauntes & gave direction to buy ginger, Cassia fistula, sugers & other goodes to the use of the said Marchauntes viz. the parties plaintiffes in this cause. And he propounds as above.

8. ITEM that in the yeres & monethes aforesaid or in some or one of them by the appoyntment of the said Marchauntes & with the Consent of the said Erricus & Vandemate Jerimie de Stemwinckle dutchman had the goverment & disposicion of all the goodes & ladinge in that shipp the Fortune of Armewe, & the rather to gyve Colour of their passage for St. Domingo & the Indies & to no other intent & purpose but that they might passe without suspect & daunger of the Spaniards Anthonio de la Samora was appoynted pilote of the said shipp called the Fortune of Armewe. And he propounds as above.

9. ITEM that the said shipp the Fortune of Armew & goodes in the yeres & monethes aforesaid or in some one of them were directed to Petro Ortro Sandawall a Merchaunt dwellinge in St. Domingo, & that Petro Ortro Sandawall is a man of great Commaund & aucthoritie in the Indias & that hee is a most deere & familier freind to the said Erricus, & was the yeres & monethes aforesaid or some of them factor in the Indias for the said Erricus & Vandemate or to one of them & that by meanes of the said Erricus & Vandemate & Ortro Sandawall or some or one of them the said Williamson & Companie viz. the Marchauntes plaintiffes in this Cause have adventured & doe at this tyme use the trade of the Indias notwithstanding anie prohibition or restrainte to the Contrarie. And he propounds as above.

10. ITEM that by meanes of the said Erricus & Vandemate & Ortro Sandavall or some or one of them the parties plaintiffes in this Cause have made one voyadge alreddie & wherein the said

[1] Valance.

Anthonio de la Samora was pilote into the Indies aforesaid, & over & besides the shipp & goodes in Controversie there is at this present a shipp provyded to the like voyadge directed as aforesaid belonginge to the said plaintiffes & other Marchauntes of England.[1] And he propounds as above.

11. ITEM that accordinge to such direction as was given to the said Ortro Sandavall by the said Erricus & Vandemate or by one of them there was provided & laded the monethes & yeres aforesaid or in one of them in the Indies to the use & Accompt of the said Marchauntes in the said shipp Called the Fortune at St. Domingo 1350 kintalls of ginger, 82 Chestes of Sugar 24 hogshedes of Cassia fistula & 400 kintalls of Guacum Woode,[2] & that the said Stemwinckle had the Custodie & Carriage of the said goodes for & to the use of the said Merchauntes.[3] And he propounds every other intervening or smaller number down to ten kintalls of ginger, ten chests of sugar, ten kintalls of guacum wood and ten hogsheads of cassia fistula and such and so great a number as shall be proved in the outcome of this cause by lawful proofs or the admission of the principal party. And he propounds as above.

12. ITEM that at the tyme of the ladinge of the shipp Called the Fortune of Armew in the Indies as aforesaid & at the time of the takinge of the said shipp by Captaine West and his associates there were in her of Dutchmen to the number of 10 or 12 persons besides diverse Spaniardes to give Colour to that trade, & that at the time of the takinge of the said shipp the principall officers belonginge thereunto were Dutchmen.[4] And he propounds every other intervening or smaller number down to three men and such and so great a number as shall be proved in the outcome of this cause by lawful proofs or the admission of the principal party. And he propounds as above.

13. ITEM that the said Captaine West & Companie had in the said shipp Called the Fortune all the Writinges Charterparties

---

[1] Peter Le Bee deposed to this article that 'an other shippe of holland whereof Jacob Branso Smallinge and Jasper Moreman are parteowners is nowe of late sente for Spaine with direction to be addressed from thence to St Domingo'.
[2] Guaiac wood, from the *guaiacum officinale*, a native of the West Indies, better known as *lignum vitae*.
[3] The rest of the article is in Latin.
[4] The rest of the article is in Latin.

billes of ladinge & bookes of affraightment of for or concerninge the goodes wares & Marchandizes laden in the said shipp, & that at this present they remaine in the possession & disposition of the said Captaine West & his Companie, Thomas Cordall, William Garraway, [Nicholas]¹ Farrer Christopher Baker or Thomas Middleton or one of them, & that by the said wrytinges Charterparties, billes of ladinge bookes & affraightment all & singuler the Contentes afore specified doe & may appere. And he propounds as above.

14. ITEM in the yeres & Monethes aforesaid or in some or one of them the foresaid Thomas West was Captaine of the shipp Called the Rose Lion of London & so commonlie accompted reputed and taken, & that in the yeres & Monethes aforesaid or in some or one of them the said shipp of Armewe called the Fortune was taken by force by the said Captaine West & his Companie nere St. Domingo in the Indies, & at the takinge thereof the said goodes and Marchaundizes mentioned as afore to bee laded in her at the Indies to the use & Accompt of the parties agent in this Cause were in the said shipp the Fortune of Armewe, & that the said Stenwinckle & other dutchmen were on borde the said Fortune at the time of the takinge of her & had the Custodie and Carriadge of the said goodes for the use and to the Accompte of the Marchauntes plaintiffes in this Cause & were forceablie spoyled thereof. And he propounds as above.

15. ITEM that the said Captaine West & his Companie fraudulentlie & with a purpose & intent to deceyve the foresaid Marchauntes at the time of the takinge of the said shipp Cast over borde the said Stenwinckle & others of the dutchmen or otherwise did presentlie putt out all the dutchmen that were in her & Caused them to be sett on land in the Iland of St. Domingoe aforesaid. And he propounds as above.

16. ITEM that the said shipp called the *Fortune* of Armewe, with all and singular the goods, wares and merchandise in her safe and in good condition, and particularly the goods above mentioned belonging to the aforesaid merchants, sailed to this realm of England and came into the possession, hands and disposition of the same West, or of the aforesaid Cordell, Garrawaie,

¹ The Christian name is omitted and a gap left in the MS.

Farrer, Baker and Middleton or another of them. And he propounds as above.

17. ITEM that the said ship called the *Fortune* of Armewe, with all and singular her equipment and furniture whatsoever, was at the time of her capture worth, in the common estimation, £2000, every kintall of ginger was worth £8, every chest of sugar £15, every hogshead of cassia fistula £10 and every kintall of guacum wood 20s in lawful English money; and he propounds every other intervening or smaller sum down to £500 for the ship and her equipment and furniture, 40s for each kintall of ginger, £5 for each chest of sugar, 40s for each hogshead of cassia fistula and 5s for each kintall of guacum wood and such and so great respective sums as shall be proved in the outcome of this cause by lawful proofs. And he propounds as above.

18. ITEM that the freight charges (for other goods, wares and merchandise in the ship at the time of capture, over and above the goods above mentioned belonging to the aforesaid merchants) owing to the aforesaid John Spirincke and Rowland Fawkner for the transportation of the same extend in the common estimation to the sum of £2000 in lawful English money. And this party propounds every other intervening or smaller sum down to £100 and such and so great a sum as shall be proved in the outcome of this cause by lawful proofs. And he propounds as above.

19. ITEM that the said Thomas West was often and on repeated occasions or at least once requested and called upon by the said plaintiffs to pay, transfer, restore and deliver to the said plaintiffs the said ship, the said goods, wares and merchandise and the aforesaid freight charges or otherwise to compound the debt with the said plaintiffs for the same, but he expressly or at least tacitly refused to perform the premisses, or at least more justly deferred and at present defers doing so. And he propounds as above.

20. ITEM that the said plaintiffs by reason of the premisses have suffered damages, over and above the principal, up to the sum of £3000 in lawful English money; and he propounds every other intervening or smaller sum down to £40 and such and so great a sum as shall be proved in the outcome of this cause by lawful proofs. And he propounds as above.

21. ITEM that the said Thomas West was and is a subject of this realm of England and for that reason is well known to be subject to the jurisdiction of this court. And he propounds as above.

22. ITEM that all and singular the premisses were and are true, well-known and manifest and discussed by the general public. Wherefore, having made oath as required by law in this behalf, this party asks that right and justice be done and given to him and his party, and that the said Thomas West be condemned in the ship, together with her equipment and furniture and the goods libellate, as well as in the aforesaid freight charges and damages and in the legal expenses incurred and to be incurred by and on behalf of the party of the plaintiffs, and that, being so condemned, he may be obliged and compelled to make due payment and restitution of the same by you and your definitive sentence or final decree, O judge aforesaid; and [the party] propounds the premisses jointly and severally, not binding himself to proof of all and singular the premisses nor to unnecessary proof of what is alleged, but he will maintain his claims so far as he shall prove the premisses, in all things always saving the benefit of the law and humbly craving your attention in this cause, O judge aforesaid.

Thomas Crompton.

158. Spirincke contra West: deposition of William Starre[1]

Johannes Spirincke et alii contra Thomam Weste. 4 testis actorum.

WILLIELMUS ARENSON STARRE de Delph in hollandia mercator ubi natus extitit, annos agens xxxv vel circa Testis in hac parte productus iuratus et examinatus Dicit quod Johannem Spirincke per xij annos Roulandum Fawconer, Willielmum Williamson et Johannem Cornelium Corffe per sex annos noverit Petrum Vanake non novit, et Thomam Weste per mensem etiam noverit ex visu.

Ad primum articulum libelli in hac causa dati ad interpretationem Francisci Marquino ad fideliter interpretandum iurati affirmat that the articulate John Spirincke & Rowlande Fawconer beinge factors at midleboroughe for william williamson John

---

[1] H.C.A. 13/31, 2 October 1595. Fourth deposition on the libel.

which tooke the said shipp the Fortune by force after good fighte made on both p*a*rtes.[1] Ac al*ite*r nescit.

Ad xv nescit deponere.

Ad xvj deponit veru*m* esse that the said shipp the Fortune was broughte in saffety to Plimouth with her whole ladinge by Thomas Weste & his company who still hould the possession of all. Ac al*ite*r nescit.

Ad xvij affirmat that the said shipp with her tacle & furniture did stande this ex*amina*te & his p*a*rtners in two thowsand poundes ster*ling* at her goinge from Civill towardes St Domingo on the said viadge and mighte be made worse duringe the viadge by two hundreth poundes, soe as he accompteth the shipp with her furniture to be worth xviij C^{ll} ster*ling* when she was taken. And he knoweth that a kintall of ginger is nowe worth vj^{ll}, a Cheste of St Domingo suger, xv^{ll}, a hogshed of Cassia fistula ix^{ll} and a kintall of guacu*m* woode xx^s and soe much this ex*amina*te would nowe geve for such goodes. Ac al*ite*r nescit.

Ad xviij nescit deponere For that he knoweth not as yet howe muche goodes was in the shipp the Fortune more then the goodes laden for the said plaintiffes.

Ad xix, xx et xxj refert se ad prius d*ic*ta et ad iura.

Ad ult*imu*m dicit predeposita p*e*r eu*m* esse vera.

Ad Interrogatoria primo loco data.

Ad primu*m* respondet he came out of Holland in June or July laste. And the Fortune in question was builte in northe Hollande aboute vij or viij yeares paste as he hath herde but who builte the said shipp he knoweth not.

Ad secundu*m* respondet he never sawe the Fortune but once at Armewe w*hi*ch was aboute the ende of november was xij monethes.

Ad tertiu*m* respondet the Fortune departed from Civill towardes St Domingo in February or m*a*rche was xij monethes as he remembreth his l*ett*res doe importe but howe many spaniardes wente in her he knoweth not.

Ad quartu*m* respondet the said shipp the Fortune sayled from middleboroughe towardes Civill in December nexte com*m*inge

---

[1] A statement which he completely contradicts in his reply to the fifteenth interrogatory.

& his said partners by lettres thereof Affirminge that yt ys most true, that this examinate and his said partners by the favor & helpe of the said Henricus Vandemate & Sandevall doe use the trade of Spaine & the Indies, and a yeare & a haulfe before the sendinge of the Fortune on this last viadge they sente one other shippe on the like viadge and nowe with in this moneth they have also sente an other shipp directed to the said Henricus & Vandemate to passe for St Domingo.

Ad decimum attestatur contenta eiusdem verissima esse Reddendo rationem ut supra & that Anthony de Samora was pilott of the other shipp which thre yeares past & uppwardes they sente for St Domingo & came home with ginger & other goodes to theire greate advantage.

Ad undecimum affirmat that this examinate & his said partners had advise by lettres from John Henricus longe before the takinge of the said shipp the Fortune or eany newes thereof, that there was laden at St Domingo on borde the said shipp for the accompte of the said merchantes of holland & Zealand 1350 kintalls of ginger 82 Chestes of suger 24 hogsheades of cassia fistula & 400 kintalls of guacum woode and thereuppon this examinate & his partners gave order to Roberte de la Barre theire factor to register the same in this Courte & to gett pasporte of the Lord Admirall for the said shippe & ladinge, that if the shipp should happely be taken, yt mighte appeare that soe much of the said shipps ladinge was for theire accomptes. Ac aliter dicit se nescire.

Ad xij dicit he knoweth there were both spaniardes & duche men in the said shippe the Fortune when she was taken as he hath by lettres understoode. Ac aliter nescit.

Ad xiij dicit he is certenly persuaded that yt will appeare by the bookes of ladinge of the Fortune made at St Domingo that the said goodes were consigned to John Henricus & Egbert Vandemate factor to this examinate & his said partners and he hath herde that Captaine West hath the said bookes. Ac aliter nescit.

Ad xiiij affirmat he certenly knoweth that all the goodes laden at St Domingo on borde the Fortune of Armewe & specified in the xj[th] article before were laden for the accompte of this examinate & his said partners For the said John Henricus wrote them soe much before the takinge of the said shipp. And he understandeth that Thomas West was Captaine of the shipp there both in receavinge of theire merchandizes, and makinge returne thereof of this examinates knowledge who is in company with them all savinge the said Vanake who laded goodes in the shipp but was not partner and in company with them ut dicit. And for theire factors they are well knowen & reputed For as he sayth they had annis articulatis in theire handes goodes & moneyes to the valewe of ten thowsand belonginge to the said plaintiffes and yet they have xvC^{li} worth of this examinates goodes in theire handes.

Ad sextum affirmat eundem continere veritatem Reddendo rationem scientie that he well knoweth the articulate persons Savinge Peter Vanake who is of Amsterdam but not knowen to him in person & that they are verey good merchantes of holland & Zealand and Inhabitantes thereof & doe use the helpe and assistaunce of the said John Henricus and Egbert Vandemate for theire trade at St Lucar & Civill and in the Indies of his knowledge who as a partner with them hath receaved his parte of such goodes belonginge unto him as he hath adventured for those partes and hath come consigned from the said Henricus and Vandemate theire factors at Civill.

Ad septimum dicit he knoweth that accordinge to the order & direction of the plaintiffes aforesaid & this examinate a partner with them the said John Henricus & Egbert Vandemate with the prosedewe[1] of the said goodes did lade the articulate shipp the Fortune at Civill with oyles, wynes linnen clothe and other goodes for the use of this examinate & his partners aforesaid, and sente the same for St Domingo in the Indies with order to relade ginger cassia fistula suger and other goodes there for theire use & accompte, as the said John Henricus and Egbert Vandemate certified this examinate & his partners by his lettres and accomptes after the dispatchinge away of the said shippe, and that they had appointed Anthony de Samora pilott of the said shipp for the said viadge.

Ad octavum nescit plura dicere quam prius dictum est.

Ad nonum dicit he certenly knoweth that John Henricus & Egbert Vandemate did consigne the said shipp & goodes to Petro Ortes Sandevall a ritche merchante & theire good freinde dwellinge in St Domingo as they have certified this examinate

---
[1] Proceeds.

Cornelius Corffe, this examinate & others theire partners did in the yeare 1593 by theire order & commission buy the articulate shippe the Fortune of Armewe with her tacle & furniture at Armewe, and reserved a parte therein to them selves whereby he certenly knoweth that the said John Spirincke Rouland Fawconer william williamson John Cornelius Corffe this examinate & others theire partners were ever since the said buyenge of the said shippe true & lawfull owners & proprietaries thereof and soe accompted & knowen.

Ad secundum affirmat eundem continere veritatem ex sua certa scientia For that he is an Inhabitante of Delphe & knoweth that the States of Holland & Sealand & theire subjectes have byn tyme out of minde in good leage & amity (as the intercourse & free trade showeth) with the Queenes majesty & her pregenitors and theire people, & that there is not neyther hath byn duringe his remembraunce eany hostility or warrs betwixte them.

Ad tertium et quartum articulos deponit verum esse That aboute the moneth of December 1593, Rouland Fawconer by the order & commission of william williamson, John Cornelius Corffe Peter Vanake this examinate & others theire partners did furnishe & sett out the said shipp the Fortune from Armewe laden with sondry barrells of nayles valnzes and other goodes and consigned them to John Henricus & Egbert Van de mate his sonne in lawe dwellinge at Civill with order to make sale of those goodes and others remayninge in theire handes & therewith to relade the said shipp with other merchandizes for theire accomptes & to sende her to St Domingo in the west Indies at theire adventure, Which he knoweth to be true For that he was & is a parte owner of the said shipp & a parte lader thereof also and gave his consente and directions as the reste of his partners did for the makinge of the said viadge.

Ad quintum dicit verum esse that the Fortune aforesaid arrived in savety at St Lucar in Spaine with the said merchandizes aboute the moneth of February followinge the settinge furth of the said shipp as this examinate was then advised by lettres from thence, And he affirmeth truth yt is that the said John Henricus & Egbert Vandemote at that tyme & longe before were the factors of the said william williamson, John Cornelius Corffe this examinate & Peter Vanake at Civill & did theire busines

THE *ROSE LION*, 1594-5

shall be two yeares and was laden with nailes, valnzes & other goodes of sondry sortes consigned to be delivered at St Lucar to John Henricus & Egbert Vandemate of his certaine knowledge beinge a parte owner & parte lader thereof.

Ad quintum respondet negative For of his certaine knowledge the said shipp the Fortune had noe corne in her when she arrived laste in Spaine nether was she taken or stayed by the Lantatho[1] or eany other officer of the kinge of Spaine duringe the whole viadge but he hath herde that before this respondente & partners boughte the said shipp, she was in an other viadge taken in the straightes by the Lantatho laden with corne, and confiscate.

Ad sextum respondet negative aliter quam prius responsum est.

Ad septimum respondet he never sawe John Henricus, but this respondente hath written many lettres unto him & receaved many lettres from him. And he maketh accompte he is an old maried man & hath lived many yeares there For that he hath maried daughters in Spaine & namelye Egbert Vandemate hath maried one of his daughters. Ac aliter respondet se nescire.

Ad octavum respondet he knoweth that John Henricus was borne in Harlam in Holland For he hath certificates thereof from the towne of Harlam. But whether he be a denizen of Spaine or naturalized there he knoweth not, nether hath herde, nether can declare whether he be accompted there for a subjecte of the kinge of Spaine. But yt may be thoughte he is soe accompted For that he hath dwelled soe longe in Spaine and maried daughters there.

Ad nonum respondet Egbert Vandemate dwelleth in Civill and hath maried the daughter of the said John Henricus in Spaine, but howe longe he hath dwelled there or whether he be a subjecte of the kinge of Spaine or naturalized there or soe accompted he knoweth not Ac aliter respondet negative For as he sayth he knoweth not the said Egbert Vandemate but by lettres.

Ad decimum respondet negative Savinge that he understood by lettres and accomptes sente from the said John Henricus that he laded oyles wynes & other goodes in the Fortune at Civill consigned for St Domingo for the accompte of the respondente & his partners.

Ad undecimum respondet that John Henricus or Egbert

---
[1] *Adelantado.*

Vandemate have not had eany Commission from this respondente or eany his partners to deale for them in Spaine or the Indies, but only they have from tyme to tyme geven them order by theire lettres to receave theire goodes and ymploy them for the Indies and make returne accordinglye, Ac aliter respondet negative.

Ad xij respondet he knoweth that Hollanders & Zelanders doe covertly trade to the Indies under the names of some assured freindes in Spaine otherwise they could not trade thither without daunger of confiscation and he beleveth that none but the kinges subjectes may trade to the West Indies openly but he knoweth that under color of freindes in Spaine many doe trade thither as this respondente & his partners have don.

Ad xiij respondet negative.

Ad xiiij respondet he herde by lettres sente him from John Henricus that Anthony de Samora was pilott or master of the said shipp the Fortune for the Indies & that the gonners were duchmen Ac aliter respondet se nescire, but thinketh the principall officers were spaniardes.

Ad xv respondet he hath herde that the Fortune was taken nere St Domingo & suffered to be taken most shamefully with smale fighte. Ac aliter respondet se nescire.

Ad xvj respondet he doth not knowe nether hath herde of what nation Petro Ortes Sandevall is borne, but he dwelleth at St Domingo as he understandeth Ac aliter respondet se nescire.

Ad xvij respondet et credit that none of the plaintiffes have seene the said Petro Ortes Sandevall or geven him eany commission to deale for them in the Indies Ac aliter respondet negative.

Ad xviij respondet he certenly knoweth that noe parte of the Fortune eyther at her goinge from Civill, or comminge from St Domingo did belonge to eany subjecte of the kinge of Spaine. But what goodes were laden in her eyther in Spaine or at St Domingo for the use and accompte of Diego Peres de Porres, John Henricus, John Ortise or Petro Alvares or eany other subjecte of the kinge of Spaine he knoweth not.

Ad xix respondet he herde from John Henricus that Petro Ortes Sandevall boughte & laded the said goodes at St Domingo into the Fortune.

Ad xx respondet he expecteth the recovery of his goodes taken in the Fortune & his parte of the Fortune For that he is partner w*ith* the plaintiffes both in shipp & goodes, if they recover but howe much his p*ar*te com*m*eth unto he knoweth not as yet.

Ad xxj r*es*pondet negative.

Ad xxij r*es*pondet he knoweth not that the Fortune was ever at Cales[1] in Spaine, but he knoweth that Jacob Johnson Fortune caried the said shipp from Armewe to Civill this laste viadge.

Ad xxiij r*es*pondet he knoweth that the Fortune was newe trimmed and sheathed in leade at Civill by the said John Henricus accordinge to order geven him by this respondente & his p*ar*tners and at theire cost*es* & chardges. And he thinketh the said shipp remayned at Civill aboute two monethes before she dep*ar*ted for St Domingo. Ac al*ite*r r*es*pondet se nescire.

Ad xxiiij r*es*pondet the Fortune was never at Cales to his knowledge Ac al*ite*r r*es*pondet se nescire. But if eany duch men continued in the shipp at Civill this respondente & his p*ar*tners must beare the chardges of them he is most assured when accompt*es* for that viadge are cleared betwixte the said Henricus & them.

Ad xxv r*es*pondet that this respondente & his p*ar*tners gave order to John Henricus to sheath the Fortune in leade For that the shipp before sente by them to St Domingo was greatly impayred by wormes & he hath herde that other duch men have sheathed theire shippes with leade & there lieth a duch shipp in this River of Thames soe sheathed.[2] Ac al*ite*r r*es*pondet se nescire.

Ad xxvj r*es*pondet that Jacob Johnson Fortune wente m*as*ter of the Fortune at her laste goinge from Armewe & had aboute xx duch men with him at his goinge away what theire names were or where they dwell he knoweth not For the m*as*ter shipped them, and they broughte the said shipp to Civill, and aboute trimminge of the shippe there the said John Henricus & the shipper[3] fell out For the shipper said he was to adventure his liffe in the viadge & therefore he would have her trimmed after his will, and John Henricus would not suffer yt, but would tryme her as he thoughte out and by that occasion they fell out & the shipper & his company for the most p*ar*te forsooke the shipp otherwise they had gone to St Domingo in her For soe the shipper was appointed at Armewe. Ac al*ite*r r*es*pondet se nescire.

[1] Cadiz.
[2] The Caribbean waters swarmed with the teredo-worm, which could riddle a ship's hull in a single voyage.
[3] Skipper.

Ad xxvij respondet negative.
Ad ultimum reddit causas scientie sue ut supra.

Ad Interrogatoria secundo loco data.

Ad primum respondet there wente not one man from Armewe in the Fortune at her last goinge thence, that was of Andwerpe or eany other place under the subjection of the spanish kinge Ac aliter respondet negative.

Ad secundum responsum est supra that the master of the Fortune was putt furth by John Henricus at Civill uppon the fallinge out for the cause before sett downe.

Ad tertium respondet he knoweth there was noe corne caried outwardes in the Fortune from Zealand for Spaine this laste viadge that ever he knewe or hearde of, but knoweth that her ladinge of merchandizes was dischardged at St Lucar or Civill as he remembrethe Ac aliter respondet negative.

Ad quartum respondet the shipp was appointed to saile from Armewe to Civill & from thence to St Domingo, & the same viadge she performed.

Ad quintum respondet negative aliter quam prius responsum est that he hath herde the said shipp the Fortune was taken by the Lantatho of Spaine in a former viadge before this respondente & his partners were owners of here.

Ad sextum respondet negative.

Ad septimum respondet the Fortune and her ladinge was taken by Captaine west before the moneth of May laste and Captaine Weste and his partners have ever since the takinge helde the possession thereof.

Ad octavum respondet that a xvj[th] parte of the Fortune doth properly belonge to this respondente, and a parte of the ladinge belongeth also to him for soe much as two drifattes conteyninge 160 peeces of valenze sente in the Fortune, and the returne of certaine lynnen cloth sente before by him to John Henricus, commeth unto. But howe much the goodes laden in the Fortune at St Domingo for him be, he knoweth not untill he shall receave his accompte from John Henricus for the same.

Ad nonum respondet he is one of the plaintiffes that presenteth this cause and at his chardges & his partners the same is prosecuted and soe shalbe untill an ende be had thereof, and for his parte he broughte fifty poundes with him to maintayne the suite & doth disburse the money aboute the same.

Ad decimum respondet that this respondente beinge borne at Delphe, John Baptista de Moy, Charles le Clarcke Nicholas van Egmont of Collen merchantes where they have dwelled ever since Andwerpe was geven over to the Spaniarde, but beinge borne at Andwerpe as he belevethe are partners in the goodes taken in the Fortune and are mente & intended to be socii[1] with the plaintiffes, and John Baptista de Moy is this respondentes brother in lawe For this respondente maried his sister and he hath a xvjth parte in the said shipp the Fortune properly belonginge unto him. Also Nicholas Rippett of Hamboroughe merchante but borne at Andwerpe, Nicholas Halse of Delphe merchante but borne at Harlem and nowe bankerupte were partners in the said goodes and are copertners with them in the prosecution of this cause and every of them exceptinge the said Halse who is bankerupte doe contribute to the chardges thereof. And other partners there are not in the goodes claymed by this suite to his knowledge, neyther are eany of them eany subjectes of the kinge of Spaine or abidinge within eany of the dominions of the kinge of Spaine that have or clame eany property in the said goodes for the which this suite is commensed Ac aliter respondet se nescire.

Ad ultimum reddit causas scientie sue ut supra.

159. Spirincke contra West: West's allegation[2]

23 September 1595.

On which day the said Clerke junior as lawful proctor of the said Thomas West in the best form and to every effect of the law that can howsoever follow thereupon alleged severally as follows.

John Sperincke, Rowland Fawkner, William Williamson, John Cornelius Corffe, Peter

1. First, that before the capture of the ship and goods in controversy in this cause, namely the ship called the *Fortune* and the goods captured in her by the ship called the *Rose Lion* of London and the aforesaid Thomas West captain of the said ship and his

---

[1] Partners.

[2] H.C.A. 24/63, no. 168. The preliminaries, the first four items, the last item and various phrases elsewhere have been translated from the Latin. The document is not endorsed.

Vanake and associates contra Thomas Weste. Clerke senior: Clerke junior.[1]

associates, and especially in the months of October, November, December, January, February and March in the year of our Lord one thousand five hundred and ninety four by the computation of the Anglican church, and in all and singular or in any of the said months, the aforesaid ship called the *Rose Lion* and the aforesaid Thomas West, captain of the said ship, and his associates were sufficiently authorised to make reprisals against the king of Spain and his subjects and their goods and ships; and the said Thomas West had power and authority to sail in the said ship and with her to take, seize and possess to his own profit and that of the owners and setters forth of the same ship and of the sailors and soldiers in her and of others having an interest in her any ships and goods, wares and merchandise whatever of the King of Spain or of some or all and singular of his subjects. And he propounds severally, conjointly and separately.

2. Item that at the time of the capture of the aforesaid ship called the *Fortune*, the aforesaid Thomas West and his company, being in the said ship called the *Rose Lion* of London and in pursuit of their letters of reprisal, in the Indies not far from a place called Santo Domingo, came upon the said ship called the *Fortune*, then lately departed from the port of Santo Domingo, and by virtue and authority of their letters of reprisal aforesaid attacked and at length took the same ship and the goods laden in her, and did this in the month of January last elapsed and since that time continuously have held and possessed the said ship called the *Fortune* and the goods laden in her. And he propounds as above.

3. Item that in the months of May, June and July 1594, or in any of the said months or thereabouts, the said ship called the *Fortune* was set forth and sent upon an Indian expedition, or for the making of a voyage and navigation from the port of Seville in Spain to the port of Santo Domingo in the West Indies, and that before undertaking that voyage the said ship in the port of Seville aforesaid was improved, repaired and suitably made ready for undergoing that voyage, and among other things her hull was sheathed with lead (viz. she was sheathed in leade),[2] at the expense and command of John Henricus or Erricus, Diego Peres

---

[1] Names of the proctors of the respective parties.
[2] The words in brackets are in English in the MS.

de Porras, John Ortys and Peter Alvares or their factors and deputies or perhaps other subjects of the King of Spain, and that no others but Spaniards doe use to sheath their shippes in leade especially noe Zelanders or Hollanders doe ev*er* sheath their shippes in leade or have used so to doe.[1] And he propounds as above.

4. Item that those goods which were exported in the said ship from the port of Seville to the port of Santo Domingo in the aforesaid voyage were bought, made ready and loaded into the said ship called the *Fortune* by inhabitants of the city of Seville or other subjects of the King of Spain, and that the goods also laden in the said ship and being there at the time of capture of the said ship were laden in the same in the port of Santo Domingo aforesaid by Spaniards or subjects of the King of Spain to the profit and account of subjects of the said King, and that the rule, care and custody of the said ship called the *Fortune* and of the goods in her while she remained in the aforesaid voyage, and especially at the time when the said ship was captured by the aforesaid Thomas West and his company, were the responsibility of Spaniards or subjects of the King of Spain, and especially at the time when the ship was taken there were in her seventy Spaniards or subjects of the King of Spain, or sixty or fifty or thereabouts, among whom a certain Christovall de Castilianos was then captain or commander of the said ship, Antonio de Samora was master of the said ship, Gasper Alvares was pilot of the said ship and John de Otro was purser of the said ship, and all and singular and any of these and others who were officers in the said ship in the aforesaid voyage before the capture of the same ship were Spaniards or subjects of the King of Spain, and for and as such were generally held, taken and reputed. And he propounds as above.

5. Item that if by chance any Dutchmen were in the said ship at the aforesaid time, these were men without any authority or command in the said ship called the *Fortune* viz. they were such as had in the said shippe but meane places or Roomes, and such as in their places, and in the said shippe served the Spaniard*e*s, and were put in and placed therin to serve by Spaniard*e*s, namely they were of noe better places in the shippe nor served in other Roomes, but as gun*ne*res, Carpenters, and one of them for

[1] The words 'doe use ... so to doe' are in English in the MS

Barbor or Surgeon and they were but fewe in number, viz. not above five, six, seaven or eight persons, and the possession of the said fortune and of her Ladinge at and before her takinge was in the said Spaniardes and at their direction, and not in the said Dutchmen and so it was commonly confessed, saied reputed and taken at the takinge of the said shippe, and before and since. And he propounds as above.

6. Item that the Dutchmen which were and served in the said shippe called the Fortune at the Tyme aforesaid were all or most of them placed in her against their willes, viz. they were pressed or commaunded to goe in her by spaniardes or sutch as were subjectes to kinge[1] & have or were to have their hires or wages for theire service of them, and so much in effect they Confessed after the takinge of the said shippe, in so much as all or most of them refused to passe away after the shippe was taken with the Spaniardes taken in the said shippe, and by theire owne Requeste entreatie and peticion obteyned a Carvell of Captaine weste to goe in and Reviled and Cursed the Spaniardes, and threatned to be Revenged of them, for forcinge them on that viadge, and saied they wold make themselves Rich upon some Spaniardes before they had done or the like in effecte. And he propounds as above.

7. Item that one of the Dutchmen which was in the fortune when she was taken as aforesaid was a Surgeon, and after the takinge of the said shippe, he beinge Commaunded by Captaine west to dresse the woundes of the hurte Spaniardes who were wounded in the fight before the takinge and yealdinge up of the said shippe, he denied a great while to doe it, and Cursed and Banned them, and Called them Dogges, and saied yf the said Captaine west wold he would cut or helpe to Cutt all their throates, and saied that they fetched him on bord, and forced him to serve on that viadge perforce, and againste his will, or the like in effect: and indeed had not Captaine weste forced him, he wold not have put his hand to helpe or dresse the said wounded Spaniardes. And he propounds as above.

8. Item that at the takinge of the said fortune, and at her comminge to and departing from Sancto Domingo and also at her departure from Civill, she was the shippe of Spaniardes or subjectes to the kinge of Spaine and a shippe of Civill, and so

[1] To the King of Spain.

the ladinge delivered to the Generall togeather with the pursers booke whereby the premisses did appeare to be true. Affirminge moreover that John Ortis & Peter Alvares dwellers in St Domingo and sondry other merchantes of that place did lade all the goodes which were laden on borde the said shipp the Fortune at St Domingo this laste viadge and consigned them to Civill For the use & accompte of Spaniardes to his knowledge For as he sayth he sawe the said goodes laden at St Domingo and also sawe the Register booke and pursers booke of all the ladinge taken in there whereby he knoweth the premisses to be true, and that both shipp & goodes were continually from the ladinge untill the tyme they were taken under the chardge possession and commaundemente of Spaniardes & portingalls, & the viadge was wholy ordered & ruled by them as namely *Christ*ofer Castilianos was Captaine Anthony de Samora master, Gasper Alvares pilott John de Ustrio purser and all the other officers of the shipp were spaniardes & portingalls of his certaine knowledge beinge one of the company of the same shipp when she was taken, and thereby knoweth the premisses to be true & that there were xliij spaniardes & portingalls mariners and ten spaniardes passingers, and seven duchmen in the said shippe at the tyme of her takinge.

Ad quintum affirmat there were only seven duchmen in the said shippe the Fortune whereof one was master gonner an other Carpenter an other Surgion & the rest gonners, and all they were at the commaunde of the Captaine & master, and did not beare eany commaunde rule or aucthority in the said shipp of his knowledge or over the goodes but the spaniardes ruled ordered & commaunded all of his sighte & knowledge.

Ad sextum dicit he was presente when as the master gonner beinge a Fleminge intreated of John Henricus that he & some other duche men mighte be shipped in the said shipp the Fortune for the said viadge, and therefore knoweth they served voluntarily for theire wages without presse or compulsion, And after the shipp the Fortune was taken, foure of them begged a Carvell of Captaine Weste to saile away in For that they feared to returne to St Domingo with the Spaniardes Ac al*iter* dicit se nescire.

Ad septimum deponit verum esse that the Flemish Surgion after the takinge of the Fortune beinge commaunded by Captaine Weste to dresse some of the Spaniardes that were wounded,

examinatus dicit quod Thomam Weste a tempore capture navis controverse noverit agentes non novit.

contra Thomam Weste.

Ad primum articulum materie ad interpretationem Francisci Marquino et Johannis Sozer ad fideliter interpretandum iuratorum affirmat se nescire.

3 testis super materia West.

Ad secundum affirmat that on newe yeares day laste accordinge to the computation of England the articulate shipp the Fortune was taken nere St Domingo in the Indies by Thomas Weste Captaine of the Rose Lion of London & his company and ever since the said Weste & his company have helde & possessed the said shipp & her ladinge as prize of this examinates knowledge who was one of the mariners of the Fortune when she was taken & came for England in the Rose Lion in company of the Fortune.

Ad tertium affirmat verum esse that the said shipp the Fortune was trimmed amended and sheathed in leade in Aprill 1594 at Civill by John Henricus & Diego Peres de Porras to make a viadge from thence to St Domingo in the West Indes by the direction of the said merchantes Which he knoweth to be true For that he sawe the said shipp a trimminge and sheathinge & when she was haulfe laden she wente to St Lucar to take in the rest of her ladinge & there this examinate was hired by Christofer Castilianos Captaine & Anthony Samora master to saile in the said shipp for St Domingo and at St Lucar this examinate sawe John Henricus & Diego Peres de Porras on bord the shipp & pay such chardges as fell due for ladinge of the goodes & bringinge them in barckes from Civill. And sayth that such shippes as goe from Civill to St Domingo are commonly sheathed in leade to avoide the daunger of wormes which otherwise would hazard such shippes and theire ladinges greatly Ac aliter nescit.

Ad quartum attestatur he knoweth that noe others but subjectes of the kinge of Spaine may trade for St Domingo by the lawes of Spaine without confiscation of shipp & goodes, and therefore knoweth that all the goodes that were putt on borde the Fortune at Civill & St Lucar this laste viadge were boughte provided & laden by Spaniardes & Inhabitantes of Civill subjectes of the kinge And geveth a reason further of his knowledge therein that when the generall of the Fleete came on borde to visite the shipp & the company he sawe the Register booke of all

Countries subjecte to the said kinge within the Tyme aforesaid and traded or used to trade in the west Indies, and had or gott all or the most part of his substance and goodes in Spaine Portingale or the Indies, and none or very litle out of the kinge of Spaines Dominions: and for a subjecte or one naturalized or a denizen to and under the said kinge he hath byn and is commonly Reputed and taken. And he propounds as above.

11. Item that it hath byn by the space of xl^{ty} xxx^{ty} or xx^{ty} yeares last paste and so is at this present a thinge prohibited for any to trade in the west Indies but onely for Spaniardes and for such as be subjectes or naturalized or denizons under the kinge of Spaine, and such onely and none other have byn within the said Tyme and are permitted there to trade and this is true, public and well known. And he propounds as above.

12. Item that at the departure of the said shippe called the fortune from Sancto Domingo there passed from thence in her company for Civill two other shippes belonginge to Spaniardes, and for that viadge the said fortune was made Admirall or generall of all these three shipes, and a Spaniard was placed in her who was appoynted the generall of all those shippes, and to him and his order the same thre shippes and their Company in that viadge were to obey, and the said Fortune as well at her goinge from Civill as from Sancto domingo in the foresaid viadge was Regestred and Recorded in the Kinge of Spaine his offices to be of Civill. And he propounds as above.

13. Item that all and singular the premisses were and are true, well-known, manifest, etc., wherefore, having made oath as required by law in this behalf, this party of the said Thomas West asks that right and justice be done and given to him in the premisses and whatsoever concerns them, not binding himself, etc.[1] humbly craving your attention, O Judge.

160. *Spirincke* contra *West: deposition of Bennet Boetto*[2]

Johannes Spirincke et socii

BENNETUS BOETTO de Berselonetta in Savia[3] nauta annos agens xxvj vel circa testis in hac parte productus iuratus et

[1] [*Sic.*]
[2] H.C.A. 13/31, 3 October 1595. Third deposition on the allegation. Signed 'Beinet Bouet'.
[3] Savoy.

held named and accompted, and the said shippe (yf she had not byn taken) had with such ladinge as she tooke in at sancto Domingo Retourned againe to Civill in Spaine, and had there discharged, and so it was appoynted she should have done. And he propounds as above.

9. Item that yf the said shippe called the fortune were ever of Armewe (which this party does not admit, but utterly denies, except in so far as may be to the advantage of him and his party) yet the said shippe by the space of Ten, nine, eight, seven six, five or fowre monethes before her departure from Civill in the viadge aforesaid was taken by the Lantatho or some other officer or subjectes of the kinge of Spaine as she was passinge with Corne for the streightes in the Company of a French shippe or vessell and she was taken away from the Flemenges and owt of their possession, yf they ever possessed her (which this party denies except in so far as it may be to his advantage) and with her ladinge she was confiscated and at lenght after she had lien at Poyntall in the Bay of Cales some five fowre or thre monethes after her takinge, she was passed over and sold to certaine subjectes of the kinge of Spaine, and namely to John Henricus Diego Peres da Porrus, John Ortys, and Petro Alvares, and they all and everie of them were and are spaniardes or subjectes of the kinge of Spaine, and or she was so sold to some others beinge subjectes to the kinge of Spaine, or to the use of some others beinge subjectes to the kinge of Spaine, and for the space of viij vij six or five monethes before her goinge from Civill on the viadge aforesaide the said fortune had noe Dutchmen in her, at leaste she was in the possession and at the disposicion and order of Spaniardes or others beinge subjectes to the kinge of Spaine, and reputed and taken to be their proper shippe, and so was in deede. And he propounds as above.

10. Item that John Erricus or Henricus aforesaid is a dweller in Spaine, and was there, or in the Indies married to a woman beinge then a subjecte of the kinge of Spaine, and in Spaine or the Indies hath dwelte and kepte howse and family these Thirtie, Twentie, fyfteene or Ten yeares before the departure of the said shippe from Civill towardes Sancto Domingo, and so longe he hath byn and is a subjecte or naturalizado or Denizon to and under the kinge of Spaine, and he hath borne office in the

as is demaunded by the Hollanders to be laden for theire accompte in this shippe.

Ad xix respondet negative.

Ad xx respondet there were only vij Fleminges when she was taken whereof one was a gonner an other a surgion & an other Carpenter, and he knoweth that they had noe office or rule in the shippe or commaunded therein more then to doe theire offices as the Spaniardes commaunded them Ac aliter respondet negative.

Ad xxj respondet he knoweth that Captaine West had the Register booke & pursers booke of the whole ladinge of the Fortune & such other writinges as were in the shippe For this respondente sawe these two bookes in Captaine Westes possession who hath them nowe he knoweth not.

Ad xxij respondet he knoweth that Captaine West & his company tooke the Fortune & her ladinge by force nere St Domingo havinge in her all such goodes as were laden at St Domingo Ac aliter respondet negative.

Ad xxiij respondet negative Savinge that vij Duch men were in the Fortune when she was taken but had noe commaunde or rule therein ut prius responsum est.

Ad xxiiij respondet foure duch men were putt into a Carvell by Captaine West, & thre were sent ashore to St Domingo with the spaniardes Ac aliter respondet negative.

Ad xxv respondet it is unpossible for Hollanders or Zelanders to trade in the Indies without losse of all theire goodes if yt should be knowen Ac aliter respondet negative.

Ad xxvj he hath not byn instructed taughte or conferred with what to speake, For as he sayth he would not for all the worlde speake eany thinge against the truth & his conscience. And sayth he was never examined before this tyme touchinge this cause, neyther hath receaved eany thinge of Captaine Weste or eany other englishe men savinge had his meate & drincke on shipp borde whiles the goodes were landinge, and since he hath mayntenaunce of meate & drincke bye the merchantes that are interested in the goodes broughte in the Fortune.

Ad xxvij respondet that the Fortune was simply boughte as he verely beleveth by John Henricus for his owne use & his partners to make the said viadge to the Indies of the Lantatho of Spaine at Pointall, and there Diego Peres de Porras partner with the said

his dominions unlesse they color theire trade under the names of some dwellinge in Spaine Ac aliter respondet se nescire.

[To the tenth and eleventh he replies negatively]

Ad xij respondet he knoweth there wente noe such man as Jerome van Stenewincle in the Fortune from Civill, nether had he or eany other duch men eany possession chardge or disposition of eany goodes laden in the Fortune outwardes or homewardes. For this respondente beinge a mariner in the shipp must needes have seene or knowen such thinge if yt had byn, duringe the whole viadge. Ac aliter respondet negative.

Ad xiij respondet the shipp the Fortune & her ladinge were consigned to Petro Ortes Sandavall & others merchantes of St Domingo, and they receyved the goodes of this respondentes knowledge.

Ad xiiij respondet he knoweth that Petro Ortis hath byn Ruler or Judge of the Courte at St Domingo, and the shippes comminge & goinge must have license to lade & unlade of him, and he is a man of greate commaunde at St Domingo of his certaine knowledge and a deere frende to John Henricus, by reason that the said Henricus was broughte upp in the house of the said Petro Ortis or his fathers house, and John Henricus and Petro Ortis are partners in trade of merchandizes, and the said Petro Ortis ys called Don Pedro at St Domingo & rideth with foure negros attendant uppon him. Ac aliter respondet se nescire.

Ad xv respondet negative.

Ad xvj respondet negative Savinge he knoweth that Anthony Samora wente master of a shipp to St Domingo for John Henricus & other merchantes of Civill the yeare before this laste viadge.

Ad xvij respondet negative.

Ad xviij respondet negative For there were only laden on borde the Fortune at St Domingo 3000 kintalls of ginger, 230 Chestes of suger or thereaboutes, 11 serons[1] of cassia fistula conteyninge aboute fyve kintalls & one haulfe thereof apperteyned to the Boateswaine, & the reste to Johan Egualo a mariner, and aboute 100 kintalls of guacum woode which belonged to the mariners, and he knoweth there was noe cassia fistula or woode in the shipp that belonged to eany merchantes much lesse soe much

[1] Baskets, probably made of wood and hide.

of his daughters with him beinge at women's state & mariadgeable And he sayth that by reason of his the said John Henricus longe dwellinge in Spaine he is a subjecte of the kinge of Spaine & soe accompted & taken of this ex*amina*tes knowledge and in that regarde he useth trade to the west Indies and there hath gotten all his substaunce and as he tould this ex*amina*te he came from the Lowe Cuntreyes when he was a childe. Ac al*iter* nescit.

Ad xj affirmat he knoweth that noe others but Spaniard*es* may trade to the West Indies, For a portingall without license from the kinge & the contractation house may not cary a shipp to the west Indies or trade there, and soe yt is notorious and well knowen in Spaine & many other cuntreyes. And this ex*amina*te by reason of his abode in Spaine hath had knowledge & experience thereof.

Ad xij affirmat veru*m* esse That two other spanishe shipps came from St Domingo in company of the Fortune, & the Fortune was appointed Admirall, and one Don Frederico was placed therein for Generall to geve direction, and com*m*aunde over all the said thre shippes of this ex*amina*tes knowledge. Affirminge that he sawe the Fortune registred both at Civill and St Domingo to be of Civill.

Ad xiij dicit predeposita per eu*m* esse vera.

Ad Interrogatoria.

Ad primu*m* respondet he was borne in Barsenoletta in Savoia, and hath dwelled in malego, mutrilla & Cales[1] theise fyve yeares space paste and is a mariner & liveth by the sea, and wissheth the Englishe men the rather to obtaine in this suite because they won the good*es* by fighte & force, & the Fleminges would nowe gett them by word*es*.

[To the second, third, fourth and fifth he replies negatively][2]

Ad sextu*m* res*p*ondet negative Savinge that John Henricus is a Fleminge borne but by reason of his mariadge & longe livinge in Spaine he is a subjecte of the kinge of Spaine.

[To the seventh and eighth he replies negatively]

Ad nonu*m* res*p*ondet he knoweth that hollanders & Zealanders may not use trade in Spaine & other places of the kinge of Spaine

---

[1] Málaga, Motril and Cadiz.
[2] 'Ad secundum respondet negative,' etc.

refused to doe yt, & cursed them callinge them dogges & sayenge nowe the tyme was come that he could revenge him selfe uppon them for misusinge of him at St Domingo of this ex*aminate*s knowledge. Ac al*iter* nescit.

Ad octavum dicit he knoweth that the said shipp the Fortune was a spanishe shipp & belonginge to John Henricus Diego Peres de Purras of Civill John Ortis & Peter Alvares of St Domingo at such tyme as she was taken, For he sawe her Registred to belonge unto them. And he knoweth that the said shippe was appointed to saile to Civill & dischardge there if she had not byn taken For this ex*aminate* was hired to saile to St Domingo & backe againe to Civill.

Ad nonu*m* attestatur he well knoweth that aboute viij or nyne monethes before the said shipp the Fortune wente from Civill this laste viadge bounde for St Domingo, the same shipp the Fortune was taken in the straightes laden with corne by the Lantatho of Spaine, and both shipp & goodes confiscated, & caried to Cales & there dischardged and afterwardes the said shipp the Fortune was caried to Pointall & there remayned haled on dry lande v or vj monethes & then was boughte by John Henricus & Diego Peres de Purras of Civill and by them caried upp to Civill & there trimmed & sheathed for the said viadge to St Domingo. And this he knoweth to be true For that he was a mariner in a frenche shipp of Nisa in Province which was likewise taken & confiscate the same tyme by the said Lantatho, and sawe the Fortune taken, and was carried to Pointall in company of the Fortune & there remayned untill both the Fortune & the French barcke were boughte at one tyme & caried upp to Civill. Soe as he knoweth that the Fortune remayned continually at Pointall from the tyme she was taken by the Lantatho untill she was boughte & caried to Civill to be trimmed for the said viadge for St Domingo, and duringe all that tyme he sawe & well knoweth that noe duchmen remayned in the Fortune or had to doe with her.

Ad decimu*m* deponit that John Henricus is a dweller and Inhabitante of Civill and was maried at St Domingo to a spanishe woman before he came to dwell at Civill, and he hath herde him say that he hath dwelled at Civill xxx yeares, and at the departure of the shipp the said Henricus came to St Lucar & broughte two

Henricus tooke possession of the said shippe which was delivered him by the Lantatho in this respondentes presence who tooke him by the hand & gave him possession. But what money was paid for the said shippe he knoweth not.

Ad xxviij respondet verum esse That most of the shippes which goe for St Domingo are sheathed with leade if the owners be of ability to doe yt and they finde good proffitt by yt of his knowledge.

Ad xxix respondet the master and pilott were sicke & the Captaine was hurte soe as they could not be broughte into Englande without daunger of theire lives, and the Purser sayd he would rather be hanged then broughte into England, and soe was sente away and sondry other of the principall Spaniardes came away in a boate out of the prize And sayth that foure of the duch men begged a Carvell of Captaine Weste and therein wente away & the other thre would not goe with them but were putt a shore with some of the Spaniardes Ac aliter respondet se nescire.

Ad xxx respondet he was a common mariner in the Fortune & had noe office therein. Ac aliter responsum est supra.

Ad xxxj respondet he hath remayned at Plimouth and in London ever since he came to Englande, and hath not byn verey well dealte withall for apparell for that he hath not had eany geven him, but for meate & drincke he hath had sufficiente at the appointemente of the English merchantes.

Ad xxxij respondet he is of the Christian romishe religion, and well knoweth what a oath is, and maketh accompte of an oath to be damnation if yt be wrongfully taken, and that an oath geven in England is of as greate force as in eany other place and soe he beleveth For although there be sondry religions yet there is but one god that will revenge perjury as he beleveth And sayth if yt were knowen in Spaine that he should take a false oathe in England he should eyther be burned or hanged as he beleveth.

Ad ultimum reddit causas scientie sue ut supra.

161. Spirincke contra West: sentence against the plaintiffs[1]

IN THE NAME OF GOD AMEN there having been heard, seen, perceived and fully and speedily discussed by us Julius

---

[1] H.C.A. 24/65, no. 115. Endorsed: 'Johannes Spirincke et alii contra Thomam

Caesar, doctor of laws, legally constituted lieutenant, judge or president of her majesty's High Court of Admiralty, the merits and circumstances of a certain civil and maritime cause, which before us in suit between John Spirincke, Rowland Fawkner, William Williamson, John Cornelius Corffe and Peter Vanake, foreign merchants, and associates as plaintiffs on the one hand and Thomas West captain of the ship called the *Rose Lion* as defendant on the other has for some time been proceeding and up to the present remains undecided, the aforesaid parties through their proctors lawfully appearing before us in trial, and the party of the said Thomas West that sentence be given and justice be done for his party, and the party of John Spirincke, Rowland Fawkner, William Williamson, John Cornelius Corffe and Peter Vanake and associates that justice also be done for their party at once respectively pleading and claiming; And the whole and entire proceedings had and done before us in this cause having first been scrutinized and carefully reviewed by us; And having lawfully observed all that should be observed in this case, we consider we should proceed to the delivery of our definitive sentence or final decree in this cause, and do proceed in the following manner: Wherefore, through what has been done, deduced, alleged, proved, and likewise admitted in this cause we have discovered and clearly found that the party of the aforesaid plaintiffs have not sufficiently founded and proved their intention as elaborated in the libel given by them in this cause, of which libel the terms are thus as follows—'In dei nomine Amen coram vobis venerabili et egregio viro nostro Julio Cesar legum doctore supreme curie Admi*ralita*tis Anglie locumtenente, iudice, etc. pars proborum virorum Joh*ann*is Spirincke, Rolandi Fawkner, Willi*el*mi Williamson, Joh*ann*is Cornelii Corffe, Petri Vanacke et sociorum contra et adversus Thomam West, capitaneum, ac contra quemcunque alium sive quoscunque alios, etc.', which particular libel we wish to take and do take as read and inserted here, but have failed and do fail in the proving of the same; and wherefore also we have discovered and clearly found that the party of the aforesaid Thomas West the said captain has suffi-

Weste, Clerke Se*n*ior: Clerke J*un*ior.—Dat*um* apud Sowther. Crastino Andreae ap*ost*oli. Viz. die Jovis Primo Decembris 1597.' The sentence is signed by Julius Caesar. Translated.

ciently and to the full, as far as is to be pronounced below, founded and proved his intention as elaborated in a certain allegation on his part given and propounded in this cause, of which allegation the terms are thus as follows—'Quo die dictus Clercke nomine partis nostrae ac ut procurator legitimus dicti Thomae West omni meliori modo necnon ad omnem iuris effectum exinde quovismodo sequi valen*tem* allegavit articulatim prout sequitur etc.', which particular allegation we wish to take and do take as read and inserted here, and that nothing effectual on the part and behalf of the aforesaid John Spirincke, Rowland Fawkner, William Williamson, John Cornelius Corffe, Peter Vanake and their associates has been or is in this behalf objected, elaborated, alleged, propounded and proved which does destroy or in any way weaken the case of the said Thomas West on his part. THEREFORE we Julius Caesar, doctor of laws, the judge aforesaid, having first invoked the name of Christ and turning our eyes to God alone and according to and with the advice of the learned men whom we have consulted in this cause, pronounce, decree and declare that the said Thomas West should be freed and absolved and ought by right to be freed and absolved from the instance and petition of the said John Spirincke, Rowland Fawkner, William Williamson, John Cornelius Corffe, Peter Vanake and associates as elaborated, narrated and propounded in the libel submitted on their behalf, and that perpetual silence should be imposed and ought by right to be imposed upon the same John Spirincke, Rowland Fawkner, William Williamson, John Cornelius Corffe, Peter Vanake and associates in respect of the matters elaborated, narrated and propounded as aforesaid, and we do thus free and absolve and impose by these presents. Further we do pronounce, decree and declare that the ship called the *Fortune* captured by Thomas West captain of the *Rose Lion* and his company and all and singular the goods and merchandize in her at the time of her capture belonged to subjects of the King of Spain, and that the same goods and merchandizes were laded into the same ship at the city of Santo Domingo in the Indies by subjects of the said King for the profit and account of subjects of the said King, and that the same ship and goods were legitimately captured in the Indies by authority of letters of reprisal lawfully granted to the said Thomas West, and that the same ship, her equipment and furniture, together with all and singular the goods and merchandizes captured in the same should be adjudged and ought to be adjudged as lawful prize to the owners and proprietors and setters forth and to the captain, master and sailors of the said ship called the *Rose Lion*, and thus by these presents do we adjudge. And by this our definitive sentence or this our final decree, which we bring and promulgate in these writings, we condemn the said John Spirincke, Rowland Fawkner, William Williamson, John Cornelius Corffe, Peter Vanake and their associates in lawful expenses incurred on the part and behalf of the aforesaid Thomas West made or to be made in this cause and by reason of the same and paid by him or his party. We reserve to ourselves or to another judge competent in this cause the taxation or assessment of the costs.

CHAPTER XVIII

THE VOYAGE OF PRESTON AND SOMMERS
1595

THE last of our voyages, that of Amyas Preston and George Sommers, is better known than any of those we have examined, perhaps on account of its connection with Raleigh's famous Guiana expedition of the same year. The report of the voyage published by Hakluyt[1] was written by Robert Davie, in all probability the same as the Robert Davis who was master of the *Bark Raleigh* in Gilbert's 1583 voyage; the same as the Robert Davies of Lyme, owner and captain of the *Lyme*, the *Son* of Lyme and the *Revenge* of Lyme, whose prize goods were delivered to Raleigh in 1591; the same as the Captain Davies on whose behalf Raleigh interceded with Sir Robert Cecil in 1594.[2] His connection with Raleigh is obvious enough; his connection with Preston was possibly an independent one, as both men had more than a little interest in the privateering enterprise of the port of Lyme. To Davie's account can be added one or two brief references in Spanish despatches to the presence of the English off La Margarita, and two Spanish accounts of the capture of Caracas.[3]

The two leaders are interesting minor figures in the Elizabethan maritime scene. Preston came from a family which had been settled for many generations at Cricket, in Somerset.[4] In 1585 he took part, with Bernard Drake, in fitting out the *Golden Riall* of Topsham for a voyage to Virginia, to follow up Grenville's expedition. The ship sailed in June and Preston went with her, but she was now bound, on the Queen's and Raleigh's

[1] Document 162.
[2] Harleian MS 598, f. 14; H.C.A. 14/28, no. 58; H.C.A. 25/3 (9), 20 May 1592; S.P. Dom. Eliz., ccxlviii, no. 4; Quinn, *Gilbert*, p. 396; *Roanoke Voyages*, p. 154.
[3] Documents 163–6.
[4] *D.N.B.*

instructions, not for Virginia, but for Newfoundland. On the way out a Portuguese prize was taken and Preston was sent back in command. Further prizes were taken by Bernard Drake, and the venture as a whole was highly successful, but Preston had to go to law and eventually to the Privy Council itself to secure the return of the money he had invested and a proportionate share of the profits from Sir John Gilbert and Sir Walter Raleigh.[1]

Preston was again privateering—in the *Eleanour* of Weymouth—in 1587,[2] and served with distinction in the Armada campaign.[3] The following year he sailed with Cumberland to the Azores.[4] Here, during October, gathered numerous privateers, among them Preston's own *Julian* (sometimes called the *Flyboat*) of Lyme, under the command of one George Sommers, the Dorsetshire seaman who was later to give his name to the Bermudas or Somers Islands. Sommers was also associated with Lyme: he had been born in or near there in 1554 and was to represent the borough in Parliament from 1604 until his death in 1610.[5] At the Azores the *Julian*, with her own pinnace the *Delight*, and in company with the *Swiftsure* of Chichester (owned by George Raymond) and the *Unicorn* of Barnstaple (owned by the merchant William Morcomb), took two very rich prizes, worth together some £30,000. Preston and Sommers were dissatisfied with the share of prize goods allotted them and sued Morcomb and Raymond; nevertheless they must have made a substantial profit on the venture.[6] Nothing further, save the legal reverberations of this dispute, is heard of the two partners until their famous exploit of 1595.[7]

It may be thought strange that Preston should have consented

---

[1] *Roanoke Voyages*, pp. 172–3, 234–42; Harlow, *Raleigh's Guiana*, p. xxviii.

[2] H. J. Moule (ed.), *Descriptive Catalogue of the Charters, Minute Books and other Documents in the Borough of Weymouth and Melcomb Regis, 1252–1800* (1883), pp. 160–1.

[3] Laughton, *Defeat*, II, 57–8.   [4] *Monson's Tracts*, I, 234.   [5] *D.N.B.*

[6] 'Elizabethan Privateering', pp. 298–300.

[7] Sommers was formerly associated with Raymond as master of his *Lion* of Chichester in 1584 (H.C.A. 13/25, 17 April 1584). He also had an interest in Raymond's *Swiftsure* of Chichester (H.C.A. 13/26, 6–11 May 1587) and joined with John Young of Chichester in a privateering venture (Lansdowne MS 115, f. 196). Preston and Sommers alike achieved distinction after 1595 in the Queen's ships, the former being knighted in the Cadiz expedition, the latter by James I in 1603. Both played active parts in the early Virginia Company (*D.N.B.*; Brown, *Genesis of the United States*, I, 46–63, 209–28; II, 1018–19).

to co-operate with Raleigh after the dispute between them in the later eighties, and it is not unlikely that he did so with some reluctance. Raleigh left the English coast on 6 February 1594/5, and on the 22nd Preston wrote to Sir Robert Cecil:[1]

'I understand by my brother, Hugh Preston, that you made a doubt of my going to sea with Sir Walter Raleigh, for that it was generally given out to the contrary. If my business had been in any reasonable forwardness (as it was altogether imperfect at his departure) I would not have been an inch behind, as well to satisfy your intent herein, as for the better performance of matters already determined. Yet nevertheless (if God permit) we shall meet again at a place appointed, where I know he doth earnestly expect my coming, and have his directions to that effect. I have here four ships and a pinnace, and am able to land 300 strong, and will by all means possible find him forth as soon as wind and weather give me leave to proceed forward.'

This letter, with all its denial of the general rumour, is not very convincing when set against Davie's account, which shows that Preston did not leave until 12 March, though he was ready a month before and lay in Plymouth harbour waiting for Captain Jones. If Raleigh sailed without Preston, why not Preston without Jones? There may have been other reasons, but it is significant that none are mentioned—not even adverse weather. Once at sea, Preston made no haste, perhaps because he was already persuaded he would be too late for the rendezvous at Trinidad; at any rate the decision to attack Puerto Santo made that certain.[2]

Preston's was not an ordinary privateering force. Like Raleigh's, it contained a large contingent of soldiers, the leaders of which were probably gentlemen. It was a force designed for land operations, the capture of enemy shipping being only a secondary (though important) object. This explains the successes at Puerto Santo, Caracas and Coro, though credit must be given to Preston for bold, but by no means foolhardy, leadership. The attack upon the city of Santiago de León de Caracas was indeed a bold stroke. The city was situated some miles inland in a posi-

---

[1] *Cal. Salis. MSS*, v (1894), 115.
[2] Raleigh generously blamed providence, though he also implied some error of judgement on Preston's part (Harlow, *Raleigh's Guiana*, p. 16).

tion almost inaccessible from the sea, for between the small port of La Guaira and the city itself lay a formidable range of mountains, through which the only fairly easy route could be held by by determined defenders against almost any force. The alternative route across the mountains was both arduous and dangerous. The first Spanish account of Preston's attack[1] shows that he realised that if the Spaniards offered resistance to his advance by this alternative route he could only hope, at the best, to retire without loss. This conclusion is underlined by the later Spanish narrative, written by Fray Pedro Simón and published in 1625,[2] which was probably based upon accounts the author had heard from the lips of participants. The better-known narrative by Oviedo y Baños, published in 1723,[3] was obviously based primarily upon Simón, though as a citizen of Caracas the later writer seems to have had access to some additional material. His literary pretensions and patriotism, however, moved him to inflate and distort the whole incident. The poor cripple Villalpando becomes a foul traitor, the foolhardy Alonso Andrea a romantic hero; the English are transformed into generous cavaliers, and their leader, the anonymous corsair, into the fearsome El Draque. Even the municipal magistrates become masters of strategy and tactics. Thus are historical legends created.

For the rest, there is no avoiding the conclusion that neither Preston nor his country gained anything worth while by this expedition. The towns taken were not places of great importance and burning them did no serious harm to the Spanish Empire. The amounts gained in loot and ransom must have been small in comparison with the cost of the venture, for there is little mention of prizes and on land the Spanish removed their valuables out of reach. Effective co-operation with Raleigh, on the other hand, might have produced some considerable result. The dissipation of English endeavours, typical of the whole period since 1588, was particularly marked in this year of 1595, when this wave of unco-ordinated depredations upon the Spanish Empire reached its rather feeble climax.

* * *

[1] Document 165, which makes it clear that the city was warned.
[2] Document 166.
[3] See footnotes to document 166.

Margarita & the maine, called Coche. We came neer it in the night with our ships within some 3 leagues, & there ankered under the maine side, and about midnight we manned our pinnesses & boats, and in the morning about breake of day, we landed on the yland, wherin are few or none inhabitants, but they commonly come from Margarita in boats on the munday, and remaine there fishing for pearles untill the saturday, and then returne & cary al that they have taken to Margarita. Here we tooke some few Spaniards and Negros their slaves with them, and had some smal quantitie of pearls. We remained on this iland the 20 and 21, in which time we went a fishing with our seine, and tooke good store of mullets and other fish, and amongst the rest drew a shore in the seine a fish called by the Spaniards Lagarto, and by the Indians Caiman, which is indeed a Crocodile, for it hath 4 feete and a long taile, and a wide mouth, and long teeth, & wil devour men. Some of these Lagartos are in length 16 foot, some 20 foot, and some 30 foot: they have muske in them, and live as wel on the land, as in the water. The 21 of May we departed for Cumana, thinking to have gotten in that night to have landed: but the current striketh so strong out of the bay that we could not recover the towne till day light. In the morning we espied 2 sailes before the towne, but could not fetch them. Here we plied too and againe in the sound all the forenoone, but could not get up so farre as the towne. These 2 sailes came roome to us, after they saw that we were at an anker, & came somewhat neere us, and sent their skyphs abord our admiral. They were 2 flieboats of Middleburgh which traded there, & had secretly advertised the country of our comming, to our great hinderance: but we knew it not at our first arrivall. Here they of Cumana perceiving that we would land, came to parle with us, and tolde us, if we would land, we might easily take the towne, for they ment not to withstand us, but that they had caried all their goods into the mountaines, but, if we would not land to burne and spoile the towne, they would give us some reasonable ransome, and any victuals that we wanted. So our general agreed with them, received their ransome, and departed without landing. But at our first arrival in this bay, our generals long boat was sent forth wel manned, and tooke 3 Caravels, but found litle or nothing of value in them: saving in one were some sides of bacon, and some maiz

Certaine Spaniards and Negros taken in the yle of Coche where they fish for pearle.

Two flieboats of Middleburgh forewarne the Spaniards of our comming.

The towne of Cumana ransomed. Three Caravels taken.

Willis.[1] The 9 of April we al departed for Tenerif to seeke captaine Preston: and standing over towards Tenerif, the 9 day at night I came into captaine Sommers ship. The 10 in the morning we brake our maine yard, yet we recovered Tenerif, & the same day towards night we ankered under the southside of the same. There I went aland in our boat, & found 3 or 4 fisherboats, and brought one of them off. The rest bulged themselves.[2] Here we rode to mend our yard til the 11 at night: then we set saile to find captaine Amias Preston: and standing towards Gomera, the 12 in the morning we had sight of him. Then we thought to have landed in Gomera: but the wind blew so much, that we could not. So we departed altogether with joy the 13 of April, & set our course for the West Indies. And the 8 of May next ensuing, we arrived at the yland of Dominica. In all which time nothing happened unto us saving this, that the 18 day of April at midnight, our admiral lost her long boat in towing. We staied at Dominica til the 14 of May, to refresh our sicke men. Here the Indians came unto us in canoas made of an whole tree, in some wherof were 3 men, in some 4 or 6, & in others 12 or 14, and brought in them plantans, pinos, and potatos, and trucked with us, for hatchets, knives, & smal beadstones. Here in refreshing of our men, we found an hot bath hard joyning to a cold river side: wherein our sick men bathed themselves, and were soone recovered of their sicknesses. This is a goodly yland, and something high land, but al overgrowen with woods. The 14 we departed from thence, & the 16 sailing Southwestward, we had sight of Granada, but landed not there. The 17 we arrived at the Testigos & ankered there, and consorted with the 3 ships of Hampton, wherin captaine Willis was. The 18 we landed our men & tooke view and muster of all, & the same night set saile away. The 19 we had sight of Margarita, where the Spaniards by their Indians fish for pearle: we stood in very neere the rode, but saw nothing there. Therefore we went no further in, but stood from it againe.[3] The same day toward night, we had sight of a litle yland, betweene

Dominica.

An excellent holesome hot bath found in Dominica.

The yles called Testigos.

---

[1] This was Captain Moses Willis in the *Archangel* of Southampton, owned by the leading Southampton shipowner, Thomas Heaton. He arrived home with some West Indian prize goods in October (Harleian MS 598, f. 36).

[2] Bulge—to take in water, to leak.

[3] Compare the Spanish version (document 163), which claims that the English retired when met with artillery.

ENGLISH PRIVATEERING VOYAGES

long boats to land his men & to force the same: but the people were on shore in warlike array, with baricados & trenches made, ready to withstand them. Whereupon, considering the great danger, and disadvantage of the place, he caused his people to returne abord againe. And the next morning 3 or 4 houres before day, he landed in a place of greater security, with 60 men onely, who lay closely in a chapel, to defend themselves from the raine til break of the day, and so marched forward upon the backs of their enemies, which kept their baricados upon the shore. By this time the enemie was 500 strong. But, being so suddenly surprised, after some resistance of our muskets, when they saw our pikes approch, and had tasted somewhat of their force they began to flee into certaine thickets & shrubs, thinking from thence to gall our men: but with very litle or no losse at all, our men dislodged them of that place also. Hereupon, they all fled toward the chiefe towne of the yland: but once again they thought to make a new stand at a certaine house by the way, from whence they were repulsed by captaine Roberts. So in the flight part of them were slaine, and an ensigne, which one captaine Harvey an English man had lost not long before, was recovered: and the chiefe towne it selfe was by our men wholly woon and possessed. But before the entrance of our men they had conveighed their wives, their children, and the rest of their goods into an exceeding high hil which standeth neere the towne, and could not be conquered, but with exceeding losse. Although they sent divers times to redeeme their towne, which was very faire and large, yet in regard of their crueltie and treachery, which they used towards captaine Harvey and his people, captaine Preston would shew them no favour, but utterly burnt their towne to ashes, and sent his men to wast the rest of their villages of the yland, preferring the honour & just revenge of his country men, before his owne private gaine, & commodity. And so with small pillage and great honour he retired in safetie and all his small company with him, from the conquered yland unto his ship. But we in our ship met not with him, until the 12. of April following. We therefore in the Derling pursuing our voiage, had sight of the yles of the Canaries the 6 of April, and the 8 of the same, we watered on the South-eastside of the grand Canaria. There we met with capt. Sommers, & his pinnesse, & 3 ships of Hampton, in one whereof was cap.

The yle of Puerto Santo taken and the chiefe towne in it burnt.

They water upon the grand Canaria.

162. Robert Davie's account of Preston's voyage[1]

The victorious voyage of Captaine *Amias Preston* now knight, and Captaine *George Sommers* to the West *India*, begun in March 1595. Wherein the yle of *Puerto Santo*, the yle of *Coche* neere *Margarita*, the fort and towne of *Coro*, the stately city of *S. Iago de Leon* were taken sacked and burned, and the towne of *Cumana* ransomed, & *Jamaica* entred. Written by *Robert Davie* one of the company.

Captaine Amias Preston, and captaine Sommers, both valiant gentlemen & discreet commanders, lying ready with two tall ships, the Ascension and the Gift, and a small pinnesse at Plimmouth, for the space of a moneth attending the comming of captaine Jones their consort, which in al that time, through the bad dealing of those which he put in trust, could not make his ship in readines, according to his appointment, the 12. of March 1595. set forward on their voyage for the West Indies. We with captaine Jones in the Derling,[2] and Captaine Prowse in the Angel,[3] followed after them the 19. of the said moneth. The last of March, captaine Preston by giving chase to a saile, was separated from captaine Sommers, and his pinnesse, so that they utterly lost sight ech of other: whereupon captain Preston in his ship alone, resolved to surprise the yle of Puerto santo, and shortly after came before the same. This yland standeth in the Northerly latitude of 33. degrees, and lieth to the Northward of the yle of Madera, and is inhabited by old souldiers, which the kings of Portugal were wont to reward for their former olde services, by placing of them there. This yland is rich in corne, wine, & oile: and hath good store of sheep, asses, goats & kine: they have also plenty of foules, fishes & fruits. Captaine Preston comming before this yland with one ship only sought with 2.

---

[1] *Principal Navigations*, III (1600), 578–83; X (1904), 213–26.

[2] Presumably Raleigh's *Darling*, used by Keymis the next year and set forth by Raleigh and Cecil in 1598 (H.C.A. 13/33, 10 June 1598; S.P. Dom. Eliz., cclxviii, no. 95).

[3] The *Angel* of Southampton, owned by Richard Goddard and Laurence Prowse, was set forth under Captain William Prowse in 1593 and 1594. The Prowses were responsible for many privateering ventures from Southampton ('Elizabethan Privateering', p. 282); Laurence was the promoter, though on occasions an active participant; William Prowse, the man in question here, is only mentioned as master or captain in the various ventures.

General required 30000 ducats. Whereunto he replied that it was very much. So having had some other conference together, hee shewed him that hee had bene a souldier in Flanders a long time, and now was sent thither by his kings commandement. Among other things our General demanded of him, what the reason was they had not walled the citie, being so faire a thing as that was. The Spaniard replied, that hee thought it to bee stronger walled than anie citie in the world, meaning, by those huge & high mountains which the enemie must passe over before he can approch it; which we found very true. Thus with many other faire speeches, he tooke his leave for that day, and told our Generall, that he would go speake with the governour: (but it might be himselfe, for any thing we know) howbeit because our General had granted him free comming and going, he suffred him to depart: who before his departure, requested to have a token of our General, that he might shew to the Governour how he had spoken with us, or else he doubted, that he would not beleeve him. Whereupon our General gave him a piece of 12 pence: so he departed and promised the next day by ten of the clocke to returne unto us with an answere: in which meane time nothing befel. The next day being the 2 of June, at his houre appointed, he returned with his Indian running by his horses side. So he was brought to the Generall, and there remained till after dinner, and dined in his company in the governours house that was. The dinner ended, with the best entertainement which could be given him, they communed again about the ransome of the citie. Our General proposed his old demand of 30000 ducats. The Spaniard first proffered him 2000, then 3000, last of all 4000, and more he would not give. Our General counting it a small summe of money among so many, did utterly refuse it. So the Spaniard departed. But before his departure our general told him, that if he came not to him again before the next day noone, with the ransome which he demanded, he would set all on fire. That whole day past, and the night also without any thing of moment, except some shew of assault, by their approching towards our Corps du guard, and retiring backe againe. The 3 day being come, in the morning some of our company went forth, a league or more from the towne, & some two leagues and more unto certaine villages thereabout, & set them on fire: but the enemy

Certain villages about Sant Iago fired.

raine ceased, and going downe a little further, on the toppe of a hill we saw the towne not farre distant from us. Here we all cleared our muskets: and when our colours came in sight, we discharged a second volee of shot to the great discouragement of the enemie. Thus we marched on a round pace. The enemie was in readinesse a little without the towne to encounter us on horsebacke. Being nowe fully descended from the mountaines wee came into a faire plaine champion fielde, without either hedge, bush or ditch, saving certaine trenches which the water had made, as it descendeth from the mountaines. Here we set our selves in a readinesse, supposing the enemie would have encountered us: but having pitched our maine battell, and marching forward a good round pace, captaine Beling, and captaine Roberts tooke ech of them some looseshoot, and marched in all hast toward the enemie before the maine battell, wherein was our generall with capt. Sommers and came to skirmish with them: but it was soone ended: for the enemie fled. One Spaniard was slaine in this skirmish, and not any one of our companies touched either with piece or arrow, God be thanked. We soone marched into the towne, and had it without any more resistance: but there we found not the wealth that we expected: for they had conveyed all into the mountaines, except such goods as they could not easily cary, as wine, and iron, and such things. By three of the clocke in the afternoone the 29 of May, we entred the citie. Here we remained until the 3 of June without anie great disturbance, saving sometime by night they would come on horse-backe hard unto our Corps du guard, and finding us vigilant, and readie for them, would depart againe. *The Citie of S. Iago de Leon taken the 29. of May.*

The first of June, there came a Spaniard neere unto us alone: the Corps du guard perceiving him, called our General, who soone came towards him: but before he approched, the Spaniard made signes that he should lay aside his armes: which he refused to doe, but promised as he was a souldier, if he would come, hee should have free passage. Upon which promise hee came to him on horse-backe, and our General brought him within the towne, and there communed with him. Who demanded what he ment to do with the towne: he answered that he meant to remaine there and keepe it; or if he did depart from it he would burne it. The Spaniard then demanded, what the ransome of it should be. Our

and Guiny-wheat. Here we staied til the 23 of May, & in the evening we set saile, and departed from thence. And the 26 of the same we thought to have landed at a fort that standeth by the sea-coast in the Caracos, as you go for S. Iago. This is a marveilous high land, as high as the pike of Tenerif. We could not land here over night, by reason of the roughnes of the sea, which goeth in that place, & there is but one litle creeke against the fort, to come in with your boat. So, we perceiving no fit place to land, by reason of the sea, stood away some league to the West-ward, about a litle head-land, there we ankered al night: and the 27 in the morning we all landed in safety, none resisting us. Then we presently set our selves in aray, and marched toward the fort, & tooke it without any resistance. Here we remained al the rest of this day until the 28, about three of the clock in the afternoone. *A fort nere the Caracos taken.*

We found nothing in this fort but a litle meale, or 2 or 3 tunnes of wine, which by reason of some disorder amongst the company overcharging themselves with the wine, our general for the most part caused to be spilt. While we remained here, some of our company ranging the woods, found the governor of the fort where he lay asleepe, brought him to our general: who examined him touching the state of the citie of S. Iago de Leon. Who declared unto us that they had newes of our comming a moneth before, and that they of the towne had made preparation for our comming: and that if we did go the common beaten way, it was never possible for us to passe, for that they had made in the midst of the way betweene this fort and the said city, an exceeding strong baricado on the top of a very high hil, the passage being not above 25 or 30 foot in bredth, & on each side marveilous steep-upright, and the woods so thicke that no man could passe for his life: which indeed at our returning backe we found to be true. Upon which speeches our general demanded of him if there were not any other way: who answered, there is another way marveilous bad and very ill to travel which the Indians do commonly use: but he thought that the Spaniards had stopt the same, by cutting downe of great trees and other things, as indeed they had. This Spaniard was a very weake and sickly man not able to travel, so our generall sent him abord his ship, & there kept him. In the taking of our 3 small Caravels at Cumana, we had a Spaniard in one of them that had traveiled these wayes to the *All our actions betrayed by dangerous spies out of England.*

citie of S. Iago. He told us he would cary us thither by any of both these wayes, if afterward we would set him at libertie: the which was granted. While we remained at the fort by the waters side, the Spaniards came downe unto us by the great & beaten way on horsebacke, who being discovered, our generall sent out to meete them captaine Roberts with some 40 or 50 musketeirs, who came to skirmish with them, but they would not stay. The same day in the afternoone we marched forth toward S. Iago, & tooke the Indians way called The unknowen way. In our march we came to divers Indians houses, which we never hurt, but passed by and left them untouched: but the Indians were all fled into the woods, and other places, we know not whither. We marched until it was night over such high mountaines, as we never saw the like, and such a way as one man could scarse passe alone. Our general being in the forward, at length came whereas a river descended downe over the mountaines, and there we lodged all that night. Here in going this way, we found the Spanish governours confession to be true: for they had baricadoed the way in divers places with trees, & other things in such sort, that we were driven to cut our way through the woods by Carpenters, which we caried with us for that purpose. The next day being the 29 of May early in the morning we set forward to recover the tops of the mountaines: but (God knoweth) they were so extreeme high and so steep-upright, that many of our souldiers fainted by the way: and when the officers came unto them, and first entreated them to goe, they answered, they could goe no further. Then they thought to make them goe by compulsion, but all was in vaine: they would goe a little and then lie downe, and bid them kill them, if they would, for they could not, nor would not goe any further. Whereby they were enforced to depart, & to leave them there lying on the ground. To be short, at length with much ado we gat the top of the mountaines about noone: there we made a stand til all the company was come up, and would have stayed longer to have refreshed our men: but the fogge and raine fell so fast, that wee durst not stay. So wee made hast to descend towards the towne out of the fogge and raine: because that in these high mountaines by report of the Spaniards themselves, it doeth almost continually raine. Assoone as we were descended downe neere halfe the way to the towne the

never came to resist them, so they returned backe againe safe into the towne, and brought certaine Indian prisoners with them, among whom there was one which spake broken Spanish, which being examined, confessed unto us of his own accord, how the General had sent to the other towns thereabout for aide, and that he thought they would be there with him that day. When we understood this, we grew into some distrust of the Spaniards trechery, and thought upon the messenger, how he had used long delayes with us: wherupon we were commanded presently, every man to make ready to depart, and to fire the citie: which foorth- *The citie of S. Iago burned.* with was done. And after we had seene it all on fire, & burnt to ashes, we tooke our leaves and so departed, & marched away that day being the 3 of June, not that way we came, but by the great beaten way. And when we had marched halfe the way towards the waters side, we came unto that strong baricado which they had made, and there lay all that night. Here we found the Spanish captaines word to be true which we tooke at the fort by the waters side: for this baricado was of such force, that 100 men in it wel furnished, would have kept backe from passing that way 100000: first by reason of the huge and high mountaines, next the steepenes of them, on both sides, last of all in regard of the fine contriving of it with the large trenches, and other munitions, which I cease to recite. The fourth day of June in the morning wee departed from thence: but before our departure, wee overthrew on the one side of the steepe hill two bases of yron, which we found there planted by the enemie, and so set forward toward our ships, and by 12 of the clocke came to the waters side, and there remayned in the fort which wee had taken before, untill the fift day at night: in which time we laded some small quantity of hides, and Salsa-perilla, which we found there at our first landing. So the fift day at night we departed from thence, to goe to a towne called Coro: but before wee departed, wee set fire in the fort, and *A fort and certain Indians houses by the waters side burnt* all the Indians houses that were about it, and burnt them. Then we set sayle, and standing along the coast, our Spanish guide signified unto us, that there were foure sayles of ships about five leagues from thence, in a place called Checherebiche, and Caio, and Maio.[1] So the 6 day in the morning we were thwart of the

[1] Chichiriviche, about half way between Caracas and Coro, and a great deal further than five leagues from either. The alternative names given presumably refer to the numerous cays in the neighbourhood.

place, and there our generall sent away his long boate with captaine Sommers, unto those places, where they found 3 of the
ships: but the Spaniards had conveyed their sailes ashore into the
woods, so that they could not bring them off, but set fire in them
and burnt them. From hence we stood along the shore, sailing
untill the ninth day of June, on which day toward the evening we
imbarked our selves in our pinnesses and small caravels, to land
at Coros: but we had none that knew the place certainely: wherefore we ankored that night some two leagues to the Eastward of
it, and in the morning I went on land, and nine more with me, to
see if we could discover the towne, but we could not, wee went
above a league up into the countrey, but could not see any village or towne. So returning backe, wee met our Generall, with
divers others which came ashore with him, with whom we
marched into the countrey againe, but could see nothing, & so
returned. At the water side captaine Prowse died. There we
remained all that day on land, by reason the wind blew so much
that wee could not get aboord untill the evening. After our
comming aboord a boat which we sent into the bay, returned and
brought us newes, that there rode a barke within the bay, and by
all likelyhood the towne should be there. So presently our
Generall went into the bay with the Derling and some of the
small caravels. The tenth day in the morning, the rest of our
shipping came into the bay, and our men landed the same day,
about 10 or 11 of the clocke in the night, & so marched on
toward the towne: but in the way they had made baricados, and
kept them very strongly. Notwithstanding the courage of our
men was such, as that they feared nothing, and forced them to
leave their forces, and flie. Having wonne this baricado they
there remained untill the next day being the 11 of June, and then
early in the morning they marched on towards the towne, where
by the way, the enemie often times came to skirmish with them,
but alwayes fled. In fine they wan the towne without any great
losse of men, God be thanked. Having gotten the town, they
found nothing in it at all; for they had intelligence from Sant
Iago, how wee had used them before, which caused them to
convey all their goods into the mountaines and woods: finding
nothing in it, our Generall caused it to be set on fire, thinking it
not good to remaine there, but to returne againe, backe to the

Three Spanish ships burnt.

A baricado woon.

The towne of Coros taken & burnt.

ships: and the greatest cause was by reason of the departure of captaine Sommers: who the day before in a most furious tempest, being in the pinnesse, with some 50 men at anker, had his cables broken and lost all his ankers, and so was faine to put to sea to save himselfe, otherwise they had bene in danger of perishing. Thus our General and his company, returned backe againe the twelfth day and imbarked themselves, and departed away with all speede to seeke captaine Sommers. The 13 toward night, hee came where captaine Sommers was, and found him riding, but not by anie ankers, but by two bases, which they had made for to stay their barke by: at which meeting the company was very glad. Then they determined to go into a mighty great bay, to a towne called Laguna:[1] but the bay was so deepe and should[2] withall, that we returned backe againe, after wee had stood in two daies & a night. So we sayled over toward the Isle of Hispaniola the sixteenth of June: and the twentieth day we saw it. The 21 we ankored under Cape Tiburon. Here we watered, and stayed untill the 25 of the same. After our departure out of the bay of Laguna, a great sicknes fell among our fleete, and there died about eighty men of the same. This sicknesse was the fluxe of the bellie,[3] which is a common disease in that countrey. We remayned about this Island untill the eight and twentieth of this moneth. Then we departed from thence, and the second of July arrived at the Island of Jamaica. Before our comming hither, the three ships of Hampton had forsaken us, and left our company. And the Derling wherein was captaine Jones, was sent to discover some other secret matter, in which discovery the valiant gentleman ended his life. So our whole fleete was now but our generall, with captaine Sommers, and a small pinnesse. We stayed at this Isle of Jamaica until the sixt of July, in which meane time we landed to see if we could kill any beeves, but we could not, they were so wild: here is great store of them, and great plenty of fresh-fish. We departed hence the 6 of July, and passed by the Islands, called Caimanes, and the Isle de Pinos, and the 12 of the said moneth by Cape de Corrientes where we watered, and the same night, wee set saile towards the cape of S.

The bay of Laguna

Hispaniola.

Jamaica.

The death of captaine Jones.

Cape de corrientes.

[1] A place of this name no longer exists in the region. It was evidently situated on the shore of Lago de Maracaibo.
[2] Shoaled.
[3] Dysentery.

ENGLISH PRIVATEERING VOYAGES

Anthony, being the westermost part of the Isle of Cuba. The 13 day in the morning we were under this cape, and the same day we met with the honourable knight, Sir Walter Ralegh, returning from his paineful, and happie discovery of Guiana, and his surprise of the Isle of Trinidad. So with glad hearts, wee kept him and his fleete of three ships company till the twentieth day at night, what time we lost them. In all which time nothing of moment fell out, save that we gave chase to a couple of frigats, but could not fetch them.

Afterward we plyed to recover Havana, untill the five and twentieth of July: then we set our course for the head of the Martyrs,[1] the 27 we were in sight of them. The 28 wee entred the gulfe of Bahama: then we set our course homeward toward Newfoundland, but we could not fetch it, but were on the Banke, and tooke fish there the 20 day of August. The same night we set sayle to come home, by reason the wind was contrary to goe in with Newfoundland. So the tenth day of September, we arrived in safety (God be thanked) in Milford haven in Wales, having performed so long a voyage in the space of sixe moneths, or somewhat lesse.

The Banke of Newfoundland.

163. Preston at La Margarita: Spanish report[2]

On 26 May[3] the lookouts I have posted on top of a mountain reported six armed ships and four others a little smaller to be steering for this island and this port. I assembled my men and deployed them as was advisable, because never before have as many ships as this been seen here together. At two in the after-

[1] *La Cabeça de los Martires*, northeast of Havana, an important landmark for navigators making from Havana for the Florida Channel.

[2] Pedro de Salazar, governor of La Margarita, to the crown, Margarita, 4 June 1595 (A. de I. 54–4–6, Santo Domingo 184. 1 *pliego*. Original). Extract. A copy of the entire document appears with a translation in the Venezuela Papers (Add. MS 36316, ff. 126–32). The earlier part of the document describes the defensive preparations against corsairs: 'The danger is this, that since the beginning of May there are never wanting corsair ships in a port of this island called Port Moreno, whence with their launches they sail to the mainland. This is at a distance of two leagues from this city. In the principal port of this island I have built a platform on a neck of land, and I am now building in great haste a fort, and the corsairs are so expert and carry such pilots that they have it measured by palms.' The part of the document following our extract is a plea for reinforcements.

[3] 19/29 May according to Davie.

noon they attempted the harbour in small craft and pinnaces, but God permitted us to defend ourselves in such manner that they had to retire before our artillery.[1] They remained in sight that day. That night I had word that they had captured one Licentiate Arze, a resident here, who was coming from Cumana, and that they had also taken a caravel from Puerto Rico. I understand that their prisoners informed them into what good shape I have put this place, for they sailed on a course for Cumana.

164. Preston followed by Raleigh at La Margarita: Spanish report[2]

Sire

God, the great protector of all things, is wont to extend His hand where most required. When we were in the direst need, by your majesty's order there arrived in this island Captain Pedro de Salazar, who (without resting two days on land after his wearisome journey) proceeded to the ports to undertake and direct their defence against the enemy. He very shortly thereafter received two despatches from your majesty ordering him to place this island on its guard. He has done so, losing not a moment by day or night. Ever since he arrived he has attended personally to the closing of roads and the digging of trenches along those ways by which the enemy might approach. He has taken other defensive measures, as becomes an old soldier experienced in war.

This accomplished, there appeared nine ships which came to our port, and on arriving learned that he was our governor. They did not anchor, but set sail and went away.

A few days later came the Duke of Cornwall,[3] who dropped anchor in the harbour. He came intending to land men, to which end he reconnoitred the port that night. Since everybody was on

---

[1] Davie makes no mention of any resistance, and for the English withdrawal offers the excuse that they could see nothing in the harbour.
[2] Gerónimo Campuzano to the crown, La Margarita, 8 July 1595 (A. de I. 54-4-6, Santo Domingo 184. 1 *pliego*. Original). Extract. A translation of the document appears in the Venezuela Papers (Add. MS 36316, ff. 133-6). The remainder of the letter merely repeats its praises of the governor's work.
[3] Raleigh was lord-lieutenant of Cornwall.

the alert, two pieces of artillery were fired upon him from a fort which is just being finished. His pinnace returned to its general to report.

After daybreak this pinnace came back to the land and there was some conversation. Those on shore informed the English that the governor here had served in Flanders and was Captain Pedro de Salazar and had put the place into such shape that if they landed it would cost them dear, for he would kill as many as set foot on land. These reasons moved them to withdraw. When their general learned who was governor here he lost his desire to land men, and made sail, which was universally regretted, because under so renowned a fighter all the residents here have experienced a revival of spirit, so that had the Englishman decided to land men, there is no doubt that he would have reshipped none of them.

165. Preston at Caracas: Spanish report[1]

After what had happened in Trinidad respecting Berrio, a soldier escaped from there. He was called Juan de Mumpabila and was a Frenchman. He arrived and took shelter at Caracas and went up to the city of Santiago de Leon, where he reported what had occurred to him in the island of Trinidad, and how the Englishman Guaterral was coming with a large force, with the purpose of burning and destroying all the ports on the coast, and that he would go up to the city of Santiago de Leon to plunder it; and as it possesses so many natural fortifications on account of the difficult passages and roads through which it is reached, they heeded little what the soldier said, as they held it impossible for the corsair to reach the city. They also took little care to defend it.

It happened that Ames Preston, an Englishman who left England with a squadron of nine vessels in pursuit of Guaterral, got ahead of him while Guaterral was detained in the island of

[1] Licentiate Pedro de Liaño to the crown, La Margarita, 13 April 1596 (A. de I. 54-4-6, Santo Domingo 184. Original). Extract. A copy of the entire document, which is a long report of the activities of Sir Walter Raleigh, prefaced by some account of the extensive barter carried on by Flemish and English ships at Cumaná and La Margarita, appears with a translation in the Venezuela Papers (Add. MS 36317, ff. 36-49 and 51-79). A part of what is now published has already been printed in Harlow, *Raleigh's Guiana*, pp. 124-5.

Trinidad and the River Orinoco. He went to the port of Cumana, where he received information that some English, who were anchored there, were bartering their merchandise with the people of Cumana, and that Guaterral was coming to destroy and burn the city. On account of this he left that capture to him, and went to the port of Guaira in the province of Venezuela, where he landed three hundred men with their flags. Although information reached the city of Santiago de Leon that the enemy was ashore and was marching towards the city, no one went out to oppose them: nor was there any order, government or defence to be found in any part. The English continued marching for half the distance, being then so tired that they could not advance further, rested and took food. Perceiving the difficulties of the roads, they wished to return. For their general had given them orders that if they found any kind of defence, they were to return, and if not, that they should inform him of what passed there, so that he might assist them. He sent them help and told them that since they had met with no opposition so far, they could go up to the city of Santiago de Leon, or as far as they met with no resistance. They then went up by a difficult path and entered the city of Santiago de Leon on Thursday, the 8th of June 1596,[1] without being opposed by anyone. They found very little property to take, because the inhabitants had taken everything with them excepting wines, flour and other provisions, which they consumed, much to their own satisfaction. They remained in Santiago de Leon from the Thursday the 8th of June until the following Monday. During this time they met with no trouble and were as undisturbed as in their own homes. On the Monday morning thirty Englishmen set out to reconnoitre the district. They burned some cattle ranches and returned with the horses and tame mules which they had found. They also set fire to the city, burning a part of the principal church and some houses.

They left an English youth in the city, under pretext that he had deserted and did not wish to go with them. It has since been ascertained that it was done in order that he might learn the Indian language and acquaint himself with the country. The English returned safely on board, although they had to travel by difficult roads and passages. They embarked their spoils and

[1] [*Sic*.] The report itself was written in 1596, but the events occurred in 1595.

carried them away, among which were a hundred quintals of sarsaparilla and five hundred hides which they had found hidden in the road. They then went on along the coast until they reached the city of Coro. They plundered and burned it without meeting any resistance. This carelessness and neglect of the inhabitants deserves due punishment, so that in future they may be compelled to live with greater precautions.

166. A later Spanish account of the capture of Caracas[1]

We must pause in our story to narrate what happened in the year 1595 in the city of Caracas, or Santiago de Leon. In the month of June there arrived an English corsair[2] with five or six ships at the port of Guiacamacuto, two leagues from the city and one league to the east of Guaira. About five hundred men landed without meeting resistance, and arriving at the native settlement about a musket shot away, they found it empty, for the Indians had taken refuge in the bush. They encountered only a single Spaniard, called Villalpando, in a house there, who, because he was crippled,[3] had not followed the example of the Indians. From this man they sought information about the country and, the better to make him tell the truth, they put a rope round his neck as if to hang him, so that in anguish he cried out to them to stop; and he guided them by a hidden path to the city, so that they could capture it by surprise. By this track it was about a league to the summit of the *cordillera* and another from there to the town, a difficult route, more of a cat-walk than a path for men. By this way the English marched, well-armed, with their guide, until

[1] Fray Pedro Simón, *Noticias Historiales de las Conquistas de Tierra Firme en las Indias Occidentales* (Bogotá, 1882), I, pt. i, 359–60. Translated. This work was first published in 1625 at Madrid. The writer spent much time in Venezuela and was collecting material for his book for some years before its publication. Cp. Don Joseph de Oviedo y Baños, *Historia de la Conquista y Población de la Provincia de Venezuela* (Madrid, 1723), ff. 377–9. The author, himself a citizen of Caracas, had some knowledge of minor details omitted by Simón, but in point of truth his account is much inferior. He says that, in the absence of Don Diego de Ossorio, the defence was organized by the municipal magistrates, Garci-Gonçález de Silva and Francisco Rebolledo.

[2] Oviedo y Baños says *El Draque.*

[3] Oviedo y Baños: 'who was either unable, through infirmity, or unwilling, to withdraw.' Earlier he simply refers to 'the traitorous spirit of a base man'.

INDEX

Bailye, Noe, deposition, 146
Baker, Christopher, 338, 343, 350–1
Baker, Henry, 302–4
Baker, Robert, 285, 292, 295
Banda del Norte (Hispaniola), 29
Bantam, 99, 220
Barahona, 284, 296
Barbary, 26, 65, 98, 101, 171, 189
Barbaterre (Barbotière), Captain, 287
Barbor, John, 164
Barcelonette (Savoy), 366, 370
Barker, Captain, 151
Barker, Andrew, 27
Barker, Edmund, 284–5, 287–91
Barlow, Arthur, 61
Barlowe, Thomas, 152
Barnestrawe, Captain, 25
Barnsley, Nicholas, 118
Barnstaple, 89, 92–3, 153, 159, 161, 327
Baron, George, 341–3
Barre, Robert La, 340, 355
Barrett (alias Frost), Robert, 175–176, 211–12
Barry, 62, 84
Barwick, John, 111
Bassett, George, 152
Bateman, William, 112
Battle, John, 158
Bayaha, 38, 296
Bayning, Paul, 21, 32, 60, 64, 81–3, 338
Bayonne, 223
Bazán, Alonso de, 175–6, 305
Bazán, Juan Caballero de, 190, 240–1, 250, 269, 272
  statement of, 273–4
  letter of, 274–7
Bedford, John, 226, 229
Bee, Peter Le, 340, 349
Beling, Captain, 387
Bendes, William, 95, 97, 106
  deposition, 151
Bense, Edmund, 55

Benson, John, deposition, 47–8
Bermuda I., 288, 298, 302, 378
Berrio, Antonio de, 394
Berselonetta, *see* Barcelonette
Bery, Thomas, 165
Best, Richard, 299, 306–7
Bickford, Richard, deposition, 310–12
Bideford, 26
Bird, John, 26, 163, 345
Blackwall, 55
Blanco, Cape, 61, 65
Bland, George, 87, 90–1, 93
Blanford (Dorset), 153
Blondell, John, 94
Boca del Dragone, 287
Bodman, Thomas, 57, 230
Boetto, Bennet, deposition, 366–373
Boise, Matthew, 285, 291
Bonacca I., *see* Guanaja
Bond, John, 326
bonds for good behaviour of privateers, 4–5, 8, 27, 40, 42, 209, 211, 308, 335
  full text of, 178–9
  summaries of, 179–80, 195–6, 217, 229–30
Boreman (Bowerman, Burman), Simon (senior), 209–10, 213, 216–17
Boreman, Simon (junior), 210
Bostocke, John, 311–12
Boteler, Nathaniel, 26
Bountainace (Boniface?), Captain, 94
Bourel, John, 111
Brading (Isle of Wight), 155–6
Bradshawe, Robert, 164, 211
Bragg, 118, 326
Bragge, James, 185, 196, 336–7
  deposition, 332
Branford (Brentford, Middx.), 47
Bratholt, James, 106
  deposition, 147–8
Brazil, 65, 67, 210, 259

400

INDEX

Aarayman, Port, 258
Abraham, Robert, 50–5, 173–83
   deposition, 53–5
Acosta, Fray Jorge de, 269
Acton, Andrew, 340
Acton, Thomas, 62–3
   deposition, 78–9
Adams, Richard, 61, 63–4, 79
Adelantado, 357, 360, 365, 369, 372–3
Adey, John, 338, 343
Admiralty, High Court of, 1–16 *et passim*
Aguada, La, 186, 189
Aguanovo, 187, 197
Aguava, *see* Guava
Aguirre, Lope de, 225
Agustín, Juan de, 103, 114
Alarte, Nicholas, 313–14
Alderney I., 67
Allberry, Robert, 204
allegations, 12, 63, 81, 105–6, 285, 291–5, 340
   full translation of, 361–6
   see also materiae
Allett, Richard, 338, 341, 343
Alonso, Melchior, 104, 115
Alvarado, Gregorio, 316
Alvarez, Gaspar, 363, 368
Alvarez (Alvez), Pedro, *see* Pedralves
Amadas, Philip, 61
Ames, Alfonso, 313–14
Amsterdam, 344, 354
Ancon de Refriegas Point, 256, 258
Andalusia, 113
Andrea de Ledesma, Alonso, 380, 397
Andres, Thomas, 224
answers (*responsa personalia*), 11, 14–15, 63–4, 84, 105–6

Anthonison, Edward, deposition 112
Anthony, Elias, 106
Anthony, Peter, 106
Antonio, Don, 86, 154–5
Antwerp, 339, 360–1
Appleby Castle, 242
Appledore, 26
Arauco, 65
Araya, Punta de and Port, 38, 243, 257–60
Archer, John, 345
Arencibia, Don Sebastián de, 331–6
Arenson, William, *see* Starre
Arica, 63
Armentières, 113
Arnemuiden (Armew), 344–51, 353, 355–6, 359–60, 365
Aruba I., 248
Arundel, 160
Arze, Licentiate, 393
Ashton (Devon), 59
Asunción, 31, 228, 233, 244, 247
Aurikes, John, *see* Henricus
Austyn, Robert, 93
Avana, Pedro de, 43
Aveiro, 224
Ayala, Gregorio de, 239, 250, 273–9
Azores Is., 8, 16, 41–2, 52, 61, 67, 100, 155, 178, 241, 252, 275, 327–8, 339, 378
   Newport at, 187–8, 195, 201–6
Azua, 270, 284, 296–7
   see also Puerto Viejo de Azua

Bagge (Badge), Michael, 193, 205–6
Bahama, Gulf or Channel of, *see* Florida

the port returned to the city with some Indian bowmen and used many stratagems to trap the enemy by night and day, making them pay with many lives for their capture. With all this, they could not expel him from the city for eight days, in which time he destroyed and burned several houses, without daring to go out to the farms, fearing the poisoned arrows of the natives: these he experienced to his cost in ambushes which were set upon the road. At the end of this time they made for their ships, in which they set sail, leaving the city at last delivered of the enemies of the Catholic Faith.

they surmounted the top and had sight of the city; where, since they seemed to need him no longer, they hanged him, saying that he, who had betrayed his country, deserved that fate, according to the proverb that evil may do good, but not to the doer.

News had been brought to the city by Indians that the enemy had landed, but it was not realised that he would come by that path, for it was thought that he would not dare to come inland except by the ordinary road from the port of La Guaira. The greater part of the soldiers and captains to be found in the town therefore went along this road with their arms to oppose the enemy's entrance. But meanwhile the English, coming down from the heights to a point half way along the road which runs from the town (since the road was shorter and easier), hoisted their flags, formed themselves into battle array and arrived in good military order at the city, which was defenceless because all the soldiers had left. And thus one man alone, called Alonso Andrea, went out with his weapons and his horse to make a rash attempt to oppose them, one alone against four hundred well-armed men. They cut him to pieces[1] immediately and entered the town, where they found few or no people except some women and slaves, for all had taken hasty flight as best they could to the farms and the bush, taking what little clothing, jewels and gold they could manage in their haste to carry away. Thus the English found plenty to lay their hands on—clothing and merchandise, wine and furniture in the houses, and large quantities of flour. They fortified themselves in the church and the main buildings around it, whence they sallied forth for pillage, though not without danger, for the soldiers and citizens who had gone to

[1] In Oviedo y Baños this incident is rendered: 'Only Alonso Andrea de Ledesma, though of an advanced age, deeming it against his reputation to turn his back on the enemy without giving proof of his valour, moved rather by temerity than courage, mounted his horse and with his spear and shield went out to meet the corsair who, marching with all his flags flying, advanced towards the city. Although El Draque, struck by the bravery of so honourable an action, gave express orders to his soldiers that he should not be slain, they nevertheless, seeing that he pressed forward his horse, trying with repeated strokes of his spear and at the risk of his life to prove the courage which set him on, shot several harquebuses at him, so that he fell dead, to the pity and sorrow even of those same corsairs, who, to honour the dead man, took the body to the city with them to give him a grave, as they did with all the ceremonies which soldiery are wont to use to honour the funerals of their leaders.

INDEX

Denbigh Castle, 339
Deptford, 182
Devereux, Walter, 1st Earl of Essex, 219
Dias, Edward, 340
Díaz, Alexos, 268
Díaz, Domingo, deposition, 259–260
Die, Richard, deposition, 163
Dieguillo el mulato, *see* Reyes, Diego de los
Dieppe, 290–2
Dix, John, 238
Dobson, Ellis, 59, 63
   deposition, 79
Dobson, Henry, 106
Dockerey, Nicholas, 100
   deposition, 149–51
Doctors' Commons, 10
Domingos, John, 312
Domínguez, Juan, 268
Dominica I., 29, 88, 100, 150, 186, 189, 194, 197, 211, 213, 288, 383
Donning, Francis, 64
Dornel, Emmanuel, 71
Douglas, John, 220
Dover, 189, 216
Dowglas, John, 57
Downing, Rowland, 64
Downs, the, 213
Downton, Nicholas, 89
Drake, Bernard, 377–8
Drake, Sir Francis, 36, 63, 188, 219, 240, 266, 275, 380, 396–397
   in 1585–6, 35, 62, 165, 238
   in 1587, 18, 41, 156, 175, 185, 219, 284, 378
   in 1595, 1, 36
Draper, Richard, 100, 128, 135, 139, 159
Drapers' Company, 338
Drewe, William, 106
   deposition, 147
Dudley, Sir Robert, 1, 35, 61–2, 310, 325

Dudson, William, 162
Duffield, John, 105
Dulce, Golfo and Rio, 38, 219, 252, 282–3, 310, 324–5
Dunkirk, 210
Dutch salt-lading, 38
Dutch trade in W.I., *see* Trade

East Country, 79
East India Company, 32, 39, 41, 99, 210, 220, 338–9
East Indies, 59, 80 284
East Smithfield, 147
Edwards, Thomas, 59, 62–3
   depositions, 72, 80–1, 84–5
Egmont, Nicholas van, 361
Egualo, Johan, 371
Eguiça, Pedro de, 283, 315
El Dorado, 219
El Passaje, 213
Elizabeth, Queen, 3, 6, 35, 59, 84, 87, 90–1, 107, 167–8, 178–83, 205, 217, 221, 230, 253, 295, 302, 305, 310–11, 331, 343, 346, 353, 374, 377
Elliott, Edward, 57
Ellis, John, 61–2, 65, 83–4
Elsemore, William, 173, 179
English Channel, 158, 210
Enkhuizen (Holland), 112
Erricus, John, *see* Henricus
Essex, Earl of, *see* Devereux
Estridge, John, 204
   deposition, 205–6
Exeter, 72, 80, 84
Exmouth, 44

Fajardo, Don Luis, 336
   report to crown, 333–4
Falmouth, 171–2
Farley, Robert, 217
Faro (Portugal), 259
Farrar, Nicholas, 338, 341, 343, 350–1
Farrier, Edward, 299
Favell, Thomas, 188

404

INDEX

Cologne, 361
Coloma, Don Francisco, 333, 336
   report to, 300–3
Collomber, Stephen, deposition, 117
Comayagua (Honduras), 321, 324
Combe, William, 71
commission of stay and arrest, 174, 183
commissions for privateering, special, 6, 59, 86, 98, 138, 142, 154, 155
Condé, Henri de Bourbon, Prince of, 98, 138, 142
consortships, 16, 34, 52, 89, 100, 102, 105, 121–72, 174, 202, 299, 302–4, 310–11, 313–14, 379, 381
contempt, 6, 84, 164
Contratación, Casa de, 233, 370
Cordell, Thomas, 21, 32, 152, 161, 338, 341, 343, 350
Corffe, John Cornelius, 345–76
Cork, 26
Coro (Venezuela), 31, 175, 275, 379, 389–91, 396
Corral, Don Francisco de, 334–5
Corrientes, Cape, 19, 34, 100–2, 107–13, 128, 131, 134, 139, 145–6, 150, 158, 163–4, 166, 214, 251, 334–5, 391
Corro, Andrés de, 282
Corugna, the (Cuba), 214
Corvo I., 203
Costo, Anthony, 223
Cotton, Edward, 164
Covert, Thomas, 89
Coxe, Alexander, 328
Cradell, William, deposition, 160
Crampton, Roger, 285–6
   deposition, 291–5
Craston, William, 95–172
   depositions, 157–8, 172
Creame, Charles, 111
crews of privateers
   numbers, 7, 17, 24, 65, 174, 185, 210, 216, 379

character, 8, 22–8
wages, 10, 20, 22, 28, 73, 144, 364
pillage, 20, 25–6, 47, 97, 100, 106, 121, 130, 135, 137, 139, 141–2, 188, 198, 254–5
thirds, 20, 27–8, 121–31, 138, 142, 151, 327
Cricket (Somerset), 377
Crokes, John, deposition, 55–6
Crompton, Thomas, 170, 304, 352
Crooke, John, 86–7, 90–1
Cuba, 37, 194, 288, 392
   in 1588, 41–3
   in 1589, 51–6
   in 1591, 95–166
   in 1592, 176, 210–18
   in 1593, 223
   in 1594, 251–2, 286, 295, 299, 304–7
   in 1595, 330–336
Cumaná, 31, 38, 234–5
   Langton at, 238–9, 247–8, 255–260
   Preston at, 381, 384–5, 393–5
Cumanagoto, Province of, 256
Cumberland, Earl of, *see* Clifford
Curaçao I., 248
Currea, Ludovicus, 340

Daca Davila, Juan, 279
Daniel, Anthony, 98, 133
Dartmouth, 106, 157, 195, 203, 205, 207, 211, 216, 218, 298, 302
Davie, Robert, *see* Davies, Robert
Davies, 286
Davies, Geoffrey, 341
Davies, Robert, 377, 379, 381–93
Davis, John, 71
Davis, Robert, *see* Davies, Robert
Davys, James, 83
Decuval (Decqueville), François, 291–4
Delft (Holland), 352–3, 361
Delgado, Gregorio, 282
Delinyhamo (Cuba?), 223

403

INDEX

Carey, Sir George, 2nd Lord Hunsdon, 19, 21–2, 28, 33–4, 87
  1588 venture, 40, 43
  1590 venture, 86–94
  1591 venture, 95–166
  letter of, 119–20
  other ventures, 138, 155–6, 159, 161–2
Carey, Henry, 1st Lord Hunsdon, 59, 76, 87
Caribs, 189, 383
Carie, Paul, 71
Carleill, Christopher, 340
Carmarden, Richard, 103
Carsate, Licentiate Diego, 324
Cartagena, 107, 175, 189, 191–2, 266, 279, 281, 296, 312, 314
Casatho, Francisco, 312–13
Castellanos, Miguel de, 263
Castilianos, Cristóbal, 363, 367–8
Catalán, Anton, 240, 269–74
  letter to, 274–7
Cathay, 61
Caucedo, Point (Hispaniola), 239, 250, 271, 280
Cave, John, 118
Cavendish, Thomas, 59, 63, 143, 164, 167, 340
Cawson, Richard, 173, 179
Cecil, Sir Robert, 286–7, 377, 379, 381
Cecil, William, Lord Burghley, 95, 201, 340–1, 344
Cecicepi (Hispaniola), 276
Cestin, Luis, 334
Challice, John, 105, 154
Charing Cross, 80
Cherbourg, 67, 310
Chichester, 86, 90, 149, 156, 162, 378
Chichiriviche (Venezuela), 389–390
Chidley (Chudleigh), Elizabeth, 63–4, 72–4, 78–85
Chidley, John, 6, 20–22, 24, 32–3, 59–85, 287

Chidley, manor of, 60, 65
Chile, 65
Chirk Castle, 339
Cholmley, Thomas, 246
Chorrera, Rio (Havana), 211, 215, 218
Ciria, Catalina de, 278
Clanton, manor of, 60
Clarck, Alexander, 311–12
Clarcke, Charles le, 361
Clement, William, 111
Clercke, John, 105
  deposition, 167–9
Clerke, Francis (senior), 81, 345, 362, 374
Clerke (junior), 345, 361–2, 374–375
Cletherow, Sir Christopher, 50
Cletherow, Henry, 21, 50
  and *Black Dog*, 50–1
  and Chidley, 59–60, 72
  and Watts, 98, 112
  and Newport (1592), 185, 195–196, 204, 206
  and Burgh, 226, 229–30
  and Newport (1594), 298–9, 302–3
Clifford, Lady Anne, 238
Clifford, George, 3rd Earl of Cumberland, 6, 18–19, 21–2, 35, 41, 89, 99, 174, 212, 284, 311
  venture of 1593–4, 236–83
Clothworkers Company, 40, 95, 98, 120, 148
Cobb, Robert, 21, 147, 163, 345
  1591 venture, 98–104, 112–19
  1592 venture, 185, 196–7, 204, 206
  1593 venture, 226, 229
  1594 venture, 298, 302
Coche, Thomas, 105, 173–83
Coche I. (La Margarita), 381, 384
Cocke, Abraham, 89
Cocke, George, deposition, 166
Cocke, Laurence, 216, 218
Coken, John, 98

INDEX

Bridgewater, 156
Bristol, 17, 19, 60, 65, 68, 84–5, 106, 123, 129, 131, 145, 156, 185, 201, 211, 213, 215
Broad Clist, manor of, 60
Brooke, John, 112
Brough, John, 98, 99–128, 159, 175, 298, 302
  deposition, 144–5
Browne, Mr, 312
Browne, Thomas, 71
Bry, Theodor de, 223
buccaneers, 38, 249
Burd, John, *see* Bird
Burgh (Burrows, Burroughs), Sir John, 22, 31, 33, 195, 201–4, 225–35
Burgh, Thomas, 5th Lord Burgh of Gainsborough, 225
Burgh, William, 4th Lord Burgh of Gainsborough, 225
Burghley, Lord, *see* Cecil
Burgley (Burley), John, 119
Burlings, the (off Portugal), 25, 299
Burnet, Robert, 61, 65, 68
Burton, Edmond, 185, 196, 204
Bush, Richard, 68
Butcher, John, 112
Bygate, William, 163, 185, 195–6, 204

Caballos, Puerto de, 19, 30, 33–4, 38, 215, 219, 238
  Newport at (1592), 187, 192, 198
  Langton at, 241–2, 251–3, 281–283, 300, 315
  Newport at (1594), 298, 300–2, 315, 321
  Parker at (1594), 308–24
  Parker at (1595), 324–5
Cabañas (Cuba), 34, 211, 215, 331, 334–5
Cacui (Hispaniola), 277
Cade, John, 92
  deposition, 93–4

Cadiz, 18, 40, 100, 113, 175, 185, 210, 219, 225, 284, 359, 365, 369, 370, 378
Caesar, Dr Julius, 53, 81, 84–6, 91, 93, 116, 120, 132–3, 143, 145–9, 151–3, 156–8, 160, 162–5, 177, 196, 205, 217, 253, 305–7, 310, 327, 331–2, 345, 352, 366
  relations with Lord Admiral, 3
  fees, 7
  letters to, 7, 87, 104, 119–20, 176–7, 181–2, 183, 195, 216, 229, 341, 344
  views on pillage and Barbary traffic, 26
  notes on prize goods, 51
  suspicion of corruption, 105
  letters of, 209
  sentences of, 221–2, 302, 314–315, 336–7, 343, 373–6
  case notes of, 285–6, 291–2
Caen, 27
Caicos Passage, 29, 291
Caiman Is., 214, 391
Caio (Venezuela), 389
Cales, *see* Cadiz
Calvete, Juan de, depositions, 114–16
Camacho, Antonio, deposition, 258–9
Campeche, 53, 324
Campion, Thomas, 63
  deposition, 79
Campos (a negro), 262
Campuzano, Gerónimo, report to crown, 393–4
Canary Is., 29, 41, 65, 67, 100, 169, 172, 174–5, 189, 213, 243, 248, 282, 328, 382–3
Cantin, Cape, 189
Cape Breton I., 97
Capilla, Don Pedro de, 279
Caracas, Santiago de León de, 31, 233, 275, 377, 379–81, 385–390, 394–8
Cardoza, Thomas, 117–18

INDEX

Fawkner, Rowland, 345–76
Fécamp (Feckamb), 94
FeeWilliams, *see* FitzWilliams
Felipe, Diego, 266, 269
Felix, M., 290
Fenner, Edward, 154
Fenner, John, 224
Fenton, Edward, 156
Fernández de Puga, Alonso, 266
Fernández de Santana, Juan, 267–268
Fernley, Thomas, 64
  deposition, 82
Fiche, Philip, *see* Finche
Figueroa, Baltazar de, 279
Finche, William (possibly William Parker), 220, 240–1, 274–7
Fingest (Bucks), 152
firearms
  cast pieces or ordnance, 7, 15–16, 26, 55, 80, 88, 126–7, 134, 143, 163, 177, 210, 216, 239, 253, 270, 282, 285, 290, 296–7, 300, 306, 324, 394
  calivers, 17–18, 58, 74–5, 84, 252
  falcons, 17, 19, 57, 108, 111, 231, 251
  minions, 17, 19, 57, 231
  muskets, 17–18, 58, 74–5, 84, 107, 109, 184, 206, 231, 258–260, 263, 266, 293, 333, 386
  sakers, 18–19, 76, 84, 111, 132, 231, 251
  harquebuses, 18, 231, 266, 301, 323, 397
  demi-culverins, 18, 75–6, 251
  culverins, 18, 59, 231, 251
  port-bases, 19, 111
  value of, 20, 51
  fowlers, 75–6
  demi-cannon, 213
  bases, 232, 389, 391
  cannon, 263
Fishbourne, Richard, 151
Fisher, John, 51

  deposition, 56
FitzWilliams, Robert, 24, 40–9
fleets, Spanish
  Tierra Firme, 29, 192, 212
  New Spain, 29, 101, 103, 212, 266, 283, 334
  armadas, 36, 101, 107–8, 128, 133, 158, 161, 164, 166, 211, 215, 283, 331–7
  Santo Domingo, 42, 89, 102–3
  Honduras, 241, 252–3, 281–3, 300, 315, 317, 325
Fleming, Giles, 59, 63, 78–80
Flores, Luis Alfonso, 192, 334
Flores I., 201, 203, 254
Florida, 88, 102, 187, 193–5
Florida, Cape or Point of, 193, 288
Florida Channel (Gulf of Florida), 29, 193–4, 212, 234, 252, 288, 392
Florida Keys, 193
Flushing, 339
Fortune, Jacob Johnson, 359
Frances, Robert, 205
Franciscus, Martin, 113
Frederico, Don, 370
French privateering in W.I., 310–25
  see also Leaguers
French trade in W.I., *see* Trade
Fricke, William, *see* Parker
Fridde, Robert, *see* Thread
Frier, William, 71
Frost, Robert, *see* Barrett
Froude, John, deposition of, 154–5
Froward, Cape, 66, 70
Furner, Simon, 59, 63
  deposition, 72

Gaffey, Nicholas, 94
Gall, John, 95, 97, 120–6
Gardener, Thomas, 185, 196, 204
Garrachico (Tenerife), 132, 267
Garraway, William, 338, 341, 344, 350

INDEX

Gayer, John, 223–4
Geare, Michael, 21, 23–4, 32, 34, 36, 212, 326
   in 1588, 40–1
   in 1591, 95–172
   depositions, 160–1, 331–2
   in 1595, 330–7
Gibson, Ralph, deposition, 165–6
Giddy, William, 64
Giggs, Edmund, 112
Gilbert, Sir Humphrey, 185, 225, 377
Gilbert, John, 225
Gilbert, Sir John, 222, 225, 378
Gilbert, Thomas, deposition, 161–2
Glover, Richard, 82–3
Goave, *see* Guava
Goddard, Anthony, 343
Goddard, Richard, 153, 381
Godfrey, Thomas, 111
Godmeston, 216–17
Gomera I. (Canaries), 383
Gómez de Abraunca, Licentiate Alvar, 309, 324
Gonaïves, Port, *see* Guanahibes
Gonsálvez, Stephen, deposition, 223–4
González, Alejo, 266
González, Alonso, 240
   deposition, 269–72
González, Antonio, 266
González, Manuel, 277
González Urraco, Benito, 282
Gore, Walter, 105
Gracia, Antonio, 312, 314
Grand Caiman I., 214
Grand Canary I. (Gran Canaria), 213, 381
Grand Goâve, Ile du, 190, 197
Grande, Martín de la, *see* Ygararan
Gravesend, 131
Grays Inn, 73
Great Comoro I., 51
Greenwich, 87, 183, 344
Gregorio, Santiago de, 322–3
Grenada I., 383

Grenville, Sir Richard, 42–3, 377
Grey, Ralph, 111
Grimesby, John, 165
Grippe, Cuthbert, 98–9, 117, 185, 196, 226, 229
Grocers Company, 339
Groves, Thomas, 230
Guadeloupe I., 100, 145
Guaira, La (Venezuela), 380, 395–7
Guanabo I. (Hispaniola), 186, 314
Guanahibes (Hispaniola), 314, 339
Guanaja I. (Gulf of Honduras), 310, 325
Guatemala, 300, 309, 317, 321–2, 324–5
Guava (Hispaniola), 186–7, 191, 197
Guernsey I., 92
Guerrero, Ensign, 333
Guiacamacuto (Venezuela), 396
Guiana, 225–8, 340, 377, 392
Guinea, 17, 189, 213
guns, *see* firearms
Gutiérrez Flores, Francisco, 235, 255–60
Gutiérrez Flores, Dr Pedro, 233, 235

Haarlem, 357, 361
Hagthorpe, John, 16
Hakluyt, Richard, 1, 50–1, 60, 63–4, 106, 184, 209–10, 219, 284, 377
   extracts from, 52–3, 65–71, 107–12, 188–95, 213–16, 287–91, 381–92
Halse, Nicholas, 361
Hammond, Thomas, deposition, 307
Hampton, John, 188
Hampton, *see* Southampton
Hampton Court, 229
Hancocke, Benjamin, 117
Hanger, George, 286, 291

INDEX

Hankyn, Harry, 158
Harding, Thomas, 98
Hareward, William, 216, 229
Hariot, Thomas, 220
Harvey, Captain, 382
Harwich, 156, 185, 189–90, 196, 205
Hatillo de las Cabras (Hispaniola), 269–70
Hato de las Cabras (Hispaniola), proceedings at, 269–72
Hattomanico (Hispaniola?), 220
Havana, 25, 29, 35–6, 42, 89, 92, 101–2, 112, 117–18, 220–3, 266, 279, 281, 315, 317, 322, 325, 328, 392
  in 1589, 51, 53–4
  in 1591, 103, 114–16, 123–32, 135–45, 147, 149–52, 155–61
  in 1592, 173, 176, 211–17
  in 1594, 251–2, 286, 295, 299, 304–7
  in 1595, 330–6
Havre, Le (Havre de Grace), 91–94, 180–2, 254–5, 285–6, 290–5
Hawes, Sir James, 40
Hawkins, Sir John, 5, 35–6, 50, 56, 174, 181, 340
Hawkins, Richard, 21, 25, 56, 340
Hawkins, William, 80
Hawlse, Matthew, 24, 68–71
Heale, John, 168
Hearle, John, 64
  depositions, 82–4
Hearne, Samuel, deposition, 49
Heaton, Thomas, 21, 162, 166, 383
Henricus, John, 341–3, 346–9, 353–73
Henry IV, King of France, 155, 174, 181, 286, 294
Heore, William, 111
Hernandes, Domingo (mariner), 104, 116
Hernández, Alonso, 269
Hernández, Domingo (notary), 260
Hernández, Manuel, 283
Hernerowe, Francisco, 104, 116
Hertford, Earl of, *see* Seymour
Hicacos Point (Cartagena), 175
Hickman, Edward, deposition, 48–9
Hill, Arthur, 166
Hill, William, 230
Hilliard, Oliver, 157
Hills, Phillip, 145
Hispaniola, 29, 37–8, 53, 88, 101, 117–19, 185–7, 189–91, 197–198, 220, 239–41, 248–51, 265–81, 285, 288, 290–2, 296–7, 325, 331–2, 336–7, 350, 391
Hodgkins, Richard, 68
Holliday, William, 25, 165
Honduras, 29, 38, 211, 218, 283, 298, 309, 316, 320, 322, 334
Honduras, Bay or Gulf of, 187, 189, 191, 194, 198, 215, 241, 251–2, 324–5
Honduras, Cape (Trujillo Point), 283, 315–17
Hone, Dr John, 113–15, 292, 310
Honfleur, 91–2
Hooke, Anthony, deposition, 148–9
Hordoñez (Cumaná), 258
Hore, John, 175, 180
Houghton, Peter, 185, 204, 230
Houldships, Thomas, 111
House of Trade, *see* Contratación
Howard, Lord Charles, baron of Effingham, Lord Admiral, 84, 87, 105, 181–2, 219, 326
  rights and duties as Lord Admiral, 3–16, 26–7
  warrants for issue of letters of reprisal, 7–8, 98, 176–7, 195, 209, 216, 229
  private ships of, 18, 21, 155–6, 160, 164, 166
  ex officio proceedings of, 84, 196–201, 205–6, 331–2
  letter from, 344

INDEX

Howard, Lord Charles—*continued*
  see also bonds for good behaviour of privateers, letters of reprisal, passports, etc.
Howard, Lord Thomas, 18, 21, 61
  action against Watts, 100, 105–106, 167–72
  1592 venture, 173–83, 215
Howe, Roger, 209–10, 213, 216–17
Hubbard, Captain, 153
Hughes, John, 55
Hull, 146
Hungate, Richard, 71
Hunsdon, 1st and 2nd Lords, see Carey
Huntlowe, Osborne, 42
  deposition, 47
Hurde, Captain, 150
Hutchins, Richard, 220–3, 310, 314
Hutton, Robert, 299, 303

Inchingham, George, 285–6
India, 296–7
Indians, 66, 70, 187, 193–4, 256–257, 281, 287, 289–90, 321, 383–6, 388–9, 396–8
interlocutory sentences, 8–9, 14, 104, 112, 114, 117, 174, 180, 223, 298, 328
  full translation of, 221–3
  summaries of, 302, 314–15, 336–7, 343
interrogatories, 11, 15, 46–9, 63, 72, 80, 105–6, 127, 132, 138, 143–7, 149–54, 156–66, 169, 172, 205–8, 286, 291–2, 299, 337, 340, 356, 360, 370
Ipswich, 79, 193, 205
Irish, William, 1590 voyage, 86–94, 153, 159
  depositions, 91–2, 158–60
  1591 voyage, 95–172
Ironmongers Company, 50
Islands, the, see Azores
Ivey, William, 25

Jamaica, 29, 37, 214, 241, 251, 254, 381, 391
James I, King, 378
James, Thomas, 185
Janico (possibly Monte Cristi), 223
Jennings, Richard, 340
John, Captain, 241, 273
Johns, Thomas, 188
Jolliffe, Henry, 162
Jones, Captain, 379, 381, 391
Jones, Nicholas, 74
Jones, William, 98, 185, 195–6, 204
Jorge, Antonio, 324
Juan, Pedro, 271
Justinián, Pedro Juan, 266

Kayns, Richard, 204
Keble, Robert, 24, 28, 185, 195, 202, 205–6
Kedgell, Henry, 185, 196, 198–200, 226, 228–9
Kendall, Abraham, 62–3, 82–4
Kennell, George, 95, 97, 100–2, 135, 137, 139, 211–12, 215
  deposition, 163–4
Kenneye, John, deposition, 93
Ketchman, Edmund, 340
Keyball, Robert, see Keble
Keymis, Lawrence, 381
King, Master, 143
King, William, 33, 98, 101, 107–111, 184, 186
  1592 voyage, 209–18
Kingsnode (Kingson), Roger, 22, 40–49, 50–58
Kinsale, 309, 311–12

Lagonasho, 314
Laguna (Hispaniola), see Yaguana
Laguna (Maracaibo), see Maracaibo
Lancaster, James, 23, 36, 41, 51, 99, 156, 210, 250–1, 284–5, 287–91, 338
Lancerota I. (Canaries), 213

INDEX

Land's End, 85
Lane, Ralph, 62, 189
Lane, William, 33, 36, 326
  in 1591, 95–172
  depositions, 120–31, 295
  in 1593, 211–12, 215
  in 1594, 284–97
Langton, James, 22, 30–34, 190, 234, 236–83, 284–5, 296–7, 300–1, 308, 315, 317
Lawles, John, 307
  deposition of, 306
Leaguers, 32–33, 86, 90–4, 174, 178, 180–3, 251, 254–5, 285–6, 291–5
Leckland, Edward, 326
Lee, Francis, deposition, 143–4
Lee, Ralph, 95–172
  deposition, 132–43
Leigh, Charles, 97
Leigh (Lee) (Essex), 145, 166
Léogane, *see* Yaguana
León, Manuel de, 283, 315
letters of reprisal, 6–8, 31, 41, 47, 53, 56, 90–1, 120, 133, 138, 143–6, 149–52, 154, 156–66, 170, 184, 197, 221, 226, 292, 295, 302–3, 313, 327, 331, 343–4
Levant, 175, 338
Levant Company, 18, 41, 338–9
Lewes, Richard, 64, 82–4
Leyva, Don Luis de, 263
Liaño, Licentiate Pedro de, report to crown, 394–6
libels, 11–12, 50–1, 63–4, 79, 83, 105–6, 132, 143, 146, 151–6, 158, 162, 167, 306–7, 340, 352
  summaries of, 44, 78, 82
  full translation of, 345–52
libels files, 13–14, 16
Lima y Meneses, Francisco de, 263
Limehouse, 23, 44, 97, 99, 151, 160, 163–4, 166, 185, 205, 215, 217, 302, 305, 326–7, 330, 332

Linewray, John, 105
Lisbon, 155, 189, 328
Lisle, Nicholas, 98, 101, 111
Liverpool, 253
Locke, John, 24, 193, 204–6
Logan, Marmaduke, 100, 106, 158
  deposition, 146
Loggins, William, 45
London, 19–21 *et passim*
London Bridge, 24
Londonderry Company, 339
Longe, William, 59, 74
López, Diego (prisoner), deposition, 117
López, Diego (ship's boy), deposition, 266–9
López, Melchior, 261
López, Melgarejo, 279
Luce, Matthew, 220–3
Lyme (Dorset), 377–8

Mabbile, Nicholas, 94
Mabbile, Peter, 94
Macanao, El (La Margarita), 256
Mace, William, 50–8
Madeira I., 223, 381
Magellan Straits, 65–8, 70
Magoths, William, 60–2, 64, 71, 73
  account of Chidley's voyage, 65–8
Main, Spanish, *see* Tierra Firme
Maio (Venezuela), 389
Major, M., 111
Málaga, 370
Maldonado, Don Francisco, 262
Maldonado Barnuevo, Don Juan, 281
  report by, 305–6
  report to, 315–16
Mallen de Rueda, Licentiate Pedro, 317
Manby, Francis, 59–60, 72–4
Manby, William, 63, 72–4
Mansfield (Mansford), Stephen, 50–1

INDEX

Mansell, Robert, 105
Manso de Contreras, Licentiate Francisco, 260–5, 310
Maracaibo, Lago de, 391
Margarita, La, I., 29, 34, 38, 175, 248, 261–2, 266, 275, 296
   Burgh at, 225–35
   Langton at, 238, 242–7, 256
   Preston at, 377, 381, 383–4, 392–3
   Raleigh at, 393–4
Marmolejo, Francisco, 267
Marquino, Francis, 113, 116, 352, 367
Marracava, Rio de (Hispaniola), 249
Marshall, Richard, 63
Martín, Antonio (prisoner), deposition, 220–1
Martín, Antonio (pilot), 238, 243, 252, 262–3, 271, 274, 278
Martín, Diego, 223
Martin, William, 71
Martín de Angulo, Diego, 187
Martinique (Martinino) I., 243, 260
Martires, La Cabeza de los, 392
Mary, Queen, 86, 150
Matanzas (Cuba), 102–3, 135, 159, 211, 214
materiae, 12, 80, 105, 120, 131–2, 144–9, 151, 157, 160–1, 163, 165–6, 170, 172
Matthewson, Bartholomew, 326
May, Henry, 284, 287–8
Maynard, Edmund, deposition, 93
Mead Hole (Isle of Wight), 26, 51
Mediterranean, 17, 51, 338
Melton (Leics.), 120
Menciana, Doña, 277
Menéndez de Valdés, Diego, 88
Menéndez Marqués, Pedro, 42
Meneses, Dr Simón de, 267, 273, 297
Mercers Company, 338
Merchants Adventurers Company, 339

Merrick, Andrew, 61, 65, 68, 85
Merrick, Hugh, 184–208
Merrick, Simon, 60, 62
   deposition, 85
Mexico, Bay of, 52, 300, 306–7
Michell, Stephen, 23–4
   1591 venture, 95–172
   depositions, 131–2, 170–2
Michelson, Arthur, 50, 53, 55–7
Michelson, William, 50–8
Middleburgh (Zeeland), 384
Middleton, David, 330
Milford Haven, 26, 392
Miller, Richard, 201
Milton, Thomas, 230
Mincing Lane (London), 339
Minehead (Somerset), 64
Molliffe, Harry, 305
Mona I., 176, 190, 214, 248, 284–285, 287, 289–90, 292, 296
Monson, Sir William, 24, 31, 34, 226, 236
Monte Cristi (Hispaniola), 223
Montero, Juan, 266–72
Monville de Hage, *see* Omonville-la-Rogue
Moorecocke, Richard, 118
Morcomb, William, 378
More, John, 21, 32, 99
   and Newport's 1591 voyage, 98–9, 117
   and Newport's 1592 voyage, 185–6, 195–6, 204, 206
   and King's voyage, 209–10, 213, 216–17
   and Burgh's voyage, 226, 229–230
   and Newport's 1594 voyage, 298, 302
   and Ridlesden's voyage, 326
Moreman, Jasper, 210, 340, 349
Moreno, Port (La Margarita), 392
Morgan, Sir Matthew, 11, 300, 306–7
Morrice, John, 71
Motril (Spain), 370
Mott, John, 100

INDEX

deposition, 145
Mounte, Peter de, 94
Mountfield, *see* Omonville-la-Rogue
Mounts Bay, 26
Moy, John Baptista de, 361
Mucheron, Peter, 340
Mumpabila, Juan de, 394
Muñon, Antonio, deposition, 234
Musgrave, Edmund, 205–6
Myddelton, Sir Hugh, 339
Myddelton, John, 32–3, 36, 175–176, 180, 212, 273, 299, 302–6
Myddelton, Richard (senior), 339
Myddelton, Richard (junior), 175
Myddelton, Roger, 339
Myddelton, Thomas, 21, 32, 103, 175, 338–41, 343, 345, 350–1
Myddelton, William, 175

Naflora, Nicholas, 331, 337
Navarre, Henry of, *see* Henry IV
Navarro, Antonio, 103
navy, Royal, *see* Queen's ships
negroes, 186, 189–90, 197, 213–214, 218, 234, 245, 249, 262, 275–8, 292, 371, 384
Neiba Bay (Hispaniola), 284
New Branforde (Brentford, Middx.), 47
New Spain, 114–15, 241, 275, 278 *see also* fleets
Newfoundland, 33, 42–3, 45, 47, 89, 91–4, 151, 167, 174, 181, 287–8, 309, 311, 378, 392
Newhaven, *see* Havre
Newport, Christopher, 23–4, 32, 35, 38, 89, 99, 241, 274, 326, 330
    1591 venture, 98–101, 104, 117–19
    1592 venture, 30, 33–5, 184–208, 212–13, 308, 324
    1593 venture, 225–35
    1594 venture, 298–304, 308, 315, 320–2

Newport (Isle of Wight), 154, 162
Newton, John, 98–9, 163, 167, 175, 180, 185, 196, 204
Nice (Provence), 369
Nigua (Hispaniola), 277
Noe, John la, 291
Norris, John, 89, 153
Norris, Sir Thomas, 311–12
Northumberland, Earls of, *see* Percy
Norumbega (Normanbege), 43, 48
Notre Dame, Bay of (Newfoundland), 89, 91–2, 94
Nueblas Is., 289

Ocoa (Hispaniola), 30, 186, 190, 197, 220, 238–42, 250, 267–271, 274, 278, 284
Odell, Roland, 60, 63, 72, 78–9
Oker, John, 100, 135–9, 146, 159
Old Channel (Cuba), 29, 41–3, 103, 155, 214
Olderney de Barges, *see* Oléron
Oléron I., 174, 180, 183
Omonville-la-Rogue (France), 67, 85
Oporto (Portugal), 223, 312
Oran, Juan, 277
Orange, William of Nassau, Prince of, 98, 138, 142
ordnance, *see* firearms
Organos, Los (Cuba), 295, 299
Orinoco, River, 41, 310, 395
Ortes Sandavall, Pedro, 342–3, 348, 354–5, 358, 371
Ortys (Ortise), John, 358, 363, 365, 367–9
Osleworth (Gloucs.), 82
Ossorio, Don Diego de, 396
Ostias, Port (Cumaná), 257–9
Otro, John de, *see* Ustrio
Oughtred, Henry, 167
Oviedo y Baños, Don Joseph de, 380, 396–7

411

INDEX

Pacific Ocean, *see* South Sea
Padilla, Adriano de, 279
Pallasus (a merchant), 117–18
Palmer, Sir Henry, 209–10, 213
Pampatar (La Margarita), 233
Pantoxa, Captain, 211
Parcke, Denise de, 92
Paria, Gulf of, 287
Parker, William, 32–4, 212, 240–241, 274, 277
  voyages of 1592–3, 219–24
  voyages of 1594–5, 308–25
passports, 292, 355
Paul, John, 185, 188, 196, 203–4, 206–8, 238
Paz, Agustín de, 103, 115
Pedernales Point (Hispaniola), 267
Pedralves (Pedraldes, Pedro Alvarez), Gerónimo, 279, 342–3, 358, 362, 365, 367–9
Pells, John, 111
Penguin I. (Magellan Straits), 66, 68, 70
Peralta, Pedro de, 262
Percy, Sir Henry, 8th Earl of Northumberland, 238
Percy, Lady Mary, 238
Percy, Sir Thomas, 7th Earl of Northumberland, 238
Pérez, Alonso, 233
Pérez, Diego, 238, 240, 243, 265–266, 271–2, 274
Pérez, Luis, 261, 263–5
Pérez Chinana, Alonso, 268
Pérez de Porras (Purras, Purres, etc.), Diego, 341–3, 358, 362–3, 365, 367, 369, 372
Peritha, John, 341–3
Pernambuco (Brazil), 99, 338
Perou (N. and W. Hispaniola), 285, 291–2
Perry, Abicocke, 95, 132
Perryman, James, 209, 216–17
Persaye (Persett), William, 210
Peter, a Breton, 68, 71

Philip II, King of Spain
  mentioned, 8, 22, 36, 66, 90–1, 107, 111, 114–15, 120, 133, 164, 169, 177–9, 195, 198, 209, 216, 218, 222–3, 229, 239, 252–3, 255, 267, 282–3, 302, 304, 314–16, 318, 327, 337, 342–3, 357–8, 360–7, 370, 375, 388
  reports to, 37–8, 233, 235, 265–6, 277–81, 295–7, 309, 321–5, 333–6, 392–6
Phillips, John, 312–14
Philpott, Robert, 106
Pie, John, 112
Piedras, Punta de (Rio de la Hacha), 263
Pigott, Thomas, 118
pillage, *see* crews of privateers
Pimentel, Don Antonio, 280
Pinchbacke, Thomas, deposition, 305
Pinos, Isla de, 391
piracy, 28, 32, 41, 87, 196, 217, 229
  prosecutions for, 9, 10, 15, 97, 100, 284
  notorious pirates, 105, 154, 238, 309
Pitts, Christopher, 156
Plate, River, 65, 67
Plymouth, 17, 19, 51, 53–4, 56, 61, 65, 100, 103, 106, 112–13, 131, 151–2, 165, 168–9, 177, 181, 188, 219–24, 240, 252–253, 277, 286, 295, 308–10, 312–15, 338, 340–3, 356, 373, 379, 381
Pocombe, Edward, 47
Pocombe, John, deposition, 44–7
Pollard, Edward, deposition, 165
Polwhele, Thomas, 59, 61–5, 72–74, 78–80, 165
Poole (Dorset), 201
Port Desire, 65–6
Port Famine (Magellan Straits), 66, 68, 71

INDEX

Porter, Giles, 105
Portland Castle, 74
Portsmouth, 86, 89, 242
Pouce, John, depositions, 115, 116
Pousley, William, 106
Poyntell, Richard, 341
Poyntz, Ferdinand, 339
Preston, Amyas, 22, 30–1, 33, 326, 377–98
Preston, Hugh, 379
Price, Walter, 106
Pring, Martin, 15
prisoners
   Spanish and Portuguese, 8, 9, 30, 112–18, 199, 203, 220–1, 223–4, 250, 280, 312–13, 341–3, 363, 368, 372–3, 393
   English, 32, 36, 175–6, 250, 290, 296–7, 299, 305–6, 331, 333–4
privateering ventures
   number of, 16, 35–6, 52, 95
   financing of, 20–2, 32, 40–1, 50, 59–61, 72–4, 78–82, 85–87, 95–9, 184–5, 204, 209–210, 226, 298, 326, 330, 338, 340, 377–8
   profitability of, 31–4, 38–9, 51, 104, 176, 188, 212–13, 220, 241, 309, 327, 331, 340, 380
Privy Council, 3, 4, 6, 8–9, 59, 64, 176, 195, 216, 229, 344, 378
prizes and prize goods, 29–35 *et passim*
   tenths of, 4–5, 8, 27, 56, 89, 179, 187, 196, 217, 223, 229, 241–2, 326–8, 331
   customs duties on, 5, 27, 59, 97, 196, 217, 229, 311–12, 327, 331
   embezzlement of, 5, 26–7, 97, 103, 106, 147, 150, 160, 188, 196–201, 206–8, 300, 305–7, 309, 311–12, 330–2, 337
   appraisements of, 8–9, 14, 33, 58, 90, 104, 118–19, 179, 182, 344–5

French, captured by English, 33, 42, 47, 174, 180–3, 285, 291–4
Portuguese, captured by English, 189, 213, 243, 258–60, 298, 302, 328, 378
   order for delivery of, 222–3
   see also crews of privateers, interlocutory sentences, etc.
Proude, Roger, deposition, 112
Prowse, Laurence, 162, 381
Prowse, William, 381, 390
Pueblo del Mar (La Margarita), 233–4
Puercos, Rio de (Cuba), 214, 336
Puerto Bello (Panama), 220
Puerto Plata (Hispaniola), 38, 248
Puerto Rico, 27, 37, 88–9, 100, 145, 164, 189–90, 197, 213, 218, 236, 238, 251, 265, 289, 331–2, 393
Puerto Santo (Madeiras), 379, 381–2
Puerto Viejo de Azua (Hispaniola), 268
Pulford, John, 170, 182
Purchas, Samuel, 219, 236, 242
Purey, Henry, 61, 64

Queen's ships, 18, 24, 27–8, 36, 50, 100, 165, 167–72, 174, 181–2, 210, 219, 378
   see also ships
querelae, 6, 8–9, 50, 53–6, 63–4, 72, 81–2, 84, 90–4, 112–16, 174, 180–1, 217–18, 253–5, 295, 304–5

Raleigh, Sir Walter, 18–19, 21–2, 35–6, 59, 61, 167, 212
   and Watts' 1591 venture, 97–8, 104
   and Parker, 219–20
   and Burgh's venture, 225–8
   Guiana voyage, 340, 377–81, 392–5

INDEX

Ramirez, Diego, 281–3, 300, 309, 315, 317, 320
Ramirez, Francisco, 274–5, 278
Randall, John, 211
ransom, 54, 186–7, 190, 197–8, 239, 249–50, 252–3, 271, 273–8, 281, 301, 331, 337, 380–1, 384, 387–9
Ratcliffe, 23, 51, 53, 56, 63–4, 73, 79, 93, 98–9, 160–1, 163–4, 185, 209–10, 213, 217, 285, 291, 302, 305
Ravens, Henry, 298, 303
Raymond, George, 51, 62, 156, 160, 250, 284, 292, 378
Raymond, Jeremias, 308, 310–11, 313–14, 317, 325
Ré, Ile de, 174, 183
Reade, John, 68
Rebolledo, Francisco, 396
recognizances, *see* bonds for good behaviour of privateers
Requests, Court of, 326
responsa personalia, *see* answers
Reyes, Diego de los, 309, 317, 320, 322
Reynolds, Henry, 176, 182
deposition, 180–1
Ribera, Diego de la, 101
Riberon (a Spanish shipowner), 282
Ribrowle (master of Spanish ship), 113
Richards, William, 209, 216
Rider, John, 63
Ridlesden, John, 34, 161, 326–9
deposition, 327–9
Ridlesden, Stephen, 130, 326
Righte, Walter, 179
Rio de la Hacha, 29, 175, 239, 248, 260–5, 269, 310
Rippett, Nicholas, 361
Roanoke I., 112, 189
Roberts, Captain, 382, 386–7
Roberts, Henry, 211–13, 215
Roberts, William, 106
Robinson, James, 63, 77

deposition, 73
Robinson, Richard, 236, 242
Robson, Peter, 305
Roche, Richard, 311
Roche, Thomas, 155
Rochelle, La, 180, 183, 254–5
Rodríguez, Balthasar, 104, 115
Rodríguez, Francisco, 315
Rokerell, John, 94
Rotherhithe, 23, 97, 145–6, 157
Rouen, 94, 292
Royal, Thomas, deposition, 156–157
Ruiz, Alonso, 279
rutters, 1, 62, 220
Rye (Sussex), 214, 218, 291

Sable, Cape (Florida), 193
Saffron Walden, 167, 174, 177
St Albans (Herts.), 48
St Clement Danes, 79
St Katherine's by the Tower, 23
St Kitts I., 100, 158
St Lucia I., 243
St Martin (Poitou), 180–1
St Nicholas, Bay of (Hispaniola), 248
St Nicholas, Cape (Hispaniola), 29, 285, 288, 291
St Vincent, Cape (Portugal), 151, 211, 213
Salazar, Pedro de, 38, 392–4
Salde, Isabel de la, 210
Saltash, 153
Saltonstall, Richard, 339
Samora, Antonio de la, 348–9, 354, 358, 363, 367–8, 371
San Antonio, Cape, 29, 51, 54, 56, 101–2, 110, 164, 176, 210, 214, 241, 251, 266, 283, 310, 316, 325, 334–5, 391–2
San Juan de Ulua (New Spain), 114–15
San Lucar, 113, 233, 347–8, 353–354, 360, 367, 369
San Pedro (Honduras), 301, 316–317, 320

INDEX

ships named—*continued*
Nuestra Señora de Loreto (prize), 312–14
Nuestra Señora de Soledad (prize), 295
Nuestra Señora del Rosario (prize), 101, 117–18
Nuestra Señora del Rosario, 233
Orphante (of London), 326
Passport (of London), 150
Pegasus (of London), 95–172
Penelope, 287
Phoenix, 156
Pilgrim (of London), 18, 173–183, 211, 236–83
Pleasure (of Bristol), 185
Post (of London), 99, 147
Princesse (prize), 285–6, 291–4
Prudence (of Barnstaple), 161, 327
Prudence (of London), 95–172, 184–208, 225–35, 298–9, 302
Revenge (of Lyme), 377
Revenge (Queen's ship), 167
Riall (of Weymouth), 175, 340
Richard (of Plymouth), 219–224, 308–24
Robert (of London), 89
Robin (alias *Delight*, of Bristol), 21, 59–85
Roebuck (Cavendish's), 164
Roebuck (of London), 99, 210
Roebuck (Raleigh's), 18–19, 225–35
Rose Lion (of London), 20–1, 34, 338–76
Roseave (prize), 341
Royal Defence (of London), 338
Royal Exchange (of London), 338
St Anthony (prize), 223
St Francis (of Cuba, prize), 223
St Francis (of Seville, prize), 327–8
St Katherine, see *Katherine*
St John (prize), 103–4, 115–16, 139

Salomon (of London), 18, 175, 184, 209–18, 284
Samaritan, 99
Sampson, 203
San Juan (a canoe), 262
Santo Tomas, 334
Scorpion (of London), 326–9
Seabright (of Bristol), 156
Seadragon (of London), 152, 165
Seraphim, 99
Son (of Lyme), 377
Susan (of London), 284; see also *Wildman*
Susan Fortune, 167
Susan's Handmaid, see *Wildman's Club*
Swallow, 24, 43, 95–172
Swiftsure (Queen's ship), 51
Swiftsure (of Chichester), 156, 162, 378
Thunderbolt (of London), 52
Tiger (of London), 25
Toby (of London), 175
Trinity alias *Michael* (prize), 103–4, 106, 114, 116, 163
Unicorn (of Barnstaple), 378
Unity (of London), 155, 165
Vineyard, 339
Violet, alias *Why not I?*, 99, 326–9
Virgin (of London), 99, 184–208, 225–35
White Lion alias *Elizabeth Bonaventure*, 18, 20, 59–85, 165
Why not I?, see *Violet*
Wildman alias *Susan*, 59–85
Wildman's Club, alias *Susan's Handmaid*, 59–85
William (of Wells), 154
William Bonaventure (of Southampton), 162
Yaguana (prize), 118–19
sickness, 28–9, 62, 66–9, 74, 83, 251, 295, 383, 391
Sifrey, Robert, 79

INDEX

Fifth Part (of London), 95–172
Flight (alias *Florissant*), 21, 173–83, 211
Flying Hart, 154
Foresight (Queen's ship), 174, 180–1
Fortunatus (of London), 19
Fortune (prize), 338–76
Frances, 156
Gabriel, 43, 159
Galleon Dudley, 164, 167, 172
Galleon Fenner, 154
Galleon Leicester, 156
George Bonaventure (of London), 161, 338
Gertrude, 209, 216
Gift, 337–98
Gift of God (of Seville, prize), 102, 104, 112–13
Gift of God (Portuguese prize), 298, 302
Gift of God (of Southampton), 153
Globe (of London), 326
Golden Dragon (of London), 18, 52, 99, 163, 184–208, 225–35, 298–304; appraisement of, 230–3
Golden Lion (Queen's ship), 185
Golden Lion (of London), 210
Golden Noble (of London), 100, 167
Golden Riall (of Topsham), 326, 377
Great Delight, 164
Handmaid, 21, 330–7
Hare (of Plymouth), 152
Hare (of Southampton), 166
Harry and John, see *Hopewell*
Hope, 40–9
Hopewell (of London), 95–172; in 1597, 97
Jane Bonaventure, 209–18
Jason, see *Bark Burr*
Jewel (of London), 26, 33, 286, 298–300, 306–7

John (of London), 52, 95–172, 211, 330
John Evangelist (of London), 88
John Young (of Chichester), 149
Jonas, 98
Julian (of London), 100, 167
Julian (of Lyme), 378
Katherine (prize), 102, 104, 112–13
Lion (of Chichester), 156, 378
Lion (of Southampton), 100, 102–5, 128, 134–5, 139, 141, 144, 146, 148–9, 153, 155–6
Lion's Whelp, 155, 180
Little Delight (of London), 164
Little John, see *John*
Luisa (of Dieppe), 290
Lyme, 377
Madre de Dios (prize), 26, 33, 185, 187–8, 195, 201–4, 225–226, 230
Margaret (of London), 95–172, 184–208, 332
Margaret and John (of London), 44, 49, 130, 163
Margery, 308
Marlyn, 161
Merchant Royal (of London), 18, 51, 284, 287, 338
Mermaid (of London), 168
Michael, see *Trinity*
Michael and John (of London), 98, 185, 330–7
Mineral (of London), 18, 173–183, 211
Minion (of Southampton), 162, 169
Moon (Queen's ship), 167
Moonlight, 88, 226
Moonshine (of London), 100, 162, 175–6, 180
Muscatt, 155, 159
Neptune (of London), 185
Nuestra Señora de Esperanza, 233

INDEX

ships—*continued*
  galiot, 325
  see also Leaguers, prizes, Queen's ships, etc.
ships named
  Affection (of London), 33, 164, 175, 211, 286, 298–9, 302–6
  Aid (Queen's ship), 165
  Amity (of London), 230
  Angel (of Southampton), 153, 381
  Anne Bonaventure, 185
  Anthony (of London), 18–19, 185, 236–83
  Archangel (of Southampton), 383
  Ark Raleigh (later *Ark Royal*), 18
  Ascension (of London), 377–98
  Bark Bery (of Plymouth), 165
  Bark Bond (of Weymouth), 326–9
  Bark Brave, 157
  Bark Burr (of London), 21, 95–172
  Bark Raleigh, 377
  Bark Randall (of Weymouth), 111, 211
  Bark Young (of Southampton), 22, 33, 35, 86–94, 149, 153–154, 159
  Bergoño, 334
  Bevis (of Southampton), 154, 164
  Black Dog (of London), 1, 17, 19–20, 22, 30, 33, 50–8, 174; appraisement of, 56–8
  Blessing of God (prize), 298, 302
  Bonaventure (Queen's ship), 168
  Brave, 99
  Brave (of Isle of Wight), 119
  Canter (of Southampton), 164
  Canter (of Weymouth), see *Bark Randall*
  Catellina (prize), 220–3
  Centaur (of London), 33, 95–172, 211–12, 284–97, 299
  Centurion (of London), 152, 164, 338
  Challenger (of London), 18, 173–83, 211
  Chance, 40–9, 105, 111
  Charles, 326
  Coloma, 333
  Commander, 43
  Conception (prize), 331–2
  Conclude, 88
  Consent (of London), 238
  Content, 19, 95–172, 210
  Crane (Queen's ship), 167
  Dainty (of Plymouth), 188, 202
  Darling (of Southampton), 381–2, 390–1
  Defiance (Queen's ship), 167–8
  Delight (of Bristol), see *Robin*
  Delight (of Lyme), 378
  Delight (of Southampton), 89
  Diamond (of Bridgewater), 156
  Diamond (of Dartmouth), 341
  Diana, 150
  Discharge (of London), 143, 156, 159, 163, 338
  Discovery, 19, 21, 236–83
  Disdain, 156, 160, 166, 168
  Drake (of London), 40–9, 161, 330
  Edward (of Southampton), 164
  Edward Bonaventure (of London), 18, 21, 51, 239, 270, 279, 284–97, 338
  Eleanour (of Weymouth), 378
  Elizabeth Bonaventure (Queen's ship), 156, 167
  Elizabeth Bonaventure, see *White Lion*
  Espérance (prize), 285–6, 291–294
  Examiner (of London), 26, 40–9, 97, 161
  Exchange (of Bristol), 211, 215
  Falcon's Flight (of Barnstaple), 35, 89, 153, 159

INDEX

San Sebastián (Spain), 114–15
San Sebastián I., 67
Sánchez de Carranza, Gerónimo, 316–24
  report by, 300–3
Sanders, Gideon, deposition 155–156
Sandoval, Dr Francisco de, 324–325
Santa Cruz Road (Barbary coast), 189
Santa Fé de Bogotá, 260, 310
Santa Maria, Puerto de (Spain), 312, 313
Santa Marta (Bogotá), 175, 260
Santiago (Cape Verde Is.), 328
Santo Domingo, City of, 29, 37, 42, 88–90, 92–3, 101–3, 112–13, 117–18, 129, 136, 140, 214, 233–5, 238–40, 242, 249–50, 255, 284–5, 288, 295–7, 300, 305, 312–313, 315, 331–4, 340–3, 345, 347–50, 353–60, 362–73, 375, 392
  harassed by Langton, 265–81
Santo Domingo I., *see* Hispaniola
Saona I., 186, 190, 214, 248–9, 279, 288, 308, 313
Saphasapea (Hispaniola?), 250
Sarmiento de Villandrando, Don Juan de, 225, 228, 233–5, 262, 296
Scott, Thomas, 98, 330
seamen, *see* crews of privateers
Seapsheade, *see* Shepshed
Sebastián (mariner), 224
Seckford, Henry, 143, 151, 156, 159, 163
sentences, 12, 64, 81, 105, 181–2, 340
  full translation of, 373–6
Sepulveda, Baltazar de, 279
Severn Stoke (Worcs.), 132, 143
Severne, John, 118
Sevilla, Luis de, 282
Seville, 109, 113–16, 210, 233, 284, 312, 327–8, 331, 341–3, 347, 353–4, 356–71
Sewell, Thomas, 40, 44
Seymour, Edward, Earl of Hertford, 156–7, 209
Shellie, Laurence, 112
Shepshed (Leics.), 78
Sherley, Sir Anthony, 308
Shillinge, Andrew, 226, 229
ships
  appraisements and inventories of, 8–9, 14, 17, 56–8, 61, 63, 73, 74–7, 118–19, 179, 182, 230–3
  pinnaces, 16, 19, 30 *et passim*
  barks, 16–17, 30, 86–94, 111, 118, 131, 149, 153–9, 163–5, 213–14, 223, 251, 303, 311–313, 326–9, 340, 390–1
  galleys, 18, 37, 53–4, 107–11, 211, 215, 228, 278–9
  caravels, 30, 82, 93, 137, 156, 168, 176, 180, 197, 206, 213–14, 243, 247, 250–1, 258–60, 299, 303, 307, 310, 333–5, 337, 368, 372–3, 384–5, 390, 393
  canoes, 38, 234, 238, 244–5, 247, 252, 257–65, 269–72, 280–2, 383
  frigates, 53, 55, 109–10, 132, 157–8, 176, 186, 189–94, 197–8, 206, 220, 223, 239, 241, 251–3, 267–8, 270, 282, 296, 308–10, 313, 315–17, 324, 328–9, 332, 392
  lighters, 74–5
  flyboats, 152, 233, 334, 336, 384
  galleons, 154, 156, 164, 167, 233–4, 265, 331, 333
  canters, 164, 211, 215
  carracks, 188, 195, 201–8, 225, 230
  shallops, 213, 215, 256, 260, 265, 281–3, 300, 331, 333–6
  pirogues, 257–9
  hulk, 296, 300

INDEX

Wattes, George, deposition, 302–304
Watts, John (senior), 21, 23, 32, 39–41, 52, 176, 330, 338
   1588 venture, 33, 40–9, 161
   and Chidley's voyage, 59–60, 63, 72, 74, 80–1
   1590 venture, 1, 35, 88–9, 161
   1591 venture, 21, 24, 28, 33–4, 36, 86, 95–172
   1592 venture, 211–12, 215
   1594 venture, 284–7, 291–5, 298–307
Watts, John (junior), 40–1, 44–5
Watts, Thomas (senior), 40
Watts, Thomas (junior), 40–9
Webber, John, 179
Webster, Thomas, 51
   deposition, 56
Wells (Somerset), 154
Wentworth, Captain, 310
West, Thomas, 57, 338–76
West Country, 207
Westbury (Bristol), 68
Weste, Walter, 340
Westham (Sussex), 91, 158
Weymouth, 17, 19, 62, 67, 74, 78, 111, 175, 187, 199–201, 211, 215, 326–9, 340–1, 343, 378
White, John (artist), 43, 88, 112
White, John, 112
White, Thomas, 230
White, William, 112
Whitechapel, 49
Whitehall, 195, 216
Whitney, George, 105
Wight, Isle of, 26, 86–7, 107, 119, 149, 154–6, 158, 162

Wildes, John, 209–10, 216–17
Wilkinson, Edward, 51–3, 185, 196, 204
Williams, Henry, 311
Williamson, Master, 73
Williamson, William, 345–76
Willis, Moses, 383
Windward Passage, 29
Winter, William, 211
wintering in West Indies, 51, 103, 135, 139, 155, 159
Wood, Benjamin, 23, 61
   deposition, 73–4
   with Chidley, 61–3, 65, 73–4, 78–9
   1592 voyage, 33, 173–83, 211–212, 215
   1594 voyage, 310, 325
Woodcocke, Richard, 286
wrecks, 62, 64, 67, 85, 239, 250–1, 284–5, 289, 295–7
Wright, William, 193

Ximénez, Juan, 316–21

Yaguana, La (Hispaniola), 29–30, 38, 101, 117–18
   Newport at, 34, 185–7, 190–1, 197–8
Ybarra, Diego de, 37, 279, 296–7
Ybarra, Juan de, 281, 305–6
Ycacos, *see* Hicacos
Ygararan, Martín de, 103, 114–15
Yguamo (Hispaniola), 277
Yonge, Edward, 205–6
Yonge, John, 241
   deposition, 253–5
Young, John, 86, 90–1, 93, 378

INDEX

Tortugas Is. (near Cuba), 152, 160, 193, 214, 334
Tower Hill, 51, 53, 165
Towers, Harry, 106
Towers, William, 83
Towerson, William, 327
trade in West Indies
  English, 30, 37–8, 186, 190, 242, 269, 273, 279, 281, 285, 310, 325–6, 339, 341, 349, 395
  Dutch, 38, 339–76, 384
  French, 38, 285–7, 290–5, 325, 339, *see also* Leaguers
Tresillions, *see* Trujillo
Trinidad I., 62, 83, 175, 225–6, 287, 379, 392, 394–5
Trinity House, 26–7, 195, 330
Trujillo (Truxillo, Tresillions, Honduras), 187, 192, 198–9, 242, 281–3, 295, 308–10, 315–17, 322, 324–5
Trujillo Point, *see* Honduras, Cape
Tulier, Ludovicus, 291–4
Turner, Captain, 152, 154
Turner, Thomas, 173–83
Twitt, John, 184–6, 197–8
  account of Newport's voyage, 188–95
Twopenie, John, 112

Ulloa de Toro, Alonso de, deposition, 233–5
Ustrio (Otro), John de, 363, 368
Utilla I. (Gulf of Honduras), 325

Valerosa, Gabriel, 68, 71
Valladolid (Honduras), 316
Vanake, Peter, 345–76
Vandemate, Egbert, 346–9, 353–355, 357–8
Vaughan, Captain, 155
Vavasour, Richard, 22, 105, 173–183
Vaze, Francisco, 312–13

Vega Portocarrero, Lope de, 240, 274
  reports to crown, 265–6, 295–6
Vela, Cabo de la, 175
Velázquez, Gaspar, 318–19
Veneciano, Miguel Antonio, 283, 316
Verde, Cape, 16, 67, 299, 308, 310, 328
Vianna (Portugal), 312, 341
vice-admirals, 4, 87, 179, 312
victuals, 7, 23, 45, 74, 80, 82, 177, 210, 216, 223, 249–52
  cost of, 20
  revictualling, 29, 31, 66–7, 175, 189–92, 197, 214–15, 239, 273–6, 289, 306–7, 310–11, 324–5, 383–4, 391
  shortage of, 66–70, 252, 287–9, 306
Vides, Francisco, 272
Vides, Francisco de, 255–6
Villa Rica (New Spain), 295
Villafañe, Licentiate Baltazar de, 273
Villalpando (a cripple), 380, 396
Villaverde, Captain, 333
Viodett, M., 180, 183
Virgin Is., 100, 146, 289
Virgin Passage, 213
Virginia, 33, 35, 42–3, 48, 61, 88–9, 377–8
Virginia Company, 39, 41, 99, 220, 339, 378

Waddon, John, 162
Wally, Thomas, 226, 228, 230
Walton, William, 59–60, 85
Wapping, 23, 149–50
Wapping Wall, 166
Warne, Thomas, 226, 230
warrants
  for arrest, 9–10, 64, 81, 84, 286
  for issue of letters of reprisal, *see* Howard, Lord Charles
Waterford, 26
Waters, Edward, deposition, 162

420

INDEX

Silva, Garci-Gonçález de, 396
Simón, Fray Pedro, 380, 396–8
Simson, George, 214, 218
Skeffington, Thomas, 117
Skinners Company, 99, 284
Slingsby, Francis (senior), 238
Slingsby, Francis (junior), 22, 236–83
Smallinge, Jacob Branso, 349
Smith, John (deponent), 106
Smith, John (sailor), 112
Smith, Phillip, 157, 311
Smith, Richard, 63
Smith, Thomas, 211
Snowe (of Limehouse), 305
Snowe, William, 106
Soco, El (Hispaniola), 274
Soco, Rio (Hispaniola), 242, 249–250
Solórzano, Martín de, 283, 315
Somers Is., *see* Bermuda
Sommers, George, 22, 38, 377–98
Sotherey, Richard, 211
  deposition, 217–18
South Sea(s), 59, 63, 65–6, 70, 78, 82, 85, 219, 310, 340
Southampton, 17, 19, 33, 86–7, 89, 100, 102, 128, 146, 148–9, 152–4, 162, 164, 166, 169, 201, 327–8, 378, 381–3, 391
Southwark, 205, 374
Southwick, George, 117, 185, 196, 204, 226, 229, 326, 345
Sozer, John, 367
Sparke, John, 220–2
Spirincke, John, 345–76
Stansted Mountfichet, 339
Staper, Richard, 175
Starkey, Thomas, 147, 163, 284
  deposition, 304
Starre, William Arenson, 345
  deposition, 352–61
Stemwinckle, Jeremy, 348–50, 371
Stepney, 330
Stephens, Edward, 230
Steveington, Thomas, 112

Stockes, Thomas, 340
Stokes, John, 21, 98, 286, 299, 330–1, 336
Stokes, Magdalene, 336
Stokes, Roland, 98
Stokes, Thomas, 331, 333
Stonier, Peter, 87–8
Stoning, Andrew, 71
Stopes, James, 172
Street, Walter, 68–70
Sydenham, George, 64
Symes, Randall, 98

Tampa Bay (Florida), 194
Taverner, William, 211
Tavira (Portugal), 224
Tayler, John, 201
Tello de Guzmán, Don Francisco, 233
Tenerife I., 101, 131, 267, 312, 314, 383, 385
tenths, *see* prizes
teredo worm, 21, 359, 367
Testigos Is., 383
Texeda, Juan de, 25, 28, 36, 211–212
Thames, River, 24, 359
Thompson, Captain, 202
Thornton, Giles, 111
Thread (Fred, Fridde), Robert, 184–208
  deposition, 196–201
Tiburon, Cape (Hispaniola), 27, 88–9, 150, 153, 186, 190, 214, 220, 248, 288, 391
Tierra Firme (Spanish Main), 29, 33, 109, 175–6, 238–9, 247–248, 266, 325, 279–80, 384–391, 394–8
Tilley, John, 150
  deposition, 151–2
Tilley, Robert, deposition, 153–4
Tomlyn, John, 173, 178
Topfield, Henry, 345
Topsham, 377
Torrosillio, Point, *see* Caucedo
Tortuga I. (Venezuela), 244